RHS
GARDEN
FINDER
2004-2005

EDITOR
CHARLES QUEST-RITSON

A Dorling Kindersley Book

LONDON, NEW YORK, MUNICH, MELBOURNE, DELHI

First published in Great Britain in 2004 by
Dorling Kindersley Limited
80 Strand, London WC2R 0RL

A Penguin company

1 3 5 7 9 8 6 4 2

Note: whilst every care has been taken to ensure that the information
contained in this directory is both accurate and up-to-date, neither the
author, the Royal Horticultural Society nor the publisher accept any
liability to any party for loss or damage occurred by reliance placed
on the information contained in this book or through omission
or errors, howsoever caused.

A CIP catalogue record for this book is available from the British Library.

ISBN 1 4053 0349 2

The opinions expressed in this work are the opinions of the author and
not of the publishers or the Royal Horticultural Society.

Produced for Dorling Kindersley Ltd by
COOLING BROWN

Printed and bound in England by Clays Ltd, St Ives Plc

Back cover photographs (from top): Flower-Pot Man at Plant World Botanic
Gardens, Devon; *Rosa hemisphaerica* at Mottisfont Abbey, Hampshire; garden
visiting at Barrington Court, Somerset; glasshouse at Goodnestone Park, Kent;
wire geese at Burton Agnes, East Yorkshire; pumpkins at Belmont Park, Kent.
Front cover photographs: formal garden at Brodsworth Hall & Gardens, South
Yorkshire; rococo statue at Nymans, West Sussex.
Spine photograph: autumn leaves in the Winter Garden at
RHS Garden Rosemoor (Stephen Record)
All pictures except spine photograph Charles Quest-Ritson, 2003.

Discover more at
www.dk.com

Join the Royal Horticultural Society

- Free entry with a guest to RHS gardens; Wisley, Rosemoor, Hyde Hall and Harlow Carr
- Free access to over 100 inspirational partner gardens at selected periods
- Privileged entry and reduced rate tickets for RHS flower shows, including Chelsea
- Free gardening advice service
- Free monthly edition of *The Garden* magazine
- Reduced price tickets to hundreds of RHS workshops, events and lectures around the UK
- Free seeds (Please note this will occur a small postage and packaging charge)

Take advantage of the £5 membership saving and pay only £35

To join call **0845 130 4646** quoting ref 1998, or complete the application form overleaf.   **www.rhs.org.uk**

The UK's leading gardening charity, working to advance horticulture and promote good gardening

Membership application form

Simply complete and detach this form enclosing your payment.
Please allow 28 days for the delivery of your members pack.

In becoming a member of the RHS, I understand that information relating to my membership will be passed to carefully selected third parties for processing purposes only and that I will receive information from the RHS relating to RHS events and products. I understand that the RHS will not sell my details to anyone.

Royal
Horticultural
Society
200 YEARS

1 MEMBERSHIP TYPE

[ ] Individual Membership - £~~40~~ £35   D.O.B (dd/mm/yy) [ ][ ] [ ][ ] [ ][ ]

2 MEMBERS DETAILS

Title _____ Surname _____ Initial(s) _____

Address _____

Postcode _____

Daytime tel no. _____ Email _____

3 TOTAL SUBSCRIPTION £ [_____]

For membership enquiries, please call **0845 130 4646**
(Lines open 9am-5pm, Monday to Friday)

HOW DOES PAYING BY DIRECT DEBIT HELP BOTH THE RHS AND YOU AS AN RHS MEMBER?
Payments by Direct Debit reduces our administration costs and enables us to use more of your subscription rates to support our charitable horticultural work. Many of our members find Direct Debit helpful since it is such a safe and convenient method of payment.

4 PAYMENT

Instruction to your Bank or Building Society to pay by Direct Debit

DIRECT Debit

Name(s) of account holder(s)

_____

Originator's number [9][9][8][9][7][9]

Bank sort code (from top right hand corner of your cheque)

[ ][ ] [ ][ ] [ ][ ]

Bank/Building Society account number

[ ][ ][ ][ ][ ][ ][ ][ ]

Instruction to your Bank/Building Society
Please pay The Royal Horticultural Society Direct Debits from the accounts detailed in the instruction subject to the safeguards assured by the Direct Debit guarantee. I understand that the instruction may remain with The Royal Horticultural Society and if so, details will be passed electronically to my Bank/Building Society.

Bank/Building Society details

The Manager   BANK/BUILDING SOCIETY   Signature

Branch name   Date

BANK AND BUILDING SOCIETY MAY NOT ACCEPT DIRECT DEBITS INSTRUCTIONS FOR SOME TYPES OF ACCOUNTS. UK BANK ACCOUNTS ONLY.

Payment by Credit or Debit card

Card number [ ][ ][ ][ ][ ][ ][ ][ ][ ][ ][ ][ ][ ][ ][ ][ ][ ][ ][ ]

Issue No. (Switch only) [ ][ ] Expiry date [ ][ ] / [ ][ ]

Signature _____   Date _____

Payment by cheque
Please make cheques payable to: **The Royal Horticultural Society for** £ [_____]

This offer applies to Individual Membership only. This offer cannot be used in conjunction with any other offer. This offer is valid until 31/10/04. The Direct Debit seed voucher offer does not apply to those living in Australia. In this circumstance a gift of similar value will be sent instead.
Registered Charity Number: 222879

1998

CONTENTS

KEY TO SYMBOLS

(P) Parking available   (+) Plants for sale

(dog) Dogs permitted   (gift) Gift Shop

(WC) Toilet facilities   (restaurant) Restaurant

(disabled) Access for the disabled   (cup) Light refreshments

INTRODUCTION

Garden visiting

Welcome to the new edition of *The RHS Garden Finder 2004–2005*. This is a companion volume to the *RHS Plant Finder*. The *RHS Plant Finder* tells you where to find the right nurseries for plants: *The RHS Garden Finder 2004–2005* will tell you where to see the same plants growing in gardens which are open to the public. This is all the more important now that membership of the Royal Horticultural Society brings free access for its members to more than 100 gardens up and down the United Kingdom and abroad.

The aim of this book is to supply sufficient detail to enable readers to decide if and when to plan a visit. The list is not exhaustive. It offers a selection of the different types of garden which are open to the public: ancient and modern, large and small, public and private. We welcome suggestions for additions, deletions or alterations to entries (please e-mail us at *questritson@aol.com*). All major gardens which are open regularly are listed as a matter of course. These include many gardens of the National Trust and the National Trust for Scotland as well as botanic and public gardens and those attached to stately homes. But many gardens do not open to visitors regularly: the National Gardens Scheme lists over 3,500. In this book you will find a selection of these gardens which open only once a year or by appointment. Some guides would omit them on the grounds that it is not worthwhile to give publicity to gardens which so few people can visit but, if a good garden is seldom open, it is all the more important to know when the opportunity to see it will arise. This book also concentrates upon gardens with plants: some of the great historic gardens of the 18th century have comparatively brief descriptions, because their landscapes are rather short on horticultural content. On the other hand, some of the best gardens for plants are those which have large 'living collections' for teaching purposes – botanic gardens, and those attached to horticultural colleges. They are among the most interesting for garden-lovers to visit.

Nurseries

Because this book is plant-led, it also includes about 150 leading nurseries. Almost all have a demonstration garden attached to them, just as most gardens have a nursery or plant stall. This is a recent development – it started about 20 years ago – but is now quite normal: visitors to a nursery like to see plants growing in a garden before making their purchases, and visitors to a garden like the opportunity to buy some of the plants they have seen there. It would not be right to exclude the inspirational series of model gardens at Bridgemere in Cheshire, Barnsdale in Leicestershire or the National Garden Exhibition Centre in Co. Wicklow just because they are attached to a commercial enterprise that sells plants.

How to use this book

Gardens are listed by county or region (for Scotland), and then alphabetically by name. The order is England, Scotland, Wales, Channel Islands, Northern Ireland and the Republic of Ireland. In general, we have stuck to the familiar 1974 counties of England and Wales and to the Scottish regional divisions. There are three exceptions: the county of Avon has been redistributed between Gloucestershire and Somerset, Cleveland has been included with North Yorkshire, and Humberside has been split between Lincolnshire and the East Riding of Yorkshire. We have also divided Hereford & Worcester into its two component parts again. We have been careful to ensure, so far as possible, that gardens are listed in the counties or region in which they actually lie, which is not always the county or region their postal addresses suggest, or where their owners believe themselves to live. Thus the Savill Garden lies in Surrey, even though most of Windsor Great Park is in Berkshire, and the gardens at Burford House near Tenbury Wells are neither in Herefordshire nor in Worcestershire, but across the border in Shropshire. To find out about a specific garden, turn to the index at the back: it should take you straight to the page you need.

Practical details

Our source for practical information about directions, opening times, admission charges, parking, lavatories, disabled facilities and refreshments has been the owners or their staff, backed up by our own enquiries where appropriate. The accuracy of these details is not guaranteed, but is believed to be correct at the time of going to press. We rely to a great extent on information which has been submitted to us by third parties. Not everyone who was approached has replied – or replied in time – and this explains some gaps. We very much regret having to drop a number of important gardens which have failed to reply to our requests for an 2004 update. These include Glebe Cottage Plants (Carol Klein), Norfolk Lavender, Probus Gardens, Sheffield Botanical Gardens, the University of Durham Botanic Garden, and West Green House (Marylyn Abbott) – all of which we hope to have back in the book next year. A paperless version of the book is on-line as part of the Royal Horticultural Society's website (*www.rhs.org.uk*) and updates will be made as and when they are available. Inclusion in this book or on the society's website, or exclusion from either of them, should not be construed as a recommendation or condemnation. And, though this book carries the Royal Horticultural Society's endorsement, its comments and opinions are the editor's, and his alone.

Contacting gardens

In order to assist readers with special needs, or who are hoping to arrange a group visit by special appointment, we list the telephone and fax numbers to which enquiries should be directed. In many cases this is the private telephone line of the owners: readers are urged to respect their privacy. If telephone and fax numbers have been omitted, this is because the owners prefer to receive such requests by letter. Next year we hope to carry e-mail addresses too.

Websites

There has been a great increase recently in the number of gardens and nurseries with dedicated internet sites. Many are beautifully designed and extremely informative. They help to attract visitors, especially groups from gardening clubs and tour operators. Please remember that website addresses change frequently and inexplicably. We have checked all the hundreds in this book during the autumn of 2003 and have only included those which are up and running and seem to us to offer useful information. Many websites are of excellent quality: some of the nursery sites permit on-line ordering. Others exist only as registered names: we have omitted them.

Visiting times

Many gardens are attached to other attractions – most typically, a house which is also open to the public. The visiting times we have given relate only to the garden.

Please remember that most gardens have a last admission time. Typically it will be 30 or 45 minutes before they close, but it can be much longer. Remember, too, that a pre-booked group can often make a visit at a time or season when the garden is not open to individual visitors.

Prices
As with times, so with prices. The admission prices we have given relate only to the garden. If the house or some other attraction is open at the same time, a supplement may be payable. Some owners insist on you buying a full ticket, notably the National Trust at Clandon Park and Hatchlands and Tussauds Group at Alton Towers and Warwick Castle, though most are more reasonable. It is true that some gardens may seem rather expensive but, generally speaking, the market rules of supply and demand apply and you get what you pay for. And it should be said that for every garden which is over-priced there are ten inspirational plantsman's gardens, run by their owners on a strictly non-commercial basis, where you can be certain of wonderful flowers, good design and a genuine welcome.

Many gardens offer special rates to groups and, if details are not given, it may be worth asking whether a reduction is available and what minimum number is acceptable. Please remember, however, that not all gardens permit parties: popular gardens which already suffer from wear and tear may not welcome increased visitor numbers. Special rates for families are sometimes available, especially at larger gardens attached to stately homes, where the garden is only one of many entertainments offered to the visitor. There are endless permutations on the numbers of adults and/or children which constitute a 'family' and the age at which a child becomes an adult and has to pay the full entry price. Season tickets are sometimes available, and

good value for people who live near a large garden or stately home.

Entrance fees vary, and a few owners have told us that they may increase fees in the middle of the season. Some have a high season for a month or so – like Exbury in Hampshire, and Leonardslee in West Sussex in spring. Others have a special day of the week or open days for charity when the entrance fee is higher. A few owners had not yet fixed their 2004 times or admission charges by the time we went to press and we have therefore indicated that the times or prices quoted are for 2003. All entrance fees are, in any event, liable to be changed: visitors would do well to take more money than they think they will need. Some gardens have honesty boxes, and it is also important to take lots of change, so that you are not forced to choose between paying too much and paying too little.

It is worth remembering that National Trust members are usually admitted free to Trust properties. Readers are strongly recommended to join the National Trust in any event: its portfolio of blue chip gardens is so comprehensive that no garden tour is complete without a visit to one or more of its properties.

Facilities
This guide uses a variety of symbols to show whether a garden has such facilities as public conveniences or plants for sale. We have indicated whether parking is available: this may be at the garden itself or on a public road very close to it. Parking may be at some distance from the house. At Saltram, in Devon, it is 500 yards away, and this is by no means exceptional. You can however expect better parking facilities at a popular property which offers a wide range of entertainments than at a small plantsman's garden in a country lane.

It is often a condition of admission that no photograph taken within the garden may be sold or used for public reproduction without the consent of the property owner. Some forbid photography altogether. Corporate owners like the National Trust or English Heritage do not welcome dogs at their properties, except guide dogs. Some restrict dogs to particular areas of a property, like the car-park, or the woods and parkland rather than the garden proper. Private owners are generally better disposed, though visitors should remember to keep their dogs on leads. A few owners – like the Howards at Castle Howard – go out of their way to say that dogs are actually welcome, but not all have shaded areas for parking.

Disabled visitors

We have generally indicated which gardens are suitable for disabled people, though it is important to stress that access may only be partial. Often an area around the house or entrance is accessible for people in wheelchairs, but the more remote parts of the garden are quite unsuitable. It is best to ring before your visit to check. The same is true of other disabled facilities. We have not specified the nature of those facilities, but in most cases it includes lavatories and ramps which are suitable for the wheelchair-bound. It is best to enquire in advance of a visit if particular items of special equipment are required. The National Trust is especially good at adapting its properties to accommodate the needs of disabled visitors.

Size of gardens

We have asked owners to indicate the size of their garden and the number of people who work in it. Taken together, these two statistics help to suggest how intensively a garden is worked and how long you need to allow for your visit. The number or gardeners must be interpreted flexibly. Some owners have told us how many paid gardeners they employ: others have included their own contributions and based their figure on how much time they and their family give to the garden.

The NCCPG

Four common abbreviations are used freely throughout the text: RHS for the Royal Horticultural Society, NGS for the National Gardens Scheme, SGS for Scotland's Garden Scheme, and NCCPG for the National Council for the Conservation of Plants and Gardens. We have noted the NCCPG National Collections which are held at the gardens and nurseries we list and supplied a separate index of them towards the end of the book. Not all genera are the subject of a National Collection: there are still some horticulturally important groups of plants which have not yet been seriously collected and studied under the auspices of the NCCPG. Other genera have been split into a number of different collections. This is particularly necessary in the case of such a large genus as *Rhododendron* or those, like *Euphorbia*, which require a great variety of growing conditions. Moreover, the NCCPG has wisely introduced a system of duplicate collections to insure against the risks which face every collection of rare plants. The need to maintain duplicate collections and split large genera explains why certain names occur several times in the list of National Collections towards the end of the book. The list of National Collections on the NCCPG website (*www.nccpg.com*) is updated fairly regularly.

Champion trees

For most gardens, we give a brief list of Features. These include general information like 'good collection of trees' and more specific facts like 'tallest *Quercus cerris* in the UK'. Occasionally we have added some features which are not strictly plants, but do add enormously to the character of a garden. Information about outsize trees is taken principally from the records kept by that excellent organisation the Tree Register of the British Isles (see www.tree-register.org). There are two ways of measuring trees: height and girth.

Sometimes the tallest specimen will also have the thickest trunk – but not always. Both the tallest and the biggest can claim to be the champion tree, and we have sometimes made this distinction when noting record breakers in gardens. Tree measurements can never be fully up to date: some records have not been verified since the great gales of 1987 and 1990.

The editor is very grateful to the many people who have helped in the compilation of this work. First and foremost he thanks all the garden owners, nurseries, horticulturists, colleges, societies and everyone else who has responded to his requests for information. He is greatly indebted to them, and regrets that it is not always possible to give each the personal attention which is their due. Particular thanks go the staff in the regional offices of the National Trust. Special thanks are also due to Susanne Mitchell, Geoff Hodge, Brent Elliott and others at the Royal Horticultural Society. The editor also acknowledges the considerable input of others who have worked with us on this project: John Hodgson, David Lamb, Peter Cooling and our colleagues at Dorling Kindersley. Finally thanks are due for their endeavours to Brigid and Madeline Quest-Ritson and Christopher and Katharine Blair.

Charles Quest-Ritson, Editor, *The RHS Garden Finder*, P.O. Box 673, Salisbury, Wiltshire. SP3 4BU. questritson@aol.com

GARDENS
TO
VISIT

GARDENS
OF
ENGLAND

The purpose of this short introduction is to highlight some of the considerations which apply to gardens in England, but not to those in other parts of the UK or abroad. The first point to make is that gardens and gardening are essentially an English phenomenon. England has always taken the lead in horticultural matters within the British Isles, and gardening is still – to some extent – one of our most important cultural, artistic and scientific exports. Within England there are differences of garden emphasis and style between regions. Alpine gardening has many followers in the north of England; Cornish gardens tend to be rhododendron woodland gardens; the smart designers tend to practise in and around London. Gardening is probably at its strongest as a national pursuit in the south-east of the country, where more than half the Royal Horticultural Society's members live. But there are good gardens of every kind open to the public in every part of the country. In fact they are also fairly evenly distributed throughout England, except perhaps for the east Midlands, which has fewer good gardens than its rich agriculture might suggest. Gardens and garden-making depend as much upon social and economic circumstances as upon soil and climate.

A word about the grading of historic gardens is needed. During the 1980s, English Heritage's predecessors compiled a register of gardens and parks of special historic interest. The aim was to draw attention to the nation's heritage, so that designed landscapes were not overlooked, for example in plans for new development. There are three gradings, each of which assesses the historic layout, features and architectural ornaments. Grade I parks and gardens are 'of exceptional interest'; Grade II* parks and gardens are 'of great quality'. Grade II – parks and gardens are 'of special interest'. These gradings reflect the importance of a particular garden or park and compare it with others in England as a whole. The register is in 46 parts, one for each of the 1974 English counties, and copies are available from English Heritage. The information they contain about the individual gardens is very comprehensive. It covers the site, area, dates and designers of key surviving elements, surviving features of the garden or park, and other interesting aspects such as historic associations.

The best source of reference for plants and nurseries is the annual publication *RHS Plant Finder*. It shows where the main concentrations of nurseries are – in Surrey, for example – and where there are few, like northern Cornwall. It lists only a handful of garden centres, which is a pity because most people buy their plants at local garden centres rather than specialist nurseries. There is no publication which tells you where to find a good garden centre, though the Garden Centre Association does have a very helpful searchable website (*www.gca.org.uk*). The advantage of buying from one of its 150 members is that all are subject to annual inspections by an independent auditor and must satisfy stringent standards to remain members. The only guide to garden centres of which we know is the *Gardeners' Atlas* published by Paragraph Publishing: the 2003 edition cost £12.99. We have sometimes found that its maps are not as accurate as they ought to be, but it does at least list over 4,500 places of gardening interest of every kind.

The starting point for garden visiting English gardens must be the 'Yellow Book' which the National Gardens Scheme publishes annually in February under the full title *Gardens of England & Wales Open to the Public*. The Yellow Book is a best seller. Its sales immediately after publication exceed 5,000 copies per week, three times the success rate of its nearest rival among best-selling paperback reference books. It is wonderfully comprehensive and totally undiscriminating. The owners write their own garden entries, with the result that a really good garden may come across as self-deprecatingly boring, while an exciting description can often lead to disappointment. Beware of self-publicists: you can usually spot the hype. The Yellow Book lists over 3,500 gardens and is the single most important guide to visiting gardens in England and Wales, and the least expensive. Copies of *Gardens of England & Wales Open to the Public in 2004* will be available as from the end of February 2004.

Members of the RHS enjoy free entry to many gardens throughout England. Some are free throughout the year: others for only a month or so. It is important that members should note carefully when they may expect free entry and when they may not. In most gardens the privilege applies only to members of the RHS not to any guests who accompany them. Nevertheless, it is an impressive list and a major benefit of membership. The list has grown considerably in recent years, and the Royal Horticultural Society hopes to expand it yet further.

In addition to its Free Access gardens, the Royal Horticultural Society has a system of running lectures at a number of Nurseries and Garden Centres in England, most of which are listed in this book, with a note of how to find out further details. The Society's own *Members' Handbook 2004* gives full details of these and of the many lectures, demonstrations, workshops, garden walks and other events held at RHS Partner Colleges.

BEDFORDSHIRE

Both the Grade I gardens in Bedfordshire – Woburn Abbey and Wrest Park – are open to the public. Few of its other important gardens remain open to visitors, though every garden-visitor should seek out the gloriously eccentric Swiss Garden (Grade II*). The headquarters of the Royal Society for the Protection of Birds, The Lodge at Sandy, is also rated as a Grade II garden and open daily throughout the year. Shuttleworth College at Old Warden is now a RHS Partner College, but Bedfordshire is otherwise horticulturally underdeveloped. It is not over-endowed with arboreta, though Woburn has a fine collection of trees: there are a number of record-breakers there, as well as at Swiss Garden, Toddington Manor and Wrest Park. Surprisingly few private gardens open for the National Gardens Scheme and the county has no National Collections. There are few nurseries too: best known is Blom's Bulbs at Melchbourne, close to the border with Northamptonshire, but it is not open to visitors. One para-horticultural curiosity worth seeing is the 'Tree Cathedral' near Whipsnade Zoo.

The Manor House

CHURCH ROAD, STEVINGTON, BEDFORD, MK43 7QB

Tel 01234 822064 **Fax** 01234 825531
Website www.kathybrownsgarden.homestead.com
Location 5 miles north-west of Bedford, off A428.
Opening hours 2 pm – 6 pm; 16 May, 13 June & 1 August. Plus 6 pm – 9 pm on 30 June, with music. And groups at other times by appointment.
Admission fee Adults £3.50; Children free.

This is a very interesting newish garden – the owners moved here in 1991 and have designed and planted it with a sense of style that is contemporary rather than nostalgic. Kathy Brown is a garden-writer and cookery-writer, and these interests have overlapped in such titles as *The Edible*

Flower Garden (1999). But she has also written books about container gardening, bulbs and cottage gardening – all of which have to some extent been worked out in the garden here. She is very good on structure: the French garden is an essay in formal design. It starts right outside the house, with a terrace that has a *gâteau* of tiles and stone at its centre: box cones and gravelled parterres lead down to a circular fountain. Planting is another of her skills: the containers are exuberantly filled with all kinds of unconventional material including succulents and other exotics. Elsewhere are masses of bulbs, some in grass and others in beds which may later be filled with herbs and roses. Some 60 late-flowering clematis extend the season alongside rambling and climbing roses. Gazebos, pergolas, a parterre leading to a wildflower meadow with a prairie planting of grasses at the centre, a cottage garden and a wisteria walk are among the many other features. Definitely a garden to see now and return to in future, as it develops.

Features good modern design; bulbs; old roses; clematis; wildflower meadow; containers; succulents; grasses; cream teas.

Owned by Simon & Kathy Brown
Number of gardeners owners only
Size 1.6ha (4 acres)

Seal Point

7 WENDOVER WAY, LUTON, LU2 7LS

Tel 01582 611567
Location North-east Luton: turn north off Stockingstone Road (A505) into Felstead Way, then second left.
Opening hours By appointment in advance, for individuals and groups.
Admission fee Adults £2.50.

This small town garden on a difficult site has been much praised: 'this garden is definitely different!' says Mrs Johnston. It manages to combine a large number of different features with an overall oriental theme, including a bonsai garden arranged on a slate moraine. Plants are important too: the trees are well-chosen for their ornamental effect, and the Johnstons use foliage plants and grasses to intensify the dramatic impact of the plantings. Mrs Johnston was BBC Gardener of 1999 for the south-east region: she made all the ornaments in the garden herself. A new, nature-friendly copse has recently been planted.

Features interesting design; grasses; light refreshments.

Owned by David & Danae Johnston
Number of gardeners owners only
Size 0.4ha (1 acre)

Swiss Garden

OLD WARDEN, BIGGLESWADE, SG18 9EA

Tel 01767 627666 **Fax** 01767 626391
Website www.bedfordshire.gov.uk
Location 1½ miles west of Biggleswade.
Opening hours 10 am – 5 pm (4 pm from November to March); daily; all year. For NGS on 27 March & 18 September.
Admission fee Adults £3; Concessions £2.

The Swiss Cottage in the Swiss garden was built in the 1820s for Lord Ongley – the guidebooks call it 'an outstanding example of the Swiss picturesque' – but most of the rustic, gothic, landscape garden we see today was largely developed by the Shuttleworth family in the 1870s. It is a remarkable relic: a picturesque pleasure ground of winding paths and sinuous waterways, little cast-iron bridges and romantic huts, Pulhamite rockwork and thatched curiosities, quaint kiosks and soaring ironwork arches, gullies and ferneries, vast conifers and cheerful rhododendrons, and an early grotto-glasshouse (note the small panes of glass) planted as a fernery. In short – most enjoyable to visit.

Features picturesque landscape; rhododendrons; Pulhamite grotto; fernery; Swiss cottage; publications and souvenirs shop; restaurant at nearby Shuttleworth Collection.

Owned by Bedfordshire County Council as lessee
Number of gardeners 2
Size 3.6ha (9 acres)
English Heritage Grade II*

Toddington Manor

TODDINGTON, LU5 6HJ

Tel 01525 872576 **Fax** 01525 874555
Location Signed from Toddington village.
Opening hours 11 am – 5 pm; 31 May. Plus pre-booked group visits in June & July.
Admission fee Adults £3.50; OAPs £2.50; Children £2.

This garden is now in its prime, and has all been made by the owners since 1979 around some magnificent old trees. It has some excellent features, notably a lime avenue which leads into a cherry walk, and a wonderfully high standard of maintenance. The walled garden has long beds of delphiniums and peonies and a fine garden of herbs (culinary, medicinal and insect-repelling), while the double herbaceous border has recently been extended and is now 100m long and 6m wide. There is also a good modern rose garden of white and yellow floribundas interplanted with philadelphus. Further away from the house are a wild garden and three small ponds: visiting children may borrow nets to go dipping.

Features woodland walks; roses (mainly old-fashioned); herbs; mature conifers; good herbaceous borders; largest *Tilia* 'Petiolaris' in the British Isles.

Owned by Sir Neville & Lady Bowman-Shaw
Number of gardeners 2
Size 2.4ha (6 acres), plus 8ha (20 acres) of woodland

Woburn Abbey

WOBURN, MK17 9WA

Tel 01525 290666 **Fax** 01525 290271
Website www.woburnabbey.co.uk
Location 1½ miles from Woburn on A4012.
Opening hours 11 am – 4 pm; daily; 13 March to 31 October. 11 am – 4 pm; Saturdays & Sundays.
Admission fee Park: £2 per car.

Woburn may not have the reputation of being a gardeners' garden, but Humphry Repton, who designed the park, considered it one of his finest achievements. The deer park is home to ten different types of deer: one is the Muntjac deer from China, some of which escaped during World War II and have spread through much of England. Nearer the house are a pinetum and a quercetum (a collection of oaks), cedars, redwoods, huge swamp cypresses and such rarities as mature specimens of the hardy 'rubber tree' *Eucommia ulmoides* and *Acer triflorum*. Elsewhere are lily ponds, fritillaries, wild orchids and masses of naturalised *Narcissus* – more than 100 daffodil cultivars. The private gardens are simple and formal, mainly 19th-century and Italianate, but they include a circular hornbeam maze with a Chinese pavilion at its centre, herbaceous borders, a rose garden, a camellia house, and lots of good statues.

Features mature conifers; fine collection of trees; deer park; tallest *Zelkova sinica* (17m.) in the British Isles; two shops; lunches & teas.

Owned by The Duke of Bedford
Number of gardeners 6
Size 16.8ha (42 acres)
English Heritage Grade I

Wrest Park

S<small>ILSOE</small>, MK45 4HS

Tel 01525 860152 (weekends)
Website www.english-heritage.org.uk
Location ½ mile east of Silsoe.
Opening hours Dates, times and prices of admission are currently under review; please ring 01525 860152 or check the website for details.

The 'English Versailles' is dominated by a graceful long canal which runs down to the classical domed pavilion built by Thomas Archer in 1710. Capability Brown came here later, but worked around the earlier design. The house came later still, in the 1830s. Many historic garden buildings have survived, some from as far back as the 1730s and others from the 19th century, including the orangery, the Mithraic altar, the bowling green house and the Chinese temple and bridge. In the walled garden and around the house are a rose garden, bedding displays and glasshouses. In the park are handsome specimen trees, including a fine example of the purple-leaved birch (*Betula pendula* 'Purpurea').

Features grand parterres; long vistas; largest pink chestnut (*Aesculus* x *carnea*) in the British Isles; gift shop; light refreshments.

Owned by English Heritage
Size 36ha (90 acres)
English Heritage Grade I

BERKSHIRE

Even in its attenuated post-1974 shape, Berkshire is well provided with good gardens. Few of its great historic gardens and landscapes are open to the public, though Berkshire's only Grade I landscape, Windsor Great Park, is of course open all the time, while Inkpen House and Lutyens's masterpiece Folly Farm (both Grade II*) open for the National Gardens Scheme. There are good specimen trees in Windsor Great Park and the grounds of Eton College. Nurseries are less common than garden centres: Henry Street Garden Centre at Arborfield is one of the more individual ones, with a special line in roses. Berkshire has comparatively few National Collections, though the Crown Estates have no less than nine of them at the Savill Gardens and Valley Gardens, just over the border into Surrey.

Englefield House

ENGLEFIELD, THEALE, READING, RG7 5EN

Tel 0118 930 2221 **Fax** 0118 930 3226
Website www.englefield.co.uk
Location On A340, 1 mile from M4 Jct 12.
Opening hours 10 am – 6 pm; Mondays (plus Tuesdays – Thursdays from 1 April to 1 November); all year.
Admission fee Adults £3; Children free.

Ⓟ ♿

The garden at Englefield descends dramatically from the hill above the house through open woodland where mature native trees like oak and beech are mixed with Victorian conifers. The underplanting was begun in 1936 with advice from Wallace & Barr and has continued ever since. Here are tremendous collections of camellias, rhododendrons, eucryphias, acers, magnolias, cornus, davidias, davidias, azaleas (many of them the nearly extinct Ghent varieties) and other unusual trees and shrubs. A grotto has lately been built at the top of the stream, lined with a mosaic of different pine cones. There are drifts of daffodils and other spring and summer bulbs and wonderful autumn colour. Grey stone balustrades and wide staircases, built in 1860, enclose the lower terraces. Here are formal plantings, mixed borders, roses, topiary, wide lawns, water-features, small enclosed areas (some lately paved and pebbled), and a children's garden with hidden jets of water from four small statues. A walled kitchen garden has recently been restored producing many varieties of fruit, vegetables, herbs and flowers. The garden is enclosed by a deer park, with magnificent views over the lake and surrounding countryside.

 Features woodland garden; roses (mainly old-fashioned); rhododendrons & azaleas; daffodils; good herbaceous borders; deer park.

Owned by Sir William & Lady Benyon
Number of gardeners 3
Size 3.6ha (9 acres)
English Heritage Grade II

Foxgrove

SKINNERS GREEN, ENBORNE, NEWBURY, RG14 6RE

Tel 01635 40554
Location On western edge of Skinner's Green.
Opening hours 10 am – 4 pm; 21 February. For snowdrops. Groups welcome by appointment.
Admission fee Adults £2; Children free.

Foxgrove is a plantsman's garden, linked to Louise Peters' nursery next door: Audrey Vockins is her aunt. Bulbs, alpines and herbaceous plants are Audrey's great interest. The hellebores, crocus and snowdrops give a great display in early spring. There are good shrubs (including more than 50 daphnes), roses and handsome small trees too. Louise's nursery is open from 10 am to 5 pm from Wednesday to Sunday but closed in August. It carries an interesting range of hardy and cottage garden plants, including several new *Saxifraga* cultivars from the Czech Republic. Its speciality is snowdrops, which are sold by mail order 'in the green'. Other specialities – worth visiting the nursery to see – are hellebores, grasses and penstemons, and some newly-planted herbaceous borders. Louise Peters' planted-up troughs have been a great feature of RHS spring flower shows recently.

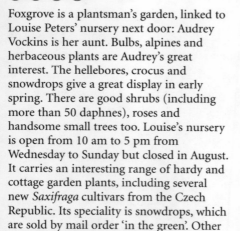**Features** snowdrops; good herbaceous borders; primulas; spring bulbs; cyclamen & colchicums in autumn; bluebells; bank garden; tea & cakes.

Owned by Miss Audrey Vockins
Size 0.8ha (2 acres)

Frogmore Gardens

THE HOME PARK, WINDSOR CASTLE, WINDSOR, SL4 2JG

Tel 01753 869898 **Fax** 01753 832290
Location Access varies: please contact 01753 869898 ext. 2347.
Opening hours Not available as we went to press.
Admission fee Adults £3; Children free in May. Adults £5.20; Children £3.20 in August. (2003 prices).

Frogmore was for many years a royal residence: most of the house dates from the reign of George III. The grounds were first laid out in 1793, when the lake was excavated and the spoil used to create a series of mounds and banks. The many garden buildings include a gothic temple, an Indian kiosk, a tea house, the Duchess of Kent's mausoleum and the Royal Mausoleum where Queen Victoria and Prince Albert lie. Nearby, but closed to visitors, is a cemetery where many members of the royal family have been interred since the middle of the 19th century. During the 1920s and 1930s, the gardens were extensively developed by the planting of ornamental trees and shrubs, underplanted by bulbs. The May openings are less expensive than the August ones, because the price for the latter includes a visit to the house. The house may also be visited in May, but there is a separate charge for it then.

Features historic landscape & buildings.

Owned by H.M. The Queen
Number of gardeners 5
Size 14ha (35 acres)
English Heritage Grade II*

The Living Rainforest

HAMPSTEAD NORREYS, THATCHAM, RG18 0TN

Tel 01635 202444 **Fax** 01635 202440
Website www.livingrainforest.org
Location Signed from Jct 13 on M4. From A34 southbound, follow signs to East Ilsey, then Hampstead Norreys.
Opening hours 10 am – 5.15 pm; daily; all year. Closed 25 & 26 December.
Admission fee Adults £4.95; Concessions £4.25; Children £3.25.

The Living Rainforest consists of two large landscaped glasshouses, computer-set to create two different rainforest climates. Each has a thickly planted collection of exotic plants of every kind, many of them rare or endangered. There is a particularly fine and near-comprehensive collection of tropical aroids, including the epiphytic *Anthurium warocqueanum* from Colombia and the terrestrial *A. watermaliense* from Costa Rica. The flowering plants are wonderful in winter when the tropical orchids flower, and in spring when the jade vine (*Strongylodon macrobotrys*) flowers for several months – it has even set seed here. Later, in the summer, *Victoria amazonica* becomes one of the great attractions when it fills one of the pools. But the Living Rainforest is fascinating whatever the season or the weather outside, and there are tropical monkeys, butterflies and birds too.

Features tropical plants from the Amazon basin and around the world; gift shop; refreshments.

Owned by The Living Rainforest
Number of gardeners 2
Size 1,860 sq.m. (20,000 sq.ft.) under glass

Old Rectory

BURGHFIELD, RG3 3TH

Tel 0118 983 3200
Location Right at Hatch Gate Inn & first entrance on right.
Opening hours 11 am – 5 pm on 6 June for NGS. Groups at other times by appointment.
Admission fee Adults £2.50; Children free.

This highly acclaimed garden was designed by Ralph and planted by Esther Merton, a first-rate plantswoman who knew exactly what she wanted to achieve. She had a very good eye for plants, and collected them herself all over the world, as well as exchanging gifts with her gardening friends throughout Britain. Her legacy includes wonderful roses, lush summer pots, quantities of spring bulbs (some of them rare), tiny alpines and unusual hellebores – all of them extremely well grown. The *tour de force* is a double herbaceous border where plants build up their impact through repetition, backed by yew hedges which get taller towards the end, to cheat the perspective. It leads to a pool framed by dense plantings of strong foliage – ferns, hostas, maples.

Features snowdrops; rock garden; plantsman's collection of plants; good late herbaceous borders; stone troughs; exotic displays in tubs; hellebores; lilies; teas.

Owned by A.R. Merton
Number of gardeners 2
Size 1.8ha (4½ acres)

Scotlands

COCKPOLE GREEN, WARGRAVE,
READING, RG10 8QP

Tel 01628 822648
Location Between Cockpole Green & Warren Row,
in triangle between the A4130, the A321 & the A4.
Opening hours By appointment; groups welcome.
Admission fee Adults £3.

The garden at Scotlands has been made by
the owners over many years. The 17th-
century house is an early barn conversion
and the lawns in front run down to a small
lake with a fine swamp cypress (*Taxodium
distichum*) on one side and a pinewood
summerhouse after the style of Repton on
the other. Further down still are more
ponds, a waterfall and waterside plantings in
a woodland garden where azaleas, camellias
and pieris are underplanted with naturalised
bluebells and primroses. The kitchen garden
is partially walled, with an 18th-century
design brick-and-flint gazebo and planted
with rather more flowers than vegetables: a
formal herb garden and a rose garden are
each more prominent than edible crops. It is
formally laid out in such a way that you
appreciate the dynamism of the design but
linger among the plants. There is one other
very handsome lay-out – a lawn with an
oval swimming pool in the centre, backed
by yew hedges which are stepped and
staggered like a stage-set. Swimming pools
are difficult to fit into a garden: this one is
very well integrated. The colours are
enhanced by small semicircular herbaceous
borders and terracotta tubs planted with
colourful bedding plants.

Features good design; good plants; all
on a handsome scale; fine trees,
especially grey cedars, chestnuts and copper
beeches.

Owned by Michael Payne
Number of gardeners 1
Size 1.6ha (4 acres)

BUCKINGHAMSHIRE

Buckinghamshire is wonderfully stocked with large estates and grand, historic gardens. All three Grade I landscapes – Cliveden, Stowe and West Wycombe Park – are regularly open to the public, as are the two Rothschild gardens at Ascott and Waddesdon. These estates also have many fine trees. The National Gardens Scheme is active in the county, and lists over 80 gardens to visit, often in village clusters. Dorneywood Garden at Burnham is particularly worth seeing on its all-too-rare openings for the National Gardens Scheme. There are comparatively few National Collections in the county, though the *Pleione* species and hybrids at Butterfields Nursery in Bourne End have long been a feature of RHS shows.

Ascott

WING, LEIGHTON BUZZARD, LU7 0PS

Tel 01296 688242 **Fax** 01296 681904
Website www.nationaltrust.org.uk
Location ½ mile east of Wing.
Opening hours House & garden: 2 pm – 6 pm; Tuesday – Sunday; 16 March to 30 April & 1 to 31 August. Garden only: Tuesday – Thursday; 4 May to 29 July. And 3 May & 23 August for NGS.
Admission fee Garden only: £4 Adults; £2 Children.

Ⓟ ⓦⓒ ♿ 🌳

Ascott is an opulent late-Victorian extravaganza. It was largely planned by Leopold de Rothschild and planted with trees and shrubs supplied by Sir Harry Veitch. The Dutch garden, the Venus garden and the topiary sundial date from this period – roughly 1880-1920. The topiary sundial is famous: its Roman numerals are planted in box and the gnomon at the centre is made of golden yew grafted onto green Irish yew. The motto – in Latin – reads 'Light and shade by turn, but love always'. Much in these old gardens has been restored, re-made and re-planted in recent

years. The bedding in the Dutch garden relies heavily upon the sumptuous leaves of coleus (*Solenostemon* cvs.), cannas and the ornamental cabbage 'Tokio': all were popular 100 years ago. Other parts of the garden have been re-designed in a more modern idiom. The 'long walk' now has a serpentine shape. The old fern garden has been replanted as a box parterre and is now known as the sunken garden. And there is a new 'planet topiary garden', built to resemble the astrological symbols of the 12 planets and showing their position in the sky at the very moment Sir Evelyn and Lady de Rothschild were each born. But there are fine old trees, and new plantings too, including a young collection of modern magnolias and groups of *Davidia involucrata*, *Aesculus indica* and *Juglans nigra*.

 Features woodland garden; topiary; mature conifers; good herbaceous borders; spring bulbs; Dutch garden; tallest *Cedrus atlantica* 'Aurea' in the British Isles.

Owned by The National Trust
English Heritage Grade II*

Blossoms

COBBLERS HILL, GREAT MISSENDEN, HP16 9PW

Tel & Fax 01494 863140
Location 2½ miles north-west of Great Missenden by Rignall Road, signed Butlers Cross, to Kings Lane about 1 mile on right, then to top of Cobblers Hill. Right at yellow stone marker and right after 50 yards.
Opening hours By appointment only.
Admission fee £2 for National Gardens Scheme.

The bones of this fascinating plantsman's garden go back to 1925 when a previous owner started to plant up a four-acre field and an acre of beech wood filled with bluebells. Dr and Mrs Hytten have lived here since 1975 and have benefited from the substantial windbreaks planted in the 1920s and 1930s. Having once been open – there is still a fine view of the Misbourne Valley – Blossoms is essentially a woodland garden now, with an established apple orchard and some lusty specimen trees including a liquidambar and a fern-leaved beech *Fagus sylvatica* 'Asplenifolia'. The Hyttens have thickened up the woodland themselves and made good collections of maples, eucalyptus and willows, together with some more unusual trees, such as *Tetradium daniellii*, *Davidia* and *Metasequoia*. Add on a herbaceous border, shrub borders (including some interesting new shade-lovers), a scree garden, a rock garden, a rare collection of herbaceous plants, a cutting garden, a number of very large climbing roses, a small lake, smaller ponds, patios and statues (mostly wood-carvings) – and the scale and variety of the owners' achievement will be apparent. The owners say that spring and autumn are the best seasons, but like all good plantsman's gardens there is lots of interest throughout the year.

 Features a plantsman's collection of good plants; woodland walks; trees, ponds & wooden sculptures; rock garden; good herbaceous borders; teas by arrangement.

Owned by Dr & Mrs Frank Hytten
Number of gardeners owners only
Size 2ha (5 acres)

Butterfields Nursery

HARVEST HILL, BOURNE END, SL8 5JJ

Tel 01628 525455
Location Off B476.
Opening hours 9 am – 5 pm (usually).

Butterfields Nursery has two very different specialities: pleiones and dahlias. Ian Butterfield is far and away the most important breeder and seller of pleiones, having bred and selected forms and hybrids for many years – and creates quite a sensation when he exhibits at shows like the Chelsea Flower Show. Two-thirds of all the species, hybrids, forms and grexes of pleiones sold in England are unique to Butterfields Nursery. The dahlias are chosen primarily as garden plants and range across all the classes.

NCCPG National Collections *Pleione*

Campden Cottage

51 CLIFTON ROAD, CHESHAM BOIS, AMERSHAM, HP6 5PN

Tel 01494 726818
Location Signed from A416 between Amersham on the Hill & Chesham.
Opening hours 2 pm – 6 pm; 29 February, 21 March, 18 April, 16 May, 13 June, 18 July, 15 August, 12 September & 10 October.

Admission fee Adults £1.50; Children free.

This plantsman's garden crams a vast number of rare and interesting plants into its half acre and, like all good gardens, has lots to enjoy at every time of the year. The owner has given the garden a good structure and placed plants together to show the contrasts and harmonies of their colours and shapes. She says they are busiest at their early spring openings, when people come to see the hellebores.

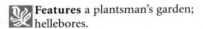**Features** a plantsman's garden; hellebores.

Owned by Mrs P. Liechti
Number of gardeners 1
Size 0.2ha (½ acre)

Chenies Manor

CHENIES, RICKMANSWORTH, WD3 6ER

Tel & Fax 01494 762888
Location Centre of Chenies village.
Opening hours 2 pm – 5 pm; Wednesdays, Thursdays & Bank Holidays; April to October. Plus special plant sale on 18 July from 10 am to 5 pm (£4.50).
Admission fee Garden only, £3; House & garden, £5.

The richly planted gardens at Chenies Manor are full of variety but designed to complement the Elizabethan house. Their most spectacular period is spring – April and early May – when 300 different cultivars of tulip come into flower in and around the sunken garden, modelled on Hampton Court. All come from Bloms and all are clearly labelled: each is grown in groups of 10 to 50 bulbs and offers a wonderful opportunity to learn about tulips. Last autumn (2003) they planted thousands of

daffodils. Later comes the summer bedding, interspersed with herbaceous plantings – red dahlias with white forms of *Campanula latiloba*, for example. And there are colour borders everywhere: one very easy but effective one mixes *Alchemilla mollis* with catmint and *Sisyrinchium striatum*. Add in a physic garden for herbs, a grass labyrinth, a yew maze, and some beautiful old lawns and yew hedges, and you have a garden of great harmony.

Features bulbs; topiary; herbs; fruit; physic garden; award-winning maze; tea, coffee, home-made cakes.

Owned by Mrs A. MacLeod Matthews
Number of gardeners 1, plus family
Size 1.8ha (4½ acres)
English Heritage Grade II*

Cliveden

TAPLOW, MAIDENHEAD, SL6 0JA

Tel 01628 605069 **Fax** 01628 669461
Website www.nationaltrust.org.uk
Location 2 miles north of Taplow, M4 Jct 7.
Opening hours 11 am – 6 pm (4 pm in November & December); daily; 15 March to 23 December.
Admission fee Adults (Grounds) £6.50; Children £3.20.

Cliveden is a vast (and very important) landscape garden, filled with whatever money could buy: balustrading from the Villa Borghese in Rome, the dramatic 'Fountain of Love' and a huge parterre below the house. The best parts are the Arcadian ilex wood, quite magical, and newly restored rose garden, originally made by Geoffrey Jellicoe in 1932. But allow lots of time to visit this garden of wonders.

Features woodland garden; snowdrops; roses (mainly modern); fruit; good herbaceous borders; bluebells;

good autumn colour; tallest *Juglans cinerea* (24m.) in the British Isles; National Trust shop; light refreshments and meals.

Owned by The National Trust
NCCPG National Collections *Catalpa*
English Heritage Grade I

Hartwell House

OXFORD ROAD, AYLESBURY, HP17 8NL

Tel 01296 747444 **Fax** 01296 747450
Website www.hartwell-house.com
Location 2 miles from Aylesbury, on A418 towards Oxford.
Opening hours For guests of the hotel.
Admission fee Free to patrons.

The gardens at Hartwell House were was laid out early in the 18th century, in the formal style. When they were landscaped by Richard Woods (a follower of Capability Brown), most of the garden buildings were retained, in particular a gothic tower and pavilion by James Gibbs. The modern gardens are especially fine in springtime, with hosts of snowdrops, daffodils, winter aconites, primroses and anemones. In the orchard old varieties of apples are grown, while the walls of the former kitchen garden support apricot, peach, pear and plum trees – the same cultivars as were originally planted in 1868. Flowers for the house and fresh herbs for the kitchen are grown in Hartwell's gardens. This year (2004) will see the completion of the Sir William Lee folly bridge.

Owned by Historic House Hotels Ltd.
Size 36ha (90 acres)
English Heritage Grade II*

Hughenden Manor

HIGH WYCOMBE, HP14 4LA

Tel 01494 755573 **Fax** 01494 474284
Website www.nationaltrust.org.uk
Location 1½ miles north of High Wycombe.
Opening hours 12 noon – 5 pm; Saturdays & Sundays in March; then Wednesday – Sunday plus Bank Holidays from 31 March to 31 October.
Admission fee Garden only £1.70; Children 80p. Park & woodland free.

Hughenden is not a great garden, but interesting for its association with Disraeli. The garden was made by his wife in the 1860s and has a classic gardenesque planting of specimen trees on the North Lawn and a more Italianate design on the southern side. The National Trust has restored it, using photographs taken in 1881, so that the parterres are once again planted with Victorian annuals and bedding.

Features good herbaceous borders; 61 old apple varieties; rolling parkland; formal Victorian parterres with bright bedding out as in Disraeli's day; National Trust shop; new stableyard restaurant.

Owned by The National Trust
English Heritage Grade II

Lower Icknield Farm

LOWER ICKNIELD WAY, GREAT KIMBLE, AYLESBURY, HP17 9TX

Tel & Fax 01844 343436
Location On B4009 between Great Kimble & Longwick.
Opening hours 9 am – 5.30 pm; daily; all year. Closed from Christmas to New Year.
Admission fee Free.

The display garden attached to Lower Icknield Farm Nurseries is best from July to September. The structure comes from hardy perennials, but supplemented by tender perennials and annuals. These include *Argyranthemum* (they used to have a National Collection), and tender salvias – mainly the Mexican species like *S. greggii* and the *S.* x *jamensis* hybrids. All the plants they sell are raised on the nursery – none is bought in – and they sell no sundries apart from their own brand of growing compost. Plants are what they raise, and there is a succession of half-hardy patio- and house-plants for sale throughout the year, as well as hardy bedding and a good range of unusual hardy perennials.

Features good display garden; salvias; argyranthemums.

Owned by Mr & Mrs J. Baldwin
Number of gardeners 1
Size 2ha (5 acres)

The Manor House

BLEDLOW, PRINCES RISBOROUGH, HP27 9PB

Tel 020 7584 4243 **Fax** 020 7823 1476
Location Off B4009.
Opening hours 2 pm – 6 pm; 2 May & 20 June for National Gardens Scheme. And by appointment.
Admission fee £4.50.

This is one of the greatest gardens of our times: beautifully planted and well maintained, it has all been made on thin chalk soil since 1969. There are four parts: first, the garden 'proper' round the house, enclosed by hedges of beech, hornbeam or yew. Best is the armillary garden, an exercise in topiary with the sphere at its centre, surrounded by four cubes of yew, smaller hedges and labels of box. Next comes the walled garden with a gazebo in the centre whose eight trellised posts are planted with clematis and rambling roses. The central grass walk is lined with apple trees trained as spheres around a wire globe: they rise from parterre boxes of teucrium, each planted with a different herb – sage, chives, Greek oregano and so on. The third part of the garden is quite different – two-and-a-half acres of sculpture garden started in 1991 and already remarkably mature. The land has been contoured to maximise the movement of the surface, and give contrasts of height and depth. Its fluid modern design is a great foil to the formal gardens around the house. The presiding spirit is a life-size gorilla by Michael Cooper. The fourth part of the garden is different again – four acres of water garden, started in 1979 on the site of three old watercress beds. The thirteen springs which issue from its sides are the headwaters of the River Lyde, a tributary of the Thames. The steep valley sides are thickly planted with shrubs and herbaceous plants. A wooden walkway, Japanese in style, takes you round the edge of the lakes at the bottom. The muddy banks are planted with candelabra primroses, gunneras, hostas and astilbes. Unlike the rest of the garden, this part is open daily (and free) from dawn to dusk.

Features good herbaceous borders; sculptures; new water feature by William Pye.

Owned by Lord & Lady Carrington
Number of gardeners 3
Size 3.6ha (9 acres)

Stowe Landscape Gardens

STOWE, BUCKINGHAM, MK18 5EH

Tel 01280 822850 **Fax** 01280 822437
Website www.nationaltrust.org.uk
Location 3 miles north-west of Buckingham.
Opening hours 10 am – 5.30 pm or dusk (last admissions 4 pm); Wednesday – Sunday plus Bank Holiday Mondays; 28 February to 31 October. Plus 10 am – 4 pm; Saturdays & Sundays; 6 November to 27 February 2005. Closed 29 May, 24 & 25 December. Garden may close in bad weather.
Admission fee Adults £5.50; Children £2.70.

This mega-landscape is considered by some the most important in the history of gardens. William Kent designed the Temple of Venus (1731), the Shell Bridge (1733), and the highly original Temple of British Worthies (1734) which has statues of Alfred the Great, the Black Prince, Queen Elizabeth, John Milton and twelve further historic persons. Capability Brown laid out the Grecian Valley in the 1740s: it was while he was head gardener at Stowe that he developed his skill in simplifying formal gardens and creating the distinctive curves and contours which we now recognise as an essential feature of the English landscape garden. The National Trust has undertaken extensive restoration and renovation since it took over in 1989. Go if you have not been already, and go again if you have: from the start, Stowe was a highly fashionable garden with a political message. Stomp round slowly, and contemplate the history and symbolism of each feature. Read the National Trust's excellent guide and then go round again, this year, next year, every year, and commune with the *genius loci*.

Features tallest *Fraxinus angustifolia* var. *lentiscifolia* (24m.) and largest **x** *Crataemespilus grandiflora* (9m.) in the British Isles; National Trust shop; light meals.

Owned by The National Trust
English Heritage Grade I

Turn End

TOWNSIDE, HADDENHAM, AYLESBURY, HP17 8BG

Tel 01844 291383/291817
Location Turn at Rising Sun in Haddenham, then 300 yards on left. Park in street.
Opening hours 2 pm – 5.30 pm; 4 April & 3 May for NGS. Groups by appointment. House & garden open one day in June: ring for details.
Admission fee Adults £2.50; Children £1.

Peter Aldington was once a young architect, much influenced by Le Corbusier and James Stirling. In 1963 he and his wife bought this plot and built their house – a modern architectural classic, much photographed, cited, visited and copied (and now listed). Aldington believed that his job as an architect was to make connections and create forms which enclosed spaces for people to use and enjoy. He then set out to apply the same principles to his garden, drawing upon his love of textures and materials to design and plant it. The garden, like the house, became one of the most acclaimed to be made in the latter half of the 20th century. Over the years he was able to increase its size by small additions. It still covers less than one acre, but never was space so used to create an illusion of size. A brilliant series of enclosed gardens, sunken or raised, sunny or shady, each different and yet harmonious, contrasts with lawns, borders and glades. The story is told in *A Garden & Three Houses* by Jane Brown (Garden Art Press, 1999). Visitors are requested to park well away from the house.

Features brilliant design – a series of spaces; rock garden; a plantsman's collection of plants; ferns; grasses; refreshments on NGS days.

Owned by Mr & Mrs Peter Aldington
Number of gardeners 1
Size 0.4ha (1 acre)

Waddesdon Manor

AYLESBURY, HP18 0JH

Tel 01296 653203 **Fax** 01296 653237
Website www.waddesdon.org.uk
Location A41 Bicester & Aylesbury; 20 miles from Oxford.
Opening hours 10 am – 5 pm; Wednesday – Sunday & Bank Holiday Mondays; 5 March to 23 December. Opens at 11 am from 3 November to 23 December.
Admission fee Grounds only: Adults £4; Children £2. RHS members free in March, September & October.

The garden at Waddesdon was laid out in the 1870s and 1880s for Baron Ferdinand de Rothschild by the French landscape designer Elie Lainé. This involved levelling the crown of a hill, planting it with mature trees and creating the drives, banks and formal gardens which were essential to the design. The result is one of the finest Victorian gardens in Britain, which has been meticulously restored since 1990 by Lord Rothschild, working in conjunction with the National Trust. A grand park, splendid formal gardens, a rococo aviary and extravagant bedding are the first fruits of his work. Formal bedding in the parterres is a Waddesdon speciality.

Features daffodils; good herbaceous borders; magnificent bedding; spring walk with 80,000 crocuses; gift & wine shop; tea-room.

Owned by The National Trust
Number of gardeners 11
English Heritage Grade II*

West Wycombe Park

WEST WYCOMBE, HP14 3AJ

Tel 01494 513569
Website www.nationaltrust.org.uk
Location West end of West Wycombe on A40.
Opening hours 2 pm – 6 pm; Sunday – Thursday; April to August.
Admission fee Adults £2.70; Children £1.30.

This park, with a lake in the shape of a swan, was made by Sir Francis Dashwood between 1735 and 1782, in a rococo style that was modified by later generations. It has been well restored and embellished by modern additions, including three modern eye-catchers designed by Quinlan Terry.

Owned by The National Trust
English Heritage Grade I

CAMBRIDGESHIRE

Cambridgeshire has a good number of historic gardens. Though only Wimpole Hall is rated as Grade I, there is a great cluster of Grade II* and Grade II landscapes in Cambridge itself: these include the Botanic gardens and the following colleges – Christ's, Emmanuel, King's, Queen's, St John's and Trinity (including Trinity Hall). The Backs are also rated Grade I – and one of the few places in the country where the strange but beautiful parasite *Lathraea clandestina* has naturalised (RHS Garden Wisley is another). The Cambridge University Botanic Garden has by far the most exciting and comprehensive collection of plants in the county, especially for those trees which grow particularly well in the dry climate: many are the tallest of their kind in the British Isles. The National Gardens Scheme is well-supported in Cambridgeshire, and has quite a number of villages where several smaller gardens open together. In Cambridge itself, several colleges open for the National Gardens Scheme, including Clare, Emmanuel, King's, Newnham, Selwyn and Trinity. The county is thinly supplied by nurseries and garden centres, but Monksilver Nursery is a magnet for keen plantsmen and of international importance as a source of rare plants. Cambridgeshire has its fair share of National Collections – here too the lead is set by the University Botanic Garden with no less than nine National Collections from *Alchemilla* to *Tulipa*.

Abbots Ripton Hall

ABBOTS RIPTON, PE28 2PQ

Tel 01487 773555 **Fax** 01487 773545
Location Off B1090.
Opening hours 2 pm – 5 pm; 23 May, 27 June, 11 July, 25 July & 8 August, for various local charities. Groups of 12+ by appointment.
Admission fee Adults £3; Children (under 16) £1.50.

Humphrey Waterfield, Lanning Roper and Jim Russell all worked here, and few garden owners have had as many gardening friends

as Lord De Ramsey's parents, who made and re-made this garden over more than 50 years. The result is a garden of stylish individuality – as witness the gothic trellis work and the bobbles of yellow philadelphus – but also of great unity. The present Lady De Ramsey has retained the unity of style while replanting many of the borders. In early summer it can fairly claim to be the most beautiful garden in England.

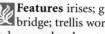 **Features** irises; grey border; Chinese bridge; trellis work; splendid herbaceous borders; tallest *Pyrus pyraster* (12m.) in the British Isles; new arboretum of rare oaks; teas.

Owned by Lord De Ramsey
Number of gardeners 1, plus 2 part-time
Size 3.2ha (8 acres)
English Heritage Grade II

Anglesey Abbey

LODE, CB5 9EJ

Tel 01223 810080 **Fax** 01223 810088
Website www.nationaltrust.org.uk/angleseyabbey
Location Off B1102, signed from A14.
Opening hours 10.30 am – 5.30 pm (last entry
4.30 pm); Wednesday – Sunday, plus Bank Holiday
Mondays; 24 March to 7 November. Plus Mondays
& Tuesdays from 5 July to 29 August. Winter Garden
open Wednesday – Sunday from 1 January to 28
March & from 10 November to 23 December.
Admission fee Gardens: Adults £4.10, but £3.25 in
winter (£3.40 as from November 2004).

Though not begun until 1926, the grounds
at Anglesey already deserve to be famous,
for they are the grandest made in England
during the 20th century. Majestic avenues
and 35 acres of grass are the stuff of them:
visit Anglesey when the horse chestnuts are
out and tulips glow in the wildflower
meadows. Large formal gardens, carved out
of the flat site by yew hedges, house the 1st
Lord Fairhaven's collection of classical and
renaissance sculpture. The winter garden
bursts with snowdrops and aconites. Then
there are smaller gardens, said to be more
intimate, where thousands of dahlias and
hyacinths hit the eye: glorious or
vainglorious, Anglesey has no match.

Features snowdrops; good herbaceous
borders; landscaping on the grandest
scale; long avenues of trees; dahlias;
cyclamen; good autumn colour; winter
walk; National Trust shop; licensed
restaurant & picnic area.

Owned by The National Trust

Number of gardeners 6
Size 39ha (98 acres)
English Heritage Grade II*

Clare College Fellows' Garden

CLARE COLLEGE, TRINITY LANE,
CAMBRIDGE, CB2 1TL

Tel 01223 333200 **Fax** 01223 333219
Website www.clare.cam.ac.uk
Location Enter from Clare Old Court off Trinity
Lane, or from Queens Road.
Opening hours 10 am – 4.30 pm; daily; April to
September.
Admission fee £2.

Two acres of views and vistas, walks and
Hidcote-style enclosures filled with exquisite
spring bulbs, spectacular hot-colour borders
dating from the 1950s and herbaceous
borders. The Fellows' Garden was largely
laid out from 1947 onwards by Professor
Nevill Willmer, who died in 2001 aged 98.
The features include a newly replanted
(2003) pond garden, a scent garden, a new
Victorian-style sub-tropical garden and fine
examples of taxodiums, metasequoias and
Tilia 'Petiolaris'. Willmer was extremely
skilful in his manipulation of perspective
and colour. Elizabeth Banks has recently set
out a ten-year plan to restore some of the
original features which have been lost over
the years. The garden is rather low-lying and
has suffered much from flooding (in
October 2001 & 2002, for example), so
please telephone the porter's lodge on 01223
333200 before making a visit.

Owned by The Master & Fellows
Number of gardeners 2
Size 0.8ha (2 acres)
English Heritage Grade II*

Cambridge University Botanic Garden

BATEMAN STREET, CAMBRIDGE, CB2 1JF

Tel 01223 336265 **Fax** 01223 336278
Website www.botanic.cam.ac.uk/
Location Entrance on Bateman Street, 1 mile to the south of the city centre & 5 mins from railway station.
Opening hours 10 am – 4 pm in winter, (5 pm in spring & autumn, 6 pm in summer); daily, except 25 December to 1 January.
Admission fee Adults £2.50; OAPs & Children £2.

This exceptionally attractive botanic garden is essential visiting for any garden lover who does not already know it. It has so many good and interesting features that you could spend all day here and not be bored. Cambridge's is also one of the most beautiful and best maintained botanic gardens in the country. The limestone rock garden is one of its major attractions, where the plantings are arranged geographically. It overlooks the small lake whose surface is covered by waterlilies. Late spring is the time to see the nearby woodland garden. Here are fine tree specimens, including *Dipteronia sinensis*, *Tetracentron sinense* and the hardy paw-paw *Asimina triloba*, and a dawn redwood (*Metasequoia glyptostroboides*) grown from the original introduction of seed into the UK in 1948. Along the sides of the little stream which runs through the wood are candelabra primulas, astilbes, irises and a bed of the giant horse tail *Equisetum telmateia*. Late spring is also the time to see the horse chestnuts in flower, the Persian lilacs and the National Collections of shrubby *Lonicera* and *Ribes*. The garden has a very good collection of peony species, which are in some places interplanted with its hardy geraniums: perhaps one reason why the garden is so attractive is that its National Collections are of supreme horticultural

value. The garden also maintains two acres of (mainly herbaceous) systematic beds, a feature which was created by the first curator Andrew Murray in 1845. It contains some 1,600 species, belonging to 98 families and growing in 157 beds: it is both historically important and beautiful in its design. A more modern addition is the genetic garden, whose scientific purpose is to demonstrate the natural effects of genes on plant morphology. Everywhere, too, are wonderful trees: was there ever a tree more beautiful than the type specimen of *Quercus* 'Warburgii'? The winter garden, planted in 1978, is the best in England, and draws on stems, leaves, bark and flowers to create its unique beauty. The superb series of linked glasshouses are a blessed sanctuary to horticulturally smart undergraduates during the cold months of an East Anglian winter, but every aspect of the garden's existence is educationally aware and it goes out of its way to attract and interest school-children too.

Features good herbaceous borders; important rock garden; species roses; dry garden; genetics garden; British wild plants; winter garden; tallest *Catalpa* x *erubescens* 'Purpurea' (11m.) in the British Isles (and 21 other record trees); shop in summer months; light refreshments.

Owned by University of Cambridge
Number of gardeners 18
Size 16ha (40 acres)
NCCPG National Collections *Alchemilla*; *Bergenia* (species & primary hybrids); *Fritillaria* (European species); *Geranium* (species & primary hybrids); *Lonicera* (shrubby species & primary hybrids); *Ribes* (species & primary hybrids); *Ruscus*; *Saxifraga* (European species); *Tulipa* (species & primary hybrids)
English Heritage Grade II*

Crossing House Garden

MELDRETH ROAD, SHEPRETH,
ROYSTON, SG8 6PS

Tel 01763 261071
Location 8 miles south of Cambridge off A10.
Opening hours Dawn – dusk; daily; all year.
Admission fee Donation to National Gardens
Scheme.

One of the wonders of modern gardening,
the Crossing House celebrates the
achievements of its makers since 1969, on
an unpropitious site right beside the main
railway line to Cambridge. Box-edged beds
separated by granite paths contain
thousands and thousands of different
plants, densely planted in the cottage style.
Shrubs, herbaceous plants, alpines and
bulbs are planted in the same beds, to
maximise the effect at all seasons. Peat beds,
screes, arches, topiary, pools and raised beds
are some of the features which add variety
to the most intensely and intensively
planted small garden in England. And every
few minutes a London express whizzes past.

 Features plantsman's collection of
plants.

Owned by Mr & Mrs D.G. Fuller and Mr J. Marlar
Number of gardeners owners only
Size 0.1ha (¼ acre)

Docwra's Manor

SHEPRETH, ROYSTON, SG8 6PS

Tel 01763 260235/261557
Location Off A10 to Shepreth.
Opening hours 10 am – 4 pm; Wednesdays &
Fridays; all year; 2 pm – 5 pm, first Sunday of
month from April to October. And by appointment.
Admission fee Adults £3; Children free.

This is very much a plantsman's garden,
whose lush profusion defies the dry, cold,
alkaline site. Docwra's Manor is a series of
small gardens – walled, wild, paved and so
on – each brimming with interesting plants
and good combinations. There is a sense of
abundance, whatever the season. Interesting
seedlings are encouraged and nurtured.
Everything you see has been made by Mrs
Raven since she and her late husband
bought the house in 1954. Do read John
Raven's charming and erudite *The Botanist's
Garden*, available from Mrs Raven by post
for £10 and one of the classics of 20th-
century garden-writing.

 Features plantsman's collection of
plants; good herbaceous borders;
Mediterranean plants; teas for NGS
opening.

Owned by Mrs John Raven
Number of gardeners 1
Size 1ha (2½ acres)

Elsworth Herbs

AVENUE FARM COTTAGE, 31 SMITH
STREET, ELSWORTH, CAMBRIDGE,
CB3 8HY

Tel & Fax 01954 267414
Location Smith Street is the road through the
middle of Elsworth; the garden is towards the
western end.
Opening hours By appointment.
Admission fee Free.

This is an excellent example of a small
boutique nursery attached to a National
Collection – in this case two of them,
Artemisia and *Nerium oleander*. Its range is
wide – over 50 oleanders, for example,
which is twice as many as anyone else – but
the owners do not carry large stocks, so they
are happy to propagate to order. The list of

Artemisia species is quite unique – a triumph of plantsmanship.

Owned by Dr J.D. & J.M. Twibell
Number of gardeners owners only.
Size 0.3ha (¾ acre)
NCCPG National Collections *Artemisia*; *Nerium oleander*

Elton Hall

PETERBOROUGH, PE8 6SH

Tel 01832 280468 **Fax** 01832 280584
Location A605, 8 miles west of Peterborough.
Opening hours 2 pm – 5 pm; Wednesdays; June to August. Also Thursdays & Sundays in July & August, 31 May & 30 August.
Admission fee Garden only: Adults £3; Children free.

The house is a castellated extravaganza. The Victorian gardens have been energetically restored in recent years which makes Elton highly visitable. The knot garden and the collection of old roses are the high spots, best in June and July.

Features roses (mainly old-fashioned); good herbaceous borders; fine collection of trees; handsome hedges; good colour plantings; plant centre on site; tea-room.

Owned by Sir William Proby Bt.
Number of gardeners 2½
Size 10.3ha (26 acres)
English Heritage Grade II*

Hardwicke House

HIGH DITCH ROAD, FEN DITTON, CAMBRIDGE, CB5 8TF

Tel & Fax 01223 292246
Location ½ mile east of village.
Opening hours 2 pm – 5 pm; 16 & 30 May. And by appointment.

Admission fee Adults £3; Children 50p.

This is an excellent plantsman's garden with an emphasis on herbaceous plants, roses and bulbs. The owner has a particular interest in Asia Minor, as witness an area devoted to Turkish plants and bulbs.

Features plantsman's collection of plants; good herbaceous borders; bulbs.

Owned by John Drake
Number of gardeners owner only
Size 0.8ha (2 acres)
NCCPG National Collections *Aquilegia*

Monksilver Nursery

OAKINGTON ROAD, COTTENHAM, CB4 8TW

Tel 01954 251555 **Fax** 01223 502887
Location North of Cambridge: between Oakington & Cottenham.
Opening hours 10 am – 4 pm; Friday – Saturday; March to June, & October.

This remarkable nursery is deservedly fashionable. Monksilver specialises in finding and rescuing really rare plants. They say that their areas of speciality include *Anthemis, Arum, Astrantia, Aster*, bulbs, *Euphorbia*, ferns, *Galanthus*, grasses and sedges, *Hemerocallis* species, herbaceous perennials, *Lamium, Lathyrus, Monarda*, Pink Sheet plants ('pink sheets' are NCCPG search lists), *Pulmonaria, Ranunculus ficaria, Sedum, Solidago, Vinca*, rare shrubs and trees, variegated and wild collected plants. But the truth is that they list hundreds of other plants which are equally interesting. Many nurseries claim to have 'rare and unusual' plants: in the case of Monksilver, the boast is consistently true. A fifth of the catalogue changes each year.

Owned by Alan Leslie & Joe Sharman

Netherhall Manor

TANNERS LANE, SOHAM, ELY,
CB7 5AB

Tel 01353 720269
Location In middle of Soham: turn right off the
main road into Tanners Lane.
Opening hours 2 pm – 5 pm; 4 April, 2 May, 8 &
15 August.
Admission fee Adults £1.

This is an unusual garden, worth seeing for
its individual collections of genera and plant
groups which offer something of interest at
every season. Many came from the owner's
great-grandmother, who was a herbalist.
The hellebores are good in spring: a 30-year
old bed is devoted to the true *Helleborus*
'Potter's Wheel' and another to white
seedlings from Helen Ballard. Elsewhere are
the seldom-seen *Helleborus* 'Günther Jürgl'
(one of the first of the upright-facing,
double cultivars), *H.* 'Circe' (long thought to
be extinct, but saved by Nancy Lindsay) and
H. 'Taurus'. Other goodies include *Primula
auricula* 'Duke of Edinburgh' (also once
thought extinct), florists' tulips, and a
complete collection of *Fritillaria imperialis*
cultivars. Better still is the collection of
19th-century *Pelargonium* cultivars,
including 'Turtle's Surprise', and 'Sophie
Dumaresque': all are grown from cuttings
every year. Calceolarias, heliotropes, turban
ranunculus and hyacinths are other
specialities. Some of the garden's progeny
are now finding their way into the *RHS
Plant Finder*, including *Heliotropium
arborescens* 'Netherhall White' and
Chrysanthemum 'Netherhall Moonlight'. The
one-acre garden is immaculately maintained
– its lawns are completely weedless – and
includes a neat kitchen garden area.

Features a great plantsman's garden;
hyacinths; Victorian pelargoniums;
florists' tulips.

Owned by Timothy Clark
Number of gardeners 1 part-time
Size 0.4ha (1 acre)

Peckover House & Garden

NORTH BRINK, WISBECH, PE13 1JR

Tel & Fax 01945 583463
Website www.nationaltrust.org.uk/peckover
Location Signed from Wisbech.
Opening hours Garden: 12.30 pm – 5 pm; daily;
21 March to 31 October.
Admission fee £2.75 (garden only).

Peckover is an exceptionally fine example of
a walled town garden, dating principally
from the 19th century, complete with
monkey puzzle, fernery and spotted laurel
shrubberies. It has good herbaceous
borders, Victorian bedding schemes, over 70
different roses, summerhouses and pool
gardens. Three of the orange trees in the
conservatory are 300 years old.

Features Victorian shrubberies;
orangery; fernery; good bedding;
herbaceous borders.

Owned by The National Trust
Number of gardeners 1½
Size 0.8ha (2 acres)
English Heritage Grade II

Wimpole Hall

ARRINGTON, ROYSTON, SG8 0BW

Tel 01223 207257 **Fax** 01223 207838
Website www.wimpole.org
Location On A603, south-west of Cambridge.
Opening hours 10.30 am – 5 pm; daily except
Monday & Friday (but open Good Friday & Bank
Holiday Mondays); 20 March to 31 October. Open
on Fridays in August. Also on Saturdays & Sundays
from 6 November to March 2005 from 11 am to 4
pm.
Admission fee Garden: £2.60. Park: free.

Wimpole is an important classical 18th-
century landscape where Bridgeman, Brown
and Repton have all left their mark. It has a
fine 19th-century collection of trees in and
around the park, and grand Victorian
parterres, where 72 flower-beds are arranged
as eight Union Jack patterns and brightly
arrayed with 24,000 bedding plants. There is
a lot of new horticultural interest in the old
two-acre kitchen garden, where fruit and
vegetables are grown on a big scale to supply
the National Trust restaurant, and flowers
are grown for traditional decoration. An
improving garden.

Features woodland garden; daffodils;
Chinese bridge; parterre; traditional
greenhouses in walled garden; National
Trust shop; restaurant & tea-room.

Owned by The National Trust
Number of gardeners 3
NCCPG National Collections *Juglans*
English Heritage Grade I

CHESHIRE

Cheshire has a fair number of important historic landscapes, including Adlington Hall, Arley Hall, Eaton Hall, Lyme Park and Tatton Park, but none is important enough to be accorded Grade I status by English Heritage. Nevertheless, Cheshire has a good reputation for gardens and gardening: it is a prosperous county, with sandy soils and plenty of rainfall. This makes it a good area for nurseries and garden centres; probably the best known are Bridgemere Nurseries and Stapeley Water Gardens, both at Bridgemere, where the International Water Lily Society also has its base. Collinwood Nurseries at Mottram St Andrew is one of the leading growers of chrysanthemums, with an exceptionally comprehensive list of cultivars. Other specialist nurseries are Caddick's Clematis Nursery at Thelwall and the two rose nurseries C. & K. Jones at Tarvin and Fryer's Roses at Knutsford. The National Gardens Scheme lists a fair number of middle-sized gardens: azaleas and rhododendrons are particularly popular. Reaseheath College near Nantwich is a RHS Partner College.

Adlington Hall

MACCLESFIELD, SK10 4LF

Tel 01625 829206 **Fax** 01625 828756
Website www.adlingtonhall.com
Location 5 miles north of Macclesfield off A523.
Opening hours 2 pm – 5 pm; Wednesdays; June to August. Also throughout the year by prior appointment on weekdays for groups of 20 or more: telephone the guide on 01625 820875. Charity openings on 13 June (NGS), 18 July & 15 August. Nurseryman's plant sale on 9 May.
Admission fee £5 per person; £4 for groups of 20 or more. RHS members free.

It is good to see this important historic garden regularly open to the public again, and to know that the owners are adding their own improvements in another part of the estate. These include a maturing maze, a rose garden and the 'Father Tiber' water garden. Last year (2003) saw the addition of a Penstemon Garden. Many of the historical features have been restored: some are still awaiting their turn. One of the oldest is an avenue of yews planted in 1660. An ancient avenue of lime trees, planted in 1688 to celebrate the accession of William and Mary, leads to a woodland wilderness with follies. These include a Shell Cottage (1750s), a Temple to Diana, a Chinese bridge and a Hermitage.

Features historic landscape; ancient lime avenue; woodland garden; tea-room.

Owned by Mrs C.J.C. Legh
Number of gardeners 4
English Heritage Grade II*

Arley Hall

GREAT BUDWORTH, NORTHWICH,
CW9 6NA

Tel 01565 777353 **Fax** 01565 777465
Website www.arleyhalland gardens.com
Location 5 miles west of Knutsford.
Opening hours 11 am – 5 pm; Tuesday – Sunday &
Bank Holidays; 3 April to 26 September. Plus
weekends in October.
Admission fee Adults £4.50; OAPs £3.90; Children
£2.20. RHS members free, except during special events.

Arley has pleached limes, red *Primula
florindae*, clipped ilex cylinders (10 metres
high), pretty old roses and a magnificent
collection of rhododendrons, azaleas and
rare trees and shrubs. But its claim to fame
is the double herbaceous border, backed and
buttressed by yew hedges, perhaps the oldest
in England. The arboretum has been built
by Lord Ashbrook over the last 30 years and
is underplanted with rhododendrons,
azaleas and flowering shrubs.

Features topiary; avenues; two walled
gardens; roses (mainly old-fashioned);
good herbaceous borders; shop; nursery;
lunches & light refreshments.

Owned by Viscount Ashbrook
Number of gardeners 4
Size 5ha (12½ acres)
English Heritage Grade II*

Bluebell Cottage Gardens & Lodge Lane Nursery

LODGE LANE, DUTTON,
WARRINGTON, WA4 4HP

Tel & Fax 01928 713718
Website www.lodgelanenursery.co.uk

Location Turn off A533 midway between Runcorn
& Northwich.
Opening hours Nursery: 10 am – 5 pm;
Wednesday – Sunday & Bank Holidays; mid March
to mid September. Garden: noon – 5 pm; Saturdays,
Sundays & Bank Holidays; May to August.
Admission fee Adults £3; Children free. RHS
members free. Nursery free at all times.

Lodge Lane Nursery sells more than 2,000
different herbaceous plants: it is particularly
strong on penstemons, but there are big
collections of achilleas, alliums, asters,
campanulas, digitalis, euphorbias,
geraniums, nepeta, salvias and ornamental
grasses too. Bluebell Cottage Gardens are
the nursery's show gardens, well worth a
visit in their own right. Both were started
as recently as 1993. The gardens have been
developed as a series of smaller gardens-
within-the-garden. Each has a different
theme: among them are the herb garden,
the yellow garden, the ornamental grass
garden and the scree bed. Large island beds
are used to display herbaceous plants: the
owners believe that there is nothing to beat
them for colour (and sheer garden value)
from early to late summer. The wildflower
meadow was started in 1994 – three acres of
native flowers among the grasses, including
perennial cornflowers, scabious, yarrows,
red clover and meadow cranesbill. At the
far side of the meadow are three more
acres of native woodland, carpeted with
bluebells in May. Three RHS special events
will take place during 2004: details from
020 7821 3408.

Features wildflower meadow; 3,000
different plants.

Owned by Rod & Diane Casey
Number of gardeners owners, plus a little part-
time help
Size 0.6ha (1½ acres), plus meadow & woodland
NCCPG National Collections *Inula*

Bridgemere Garden World

BRIDGEMERE, NANTWICH, CW5 7QB

Tel 01270 521100 **Fax** 01270 520215
Location M6 Jct 15 & 16: follow signs.
Opening hours 9 am – 7 pm (6 pm in winter); daily; all year except 25 & 26 December.
Admission fee Free.

More than twenty immaculate show gardens in different styles are the attraction of Bridgemere. They are intended to give you ideas on design and planting for your own garden. There is a very wide range of interesting plants for sale, too. Definitely worth a visit, whatever the season. The RHS will be running two regional lectures at Bridgemere in 2004, on 13 May & 30 September: details from 020 7821 3408.

Features woodland garden; roses (ancient & modern); rock garden; plantsman's collection of plants; herbs; plants under glass; fruit; good herbaceous borders; several shops, as well as the famous garden centre; restaurant & coffee shop.

Owned by J. Ravenscroft
Number of gardeners 3
Size 2.4ha (6 acres)

Capesthorne Hall

SIDDINGTON, MACCLESFIELD, SK11 9JY

Tel 01625 861221 **Fax** 01625 861619
Website www.capesthorne.com
Location A34, 3 miles south of Alderley Edge.
Opening hours 12 noon – 5 pm; Wednesdays, Sundays & Bank Holidays; April to October. Charity open day 4 August 2004.
Admission fee Adults £4; OAPs £3; Children £2.

There are lots of interesting things to see at Capesthorne Hall, provided you are prepared to explore the grounds and find them. Fine trees are certainly a feature: the Victorian arboretum contains some very vigorous wellingtonias and chestnuts, supplemented by recent plantings over the last 50 years. Vernon Russell-Smith designed the formal lakeside gardens in the 1960s: mixed borders of shrub roses and herbaceous plants. Along the rhododendron walk is a splendid mixture of hardy hybrids interspersed with *Rhododendron ponticum* and the sweet-scented *Rhododendron luteum.* They flourish under a canopy of tall English oaks and wild cherries. Here too are two cork trees, *Quercus suber.* By the time you have discovered the rose arbour, the avenue of American hawthorns, the ice house and the golden glade (planted to commemorate the golden wedding of Sir Walter and Lady Bromley-Davenport in 1983), you will have some measure of just how much the garden has to offer.

Features woodland garden; fine collection of trees; historic park; tea-room.

Owned by W.A. Bromley-Davenport
Number of gardeners 2

Cholmondeley Castle Gardens

MALPAS, SY14 8AH

Tel 01829 720383 **Fax** 01829 720877
Location Off A49 Tarporley-Whitchurch road.
Opening hours 11.30 am – 5 pm; Wednesdays, Thursdays, Sundays & Bank Holidays. 4 April to 26 September. Rare Plant Sale on 11 July.
Admission fee Adults £3.50; Children £1.50. RHS members free in June.

The gardens below this handsome early 19th-century castle set in rolling parkland have been redeveloped since the 1960s with horticultural advice from Jim Russell. The new plantings have been well integrated into the classical landscape and have added an entirely new horticultural dimension to the landscape. The exquisite temple garden, curling the whole way around a small lake, is breathtakingly beautiful. Highly recommended.

 Features woodland garden; rock garden; good herbaceous borders; fine collection of trees; azaleas & rhododendrons; gift shop; tea-room, light lunches, home-made teas.

Owned by The Marchioness of Cholmondeley
English Heritage Grade II

Dorfold Hall

NANTWICH, CW5 8LD

Tel 01270 625245 **Fax** 01270 628723
Location 1 mile west of Nantwich on A534.
Opening hours 2 pm – 5 pm; Tuesdays & Bank Holiday Mondays; April to October. Also 2 pm – 5.30 pm on 23 May for National Gardens Scheme.
Admission fee House & gardens: Adults £5; Children £3. National Gardens Scheme day: Adults £4; Children £2.

Ⓟ 🐎

William Andrews Nesfield designed the formal approach but the main reason for visiting the gardens at Dorfold Hall is the new woodland garden of rhododendrons and other shrubs, leading down to a stream where *Primula pulverulenta* has naturalised in its thousands. Do not miss the incredible hulk of an ancient Spanish chestnut in the stable yard.

 Features spring woodland garden; camellias; magnolias; rhododendrons & azaleas; daffodils & bluebells; good summer herbaceous borders.

Owned by R.C. Roundell
Number of gardeners 2
Size 7.2ha (18 acres)
English Heritage Grade II

Dunge Valley Hidden Gardens

KETTLESHULME, HIGH PEAK, SK23 7RF

Tel & Fax 01663 733787
Website www.dungevalley.co.uk
Location 1 mile south of Kettleshulme village: follow brown tourist signs and turn down a minor road towards Goyt Valley.
Opening hours 10.30 am – 5 pm. Thursday – Sunday in March and from 14 June to 31 August. Daily except Mondays from 1 April to 13 June. Open on Bank Holiday Mondays.
Admission fee Adults £3; Children 50p.

These hidden gardens 300m up in the Pennines are a surprise and a delight: few are so high, and fewer still so full of colour. It is not only the number of plants which gives such pleasure, but the surprise of finding so many that one might suppose too tender – embothriums, desfontainias and mahonias, for example. But there are also fine rhododendrons, old-fashioned roses and flowering borders in an almost Himalayan setting. The nursery has one of the largest selections of rhododendrons for sale in England.

 Features rhododendrons & azaleas; roses; hardy trees & shrubs; tea-room; lunches & light refreshments.

Owned by David & Elizabeth Ketley
Number of gardeners 2
Size 2.2ha (6 acres)

Granada Arboretum

JODRELL BANK, MACCLESFIELD, SK11 9DL

Tel 01477 571339 **Fax** 01477 571695
Location On A535 between Holmes Chapel & Chelford.
Opening hours 10.30 am – 4.30 pm; daily; mid-March to October. 10.30 am – 3 pm; weekdays; November to mid-March.
Admission fee £3 car park fee (pay & display).

The Granada Arboretum at Jodrell Bank was founded by Sir Bernard Lovell in 1971 with funding from the Granada Foundation. This wonderful arboretum specialises in alders, birches, crab apples, pine and *Sorbus*. Long straight drives lead spaciously into the distance. The plantings are young and vigorous, the groupings imaginative. Alas, the collections of heaths (*Erica*) and heathers (*Calluna*) became diseased and have had to be removed, but the other plantings are growing apace. A huge radio telescope dominates the site: an awesome presence.

Features shop; self-service cafeteria.

Owned by Manchester University
Number of gardeners 2
Size 14ha (35 acres)
NCCPG National Collections *Malus*; *Sorbus*

Hare Hill Garden

GARDEN LODGE, OVER ALDERLEY, MACCLESFIELD, SK10 4QB

Tel 01625 828981
Website www.nationaltrust.org.uk
Location Between Alderley Edge & Prestbury.
Opening hours 10 am – 5 pm; Wednesdays, Thursdays, Saturday, Sundays & Bank Holiday Mondays; 1 April to 30 October. Open daily from 10 to 30 May for rhododendrons & azaleas.
Admission fee Adults £2.75; Children £1.25.

Hare Hill is a woodland garden, thickly planted with trees and underplanted with rhododendrons, azaleas and shrubs by Jim Russell in the 1960s. In the middle is a walled garden which has been developed as a flower garden with a pergola, arbour and tender plants against the walls. Planting continues with new cultivars. Perhaps best in May, there are still some rhododendrons to flower with the roses in July.

Features woodland garden; rock garden; plantsman's collection of plants; good herbaceous borders.

Owned by The National Trust
Number of gardeners 1½
Size 4ha (10 acres)

Little Moreton Hall

CONGLETON, CW12 4SD

Tel 01260 272018
Website www.nationaltrust.org.uk
Location 4 miles south of Congleton on A34.
Opening hours 11.30 am – 5 pm (or dusk, if earlier); Wednesday – Sunday & Bank Holiday Mondays; 20 March to 31 October. 11.30 am – 4 pm; Saturdays & Sundays; 6 November to 19 December.
Admission fee Adults £5; Children £2.50.

Little Moreton Hall is the handsomest timber-framed house in England – an icon of domestic Tudor architecture. When the National Trust asked Graham Stuart Thomas to design and plant a suitable period garden, he specified box-edged borders with yew topiary and gravel infilling – and very fine they are too. A speciality has been made of old varieties of fruit, vegetables and herbs around the knot garden. Peaceful, charming and orderly.

 Features herbs; fruit; good herbaceous borders; restaurant – lunches, coffee, teas.

Owned by The National Trust
Number of gardeners 1
Size 0.4ha (1 acre)
English Heritage Grade I

Lyme Park

DISLEY, SK12 2NX

Tel 01663 762023 **Fax** 01663 765035
Website www.nationaltrust.org.uk
Location 6½ miles south-east of Stockport on A6, just west of Disley.
Opening hours 11 am – 5 pm (but 1 pm – 5 pm on Wednesdays & Thursdays); daily; 29 March to 30 October. Plus 12 noon – 3 pm; Saturdays & Sundays; 1 November to 18 December.
Admission fee Garden only: Adults £2.70; Children £1.40. Plus £3.80 for car (National Trust members free).

There is much of horticultural interest at Lyme, as well as the razzmatazz of a country park: traditional bedding out, two enormous camellias in the conservatory, and a Jekyll-type herbaceous border by Graham Stuart Thomas where the colours run from orange to deepest purple. Best of all is the sunken Dutch garden whose looping box and ivy parterres contain the most extravagant bedding displays. The National Trust has now assumed full control of the garden and restored the structure in line with the original Lewis Wyatt design. Lyme Park featured as Pemberley in the BBC's *Pride & Prejudice*.

 Features roses (mainly old-fashioned); good herbaceous borders; spring bulbs; bedding out; orangery by Wyatt; 'Dutch'

garden shop; restaurant & coffee shop (April to October).

Owned by The National Trust
Number of gardeners 4
Size 6.7ha (17 acres)
English Heritage Grade II*

Mellors Garden

HOUGH HOLE HOUSE, RAINOW, MACCLESFIELD, SK10 5UW

Tel 01625 573251 **Fax** 01625 572389
Location In Sugar Lane.
Opening hours 2 pm – 5 pm; 31 May & 30 August. And by appointment.
Admission fee £1.50.

This remarkable small garden was laid out in the 19th century as an allegory of Christian's journey in *Pilgrim's Progress* and originally planted only with plants that are mentioned in the Bible. Features represent such places as the Wall of Salvation, the Cave of the Holy Sepulchre, Vanity Fayre, the Dark River, the Delectable Mountains, Doubting Castle and the Celestial City. A spiritual and historical experience more than a horticultural one.

 Features refreshments by arrangement.

Owned by Mr & Mrs A. Rigby
Size 0.8ha (2 acres)

Norton Priory Museum & Gardens

TUDOR ROAD, RUNCORN, WA7 1SX

Tel 01928 569895
Location Well signed locally.
Opening hours 12 noon – 5 pm (6 pm at weekends & Bank Holidays) daily; March – October.
Admission fee Adults £4.25; OAPs £2.95.

Ness Botanic Gardens

NESTON, CH64 4AY

Tel 0151 353 0123 **Fax** 0151 353 1004
Website www.merseyworld.com/nessgardens
Location Signed off A540, Chester to Hoylake.
Opening hours 9.30 am – 4 pm (5 pm from March
to October); daily; all year. Closed 25 December.
Admission fee Adults £4.70; Concessions £4.30.
£3.70 from November to January.

Ness was the creation of a Liverpool
cotton merchant, Arthur Bulley, who
laid out the garden in 1898 and started to
plant it with new species from abroad. He
was particularly interested in Himalayan
and Chinese plants: he believed that many
could become established in cultivation in
Britain and he therefore sponsored such
plant collectors as George Forrest and Frank
Kingdon Ward. It is to Bulley that we owe
such plants as *Gentiana sino-ornata* and
Pieris formosa var. *forrestii*, and it was at
Ness that many Chinese plants were first
grown in Europe – notably the candelabra
primulas. Ness was presented to the
University of Liverpool by Bulley's daughter
in 1948 and has continued to develop as a
public amenity, a tourist attraction and a
teaching garden, while still retaining the
'feel' of a private garden. It is beautifully laid
out in a sequence of incidents: both its
design and plantings have continued to
improve year by year. The main features are
as follows: a laburnum arch; a herb garden;
a rhododendron border (long and deep)
underplanted with many lilies; an excellent
heather garden; sandstone terraces where
tender plants like *Ribes speciosum* flourish; a
rock garden with an enormous range of
different environments, south-facing and
north-facing, limestone and sandstone,
sunny, shaded and damp; a water garden; a
camellia collection; an arboretum; a willow
collection recognised by the NCCPG as a
National Collection; herbaceous borders;
and a series of glasshouses with temperate,
arid and tropical sections for such plants as
Lonicera hildebrandiana, the crown of
thorns (*Euphorbia milii*) and important
economic plants like cotton, sugar cane,
kapok and papyrus. As with all botanic
gardens, there is no end of things to see
whatever the season, and your visit can be as
short or as long as it suits. In practice,
however, Ness is one of those gardens where
you tend to spend much longer than you
intended. A £3m development plan started
in October 2003 to conserve and enhance
the plant collections and emphasise its
educational work. The Friends of Ness are
very active and the website, too, is very
comprehensive.

Features roses (mainly old-fashioned);
mature conifers; fine collection of
trees; 30-metre laburnum arch; camellia
walk; notable collections of *Sorbus*, *Betula*,
Salix & *Cotoneaster*; tallest *Alnus
cremastogyne* (3.3m.) in the British Isles; gift
shop; tea-room.

Owned by University of Liverpool
Number of gardeners 11
Size 26ha (65 acres)
English Heritage Grade II

The old walled garden at Norton Priory has a new lay-out modelled on 18th-century precedents and intended to instruct and please visitors. A cottage garden border, a medicinal herb garden and orchard rub shoulders with colour borders, children's gardens and a scented garden. Beyond are 16 acres of woodland garden with Georgian summerhouses and glades by the stream.

 Features roses (ancient & modern); rock garden; herbs; fruit; good herbaceous borders; current holder of Sandford Award; garden produce shop; refreshments at museum site.

Owned by Norton Priory Museum Trust (Halton Borough Council)
Number of gardeners 2
Size 15ha (38 acres)
NCCPG National Collections Cydonia oblonga

Peover Hall

OVER PEOVER, KNUTSFORD, WA16 9HW

Tel 01565 722656 **Fax** 01565 722611
Location 3 miles south of Knutsford.
Opening hours 2 pm – 5 pm; Mondays & Thursdays; May to September. And 15 & 16 May for NGS.
Admission fee Adults £2.

First a classic 18th-century parkland, then an Edwardian overlay of formal gardens – yew hedges and brick paths. Now Peover has modern plantings too – borders in colour combinations, a herb garden, and a rhododendron dell in the woods.

 Features topiary; roses (mainly old-fashioned); herbs; walled garden; landscaped park; rhododendrons; tea-room (Mondays only).

Owned by R. Brooks Ltd.
Number of gardeners 3
Size 10.3ha (26 acres)
English Heritage Grade II

The Quinta

SWETTENHAM VILLAGE, CONGLETON, CW12 2LD

Tel 01270 610180 **Fax** 01270 610430
Website www.wildlifetrust.org.uk/cheshire/
Location Access through the garden of Swettenham Arms.
Opening hours Dawn – dusk; daily; all year.
Admission fee Adults £2; Children £1. RHS members free.

The Quinta Arboretum was created by Sir Bernard Lovell, originator of the Jodrell Bank Radio Telescope, and is now owned by the Cheshire Wildlife Trust. The garden features more than 5,000 trees and shrubs, with beautiful views over the River Dane meanders. Grand avenues lead to the ancient woodland nature reserve with flower-rich meadows grazed by rare-breed sheep. A wonderful site to visit in all seasons. A new association with the Tatton Garden Society promises well for the future.

 Features nice young arboretum; wildflowers; woodland garden.

Owned by Cheshire Wildlife Trust
Size 16ha (40 acres)
NCCPG National Collections Fraxinus; Pinus

Reaseheath College

NANTWICH, CW5 6DF

Tel 01270 625131 **Fax** 01270 625665
Website www.reaseheath.ac.uk
Location 1 mile north of Nantwich on A51.
Opening hours 2 pm – 4 pm; Wednesdays; 19 &
26 May, & 2 June. College Open Day 11 am – 5 pm
on 23 May. Guided tours for groups at other times.
Admission fee Donation to NGS.

Reaseheath has been thoroughly replanted
recently: there is an enormous amount to
enjoy and learn here. Highlights include a
woodland garden, a model fruit garden, a
lake, a gravel garden, good bedding on the
formal terraces and splendid mixed borders.
There will be a very large number of RHS
special events at Reaseheath during 2004:
details from 020 7821 3408.

Features woodland garden;
rhododendrons & azaleas; good
herbaceous borders; fine collection of trees;
heather garden; formal bedding; Reaseheath
Garden Centre, open daily, all year; shop &
coffee lounge.

Owned by Reaseheath College
Number of gardeners 2
Size 12ha (30 acres)

Rode Hall

CHURCH LANE, SCHOLAR GREEN,
STOKE ON TRENT, ST7 3QP

Tel 01270 882961 **Fax** 01270 882962
Location 5 miles south-west of Congleton between
A34 & A50.
Opening hours 2 pm – 5 pm; Tuesday – Thursday
& Bank Holiday Mondays; 1 April to 30 September.
Plus 1.30 pm – 5.30 pm on 11 May for National
Gardens Scheme & 12 noon – 4 pm from 7 to 22
February for snowdrops.

Admission fee Garden only: Adults £3; OAPs £2.
RHS members free.

Stand on the terraces at Rode Hall and take
in the prospect: William Andrews Nesfield's
1860s rose garden and Humphry Repton's
landscape beyond. The 'pool' is nearly a mile
long and 150 yards wide. But horticulture is
also here in abundance: take the boathouse
walk past the old stew pond (pretty
marginals and a waterfall) to the wildflower
garden (terraced rock garden – early 19th-
century – *very* early for this sort of garden)
where snowdrops, sarcococcas, hellebores
(lots), ferns, primroses and soldanellas
flourish in the lee of rhododendrons. Note
the splendid Loderi crosses, which smell of
sugared almonds and extend the flowering
season into early June. Admire Professor
Pratt's scented azaleas (would that more
people knew and grew them) and note how
the plantings of rhododendron species are
being extended into the adjacent Old Wood.
Then visit the walled kitchen garden (about
two acres) and see the rows of decorative
vegetables set between cornflowers, poppies,
marigolds and flowers for drying. Espaliered
fruit trees cover the walls between 4m
abutilons: Cheshire has a mild climate. Look
inside the greenhouses and see the many
geraniums with scented leaves. And ponder
the industry of the head gardener, Kelvin
Archer, who grows over 40 cultivars of
gooseberry here and holds the world record
for the largest gooseberry fruit.

Features woodland garden; topiary;
snowdrops; roses (mainly old-
fashioned); fruit; mature conifers; ice house;
rhododendrons; grotto; laburnum walk;
fully functional two-acre walled kitchen
garden; garden produce; cream teas.

Owned by Sir Richard Baker Wilbraham
Number of gardeners 2
Size 2.4ha (6 acres)
English Heritage Grade II

Stapeley Water Gardens

LONDON ROAD, STAPELEY, NANTWICH, CW5 7LH

Tel 01270 623868 **Fax** 01270 624919
Website www.stapeleywatergardens.com
Location A51, 1 mile south of Nantwich.
Opening hours 10 am – 6 pm (5 pm in winter); daily; all year except 12 April & 25 December. Nursery opens at 9 am Monday – Saturday & 10 am on Sundays; closes at 6 pm (but 5 pm in winter, 4 pm on Sundays & 8 pm on summer Wednesdays).
Admission fee The Palms Tropical Oasis: Adults £4.35; OAPs £3.90; Children £2.50.

Part entertainment, part nursery and part display garden, the Palms Tropical Oasis is worth a visit in its own right. A long rectangular pool in the Moorish style is flanked by tall palms, strelitzias and other showy tropical flowers. The display gardens outside are fascinating all through the year, especially the water gardens where all the waterlilies grow.

Features plants under glass; collection of hardy water lilies; *Victoria regia*, the giant water lily; major nursery & garden centre; cafeteria & terrace restaurant.

Owned by Stapeley Water Gardens Ltd
NCCPG National Collections *Nymphaea*

Tatton Park

KNUTSFORD, WA16 6QN

Tel 01625 534400 **Fax** 01625 534403
Website www.tattonpark.org.uk
Location Off M6 Jct 19 & M56 Jct 7 – well signed.
Opening hours 10 am – 6 pm; Tuesday – Sunday, plus Bank Holiday Mondays; all year, but open 11 am – 4 pm from 5 October to 25 March 2005.
Admission fee Adults £3; Children £2. RHS members free. Car parking charges apply.

Humphry Repton laid out the parkland at Tatton. Joseph Paxton designed both the formal Italian garden and the exquisite fernery, claimed as the finest in the UK. Later came a Japanese garden (restored for the Japanese festival in 2001) and Shinto temple (1910), such follies as the African hut, and the mass plantings of rhododendrons and azaleas. Work on restoring the walled garden and its glasshouses continues apace. Tatton Park is wonderfully well organised for visitors, and gets better every year. Be prepared for a long and absorbing visit. The RHS Flower Show at Tatton Park will take place from 21 to 25 July 2004 (tickets from 0870 906 3810).

Features good herbaceous borders; fine collection of trees; rhododendrons & azaleas in May; biggest *Quercus* x *schochiana* in the British Isles; current holder of Sandford Award; Europa Nostra award for restored orangery & fernery; shop (closed Mondays); restaurant (closed Mondays in winter).

Owned by The National Trust (managed by Cheshire County Council)
Number of gardeners 13
Size 20ha (50 acres)
NCCPG National Collections *Adiantum*
English Heritage Grade II*

CORNWALL

Many of the great historic gardens of Cornwall are also the most interesting horticulturally. Mount Edgcumbe and Tresco are both rated Grade I gardens of national importance, while Caerhays Castle, Lanhydrock, Tregrehan and Trewithen are Grade II* and Antony, Carclew, Chyverton, Cotehele, Glendurgan, Heligan, Lamellen, Pencarrow, Penjerrick, St Michael's Mount, Trebah, Trelissick and Trengwainton are all Grade II. It is a proud list, unmatched by any other county, and evidence of how the big estates have always dominated the gardening scene in Cornwall. The county still has its own horticultural organisation, the Cornwall Garden Society: its spring show is a showcase for camellias and rhododendrons. About 80 gardens open every year for the Cornwall Festival of Spring Gardens which runs from mid-March to the end of May: details from the Cornwall Tourist Board on 01872 322900. Almost all the gardens have fine collections of trees too: those at Trebah, Tregrehan and Trewithen are particularly noted for the age and size of their specimens, while the woodlands of Caerhays contain an exceptional number of well-grown rarities. Unfortunately the great camellia garden at Trehane is now closed to the public, following a change in ownership in 2001. A new type of Cornish garden has, however, been emerging over the last 25 years, where the owners have taken advantage of the climate to grow a very wide range of newer plants: Pine Lodge, Lamorran and Bosvigo are good examples and will doubtless be followed by others. The county's National Collections reflect the opportunities which the mild climate makes possible: among them are *Escallonia* at Duchy College (a RHS Partner College), *Azara* at Trelissick, *Grevillea* at Pine Lodge and *Acacia* at Tresco. Finest of all is the National Collection of *Dahlia* at Varfell Farm at Long Rock, just off the A30, where some 2,000 species and cultivars can be seen by prior appointment (further details from 01736 711271). Cornish nurseries cater well for the local market: the Duchy of Cornwall Nursery at Lostwithiel has the largest stock of all, while tender exotica are the speciality of Trevena Cross Garden Centre near Helston and Lower Kenneggy Nurseries near Penzance. Best known is Burncoose & South Down Nurseries, a regular winner of Gold Medals for its spectacular displays of flowering trees and shrubs at RHS shows throughout the year.

Antony

<small>TORPOINT, PL11 2QA</small>

Tel & Fax 01752 812364
Website www.nationaltrust.org.uk
Location 5 miles west of Plymouth, 2 miles north-west of Torpoint.
Opening hours 1.30 pm – 5.30 pm; Tuesday – Thursday & Bank Holiday Mondays; 30 March to 28 October; also 1.30 pm – 5.30 pm on Sundays from June to August. Last admissions 4.45 pm.
Admission fee Adults £2.50; Children £1.25. Combined ticket with Antony Woodland Garden: Adults £4; Children £2.

Antony has been an historic and important garden for centuries – and every generation has left its mark. Its classic late 18th-century landscape is superb, though there is considerable debate as to whether Humphry Repton designed it or the Pole-Carews (as they were then called) listened to Repton's advice but followed little of it. The yew walk with its lead statues of a shepherd and his shepherdess and the huge Burmese temple bell, flanked by stone lanterns, date from the 19th century. Much of the horticultural interest was created by Sir John Carew Pole in the middle of the twentieth century – masses of bulbs, the lime-tree avenues, over 600 early *Hemerocallis* hybrids from the USA, a 9.2m loquat tree (*Eriobotrya japonica*) against the house, the vast cork oak (*Quercus suber*) (another record-breaker), the venerable old 'Black Walnut' (*Juglans nigra*) on the main lawn and the beautiful spring-flowering *Magnolia denudata*. The position is superb – an elevated promontory above the Tamar estuary, just across Plymouth Sound from Devon. Sir Richard and Lady Carew Pole, who now live at Antony, have continued to intensify and extend this plantsman's garden: more spring-flowering trees and shrubs have been planted, alongside the creation of gardens for summer and autumn interest. The Summer Garden is particularly effective: hybrid musk roses are underplanted with lilies, irises, phlox and peonies and its walls are covered in clematis, climbing roses, lemon-scented verbena and *Cytisus battandieri*. But there is much to see at every season – the magnolia walk in spring, the knot garden, the terraces in high summer with giant catmint (*Nepeta* 'Six Hills Giant') mingling with the floribunda rose 'Iceberg' and free-standing fig-trees *Ficus carica* 'White Marseilles' in autumn. And it is a large garden, so you need to allow a lot of time to do it justice.

Features mature conifers; good herbaceous borders; magnolias; yew hedges; tallest Japanese loquat *Eriobotrya japonica* (9.2m.) in the British Isles (and two other tree records); tea-room open at 12.30 pm.

Owned by The National Trust
Number of gardeners 3, plus 2 trainees
Size 14ha (35 acres)
NCCPG National Collections *Hemerocallis*
English Heritage Grade II

Antony Woodland Garden

<small>ANTONY HOUSE, TORPOINT, PL11 2QA</small>

Tel & Fax 01752 812364
Location 5 miles west of Plymouth, 2 miles north-west of Torpoint.
Opening hours 11 am – 5.30 pm; daily except Mondays & Fridays (but open on Bank Holidays); 1 March to 30 October.
Admission fee Adults £3.50; Accompanied Children free.

This is the 'Cornish' part of the grounds at Antony, still controlled by the Carew Pole family rather than the National Trust. It is a garden of considerable botanical interest divided into two main areas. First comes the Wilderness, a wooded area to the north-west of the house which runs down to the banks of the River Lynher. Three vistas frame the house from the river: Humphry Repton's influence is clearly apparent here. The Wilderness has been planted with trees and shrubs like Japanese maples, a tunnel of *Camellia* x *williamsii* 'Donation' and *Camellia japonica* 'Lady de Saumarez', *Magnolia obovata*, rhododendron species and hybrids including the strongly scented 'Loderi' and *R. griffithianum*. There is a conifer dell with giant redwoods *Sequoiadendron giganteum*, *Cryptomeria japonica* and *Taxus baccata* 'Dovastoniana' and three ponds cascading down a valley to the salt pans and the Bath House pond. The second area is Westdown, where the planting consists mainly of camellias of considerable variety (including the National Collection of *Camellia japonica*) interspersed with Asiatic magnolias and rhododendron species, thriving in the deep valley. The magnolias include specimens of 'Charles Raffill', *M. dawsoniana*, and *M. campbellii* subsp. *mollicomata* 'Lanarth'. The two areas are joined by the Garden Field where ornamental trees have been underplanted with flowering shrubs and daffodils. A path through deep-scented shrubs and birches completes the link along the river's edge. The Carew Poles have also commissioned several pieces of contemporary sculpture for the garden and the wider estate.

Features woodland garden; plantsman's collection of plants; mature conifers; camellias; magnolias; rhododendrons & azaleas; tea-room as for Antony (q.v.).

Owned by The Carew Pole Garden Trust
Number of gardeners 1
Size 26ha (65 acres)
NCCPG National Collections *Camellia japonica*

The Barbara Hepworth Museum & Sculpture Garden

2 BARNOON HILL, ST IVES, TR26 1TG

Tel 01736 796226 **Fax** 01736 794480
Website www.tate.org.uk/stives/hepworth.htm
Location In town centre.
Opening hours 10.30 am – 5.30 pm; daily; March to October. 10.30 am – 4.30 pm; Tuesday-Sunday; November to March. Closed 23-26 December.
Admission fee Adults £4.25; Concessions £2.25. Free to over-60s and under-18s.

Dame Barbara Hepworth's studio and garden have been run by the Tate Gallery since 1980. Hepworth died in 1975, and asked (in her will) that Trewyn studios and the subtropical garden should become a permanent setting to exhibit her works. Visiting it gives you a remarkable insight into one of the 20th century's most important sculptors.

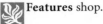**Features** shop.

Owned by Tate Gallery & Hepworth Estate
Number of gardeners 2
Size 0.2ha (½ acre)
English Heritage Grade II

Bosahan

MANACCAN, HELSTON, TR12 6JL

Tel 01326 231351 **Fax** 01326 231497
Location Off Manaccan to St Anthony Road; or uphill from Treath & first left.
Opening hours By appointment on weekdays; groups preferred.
Admission fee Adults £4; Children free.

Bosahan is a steep valley garden, dating from the 19th century but restored and revived by Christine Graham-Vivian, who is a garden designer. The collection of rhododendrons, magnolias, azaleas, conifers, camellias and tender trees is excellent. Down by the lake are good plantings of bog-plants and marginals. Bosahan is said to have been the inspiration for Daphne du Maurier's novel 'Rebecca'.

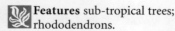 **Features** sub-tropical trees; rhododendrons.

Owned by Mr & Mrs R.J. Graham-Vivian
Number of gardeners 1
Size 4ha (10 acres)

Bosvigo

BOSVIGO LANE, TRURO, TR1 3NH

Tel & Fax 01872 275774
Website www.bosvigo.com
Location Turn off A390 at Highertown just west of Sainsbury's roundabout, then 500 yards down Dobbs Lane.
Opening hours 11 am – 6 pm; Thursdays & Fridays; 4 March to 30 September.
Admission fee Adults £3; Children (5-15) £1.

Not a typical Cornish garden, the emphasis at Bosvigo is upon herbaceous plants, chosen for their individual qualities and planted in fine colour combinations. The woodland garden is more traditional, and underplanted with snowdrops, hellebores, wood anemones, erythroniums and epimediums, but the rest of the garden is at its best in summer and keeps well into the autumn. Over the last 20 years or so, Wendy & Michael Perry have created a series of small walled or hedged garden 'rooms' around the mainly Georgian house. Each has its own colour theme: the walled garden heaves with polite blues, mauves and pinks

while another is mainly of gold and white. Reds and oranges co-exist in a 'hot' garden which, according to Patrick Taylor in the *Daily Telegraph,* 'will blow your socks off'. Many of the plants are rare, and some are sold in the small specialist nursery.

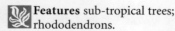 **Features** woodland garden; plantsman's collection of plants; good herbaceous borders; unusual perennials; Victorian conservatory; colour borders; excellent small herbaceous nursery.

Owned by Wendy & Michael Perry
Number of gardeners owners only
Size 0.8ha (2 acres)

Burncoose Gardens & Nurseries

GWENNAP, REDRUTH, TR16 6BJ

Tel 01209 860316 **Fax** 01209 860011
Website www.burncoose.co.uk
Location Directly on the A393 Redruth to Falmouth road between the villages of Lanner & Ponsanooth.
Opening hours 8.30 am – 5 pm (11 am – 5 pm on Sundays); daily except 25 December; all year.
Admission fee Gardens: Adults £2; Children free. Nursery free.

Burncoose Nurseries specialise in rare and unusual plants: they list over 3,500 different ones – mainly ornamental trees and shrubs – which makes them one of the best for sheer choice in all Europe. Their real specialities are camellias, rhododendrons, magnolias and conservatory plants. Burncoose has won 18 gold medals at the last 23 Chelsea Flower Shows and numerous gold medals at Hampton Court, Tatton Park and other shows. The garden is a woodland garden, carpeted with bluebells, primroses, snowdrops and wild violets in spring. Two monkey puzzles *Araucaria araucana* are over 30m (100ft) high and a *Eucryphia* x

Caerhays Castle Gardens

GORRAN, ST AUSTELL, PL26 6LY

Tel 01872 501310 **Fax** 01872 501870
Website www.caerhays.co.uk
Location Between Mevagissey & Portloe.
Opening hours 10 am – 5.30 pm; daily; 16
February to 31 May.
Admission fee Adults £5.50; Children (5-16) £2.50.
RHS members free from 16 February to 16 March.

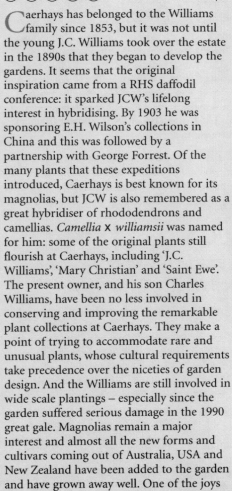

Caerhays has belonged to the Williams family since 1853, but it was not until the young J.C. Williams took over the estate in the 1890s that they began to develop the gardens. It seems that the original inspiration came from a RHS daffodil conference: it sparked JCW's lifelong interest in hybridising. By 1903 he was sponsoring E.H. Wilson's collections in China and this was followed by a partnership with George Forrest. Of the many plants that these expeditions introduced, Caerhays is best known for its magnolias, but JCW is also remembered as a great hybridiser of rhododendrons and camellias. *Camellia* x *williamsii* was named for him: some of the original plants still flourish at Caerhays, including 'J.C. Williams', 'Mary Christian' and 'Saint Ewe'. The present owner, and his son Charles Williams, have been no less involved in conserving and improving the remarkable plant collections at Caerhays. They make a point of trying to accommodate rare and unusual plants, whose cultural requirements take precedence over the niceties of garden design. And the Williams are still involved in wide scale plantings – especially since the garden suffered serious damage in the 1990 great gale. Magnolias remain a major interest and almost all the new forms and cultivars coming out of Australia, USA and New Zealand have been added to the garden and have grown away well. One of the joys

of Caerhays is to stumble upon magnificent old specimens deep in its 100 acres of woodland. Among the many rare trees are fine specimens of *Laurus azorica*, *Lithocarpus cleistocarpus*, *Lithocarpus henryi*; magnolias like *M. delavayi*, *M. nitida*, *M. robusta* and *M. salicifolia*; and such oaks as *Quercus acuta*, *Q. crassifolia*, *Q. glauca*, *Q. ilicifolia*, *Q. lamellosa*, *Q. lanata*, *Q. lodicosa*, *Q. oxyodon* and *Q. phillyreoides*. Almost all these species are known to few of us: this litany of names is a measure of the importance of Caerhays. There is much to discover, so you should allow plenty of time. And see the website – very informative.

Features woodland garden; plantsman's collection of plants; mature conifers; fine collection of trees; camellias; magnolias; rhododendrons; tallest specimen of *Emmenopterys henryi* (17m.) in the British Isles, and 37 other record-breaking trees (including eight *Acer* species); tea-room & beach shop/café in car-park.

Owned by F.J. Williams CBE
Number of gardeners 4
Size 24ha (60 acres)
NCCPG National Collections *Magnolia*
English Heritage Grade II*

nymansensis reaches 13m (40ft). Most of the ornamental plants have been planted since 1900 and the older ones have been matched in recent years by substantial additions.

Features woodland garden; rhododendrons & azaleas; plantsman's collection of plants; camellias; bluebells; magnolias; rare trees & shrubs; important nursery (major RHS gold medal winner); teas & light refreshments.

Owned by Charles Williams
Number of gardeners 1
Size 12ha (30 acres)

Carclew Gardens

PERRAN-AR-WORTHAL, TRURO, TR3 7PB

Tel 01872 864070
Location A39 east at Perran-ar-Worthal, 1 mile to garden.
Opening hours 2 pm – 5.30 pm. Sundays in April, plus 2 & 30 May. And at any time by appointment.
Admission fee Adults £2.50; Children 50p.

Ⓟ ⓌⒸ ☕

Carclew's garden first opened to the public in 1927 and has continued to do so for charity every year since then. It was once the greatest rhododendron garden in the south-west: some of the oldest rhododendrons were grown from Sir Joseph Hooker's Himalayan collections nearly 150 years ago. The many fine trees include a large ginkgo and a form of *Quercus* x *hispanica* which is *not* 'Lucombeana'. Mrs Chope has been busy replanting and restoring the garden: the waterfall has recently been repaired.

Features woodland garden; roses (mainly modern); rhododendrons; tallest *Pseudolarix amabilis* (23m.) in the British Isles; home-made teas.

Owned by Mrs Robert Chope
English Heritage Grade II

Carwinion

MAWNAN SMITH, FALMOUTH, TR11 5JA

Tel 01326 250258 **Fax** 01326 250903
Website www.carwinion.com
Location From Mawnan Smith, turn left at Red Lion, 500 yards up hill on right.
Opening hours 10 am – 5.30 pm; daily or by appointment; all year.
Admission fee Adults £3; Children free.

Ⓟ 🐕 ⓌⒸ ♿

Twelve acres of Cornish jungle, exotically thick with vast rhododendrons, camellias, *Trachycarpus fortunei*, drimys, gunneras, lysichitons, ferns, hellebores and the largest collection of bamboos in the south-west. The Towan Nursery collection of camellias and hydrangeas has recently been planted out in the garden and will add yet further interest in future.

Features woodland garden; sub-tropical plants; mature conifers; 160 species of bamboo; gunnera; bluebells.

Owned by Anthony Rogers
Number of gardeners 1
Size 4.8ha (12 acres)

Chyverton

ZELAH, TRURO, TR4 9HD

Tel 01872 540324
Location 1 mile south-west of Zelah on A30.
Opening hours By appointment at any time.
Admission fee Adults £5; Children (under 16) free. Visits are personally conducted.

Ⓟ 🐕 ⓌⒸ ☕

Chyverton started out as a Georgian landscape garden. Later owners planted a pinetum in the 1830s and the first rhododendrons in 1890. The horticultural plantings have however been very much extended since the 1920s, initially with some advice from Sir Harold Hillier (his first ever advisory visit), but latterly by the owners themselves. Nigel Holman is a distinguished plantsman: Hugh Johnson calls his garden 'a magic jungle'. Magnolias are a particular interest: several Chyverton seedlings now bear cultivar names. Many other established plants have also been grown from seed, including plants collected by Nigel Holman in China and rhododendron hybrids from Brodick. But there is much more to interest the plantsman. A lanky red-stemmed hedge of *Luma apiculata* below the house is outstanding. The planting continues and is now accompanied by the placement of statues in suitable sites.

 Features woodland garden; plantsman's collection of plants; mature conifers; magnolias, including four record-breakers; nothofagus; tallest *Rhododendron* 'Cornish Red' (16m) in the British isles; lunches & teas for parties, by prior arrangement.

Owned by Nigel Holman
Number of gardeners 1
Size 50ha (125 acres)
English Heritage Grade II

Cotehele

St Dominick, Saltash, PL12 6TA

Tel 01579 351346 **Fax** 01579 351222
Website www.nationaltrust.org.uk
Location 14 miles from Plymouth via Saltash.
Opening hours 10.30 am – dusk; daily; all year.
Admission fee Adults £4; Children £2.

Ⓟ ⓦⒸ ⊕ ⊞ ⊜

Broad Victorian terraces below the house support many tender climbers such as *Jasminum mesnyi*, while the beds beneath have wallflowers and roses. Down the wooded valley are camellias, rhododendrons

and shade-loving plants which thrive in an ancient woodland, kept damp by a small stream. The National Trust has undertaken much gentle restoration and renewal in recent years.

 Features woodland garden; topiary; roses (mainly modern); daffodils; fine collection of trees; palms; ferns; pretty dovecote; National Trust gift shop; restaurant (20 March – 31 October) for meals and drinks.

Owned by The National Trust
Number of gardeners 3, plus 2 students
Size 5.6ha (14 acres)
English Heritage Grade II

Duchy of Cornwall Nursery

Cott Road, Lostwithiel, PL22 0HW

Tel 01208 872668 **Fax** 01208 872835
Website www.duchyofcornwallnursery.co.uk
Location 1½ miles off A390 at Lostwithiel.
Opening hours 9 am – 5 pm; Monday – Saturday.
10 am – 5 pm; Sundays. Closed Bank Holidays.

Ⓟ ⓦⒸ ⓰ ⓯

The Duchy of Cornwall nursery stocks an extensive general range of all types of plants, and will interest even the most discriminating plantsman. Its policy does not compromise on quality: it offers the cultivars which it considers the best. These range from reliable old favourites to rare and recent cultivars. It was recently described as resembling 'a series of specialist nurseries in one nursery' because of the depth and breadth of its range. It is especially good on hardy fuchsias, and hopes that its collection will one day be recognised by the NCCPG. It is also one of the few nurseries which still supply bare-rooted stock in winter. There is a special tree week (27 September to 3 October 2004) when customers can visit the growing fields and label the trees they want to buy with their own names.

The Eden Project

BODELVA, ST AUSTELL, PL24 2SGE

Tel 01726 811911 **Fax** 01726 811912
Website www.edenproject.com
Location Signed from A30, A390 & A391.
Opening hours 10 am – 6 pm; daily; all year, except 24 & 25 December. Closes at 8 pm from Tuesday to Thursday in August. Closes at 4.30 pm from November to March. Last admissions 1½ hours before closing.
Admission fee Adults £11; OAPs £8; Children £4.

The promoters of this imaginative project hope to provide visitors with an understanding of the world of plants, and their importance to human welfare. The area under glass is described as being the size of 30 football pitches. One of the gigantic conservatories – all made in a disused clay-pit near St Austell – is landscaped as a rainforest, while others are Mediterranean, South African and Californian. Staples like cocoa, coffee, bananas and rubber are grown alongside plants used in paper, wine, scent and brewing. Outside are collections of camellias, lavender, sunflowers and hemp. There is plenty of hype, too, but visitors all speak enthusiastically of the experience.

 Features giant glasshouses; exotic plants.

Owned by The Eden Trust
Size 14.7ha (37 acres)

Glendurgan

MAWNAN SMITH, FALMOUTH, TR11 5JZ

Tel 01326 250906 **Fax** 01872 865808
Website www.nationaltrust.org.uk
Location 1 mile west of Mawnan Smith, close to Trebah.
Opening hours 10.30 am – 5.30 pm (last admissions 4.30 pm); Tuesday – Saturday, plus Bank Holiday Mondays; 14 February to 30 October. Closed Good Friday.
Admission fee Adults £4.20; Children £2.10.

Glendurgan is a steep, sub-tropical valley garden on the Helford River with a good collection of old rhododendrons and camellias. It also boasts an extraordinary 1830s maze of clipped cherry laurel, recently restored and best seen from the new viewing platform above. Indeed, the whole garden is almost best when viewed from the top – but the temptation to wander down and into it is irresistible.

Features woodland garden; sub-tropical plants; mature conifers; laurel maze; wild flowers; huge tulip tree; tallest *Eucryphia lucida* (13m.) in the British Isles; small shop; teas & light lunches.

Owned by The National Trust
Number of gardeners 3, plus 1 trainee
Size 14ha (35 acres)
English Heritage Grade II

Headland

POLRUAN-BY-FOWEY, PL23 1PW

Tel 01726 870243
Website www.headlandgarden.co.uk
Location Find Polruan: go to the bottom of Fore Street, along West Street, left up Battery Lane to end.

Opening hours 2 pm – 6 pm; Thursdays; 6 May to 9 September.
Admission fee Adults £2; Children £1.

A cliff garden with 500 steps, the sea on three sides and a sandy beach, Headland is a lesson in what will tolerate salt-laden winds: eucalyptus, acacias, foxgloves and junipers, but especially cacti and succulents – agaves, aloes, echeverias, sedums, lampranthus and crassulas. The design and the variety of the planting make it seem much larger than its 1½ acres and there are many stone seats tucked in between the rocky outcrops.

 Features cacti & succulents; salt-spray resistant plants; cream teas in garden.

Owned by Jean & John Hill
Size 0.5ha (1¼ acres)

Heligan Gardens

PENTEWAN, ST AUSTELL, PL26 6EN

Tel 01726 845100 **Fax** 01726 845101
Website www.heligan.com
Location St Austell to Mevagissey Road, following brown tourist signs.
Opening hours 10 am – 6 pm; daily; all year except 24 & 25 December. Closes at 5 pm from November to March.
Admission fee Adults £7.50; OAPs £7; Children £4.

Heligan calls itself 'The Lost Gardens of Heligan' but its 200 acres have been spectacularly rescued since 1990 from a jungle of neglect. The owners emphasise that it is 'definitely not just another pretty garden' but best described as a whole series of gardens within a garden. Its kitchen gardens – there are five walled gardens – are of particular interest: they contain over 300 cultivars of fruits, herbs and vegetables, some of them no longer commercially available. Many of the working buildings are once again carrying out their original functions – fruit stores, tool and potting sheds, pineapple pits, peach, vine and melon houses, manure-heated frames and the bachelor gardeners' bothies. Elsewhere is an Italian Garden, a Sundial Garden, a New Zealand Garden, and the Alpine Ravine. Newly recovered features emerge with incredible speed: recent restorations include the 22-acre lost 'jungle' valley with a large collection of Tasmanian tree-ferns and 60 bamboo cultivars. The enthusiasm of the restorers is infectious and their achievements are already substantial. The owners are brilliant at getting financial support and publicity – with the result that the garden can get very crowded. They have now turned their attention to the woodlands and wilder parts of the estate.

 Features woodland garden; sub-tropical plants; rock garden; rhododendrons & azaleas; beautiful ferny gully; splendid kitchen garden; farm shop; licensed restaurant.

Owned by Heligan Gardens Ltd
Number of gardeners 25
Size 80ha (200 acres)
English Heritage Grade II

Ken Caro

BICTON, LISKEARD, PL14 5RF

Tel 01579 362446
Location Signed from A390, midway between Callington & Liskeard.
Opening hours 10 am – 6 pm; Sunday – Friday; 28 March to 30 September.
Admission fee Adults £3.50; Children £1.

Ken Caro was started in 1970 as two acres of intensely planted formal gardens in different styles, and extended in 1993 by taking in a further two acres. It is very much a plantsman's garden with good herbaceous plants and shrubs, not at all a traditional Cornish garden. All-round colour is important here, and so are the panoramic views. The owners are flower-arrangers: look for architectural plants and original combinations.

 Features plantsman's collection of plants; mature conifers; good herbaceous borders; tea/coffee.

Owned by Mr & Mrs K.R. Willcock
Number of gardeners 2
Size 1.8ha (4½ acres)

Lamorran House

UPPER CASTLE ROAD, ST MAWES, TR2 5BZ

Tel 01326 270800 **Fax** 01326 270801
Location ½ mile from village centre.
Opening hours Not available as we went to press. 2003 times were: 10.30 am – 5 pm; Wednesdays, Fridays & the first Saturday of the month; April to September.
Admission fee Adults £4; Groups £3.50; Children free. (2003 prices).

(P) (WC)

The garden at Lamorran has been almost entirely made since 1980, on a steep site above Falmouth Bay. It is tightly designed in the Italian style, but also full of unusual plants – an English Mediterranean garden in Cornwall, say the owners, or a mainland Tresco, though it is closest to the great English garden at La Mortola on the Italian Riviera. One of their latest ventures has been a bank planted with cacti and succulents: another has seen an increase in the number of cyatheas in the garden. But tender rhododendrons from Asia are yet another interest, and plants from Australia too. The collection of unusual plants is

simply amazing: very adventurous. The planting is guided by a desire to experiment with hardiness and tempered by the aesthetic demands of the whole garden. So the garden is not a *botanic* collection, but an extremely good *horticultural* one, and the plants are chosen and placed for their decorative merit and their contribution to the whole.

 Features sub-tropical plants; plantsman's collection of plants matched to a firm design; good herbaceous borders; fine collection of trees; extensive plantings of Australian & South African plants; over 25 different palms.

Owned by Mr & Mrs Robert Dudley-Cooke
Number of gardeners 2
Size 1.8ha (4½ acres)

Lanhydrock

BODMIN, PL30 5AD

Tel 01208 73320 **Fax** 01208 74084
Website www.nationaltrust.org.uk
Location 2½ miles south-east of Bodmin.
Opening hours 10 am – 6 pm (dusk, if sooner); daily; all year.
Admission fee Garden only £4.20; Children £2.10.

(P) (WC)

Lanhydrock is a grand mansion, mainly 19th-century, with one of the best formal gardens in Cornwall – clipped yews, box parterres and bedding out, as well as large herbaceous borders which contain a good collection of *Crocosmia* (a National Collection until recently). The woodlands behind are impressive for their size and colourful rhododendrons in spring. But it is the magnolias which impress the visitor most: 140 different species and cultivars.

 Features woodland garden; topiary; good herbaceous borders; bluebells; Victorian parterres; spring bulbs; National

Trust shop; restaurant & refreshments from 15 February to 2 November.

Owned by The National Trust
Number of gardeners 5
Size 12.3ha (31 acres)
English Heritage Grade II*

Mount Edgcumbe Gardens

CREMYLL, TORPOINT, PL10 1HZ

Tel 01752 822236 **Fax** 01752 822199
Website www.gardensincornwall.co.uk
Location At the end of the B3247 in south-east Cornwall, or by ferry from Plymouth.
Opening hours Formal gardens & park: dawn to dusk; all year. House & Earl's Garden: 11 am – 4.30 pm; Sunday – Thursday; April to September. Guided tours for groups by appointment.
Admission fee House & Earl's Garden: Adults £4.50; OAPs £3.50; Children £2.25. Formal gardens & park: free.

A long, stately grass drive runs down from the house to Plymouth Sound, through oak woods interplanted with large ornamental trees. The formal gardens are right down on the waterside, protected by a clipped ilex hedge 10m high. There are no less than ten acres of gardens here, including an Italian garden (made in the 1790s), a French garden (Regency), a modern American garden, a New Zealand garden complete with geyser, a Jubilee garden, the 18th-century Thomson's Seat, an Orangery with newly acquired orange trees, and the fern dell with ivies and tree ferns. The two-acre Earl's Garden has recently been restored and planted: highlights include a 400-year-old lime-tree and a Victorian shell seat among the herbaceous borders, summerhouses and statues. Allow plenty of time to do justice to these majestic pleasure gardens.

Features sub-tropical plants; plants under glass; daffodils; good herbaceous borders; fine collection of trees; summer bedding; deer park; formal gardens; fern dell; genuine Victorian rose garden; tallest cork oak *Quercus suber* (26m.) in the British Isles; gift and book shops; Orangery restaurant in formal gardens.

Owned by Cornwall County Council & Plymouth City Council
Number of gardeners 4
Size 4ha (10 acres), plus 320-ha (800-acre) park
NCCPG National Collections *Camellia*
English Heritage Grade I

Pencarrow

WASHAWAY, BODMIN, PL30 3AG

Tel 01208 841369 **Fax** 01208 841722
Website www.pencarrow.co.uk
Location 4 miles north-west of Bodmin – signed off the A389 at Washaway.
Opening hours 9.30 am – 5.30 pm; daily; March to October.
Admission fee Adults £3.50; Children free. Groups welcome by appointment (discounts usually available).

The mile-long drive at Pencarrow leads to an avenue of rhododendrons and rare conifers before you eventually come to the pretty Anglo-Palladian house. On one side are the outlines of an Italian garden, complete with fountain, laid out in the 1830s, and next to it a great granite rock garden where vast boulders from Bodmin Moor lie strewn among the trees and shrubs. Pencarrow is famous for its conifers: an ancestor planted one of every known variety in the mid-19th century and the survivors are so venerable that the great Alan Mitchell wrote a guide to them. The monkey puzzle *Araucaria araucana* acquired its nickname when a visitor to Pencarrow,

Charles Austen, remarked to his host, after some thought, 'that tree would puzzle a monkey'. Since about 1970 the owners have steadily retrieved the garden from the state of dereliction in which it was left at the end of World War II and added a further 200 or so conifers. Recent plantings have involved the addition of over 700 of the best modern rhododendrons, 70 camellias and many other broad-leaved trees and shrubs. It is good to see the fortunes of such a distinguished garden revived.

 Features important collection of mature conifers; Italian garden; rhododendrons; camellias; great granite Victorian rock garden; blue hydrangeas; ice-house; monkey puzzle avenue; craft gallery; light lunches, cream teas.

Owned by The Trustees of the Molesworth-St Aubyn Family
Number of gardeners 3
Size 20ha (50 acres)
English Heritage Grade II

Penjerrick

BUDOCK WATER, FALMOUTH, TR11 5ED

Tel 01872 870105
Location 3 miles south-west of Falmouth, entrance at junction of lanes opposite Penmorvah Manor Hotel.
Opening hours 1.30 pm – 4.30 pm; Wednesdays, Fridays & Sundays; March to September.
Admission fee Adults £2.50; Children £1.

Ⓟ 🐕

The garden at Penjerrick was begun by the Fox family in the mid-19th century. It is a great plantsman's garden, famous in particular for its Barclayi and Penjerrick hybrid rhododendrons. Some of the original plants still survive in the peaceful woodland garden, thick with exotics: tender plants thrive in the lush, sheltered valley. The garden is recovering well from a period of neglect: it sums up all that was best about private Cornish gardens 100 years ago. Take your gumboots, and prepare for a fascinating walk.

 Features woodland garden; rhododendrons; camellias; tree ferns; ponds & bamboos.

Owned by Mrs Rachel Morin
Number of gardeners ½
Size 4ha (10 acres)
English Heritage Grade II

Pine Lodge Gardens & Nursery

HOLMBUSH, ST AUSTELL, PL25 3RQ

Tel 01726 73500 **Fax** 01726 77370
Website www.pine-lodge.co.uk
Location East of St Austell between Holmbush & Tregrehan.
Opening hours 10 am – 6 pm; daily; 12 March to 31 October.
Admission fee Adults £5 Children £3.

This modern 30-acre garden is quite unlike the typical Cornish garden. It has several distinct styles and contains over 6,000 different plants, all of which are labelled. In addition to the rhododendrons, magnolias and camellias so familiar in Cornish gardens there are Mediterranean and southern-hemisphere plants grown for year-round interest, herbaceous borders, a fernery, a formal garden, a Japanese garden, a woodland walk and shrubberies. The water features include a large wildlife pond, an ornamental pond, a lake with breeding black swans and an island, and marsh gardens. Trees are a particular interest: Pine Lodge has an acer glade, a young four-acre pinetum, and an arboretum. And a new wildflower meadow has just been planted with over 7,000 bulbs and flowers. The pace of the garden's development is very exciting and the owners' appetite for new plants grows even stronger every year.

Features woodland garden; good herbaceous borders; Japanese Garden; good water features; lots of interesting plants; garden nursery with plants from wild-collected seed; tea-room.

Owned by Mr & Mrs Raymond Clemo
Number of gardeners 4
Size 12ha (30 acres)
NCCPG National Collections *Grevillea*

Pinsla Garden & Nursery

CARDINHAM, BODMIN, PL30 4AY

Tel & Fax 01208 821339
Website www.pinslagarden.co.uk
Location Brown signs from Cardinham village.
Opening hours 10 am – 6 pm; daily; March to October. 10 am – 4 pm; Saturdays & Sundays; November to February.
Admission fee Adults £2; Children free.

Winding paths, granite boulders, unusual textures and a stone circle in the meadow: these, and the sculptures, are some of the garden features designed to 'arouse your emotions and feed your soul' at Pinsla. But there are also fine herbaceous borders, cottage-garden plantings and alpine beds – and an nursery with a good choice of herbaceous and alpine plants, ferns, bamboos and succulents.

 Features good nursery; light refreshments.

Owned by Mark & Claire Woodbine
Number of gardeners 2½
Size 0.6ha (1½ acres)

St Michael's Mount

MARAZION, TR17 0EF

Tel 01736 710507 **Fax** 01736 719930
Website www.stmichaelsmount.co.uk & www.nationaltrust.org.
Location 1 mile south of Marazion.
Opening hours Garden: 10.30 am – 5.30 pm; daily (weather & tide permitting); April & May. Plus Thursdays & Fridays from June to October.
Admission fee £2.50.

St Michael's Mount is a triumph for man's ingenuity in the face of Atlantic gales, salt spray and bare rock – with sand for garden soil. Careful experiment over the generations has enabled the owners to plant a remarkable garden of plants which resist the elements: *Luma apiculata*, Rugosa roses, correas, nerines, Hottentot figs and naturalised agapanthus. On the north side, a sparse wood of sycamores and pines gives protection to camellias, azaleas and hydrangeas. Nigel Nicolson calls it 'the largest and loveliest rock-garden in England'. There is nothing rare about the plants: the wonder is that they grow at all.

Features sub-tropical plants; natural rock garden; wild narcissus; naturalised kniphofias and agapanthus; National Trust shop; National Trust refreshments.

Owned by Lord St Levan & The National Trust
Number of gardeners 3
Size 4ha (10 acres)
English Heritage Grade II

Trebah Garden Trust

MAWNAN SMITH, FALMOUTH, TR11 5JZ

Tel 01326 250448 **Fax** 01326 250781
Website www.trebah-garden.co.uk
Location 4 miles south-west of Falmouth, signed

from Treliever roundabout at A39/A394 junction, through Mawnan Smith to garden.
Opening hours 10.30 am – 5 pm (last admission); daily; all year. Half price from November to February.
Admission fee Adults £5; OAPs £4.50; Children (5 – 15) & disabled visitors £3; Children (under 5) free. RHS members free.

Trebah has been vigorously restored and improved since the Hibberts bought it in 1980. The view from the top is magical – a beautiful, secret, wooded valley which runs right down to the Helford estuary. A stream cascades over waterfalls, through two acres of blue and white hydrangeas, and spills out over the beach. Vast trees, natural and exotic, line the steep sides, while the central point is held by a group of elegant tall palms. Glades of huge sub-tropical tree ferns mingle with giant gunneras, puyas and echiums, while along the sides and overhead is the rolling canopy of 100-year-old rhododendrons. The nursery was re-made in 2001 and a new visitor centre funded by the Heritage Lottery Fund opened in 2002. A paradise for plantsmen, Trebah is also popular with children, whose curiosity is aroused by trails, quizzes and educational games. It is a garden for all people and for all seasons – open *every day of the year*.

Features woodland garden; sub-tropical plants; plantsman's collection of plants; fine collection of trees; massed hydrangeas; lilies and candelabra primulas; extensive new plantings of palms & succulents at the top of the garden; tallest hardy palm *Trachycarpus fortunei* (15m.) in the British Isles and three other tree records; excellent nursery; private beach on Helford river; café.

Owned by The Trebah Garden Trust
Number of gardeners 8, plus volunteers & students
Size 10ha (25 acres)
English Heritage Grade II

Tregrehan

PAR, PL24 2SJ

Tel 01726 812438 **Fax** 01726 814389
Location 1 mile west of St Blazey on A390.
Opening hours 10.30 am – 5 pm; Wednesday – Sunday (except Easter Sunday); mid-March to mid-June. Then 2 pm – 5 pm on Wednesdays to end of August.
Admission fee Adults £3.50; Children free.

An old Cornish garden whose 20 acres of woodland date back 200 years and include a fine range of Victorian conservatories, tall conifers and vast, venerable rhododendrons. Tregrehan is best known for the camellias bred there by the late Gillian Carlyon, especially 'Jenefer Carlyon' which won her the Cory Cup from the RHS. But Tom Hudson's collections in warm temperate regions have also made a big impact on the garden which, under his guidance, has become an important living gene bank of known source plants.

Features woodland garden; camellias; pinetum; walled garden; sunken garden; phytogeographic planting; teas.

Owned by T.C. Hudson
Number of gardeners 2
Size 8ha (20 acres)
English Heritage Grade II*

Trelissick Garden

FEOCK, TRURO, TR3 6QL

Tel 01872 862090 **Fax** 01872 865808
Website www.nationaltrust.org.uk
Location Take B3289 off main Truro – Falmouth Road.
Opening hours 11 am – 4 pm; Thursday – Sunday; 2 January to 13 February. 10.30 am – 5.30 pm (or dusk, if earlier); daily; 14 February to 31 October. 11

am – 4 pm; daily; November & December (12 noon – 4 pm from 27 to 31 December).
Admission fee Adults £4.60; Children £2.30.

Once famous as 'the fruit garden of Cornwall' – there is a newly planted (2003) Cornish apple orchard – and still maintained by the National Trust, Trelissick is particularly colourful in August and September when the hydrangeas are in full flower. There are over 100 cultivars, some in a special walk. But venerable conifers and tender plants are also features: *Erythrina crista-galli*, cannas and hedychiums are among the many good things that over-winter outside, not to mention daffodils, rhododendrons and camellias in spring.

Features woodland garden; plantsman's collection of plants; mature conifers; aromatic plant garden; fig garden; hydrangeas; tallest tree fern *Dicksonia antarctica* (6m.) in the British Isles; gift and plant shop; refreshments.

Owned by The National Trust
Number of gardeners 4
Size 10ha (25 acres)
NCCPG National Collections *Azara*; *Photinia*
English Heritage Grade II

Trengwainton Garden

MADRON, PENZANCE, TR20 8RZ

Tel 01736 362297 **Fax** 01736 362297
Website www.nationaltrust.org.uk
Location 2 miles north-west of Penzance, ½ mile west of Heamoor.
Opening hours 10 am – 5.30 pm (5 pm in February, March, October & November) ; Sunday – Thursday & Good Friday; 15 February to 31 October.
Admission fee Adults £4.40; Children £2.20.

Trengwainton has one of the best collections of tender plants on the Cornish mainland,

all thanks to the Bolitho family who started planting seriously only in 1925. Much came from original seed from such collectors as Kingdon Ward: some rhododendrons flowered here for the first time in the British Isles, among them *R. macabeanum*, *R. elliottii* and *R. taggianum*. The plants in many Cornish gardens are past their best. Not so at Trengwainton, where many are in their prime. It is a garden to wander through slowly, giving yourself as much time as you need to enjoy its riches.

Features woodland garden; sub-tropical plants; roses (mainly old-fashioned); lilies; acacias; *Myosotidium hortensia*; tree ferns; tallest *Xanthoceras sorbifolium* (7m.) in the British Isles (and two record trees); National Trust shop; tea-room.

Owned by The National Trust
Number of gardeners 4
English Heritage Grade II

Trerice

KESTLE MILL, NEWQUAY, TR8 4PG

Tel 01637 875404 **Fax** 01637 879300
Website www.nationaltrust.org.uk
Location 3 miles south-east of Newquay – turn right off A3058 at Kestle Mill.
Opening hours 11 am – 5.30 pm (5 pm in October); daily except Tuesdays & Saturdays (but open on Tuesdays from 19 July to 12 September); 28 March to 31 October.
Admission fee House & garden £4.70.

A perfect West Country manor house with pretty Dutch gables, Trerice is unusual among Cornish gardens. It is small and comparatively formal: the design and herbaceous plantings are its best points. It is not surrounded by swirling rhododendron woodland. There is a perfect harmony between the Elizabethan architecture and the gardens. Somewhat anomalously, it boasts the largest collection of mid-Victorian to current-day lawn mowers in the country. They are both interesting and fun to visit.

**Features** colour borders; good collection of apple trees; lawn-mower museum; National Trust shop; restaurant.

Owned by The National Trust
Number of gardeners 1
Size 5.6ha (14 acres)

Tresco Abbey

ISLES OF SCILLY, TR24 0QQ

Tel 01720 424105 **Fax** 01720 422868
Website www.tresco.co.uk
Location Direct helicopter flight from Penzance, or boat from St Mary's.
Opening hours 10 am – 4 pm; daily; all year.
Admission fee Adults £8.50; Children free.

🐕 ♿ ⛲ 🏪 ☕

The sub-tropical gardens on Tresco are unique in the British Isles. They were first designed and planted by Augustus Smith in 1834: his successors have been equally passionate in their search for tender plants that will grow outside on Tresco's south-facing terraces as nowhere else in Britain. The collection is especially strong in plants from South Africa, Australia and New Zealand but, even though any account of Tresco reads like a list of plants, it is still very much an ornamental garden which strives for horticultural effect. The oldest specimens include Canary Island palms, a large number of aeoniums from both the Canary Islands and Madeira, agaves from America and puyas from Chile. Since the great gale of 1990, the gardens have been extensively replanted, with hundreds of exotic plants from Kew, all protected by extensive new shelterbelts. No matter what

time of the year, there is always a lot of colour and much of interest: proteas and acacias in winter; the shrubby foxglove (*Isoplexis sceptrum*); mesembryanthemums and agapanthus in summer.

**Features** sub-tropical plants; plantsman's collection of plants; mature conifers; cacti; succulents; South African, Australian and New Zealand plants; tallest *Luma apiculata* (20m.), *Metrosideros excelsa* (20m.) and *Cordyline australis* (15m.) in the British Isles; shop; light refreshments.

Owned by Robert Dorrien Smith
Number of gardeners 5, plus 2 students
Size 6.7ha (17 acres)
NCCPG National Collections *Acacia*
English Heritage Grade I

Trevarno Gardens & National Museum of Gardening

HELSTON, TR13 0RU

Tel 01326 574274 **Fax** 01326 574282
Location 3 miles west of Helston, signed from the junction of A394 & B3302.
Opening hours 10.30 am – 5 pm; daily; all year. Closed 25 & 26 December.
Admission fee Adults £4.75; OAPs £4.20; Children £1.50. RHS members free from 1 January to 8 April and from 1 November to 31 December.

Ⓟ ♿ ⛲ 🏪 ☕

Trevarno is an interesting new project – an old estate which has been restored and developed since 1997 and which promises to become one of the great gardens of Cornwall again. The old woodland gardens have been cleared, the lake dredged, the 19th-century Italian garden restored and the fountain conservatory refurnished. Work continues: there are plans for a series of stylishly themed gardens dedicated to the flora of different parts of the world. Meanwhile the National Museum of Gardening has a vast and fascinating collection of old garden tools and horticultural equipment of every sort; it alone is worth a long journey to see.

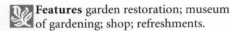 **Features** garden restoration; museum of gardening; shop; refreshments.

Owned by M. Sagin
Number of gardeners 3
Size 12ha (30 acres)

Trewidden Gardens

PENZANCE, TR20 8TT

Tel 01736 363021 **Fax** 01736 368142
Location Off A30, 2 miles west of Penzance.
Opening hours 10.30 am – 4.30 pm; Wednesday-Sunday, plus Bank Holiday Mondays; 18 February to 6 June.
Admission fee Adults £3.50; Children free.

The gardens at Trewidden have only been regularly open to the public since 2001, and there is much to see. It is essentially a springtime garden, perhaps at its best towards the end of March. The camellia collection is one of the largest (300+ cvs.) while the tree fern dell claims to have more dicksonias than any other garden in the northern hemisphere, some of them 150+ years old. Rare specimens include a venerable jelly palm *Butia capitata*, Chilean nut-tress *Gevuina avellana* and the garden's own magnolia, 'Trewidden Belle'.

 **Features** broadest *Metasequoia glyptostroboides* in UK; unusual plants for sale; light refreshments.

Owned by Alverne Bolitho
Number of gardeners 3
Size 4.8ha (12 acres)

Trewithen

GRAMPOUND ROAD, TRURO, TR2 4DD

Tel 01726 883647 **Fax** 01726 882301
Website www.trewithengardens.co.uk
Location A390 between Probus & Grampound.
Opening hours 10 am – 4.30 pm; Monday – Saturday (& Sundays in April & May); March to September.
Admission fee Adults £4.25; Children free. RHS members free from July to September.

Trewithen's setting is magnificent. Instead of the steep terraces of most Cornish gardens, there is a spacious flat lawn that stretches for 200 yards into the distance, with gentle banks of rhododendrons, magnolias and rare shrubs on all sides. It sets the tone for the garden's grandeur, which was largely the work of George Johnstone in the early years of the 20th century. Johnstone inherited Trewithen in 1904, so this is the gardens' centenary. Johnstone was a great plantsman. He subscribed to plant hunting expeditions, such as those of Frank Kingdon Ward. Note how he used laurel hedges to divide up the woodland and give structure to the garden. He also had an eye for placing plants to advantage.

Features woodland garden; rhododendrons & azaleas; plantsman's collection of plants; camellias; good herbaceous borders; fine collection of trees; magnolias; quarry garden; cyclamen; tallest *Magnolia campbellii* subsp. *mollicomata* (19m.) in the British Isles and sixteen more record-breaking tree species; excellent nursery & garden shop; tea-room with light refreshments.

Owned by A.M.J. Galsworthy
Number of gardeners 4
Size 12ha (30 acres)
English Heritage Grade II*

CUMBRIA

Cumbria came into being in 1974, an amalgam of the old counties of Cumberland, Westmorland and the northern part of Lancashire. Gardening in Cumbria is dominated by the Lake District: both Wordsworth's garden at Rydal Mount and Ruskin's at Brantwood are open to visitors. There are good historic gardens of the grander sort, too. Though few in number, almost all the most important are open to the public: Levens is rated Grade I, while Dalemain, Holker, Muncaster and Sizergh are all Grade II*. Cumbria's acid soils and the highest rainfall in England are very favourable to the growth of conifers: many of the older gardens have fine specimens of *Abies, Picea* and *Pinus,* while Muncaster also offers an extensive collection of *Nothofagus* species. The National Gardens Scheme is active in the county, and particularly successful in persuading garden-owners in and around the Lake District to open for charity. Cumbria has comparatively few nurseries, but the ones we list below are exceptionally good. The county has its fair share of National Collections, with clusters of genera at three of the larger gardens: *Halesia, Pterostyrax, Styrax, Sinojackia* and other *Styracaceae* at Holker; *Astilbe, Hydrangea* and *Polystichum* at Holehird; and *Asplenium scolopendrium, Cystopteris, Dryopteris,* and *Osmunda* at Sizergh. Cumbria Campus at Newton Rigg near Penrith is a RHS Partner College, with lectures, demonstrations and garden walks throughout the year. *www.visitcumbria.com* is a useful website.

Acorn Bank Garden

ACORN BANK, TEMPLE SOWERBY, PENRITH, CA10 1SP

Tel 01768 361893 **Fax** 01768 366824
Website www.nationaltrust.org.uk
Location North of Temple Sowerby, 6 miles east of Penrith on A66.
Opening hours 10 am – 5 pm; Wednesday – Monday; 29 March to 31 October.
Admission fee Adults £2.75; Children £1.30.

Acorn Bank claims to have the largest collection (250 cvs) of culinary and medicinal plants in the north: it was redesigned and replanted in 2002-2003. The garden is especially worthwhile in spring when thousands and thousands of daffodils fill the woodland slopes, and the fruit trees flower in the old walled garden. Best of all is the huge quince tree in the herb garden, a wondrous sight in flower or fruit.

Features woodland garden; roses (mainly old-fashioned); herbs; fruit; good herbaceous borders; spring bulbs;

woodland walk past Mill; National Trust shop; tea-room.

Owned by The National Trust
Number of gardeners 1
Size 1ha (2½ acres)

Brantwood

CONISTON, LA21 8AD

Tel 01539 441396 **Fax** 01539 441263
Website www.brantwood.org.uk
Location East side of Coniston Water, 2½ miles from Coniston, 4 miles from Hawkshead.
Opening hours 11 am – 5.30 pm; daily; mid-March to mid-November. 11 am – 4.30 pm; Wednesday – Sunday; rest of year.
Admission fee Adults £3; Children £1.

This woodland garden was laid out by John Ruskin from 1871 to 1886 but somewhat altered and neglected after his death in 1900. Working with the natural materials of the site, Ruskin developed a series of experimental gardens within the ancient woodland and on the high moorland behind. When the Brantwood Trust began the task of reclamation, it decided to restore the garden partly as it was in Ruskin's lifetime, and partly as a modern re-interpretation of his ideas, thereby continuing his work and addressing contemporary issues. The Victorian 'viewing terrace' has been restored, and Ruskin's 'zig-zaggy garden' is now looking young again. Ascending from the Purgatory of the car park, visitors reach Paradise through the levels inspired by Dante's *Divine Comedy*. So Brantwood is a garden which offers thought-provoking ideas for everyone. Below Ruskin's 'living laboratory', exotic ornamental plantings frame wonderful views across Coniston Water. There is a regular passenger ferry service from Coniston Boat-buildings: the steam yacht *Gondola* also calls from May to October.

Features rhododendrons & azaleas; daffodils; bluebells; cottage garden; extensive native fern collection; bookshop & craft gallery; plants for sale; meals, light refreshments & drinks all day.

Owned by The Brantwood Trust
Number of gardeners 2
Size 10ha (25 acres)

Dalemain

PENRITH, CA11 0HB

Tel 017684 86450 **Fax** 017684 86223
Website www.dalemain.com
Location M6 (Jct 40), A66, A592, between Penrith & Ullswater.
Opening hours 10.30 am – 5 pm; Sunday – Thursday; 28 March to 14 October.
Admission fee Gardens only: £3.50. RHS members free from 20 April to 16 May. NGS days 2 May & 12 September.

Dalemain has belonged to the Hasell family since 1679. The history of the garden starts, however, with a 16th-century terrace, of which very few remain anywhere in the British Isles. Then comes a kitchen garden with fruit trees planted 250 years ago, though the overall 'feel' of Dalemain is Edwardian. Most of the plantings are modern, including the formal knot garden and the long and richly planted herbaceous border which overlooks the park and the Lakeland Fells. The mixed borders and roses are dreamily English, particularly the Rose Walk, which boasts more than 100 old-fashioned roses. Nearby is the wild garden with drifts of meconopsis and martagon lilies in late spring, though it is fair to say that this is a garden which looks good at all seasons. Plants are well labelled and well grown.

Features woodland garden; roses (mainly old-fashioned); herbs;

meconopsis; old flower and fruit varieties; good herbaceous and mixed borders; biggest *Abies cephalonica* in the British Isles; gift shop; morning coffee, light lunches, afternoon teas.

Owned by Robert Hasell-McCosh
Number of gardeners 2
Size 2ha (5 acres)
English Heritage Grade II*

Graythwaite Hall

ULVERSTON, HAWKSHEAD, LA12 8BA

Tel 01539 531248 **Fax** 01539 530060
Website www.visitcumbria.com
Location Between Newby Bridge & Hawkshead.
Opening hours 10 am – 6 pm; daily; April to June.
Admission fee Adults £2; Children free.

Ⓟ 🐕 🆆🅲

Graythwaite shows Thomas Mawson on home ground and at his best. Formal gardens in the Arts & Crafts style by the house drop down to sweeping lawns; beyond the stream is a woodland of rhododendrons and azaleas. The yew topiary is good – some castellated and some with a mixture of green and gold cultivars.

Features topiary; roses (ancient & modern); rock garden; fine collection of trees.

Owned by Myles Sandys
Number of gardeners 1
Size 2.4ha (6 acres)

Holehird Gardens

LAKELAND HORTICULTURAL SOCIETY, PATTERDALE ROAD, WINDERMERE, LA23 1NP

Tel 01539 446008
Website www.cragview.demon.co.uk
Location 1 mile north of Windermere town, off A592.

Opening hours Dawn – dusk; daily; all year.
Admission fee Free, but donations towards upkeep are welcome.

Holehird is a demonstration and trial garden, maintained entirely by members of the Lakeland Horticultural Society. The society's aim is to 'promote and develop the science, practice and art of horticulture, particularly with regard to the conditions prevailing in the Lake District'. In practice this means an exposed site with neutral-to-acid soil conditions in a cool, wet climate. The gardens have recently been extended to about ten acres and occupy an old walled garden, rockery and the formal gardens in front of the mansion. The interesting thing for visitors is to see what flourishes: alpines, rhododendrons and azaleas, camellias, magnolias, heathers, bulbs (especially snowflakes, cyclamen and wild daffodils), gentians, hostas, meconopsis, ferns and much, much more at every time of the year. Some of the oldest plantings date back to the original owners in the 19th century.

Features woodland garden; rock garden; herbs; plants under glass; heathers; roses; hostas; ferns; Victorian garden; walled garden; spring bulbs; rhododendrons & azaleas.

Owned by Lakeland Horticultural Society
Number of gardeners about 70 volunteers
Size 4ha (10 acres)
NCCPG National Collections *Astilbe*; *Hydrangea*; *Polystichum*

Holker Hall

CARK-IN-CARTMEL, GRANGE-OVER-SANDS, LA11 7PL

Tel 01539 558328 **Fax** 01539 558378
Website www.holker-hall.co.uk
Location Jct 36 off M6, follow brown & white tourist signs.

Opening hours 10 am – 6 pm (last admission 4.30 pm); Sunday – Friday; 28 March to 29 October.
Admission fee Adults £4.50; Children £2.75. Prices subject to review. RHS members free, excluding special event days.

The 19th-century formal gardens below the house are scrumptiously planted as herbaceous borders, the first of many imaginative modern designs and plantings throughout this extensive garden. The woodland has foxgloves, rhododendrons and splendid trees: Joseph Paxton supplied a monkey puzzle and Lord George Cavendish the cedars grown from seeds he brought back from the Holy Land. The Gulf Stream enables many exotic trees and shrubs to flourish and flower which might not otherwise be hardy in this northerly climate.

Features formal & woodland gardens; roses (ancient & modern); rhododendrons; fine limestone cascade & fountain; HHA/Christie's Garden of the Year in 1991; tallest *Ilex latifolia* (15m.) in the British Isles (and two other tree records); shop; cafeteria (licensed).

Owned by Lord Cavendish of Furness
Number of gardeners 6
Size 10ha (25 acres)
NCCPG National Collections Styracaceae (incl. *Halesia, Pterostyrax, Styrax, Sinojackia*)
English Heritage Grade II*

Hutton-in-the-Forest

PENRITH, CA11 9TH

Tel 01768 484449 **Fax** 01768 484571
Website www.hutton-in-the-forest.co.uk
Location 3 miles from Exit 41 of M6 on B5305, 6 miles north of Penrith.
Opening hours 11 am – 5 pm; daily, except Saturdays; Easter to October..
Admission fee Gardens only: Adults £3; Children free.

The charm of Hutton-in-the-Forest derives from its many architectural, gardening and landscape styles which span 400 years but come together as an historic and romantic whole. The pale pink sandstone house is old, handsomely sited and built onto a mediaeval pele tower. Salvin refashioned it in the 19th century and Gilpin restored the terraces at about the same time: the fine topiary is a little later. Beyond the terraces is a woodland garden where large conifers are underplanted by billowing rhododendrons. A woodland walk with 65 different tree species surrounds the property. The walled garden, once a kitchen garden, is now the main flower garden: a double herbaceous border runs from end to end, backed by thick yew hedges. This is a very traditional garden of great serenity.

Features woodland walk; herbaceous borders in the walled garden; terraces with topiary; 17th-century dovecote; refreshments when house open, 11 am – 4.30 pm

Owned by Lord & Lady Inglewood
Number of gardeners 1
Size 4.4ha (11 acres)
English Heritage Grade II

Larch Cottage Nurseries

MELKINGTHORPE, PENRITH, CA10 2DR

Tel 01931 712404 **Fax** 01931 712727
Location In village.
Opening hours 10 am – 5.30 pm (dusk in winter); daily. Closed over Christmas.
Admission fee Free.

This nursery garden is not large, but it is backed by the longest list of plants in the

north of England, including many items which are not available from anyone else. Within the walls are a smart restaurant in the Tuscan style, and a neat Japanese-style garden. But the plants deserve a long visit to study.

 Features Japanese garden; unusual plants; nursery; restaurant.

Owned by Peter Stott

Levens Hall

KENDAL, LA8 0PD

Tel 01539 560321 **Fax** 01539 560669
Website www.levenshall.co.uk
Location 5 miles south of Kendal on A6.
Opening hours 10 am – 5 pm; Sunday – Thursday; 13 April to mid-October.
Admission fee Adults £5.80; Children £2.60.

Levens means topiary: huge overgrown chunks of box and yew. Some is said to be left over from a simple formal parterre laid out in 1694 and supplemented by golden yews in the 19th century. Some is more recent – successive generations have been good about replacing plants and restoring the garden when necessary. The arbours and high yew hedges, some of them crenellated, are spangled with *Tropaeolum speciosum* and the parterres planted annually with 15,000 plants, which makes Levens one of the best places to study the expensive art of bedding out. Well maintained.

 Features topiary; spring & summer bedding; new fountain garden; HHA/ Christie's Garden of the Year in 1994; gift shop and plant centre; light lunches & teas.

Owned by C.H. Bagot
English Heritage Grade I

Muncaster Castle

RAVENGLASS, CA18 1RQ

Tel 01229 717614 **Fax** 01229 717010
Website www.muncaster.co.uk
Location A595 1 mile east of Ravenglass on west coast of Cumbria.
Opening hours 10.30 am – 6 pm; daily; all year.
Admission fee Adults £6; Children £4. RHS members free from July to 7 November.

Visit Muncaster in May, when the rhododendrons are at their peak. Many are grown from the original seed introduced by such plant hunters as Forrest and Kingdon Ward in the 1920s and 1930s. The owners have made an excellent job of identifying them and labelling them: some have turned out to be the tallest of their kind in England. The castle was revamped by Salvin in the 1860s: stand on its wonderful long curved terrace (*very* long – half a mile) above the steep slopes and soak up the intensely romantic landscape of the Lakeland hills around. Ruskin called it 'the gateway to Paradise'. The new MeadowVole (*sic*) Maze will appeal to younger visitors.

 Features woodland garden; mature conifers; camellias; maples; masses of new plantings; bluebells; tallest *Nothofagus obliqua* (31m.) in the British Isles; lots of new plantings; two gift shops; snacks & full meals.

Owned by Mrs P.R. Gordon-Duff-Pennington
Number of gardeners 3, plus some part-time help
Size 31ha (77 acres)
English Heritage Grade II*

Rydal Mount

AMBLESIDE, LA22 9LU

Tel 01539 433002 **Fax** 01539 431738
Website www.wordsworthslakes.co.uk
Location 1½ miles north of Ambleside on A591,

turn up Rydal Hill.

Opening hours 9.30 am – 5 pm; daily; March to October. 10 am – 4 pm; daily, except Tuesdays; November to February. Closed 8 to 31 January.

Admission fee Adults £2.

Kept very much as it was in the poet's day, the garden at Rydal Mount is a memorial to William Wordsworth. He believed that a garden should be informal in its design, harmonise with the country and keep its views open.

Features daffodils; bluebells; trees; rhododendrons.

Owned by Rydal Mount Trust (Wordsworth Family)
Number of gardeners 1
Size 1.6ha (4 acres)
English Heritage Grade II

Sizergh Castle

KENDAL, LA8 8AE

Tel 01539 560070 **Fax** 01539 560951
Website www.nationaltrust.org.uk
Location 3½ miles south of Kendal.
Opening hours 12.30 pm – 5.30 pm; Sunday – Thursday; 1 April to 31 October.
Admission fee Garden only: Adult £3; Children £1.

One of the best National Trust gardens, Sizergh has lots of interest from wild daffodils and alpines in April to hydrangeas and a hot half-hardy border in September – *Beschorneria yuccoides* and *Buddleja colvilei*. Best of all is the 1920s rock garden, made of local limestone, and home to an important

(and beautiful) collection of ferns – over 100 hardy species and cultivars. Some of the 60 dwarf conifers have grown to a remarkable size.

Features good herbaceous borders; wildflower meadow; tender plants; National Trust shop; tea-room from 1.30 pm.

Owned by The National Trust
Number of gardeners 2
Size 6.4ha (16 acres)
NCCPG National Collections *Asplenium scolopendrium*; *Cystopteris*; *Dryopteris*; *Osmunda*
English Heritage Grade II*

Winderwath Gardens

WINDERWATH, TEMPLE SOWERBY, PENRITH, CA10 2AG

Tel & Fax 01768 88250
Location On A66, 5 miles east of Penrith.
Opening hours 10 am – 4 pm; Monday – Friday; March to October. Plus Saturdays 10 am – 12 noon.
Admission fee Adults £2.50; Children free.

The structure of the garden at Winderwath dates back to about 1900; the wellingtonia, cut-leaf beech and cedar date from this time. The present owner has planted extensive herbaceous beds, alpines and Himalayan species.

Features plants for sale.

Owned by Jane Pollock
Number of gardeners 2
Size 2ha (5 acres)

DERBYSHIRE

Derbyshire has no less than five historic gardens which are listed as Grade I: Chatsworth, Haddon, Hardwick, Kedleston and Melbourne. All are regularly open to the public. The National Gardens Scheme is very active in the county, with a good number of medium-sized and small gardens listed in the Yellow Book.

Nevertheless it is the larger gardens on old estates which offer the most horticultural interest. Much of Derbyshire is high and cold in winter, yet it also has some excellent nurseries and garden centres. Bluebell Nursery & Arboretum, right in the south of the county, has one of the most exciting new collections of trees and shrubs in the British Isles, while Abbey Brook Cactus Nursery in Matlock has for long been the UK's leading specialist nursery for cacti and succulents. Its five National Collections of *Conophytum, Echinopsis, Gymnocalycium, Haworthia* and *Lithops* are unmatched by any other collection holder. Begonias and gladiolus are popular in Derbyshire, and fine displays are often seen at local flower shows. Derby College at Broomfield Hall is a RHS Partner College with a wide range of workshops and lectures throughout the year: details from 01332 836600.

Abbey Brook Cactus Nursery

BAKEWELL ROAD, MATLOCK, DE4 2QJ

Tel 01629 580306 **Fax** 01629 558552
Website www.abbeybrookcacti.com
Location On A6, 2 miles north of Matlock.
Opening hours 1 pm – 4 pm; Wednesday – Friday. 1 pm – 5 pm; Saturdays, Sundays & Bank Holiday Mondays. Closed 1 January, 25 & 26 December.
Admission fee Free.

Abbey Brook is the UK's leading cactus nursery, now 90% wholesale and with 1,000,000 plants in stock. The retail list is remarkable – it offers over 2,000 cultivars, and has at least the same number again among its stock plants. The nursery is worth a visit at any time of the year – so is the website, which offers a full-colour catalogue. Cactus buffs need no introduction to Abbey Brook, but the nursery is also extremely interesting for those whose gardening interests are quite different. It displays the wonder and beauty of these plants in such a way that you cannot help responding to them – and their extraordinary diversity. There are three special open weekends for the NCCPG this year: 27 & 28 March, 29 & 30 May, and 25 & 26 September 2004.

Features restaurant/café.

Owned by Brian Fearn
Number of gardeners 4
Size 0.15ha (one-third of an acre) of glass

NCCPG National Collections *Conophytum*; *Echinopsis* hybrids; *Gymnocalycium*; *Haworthia*; *Lithops*

Bluebell Arboretum & Nursery

ANNWELL LANE, SMISBY, ASHBY-DE-LA-ZOUCH, LE65 2TA

Tel 01530 413700 **Fax** 01530 417600
Website www.bluebellnursery.com
Location 200 yards south of Smisby Church. Follow brown tourist signs to arboretum.
Opening hours 9 am – 5 pm (4 pm from November to February); Monday – Saturday; all year. 10.30 am – 4.30 pm; Sundays; March to October (NB closed on Sundays from November to February). Closed on Easter Sunday and from 24 December to 4 January.
Admission fee Adults £2.50; Children free. RHS members free.

Bluebell Arboretum & Nursery has been a stalwart supporter of RHS shows for some years now and has won many medals for its displays of rare trees and shrubs. The six-acre arboretum has expanded every year since it was first planted in 1992 and is already remarkably mature, but the owners are keen to emphasise that 'you should not expect to find a Westonbirt, Wisley or Wakehurst' yet. Nevertheless, it is a most interesting place to visit, with a fluid design and two ponds. The tallest trees are birches, alders and some tearaway poplars which have already reached 15m. Most visitors are intrigued by the many cultivars of dogwoods (*Cornus*), maples (*Acer*) and beech (*Fagus sylvestris*). Particular successes include *Morus alba* 'Pendula' and *Magnolia* 'Vulcan'. Other highlights are fine specimens of *Quercus castaneifolia* 'Green Spire' and the very rare *Quercus rhysophylla* from Mexico, and the largest collection of deciduous hollies *Ilex verticillata* in Europe. The website allows on-line ordering: the nursery sells many more plants than those listed in its excellent catalogue. Four RHS special events will take place at Bluebell Arboretum & Nursery during 2004: details from 020 7821 3408.

Features fine collection of trees & shrubs; important tree & shrub nursery.

Owned by Mr & Mrs Robert Vernon
Size 2ha (5 acres)

Calke Abbey

TICKNALL, DE73 1LE

Tel 01332 863822 **Fax** 01332 865272
Website www.nationaltrust.org.uk
Location 10 miles south of Derby on A514 in village of Ticknall.
Opening hours 11 am – 5.30 pm; Saturday – Wednesday; 27 March to 31 October.
Admission fee Adults £3.40; Children £1.70.

The 'sleeping beauty' house is not really matched by its garden, but there are interesting glasshouses in the walled garden, a 19th-century ice-house, a bothy and a kitchen garden. The drive runs along a magnificent avenue of ancient limes. In the walled garden is the only surviving Auricula Theatre, originally built to display the perfection of these beautiful 'florist's' plants. The traditional summer bedding is very well done.

Features vegetables; fruit; good herbaceous borders; dahlias; good Victorian-style bedding; deer park; horse-chestnut trees; local varieties of apples & soft fruit; National Trust gift shop; licensed restaurant.

Owned by The National Trust
Number of gardeners 3½
Size 4ha (10 acres)
English Heritage Grade II*

Chatsworth

Bakewell, DE45 1PP

Tel 01246 582204 **Fax** 01246 583536
Website www.chatsworth.org
Location 8 miles north of Matlock off B6012.
Opening hours 11 am (10.30 am from June to August) – 6 pm (last admissions 5 pm); daily; 17 March to 19 December.
Admission fee Adults £5.50; OAPs £4; Children £2.50; Family ticket £13.50.

Chatsworth sits near the bottom of a high valley on the edge of the Peak District surrounded by over 100 acres of beautiful landscaped park – the work of Capability Brown. Into this naturalistic setting successive Dukes of Devonshire have inserted formal designs, flower gardens and magnificent garden buildings. Despite their piecemeal history, the gardens at Chatsworth all come together as a single ornament for the house. They have been open to the public for nearly 200 years. The glory days of Chatsworth's garden were the 1830s and 1840s when Sir Joseph Paxton and the 'bachelor Duke' built the Emperor fountain, the rock garden (huge boulders surrounded by conifers), the arboretum, the pinetum and the 'conservative wall', which was intended to keep the heat and ripen fruit trees (and protects an enormous *Camellia reticulata* 'Captain Rawes' with trunks 80cm thick). The present Duchess has been responsible for some stylish additions such as the serpentine hedges which lead from the Victorian ring pond to a bust of the 6th Duke. Perhaps the best known features at Chatsworth today are the Great Cascade, built in about 1700 and unique in England and the Canal, dug at the same time as a formal sheet of water to set off the southern façade of the house. But there is much of horticultural interest too: a tulip tree avenue, the bamboo walk,

Victorian yews of different hues, the rose garden, the cottage garden, the kitchen garden, the blue-and-white and the orange borders and record trees like *Pinus peuce*. Chatsworth has also long been famous for its camellias and glasshouse grapes, both of which have won many prizes at RHS shows. But perhaps the greatest joy of Chatsworth is the sense, which still pervades the entire estate, that it is a private garden in which every visitor feels that he is a welcome guest.

Features woodland garden; topiary; roses (mainly modern); rock garden; rhododendrons & azaleas; fine collection of trees; pinetum; maze; tulip tree avenue; millennium planting of 100 oaks in 50 different varieties; tallest *Pinus strobus* (42m.) in the British Isles; plants for sale in stable yard; licensed self-service restaurant.

Owned by Chatsworth House Trust
Number of gardeners 21
Size 42ha (105 acres)
English Heritage Grade I

Dam Farm House

EDNASTON, ASHBOURNE, DE6 3BA

Tel 01335 360291
Location Turn off A52 to Bradley, opposite
Ednaston Lane end.
Opening hours 11 am – 4 pm on 25 April (plant
sale). 2 pm – 4 pm on 20 June & 5 September.
Visitors & parties by arrangement from April to
October.
Admission fee Adults £3; Children free.

Mrs Player (born a Loder) has made this
outstanding garden on a greenfield site since
1980. The design is firm, and the planting
exuberant. Clipped hedges enclose a series
of separate gardens which flow into each
other, but in contrast to the firm design, the
planting belongs to the cottage garden
tradition. There is a formal garden by the
house which ends in a delicate white wire
gazebo. The borders are richly planted with
the best of modern plants – *Cercis
canadensis* 'Forest Pansy' for example and
Viburnum sargentii 'Onondaga'. Clematis are
a favourite and there is a surprisingly large
number of plants which one might suppose
too tender for Derbyshire – cistus, ceanothus
and penstemons. Recent additions include a
number of magnolias and a collection of
Cornus kousa and *C. florida* forms and
hybrids. This garden is now in its prime: the
trees are semi-mature and the plants have
lost none of their youthful vigour. Rare
plants abound and are always being added,
but it is their treatment which makes the
garden such an exciting place to visit and
learn from: their planting, training and
cultivation are a model for our times.

Features roses (mainly old-fashioned);
fine collection of trees; scree garden;
young arboretum.

Owned by Mrs Jean Player
Number of gardeners part-time help
Size 1.2ha (3 acres)

Elvaston Castle

BORROWASH ROAD, ELVASTON,
DE72 3EP

Tel 01332 571342 **Fax** 01332 758751
Location 5 miles south-east of Derby. Signed from
A6 & A52.
Opening hours Dawn – dusk (Old English Garden,
9 am – 5 pm, but 4 pm in winter); daily; all year.
Admission fee Gardens free. Car park 70p
midweek, £1.30 weekends.

This is an historic garden, famous for its
spectacular lumpy, yew topiary. It has good
rhododendrons in the park, and
magnificent conifers. It was saved from
oblivion by Derbyshire County Council
some 25 years ago. The parterres have been
replaced and the walled garden replanted
with fine double herbaceous borders, good
seasonal bedding and dahlias, and renamed
the Old English Garden. However, there
remains a possibility that the estate might
soon be sold.

Features topiary; roses (mainly old-
fashioned); good herbaceous borders;
gift shop; restaurant open all year 11 am –
3.30 pm, closed Mondays.

Owned by Derbyshire County Council
Number of gardeners 6
English Heritage Grade II*

Haddon Hall

BAKEWELL, DE45 1LA

Tel 01629 812855 **Fax** 01629 814379
Website www.haddonhall.co.uk
Location 1½ miles south of Bakewell on A6.
Opening hours 10.30 am – 4.30 pm; daily; 1 April
to 30 September. Plus Thursday – Sunday in
October (closes at 4 pm).
Admission fee House & garden: Adults £7.25;
OAPs £6.25; Children £3.75.

Haddon Hall is a substantial house which dates mainly from about 1600. The gardens, however, are less than 100 years old, having been laid out by the 9th Duchess of Rutland in the 1910s and 1920s along the much older terraces. The Duchess planted formal features like yew trees to add to the structure, but her great passion was for roses, and it is for these most beautiful of flowers that the garden is now known. The collection is a good one and, though it lacks any real rarities, it is kept up to date by the addition of all the best repeat-flowering cultivars, which means that there is a good selection of modern roses among the older ramblers and Noisettes. The hybrid teas include the bright crimson 'Royal William' and pink 'Paul Shirville' and among the floribundas are yellow 'Arthur Bell' and the dark red 'The Times' rose. But shrub roses and wild rose species are also well represented. There are 60 different cultivars of delphinium in the herbaceous borders, which are supplemented by tender perennials and annuals, hardy and half-hardy. In June and July there is no more beautiful and romantic garden in England.

Features topiary; good herbaceous borders; roses of every kind; clematis; delphiniums; coffee, lunch, afternoon teas.

Owned by Lord Edward Manners
Number of gardeners 2
English Heritage Grade I

Hardwick Hall

DOE LEA, CHESTERFIELD, S44 5QJ

Tel 01246 850430 **Fax** 01246 854200
Website www.nationaltrust.org.uk
Location Signed from M1 Jct 29.
Opening hours Gardens: 11 am – 5.30 pm; Wednesday – Saturday; 31 March to 31 October.
Admission fee Garden only: Adults £3.70; Children £1.85.

The formal gardens at Hardwick are of special interest to those with a sense of history: tall hedges of hornbeam and yew, spacious and simple. In the 'Elizabethan' (actually 1970s) herb garden, thyme and chamomile, lavender, laurel and rue are supplemented by seasonal bedding and dahlias. Elsewhere are old fruit trees, a nut-garden, a mulberry avenue, old roses and modern borders in the Jekyll style.

Features good herbaceous borders; daffodils; fine hedges; mulberry walk; hollies; refreshments Wed/Thurs/Sat/Sun when Hall is open.

Owned by The National Trust
Number of gardeners 4, plus 2 trainees
Size 3.6ha (9 acres)
English Heritage Grade I

Kedleston Hall

DERBY, DE22 5JH

Tel 01332 842191 **Fax** 01332 841972
Website www.nationaltrust.org.uk
Location 5 miles north-west of Derby, signed at A38/A52 roundabout.
Opening hours 10 am – 6 pm; daily; 20 March to 31 October.
Admission fee Park & garden only: Adults £2.60; Children £1.30.

Kedleston is an important historic garden. The 18th-century landscaped park runs down to a long lake. The house is matched by a Robert Adam summerhouse in the circular garden: impressive and important. Lord Curzon moved it to its present position at the side of the lawns. The park has some splendid trees, most notably a fern-leaved beech (*Fagus sylvatica* 'Aspleniifolia').

Features roses (mainly modern); rhododendrons & azaleas; handsome

Adam orangery; National Trust shop; lunches & teas.

Owned by The National Trust
Number of gardeners 2½
Size 7ha (17½ acres)
English Heritage Grade I

Lea Gardens

LEA, MATLOCK, DE4 5GH

Tel 01629 534380 **Fax** 01629 534260
Location 3 miles south-east of Matlock.
Opening hours 10 am – 5.30 pm; daily; 20 March to 30 June.
Admission fee Adults £3.50; Children 50p; Season ticket £6; wheelchair-bound free.

These rhododendron gardens were started in 1935 by John Marsden-Smedley who was so inspired by his visits to Bodnant and Exbury that he decided to plant his own rhododendron collection. He was then aged 68: by the time he died aged 92 in 1959, the garden contained some 350 cultivars of rhododendron and azaleas. Since that time, it has belonged to the Tye family, who have continued to maintain and develop it. The standard of maintenance is extremely high and it is one of the most beautiful gardens to visit in season. Much is on a steep slope and some of the paths are narrow, but an energetic pusher should be able to negotiate a wheelchair around most of the garden: the principal areas are fairly open. There are large numbers of modern, low-growing rhododendron and azalea hybrids underplanted with naturalised bluebells. Little attempt has been made to segregate the colours but the plants are graded for height, so you stand on a path and look at a mass of rhododendrons of every imaginable hue rising from knee level right back to huge giants far behind. There have been some interesting interplantings with other plants in recent years – ornamental trees, especially conifers, and herbaceous plants like gunneras, celmisias, *Dactylorhiza foliosa* and *Meconopsis betonicifolia*. It should also be said that the garden is extremely well organised for visitors to enjoy themselves.

 Features rhododendrons & azaleas; tea & coffee shop.

Owned by Mr & Mrs J. Tye
Number of gardeners 3
Size 1.8ha (4½ acres)

Melbourne Hall

MELBOURNE, DE73 1EN

Tel 01332 862502 **Fax** 01322 862263
Location 8 miles south of Derby.
Opening hours 1.30 pm – 5.30 pm; Wednesdays, Saturdays, Sundays & Bank Holiday Monday; April to September.
Admission fee Adults £3; OAPs £2.

Melbourne is a near-perfect example of an early 18th-century garden, influenced by Le Nôtre. Terraces, circular *bassins*, palisades of limes, intersecting *allées*, lumpy old hedges and the famous yew tunnel will all fire the visitor's imagination. The lead statues (from Jan van Nost's foundry in Piccadilly in about 1710) are unique: so is the large urn known as the Four Seasons, which was originally cast for Queen Anne.

  Features rococo design; turf terracing; grand avenues; shop; refreshments.

Owned by Lord Ralph Kerr
Number of gardeners 2
English Heritage Grade I

Renishaw Hall

RENISHAW PARK, SHEFFIELD,
S21 3WB

Tel 01246 432310 **Fax** 01246 430760
Website www.sitwell.co.uk
Location 2½ miles from M1 Jct 30.
Opening hours 10.30 am – 4.30 pm; Thursday –
Sunday, plus Bank Holiday Mondays; 1 April to 26
September.
Admission fee Adults £3.75; Concessions £2.80.

The gardens at Renishaw were laid out in
around 1900 by Sir George Sitwell,
grandfather of the present owner. Sir
George was an expert on Italian gardens and
his book *On the Making of Gardens* (1909) is
a gardening classic. He applied the
principles of Italian renaissance gardens to
the garden he made at Renishaw: symmetry,
proportion, scale and shadow. What we see
today are yew hedges, pools, fountains, grass
and statues – a garden which would not be
out of place in Tuscany or the Veneto. The
plantings are modern, mainly herbaceous,
and colour-schemed, but kept within pastel
shades to emphasise the line of the formal
garden. The soft colours of old-fashioned
roses are perfect: Renishaw has three
separate rose gardens with over 1,000 roses.
In the woodland garden and against the
walls of the kitchen garden, tender plants
thrive that seldom survive in Derbyshire –
Acacia dealbata, Cytisus battandieri and
dendromecons. Renishaw is also worth
visiting in the spring, when daffodils fill the
lime avenue: they were first planted in 1680
on the advice of no lesser authority than
John Evelyn. In the recently restored
orangery, the National Collection of yuccas
is displayed against an Arizona landscape.

Features Italian garden; yew walks &
pyramids; clematis; woodland walks;
roses (ancient & modern); good herbaceous
borders; daffodils; café.

Owned by Sir Reresby Sitwell
Number of gardeners 4
Size 2.8ha (7 acres) formal gardens, plus
woodlands
NCCPG National Collections *Yucca*
English Heritage Grade II*

DEVON

No county has such an abundance of good gardens and nurseries as Devon: Devonians maintain that it is the best place in the world for gardening with plants. Rich soils ('Devon acres') and high rainfall make for excellent growth, but the county's microclimates are immensely variable, from the cold, windswept uplands of Dartmoor to valleys along the southern coast which are virtually frost-free. The Royal Horticultural Society's West Country flagship at Rosemoor shows what can be done to develop a major horticultural garden in little more than 10 years. And there is no private garden in England to match the lifetime achievements of the late Dr Smart at Marwood Hill, now well maintained by his nephew. Devon has some fine general nurseries and garden centres, like Hill House near Ashburton, but surely no county ever had such an abundance of specialist nurseries. Their specialities include hostas (Roger and Ann Bowden near Okehampton), rare perennials (Carol Klein's Glebe Cottage Plants), violets (Devon Violet Nursery at Rattery), rare trees (Thornhayes Nursery near Cullompton) and penstemon (Shirley Reynolds at Seaton). Devon has more National Collection holders than any other county, including many tender genera like *Azara* and *Agapanthus*. There are comparatively few top-class historic gardens and – such as they are – they tend to date from the 19th century like Bicton. Nevertheless the history of Devon gardens is extremely well documented and the Devon Gardens Trust has a large and vigorous membership. Bicton, Killerton and Endsleigh have splendid collections of old trees: in Edwardian times the avenue of monkey puzzles (*Araucaria araucana*) at Bicton was one of the wonders of English horticulture. Bicton College of Agriculture is a RHS Partner College. The National Gardens Scheme also does exceptionally well in Devon, with more gardens open for its charities than anywhere else in the south-west. Deep narrow lanes and inadequate signage are problems for garden-visitors. Nevertheless, Devon remains a county of horticultural superlatives.

Arlington Court

ARLINGTON, BARNSTAPLE, EX31 4LP

Tel 01271 850296 **Fax** 01271 851108
Website www.nationaltrust.org.uk
Location 8 miles north of Barnstaple on A39.
Opening hours 10.30 am – 5 pm; Sunday – Friday;
28 March to 31 October. Plus 10.30 am – 4.30 pm
on Saturdays from 1 July to 31 August.
Admission fee Gardens only: Adults £4, but £2.60
on Saturdays in July & August.

Arlington offers mature parkland on a level
site in front of a fine Georgian house. It has
a pretty Victorian formal garden: herbaceous
borders and basket beds with bedding plants
on three grass terraces around a handsome
conservatory. In the walled garden, recently
part-restored, 19th-century fruit and
vegetables grow alongside local cultivars.

Features mature conifers; huge old
rhododendrons; National Trust shop;
restaurant & tea-room.

Owned by The National Trust
Number of gardeners 2
Size 12ha (30 acres)
English Heritage Grade II

Bicton Park Gardens

EAST BUDLEIGH, BUDLEIGH
SALTERTON, EX9 7BJ

Tel 01395 568465 **Fax** 01395 568374
Website www.bictongardens.co.uk
Location On B3178 between Budleigh Salterton &
Newton Poppleford.
Opening hours 10 am – 6 pm (5 pm in winter);
daily except Christmas Day.
Admission fee Adults £4.95; OAPs £3.95; Children
£2.95; Dogs £1. (2003 prices). RHS members free in
March and November.

There is lots to see at Bicton, including the
Italian Garden, American Garden,
Mediterranean Garden, and Stream Garden,
as well as the classical orangery, three walled
gardens, a hermitage; and the finest pre-
Paxton palm house, built from 18,000 tiny
panes of glass. The trees are important and
impressive: they include 25 champions.
There are collections of dwarf conifers, roses
(ancient and modern) and ferns. Colour
comes from fine camellias, magnolias,
azaleas and rhododendrons. A rugged
Wisteria sinensis is thought to be Britain's
oldest at over 180 years. And there is a
narrow-gauge railway to chug you through
the Pinetum and lakeside areas.

Features woodland garden; roses
(ancient & modern); plantsman's
collection of plants; plants under glass;
mature conifers; good herbaceous borders;
fine collection of trees; tallest Grecian fir
Abies cephalonica (41m) ever recorded in the
British Isles; garden shop; restaurant.

Owned by Simon & Valerie Lister
Number of gardeners 6
Size 25ha (63 acres)
English Heritage Grade I

Ann & Roger Bowden

HOSTAS, STICKLEPATH, OKEHAMPTON,
EX20 2NL

Tel 01837 840481 **Fax** 01837 840482
Website www.hostas-uk.com
Location Near Okehampton, in centre of
Sticklepath, near turning signed 'Skaigh'.
Opening hours By appointment only. Garden open
for NGS: 10.30 am – 5 pm; 24 & 25 April and 5 & 6
June.
Admission fee Adults £2; Children free.

Ann and Roger Bowden know everything
there is to know about hostas: they are the

UK's leading ambassadors for these useful and easy-to-grow beauties. They sell them from a handsome catalogue with excellent photographs. Prices are fair and range from £3 for basic species to £15 for the latest imported hybrids. But the choice is magnificent: some 400 different hostas, of which a large number are new or re-introduced. Their garden at Cleave House in Sticklepath (NB there are two Sticklepaths in Devon – this is the Okehampton one) has been developed over the last 30 years with mixed plantings for year-round interest. But the display beds for their National Collection of hostas are here too – an incredible 1,000 cultivars.

Owned by Mr & Mrs Roger Bowden
Size 0.4ha (1 acre)
NCCPG National Collections *Hosta* (modern hybrids)

Buckland Abbey

YELVERTON, PL20 6EY

Tel 01822 853607 **Fax** 01822 855448
Website www.nationaltrust.org.uk
Location Signed from A386 at Yelverton.
Opening hours 2 pm – 5 pm; Saturdays & Sundays; 14 February to 21 March. 10.30 am – 5.30 pm; Friday – Wednesday; 27 March to 31 October. 2 pm – 5 pm; Saturdays & Sundays; 6 November to 19 December.
Admission fee Adults £2.90; Children £1.40. Free in winter.

Originally a Cistercian Abbey, then the house of Sir Francis Drake, the main interest for garden lovers is the charming herb garden along the side of the Great Barn. It has over 50 different culinary and medicinal herbs. The new Elizabethan garden has topiary bushes, box-edged beds, plants from Tudor times and a small orchard of old fruit cultivars.

Features herbs; current holder of Sandford Award; refreshments.

Owned by The National Trust
Number of gardeners 1½
Size 1.2ha (3 acres)

Burrow Farm Gardens

DALWOOD, AXMINSTER, EX13 7ET

Tel 01404 831285 **Fax** 01404 831445
Website www.burrowfarmgardens.co.uk
Location Turn north off A35 at Taunton Cross: follow brown tourist signs for ½ mile.
Opening hours 10 am – 7 pm; daily; April to September.
Admission fee Adults £3.50; Children 50p.

There are nearly ten acres of plantsmanship at Burrow Farm Gardens, and long views over the sweeping hills. A formal pergola walk is lined with shrubs and climbing roses, while the woodland garden is underplanted with rhododendrons, azaleas and interesting herbaceous plants. The candelabra primulas have naturalised all through the bog garden. And the garden is still growing – both in its size and in the intensity of its planting. A recent addition was the rill garden, lined with luxuriantly colour-themed plantings of shrubs and unusual herbaceous plants.

Features plantsman's collection of plants; woodland garden; morning coffee, light lunches, teas.

Owned by Mr & Mrs J. Benger
Number of gardeners 2
Size 4ha (10 acres)

Castle Drogo

DREWSTEIGNTON, EX6 6PB

Tel 01647 433306 **Fax** 01647 433186
Website www.nationaltrust.org.uk
Location Drewsteignton village: signs from A30 &
A382.
Opening hours 10.30 am – 5.30 pm or dusk; daily;
all year.
Admission fee Adults £3.15; Children £1.60.

This is a major 1920s garden, made to
match the last castle built in Britain – a
granite vanity which was one of Lutyens's
most remarkable works. The gardens too are
grand and grandiose and, up on the edge of
Dartmoor, the highest gardens owned by the
National Trust. They are mainly within a
large enclosed area, tightly hedged against
the wind by thick, clipped yew. The design is
formal and terraced with granite steps and
walls. Both the rose garden (planted with
Hybrid Teas and Floribundas) and the vast
and vivid herbaceous borders are a contrast
with the austere castle on its windy bluff.
Weather-beaten, lichen-heavy Japanese
cherries, rhododendrons and acers survive
in the woodland spring garden on the
slopes below.

Features woodland garden; roses
(ancient & modern); rock garden; good
herbaceous borders; National Trust shop;
self-service tea-room; waitress-service
restaurant.

Owned by The National Trust
Number of gardeners 2½
Size 5ha (12½ acres)
English Heritage Grade II*

Clovelly Court

CLOVELLY, BIDEFORD, EX39 5SZ

Tel 01237 431200 **Fax** 01237 431205
Website www.clovelly.co.uk
Location Signed in village.
Opening hours 10 am – 4 pm; daily; March to
October.
Admission fee Adults £1.50; Children 20p. RHS
members free in March & October.

Clovelly Court Garden is a classic example
of the Victorian Kitchen Garden tradition.
Lean-to greenhouses with original manual
levers house apricots, melons, peaches,
nectarines, a vine, citrus and a fig tree. New
espalier fan and cordon trees line the walls
enclosing the garden, which also shelter the
vegetables grown organically and in
rotation. Flower borders form the lower half
of the walled garden. From the village of
Clovelly a woodland walk know as the Long
Walk leads an elegant and beautiful path to
the gardens. Many tender plants flourish
within the unique maritime microclimate of
the gardens.

Owned by The Hon. John Rous
Number of gardeners 1, plus 3 part-times
Size 0.6ha (1½ acres)

Coleton Fishacre Garden

COLETON, KINGSWEAR, DARTMOUTH,
TQ6 0EQ

Tel 01803 752466 **Fax** 01803 753017
Website www.nationaltrust.org.uk
Location 3 miles from Kingswear off Lower-Ferry
Road.
Opening hours 11 am – 5 pm; Saturdays &
Sundays in March. 10.30 am – 5.30 pm (or dusk, if
earlier); Wednesday – Sundays & Bank Holidays; 31

March to 31 October.
Admission fee Adults £4.10; Children £2. RHS members free.

The Lutyens-style house at Coleton Fishacre was built by Oswald Milne for Sir Rupert and Lady Dorothy D'Oyly Carte in 1925. Rare bulbs flourish in the warm terraces which surround it. The woodland garden, thickly planted with rhododendrons, azaleas and camellias, crashes down a secret valley to the sea. A stream runs down the valley, dammed to make small pools along the way, where damp-loving perennials luxuriate. Almost frost-free, the range and size of Southern Hemisphere trees and shrubs is astounding – *groves* of mimosa, for example.

Features woodland garden; sub-tropical plants; plantsman's collection of plants; good herbaceous borders; rhododendrons; rare trees; tallest *Catalpa bungei* in the British Isles (and two other record trees); interesting new plantings in the 'Holiwell' area; visitor reception area & tea room.

Owned by The National Trust
Number of gardeners 3
Size 10ha (25 acres)
English Heritage Grade II

Dartington Hall

DARTINGTON, TOTNES, TQ9 6EL

Tel & Fax 01803 862367
Website www.dartington.u-net.com
Location 2 miles north-west of Totnes.
Opening hours Dawn – dusk; daily; all year. Groups by prior appointment only. For NGS on 25 April & 16 May.
Admission fee Donation (£2 suggested).

Dartington is one of the best examples of grand mid-20th century gardening in England: it was restored and improved with American money at a time when few Englishmen could afford to spend on such a scale. Some famous designers are associated with it: Beatrix Farrand designed the courtyard and influenced the woodland plantings. Percy Cane built the long staircase, and opened up some of the long vistas. Henry Moore deposited a reclining woman. The scale is magnificent, and wholly appropriate to the house and landscape. The grassy 'tiltyard', planted with Irish yews known as the 'twelve apostles', is now considered iconic. The gardens are very well maintained and full of horticultural interest, but the detail is never allowed to obscure the greater scheme of it. Dartington also has fine mature trees and some interesting modern additions like the quietly contemplative Japanese garden.

Features woodland garden; topiary; magnolias; rhododendrons; camellias; dry-landscape Japanese garden.

Owned by Dartington Hall Trust
Number of gardeners 4
Size 11.1ha (28 acres)
English Heritage Grade II*

Docton Mill

LYMEBRIDGE, HARTLAND, BIDEFORD, EX39 6EA

Tel & Fax 01237 441369
Website www.doctonmill.co.uk
Location Take road from Hartland to Stoke & follow signs towards Elmscott.
Opening hours 10 am – 6 pm; daily; March to October.
Admission fee Adults £3.50; OAPs £3; Children (under 14) £1. RHS members free in March & April, September & October, and on Saturdays in between.

The main attraction at Docton used to be a working water mill. It is still a great draw, but the garden has a stronger pull nowadays. The new owners have made many improvements. First they planted up a small field with magnolias (25 cultivars) and flowering shrubs. In 2001 they filled a large new glasshouse. Much of the garden is natural bluebell woodland, into which shrubs like rhododendrons have been planted over the last 20 years. But there is also a fine bog garden (candelabra primulas in late spring) and a collection of old roses underplanted with herbaceous and ground-cover plants.

Features apple orchards; new David Austin rose bed; some young magnolias; light refreshments & cream teas.

Owned by Mr & Mrs J. Borrett
Number of gardeners 2
Size 3.4ha (8½ acres)

Escot

OTTERY ST. MARY, EXETER, EX11 1LU

Tel 01404 822188 **Fax** 01404 822903
Website www.escot-devon.co.uk
Location Signed from Fairmile.
Opening hours 10 am – 6 pm; daily; all year.
Admission fee Adults £4.95; OAPs & Children £3.50; under fours free. Reduced rates from November to March.

Escot is a elegant Regency house, with distant views to East Hill: Capability Brown advised on the prospect. The walled garden has a pretty collection of climbing roses, and a few old shrub roses too. The woodlands around the house are full of good Victorian rhododendrons, a hardy fernery, some good 19th-century trees (holm-oaks, purple beech, cedar & wellingtonias) and good new plantings.

Great efforts have been made to make Escot fun for the young – not just animals, fish and birds, but also trails, a grass maze, a collection of upside-down trees and a cork oak hung with bottles by Ivan Hicks. It is fairly wild and roughly maintained, and is not a place for sensitive horticulturists, but brilliant for children.

Features snowdrops; rhododendrons & azaleas; mature conifers; bluebells; water-plants for sale; home-cooked lunches & cream teas.

Owned by John-Michael Kennaway
Number of gardeners 1
Size 10ha (25 acres)

Exeter University Gardens

EXETER, EX4 4PX

Tel 01392 263059 **Fax** 01392 264547
Website www.ex.ac.uk
Location 1 miles north of city centre: gardens throughout the main campus.
Opening hours Dawn – dusk; daily; all year.
Admission fee Free.

From the horticultural point of view, Exeter has the most interesting university campus in England: the gardens are educational, attractive and important. At the centre are the gardens around Reed Hall, laid out by Veitch in the 1860s at the then phenomenal cost of £70,000. This explains the framework of splendid mature trees and shrubs which give such character to the whole site – especially conifers, rhododendrons, magnolias and hardy palm trees. Modern plantings have kept pace: there is a particularly fine collection of Australasian plants including acacias, callistemons and eucalyptus. Other tender plants that grow outside include *Albizia*

The Garden House

BUCKLAND MONACHORUM, YELVERTON, PL20 7LQ

Tel 01822 854769 **Fax** 01822 855358
Website www.thegardenhouse.org.uk
Location Signed off A386 on Plymouth side of Yelverton.
Opening hours 10.30 am – 5 pm; daily; March to October.
Admission fee Adults £4.50; OAPs £4; Children £1.

The Garden House was first developed by the late Lionel Fortescue, a retired Eton 'beak' between 1945 and 1981. The setting is awesome: a ruined ecclesiastical site on the edge of Dartmoor, with stupendous views. Fortescue was responsible for much of the design and planting as we still see it in the walled garden. He was a great plantsman and insisted upon growing only the best forms and cultivars. He also believed that plants should be well fed and firmly controlled: they still flourish on the treatment and Fortescue's plantings have continued to fulfil their early promise. Over the last 20 years, however, the Garden House has developed in quite a different way under the guidance of the curator Keith Wiley. He has developed six acres of inter-connected gardens, each dedicated to a single theme. The South African garden is intended to replicate the spring flowering of the South African veldt, though mixed with some Californian annuals which pick up the same bright colours – eschscholtzias among the arctotis and osteospermums: it is probably best in July and August. Nearby is the quarry garden where natural outcrops have been covered with such plants as rock roses and creeping thymes around a series of ponds fed by a waterfall. The Cretan cottage garden is a pan-European wildflower meadow where the native campions and ox-eye daisies are joined by such plants as

Alchemilla mollis and astrantias. There is an maple glade underplanted with thousands of naturalised crocus in March, followed by azaleas in April and May: the autumn colour is spectacular. Elsewhere are a lime avenue, a spring garden, a herbaceous bed, a wisteria bridge, a peat garden and a bulb meadow . But this is a garden in an active state of evolution, full of new features and stimulation at every time of the year.

Features plantsman's collection of plants; good herbaceous borders; alpine bank; flowering cherries; wisterias; a developing naturalistic extension with *Acer* glade, spring garden, quarry garden, wildflower meadow & South African garden tea-room with light lunches.

Owned by Fortescue Garden Trust
Number of gardeners 5
Size 4ha (10 acres)

julibrissin, cacti like *Opuntia humifusa* and the beautiful parrot-bill plant (*Clianthus puniceus*) from New Zealand. The gardeners also practise with great artistry the Victorian art of bedding out.

Features tender plants; heathers; summer bedding; conifers; rhododendrons.

Owned by The University of Exeter
Number of gardeners 25
Size 100ha (250 acres)
NCCPG National Collections *Azara*

Gidleigh Park Hotel

CHAGFORD, TQ13 8HH

Tel 01647 432367 **Fax** 01647 432574
Website www.gidleigh.com
Location 20 miles west of Exeter. Approach from Chagford: do NOT go to Gidleigh.
Opening hours Guests of the hotel & restaurant only.
Admission fee Free to hotel & restaurant clients.

(P) (wc) (☕)

Gidleigh has 45 acres of established woodland on the edge of Dartmoor. Many of the rhododendrons and conifers were planted in the 19th century and are wonderfully mature. Around the Tudorised house – now a top hotel – is a 1920s garden. Below is a fine 1930s water garden. The garden contains nothing very rare or special, but the position is stupendous and the sense of space, even grandeur, is enhanced by immaculate maintenance. The hotel and restaurant have received innumerable awards over many years. Finding it needs careful map-reading: in Chagford Square turn right at Lloyds Bank and, after 150 yards, take the first fork to the right and follow the lane for two miles to its end. The excellent website includes a virtual tour of the garden.

Features woodland garden; delicious food in Hotel.

Owned by Paul Henderson
Number of gardeners 4
Size 18ha (45 acres)

Gnome Reserve & Wild Flower Garden

WEST PUTFORD, BRADWORTHY, EX22 7XE

Tel 01409 241435
Website www.gnomereserve.co.uk
Location Between Bideford & Holsworthy, signed from A39, A386 & A388.
Opening hours 10 am – 6 pm; daily; 21 March to 31 October.
Admission fee Adults £2.45; OAPs £2.20; Children £1.90.

There are four reasons to visit this remarkable conservation centre which has been featured on television more than 60 times: first, the two-acre gnome reserve in a beech wood with a stream; second the two-acre pixies' wildflower meadow, with 250 labelled species; third, the kiln where pottery gnomes and pixies are born; fourth, the museum of rare early gnomes. A large slice of gardening history is displayed in this garden and its museum, while the wildflower meadow is one of the best in the country.

Features wildflower meadow; large shop selling gnomes; sandwiches, drinks & ice-creams.

Owned by The Atkin Family
Number of gardeners 3
Size 1.6ha (4 acres)

Greenway

GREENWAY ROAD, GALMPTON,
CHURSTON FERRERS, TQ5 0ES

Tel 01803 842382 **Fax** 01803 661900
Website www.nationaltrust.org.uk
Location 6 miles east of Brixham, on the Dart estuary.
Opening hours 10.30 am – 5 pm; Wednesday – Saturday; 3 March to 9 October.
Admission fee £3.90, but £3.25 for visitors arriving on foot, bike or public transport.

Greenway is one of the National Trust's newest acquisitions, with a wonderful collection of subtropical exotica: among the best specimens are mimosas, clianthus, myrtles, mahonias and puyas. The collection of camellias (over 200 different cultivars, most of them in the sensational camellia walk) is exceptional, and there are more than 50 different *Eucalyptus* species. All visitors intending to arrive by car must telephone 01803 842382 to book a parking space before arriving at this property (the morning of the day in question is usually all right). Visitors arriving without having booked a parking space will not be admitted. There are no parking spaces on the narrow country lanes leading to the property.

 Features camellias; subtropical plants; eucalyptus; café.

Owned by The National Trust
Number of gardeners 3
Size 13ha (33 acres)

Higher Knowle

LUSTLEIGH, NEWTON ABBOTT,
TQ13 9SP

Tel 01647 277275 **Fax** 0870 131 5914
Location 3 miles north-west of Bovey Tracey.

Opening hours 2 pm – 6 pm; Sundays & Bank Holiday Mondays; 28 March to 31 May.
Admission fee Adults £2.50; Children free.

Higher Knowle was built by a pupil of Lutyens on a wooded slope on the south-eastern edge of Dartmoor: a stream flows down towards the Bovey valley – the views are stupendous. The first plantings date from the late 1950s – mature azaleas and magnolias around the house. The present owners bought the property in 1966 and have since planted up the lower woodland area with camellias, modern magnolias and rhododendrons. Bluebells, primroses and huge boulders of natural granite add to its charm, especially in spring.

Owned by Mr & Mrs David Quicke
Number of gardeners owners only
Size 1.2ha (3 acres)

Hill House

LANDSCOVE, ASHBURTON, NEWTON
ABBOT, TQ13 7LY

Tel & Fax 01803 762273
Website www.hillhousenursery.co.uk
Location Off A384, follow signs for Landscove.
Opening hours 11 am – 5 pm; daily; all year (including bank holidays). Closed 15 December to 9 January.
Admission fee Free.

This Victorian Old Vicarage was made famous by Edward Hyams' *An Englishman's Garden* but for many years now it is has been the centre of a distinguished plantsman's nursery. Family-owned and family-run, the three-acre nursery has an excellent range of unusual or 'hard-to-find' plants – a list of over 3,000 in all, most of them available at any one time. In the glasshouses are handsome large specimens, particularly of fuchsias and passion flowers. Most of the stock is raised in the nursery. Raymond Hubbard also breeds plants: this is where *Nemesia* 'Bluebird' originated. He is also the breeder of *Dianthus* 'Old Mother Hubbard', *Plectranthus argentatus* 'Hill House' and *P. ciliatus* 'Sasha'.

Features mature conifers; daffodils; cyclamen and snowdrops; herbaceous borders; pond garden; conservatory; garden shop; tea-room (home-made cakes) March to September.

Owned by Raymond & Matthew Hubbard
Number of gardeners 2 part-time
Size 1.2ha (3 acres)

Killerton

BROADCLYST, EXETER, EX5 3LE

Tel 01392 881345 **Fax** 01392 883112
Website www.nationaltrust.org.uk
Location West side of B3181, Exeter to Cullompton Road.
Opening hours 10.30 am – dusk; daily; all year.
Admission fee Adults £4.20; Children £2.10.
Reduced rates in winter.

Killerton is an historic giant among gardens. Its long connections with Veitch's Nursery have bequeathed it a great tree collection. These include innumerable record-breaking specimens, many from collectors' seed, though one's sense of awe may be a little spoilt by droning traffic on the M5.

Features snowdrops; rock garden; rhododendrons & azaleas; daffodils; fine collection of trees; bluebells; tallest *Ostrya carpinifolia* (22m.) in the British Isles (and eight further record trees); magnolias; drifts of *Crocus tommasinianus*; National Trust shop; small well-run plant centre; waitress-service restaurant and self-service tea-room.

Owned by The National Trust
Number of gardeners 5
Size 8.7ha (22 acres)
English Heritage Grade II*

Knightshayes Garden

TIVERTON, EX16 7RG

Tel 01884 254665 **Fax** 01884 243050
Website www.nationaltrust.org.uk
Location Off A396 Tiverton – Bampton Road.
Opening hours 11 am – 5.30 pm; Saturdays & Sundays; 28 February to 21 March. Then daily; 27 March to 31 October.
Admission fee Adults £4.80; Children £2.40.

Knightshayes is a garden in a wood – one of the best of its kind in the world. Much of the original canopy is there – notably some very fine oaks – but it is now supplemented by magnolias, birches, nothofagus and sorbus. The garden unveils as a series of walks and glades, with beautiful rhododendrons, camellias and rare shrubs underplanted by hellebores, erythroniums, foxgloves, cyclamen and bluebells. Closer to the house are the stately formal gardens, enclosed by immaculately clipped yew hedges. Here alpine treasures and small bulbs grow in raised beds. The old bowling lawn is filled by a vast circular pool and a single weeping pear, *Pyrus salicifolia* 'Pendula', which is pruned to thin out its canopy of branches. The walled garden, near the stables, is being restored and run organically. In the surrounding park is a very fine collection of trees, including several record breakers. The Douglas firs are particularly impressive.

Features woodland garden; topiary; good herbaceous borders; hellebores; cyclamen; bulbs; peat beds; centenary planting of 100 trees along visitors' entrance; tallest *Quercus cerris* (40m.) in the

British Isles; National Trust shop; licensed restaurant; coffee, lunch & teas.

Owned by The National Trust
Number of gardeners 6
Size 20ha (50 acres)
English Heritage Grade II*

Lukesland

HARFORD, IVYBRIDGE, PL21 0JF

Tel 01752 893390 **Fax** 01752 896011
Location 1½ miles north of Ivybridge on the Harford road.
Opening hours 2 pm – 6 pm; Wednesdays, Sundays & Bank Holiday Mondays; 13 April to 13 June. Also on 21 & 28 March and 4 April.
Admission fee Adults £3.30; Children free. £2.60 on 21 & 28 March and 4 April.

  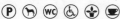

Lukesland is a woodland garden in a stream-fed valley on the southern edge of Dartmoor: it offers the perfect conditions for growing rhododendrons, azaleas and many other flowering shrubs. The house and the earliest plantings date from the 1880s, but most of what we see now has been planted by the Howells since 1975. The family's policy is to try to regenerate poor or over-mature areas, so that the quality and display of plants are improved: during the 1990s, for example, they planted a good selection of late-flowering rhododendrons at the north end of the pinetum. Here too, in 1992, they built a striking reverse suspension bridge, designed by the Scottish architect Sir James Dunbar-Nasmith. The many paths and bridges crossing the stream open up different views as you progress through the garden. The fine examples of rhododendron species include the large-leafed *R. sinogrande*, *R. macabeanum*, *R. falconeri* and *R. arizelum*. The Exbury hybrids include 'Cornish Cross', 'Hawk

Crest' and 'Jalisco'. Youngish camellias are already making an impact, while other good shrubs include *Drimys lanceolata*, *Michelia doltsopa*, hoherias and eucryphias. There are some very fine specimen trees: *Ginkgo biloba* at 22m, *Davidia involucrata* var. *vilmoriniana* planted in 1936 and now a broad 17m specimen, and a magnificent *Magnolia campbellii* planted at the same time and now about 23m high – its exceptionally wide spread makes it one of the largest in the country.

Features small pinetum; rhododendrons & azaleas; stream, ponds & waterfalls; tea-room (from 11 April)

Owned by Mrs R. Howell
Number of gardeners family, plus part-time help
Size 6ha (15 acres)

Mothecombe House

HOLBETON, PLYMOUTH, PL8 1LA

Tel 01752 830444
Location 10 miles south-east of Plymouth; signed from A379.
Opening hours 2 pm – 5 pm; 21 March; 18 April; 1, 2 & 30 May; 13 & 27 June; 11 July; & 3 October.
Admission fee Adults £3.

Mothecombe is a beautiful, unspoilt estate which runs down to the sandy shore. The walled garden has fruit, vegetables, flowers and borders. In the woodlands are spring bulbs, a camellia walk, flowering shrubs and a bog garden as well as a stream and large pond. And masses of bluebells.

Features nursery plant sales; teas.

Owned by Mr and Mrs A. Mildmay-White
Number of gardeners 2
Size 6ha (15 acres)

Marwood Hill Gardens

MARWOOD, BARNSTAPLE, EX31 4EB

Tel 01271 42528
Website www.marwoodhillgarden.co.uk
Location Signed from A361 Barnstaple to Braunton Road.
Opening hours Dawn – dusk; daily; all year except Christmas Day.
Admission fee Adults £3.

Marwood Hill is a remarkable plantsman's garden, conceived on a grand scale and fast maturing, though it is still expanding along the long sheltered valley which gives such vigorous growth to its plants. Its is a tribute to the energy, determination and sheer plantsmanship of the late Dr Smart, who died in 2002. Marwood Hill is exciting for its scale and variety: there is no better place in the South West to learn about plants of every kind, especially as all the plants are clearly labelled. It is moreover a garden of year-round interest. Late in the year, *Galanthus reginae-olgae* flowers with the last of the *Cyclamen hederifolium*: these are followed in midwinter by many other snowdrops and *Cyclamen coum*. There is a wonderful collection of camellias at this season too – some in the open, and others (huge bushes of Reticulata Hybrids) under glass. Magnolias are numerous, including many of the Jury hybrids from New Zealand, the dark form of *M. campbellii* called 'Betty Jessel', *M. sprengeri* var. *diva*, *M. dawsoniana*, *M.* x *wieseneri* and the home-grown 'Marwood Spring'. Many are underplanted with drifts of narcissi. Come the spring, and the pergola draped with 12 different wisterias starts into flower (the colour is extended by interplanted clematis and climbing roses) and the walled garden begins to make an impact with ceanothus, *Clianthus puniceus* and the poppy bush (*Dendromecon rigida*). In early summer the bog garden comes into its own, starting with drifts of candelabra primulas and continuing with astilbes from the National Collection: in fact the bog garden is full of colour right through until autumn. Hydrangeas are another success story: a very large number of cultivars is planted throughout the garden. As the soil is acid, the 'mopheads' come out in many shades of blue, alongside the cultivars of *Hydrangea paniculata* (Dr Smart considered 'Pink Diamond' one of the best) and *Hydrangea quercifolia* whose oak-shaped leaves change to brilliant colours in autumn. Leaves and bark are important elements of the garden: Dr Smart planted the birches close to the eucalyptus so that the contrasts of bark can be enjoyed together – he planted large numbers of both *Betula* and *Eucalyptus* species. He also had a high regard for the seldom-seen *Amomyrtus lechleriana* in the walled garden. And there is a fine collection of rhododendrons, including large plants of *R. macabeanum*, *R. sinogrande*, *R. eximium*, *R. arizelum*, *R. arboreum* and *R.* 'Sir Charles Lemon'. There are additions and improvements every year: 2004 sees the start of a three-year project to plant up the hilltop with four acres of prairie garden – grasses, perennials and flower meadows among the eucalyptus.

Features a supreme example of a plants-man's collection of supreme plants; roses (mainly old-fashioned & climbers); rhododendrons & azaleas; plants under glass; daffodils; good herbaceous plants; fine collection of trees; alpine plants; birches; *Eucalyptus*; camellias; hebes; teas, April – September, Sundays & Bank Holidays only.

Owned by Dr J.A. Snowdon
Number of gardeners 4
Size 8ha (20 acres)
NCCPG National Collections Astilbe; *Iris ensata*; *Tulbaghia*

Nicky's Rock Garden Nursery

BROADHAYES, STOCKLAND, HONITON, EX14 9EH

Tel 01404 881213
Location 6 miles east of Honiton, off midpoint of north-south road between A30 & A35.
Opening hours 9 am – dusk, daily. Please telephone first.
Admission fee Free.

This nursery is one of few in the south-west which specialise in alpines. The owners are keen plantsmen and almost everything can be seen growing in their show garden, which is small and not always tidy. However, it is always worth rooting round the sales beds, where there are treasures to find at very moderate prices. The owners enjoy looking at the garden with visitors and talking about the plants.

Features rockeries; troughs; scree; raised beds.

Owned by Bob & Diana Dark
Number of gardeners owners
Size 0.2ha (½ acre)

The Old Glebe

EGGESFORD, CHULMLEIGH, EX18 7QU

Tel & Fax 01769 580632
Location South (& uphill) of Eggesford station for two-thirds of a mile; right into bridleway.
Opening hours 2 pm – 6 pm; 15, 16, 22 & 23 May for National Gardens Scheme. All customers by appointment.
Admission fee Adults £2 & Children £1 on NGS days.

This is a great rhododendron collection, well-known to the *cognoscenti*. Nigel Wright grows over 6,000 plants and 750 different cultivars, and his nursery sells over 200 of them. It is one of the best lists in the UK. The house is an old rectory, with fine lawns, mature trees, walled herbaceous borders, a bog garden and a small lake.

Features rhododendrons.

Owned by Mr & Mrs Nigel Wright
Number of gardeners 4 part-time
Size 2.8ha (7 acres)

Orchid Paradise

BURNHAM NURSERIES, FORCHES CROSS, NEWTON ABBOT, TQ12 6PZ

Tel 01626 352233 **Fax** 01626 362167
Website www.orchids.uk.com
Location Brown signs from A382 between Newton Abbot & Bovey Tracey.
Opening hours 10 am – 4 pm; daily, except Christmas & New Year.
Admission fee Adults £2; Children free.

The Rittershausens are famous for their orchids – their books, their expertise, their exhibits and the range of what they grow and sell. The display houses are open all year – a place of pilgrimage for beginners and experts alike, and a feast for the eyes whatever the weather outside.

**Features** orchids for sale; tea, coffee & light refreshments.

Owned by Sara Rittershausen

Overbeck Museum & Garden

SHARPITOR, SALCOMBE, TQ8 8LW

Tel 01548 843238 **Fax** 01548 845020
Website www.nationaltrust.org.uk
Location 2 miles south of Salcombe.
Opening hours 10 am – 7 pm (or dusk, if earlier);
daily; all year.
Admission fee Adults £3.40; Children £1.70.

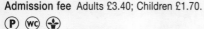

Overbeck has a small, intensely planted,
almost jungly garden, perched above the
Salcombe estuary. The formal terraces
(rather 1930s) are stuffed with interesting
tender plants: *Musa basjoo*, phormiums,
agapanthus, self-sown *Echium pininana* and
every kind of South African daisy, all held
together in a framework of hundreds of
Trachycarpus palms.

Features sub-tropical plants; bluebells;
palms; mimosas; cyclamen; *Magnolia
campbellii*.

Owned by The National Trust
Number of gardeners 2
Size 2.4ha (6 acres)
English Heritage Grade II

Paignton Zoo & Botanical Gardens

TOTNES ROAD, PAIGNTON, TQ4 7EU

Tel 01803 697500 **Fax** 01803 523457
Website www.paigntonzoo.org.uk
Location On A385 Totnes Road, 1 mile from
Paignton.
Opening hours 10 am – 6 pm (or dusk, if earlier);
daily; all year. Closed 25 December.
Admission fee Adults £8.50; OAPs £7; Children
£6.20.

Once a private garden devoted to blue-
flowered and blue-leaved plants, this is now
an inspiring combination of zoo, botanic
collection, public park and holiday
entertainment. Themed plant collections are
one of its more recent features: among them
are economic plants, medical plants;
Mexican oaks; palm species. There are
tropical, temperate and desert-plant
glasshouses.

Features mature trees & shrubs;
unusual exotics; glasshouses with
tropical plants; shops; large self-service
restaurant.

Owned by Whitley Wildlife Conservation Trust
Number of gardeners 6
Size 30ha (75 acres)

Plant World Botanic Gardens

ST MARYCHURCH ROAD, NEWTON
ABBOT, TQ12 4SE

Tel 01803 872939 **Fax** 01803 875018
Website www.plantworld-devon.co.uk
Location Follow brown tourist signs from Penn Inn
roundabout at Newton Abbot, at end of A380 dual
carriageway from Exeter.
Opening hours 9.30 am – 5 pm; daily; April to
September.
Admission fee Adults £2; Children free.

This plantsman's nursery sells a selection of
alpines, perennials and shrubs. There is an
illustrated seed list with fresh material from
the gardens and some interesting collected
species. The National Collection of *Primula*
extends only to the Cortusoides section of
the genus, but the nursery used to collect
the Capitatae and Farinosae too, and it still
grows many from those sections. The
mature four-acre gardens are planted out as
special habitat zones representing the five

continents. They burgeon with rare trees and shrubs: worth a long journey to visit in their own right.

 Features many good plants; innovative design; small self-service café.

Owned by Ray Brown
Number of gardeners 2
Size 1.6ha (4 acres)
NCCPG National Collections Primula (Cortusoides section)

Pleasant View Nursery & Garden

TWO MILE OAK, DENBURY, NEWTON ABBOT, TQ12 6DG

Tel 01803 813388
Location Off A381 at Two Mile Oak pub towards Denbury: then ½ mile on the left.
Opening hours Garden: 2 pm – 5 pm; Wednesdays & Fridays; May to September. Nursery: 10 am – 5 pm; Wednesday – Friday; mid March to end of September.
Admission fee Adults £2.50.

This garden is a remarkable achievement: the collection of trees and shrubs is exceptionally comprehensive – enough to be called an arboretum – and it has all been achieved from open pasture since 1988. Ceanothus and abelias flourish despite being some way inland from the south coast. The nursery has lots of interesting shrubs, both for garden planting and for conservatories, with a special emphasis upon salvias from the National Collection. Pleasant View is the only place to offer some of the rarer species of every kind from all over the world. There will be a special *Salvia* open day on 29 June – booking essential.

Owned by Mr & Mrs B.D. Yeo
Size 1.6ha (4 acres)
NCCPG National Collections Abelia; Salvia

Powderham Castle

EXETER, EX6 8JQ

Tel 01626 890243 **Fax** 01626 890729
Website www.powderham.co.uk
Location Off A379 Dawlish to Exeter Road at Kenton.
Opening hours 10 am – 5.30 pm; Sunday – Friday; 4 April to 2 October.
Admission fee Adults £6.90; OAPs £6.40; Children £3.90. Charges include guided tour of Castle, but there are plans to introduce a 'garden only' ticket this year.

Powderham is not a major garden, though it has some good trees – notably the cork oak (*Quercus suber*) and its Devon hybrid *Q.* x *lucombeana*. Nevertheless the 18th-century landscaped park is serenely English, the woodland garden is stupendous in March and there is a cheerful modern rose garden all along the front of the house. The greenhouses in the Victorian walled garden are now back in commission after recent restoration.

 Features roses (mainly modern); good trees in park; plant centre; licensed restaurant.

Owned by Earl & Countess of Devon
Number of gardeners 3
Size 22ha (55 acres), including grounds
English Heritage Grade II

R.D. Plants

HOMELEA FARM, TYTHERLEIGH, AXMINSTER, EX13 7BG

Tel 01460 220206
Location On A358, just inside the county boundary.
Opening hours 9 am – 1 pm, 2 pm – 5 pm, March to June. Closed on Mondays. Phone first (between 8.30 am & 9.30 am only). Also by appointment for hellebores in February.

This nursery specialises in good herbaceous plants and has an especially good list of plants for damp and shady places – woodlanders from all over the world. It is particularly strong on modern developments of *Helleborus orientalis* – including doubles and anemone-centred forms.

Owned by Rodney Davey & Lynda Windsor

Rowden Gardens

BRENTOR, TAVISTOCK, PL19 0NG

Tel & Fax 01822 810275
Location 1 mile west of North Brentor.
Opening hours For NGS (see Yellow Book) and by prior appointment.
Admission fee £1 for charity.

Rowden Gardens is a nursery with a show garden attached. Its speciality is aquatic plants, and the remarkable thing about the garden is that it planted around thirteen, old, disused water-cress beds – long, rectangular tanks, each resembling a canal. More than 3,000 different plants grow in the garden, which provides the propagating material for the nursery. As well as the four National Collections, there is a good choice of waterlilies and *Iris ensata* cultivars, many of them raised by the nursery. Its list of non-aquatic herbaceous plants now totals nearly 2,000 cultivars, with a particularly strong hand of grasses, ligularias, rheums and rodgersias. But Rowden is also *the* place for celandines and water irises. From its National Collections it grows and offers for sale more species and cultivars than anyone else in Britain. The nursery prides itself on being an introducer of new plants. Until recently it was also a regular exhibitor at RHS shows, where its displays were always much admired for their variety.

Owned by John Carter
Number of gardeners 2
Size 0.4ha (1 acre)
NCCPG National Collections *Caltha*; *Iris* (*fulva*, *pseudacorus*, *versicolor*, *virginica* & *laevigata* cvs); *Polygonum* (i.e. *Fagopyrum*, *Fallopia* & *Persicaria*); *Ranunculus ficaria*

Saltram

PLYMPTON, PLYMOUTH, PL7 3UH

Tel 01752 333500 **Fax** 01752 336474
Website www.nationaltrust.org.uk
Location 2 miles west of Plympton.
Opening hours 11 am – 5 pm; Saturday – Thursday (plus Good Friday); 27 March to 31 October. 11 am – 4 pm; Saturday – Thursday; 1 November to 31 March 2005.
Admission fee Adults £3.30; Children £1.60.

Twenty acres of beautiful parkland, whose huge and ancient trees are underplanted with camellias and rhododendrons. Best in spring when the daffodils flower in hosts.

Features rhododendrons & azaleas; camellias; parkland; handsome orangery; lime avenue; 'melancholy' walk; tallest *Acer palmatum* 'Osakazuki' (13m.) in the British Isles National Trust shop in stable block; licensed tea-room.

Owned by The National Trust
Number of gardeners 3
Size 8ha (20 acres)
English Heritage Grade II*

RHS Garden Rosemoor

GREAT TORRINGTON, EX38 8PH

Tel 01805 624067 **Fax** 01805 624717
Website www.rhs.org.uk
Location 1 mile south of Torrington on A3124 (formerly B3220).
Opening hours 10 am – 6 pm (but 5 pm October to March); daily; all year except 25 December.
Admission fee Adults £5; Children £1; Groups (10+) £4. RHS members (plus one guest) free.

The Royal Horticultural Society's garden at Rosemoor has proved a great success. When Lady Anne Palmer gave it to the Society in 1988, few people imagined that it would develop into such a major tourist attraction. The setting certainly helped – the Torridge valley is unusually wooded and sheltered – and Lady Anne's original garden was full of good plants, but the achievement is entirely due to the Society's good management and its original garden masterplan. This was effectively recognised last year when the garden was awarded the accolade "Large Visitor Attraction of the Year 2003" for the South-West. Rosemoor is now an all-year garden, with a great variety of designs, styles, plants and plantings in both its formal 'rooms' and in the more natural parts. Its is therefore a good place for ideas and inspiration at every season. The Winter Garden is designed to show what can be done fill a garden with colour and interest during the colder months. The alpine display house provides colour and interest all the year round. Two major features for the summer and autumn months are the Queen Mother's Rose Garden, for modern roses, and its companion Shrub Rose Garden containing 130 cultivars. The two colour-themed formal gardens provide strong contrasts: the Spiral Garden has cool, soft, pastel colours while the Square Garden contains 'hot'

plantings. The cottage and herb gardens are more informal, but separated by the *potager* with its decorative vegetable planting. Leaf form and colour dominate in the foliage garden while the model gardens demonstrate three contrasting design solutions for the average domestic plot. Other attractions include the stream and bog garden; the lake; large areas of parkland and the arboretum. An enormous number of events, shows, workshops, lectures, demonstrations and gardens walks take place at Rosemoor all through the year: for details see the Society's website.

Features woodland garden; roses (ancient & modern); plantsman's collection of plants; stream and bog garden; foliage garden; colour theme gardens; fruit and vegetable gardens; herb garden; cottage garden; tallest *Eucalyptus glaucescens* (21m.) in the British Isles (and seven further record trees); good range of book & gifts; plant centre; licensed restaurant.

Owned by The Royal Horticultural Society
Number of gardeners 16, plus 40 volunteers
Size 16ha (40 acres)
NCCPG National Collections *Ilex; Cornus*

Sherwood

NEWTON ST CYRES, EXETER, EX5 5BT

Tel 01392 851216 **Fax** 01392 851870
Location 2 miles south-west of Newton St Cyres, at the end of a signed road.
Opening hours 2 pm – 5 pm; Sundays; all year.
Admission fee Adults £2.

This is an important rhododendron and magnolia garden with much more than the collection of Knap Hill azaleas to see and enjoy. The magnolias are good, and there are handsome collections of buddlejas, berberis, cotoneasters, hydrangeas and maples which take the garden through, with late-summer flowering and fine autumn colour, to the end of the year.

Features rhododendrons; magnolias; good collection of ornamental shrubs.

Owned by Sir John & Lady Quicke
Number of gardeners 1½
Size 5.6ha (14 acres)
NCCPG National Collections *Rhododendron* (Knap Hill azaleas); *Magnolia*

Tapeley Park

INSTOW, EX39 4NT

Tel 01271 342558 **Fax** 01271 342371
Location Off A39 between Barnstaple & Bideford.
Opening hours 10 am – 5 pm; daily, except Saturdays; 14 March to 31 October.
Admission fee Adults £4; OAPs £3.50; Children £2.50. RHS members free 8 June – 8 July.

Tapeley's fame rests on its fine Italianate formal garden laid out on several levels in about 1900 and planted with such tender plants as *Sophora tetraptera* and *Myrtus*

communis subsp. *tarentina*. Beyond are palm trees and a rhododendron woodland: worth exploring. All parts are undergoing restoration and replanting with advice from Mary Keen and Carol Klein.

Features woodland garden; plants under glass; fruit; gift shop; licensed lunches & cream teas.

Owned by NDCI Ltd.
Number of gardeners 2½
Size 20ha (50 acres)
English Heritage Grade II*

Thornhayes Nursery Ltd.

DULFORD, CULLOMPTON, EX15 2DF

Tel 01884 266746 **Fax** 01884 266739
Website www.thornhayes-nursery.co.uk
Location 10 minutes from M5, Jct 28.
Opening hours 8 am – 4.30 pm; Monday – Friday.
Admission fee Free.

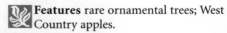

This nursery (retail and wholesale) was founded in 1991 with the aim of growing a wider range of ornamental and fruit trees than was generally available in the West Country. Thornhayes has some interesting ornamental trees: they include *Fitzroya cupressoides*, *Betula* 'Conyngham' and good collections of sorbus, pyrus and crataegus: dendrophiles should take a closer look. Hard-to-get West Country apples for cider, cooking and eating are another speciality: these include 'Chorister Boy', 'Peter Lock' and 'Royal Somerset'.

Features rare ornamental trees; West Country apples.

Owned by K. D. & P. M. Croucher
Size 5.2ha (13 acres)

Ugbrooke Park

CHUDLEIGH, TQ13 0AD

Tel 01626 852179 **Fax** 01626 853322
Location Signed off A380.
Opening hours 1.30 pm – 5.30 pm; Tuesday –
Thursday, & Sundays; 11 July to 2 September.
Admission fee Adults £3.

Ugbrooke's main claim to fame is the
beautiful landscaped park laid out by
Capability Brown in about 1770 and utterly
unspoilt since then. His ponds and lakes still
make for one of the best walk-arounds in
Devon. In the park are mature specimens of
Spanish chestnut, Turkey oak, holm oak and
that West Country speciality *Quercus* x
hispanica 'Lucombeana'. However, the
gardens have been taken in hand in recent
years, and now offer much to enjoy,
including a rose garden, a maze, a small
fernery, a lavender-and-box parterre, a
hydrangea walk and a Spanish garden.

Features landscaped park; fine trees;
attractive new gardens; tea-room.

Owned by Clifford Estate Company
Number of gardeners 3
Size 2 ha (5 acres), plus 40ha (100 acres) park
English Heritage Grade II*

DORSET

Both Dorset's Grade I gardens – Abbotsbury and Athelhampton – have plenty of horticultural interest to offer their visitors as well as their historic importance. Abbotsbury has an especially good collection of old trees, including several UK record-holders. Minterne and Forde, too, are good for specimen trees, while one of the tallest specimens in the British Isles of the dawn redwood (*Metasequoia glyptostroboides*) is a twin-stemmed specimen more than 25m high in Bournemouth's Central Park. Most of Dorset's leading nurseries are close to the coast – the chalk hinterland can be cold in winter – and there is a cluster of eminent nurseries on the sandy soils in the southeast of the county. The National Gardens Scheme is very well supported and lists well over 100 gardens – a remarkable number for such a small county. The NCCPG has a very active group in the county, but there are comparatively few National Collections – among them *Hoheria*, *Ceanothus* and *Penstemon* – all benefiting from the mild climate along the Dorset coast. Kingston Maurward is a RHS Partner College: the estate once belonged to Sir Thomas Hanbury, who gave Wisley to the Royal Horticultural Society.

Abbotsbury Sub-Tropical Gardens

ABBOTSBURY, WEYMOUTH, DT3 4LA

Tel 01305 871387 **Fax** 01305 871902
Website www.abbotsbury-tourism.co.uk/gardens.html
Location B3157, on coast, in village.
Opening hours 10 am – 6 pm (dusk in winter); daily; all year. Closed 1 January, 25 & 26 December. Free to RHS members from January to February & from October to December.
Admission fee Adults £6.50; OAPs £5.80; Children £3.75. RHS members free from October to February.

Abbotsbury is a woodland garden of splendid trees and shrubs of great rarity which has enjoyed a spectacular renaissance in recent years. Palms, eucalyptus, pittosporum and camellias all grow lushly in the sheltered valley and romantic walled garden. Among the trees are many exceptionally large specimens of species that are normally too tender to grow even in southern England – including *Buxus balearica*, *Ilex fargesii*, *Photinia nussia*, *Picconia excelsa*, and *Pittosporum crassifolium*. As well as the collection of hoherias, the gardens' comprehensive display of large-leaved hebes was until quite recently designated a National Collection by the NCCPG. There has been a lot of good planting in recent years, including many new species introduced by such collectors as Roy Lancaster. A stylish Visitors' Centre designed as a Colonial Teahouse and an excellent nursery make for added value.

 **Features** fine collection of trees; magnolias; candelabra primulas; rare trees; free-standing loquat *Eriobotrya japonica*; excellent collection of rare trees and shrubs; camellias; rhododendrons & azaleas; bluebells; sub-tropical rarities; tallest English oak *Quercus robur* (40m.) in the British Isles; five other record trees; shop; restaurant.

Owned by Ilchester Estates
Number of gardeners 5
Size 8ha (20 acres)
NCCPG National Collections *Hoheria*
English Heritage Grade I

Athelhampton

DORCHESTER, DT2 7LG

Tel 01305 848363 **Fax** 01305 848135
Website www.athelhampton.co.uk
Location 5 miles east of Dorchester, off A35 at Northbrook-Puddletown junction.
Opening hours 10.30 am – 5 pm; Sunday – Thursday; March to October. Plus 10.30 – dusk on Sundays from November to February.
Admission fee Garden only: £5.50.

Ⓟ ⓦⓒ ♿ ⚘ 🎁 ☕

Inigo Thomas designed these gardens about 100 years ago as the perfect complement for the perfect manor house. Sharply cut pyramids of yew, a long canal with water-lilies, and rambling roses in early summer are some of the main features, alongside tulips, magnolias and clematis. The overall effect is most satisfying and harmonious.

Features gazebos; beautiful walls and hedges; topiary; winner of HHA/ Christie's Garden of the Year Award for 1997; two *Metasequoia glyptostroboides* from the original seed; shop; restaurant; refreshments.

Owned by Patrick Cooke
Number of gardeners 3
Size 4ha (10 acres)
English Heritage Grade I

Bennetts Water Lily Farm

WATER GARDENS, PUTTON LANE, CHICKERELL, WEYMOUTH, DT3 4AF

Tel 01305 785150
Website www.waterlily.co.uk
Location 2 miles west of Weymouth, signed off B3157 Bridport road.
Opening hours 10 am – 5 pm; Tuesday – Sunday; April to August. 10 am – 5 pm; Tuesday – Saturday; September. Open on Bank Holidays.
Admission fee Adults £5.50; OAPs £5.20; Children £3.25.

Ⓟ ⓦⓒ ♿ ⚘ ☕

Bennetts Water Lily Farm is the leading nursery in the south-west for aquatic plants: waterlilies, pond plants and marginals in abundance. The flowering season is from to June to late September, which coincides with the tourist season. The gardens have been developed as a visitor attraction: thousands of waterlilies and a 'Monet' bridge.

**Features** waterlilies; tea-room; museum.

Owned by J.L. & A.J. Bennett
Number of gardeners 4
Size 2.4ha (6 acres)
NCCPG National Collections *Nymphaea*

Chettle House

CHETTLE, BLANDFORD FORUM, DT11 8DB

Tel & Fax 01258 830858
Location 6 miles north of Blandford; 1 mile west of the A354.

Opening hours 11 am – 5 pm; first Sunday of each month; May to September. Groups by appointment.
Admission fee Adults £3.50; Children free.

Chettle House is stunning – built by Thomas Archer in the 1710s and actually improved in the 1840s: it is full of beautiful architectural detail. The gardens are old and formal in structure, but have been re-planted in the English style since about 1970. A croquet lawn fringed by herbaceous plantings fills the foreground to the park, while the borders in the main garden surround a sunken lawn. The plantings are effective, and include a variegated liriodendron, a stauntonia growing over an old yew, a holboellia, a small rose garden, a fine display of *Campsis* in late summer, some 60 clematis cultivars and 23 cultivars of lonicera. A walnut planted in 1957 is already nearly 60ft high. This garden is the original home of the very pretty (and popular) *Campanula persicifolia* 'Chettle Charm' which is white with a blue edge. But the really inspirational thing about the garden is that it is all maintained by the husband-and-wife owners who inherited the estate in 1967 and have devoted themselves to restoring both house and garden.

Features fine borders; small tea-room.

Owned by Patrick & Fiona Bourke
Number of gardeners owners only
Size 1.6ha (4 acres)

Chiffchaffs

CHAFFEYMOOR, BOURTON,
GILLINGHAM, SP8 5BY

Tel 01747 840841
Location At Wincanton end of Bourton, off A303.
Opening hours 2 pm – 5 pm; Wednesdays & Thursdays; March to October. Plus 14 & 28 March; 11 & 25 April; 2, 16 & 30 May; 13 & 27 June; 18

July; 29 August; and 19 September.
Admission fee Adults £2.50; Children 50p. RHS members free from April to October.

A pretty cottage, with an excellent small nursery attached, and just off the A303. Started in 1978, the garden has a flowing design, exploits a great variety of habitats and burgeons with good plants. Spring bulbs, herbaceous borders, shrub roses, lilies and clematis are among its key features. A bluebell-lined path leads to the woodland garden, which boasts a splendid collection of rhododendrons, drifts of daffodils and candelabra primulas, and yet more carpets of bluebells. It was originally a dank and scrubby alder copse – on a spring line – but the Potts have cleared it, drained it and planted ornamental trees and shrubs, with autumn colour in mind as much as spring flowers. Here are about a dozen cultivars of *Liquidambar styraciflua* and groups of *Disanthus cercidifolius*, as well as magnolias, meconopsis, maples and gunneras. The nursery is open at the same times as the garden.

Features woodland garden; plantsman's collection of plants, designed for all seasons; spring bulbs; dwarf rhododendrons; excellent nursery attached; refreshments for groups (15+), by appointment.

Owned by Mr & Mrs K.R. Potts
Number of gardeners part-time help
Size 1.4ha (3½ acres), including woodland

Compton Acres Gardens

CANFORD CLIFFS ROAD, POOLE,
BH13 7ES

Tel 01202 700778 **Fax** 01202 707537
Website www.comptonacres.co.uk
Location Well signed locally; brown tourist signs.

Opening hours 9 am – 6 pm (or sunset, if earlier); daily; all year. Closed 25 December.
Admission fee Adults £5.95; OAPs £5.45; Children £3.95. RHS members free.

Very touristy, very Bournemouth and very 1920s, Compton Acres offers ten totally unconnected but highly entertaining gardens, all in different styles but joined by tarmac paths. They include an Egyptian Court garden, the Spanish water garden, the Roman gardens and the Canadian Woodland Walk. Best are the Italian garden and the stupendous Japanese Garden. The gardens are undergoing extensive renovation and replanting, and the views across Poole Harbour have been opened out again. The atmosphere is still fairly commercial, but the standards of maintenance are among the highest in any garden: no visitor could fail to be cheered up by the bravura of it all.

Features conifers; rock plants; modern roses; woodland walks; sub-tropical plantings; several shops; plant centre; tea-room & light lunches.

Owned by Red Sky Leisure Ltd
Number of gardeners 5
Size 4ha (10 acres)
English Heritage Grade II*

Cranborne Manor

CRANBORNE, WIMBORNE, BH21 5PP

Tel 01725 517248 **Fax** 01725 517862
Website www.cranborne.co.uk
Location 10 miles north of Wimborne on B3078.
Opening hours 9 am – 5 pm; Wednesdays; mid-March to September.
Admission fee Adults £3.50; Concessions £3; Children 50p. RHS members free.

Much of the garden at Cranborne is modern, laid out and planted by Lady Salisbury in the 1960s and 1970s. The Jacobean-style features are designed to complement the old house, which dates principally from the early 1600s, and to remind us that the first gardener was John Tradescant the Elder. You enter the garden through a large (and excellent) garden centre, passing through a small walled kitchen garden where apple trees are trained as five-foot espaliers. Espaliered apples appear almost as a *Leitmotif* in many other places in the garden. Everywhere are neat yew hedges and a little topiary. There are no horticultural rarities, but bulbs and polyanthus in spring and a cyclamen bank in autumn, and everywhere a sense of spaciousness, order and age. The classic view is of the narrow cottage-garden walk, backed by more apple-trees, leading towards the pretty flint church. Cranborne also has some fine old trees, notably beeches, limes and a vast low-branching ilex close to the house. You exit along an attractive double border, with windows cut into the yew hedge on one side, and finally through a herb garden.

Features topiary; roses (mainly old-fashioned); good herbaceous borders; Jacobean mount; new lavender garden (22 cultivars); garden centre; tea-room.

Owned by The Marquis of Salisbury
Number of gardeners 2½
Size 3.2ha (8 acres)
English Heritage Grade II*

Dean's Court

WIMBORNE, BH21 1EE

Tel 01202 882456
Location 2 mins walk from central Wimborne.
Opening hours Sundays, 2 pm – 6 pm; Mondays 10 am – 6 pm. 11 & 12 April; 2, 3, 30 & 31 May; 29 & 30 August; 12 September.
Admission fee Adults £2; OAPs £1.50; Children 50p.

There are some very fine old trees in the lawns and wild gardens around Dean's Court, but the most interesting part is the mellow walled garden with its long serpentine wall. Here are fruit, flowers and vegetables, traditionally grown without artificial fertilisers, pesticides or herbicides. In front of the house is a small formal herb garden.

 Features monastery fishpond; good trees; all organic; herb garden; old roses; organic herb plants and vegetables; cream teas.

Owned by Sir Michael & Lady Hanham
Number of gardeners 4
Size 5.2ha (13 acres)

Edmondsham House

EDMONDSHAM, WIMBORNE, BH21 5RE

Tel 01725 517207
Location Off B3081 between Cranborne & Verwood.
Opening hours 2 pm – 5 pm; Wednesdays & Sundays; April to October.
Admission fee Adults £1.50; Children 50p.

The walled garden (one of the walls is of cob construction) is maintained organically, with beautiful herbaceous borders – go at midsummer to see the many hardy geraniums, or in August for the vast patches of white crinums. It is intensively cultivated and brims with interesting vegetables and fruit houses. There are fine trees around the main lawns and masses of spring bulbs.

 Features grass cockpit; herbaceous borders; fine kitchen garden; herbs; old roses; old grass cockpit; spring bulbs.

Owned by Mrs Julia E. Smith
Number of gardeners 1, plus 3 part-time
Size 2.4ha (6 acres), plus 0.4ha (1-acre) walled garden)

Forde Abbey

CHARD, TA20 4LU

Tel 01460 221290 **Fax** 01460 220296
Website www.fordeabbey.co.uk
Location 4 miles south-east of Chard.
Opening hours 10 am – 4.30 pm; daily; all year.
Admission fee Adults £5.25; OAPs £4.75; Children free. (2003 prices). RHS members free from October to February.

The gardens of Forde Abbey surround the 12th-century Cistercian Monastery, a rambling private home since 1650, part Jacobean and part Gothic. They extend over 30 informal acres, with plants of interest and beauty throughout the year, set off by ancient and mellowed stone walls. Trees survive from 1700, although much has been planted in recent years: rhododendrons, azaleas, acers, magnolias, irises, meconopsis and candelabra primulas. But there are also mature Victorian conifers (*Sequoia sempervirens* and *Calocedrus decurrens*), lakes, ponds, streams, cascades, bogs and such oddities as a Beech House.

 Features good herbaceous borders; fine collection of trees; rock garden planted by Jack Drake; Ionic temple (Ham stone); seventeeth-century vistas; bog garden; working kitchen garden; HHA/Christie's Garden of the Year in 1993; tallest *Cornus controversa* (16m.) in UK; gift shop; plant centre; cafeteria.

Owned by The Trustees of the G D Roper settlement
Size 12ha (30 acres)
English Heritage Grade II*

C. W. Groves & Son

NURSERY & GARDEN CENTRE, WEST
BAY ROAD, BRIDPORT, DT6 4BA

Tel 01308 422654 **Fax** 01308 420888
Website www.cwgrovesandson.co.uk
Location South of town centre, by river, next to the
Crown roundabout on A35.
Opening hours 8.30 am – 5 pm; Monday –
Saturday. 10.30 am – 4.30 pm; Sundays.

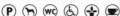

This modern, up-to-date garden centre
(rose beds, Koi carp etc.) also has a
traditional nursery attached. Founded in
1866 by the present owner's great-great-
grandfather, it specialises in Sweet Victorian
Hardy & Parma Violets. These are available
from the garden centre as well as by mail
order and include a large number of rarities.

 Features old-fashioned violas; café
with home cooking.

Owned by Clive & Diana Groves

Ivy Cottage

ALLER LANE, ANSTY, DORCHESTER,
DT2 7PX

Tel & Fax 01258 880053
Location Midway between Blandford & Dorchester.
Opening hours 10 am – 5 pm; Thursdays; May to
September. Groups welcome by appointment at
other times. Picnickers welcome.
Admission fee Adults £2.50; Children free.

This cottage garden has been made (and
immaculately maintained) by the present
owners since the mid-1960s and is crammed
with interesting things, particularly
moisture-loving plants. Springs and
streams, combined with greensand soil,
multiply the possibilities – drifts of marsh
marigolds, astilbes and candelabra primulas.

Many are chosen with wildlife in mind,
especially birds, butterflies and bees. The
kitchen garden is good, too.

 Features plantsman's collection of
plants; good herbaceous borders; small
kitchen garden.

Owned by Anne & Alan Stevens
Number of gardeners owners only
Size 0.7ha (1¾ acres)

Kingston Lacy

WIMBORNE MINSTER, BH21 4EA

Tel 01202 883402 **Fax** 01202 882402
Website www.nationaltrust.org.uk
Location 1½ miles from Wimborne on B3082 to
Blandford.
Opening hours 10.30 am – 6 pm; daily; 20 March
to 31 October. Then 10.30 am – 4 pm; Friday –
Sunday; 5 November to 19 December. And 10.30
am – 4 pm; Saturdays & Sundays; 5 February to 20
March 2005.
Admission fee Adults £3.60; Children £1.80.

The magnificent home of the Bankes family
sits among 250 acres of parkland, filled in
all directions as far as the eye can see with
single specimen trees of great spread –
beech, oak and chestnut. Nearer the house
are a wonderfully gloomy cherry laurel
walk, a lime avenue, and a cedar avenue
planted piecemeal over the centuries to
commemorate visits by everyone from the
Duke of Wellington to the Kaiser. Next to
the house is a pretty formal garden, first laid
out in 1899 and still planted with the
original scheme of pink begonias and blue
heliotrope in summer. Nearby is a fern
garden with 25 cultivars under a canopy of
hollies, aucubas and yews: gravel paths run
between irregularly shaped raised beds
planted with male ferns and hart's tongues.
There is little of floral interest apart from

snowdrops and daffodils in spring and some pretty roses near the stables restaurant – notably 'Cardinal Hume' and 'Anna Zinkeisen' – in summer. There are also many handsome trees, including a cut-leaved beech and several Lebanon cedars. The garden ornaments are however exceptional: they include an Egyptian obelisk (Ptolemy VII) and some first-class 19th-century marbles from Italy.

**Features** snowdrops; mature conifers; Victorian fernery; Dutch parterre; huge cedars of Lebanon planted by visiting royalty; shop; licensed restaurant.

Owned by The National Trust
Number of gardeners 4, plus 2 part-time
Size 12ha (30 acres)
NCCPG National Collections *Anemone nemorosa*; *Convallaria*
English Heritage Grade II

Kingston Maurward Gardens

KINGSTON MAURWARD COLLEGE, DORCHESTER, DT2 8PY

Tel 01305 215003 **Fax** 01305 250001
Website www.kmc.ac.uk
Location 1 mile east of Dorchester from A35: signed.
Opening hours 10 am – 5.30 pm (or dusk, if earlier); daily; 6 January to 23 December.
Admission fee Adults £4; Children £2.50; Family £12.50. RHS members free.

Ⓟ ⓌⒸ ♿ ⚘ 🍽

Kingston Maurward belonged to the Hanbury family who owned La Mortola on the Riviera, and laid out the formal garden here in the Arts & Crafts style (with an Italianate overlay) in the 1920s. The parkland is older – a rolling 18th-century landscape. Much of the present planting is modern. The 'Grecian' temple was restored

in 2000, and the hardy salvias in the National Collection have just been planted in a new parterre. The old kitchen garden is a splendid modern teaching garden with innumerable demonstrations of what can be grown in Dorset. Highly instructive. There will be fifteen RHS special events at Kingston Maurward during 2004: details from 020 7821 3408.

Features cyclamen; autumn crocus; fine borders; daffodils; topiary; parkland; cakes & drinks.

Owned by Kingston Maurward College
Number of gardeners 6
Size 14ha (35 acres)
NCCPG National Collections *Penstemon*; *Salvia*
English Heritage Grade II*

Knoll Gardens

STAPEHILL ROAD, WIMBORNE, BH21 7ND

Tel 01202 873931 **Fax** 01202 870842
Website www.knollgardens.co.uk
Location Signed from B3073 at Hampreston.
Opening hours 10 am – 5 pm (or dusk if earlier); Wednesday – Sunday; closed over Christmas & New Year period.
Admission fee Adults £3.50; OAPs £3; Children £2. RHS members free from April to October.

Ⓟ ⓌⒸ ♿ ⚘ 🍽

This garden was once an intimate and enclosed collection of tender exotics, many of them Australian trees and shrubs which now form the framework for extensive newer plantings. It was here, too, that the first owner, John May, bred the hybrid *Phygelius* x *rectus* 'African Queen'. The modern plantings have come together well and provide much to admire: this is a garden to interest the plantsman as much as the less horticulturally minded. The many different areas, winding pathways, and constantly changing views give an impression of a much larger area than its four acres. The owners continue to develop the garden and its plant collections, particularly of hardy perennials and grasses – in which the adjoining nursery specialises. There is a fine open area of lawn at the bottom which gives onto the gravel garden. The garden is maintained to a high standard. New for 2004 are some plantings in 'the modern naturalistic style'.

 Features rock garden; mature conifers; good herbaceous borders; *Eucalyptus*; gravel garden; ornamental grasses.

Owned by John & Janet Flude, & Neil Lucas
Number of gardeners 2
Size 1.6ha (4 acres)
NCCPG National Collections *Ceanothus* (deciduous); *Pennisetum; Phygelius*

Macpennys Nurseries

154 BURLEY ROAD, BRANSGORE, CHRISTCHURCH, BH23 8DB

Tel 01425 672348
Website www.macpennys.co.uk
Location On the Burley Road, on the north-west edge of Bransgore.
Opening hours 9 am – 5 pm; Monday – Saturday. 12 noon – 5 pm; Sundays. Closed at Christmas & New Year.
Admission fee Donation to NGS.

This long-established nursery ('old-fashioned' in the best sense) has a reliable general range across the plant spectrum, plus a few rarities. It is particularly good for conifers, rhododendrons and shrubs. The large woodland garden next to the nursery is open for the National Gardens Scheme and full of interesting plants. Many have grown to a considerable size. The garden is perhaps at its best in late spring, when the rhododendrons and azaleas overlap with the last camellias.

Owned by Mr & Mrs T.M. Lowndes
Size 1.6ha (4 acres)

Mapperton Gardens

BEAMINSTER, DT8 3NR

Tel 01308 862645 **Fax** 01308 863348
Website www.mapperton.com
Location 2 miles south-east of Beaminster.
Opening hours 2 pm – 6 pm; daily; 1 March to 31 October.
Admission fee Adults £4; Children £2 (under 5, free). RHS members free.

Mapperton has spectacular hanging gardens that you see laid out in their entirety from the lawn beside the house. First comes an enchanting steep formal valley-garden, running down from a pinnacled orangery to a handsome pool surrounded by Italianate terracing and gardens of clipped yew. Below are a 17th-century summer house, two canals and finally a long dell garden, with an excellent collection of spring-flowering trees and shrubs, some of them rare and many with good autumn colour.

 Features terraced design; topiary; fine collection of trees; small gift shop; licensed café.

Owned by The Earl & Countess of Sandwich
Number of gardeners 3
Size 5.6ha (14 acres)
English Heritage Grade II*

Melbury House

MELBURY SAMPFORD, DORCHESTER, DT2 0LF

Tel 01935 83222 **Fax** 01935 83929
Location 6 miles south of Yeovil, opposite turning to Stockwood.

Opening hours 13 & 27 May, 10 & 24 June, 8 & 22 July, and 12 August.
Admission fee Adults £4; Concessions £3.

Melbury has belonged to Mrs Townshend's family since at least the 15th century; much of its charm and importance are the result of a willingness not to change things. The deer park, for example, is maintained as it was when first enclosed in 1546. The garden's great glory is the collection of mature trees, including at least four record-breakers – *Fagus sylvatica* 'Albovariegata', *Quercus macranthera*, *Quercus pyrenaica* and the English oak known as 'Billy Wilkins'. But there is much more to admire, including a well-run, traditional, walled kitchen garden supplying fruit, vegetables and flowers to the house.

Features deer park; record-breaking trees; teas.

Owned by The Hon. Mrs Townshend
Size 16ha (40 acres)
English Heritage Grade II*

Minterne

MINTERNE MAGNA, DORCHESTER, DT2 7AU

Tel 01300 341370 **Fax** 01300 341747
Location On A352 Dorchester/Sherborne road, 2 miles north of Cerne Abbas.
Opening hours 10 am – 7 pm; daily; 1 March to 10 November.
Admission fee Adults £3; Children free.

A woodland garden, best in spring, and well integrated into the park around the handsome Edwardian house. The valley was landscaped in the 18th century with a series of small lakes and cascades. The oldest rhododendrons came from Hooker's collection, but the remarkable Lord Digby (father of the present owner) supported Farrer, Forrest, Rock and Kingdon Ward, which makes Minterne one of the best Himalayan collections. The circular walk down a greensand valley to the woodland stream and back again is ravishing: magnolias and Japanese cherries are underplanted with camellias and azaleas, while candelabra primulas and astilbes line the pools at the bottom. The fine collection of trees includes exceptional specimens of *Corylus avellana* 'Heterophylla' and *Cercidiphyllum japonicum*, while the many handkerchief trees (*Davidia involucrata*) are sensational in late May.

Features cherries; cyclamen; *Lathraea clandestina*; rhododendrons & azaleas; fine woodland walks; tallest *Chamaecyparis pisifera* 'Filifera' (25m.) in the UK.

Owned by Lord Digby
Number of gardeners 2
Size 11.5ha (29 acres)
English Heritage Grade II

Snape Cottage

CHAFFEYMOOR, BOURTON, SP8 5BY

Tel & Fax 01747 840330
Website www.snapestakes.com
Location At west end of Bourton, ½ mile up Chaffeymoor Hill.
Opening hours 10.30 am – 5 pm; Wednesdays; April to July, plus September. Also 22 & 29 February for snowdrops.
Admission fee Adults £2.50; Children free.

This small but atmospheric cottage garden is crammed with thousands of plants and organically managed to attract wild life. It is therefore especially inspirational for visitors who garden with plants in a small space. Plant specialities include hellebores, narcissi, pulmonarias, auriculas, geraniums,

Sticky Wicket

BUCKLAND NEWTON, DORCHESTER, DT2 7BY

Tel & Fax 01300 345476
Website www.stickywicketgarden.co.uk
Location 11 miles from Dorchester & Sherborne.
Opening hours 10.30 am – 8 pm; Thursdays; June
to September. Plus 20 June & 15 August for
National Gardens Scheme (2 pm – 8 pm). And by
appointment at other times.
Admission fee Adults £3; Children £1.50.

Sticky Wicket is a highly original garden and worth revisiting frequently. The owners are both designers and conservationists, and their devotion to ecology guides their garden-making: they understand the need to attract birds, insects and other wild life. Yet it is also one of the most photographed and admired of modern gardens, because of the subtlety and integrity of Pam Lewis's colour combinations. She and her husband began the garden in 1987 but the plantings are constantly reworked, so that you find new compositions and combinations every year. Berrying trees and shrubs and those with interesting winter stems are supplemented by plants chosen for their scent, decoration and usefulness to wildlife. The planting is increasingly naturalistic and draws upon a choice of native British plants. There are four principal wildlife gardens: the Frog and Bird gardens where ponds, bird baths, nesting boxes and feeders are thickly incorporated into the design, to attract wildlife close to the house where they can be seen; the beautiful Round Garden, whose colours move from pastel tints to richer hues and back again, but where the plants are chosen for the nectar and pollen they offer to insects; and the White Garden, where ornamental grasses and flowers in loosely planted borders echo the grassy effect of the meadows beyond. The half-acre wildflower meadow, started in 1997, was sown with seed of local provenance and is managed as a traditional hay meadow, at its most glamorous in June and July. Throughout the garden, information boards explain how the Lewises preach and practice 'gardening in tune with Nature'. This is expanded in Pam Lewis's excellent book *Making Wildflower Meadows* [Frances Lincoln, 2003].

Features wide collection of interesting plants; strong ecological interest; many ornamental grasses; good colour associations; tea, coffee & home-made cakes.

Owned by Peter & Pam Lewis
Size 1ha (2½ acres)

dianthus, irises and asters, but perhaps the most impressive collection is of snowdrops (*Galanthus* species and cultivars) – over 250 different ones. There is a special emphasis on plant history and the conservation of 'old' cultivars of every sort.

 Features lots of plants for plantsmen.

Owned by Mrs A .Whinfield
Number of gardeners 1
Size 0.2ha (½ acre)

Stapehill Abbey

276 WIMBORNE ROAD WEST, STAPEHILL, WIMBORNE, BH21 2EB

Tel 01202 861686 **Fax** 01202 894589
Location Signed from A31.
Opening hours 10 am – 5 pm; daily; Easter to September. Plus 10 am – 4 pm; Wednesday – Sunday; February to Easter & October to December.
Admission fee Adults £8; OAPs £7; Children £4.50.

A modern leisure development with vintage tractors to admire and lots of plants to sell – rather expensive if you are only interested in seeing a garden. The design is rather uncoordinated but the individual gardens are richly planted and there are some handsome features: a small rose garden, a laburnum pergola, a water garden, a small tropical house and an extensive rock garden, more noteworthy for its size than for its plantings.

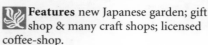 **Features** new Japanese garden; gift shop & many craft shops; licensed coffee-shop.

Owned by Stapehill Enterprises Ltd
Number of gardeners 4
Size 2ha (5 acres)

Trehane Camellia Nursery

STAPEHILL ROAD, HAMPRESTON, WIMBORNE, BH21 7ND

Tel & Fax 01202 873490
Location Between Ferndown & Wimborne, off A31. Next to Knoll Gardens.
Opening hours 9 am – 4.30 pm; Monday – Friday; all year. 10 am – 4.30 pm; Saturdays & Sundays; late February to end May. And by appointment.
Admission fee Free.

This is a wholesale and retail camellia nursery in a woodland setting. They have a wide choice of *Camellia* hybrids, plus a good range of magnolias, pieris, rhododendrons, azaleas and blueberries (plus 'pick-your-own' blueberries in August!).

 Features camellias; blueberries.

Owned by The Trehane family
Number of gardeners 3
Size 4ha (10 acres)

DURHAM

Durham is too often – and wrongly – considered a horticultural wasteland, though it is true that in the 1980s the Royal Horticultural Society had fewer members in Durham than any other English county – less than 100. Things have come a long way since then. English Heritage has drawn attention to the importance of historic landscapes like Raby Castle and the Bowes Museum, and there are now five National Collections in the county. Horn's Garden Centre at Shotton Colliery has the National Collection of coleus (*Solenostemon* cvs.) and a large collection of *Streptocarpus* and pelargoniums too. East Durham & Houghall College is a RHS Partner College.

Barningham Park

BARNINGHAM, RICHMOND, DL11 7DW

Tel 01833 621202 **Fax** 01833 621298
Location 10 miles north-west of Scotch Corner off A66.
Opening hours 2 pm – 5 pm; 23 May. And parties by appointment.
Admission fee Adults £3; Children free.

This late 18th-century landscape includes terraces, an old bowling green and a skating pond. Humphry Repton may have had a hand in it. Keen horticultural Milbanks got to work in the 1920s. They designed the splendid rock garden and diverted a stream to form cascades and pools through it. Unknown and perhaps underrated, if Barningham were in the Home Counties everyone would rave about it.

Features hillside rock garden with stream; good herbaceous borders; terraced gardens; rhododendrons; woodland walks; home-made teas.

Owned by Sir Anthony Milbank Bt.
Number of gardeners 1
Size 1.6ha (4 acres), plus 24ha (60 acres) of woodland

The Bowes Museum Garden & Park

BARNARD CASTLE, DL12 8NP

Tel 01833 690606 **Fax** 01833 637163
Website www.bowesmuseum.org.uk
Location In Barnard Castle town.
Opening hours Dawn – dusk; daily; all year.
Admission fee Free.

Twenty-one acres of Victorian splendour, now maintained by the trustees as a public amenity. The formal gardens around the fountain are good – a vast oval parterre re-made in the French style in 1982 – and mature trees pepper the park. Almost all were planted in the 1870s: some of the conifers are particularly fine. A tree trail highlights their splendour and diversity.

The museum will be housing an important exhibition called 'Northumbria Gardens Trust' from 3 April to 30 May 2004; it will highlight some of the great gardens of northern England and focus on conservation issues.

Features fine collection of trees; parterre; large monkey puzzle; gift shop; museum café.

Owned by Trustees of the Bowes Museum
Number of gardeners 1
Size 8.3ha (21 acres)
English Heritage Grade II

Crook Hall

FRANKLAND LANE, SIDEGATE, DURHAM, DH1 5SZ

Tel 0191 384 8028 **Fax** 0191 386 4521
Location Close to city centre.
Opening hours 1 pm – 5 pm. 9-12 April; Sundays & Bank Holidays in May & September; daily except Saturdays from June to August.
Admission fee Adults £4; Concessions £3.50.

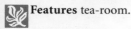

Crook Hall is a real gem of a cottage garden – very peaceful and beautiful. Ignore the trendy circular maze of cotoneaster near the entrance and make straight for the garden proper – a series of many, small, enclosed gardens with narrow paths. None of the plants are rare, but the new owners have begun to make additions. Old shrubs and hedges give structure: new underplantings supplement established colonies of campanulas and Spanish bluebells. Colour is important: the Cathedral Garden takes its inspiration from the stained glass windows. The Silver Wedding Garden is a contrast of greys, greens and whites.

Features tea-room.

Owned by Keith & Maggie Bell
Number of gardeners 2
Size 1.2ha (3 acres)

East Durham & Houghall Community College

DURHAM, DH1 3SG

Tel 0191 386 1351 **Fax** 0191 386 0419
Location Follow A177 from A1 to Durham.
Opening hours Not available as we went to press. Last year's times: 12.30 pm – 4.30 pm; daily; all year.
Admission fee Free (in 2003).

Houghall is a well-run teaching garden, originally attached to Durham's horticultural college. There is much to see here: a fine arboretum (more than 500 different trees, but rather fewer labels), an interesting young pinetum, good displays of perennial plants and shrubs (one of the best in northern England), and a wildflower meadow for summer interest. Many trials are conducted here, for example on the hardiness of fuchsias: the garden staff say that 'if it grows at Houghall it will grow anywhere'.

Features roses (mainly modern); rock garden; heathers; hardy fuchsias; seasonal bedding; young pinetum & arboretum; shop; refreshments available.

Owned by East Durham & Houghall Community College
Number of gardeners 6
NCCPG National Collections *Sorbus*; *Meconopsis*

Raby Castle

STAINDROP, DARLINGTON,
DL2 3AH

Tel 01833 660202 **Fax** 01833 660169
Website www.rabycastle.com
Location On A688, 1 mile north of Staindrop.
Opening hours 11 am – 5.30 pm; Sunday to
Friday; June to August. Plus Wednesdays &
Sundays in May & September.
Admission fee Adults £4; Concessions £3.50;
Children £2.50. RHS members free, except during
special events.

The 18th-century walled gardens at Raby
Castle are set within a 80-ha (200-acre) deer
park in the heart of Teesdale. Designers such
as Thomas White and James Paine have
worked on these magnificent gardens, which
incorporate herbaceous borders, shrub
borders, yew hedges, a conservatory, formal
rose gardens and informal heather and
conifer gardens. The gardens were
considerably altered during the 20th century
but many of the original features remain,
notably the two fine 200 year-old yew
hedges and the ornamental pond that
dominates the central garden.

Features deer park; walled garden; fine
yew hedges; gift shop; cafeteria.

Owned by Lord Barnard
Number of gardeners 3½
Size 2ha (5 acres)
English Heritage Grade II*

Westholme Hall

WINSTON, DARLINGTON, DL2 3QL

Tel 01325 730442 **Fax** 01325 730946
Location On B6274 north towards Staindrop.
Opening hours 2 pm – 6 pm; 16 May, 4 July & 12
September. For charity. And by appointment.
Admission fee Adults £2.50; Children 50p.

Westholme is a beautiful Jacobean house,
with a fine Victorian garden running down
to a brook. The McBains have restored and
revived the garden, giving it a firm structure
and good plants for every season. The old
rhododendrons, azaleas and millions of
daffodils make a magnificent display in
spring. Summer brings the lilacs and roses:
the old-fashioned rose garden is maintained
without spraying and remains remarkably
free from diseases – a great example of
sympathetic maintenance. The herbaceous
borders hold sway in autumn, followed by
masses of cyclamen and snowdrops in
winter. A long walk along an old railway
embankment planted with young trees leads
to a landscaped lake rich in wildfowl. All is
maintained by the owners' own hard work
and enthusiasm. The garden is worth a long
detour to see: would that it were open more
often.

Features roses (mainly old-fashioned);
rhododendrons; tea-room.

Owned by Mrs J.H. McBain
Number of gardeners owners only
Size 2ha (5 acres)

ESSEX

Considering its proximity to London, where fortunes have for centuries been made, Essex has few famous historic gardens: Audley End is the pre-eminent exception, and as important horticulturally as historically. It is the county's only Grade I garden. Few of the county's other historic gardens are open to the public. Essex's most famous gardener was Miss Ellen Willmott of Warley Place, Great Warley, but her house was demolished shortly after her death in 1934 and the garden (what remains of it) is now a nature reserve: arrangements to visit it may be made through Essex Wildlife Trust. It has one of Essex's few record trees, an *Umbellularia californica* 20m high. Low rainfall and hot summers define Essex gardening: Beth Chatto has made a study of dry gardening at her nursery near Elmstead Market. Other nurseries of exceptional interest to keen plantsmen are Glen Chantry and Langthorns Plantery. The National Gardens Scheme has a fair number of gardens opening for the Yellow Book, most of them medium-sized and good for seeing plants. There are 13 National Collections in the county. Writtle College near Chelmsford is a RHS Partner College, with lectures and workshops on a wide range of hands-on topics throughout the year. The garden at Hyde Hall has proved an interesting acquisition for the Royal Horticultural Society and much improved by the Society's input – new design features and many new plants.

Audley End

SAFFRON WALDEN, CB11 4JF

Tel 01799 522842/520052 **Fax** 01799 522131
Website www.english-heritage.org.uk
Location On B1383, 1 mile west of Saffron Walden.
Opening hours Garden: 11 am – 6 pm; Wednesday – Sunday, plus Bank Holidays; April to September.
Admission fee Gardens: Adults £4.50; OAPs £3.40; Children £2.30.

Capability Brown landscaped the park in 1763 but work on rejuvenating the garden at Audley End started some years ago with the parterre garden behind the house towards the Temple of Concord. This dates from the 1830s and has 170 geometric flower beds crisply cut from the turf and planted with original varieties of perennials, bedding plants and annuals for spring and summer. Nearby are the Elysian Garden, designed in the 1780s by Placido Columbani, and the Victorian pond garden in the 'picturesque' style, whose walls and pergola are clad with climbing shrubs and roses. Work continues: the kitchen garden is now run as a joint venture with HDRA as a working organic garden. It looks much as it would have done in late Victorian times with vegetables, fruit, herbs and flowers to supply the household. The cultivation is, of

Beth Chatto Gardens

ELMSTEAD MARKET, COLCHESTER, CO7 7DB

Tel 01206 822007 **Fax** 01206 825933
Website www.bethchatto.co.uk
Location 7 miles east of Colchester.
Opening hours 9 am – 5 pm; Monday – Saturday;
March to October; 9 am – 4 pm; Monday – Friday;
November to February.
Admission fee Adults £3.50; Children free. RHS
members free in February & March.

This beautiful and instructive garden was begun in 1960 and uses a very wide range of plants, mostly species, chosen for their foliage and form as much as for their flowers. Beth Chatto's planting is based largely on ecological principles, following her late husband, Andrew Chatto's lifetime research into the natural associations of garden plants. The original site was wasteland, unfit for farming and unfit for the planting of many conventional plants, especially cultivars. It had – and still has – three very different ecologies: areas of hungry sand and gravel, a clay-based spring-fed hollow and elsewhere dry shade beneath ancient oaks. Beth Chatto has developed three contrasting types of planting, based on the principle of finding the right plant for the right place, and thus turning problem areas into advantages. Around the modest house, where the soil is thin and dry, Beth Chatto used plants mostly from the Mediterranean: cistus, broom, salvias, euphorbias, potentillas, verbascums, and the tree-like *Genista aetnensis* have come together on the warm sandy slopes. A short walk leads down to a water-garden of remarkable luxuriance, made by damming the spring-fed ditch to create a series of ponds in the valley. The lush plantings are quite untypical of Essex, where rainfall averages 50 cm a year. Here are gunneras, astilbes, lysichitons, hostas, phormiums,

water-irises and the ostrich fern *Matteuccia struthiopteris*. They have a continuous background, not too intrusive, of conifers, specimen trees and shrubs – but the emphasis throughout the garden is on the herbaceous plants for which the adjoining nursery is famous. A copse has been developed as woodland garden and a canopy of young oaks underplanted with shade-lovers. Here, and in the long shady border above the water garden, are rich plantings of bulbs, woodlanders and ground cover – aconites, cyclamen, erythroniums and dicentras. The gravel garden was made in 1992 on the site of the old car park, where drought-resistant sun-lovers have been planted in a fluid sequence of island beds. Before planting, this ¾ acre of yellow sand and gravel was 'improved' with the addition of home-made compost, to give the plants a good start. Since then, however, the area has not been irrigated in any way, despite periods of drought, since it is a horticultural experiment to see which plants will survive and maybe inspire visitors who have hosepipe bans. But garden making is only one of Beth Chatto's gifts: her writings and nursery have made her famous. And the standard of maintenance is impeccable.

Features colour contrasts; gravel garden; luxuriant water gardens; woodland garden; big nursery adjacent to the garden; tea-room (seasonal).

Owned by Beth Chatto
Number of gardeners 4, plus seasonal help
Size 2ha (5 acres)

course, entirely organic. The vinehouse is one of the earliest and largest in the country, with vines over 200 years old.

Features bedding out; parterre; magnificent plane trees; organic kitchen garden; ancient trees; shop; restaurant & picnic site.

Owned by English Heritage
Number of gardeners 9
Size 40ha (100 acres), including parkland
English Heritage Grade I

County Park Nursery

384 WINGLETYE LANE, HORNCHURCH, RM11 3BU

Tel 01708 445205
Location 2½ miles from M25, Jct 29. Off Wingletye Lane, in Essex Gardens, Hornchurch.
Opening hours 9 am – 6 pm, Monday – Saturday; 10 am – 5 pm, Sundays; from March to October. Closed Wednesdays. Open in winter by appointment only.

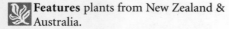

This small nursery specialises in Antipodean plants, many of them grown from native seed and not available from any other nursery in the UK. There is no show garden to speak of, but every tiny corner seems covered in pots of unusual plants – some for display and others for sale.

Features plants from New Zealand & Australia.

Owned by Graham Hutchins
NCCPG National Collections Coprosma

Easton Lodge

WARWICK HOUSE, GREAT DUNMOW, CM6 2BB

Tel & Fax 01371 876979
Website www.eastonlodge.co.uk

Location Signed from A120 at Great Dunmow.
Opening hours 12 noon – dusk; daily; February to early March (ring for exact dates) for snowdrops. Then 12 noon – 6 pm; Friday – Sunday & Bank Holiday Mondays; Easter to October.
Admission fee Adults £3.80; OAPs £3.50; Children £1.50.

The garden was laid out by Harold Peto in 1902 for the Countess of Warwick (Edward VII's 'darling Daisy'), fell into to serious neglect, and has been wonderfully restored since 1993. Much remains to be done, as the owner is the first to admit, but the Lime Grove has now been cleared and work has begun on re-paving the Italian garden. There is an exhibition of how the house was built and the gardens made.

Features cream teas in courtyard & tea-room.

Owned by Brian Creasey
Number of gardeners 2
Size 9.2ha (23 acres)
English Heritage Grade II

The Gibberd Garden

MARSH LANE, GILDEN WAY, HARLOW, CM17 0NA

Tel 01279 442112
Website www.thegibberdgarden.co.uk
Location Leave Harlow on B183. Marsh Lane is on left: follow brown tourist sign.
Opening hours 2 pm – 6 pm; Wednesdays, Saturdays, Sundays & Bank Holidays; April to September
Admission fee Adults £4; Concessions £2.50; Children free.

This was the private garden of Sir Frederick Gibberd, the master planner of Harlow New Town. It was designed as a series of distinct rooms, and filled with sculpture, pots and architectural salvage. One of the most

Glen Chantry

ISHAMS CHASE, WICKHAM BISHOPS, WITHAM, CM8 3LG

Tel & Fax 01621 891342
Location Turn off B1019 just south of A12 towards
Benton Hall golf course & Wickham Bishops:
immediately left after bridge & up track ½ mile.
Opening hours 10 am – 4 pm; Fridays &
Saturdays; 4 April to 27 September.
Admission fee Adults £2.50; Children 50p. RHS
members free.

This remarkable garden has been made
from a bare hillside since 1976: the
owners have an excellent eye for good plants
and for how to use them. You enter past a
very pretty new *potager* and through the
immaculately tidy nursery, itself a
plantsman's treasure-house for herbaceous
plants. Then you step down into the garden,
filled with endless micro-habitats, some
exploiting the opportunities offered by dry,
stony acid soil, and other defying it. Scree
beds, peat beds, raised beds and an artificial
stream are part of the story, but so is a
winding pattern of ebbing and flowing
island beds. Along the centre of these beds
are trees and shrubs which screen the two
faces from each other and make it possible
to plant both sides of a path with the same
colour. The owners also practice 'vertical
planting', which means that season after
season different displays are possible from
the same patch: in one small area, for
example, the spring-flowering fritillaries,
erythroniums and corydalis are covered in
summer by hostas, grasses and rushes. A
new bed planted with a wide selection of
grasses, interplanted with late-flowering
perennials, is maturing well. Glen Chantry is
a model of what devoted plantsmanship can
achieve: educational, functional and
beautiful all at once. There is one formal
garden near the house, white and green in
summer with 'Katharina Zeimet' and

'Iceberg' roses, campanulas, lilies,
eryngiums, alliums and geraniums, but the
rest of the garden is fluid, however
disciplined may be the controlling hand. In
fact, very little seeding around is allowed –
perhaps a few plants of Martyn Rix's form
of *Eryngium giganteum* 'Silver Ghost' –
because the planting is intended to slow you
down and stop you on your way, to admire
individual plants. Besides, the standards of
maintenance are immaculate.

Features alpines; herbaceous plants;
bulbs; special habitats; masses of
fascinating plants for plantsmen; fine
specialist nursery attached; light
refreshments.

Owned by Sue & Wol Staines
Number of gardeners owners only
Size 1ha (2½ acres)

important architectural gardens of the 20th century, it is being restored with aid from the Heritage Lottery Commission. Much of the restoration work featured in the BBC series *Hidden Gardens* in December 2002. There is an active Friends Organisation: details from Gordon Whittle on 01279 434840.

 Features good modern design; wild garden; lime avenue; 'Roman Temple' vistas; shop; light refreshments.

Owned by Gibberd Garden Trust
Number of gardeners 2 part-time plus volunteers
Size 2.8ha (7 acres)

Green Island

PARK ROAD, ARDLEIGH, COLCHESTER, CO7 7SP

Tel & Fax 01206 230455
Location Off B1029 from Ardleigh to Bromley; look out for brown signs.
Opening hours noon – 5 pm; Wednesdays & Thursdays; April to mid-October. Plus 11 & 25 April; 9, 16 & 30 May; 6, 20 & 27 June; 11 & 25 July; 15 August; 12 & 26 September.
Admission fee Adults £2.50; Children 50p.

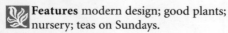

This a new garden, started as recently as 1997 and made by a garden designer on a large scale. It has a woodland garden, a pond, a bamboo dell, an orchard, a Japanese garden, a 'seaside' garden, and much else besides. But the main attractions are the fluid design, which leads you along quite naturally, and the spacious island beds, planted with a large number of herbaceous plants and shrubs. Seldom does a designer's garden display so much plantsmanship.

 Features modern design; good plants; nursery; teas on Sundays.

Owned by Fiona Edmond.
Number of gardeners 1
Size 8ha (20 acres)

Langthorns Plantery

LITTLE CANFIELD, DUNMOW, CM6 1TD

Tel & Fax 01371 872611
Location Between Takeley & Great Dunmow, signed off A120.
Opening hours 10 am – 5 pm; daily. Closed Christmas to New Year.
Admission fee Free.

Langthorns Plantery is a go-ahead modern nursery with an eye for good plants. Though best known for their wide range of hardy herbaceous plants, the owners apply their discriminating taste to all their stock – alpines, shrubs, trees and climbers, especially clematis. The garden is worth a visit in its own right but not always open, so check before you visit.

Owned by The Cannon family
Size 1.2ha (3 acres)

Olivers

OLIVERS LANE, COLCHESTER, CO2 0HJ

Tel 01206 330575 **Fax** 01206 330366
Location 3 miles south-west of Colchester between B1022 & B1026.
Opening hours 2 pm – 6 pm; 29 April; 2, 3, 6, 13 & 20 May. And by appointment.
Admission fee Adults £2.50; Children free.

Quite a modern garden, started in 1968 around three small lakes, with an eye-catching walk to one side leading down to a statue of Bacchus. Good plants and planting everywhere, from the parterres by the house to the woodland where roses and rhododendrons flourish. The main borders underwent a highly successful major re-design in 1998 and are looking very good

RHS Garden Hyde Hall

BUCKHATCH LANE, RETTENDON, CHELMSFORD, CM3 8ET

Tel 01245 400256 **Fax** 01245 402100
Website www.rhs.org.uk
Location South-east of Chelmsford, signed from
A130. Exit for the Rettendon turnpike, north through
Rettendon village and follow the brown tourist signs.
Opening hours 10 am – 6 pm (5 pm or dusk from
January to March and from October to December);
daily; all year.
Admission fee Adults £4.50; Children (6 – 16) £1;
pre-booked groups (10+) special rates. RHS
members (plus one guest) free.

Hyde Hall is the result of 40 years of
dedication, endeavour and inspiration.
The garden has also become well-known as
a plantsman's garden and for its superb
collection of roses. Both modern and old-
fashioned roses are displayed together with a
large number of climbers and ramblers, many
of which are pruned and trained in
interesting and unusual styles. The sheltered
woodland garden on the northern side is a
triumph of cultivation and there are
interesting examples of hardiness throughout:
Eriobotrya japonica, Eucalyptus urnigera and
Pittosporum tenuifolium are grown in the
open, *Buddleja officinalis* and *Crinodendron
patagua* against a wall of the yard and *Acca
sellowiana* against the house. Hyde Hall was
donated to the Society in 1993 and much
work has since been carried out. The new
Entrance Garden has a distinctive oak pergola
and water feature, with new plantings around
the Upper Pond and Hyde Hall Farmhouse.
The long herbaceous border has been
reworked – backed by new shelter hedges
of yew and tongues of yew which divide
the border into bays. In spring, there is a
delightful mix of bulbs and blossom
throughout the garden, particularly in the
old stable-yard and Hermione's Garden, and
towards the end of the year colour is provided
in large part by viburnums and crab apples
(*Malus*), both of which are particularly
noted for their autumn foliage and fruit.
Hyde Hall is a garden that continues to
grow and develop. One popular recent
development is the Dry Garden (2001), with
over 4,000 plants representing 740 different
species and cultivars of drought- and
exposure-tolerant plants from around the
world and planted in a naturalistic setting.
The aim of the Dry Garden is to show the
broad diversity and aesthetic value of plants
that can thrive without artificial irrigation.
Over the next few years Hyde Hall will
grow to 24ha (60 acres) or more. Current
development is centred on the Malus Field,
where the Millennium Avenue, 300m long
and 20m wide, was planted with *Fraxinus
excelsior* 'Westhof's Glorie' for short-term
effect and *Quercus frainetto* 'Hungarian
Crown' for 100 years hence. The Queen
Mother's Garden opened for the first time
in 2003. This area of mixed shrubs, trees
and perennials combines existing garden
areas with new plantings and hard tracks.
New for 2004 is a model garden for wildlife.
Around the 130-ha (320-acre) estate a
substantial woodland planting is being
undertaken. A new 1.5-ha (4-acre) perennial
wildflower meadow has developed well since
it was first sown during October 2001.

Features plantsman's collection of
plants; good herbaceous borders;
spring bulbs; ponds; heathers; new dry
garden of drought-tolerant plants; visitor
centre; shop; garden library; plant centre;
licensed restaurant serving hot & cold
lunches, afternoon teas, tea/coffee.

Owned by The Royal Horticultural Society
Number of gardeners 11, plus students
Size 11.1ha (28 acres)
NCCPG National Collections *Viburnum*

now. This is the garden of enthusiastic and energetic owners: an inspiration.

 Features roses (ancient & modern); bluebells; rhododendrons; fine borders; teas on 2 & 3 May.

Owned by Mr & Mrs David Edwards
Number of gardeners 2 part-time
Size 2.2ha (6 acres), plus woodland.

Rhodes & Rockliffe

2 NURSERY ROAD, NAZEING, EN9 2JE

Tel 01992 451598 **Fax** 01992 440673
Location ½ mile west of Lower Nazeing along B194; turn right into Nursery Road.
Opening hours By appointment only.
Admission fee Free.

David Rhodes and John Rockliffe have the finest collection of *Begonia* species and hybrids in Britain. Their occasional exhibits at Chelsea and other RHS flower shows have won them well-deserved gold medals and contributed immensely to popularising the genus in recent years.

Owned by David Rhodes
Number of gardeners 2
NCCPG National Collections *Begonia*

R & R Saggers

WATERLOO HOUSE, HIGH STREET, NEWPORT, CB11 3PG

Tel 01799 540858 **Fax** 01799 542900
Location On B1383 in centre of village.
Opening hours 10 am – 5 pm; Tuesday – Sunday, plus Bank Holidays; all year. Closed on Sundays from January to March.
Admission fee Free.

This garden-nursery has a wide and ever-changing stock of herbaceous plants, as well as shrubs, climbers, old-fashioned roses and trees. Many are grown from seed. The owners offer a plant-finding service. The garden is beautifully maintained and runs down to a stream.

Features unusual plants for sale.

Owned by Roger & Roslyn Saggers
Number of gardeners 4 part-time

Saling Hall

GREAT SALING, BRAINTREE, CM7 5DT

Location 2 miles north of the old A120, between Great Dunmow & Braintree, at Blake End.
Opening hours 2 pm – 5 pm; Wednesdays; May, June & July. Groups by appointment on weekdays; please apply in writing.
Admission fee Adults £2.50 (for National Gardens Scheme); Children free.

A thinking man's garden, Saling also provokes thought in its visitors. The plantsmanship is impressive, particularly the placing of trees and shrubs. Few modern gardens are conceived on such a scale, or mix classical and Japanese elements so smoothly. The moods, and the lessons, are endless.

Features 17th-century walled garden with fruit trees & borders; oriental touches; fine standing stone; Temple of Pisces, moat & water gardens.

Owned by Mr & Mrs Hugh Johnson
Number of gardeners 2
Size 5ha (12½ acres)
English Heritage Grade II

GLOUCESTERSHIRE

Gloucestershire is rich in nurseries and large important gardens. Six of its nine Grade I historic gardens (a remarkable number for one county) are regularly open to the public – Batsford Park, Frampton Court, Hidcote Manor, Sezincote, Stanway House, and Westonbirt Arboretum – while a seventh, Stancombe Park, is open by appointment. Almost all the county's Grade II* gardens also welcome visitors, including Abbotswood, Berkeley Castle, Kiftsgate Court, Miserden Park, Painswick House, Rodmarton Manor, Sudeley Castle and Westbury Court. Most have important collections of plants as well as attractive design features. Indeed, almost all Gloucestershire's leading historic gardens have been highly graded precisely because of their horticultural attractions. Rich clay soils account for some of the popularity of gardening in Gloucestershire, though the inland, upland parts of the county can be very cold in winter. It is good to note that Rosemary Verey's garden at Barnsley House, now under new ownership, is once again open to visitors. Among garden centres and nurseries, the Batsford Garden Centre has a very good general range and makes a speciality of ferns, while Hunt's Court is excellent for roses of every kind. A very large number of gardens – some 150 – open for the National Gardens Scheme though, slightly confusingly, the southern part of the county which used to belong to Avon, is still separately organised: both continue to be very successful in persuading garden-owners to open their gardens and visitors to visit them. Permission to visit HRH The Prince of Wales's garden at Highgrove House near Tetbury may be given to garden clubs and similar organisations. In addition to the world-famous Westonbirt Arboretum, there are important collections of trees at Highnam Court, Batsford Park, and Tortworth Court. The NCCPG is active in Gloucestershire and accounts for 19 National Collections.

Abbotswood

STOW-ON-THE-WOLD, CHELTENHAM, GL54 1LE

Tel 01451 830173
Location 1 mile west of Stow-on-the-Wold.
Opening hours 1.30 pm – 6 pm; 11 & 25 April, 16 May, 6 June, 11 July and 12 September.
Admission fee Adults £3; Children free.

Abbotswood is one of the most interesting gardens in the Cotswolds – very Lutyens, very photogenic – with handsome formal gardens in front of the house. A stream meanders through a magnificent rock garden set with a alpine meadows, bogs and moraines, past dwarf azaleas, primulas, lysichitons, heaths and heathers until it disappears. There is also a small, densely planted arboretum, with some unusual cultivars dating from about 100 years ago, fascinating to browse around: it is being cleared and replanted. The two-acre kitchen garden is worth the long walk on the occasions when it too is open: it has a fruit house, indoor roses and some interesting new plantings.

Features interesting topiary; fine collection of trees, including conifers; magnolias; heather garden; good borders; roses ancient & modern; good for plants; teas.

Owned by Dikler Farming Co.
Size 8ha (20 acres)
English Heritage Grade II*

Barnsley House Garden

BARNSLEY, CIRENCESTER, GL7 5EE

Tel 01285 740000 **Fax** 01285 740900
Website www.barnsleyhouse.com
Location On B4425 in Barnsley village.

Opening hours 11 am – 5 pm; 15 April; 8 & 27 May; 24 June; 22 July; 19 August; 16 September. Groups at other times by prior arrangement.
Admission fee Adults £5. But £6 on 8 May.

Rosemary Verey's famous garden was started in 1952 and more-or-less finished 25 years later. The bones were a pretty house (1697), an 18th-century wall ending in an original Gothick summerhouse & ha-ha, and some fine 19th-century trees. Her architect husband David helped with the design, and together they commissioned sculptures by Simon Verity for important focal points. The result was compact, neat, thickly planted, fairly labour-intensive – and very influential. Mrs Verey reflected the aspirations of many garden-owners in the difficult post-war years, so that when people had more money to spend again in the 1970s and 1980s, Barnsley was available to teach and inspire. The scale is surprisingly intimate – one of the garden's strengths – and the small decorative *potager* spawned many imitations. Barnsley is interesting at all seasons, particularly in early spring when it seems to have much more colour than other people's gardens, and again at midsummer rose time and when the salvias and asters flower in autumn. But it is probably at its best – and certainly at its most photographed – in late spring when the little laburnum walk and the purple alliums underneath are in flower together. The house is now an exclusive country house hotel.

Features good borders; old roses; ornamental *potager*.

Owned by Tim Haigh & Rupert Pendered
Number of gardeners 6
Size 2.2ha (5½ acres)

Batsford Arboretum

MORETON-IN-MARSH, GL56 9QB

Tel 01386 701441 **Fax** 01386 701829
Website www.batsford-arboretum.co.uk
Location Off A44 between Moreton-in-Marsh &
Bourton-on-the-Hill.
Opening hours 10 am – 5 pm; daily; 1 February to
15 November. Plus 10 am – 3 pm at weekends in
winter (hot punch on Boxing Day!). Open on New
Year's Day 2004.
Admission fee Adults £5; OAPs £4; Children £1.
RHS members free except in October.

Batsford has an openness which makes its
hillside a joy to wander through, passing
from one dendrological marvel to the next.
Begun in the 1880s, the Arboretum also has
several oriental curiosities brought from
Japan by Lord Redesdale – a large bronze
Buddha and an oriental rest-house for
instance. But the arboretum is mainly the
work of the late Lord Dulverton, who added
a large number of new plantings between
1956 and 1992. These include nearly 100
different magnolia cultivars, a
comprehensive collection of Japanese
cherries, some very beautiful conifers, and
excellent collections of such genera as *Acer*,
Betula and *Sorbus*. Some are already record-
breakers: all are in the prime of their life,
well-grown and vigorous. The
underplantings of spring bulbs are worth
seeing, but visit Batsford at any season and
you will find much to admire and enjoy.

Features mature conifers; fine
collection of trees; maple glade;
bluebells; aconites; snowdrops; tallest *Betula
platyphylla* (19m.) in the British Isles (and
12 other tree records); shop; light meals &
refreshments.

Owned by The Batsford Foundation
Number of gardeners 2
Size 22ha (55 acres)

NCCPG National Collections *Prunus* (sato-sakura
group)
English Heritage Grade I

Berkeley Castle

BERKELEY, GL13 9BQ

Tel 01453 810332
Website www.berkeley-castle.com
Location Off A38.
Opening hours 11 am – 4 pm; Wednesday –
Saturday; April to September. Plus 2 pm – 5 pm;
Sundays; April to October.
Admission fee Garden only: Adults £2; Children
£1. (2003 dates & prices).

The grim battlements of Berkeley Castle are
host to an extensive collection of tender
plants. On three terraces are *Cestrum*, *Cistus*
and *Rosa banksiae* among hundreds of plant
varieties introduced by the owner's
grandmother, a sister of Ellen Willmott. An
Elizabethan-style bowling green and a
waterlily pond fit well into the overall
scheme.

Features roses (mainly old-fashioned);
plantsman's collection of plants;
mature conifers; good herbaceous borders;
shop at Castle Farm; light lunches &
afternoon tea.

Owned by R.J.G. Berkeley
Number of gardeners 2
Size 2ha (5 acres)
English Heritage Grade II*

Bourton House

BOURTON-ON-THE-HILL, MORETON-
IN-MARSH, GL56 9AE

Tel 01386 700754 **Fax** 01386 701081
Website www.bourtonhouse.com

Location On A44, 1½ miles west of Moreton-in-Marsh.
Opening hours 10 am – 5 pm; Wednesday – Friday; 26 May to 31 August. Plus 30 & 31 May and 29 & 30 August, and Thursdays & Fridays in September & October.
Admission fee Adults £4.50; Children free.

First laid out by Lanning Roper in the 1960s, but consistently improved by the present owners, the gardens at Bourton House are both fashionable and a delight. They include a knot garden, a small *potager*, a raised pond, the topiary walk, trellis work, a croquet lawn, and borders bulging with good colour schemes – purple-leaved prunus with yellow roses, for instance.

Features topiary; good colour plantings, especially of herbaceous plants; lots of unusual and little-known plants; light lunches and home-made teas.

Owned by Mr & Mrs Richard Paice
Number of gardeners 2, plus 2 part-time
Size 1.2ha (3 acres), plus 2.8-ha (7-acre) arboretum
English Heritage Grade II

Daylesford House

DAYLESFORD, MORETON-IN-MARSH, GL56 0YH

Tel & Fax 01698 658888
Location On A436 between Chipping Norton & Stow-on-the-Wold.
Opening hours For charity. And by appointment.
Admission fee By agreement.

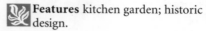

There are few better places to see a traditional well-run estate than Daylesford. The house was built by Cockerell, the architect of Sezincote, and is still surrounded by a late 18th-century landscape park, complete with lake. The handsome orangery also dates from the 1790s. The kitchen garden is a proper working garden for the production of fruit, vegetables and flowers, and includes a peach house and an orchid house. Elsewhere are a trellised rose garden and an avenue of tulip trees, planted in the 1960s with advice from Lanning Roper. New, more recent ventures include the lake temple and secret garden.

**Features** kitchen garden; historic design.

Owned by Sir Anthony & Lady Bamford
Number of gardeners 8
Size 12ha (30 acres)
English Heritage Grade II*

Dyrham Park

CHIPPENHAM, SN14 8ER

Tel 0117 937 2501 **Fax** 0117 937 1353
Website www.nationaltrust.org.uk
Location On A46, 8 miles north of Bath.
Opening hours 11 am – 5.30 pm; Friday – Tuesday; 26 March to 31 October.
Admission fee Garden only £3.20; Children £1.60.

Dyrham is fascinating for garden historians, who can study the Kip plan and trace the lines of the 17th-century formal garden which Charles Harcourt Masters turned into classic English parkland. It is not a Mecca for the dedicated plantsman, but the impressive orangery is full of colour and scent.

Features good herbaceous borders; deer park; handsome orangery; shop; tea-room.

Owned by The National Trust
Number of gardeners 2
Size 3.2ha (8 acres), plus park
English Heritage Grade II*

Eastleach House

EASTLEACH, CIRENCESTER, GL7 3NW

Tel & Fax 01367 850416
Location In middle of village.
Opening hours 2 pm – 5 pm; Fridays; June & July.
And by appointment for groups.
Admission fee Adults £5; Children free.

Eastleach House is at the top of a steep slope, and the garden has been laid out to provide enclosure and protection, while not interfering with the magnificent views. Each area is treated differently, but the garden is brought together by bold plantings like an avenue of limes, and by inspired plantsmanship. There is colour at every season: in May from the iris borders, in June from rambling roses, in high summer from spectacular herbaceous borders, and in autumn from the small arboretum.

Features good design; rich plantings; unusual plants for sale.

Owned by Mrs David Richards
Number of gardeners 3 part-time
Size 5.6ha (14 acres)

Ernest Wilson Memorial Garden

HIGH STREET, CHIPPING CAMPDEN, GL55 6AF

Tel 01386 841298
Location North end of main street.
Opening hours 9 am to dusk; daily, except Christmas day; all year.
Admission fee Collection box for donations.

A collection of plants all introduced by Ernest H. Wilson, the greatest of European plant hunters in China: Chipping Campden

was his birthplace. *Acer griseum*, *Clematis montana* var. *rubens* and the pocket-handkerchief tree (*Davidia involucrata*) are among his best-known introductions: all are represented here.

Features herbaceous borders; trees & shrubs.

Owned by Chipping Campden Town Council
Number of gardeners 1
Size 0.1ha (¼ acre)

Frampton Court

FRAMPTON-ON-SEVERN, GL2 7EU

Tel 01452 740267 **Fax** 01452 740698
Website www.framptoncourtestate.uk.com
Location Signed to Frampton-on-Severn from M5 Jct 13 (3 miles).
Opening hours By appointment all year.
Admission fee House & garden £4.50; Garden £1.

Beautiful and mysterious garden, little changed since 1750. The Dutch water garden – a long rectangular pool – reflects the orangery of Strawberry Hill Gothic design. But do also ask to see the collection of botanical water colours known as the Frampton Flora.

Features gothic orangery.

Owned by P.R.H. Clifford
Number of gardeners 1½
English Heritage Grade I

Goldney Hall

LOWER CLIFTON HILL, CLIFTON, BRISTOL, BS8 1BH

Tel 0117 903 4873 **Fax** 0117 903 4877
Website www.goldneyhall.com

Hidcote Manor Garden

HIDCOTE BARTRIM, CHIPPING CAMPDEN, GL55 6LR

Tel 01386 438333 **Fax** 01386 438817
Website www.nationaltrust.org.uk/hidcote
Location Signed from B4632, Stratford/Broadway Road.
Opening hours 10.30 am – 6 pm (5 pm in October); Saturday – Wednesday; 27 March to 31 October. Last admission one hour before closing.
Admission fee Adults £6.20; Children £3.10.

One of England's great gardens, Hidcote is an arts-and-crafts masterpiece created by the American plant-collector Major Lawrence Johnston. It was designed as a series of outdoor rooms, each with a different character and separated by walls and hedges of many different species. Hidcote therefore has a firm architectural structure – many of Lawrence Johnston's ideas came from France and Italy – combined with a great love of plants. The planting is exuberant but always considers the contrasts and harmonies which can be obtained by planting different things together. Some of the rooms are very small, like Mrs Winthrop's garden – no more than a courtyard with a potted cordyline at the centre – and others like the long walk and the great lawn give a great sense of space – though in fact the garden is no more than ten acres in size. Among the most famous features are: the mixed borders down the middle of the kitchen garden richly planted with old roses and companion plants; the red borders, which were one of the first single-colour borders in the country when first planted in 1913; the cottage garden, planted like an Edwardian flower painting where *Campanula latiloba* 'Hidcote Amethyst' is prominent; the sunken garden where a huge circular swimming pool fills a hedged compartment; and the woodland area known as Westonbirt where Johnston planted long vistas which run from end to end, but which disappear and reappear as you follow the paths back and forth. The National Trust is working on a programme of renewal and regeneration and it fair to say that Hidcote will shortly be looking better than ever.

Features woodland garden; topiary; roses (ancient & modern); rock garden; plantsman's collection of plants; good herbaceous borders; tallest pink acacia *Robinia* x *ambigua* 'Decaisneana' (19m.) in the British Isles; National Trust shop; licensed restaurant; teas.

Owned by The National Trust
Number of gardeners 7
English Heritage Grade I

Location Top of Constitution Hill: entrance on Lower Clifton Hill.
Opening hours 2 pm – 6 pm; 25 April & probably again in August (ring for dates).
Admission fee Adults £2.50; Concessions £1.50.

A Bristol merchant's extravagance, nearly 300 years ago. Ten acres in the middle of the City, with an elegant orangery, a gothic folly tower and the gorgeous Goldney Grotto, which sparkles with crystalline rocks among the shells and follies.

Features plants under glass; good herbaceous borders; holm oak hedge; many varieties of fruit; the *Chronicles of Narnia* were filmed in the grotto; cream teas in the Orangery.

Owned by The University of Bristol
Number of gardeners 6
English Heritage Grade II*

Highfield Nurseries

SCHOOL LANE, WHITMINSTER, GLOUCESTER, GL2 7PL

Tel 01452 740266 **Fax** 01452 740750
Location Off A38, ½ mile from M5, Jct 13.
Opening hours 9 am – 4 pm, Monday – Friday. Closed Saturdays & Sundays.
Admission fee Free.

Highfield is a large nursery, specialising in fruit trees and bushes: it offers a good choice of the best and most reliable cultivars. It also has a good list of roses, ornamental trees, shrubs and herbaceous plants – something for everyone, in fact. The adjoining garden centre is open 9 am – 6 pm daily (10.30 am – 4.30 pm on Sundays).

Features coffee shop.

Owned by Joan Greenway

Highnam Court

HIGHNAM, GLOUCESTER, GL2 8DP

Tel 01452 308251
Location Entrance on A40 roundabout.
Opening hours 11 am – 5 pm; first Sunday of the month; April to September.
Admission fee Adults £3; Children free.

Little remains of the original Highnam, laid out when the house was built in 1658. The garden was however very famous 100 years ago for the features designed or commissioned by Thomas Gambier-Parry in the middle of the 19th century: the terraces, the broad walk, the arboretum and, above all, the winter garden where natural stone is supplemented by Pulhamite – the largest and earliest surviving example of the artificial stone from which the rock garden at Wisley is also made. The estate was neglected for nearly 100 years, but restoration – slow and painstaking – began in 1994, so this is a garden to watch and revisit as the work continues. A new, one-acre rose garden was completed last year (2003) – 2,000 roses, underplanted with 60,000 bulbs.

Features Pulhamite rock garden; fine conifers; tallest *Quercus acutissima* and *Fraxinus excelsior* 'Jaspidea' in the British isles; historic garden in restoration; tea & cakes.

Owned by Roger Head
Number of gardeners 2
Size 12ha (30 acres)
English Heritage Grade II*

Hodges Barn

SHIPTON MOYNE, TETBURY, GL8 8PR

Tel 01666 880202 **Fax** 01666 880373
Location 3 miles south of Tetbury on Malmesbury Road from Shipton Moyne.

Opening hours For NGS: 2 pm – 6 pm; 18 & 19 April; 23 & 24 May; 20 June; 6, 7 &. 9 July. Groups welcome by appointment.
Admission fee Adults £5; Children free.

This is a large garden – six acres surrounding a converted 15th-century columbarium – all intensively planted. The terraces, courtyards and gardens are divided into rooms (surrounded either by walls or by tapestry, laurel or yew hedges) to give year-round colour. Old-fashioned rose beds are underplanted with tulips for spring and with alliums and campanulas for summer. There is a formal herbaceous border, a water garden and a swimming pool area with large planted pots. Shrub roses and climbers are another Hornby passion and are to be found winding up walls and trees. The plantings reflect a desire to create an informal feeling within a formal framework. The woodland garden is almost an arboretum of ornamental trees (especially birches, maples, whitebeams and many different magnolias), underplanted with spring bulbs. In summer the grass is left long in the wood and wildflowers are encouraged to naturalise. Hodges Barn is a garden of great energy and diversity.

Features woodland garden; topiary; roses (mainly old-fashioned & climbers); plantsman's collection of plants; good herbaceous borders; daffodils; bluebells; cyclamen.

Owned by Mrs Charles Hornby
Number of gardeners 2 part-time
Size 2.4ha (6 acres)

Hunts Court

NORTH NIBLEY, DURSLEY, GL11 6DZ

Tel 01453 547440 **Fax** 01453 549944
Location Signed in centre of village. Or turn across front of Black Horse pub & bear left for ½ mile.

Opening hours 9 am – 5 pm; Tuesday – Saturday (& Bank Holiday Mondays in spring); all year, except August. Also 13, 20 & 27 June and 5 & 12 September for National Gardens Scheme.
Admission fee Adults £2; Children & RNRS members free.

The garden at Hunts Court has been planted since 1976 by something of a horticultural rarity – a plant-loving farmer, and his wife. Keith and Margaret Marshall say they have 'the collector's touch of madness': the result is a garden which is charming, peaceful and educational. Their first love was old-fashioned roses, and they moved their garden fence out into the surrounding fields as the collection of Gallicas, Damasks and Hybrid Perpetuals began to grow: it is now the best in the west of England, and still expanding. The 450 cultivars include climbers, species and a few modern shrub roses. Many are underplanted by the Marshalls' next great passion – hardy geraniums and penstemons, each of which is represented by over 100 cultivars. The fence has been moved out several times now to accommodate a large collection of ornamental trees and shrubs, underplanted in turn by more unusual herbaceous plants. These are the stock plants for the thriving nursery they now run in their old stock-yard. It is surrounded by a fine plantsman's garden with something for all seasons, including good autumn colour and winter-flowering shrubs. But the Marshalls have just moved the fence again – to plant a mini-arboretum.

Features roses (mainly old-fashioned & climbers); roses of every kind, especially nineteenth-century cultivars; many other plants of interest to the plantsman; first-rate nursery attached; refreshments on NGS days.

Owned by T.K. & M.M. Marshall
Number of gardeners 1
Size 1ha (2½ acres)

Kiftsgate Court

CHIPPING CAMPDEN, GL55 6LW

Tel & Fax 01386 438777
Website www.kiftsgate.co.uk
Location 3 miles from Chipping Campden opposite Hidcote Manor.
Opening hours 2 pm – 6 pm; Wednesdays, Thursdays, Sundays & Bank Holiday Mondays; April, May, August & September; plus 12 noon – 6 pm on Mondays, Wednesdays, Thursdays, Saturdays & Sundays in June & July.
Admission fee Adults £5: Children £1.50.

Famous for its roses, especially the eponymous *Rosa filipes*, Kiftsgate is all about plants and the use of colour. The best example is the yellow border, where gold and orange are set off by occasional blues and purples. After some dull years, everything about Kiftsgate has revived again: new thinking, new plantings and new enthusiasm have more than restored its excellence. The latest addition (2000) is in marked contrast to the rest of the garden: the tennis court has been transformed into a contemporary water garden, full of movement and sound, by Simon Allison. Structure and form predominate here over Kiftsgate's traditional themes of colour and texture. And the garden as a whole is remarkable for its tender plants – abutilons, echiums, azaras and wonderful tree peonies in May.

Features roses (mainly old-fashioned); colour plantings; good borders; many interesting plants; tea-room in the house.

Owned by Mr & Mrs J. Chambers
Number of gardeners 2
Size 1.6ha (4 acres)
English Heritage Grade II*

Lydney Park Gardens

LYDNEY PARK, GL15 6BU

Tel 01594 842844 **Fax** 01594 842027
Location Off A48 between Lydney & Aylburton.
Opening hours 11 am – 6 pm; Sundays, Wednesdays & Bank Holidays; 21 March to 6 June. Plus daily, 2 to 7 May & 30 May to 4 June.
Admission fee £4, but £3 on Wednesdays; Children 50p.

There are fine formal gardens around the house, but Lydney is famous for its rhododendrons: a remarkable collection planted over the last 50 years is the backbone to the extensive woodland garden. And not just rhododendrons, but azaleas and camellias too – all are carefully planted to create distinct effects from March to June. The numbers are still growing, and include plants grown from collected seed and hybrids from distinguished breeders, many as yet unnamed, while others have yet to flower. Lydney is now recognised as one of the best rhododendron gardens in England.

Features rhododendrons & azaleas; woodland garden; mature conifers; deer park; daffodils; some souvenirs for sale; light teas.

Owned by Viscount Bledisloe
Number of gardeners 2, plus part-time help in season
Size 3.2ha (8 acres) of woodland garden

Mill Dene Gardens

SCHOOL LANE, BLOCKLEY, MORETON-IN-MARSH, GL56 9HU

Tel 01386 709457 **Fax** 01386 700526
Website www.gardenvisit-cotswolds.co.uk
Location First road on left as you come into Blockley from Bourton-on-the-Hill.

Opening hours 10 am – 5.30 pm; Tuesday – Friday; April to October. Plus 2 pm – 6 pm on Sundays in June and Bank Holiday Mondays. And by appointment.
Admission fee Adults £4; Children £1. RHS members free in April and October.

This Cotswold water-mill garden has been designed and planted by the owner in an English country-garden style. Steep terraces rise from the mill-pond, stream and grotto. Paths wander through the rose walk, flanked by standard 'Sander's White Rambler' roses and lavender, to the cricket lawn. At the top of the garden, the *potager* and the 'fantasy fruit garden' (all greys and blues) have the church as a backdrop and views of the hills. Three RHS special events will take place at Mill Dene during 2004: details from 020 7821 3408.

Features refreshments.

Owned by Mr & Mrs B.S. Dare
Number of gardeners 1
Size 1ha (2½ acres)

Miserden Park

MISERDEN, STROUD, GL6 7JA

Tel 01285 821303 **Fax** 01285 821530
Location Signed from A417, or turn off B4070 between Stroud & Birdlip.
Opening hours 10 am – 5 pm; Tuesday – Thursday; April to September.
Admission fee Adults £3.50; Children free.

The Cotswold house at Miserden (Jacobean, with a Lutyens addition) has wide views across the Golden Valley, while the spacious peaceful gardens lie to the side. Most were laid out in the 1920s using a 17th-century structure – a charming rose garden, a long yew walk and expansive herbaceous borders.

Recent additions include a rill and summerhouse, a parterre of lavender and hebes, a shrub border and a border of silvers and greys. Near the entrance is an interesting nursery with a stock of good herbaceous plants.

Features topiary; good trees; good herbaceous borders; martagon lilies; roses; domed yew walk; cyclamen; excellent garden nursery by entrance.

Owned by Major M.T.N.H. Wills
Number of gardeners 2
Size 5ha (12½ acres)
English Heritage Grade II*

Owlpen Manor

ULEY, DURSLEY, GL11 5BZ

Tel 01453 860261 **Fax** 01453 860819
Website www.owlpen.com
Location Off B4066 near Uley.
Opening hours 2 pm – 5 pm; Tuesday – Sunday & Bank Holiday Mondays; April to September.
Admission fee Adults £2.80; Children £1.

Owlpen is a dreamy Cotswold manor house whose loveliness depends upon its site. It has a small formal garden which was terraced in the 16th century, altered c.1720 and restored in the Old English style by Norman Jewson in 1926. Jewson planted the box parterres and topiary yews; the present owners have added the roses and herbs since 1980. The aim is to suggest an earlier garden 're-ordered conservatively' in about 1700. Owlpen is perhaps not worth a special journey by keen plantsmen, but the restaurant, the setting and the house all add up to a good place for an outing.

Features topiary; roses (mainly old-fashioned); standard gooseberries; guidebooks & postcards for sale; licensed restaurant (noon – 5 pm).

Owned by Nicholas & Karin Mander
Number of gardeners 1
Size 0.8ha (2 acres)
English Heritage Grade II

Painswick Rococo Garden

THE STABLES, PAINSWICK HOUSE, PAINSWICK, GL6 6TH

Tel 01452 813204 Fax 01452 814888
Website www.rococogarden.co.uk
Location Outside Painswick on B4073.
Opening hours 11 am – 5 pm; daily; 10 January to 31 October.
Admission fee Adults £4; OAPs £3.50; Children £2.

Years of restoration work have saved the unique rococo garden at Painswick from back-to-nature woodland. A white Venetian gothic exedra, a Doric seat, the plunge pool, an octagonal pigeon house, a gothic gazebo called the Eagle House, a bowling green, the fish pond and a gothic alcove have all been reconstructed in their original positions thanks to the efforts of Lord Dickinson and the Painswick Rococo Gardens Trust. Recent additions include the Exedra Garden (18th-century herbaceous plantings in an informal structure, best in early summer) and the kitchen garden (best in late summer). A remarkable garden and a brilliant theatrical achievement.

Features woodland garden; snowdrop wood; new plant nursery; maze; gift shop; licensed restaurant, coffee, teas & light snacks.

Owned by Painswick Rococo Garden Trust
Number of gardeners 4
Size 2.4ha (6 acres)
English Heritage Grade II*

Rodmarton Manor

RODMARTON, CIRENCESTER, GL7 6PF

Tel 01285 841253 Fax 01285 841298
Website www.rodmarton-manor.co.uk
Location Off A433 between Cirencester & Tetbury.
Opening hours 2 pm – 5 pm; Wednesdays, Saturdays & Bank Holiday Mondays; 3 May to 30 August. Plus Mondays in June & July.
Admission fee Adults £4; Children £1. RHS members free in May & August.

A splendid Arts & Crafts garden, with a strong design and exuberant planting. Simon Biddulph says there are 18 different areas within the garden, from the trough garden for alpine plants to the famous double herbaceous borders, now entirely renovated, which lead to a Cotswold summerhouse. Highly original – contemporary, but made without any contact, with Hidcote.

Features interesting plants; old-fashioned roses; topiary; much renovation and replanting.

Owned by Simon Biddulph
English Heritage Grade II*

Sezincote

MORETON-IN-MARSH, GL56 9AW

Tel 01386 700444
Location On A44 to Evesham, 1½ miles out of Moreton-in-Marsh.
Opening hours 2 pm – 6 pm (or dusk, if earlier); Thursdays, Fridays & Bank Holiday Mondays; January to November.
Admission fee Adults £3.50; Children £1 (under-5s free).

The house at Sezincote was the model for the Brighton Pavilion, and seems inseparable from the cruciform Moghul garden that sets off its Indian façade so well: yet this brilliant formal garden was designed as recently as 1965. On the other side are sumptuous borders planted by Graham Stuart Thomas and a luscious water garden of candelabra primulas and astilbes around the Temple to Surya, the Snake Bridge and Brahmin bulls. Humphry Repton had a hand in the original landscape, but the modern gardens are even more satisfying than the classical, 18th-century, parkland setting.

 Features good, bold plantings in the water garden; tallest maidenhair tree *Ginkgo biloba* (26m.) in the British Isles and 5 other record trees. These include the blue-leaved noble fir *Abies procera* Glauca Group, the weeping hornbeam *Carpinus betulus* 'Pendula' and the yellow-leaved beech *Fagus sylvatica* 'Zlatia'.

Owned by Mr & Mrs D. Peake
Number of gardeners 3
Size 4ha (10 acres)
English Heritage Grade I

Snowshill Manor

SNOWSHILL, BROADWAY, WR12 7JU

Tel 01386 852410 **Fax** 01386 842822
Website www.nationaltrust.org.uk
Location In Snowshill village.
Opening hours 11 am – 5.30 pm; Wednesday – Sunday; 19 March to 31 October. Plus Bank Holiday Mondays.
Admission fee Gardens only: Adults £3.80; Children £1.90.

The garden at Snowshill has often been praised for its changes of levels and collection of curious artefacts – an armillary sphere and a gilt figure of St George and the Dragon, for instance. Snowshill is as curious as its maker, Charles Wade, and the spooky bric-a-brac which fills his house, but many visitors find it 'charming' or 'interesting'. Snowshill was the

National Trust's first all-organic garden.

 Features unusual design; good borders; National Trust shop; restaurant.

Owned by The National Trust
Number of gardeners 2
Size 0.8ha (2 acres)
English Heritage Grade II

Special Plants

HILL FARM BARN, GREENWAYS LANE, COLD ASHTON, CHIPPENHAM, SN14 8LA

Tel 01225 891686
Website www.specialplants.net
Location Near Bath, just south of junction of A46 & A420. Not in Cold Ashton.
Opening hours Nursery open: 10 am – 5 pm; daily; March to September. And by appointment. Garden open: 2 pm – 5 pm for NGS on 17 June, 15 July, 19 August & 16 September. Plus 11 am – 5 pm on 4, 11, 18 & 25 August.
Admission fee Adults £2.

The collection of hardy plants at this connoisseur's nursery is excellent, but it is for her tender perennials that Derry Watkins's nursery is best known. Diascias, salvias, pelargoniums and streptocarpus are among her top lines, together with conservatory climbers and shrubs. A three-month visit to South Africa has introduced some interesting novelties – both plants and seeds are available. There are also one-day courses at the nursery in autumn. The new garden is open monthly for the National Gardens Scheme and a useful adjunct to the nursery. In 1996, Derry Watkins and her architect husband bought a derelict barn with three acres of steeply sloping fields. Around the barn he designed bold shapes in gravel, water and grass, terraced with dry stone walls. Then she planted it up with drifts of colour using many unusual plants (not a rose or a clematis in sight, alas). There is a 'black and white' border, a sizzling hot red-and-orange bed and a cooler lemon-and-lime slope, as well as a gravel garden, grass garden, bog garden, ponds, vegetable garden and now an orchard and a woodland walk, all set off by wonderful views down the valley.

 Features unusual plants.

Owned by Derry Watkins

Stancombe Park

DURSLEY, GL11 6AU

Tel 01453 542815
Location Off the B4060 between Dursley & Wotton-under-Edge.
Opening hours Groups by appointment.
Admission fee Adults £3; Children (under 10) £1.

Stancombe has everything: a handsome house above a wooded valley, a flower garden of wondrous prettiness, and a gothic horror of an historic Folly Garden at the valley bottom. Start at the top. Peter Coats, Lanning Roper and Nadia Jennett all worked on the rose gardens and mixed borders by the house: there is more to learn about good modern design and planting here than any garden in Gloucestershire. Then wander down the valley where the path narrows and the incline steepens to a ferny tunnel, and start the circuit of the follies, best described as an open-air ghost-train journey without the ghosts. Highly recommended.

 Features fine collection of trees; excellent borders; fine spring bulbs; lots of roses; some interesting and unusual plants.

Owned by Mrs Basil Barlow
Size 6ha (15 acres)
English Heritage Grade I

Stanway House

STANWAY, CHELTENHAM, GL54 5PQ

Tel 01386 584469 **Fax** 01386 584688
Location On B4077.
Opening hours 2 pm – 5 pm; Tuesdays, Thursdays & Saturdays; July to September. And groups by appointment. On 21 March and 18 April for NGS.
Admission fee Adults £4; OAPs £3; Children £1.

The important water-gardens at Stanway are undergoing restoration: the gravity-fed fountain is the tallest in Britain. A pyramidal folly dominates the hillside behind the house. Repairs have begun on the 170m cascade which runs down to a long still tank known as the Canal. On the way up to the top are some interesting trees and shrubs. If you have not been to Stanway for a few years, you will be amazed by the changes; worth another visit.

 Features woodland garden; mature conifers.

Owned by Lord Neidpath
Number of gardeners 1½
Size 8ha (20 acres)
English Heritage Grade I

Stowell Park

NORTHLEACH, GL54 3LE

Tel 01285 720308 **Fax** 01285 720360
Location A429 between Cirencester & Northleach.
Opening hours 11 am – 4 pm; 16 May (plus plant sale). 2 pm – 5 pm; 20 June for Royal British Legion.
Admission fee £4. No concessions. Children free.

The most important feature at Stowell is its peach house, 180ft long, which has been in constant use since the early 19th century. Nowhere in England does such a glasshouse produce fruit in the manner perfected by our Victorian ancestors. Stowell also has an historic landscape in a magnificent position, with terraced gardens in front of the house looking down over the Coln valley and landscaped woodlands dating from the 18th century. The pleached lime avenue at the entrance to the house was planted in 1983 and is now fully established. In the superb traditional walled gardens are substantial herbaceous borders and some notable plantings of old-fashioned roses.

 **Features** fine kitchen garden and glasshouses; roses; good herbaceous borders; plants for sale on 16 May only; excellent teas.

Owned by Lord Vestey
Number of gardeners 4
Size 3.2ha (8 acres)
English Heritage Grade II

Sudeley Castle & Gardens

WINCHCOMBE, GL54 5JD

Tel 01242 602308 **Fax** 01242 602959
Website www.sudeleycastle.co.uk
Location 8 miles north-east of Cheltenham B4632.
Opening hours 10.30 am – 5.30 pm; daily; 6 March to 31 October.
Admission fee Adults £5.50; OAPs £4.50; Children £3.25.

Ⓟ ⓌⒸ ♿ ⚓ ⌼ ☕

This large commercially-run garden has features by many top garden designers: Jane Fearnley-Whittingstall did the roses and Charles Chesshire replanted the 'secret garden' (originally designed by Rosemary Verey) in the Mediterranean style. The whole garden is organically managed. There are fine old trees, magnificent Victorian topiary (mounds of green and gold yew) and a raised walk around the pleasure gardens that may be Elizabethan in origin. Popular and successful.

 Features topiary; roses (ancient & modern); herbs; mature conifers; good herbaceous borders; ruins of banqueting hall, now a pretty garden; wildflower meadow; HDRA heritage seed garden; gift shop; plant centre; restaurant & tea-rooms.

Owned by Lady Ashcombe
Number of gardeners 4
Size 5.6ha (14 acres)
English Heritage Grade II*

University of Bristol Botanic Garden

BRACKEN HILL, NORTH ROAD, LEIGH WOODS, BRISTOL, BS8 3PF

Tel 0117 973 3682 **Fax** 0117 974 1929
Website www.bris.ac.uk/depts/BotanicGardens
Location Take M5 Jct 19 towards Clifton, left into North Road before suspension bridge.
Opening hours 9 am – 5 pm; Monday – Friday; all year except public holidays.
Admission fee Free, except when open for National Gardens Scheme.

Ⓟ ⓌⒸ

This is an educational and accessible garden that bridges the gap between botany and horticulture. It has the most diverse plant collection in the whole region. The Pulhamite rock garden is listed by English Heritage as Grade II, 'of special interest'. The unusual climatic conditions in its position high above the river Avon have made possible some fine new plantings of South African and New Zealand plants. The collection of *Aeonium* is the most comprehensive in the UK, and the collections of *Pelargonium* species and Central American *Salvia* species are also very good. The rare endemic *Sorbus bristoliensis* grows in a part of the garden dedicated to the flora of the Clifton Gorge. However, there is a plan under discussion to move the garden and its collections to a new site.

Westonbirt The National Arboretum

WESTONBIRT, TETBURY, GL8 8QS

Tel 01666 880220 **Fax** 01666 880559
Website www.forestry.gov.uk/westonbirt
Location 3 miles south-west of Tetbury on A433.
Opening hours 10 am – 8 pm (or dusk if earlier);
daily; all year. Visitor centre open 10 am – 5 pm;
daily; March to December.
Admission fee January to March: Adults £5; OAPs
£4; Children £1. April to 5 June: Adults £6; OAPs
£5; Children £1. 6 June to 7 September: Adults
£7.50; OAPs £6.50; Children £1. 8 September to
31 December: Adults £6; OAPs £5; Children £1.
RHS members free.

Westonbirt is the finest and largest
arboretum in the British Isles: it
contains one of the most important
collections of trees and shrubs in the world.
There are 18,000 of them, representing
4,000 species and cultivars, planted from
1829 to the present day, and covering some
600 acres of beautifully landscaped grounds.
The maple glade is famous, and so are the
bluebells in the part known as Silk Wood.
Magnificent spring displays of
rhododendrons, azaleas and magnolias,
wildflowers in summer and architectural
winter beauty are matched by the
spectacular autumn colouring for which
Westonbirt is justifiably famous. Westonbirt
is also one of the best gardens in England
for a winter walk but, with 17 miles of
paths, you can find quiet areas even in the
third week of October when the maples are
at their most colourful.

Features over 1000 species of record-
breaking trees, including 24 maples
(*Acer* species) and 16 *Sorbus*. Other
champion trees include the red horse
chestnut *Aesculus* x *carnea* at 27m; the
upright birch *Betula pendula* 'Fastigiata' at
29m; the handkerchief tree *Davidia*

involucrata at 24m; the home-sprung *Pinus*
'Holfordiana' at 36m; and the large-leaved
deciduous oak *Quercus macranthera* at 31m;
gift shop; plant centre; restaurant; cafeteria.

Owned by Forestry Commission
Number of gardeners 8
Size 240ha (600 acres)
NCCPG National Collections *Acer* (Japanese
cvs.); *Salix*
English Heritage Grade I

Features rock garden; plantsman's collection of plants; plants under glass; fine collection of trees; cistus; hebes; sempervivums; peonies; aeoniums; salvias; Chinese medical plants; rare & threatened plants of south-west Britain.

Owned by University of Bristol
Number of gardeners 6½
Size 2ha (5 acres)

Westbury Court

WESTBURY-ON-SEVERN, GL14 1PD

Tel 01452 760461 **Fax** 01452 760461
Website www.nationaltrust.org.uk
Location 9 miles south-west of Gloucester on A48.
Opening hours 10 am – 5 pm, Wednesday – Sunday & Bank Holiday Mondays; 3 March to 31 October. Daily in July & August.
Admission fee Adults £3.50; Children £1.70.

Westbury was restored in the 1970s to become the best example of a medium-sized 17th-century Dutch garden in England. An elegant pavilion, tall and slender, looks down along a long tank of water. On the walls are old apple, pear and plum cultivars. Parterres (now planted in the 17th-century style), fine modern topiary and a T-shaped tank with a statue of Neptune in the middle make up the rest of the garden, with an opulent rose garden (old varieties only, including the 'true' *Rosa moschata*) underplanted with pinks, tulips and herbs. All the plants were known to cultivation before 1720. New for 2004 is a recreated 17th-century vegetable garden. Immaculately maintained.

 Features topiary; herbs; biggest holm oak *Quercus ilex* in the British Isles.

Owned by The National Trust
Number of gardeners 1
Size 1.6ha (4 acres)
English Heritage Grade II*

Willow Lodge

GLOUCESTER ROAD (A40), LONGHOPE, GLOUCESTER, GL17 0RA

Tel & Fax 01452 831211
Website www.willowgardens.fsnet.co.uk
Location On A40, 10 miles from Gloucester & 6 miles from Ross-on-Wye: ½ mile west of Dursley Cross.
Opening hours 1 pm – 5 pm; 18, 19, 25 & 26 April; 2, 3, 23 & 24 May; 6 & 7 June; 11, 12, 25 & 26 July; 1, 2, 8, 9, 15 & 16 August. Groups and private visits by appointment.
Admission fee Adults £2; Children free.

This garden has been entirely made by the owners, enthusiastic plantsmen, since they moved here in 1987. At first they developed just an acre around the house: it remains a good garden of mixed herbaceous and shrubby plantings, with some particularly fine shade-lovers – trilliums, erythroniums and dodecatheons. Then they started to plant the adjoining field as an arboretum, underplanted with native daffodils, snowdrops and ground orchids, *Dactylorhiza* species. Among the many interesting plants here are *Sinocalycanthus chinensis* and several *Lespedeza* species; some have been collected on their travels in China and North America. The stream that runs from end to end of the garden has been used to create a bog garden (lots of different primulas) and a pond, alongside a large alpine bed. There is much to enjoy and learn throughout the garden.

 Features a good young arboretum; bog garden; maples; teas.

Owned by Mr & Mrs J.H. Wood
Number of gardeners 3
Size 1.6ha (4 acres)

HAMPSHIRE

For such a prosperous county, Hampshire has comparatively few historic gardens of the highest importance: only Hackwood Park (not open to the public) and Highclere Park (right in the north) are listed as Grade I. But Hampshire compensates with a wealth of 20th-century plantsman's gardens and nurseries. Indeed, the Sir Harold Hillier Gardens (alas, now longer called 'Arboretum') at Ampfield – the world's greatest collection of temperate trees and shrubs – was founded as recently as 1953 and grew out of the commercial activities of Hillier's Nursery. When modern gardens like Brandy Mount, Exbury, Longstock, Spinners, Longthatch and Meon Orchard are taken into account, and some of the small specialist nurseries like Blackthorn and Langley Boxwood, Hampshire emerges as one of the best places in Europe for plants and gardens, plantsmen and gardeners. The National Gardens Scheme is extremely well represented in the county, with a very large number of gardens (nearly 150 last year) opening for charity. There are many good gardens which do not open often enough for us to list in this guide: Pylewell Park, Moundsmere Manor and Conholt Park among them. And deep in the New Forest, at Rhinefield, is the best late-Victorian pinetum in southern England. The Hampshire Group of the NCCPG is strong – always a good measure of the interest in gardening with plants – with nearly 40 National Collections. And the Hampshire Gardens Trust, founded more than 20 years ago by the energy and foresight of Gilly Drummond, has been the model for every county-based gardens trust since then. Sparsholt College, between Winchester and Stockbridge, is a RHS Partner College.

53 Ladywood

EASTLEIGH, SO50 4RW

Tel 023 8061 5389
Location M3 Jct 12; along A335, right at first roundabout (Woodside Ave); 2nd right into Bosville. Ladywood is 5th on right.
Opening hours 2 pm – 5 pm; Tuesdays; 6 April to 24 August. Plus 11 am – 5.50 pm on 16 May & 6

June for NGS.
Admission fee Adults £2; Children £1.

Mrs Ward's garden is a model of how to design a very small garden to look much bigger than it really is, and then to fill it with interesting plants and attractive colour combinations. Screens and trellis-work divide up the space, and the compartments are so ornamented with decorative details that you have to stop and go round it very slowly, in case you might miss something. Contrasts of textures are another feature – brick, stone, concrete, gravel, pebbles are mixed up to maximise variety – and so are flowering plants in pots. Leaves are as important as flowers; most of the shrubs are evergreen, and chosen for their foliage. The range of herbaceous and woodland plants is truly amazing, and they are all extremely well grown. A garden to admire and learn from.

 Features plants from the garden for sale; refreshments on NGS days.

Owned by Mys Sue Ward
Number of gardeners owner only
Size 14m ½ 14m

Abbey Cottage

RECTORY LANE, ITCHEN ABBAS, WINCHESTER, SO21 1BN

Tel & Fax 01962 779575
Location On B3047, 1 mile east of the Trout Inn at Itchen Abbas.
Opening hours 12 noon – 5 pm; 2 & 3 May. And 2 pm – 5 pm; 14 April, 9 June & 16 June.
Admission fee Adults £2.50; Children free.

Abbey Cottage would be a fine garden by any standards – it has a firm design, beautiful flint-and-brick walls, good lines, interesting plants, good colour schemes and immaculate standards of tidiness – but what makes it especially interesting is that Colonel Daniell is a recent convert to organic gardening. His says that 'organic gardening was the element missing from my gardening... now the garden feels complete'. The garden is maintained as much for the pleasure of his many friends and visitors as for his own pleasure. Teas and plants for sale are available at the openings on 2 & 3 May.

 Features organic garden; good structure; excellent maintenance.

Owned by Col. Patrick Daniell CBE
Number of gardeners 1 part-time
Size 0.6ha (1½ acres)

Apple Court

HORDLE LANE, HORDLE, LYMINGTON, SO41 0HU

Tel 01590 642130 **Fax** 01590 694220
Website www.applecourt.com
Location South of New Forest, just north of A337 at Downton crossroads.
Opening hours 10 am – 5 pm; Friday to Sunday; March to October.
Admission fee Adults £2.50; Children free.

The display gardens attached to this specialist nursery (hostas, hemerocallis and grasses) are firmly designed and would be worth a visit even without plants. The white garden is especially original: at its heart is an oval-shaped lawn, surrounded by pleached hornbeams. The white plantings lie *outside* this oval of limes. Elsewhere are about 300 cultivars of *Hosta*, many of them – like the daylilies – bred in USA and offered for sale by Apple Court but by no other UK nursery. There are 400 *Hemerocallis* cultivars too, including spider and other unusual forms.

 Features tea & coffee.

Owned by Charles & Angela Meads
Number of gardeners 2
Size 0.6ha (1½ acres)

Brandy Mount House

EAST STREET, ALRESFORD, SO24 9EG

Tel 01962 732189
Website www.brandymount.co.uk
Location Left into East Street from Broad Street, 50 yards first right.
Opening hours 11 am – 4 pm; 4, 7 & 8 February. 2 pm – 5 pm; 7 March. And by appointment.
Admission fee Adults £2; Children free.

Brandy Mount is the garden of plantsmen – but plantsmen who are also distinguished cultivators and exhibitors of alpine plants. The first surprise is to find quite such a large and secluded garden so near the centre of a busy town. Then you discover that, although the underlying soil is chalky, a great variety of the rarer shade-loving plants thrive in the rich soil under the trees – as well as the snowdrops, for which the garden is famous among galanthophiles. The herbaceous borders in the sunnier parts support the many species of geranium, peonies, daphnes and spring-flowering bulbs which are happy in the warm, free-draining soil. The planting of all these areas is informal, with wide sweeps of lawn between the borders. The vegetable area has been re-organised as a formal *potager* with traditional box hedges and small beds to allow the owners to grow a greater variety of salad crops and more unusual vegetables, interspersed with flowering plants. Alpines have always been a speciality: they flourish around the terrace in front of the house, where there are over 30 kinds of smaller daphnes. Many alpines are also grown in troughs and sinks, which are organised as a group and replanted as small crevice gardens. These support many rare and tricky species which are also grown in frames and in the Alpine House. There is a fine collection of European primulas, saxifrages and dwarf narcissi. This garden is fascinating, immaculately maintained, and forever changing, as the collection of rare plants grows ever larger. Strongly recommended.

Features plantsman's garden; woodland and herbaceous plants on a chalk soil; terrace and troughs for alpines; snowdrops; daphnes; peony species; European primulas; Alpine House; extensive plant sales area full of good plants; teas (but not in February).

Owned by Caryl & Michael Baron
Number of gardeners part-time (very)
Size 0.5ha (1¼ acres)
NCCPG National Collections *Daphne*; *Galanthus*

Blackthorn Nursery

KILMESTON, ALRESFORD, SO24 0NL

Tel 01962 771796 **Fax** 01962 771071
Location 1 mile south of Cheriton, off A272.
Opening hours 9 am – 5 pm; Fridays & Saturdays;
5 March to 25 June, and 3 to 25 September. Plus
Hellebore Days 9 am – 4 pm on 13 & 14 February.

Blackthorn's plants tend to be spring
beauties: the nursery's three specialities are
hellebores, epimediums and daphnes, all of
which they breed, as well as introducing
new species. Their most striking hellebores
are semi-doubles called 'Party Dress' hybrids.
The list of epimediums is the best in
England – over 40 different names: their
rarities include a large number of collected
species like *E. fargesii* Og. 93057 and
E. franchetii 'Brimstone Butterfly' Og. 87001.
The daphnes are no less remarkable: over 50
different names, including such little-known
hybrids as *D.* x *thauma* and no less than 7
cultivars of *D.* x *hendersonii*. Their general
list of alpines and herbaceous plants is
equally exciting: they have a covetable and
ever-changing selection of good plants. For
dedicated plantsmen, a visit to Blackthorn
on an open day in February or March is one
of the social highlights of early spring: every
fellow-plantsman in the country seems to be
there too.

Owned by R. & S. White
Size 0.1-ha (¼-acre) woodland walk

Bramdean House

BRAMDEAN, ALRESFORD, SO24 0JU

Tel 01962 771214 **Fax** 01962 771095
Location On A272, between Winchester &
Petersfield.
Opening hours 2 pm – 5 pm; 29 February, 11
April, 9 May, 13 June, 11 July, 8 August, 12
September, & by appointment.
Admission fee Adults £3; Children free; for
National Gardens Scheme. Otherwise Adults £4.

The gardens at Bramdean are much
admired, and rightly so. Against a backdrop
of mature trees, two wide mirror-image
borders lead away from the back of the
house. At the end of the central axis, steps
lead to a one-acre walled kitchen garden
whose central beds are planted with a range
of herbaceous plants, roses, perennials and
bulbs. The vista runs yet further, through an
orchard under-planted with massed
daffodils to an apple-house some 300 yards
from the house. The views in both
directions are stunning.

Features climbing roses; herbaceous
plants; peonies; ornamental shrubs;
bulbs of every sort; climbing roses; clematis;
sweet peas; vegetables; fruit; tender nerines;
refreshments.

Owned by Mr & Mrs H. Wakefield
Number of gardeners 2
Size 2.6ha (6½ acres)
English Heritage Grade II

Exbury Gardens

EXBURY, SOUTHAMPTON, SO45 1AZ

Tel 023 8089 1203 **Fax** 023 8089 9940
Website www.exbury.co.uk
Location 3 miles south of Beaulieu.
Opening hours 10 am – 5.30 pm (or dusk if
earlier); daily; 28 February to 31 October. Limited
winter opening dates to be confirmed.
Admission fee Adults £4; OAPs £3.50; Children
£1. But Adults £6; OAPs £5.50; Children £1.50 in
high season (approximately mid-March to mid-June).
OAPs £5 on Tuesdays, Wednesdays & Thursdays.
RHS members free in March and October.

Rhododendrons, rhododendrons,

rhododendrons: over one million of them in 200 acres of natural woodland. More than 40 have won awards from the Royal Horticultural Society. But there are magnolias, camellias and rare trees too, many grown from the original seed introduced by famous plant collectors. A place of wonder in May, but beautiful at every time of the year. The collection of nerines which Lionel de Rothschild bred between the wars was dispersed after his death but reassembled and developed by Sir Peter Smithers in Switzerland. A few years ago he returned them to Exbury where they may be seen once again in October. A new garden has been created in the style of Piet Oudolf and James Van Sweden – huge swathes of herbaceous perennials and grasses within a strong woodland structure.

Features good herbaceous borders; candelabra primulas; rare trees; rose garden; water garden; daffodils; massive two-acre rock garden; *Nerine* hybrids; hydrangea walk; plant centre; gift shop; artist's studio; hot & cold lunches; cream teas; new tea-room.

Owned by Edmund de Rothschild
Number of gardeners 9
Size 80ha (200 acres)
English Heritage Grade II*

Fairfield House

HAMBLEDON, WATERLOOVILLE, PO7 4RY

Tel 023 9263 2431
Location East Street, Hambledon.
Opening hours 2 pm – 6 pm; 21 March & 20 June. And by appointment.
Admission fee Adults £3; Children free.

Fairfield is one of the best private rose gardens in England. Old roses and climbers were the late Peter Wake's main interest and

he grew them unusually well. The shrubs are trained up a cat's cradle of string drawn between five wooden posts. 'Charles de Mills' and 'Andersonii' are simply spectacular, while a very fine 'Climbing Mme Caroline Testout' runs up the back of the house and 'François Juranville' rambles over the canopy.

Features mature conifers; good herbaceous borders; beautifully grown roses, ancient & modern.

Owned by Mrs Peter Wake
Number of gardeners 1
Size 2.4ha (6 acres)

Furzey Gardens

MINSTEAD, LYNDHURST, SO43 7GL

Tel 023 8081 2464 **Fax** 023 8081 2297
Website www.furzey-gardens.org
Location Off A31 or A337 to Minstead.
Opening hours 10 am – 5 pm (dusk in winter); daily except 25 & 26 December.
Admission fee March – October: Adults £3.50; OAPs £2.80; Children £1.50. Reductions in winter. RHS members free from March to October.

Furzey demonstrates how woodland garden effects can be created in quite small areas. Parts are a maze of narrow curving paths running between hedges of Kurume azaleas, unforgettable in April and May, but the late summer flowering of eucryphias runs them close and the autumn colours of nyssas, parrotias and enkianthus are worth a visit in October.

Features rhododendrons & azaleas; mature conifers; camellias; bluebells; naturalised dieramas; heathers; spring bulbs; small shop; refreshments.

Owned by Furzey Gardens Charitable Trust
Number of gardeners 2 horticultural instructors with teams of students with learning difficulties
Size 3.2ha (8 acres)

Gilbert White's House

HIGH STREET, SELBORNE, ALTON,
GU34 3JH

Tel 01420 511275 **Fax** 01420 511040
Location In centre of Selborne, on B3006.
Opening hours 11 am – 5 pm; daily; 1 January to
24 December.
Admission fee Adults £4.50; OAPs £4; Children
£1.

The house was bought some years ago, and
the museum founded to commemorate the
life and work of Gilbert White, author of
*The Natural History & Antiquities of
Selborne*. The garden provides a very good
example of how a person of modest means
might construct a scaled-down landscaped
park in the mid-18th century. The flower
borders display plants and features
described by White. The 'wild' garden,
orchard and vegetable garden, with a 'wine
pipe' and a herb garden, complete the idyll.

**Features** plants associated with Gilbert
White; gift shop; tea parlour.

Owned by Oates Memorial Trust
Number of gardeners 2, plus volunteers
Size 12ha (30 acres)

Hambledon House

HAMBLEDON, WATERLOOVILLE,
PO7 4RU

Tel 023 9263 2380
Location In village centre.
Opening hours 2 pm – 5.30 pm, for NGS, and for
groups by appointment.
Admission fee Adults £2.50; Children free.

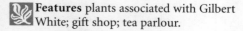

Hambledon House sits in a frost pocket on
thin chalky soil, but Mrs Hart Dyke has
created a garden which is thick with colour
all through the year. She is a great
plantswoman, but it is the placing of plants
that interests her most. Bricks walls and
hedges of beech and box divide the garden
into smaller areas. Colour, shape and form
determine where plants look best: highlights
include clematis, salvias, lavender, cistus,
grasses and a great choice of herbaceous
plants.

Features plants for plantsmen; good
colour combinations; plants from
garden for sale; home-made teas.

Owned by Captain & Mrs David Hart Dyke
Number of gardeners owners only
Size 1ha (2½ acres)

Heathlands

47 LOCKS ROAD, LOCKS HEATH,
SOUTHAMPTON, SO31 6NS

Tel 01489 573598 **Fax** 01489 557884
Location 2 miles from M27 Jct 9. Locks Road is
the main north-south road through the middle of
Locks Heath.
Opening hours 2 pm – 5.30 pm; 7 March, 11 April,
9 May & 22 August.
Admission fee Adults £2.50; Children free.

Since building his house in 1967, Dr Burwell
has filled his acre of stony soil with a
wonderful choice of immaculately grown
plants of every type. It is the embodiment of
careful plantsmanship, a garden to go round
slowly – looking, studying and thinking.
Your first sight is an eighty-metre line of
Paulownia tomentosa grown from seed in
about 1970, flowering (in May) all along the
road and thought to be the longest line in
England. Next comes *Garrya elliptica*
trained as a small tree. Round the side of the
house is a tall yew hedge, topped by a
brooding topiary peacock. The design is a
mixture of formal and informal, with a large

The Sir Harold Hillier Gardens

JERMYNS LANE, AMPFIELD, ROMSEY, SO51 0QA

Tel 01794 368787 **Fax** 01794 368027
Website www.hillier.hants.gov.uk/
Location Signed from A3090 & A3057.
Opening hours 10.30 am – 6 pm (dusk if earlier);
every day except 25 & 26 December.
Admission fee Adults £6; Concessions £5.50;
Children (under 16) free.

This is quite the most important modern arboretum in UK. The gardens have the greatest collection of wild and cultivated woody plants in the world: over 12,000 taxa in 180 acres, totalling 42,000 plants. The arboretum was established in 1953 by the late Sir Harold Hillier: Hillier's Nursery aimed at the time to offer for sale every cultivar of every tree or shrub that was hardy in the British Isles. Sir Harold himself was an active importer and collector of new species from all over the world, at a time (of relative economic depression) when few British horticulturists had the impetus to look outside the United Kingdom for plants of any kind. Every part of the arboretum is an education and a pleasure, whatever the season or weather. It has so many unique features that the visitor needs all day to see more than a fraction of its riches: the collection of poplar trees called the Populetum; more than 100 pines (*Pinus* species), including the 'big cone' pine *P. coulteri* whose cones may weigh as much as two kilos; a maple valley; the largest Winter Garden of its kind in Europe and a Gurkha Memorial Garden. But it is the sheer number of trees and shrubs here that makes the most lasting impression: every time you visit, and wherever you walk, you see interesting plants that you have never seen before. The labelling is exemplary and a helpful guide is available. Hilliers' nursery shares a car park with the arboretum.

Details of seasonal special events, workshops, evening talks, guided tours and children's activities can be obtained on request.

Features a plantsman's collection of trees and shrubs; mature conifers; also good mixed borders; 51 record trees, including 11 *Sorbus*; light refreshments.

Owned by Hampshire County Council
Number of gardeners 14, plus volunteers
Size 72ha (180 acres)
NCCPG National Collections *Carpinus*; *Cornus*; *Corylus*; *Cotoneaster*; *Hamamelis*; *Ligustrum*; *Lithocarpus*; *Photinia*; *Pinus* (excl. dwarf cvs.); *Quercus*; 'Hillier' plants

number of different habitats. Under a canopy of light oak woodland thrives a shady fernery with orchids and *Rhododendron sinogrande*. *Iris confusa* flourishes against a wall of the house. Cyclamen and bulbs are everywhere. The climate is mild – the sea is only a mile or so away – so there are hedges of griselinia, a plant of *Pittosporum* 'Garnettii' five metres high, and *Cleyera japonica* growing in the open. The vegetable garden has a new cutting garden, and an area for standing pots. In a narrow alley between tall hedges of yew and rhododendron is the National Collection of Japanese Anemones. Dr Burwell will tell you that, though first described in 1695, they were not introduced (from mainland Asia) until the 1840s by Robert Fortune. The collection has about 40 cultivars, including a seedling which will shortly be introduced as 'Heathlands Ruby'.

 Features many different habitats; a very wide range of plants of every kind; some good combinations of colour & form.

Owned by John Burwell
Number of gardeners owner only
Size 0.4ha (1 acre)
NCCPG National Collections *Anemone* (Japanese anemones)

Highclere Castle

HIGHCLERE, NEWBURY, RG15 9RN

Tel 01635 253210 **Fax** 01635 255315
Website www.highclerecastle.co.uk
Location South of Newbury off A34.
Opening hours 11 am – 6 pm; daily, except Mondays & Saturdays; 6 July to 5 September. Plus 11 & 12 April; 2, 3, 30 & 31 May; and 30 August.
Admission fee Gardens only: Adults £4; Children £1.50.

A major historic garden – when Capability Brown landscaped it in the 1770s he left intact the avenues and follies of the early 18th century, but the park is dominated now by hundreds of huge cedars. Jim Russell advised on the planting in the walled garden, though the 'Secret Garden' is not among his best. The espaliered medlars and quince trees are its best feature.

 Features rhododendrons & azaleas; herbaceous borders; good collection of cedars; long avenues; shop; good restaurant.

Owned by The Earl of Carnarvon
Number of gardeners 2
Size 240ha (600 acres) of parkland
English Heritage Grade I

Hinton Ampner House

BRAMDEAN, ALRESFORD, SO24 0LA

Tel 01962 771305 **Fax** 01962 793101
Website www.nationaltrust.org.uk
Location On A272 1 mile west of Bramdean.
Opening hours 12 noon – 5 pm; Saturday – Wednesday; 31 March to 29 September. Also 23 March.
Admission fee Adults £4.80; Children £2.40.

The gardens at Hinton Ampner were laid out by the scholarly Ralph Dutton in the middle of the 20th century with great regard to line, landscape and historical propriety. Statues, buildings, axes and views have been placed with exquisite judgement to lead you subtly along the exact route that Dutton intended. He was also careful to choose plants which would do well on chalk and then planted lots of them – using always the best forms: among them are buddlejas, lilacs, philadelphus, cotoneasters, weigelas and shrub roses. It is now one of England's best mid-20th-century gardens, maintained to a high specification.

Features topiary; daffodils; yew trees; good plants; teas & home-made cakes.

Owned by The National Trust
Number of gardeners 3
Size 5ha (12½ acres)
English Heritage Grade II

Houghton Lodge

STOCKBRIDGE, SO20 6LQ

Tel 01264 810502 **Fax** 01264 810063
Website www.houghtonlodge.co.uk
Location Off A30 at Stockbridge. Well signed.
Opening hours 2 pm – 5 pm; daily, except Wednesdays; March to September. And by appointment. Open at 10 am at week-ends and Bank Holidays.
Admission fee £5 for garden & hydroponicum. Groups at special rates. Children free.

A lovely gothic *cottage ornée* on a ledge above the River Test, with long spacious views down the river and across the water-meadows. Part of BBC's 'David Copperfield' was shot here. In the traditional walled garden are espaliered fruit-trees, herbs, a glasshouse filled with tropical orchids and a topiary known as the snorting dragon. The owner has been restoring the 18th-century shrubbery: this means clearing seedling trees to open up the view across the river and re-planting with trees and shrubs which were grown there 200 years ago. Houghton also boasts the leading hydroponic greenhouse in England, where plants are grown in nutrient-rich solutions instead of soil – salad vegetables and some 50 different herbs, as well as bougainvilleas and bananas. The garden makes a great effort to be educational and entertaining.

 Features plants under glass; daffodils; cyclamen; topiary snorting dragon; refreshments; windfall apples (free!).

Owned by Martin Busk
Number of gardeners 2 part-time
Size 2ha (5 acres)
English Heritage Grade II*

Langley Boxwood Nursery

RAKE, LISS, GU33 7JL

Tel 01730 894467 **Fax** 01730 894703
Website www.boxwood.co.uk
Location 5 miles north of Petersfield, ring for map or directions (B2070).
Opening hours 8 am – 4.30; Monday – Friday. Plus 10 am – 4 pm on Saturdays.
Admission fee Free

These specialist growers of box have a comprehensive range of box plants for hedging, edging and topiary. There are over 50 cultivars of *Buxus* in their delightful catalogue, and some yew *Taxus* also. Both are available in a wide variety of topiary shapes, from simple balls to complex crowns and animals, and (given sufficient notice) they will create individual designs. Rare free-form specimens are also offered.

 Features box, yew & evergreen topiary.

Owned by Russell Coates
NCCPG National Collections *Buxus*

Little Court

CRAWLEY, WINCHESTER, SO21 2PU

Tel 01962 776365 **Fax** 01962 776842
Location On main street through Crawley village, 300 yds from church/pond.
Opening hours 2 pm – 5.30 pm; 15, 16 & 17 February; 14, 16, 28 & 30 March; 4, 5, 20 & 21 April; 2 & 4 May; 22 & 23 June; 20 & 21 July.

Groups by appointment.
Admission fee Adults £2.50; Children free. For NGS.

Little Court fits a lot into its 1½ acres: the design allows for several distinct areas which are linked by spacious vistas and judiciously placed seats to emphasise the many views and axes. A sunken lawn, flint walls, orchards, fine trees, a copse (with a large tree-house) and a 'proper' old-fashioned kitchen garden are some of the features. The plantings are colour-themed, but some plants (like cyclamen and *Crocus tommasinianus*) have naturalised, too. The range of herbaceous plants is fairly impressive, especially hellebores, clematis and hardy geraniums. There is much to be learned and enjoyed here.

Features plantsman's plants; herbaceous perennials; teas on Sundays.

Owned by Professor & Mrs A.R. Elkington
Size 0.6ha (1½ acres)

Longmead House

LONGPARISH, ANDOVER, SP11 6PZ

Tel 01264 720386 **Fax** 01264 720786
Location 1½ miles from junction of A303 & B3048.
Opening hours 2 pm – 6 pm on 30 & 31 May. Then 11 am – 6 pm on 19 & 20 June, together with other Longparish gardens in aid of NGS. And by appointment for groups.
Admission fee Adults £2.

Longmead House is an organic showcase: Wendy Ellicock is on the council of the Henry Doubleday Research Association. She and her husband started the garden when they returned from overseas in 1987. The wildflower meadow was one of their first endeavours, begun by planting plugs into areas cleared of turf: now it provides colour from February to November. The kitchen garden has 25 deep beds, much enriched by compost. There are also wildlife areas, a woodland walk, fish pond and wildlife pond, as well as herbaceous and shrub borders, a polytunnel and greenhouse.

Features wildflower meadow; kitchen garden; all organically maintained.

Owned by Wendy & John Ellicock
Number of gardeners 1
Size 1ha (2½ acres)

Longthatch

LIPPEN LANE, WARNFORD, SOUTHAMPTON, SO32 3LE

Tel 01730 829285
Location 1 mile south of West Meon on A32, turn right by George & Falcon, & right again. 400m on right.
Opening hours 10 am – 5 pm; Wednesdays; March only. And 2 pm – 5 pm; 14, 21 & 28 March, 25 April, 30 & 31 May & 20 June for National Gardens Scheme. And at other times by appointment.
Admission fee Adults £2.50; Children free.

The Shorts have gardened at Longthatch since 1955, though in their early years they were busy with the farm around their 16th-century thatched cottage. They started to develop the garden seriously in 1968: it is now a great favourite among dedicated plantsmen. Over the years they have built up large collections not only of hellebores, but also of herbaceous plants (especially hardy geraniums), unusual trees and shrubs. Some of the trees they planted in the early days are now spectacularly mature. There are two central features: first an acre of woodland filled with wonderful small plants, from snowdrops and pulmonarias in winter through to cyclamen in late autumn; and, second, the River Meon which flows

Longstock Water Gardens

LONGSTOCK, STOCKBRIDGE, SO20 6EH

Tel 01264 810894 & 01264 810904 **Fax** 01264 810924
Website www.longstockpark.co.uk
Location 1½ miles north-east of Longstock Village.
Opening hours Not available as we went to press. 2003 times were: 2 pm – 5 pm; 1st & 3rd Sunday in the month; April to September.
Admission fee Adults £3; Children 50p. (2003 prices).

Longstock has quite the most extraordinary and beautiful water garden in England, a little Venice where dozens of islands and all-but-islands are linked by an apparently endless number of small bridges and intensely planted with water-loving plants: drifts of astilbes, primulas, kingcups, hemerocallis, musks, water irises and lilies. The ground is so soft that the islands seem to float, and a remarkable accumulation of peat has allowed such calcifuge plants as *Meconopsis betonicifolia* to flourish in this chalky valley. But the garden as a whole has an exceptional variety of habitats: parts are very dry. A seam of acid soil supports a collection of *Rhododendron orbiculare* and *R. williamsianum* cultivars and their hybrids like 'Temple Belle'. Around the perimeter are swamp cypresses and liquidambars: further away are oaks and Scots pines. On the other side of the road lies the splendid arboretum, open at the same time and with a vast collection of well-spaced specimen trees now approaching the prime of their life. Both the water gardens and the arboretum are open only rarely, so that they can be maintained principally for the benefit of partners of John Lewis, but up at the top, along a wooded drive, is an excellent nursery which is open daily throughout the year (afternoons only on Sundays). It specialises in rare trees and shrubs, but also has a constantly changing stock of other interesting plants. Nearby is a beautiful, long, rose and clematis pergola – but you need permission to see the National Collection of *Buddleja*. Every part of the Longstock estate – water gardens, arboretum, nursery and walled garden – are models of their kind, beautifully maintained and in top condition.

Features plantsman's collection of plants; good herbaceous borders; arboretum.

Owned by John Lewis Partnership
Number of gardeners 3 at water garden; 3 in arboretum
Size 4ha (10 acres) of water garden; 26ha (65 acres) in arboretum
NCCPG National Collections *Buddleja*; *Clematis viticella*

through the garden. This is supplemented by numerous spring-filled ponds throughout the garden, one of which helps to maintain the bog garden where *Gunnera manicata* and many other damp- and shade-loving plants flourish. The owners say that their best season is spring – *Narcissus* is another of their many special interests – but there is much to see throughout the year. Birds are encouraged – as is all wildlife, including the trout in the river and waterfall pool.

 **Features** a plantsman's collection of plants; primulas; meconopsis; hostas; pulmonarias; azaleas and rhododendrons; large gravel bank used as a scree bed; tea & coffee; cake on NGS days.

Owned by Peter & Vera Short
Number of gardeners owners only
Size 1.4ha (3½ acres)
NCCPG National Collections *Helleborus* (part)

The Manor House

UPTON GREY, BASINGSTOKE, RG25 2RD

Tel 01256 862827 **Fax** 01256 861035
Website www.gertrudejekyllgarden.co.uk
Location In Upton Grey village above & beside the church.
Opening hours By appointment only: 9 am – 4 pm; weekdays.
Admission fee £4, to include a copy of the guidebook & complete plant list. Groups of 20+ receive a personal guided tour.

ⓟ ⓦⓒ ⓖ ⓨ ⓔ

Ros Wallinger has restored this Jekyll garden since 1984 using the original planting plans (now at Berkeley University, California, though copies are on display at Upton Grey). She has gone to great pains to recreate it exactly in all its Edwardian loveliness. Some of the roses were extinct

here until re-introduced from private gardens in France and Italy after years of searching. The rich herbaceous borders drift from cool blues, white and pinks at either end to hot reds, oranges and yellows in the middle. There is no better place to study Gertrude Jekyll's plantings, but what makes it so special is that it is a 'young' garden again. And the restoration continues. Read more about it in Ros Wallinger's *Gertrude Jekyll's Lost Garden* (Garden Art Press, 2000).

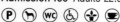 **Features** roses (mainly old-fashioned & climbers); good herbaceous borders; refreshments for groups.

Owned by Mrs John Wallinger
Number of gardeners 1, plus very keen owners
Size 2ha (5 acres)
English Heritage Grade II

Meon Orchard

KINGSMEAD, WICKHAM, FAREHAM, PO17 5AU

Tel & Fax 01329 833253
Location Take A32 north from Wickham for 1½ miles; turn left at Roebuck; ½ mile on left.
Opening hours 2 pm – 6 pm; 6 June & 25 July. Plus 1 pm – 6 pm on 5 September for NCCPG plant sale. Groups welcome by appointment.
Admission fee Adults £2.50.

ⓟ ⓗ ⓦⓒ ⓖ ⓨ ⓔ

This stylish garden is a plantaholic paradise. The emphasis is upon difficult and tender plants which look their best in late summer. An extraordinary number of plants survive the winter outside with a little protection: bananas, hedychiums, *Impatiens tinctoria* and *Dahlia imperialis* for example. The Smiths bought the property in 1986 and designed the garden as a series of interlinking paths and glades which radiate out and give the whole lay-out the impression of being much larger than it really is. It is not a quiet or refined garden, but exuberant and experimental, full of dramatic plants and contrasts. The forty or so *Eucalyptus* species in their National Collection have grown quickly and give the garden an air of maturity. Cordylines, Italian cypresses and *Ligustrum japonicum* 'Rotundifolium' also recur throughout the garden and bind it together. A vast number of pots are planted out for the summer or grouped together. Some may be put in a strategic position for only a few weeks while their flowers associate well with another plant. The owners' plantsmanship is very broad and encompasses hardy plants and alpines plants too: a laburnum hedge as you come down the drive, bulbs of every kind, a quincunx of Japanese anemones, a water garden, a pond, and hundreds of hardy trees and shrubs too. This is a most imaginative and creative garden to visit for ideas about what to grow and how to display it.

 Features southern hemisphere plants; tea/coffee & biscuits.

Owned by Dr D.J. & Mrs L.A. Smith
Number of gardeners owners, plus 3 hrs help a week
Size 0.6ha (1½ acres)
NCCPG National Collections *Eucalyptus*

Mottisfont Abbey

MOTTISFONT, ROMSEY, SO51 0LP

Tel 01794 340757 **Fax** 01794 341492
Website www.nationaltrust.org.uk
Location 4½ miles north-west of Romsey.
Opening hours 11 am – 4 pm; 6, 7, 13, 14, 20 & 21 March. 11 am – 6 pm; Saturday – Wednesday (plus Good Friday); 22 March to 2 June & 1 September to 31 October. 11 am – 8.30 pm; daily; 5 to 27 June, for the roses. 11 am – 6 pm; daily; 28 June to 31 August.
Admission fee Adults £6.50; Children £3.

The park and gardens near the house are stately: Russell Page, Geoffrey Jellicoe and Norah Lindsay all worked here. A broad chalk spring surges out in the grounds and runs down to feed the River Test. One of the London planes *Platanus* x *hispanica* near the river has two huge trunks fused together, though nobody can work out whether the two stems are on the same roots. But it is the old rose collection in the walled garden which has made Mottisfont's name. It is Graham Stuart Thomas's best known work, a collection of all the roses he has discovered, assembled, preserved and made popular through his writings. Mottisfont is surely the loveliest rose garden in Britain, but expect some temporary slippage as it is thoroughly overhauled for the first time since the walled garden was planted in 1972.

 Features roses (mainly old-fashioned & climbers); good herbaceous borders; guided walks and 'rose clinics' in season; tallest *Platanus* x *hispanica* (42m) in the British Isles; good shop selling books; licensed restaurant.

Owned by The National Trust
Number of gardeners 4
Size 11.1ha (28 acres)
NCCPG National Collections *Platanus*; *Rosa*
English Heritage Grade II

Sir George Staunton Country Park

MIDDLE PARK WAT, HAVANT, PO9 5HB

Tel 023 9245 3405 **Fax** 023 9249 8156
Website www.hants.gov.uk/countryside/staunton
Location North of Havant on B2149.
Opening hours Glasshouses 10 am – 5 pm (4 pm in winter); daily; all year. Park dawn to dusk.

Admission fee Adults £4.30; Concessions £3.90; Children £3.30. Parkland free. (2003 prices).

The historic heart of this landscape garden is a Regency walled garden, pleasure grounds and *ferme ornée*, but the local authority has also restored and developed the Victorian glasshouses as an educational resource. Here you can see useful plants like tea, coffee, pineapple, coconut palms, papyrus and rice plants, as well as such ornamentals as passion flowers, sarracenias, *Nepenthes* and strelitzias. Recent additions include a Golden Jubilee maze and puzzle garden.

Features Chinese bridge; good trees; shell-house; lakes; Regency farm; Victorian glasshouses; tea-room; light lunches & refreshments.

Owned by Hampshire County Council
English Heritage Grade II*

Spinners

BOLDRE, LYMINGTON, SO41 5QE

Tel 01590 673347 **Fax** 01590 679506
Website www.spinnersgarden.com
Location Signed off A337 between Brockenhurst & Lymington.
Opening hours 10 am – 5 pm; Tuesday – Saturday; 14 April to 14 September. Nursery & part of garden open all year.
Admission fee £2 from 14 April to 14 September; free at other times. RHS members free at all times.

Only two acres, but what a garden! Spinners is a plantsman's paradise, where the enthusiast can spend many happy hours browsing at any time of the year. The habitat plantings and plant associations are particularly interesting to study. Much of the garden is light woodland, so it has good

collections of hydrangeas, lilies, hostas, rodgersias and ferns. Peter Chappell's nursery sells an extraordinary range of good plants: you always come away with a bootful of novelties. The trilliums are of course one of the nursery's specialities: they include such rarities as *T. chloropetalum*. The list of magnolias is perhaps even more impressive: over 80 cultivars, including a great range of *M. acuminata* hybrids, Gresham hybrids and the new *M. stellata* x *liliiflora* hybrids, as well as such introductions as *M. stellata* 'Jane Platt' and *M.* x *loebneri* 'Donna'. Three RHS special events will take place during 2004: details from 020 7821 3408.

Features woodland garden; an important plantsman's garden; fine collection of trees; rhododendrons; magnolias; woodland plants; rarities and novelties; new peat beds & bog garden; biggest *Eucalyptus perriniana* in the British Isles.

Owned by Diana & Peter Chappell
Number of gardeners 1, plus part-time help
Size 1ha (2½ acres)
NCCPG National Collections *Trillium*

Steven Bailey Ltd

SILVER STREET, SWAY, LYMINGTON, SO41 6ZA

Tel 01590 682227 **Fax** 01590 683765
Location East of Hordle, not in Sway.
Opening hours 9 am – 5 pm; Monday – Saturday; all year. 10 am – 4 pm on Sundays.

This long-established nursery built its reputation on breeding and introducing carnations and pinks. Its exhibits have for long been a feature of RHS shows. The nursery shop has a good selection of bedding and summer pot plants, alstroemerias and penstemons.

Stratfield Saye House

STRATFIELD SAYE, BASINGSTOKE,
RG7 2BZ

Tel 01256 882882 **Fax** 01256 882345
Website www.stratfield-saye.co.uk
Location 1 mile west of A33 between Reading &
Basingstoke.
Opening hours 11.30 am – 5 pm (last admissions
3 pm); daily; 6 July to 1 August. Plus groups by
arrangement.
Admission fee Garden only: £3.

Not a famous garden, but there are some
fine incidents: a huge kitchen garden, a large
and cheerful rose garden, rhododendrons in
the park, and magnificent trees, including
wellingtonias, named after the Iron Duke.

Features tallest Hungarian oak
Quercus frainetto (33m.) in the British
Isles; gift shop; light refreshments.

Owned by The Duke of Wellington
English Heritage Grade II

Tudor House Garden

BUGLE STREET, SOUTHAMPTON,
SO14 2AD

Tel 023 8063 5904 **Fax** 023 8033 9601
Website www.southampton.gov.uk/
Location Bugle Street runs parallel to the High
Street in the old town.
Opening hours By arrangement for groups.
Admission fee Free.

(WC) (&)

The house and garden are both closed for
urgent repair to the house. Pre-booked
groups can however still be organised. Sylvia
Landsberg's unique reconstruction of a
Tudor garden has a knot garden, a fountain,
a secret garden and contemporary plantings
of herbs and flowering plants all crammed
into a tiny area.

Features Tudor-style knot garden;
herbs.

Owned by Southampton City Council
Number of gardeners 1
Size 30mx30m (100ftx100ft)

The Vyne

SHERBORNE ST JOHN, BASINGSTOKE,
RG24 9HL

Tel 01256 883858 **Fax** 01256 881720
Website www.nationaltrust.org.uk
Location 4 miles north of Basingstoke.
Opening hours 11 am – 5 pm; Saturdays &
Sundays; 1 February to 19 March. Then 11 am –
5 pm; Saturday – Wednesday, plus Good Friday;
20 March to 31 October.
Admission fee Adults £4; Children £2.

This historic garden has many fine features,
including a 17th-century summerhouse
which is said to be the earliest domed
garden building in England. The
horticultural interest lies in its fine old trees,
an avenue of red-twigged limes, walnuts,
and a venerable tree known as the 'Hundred
Guinea Oak' because that was the price
which a passing timber-merchant offered
for it nearly 200 years ago. In the 1960s,
Graham Stuart Thomas added herbaceous
borders and old shrub roses.

Features herbaceous borders; annuals;
good trees; wild garden; restaurant.

Owned by The National Trust
Number of gardeners 3½
Size 5ha (12½ acres)
English Heritage Grade II

Water Meadow Nursery and Herb Farm

CHERITON, ALRESFORD, SO24 0QB

Tel 01962 771895 **Fax** 01962 771985
Website www.plantaholic.co.uk
Location Just off the A272, on the B3046 to Alresford.
Opening hours 10 am – 5 pm; Wednesday – Saturday; March to July. And by appointment between August and November.
Admission fee Garden £2.50; Nursery free.

This nursery offers a good list of waterlilies – *Nymphaea* cultivars, of which they have 70 – and oriental poppies, which indicates that it is equally good for plants for wet situations and dry banks. Many of the hardy plants and herbs in the general list are unusual. The display garden is beautifully laid out – the nursery offers a design and landscaping service – and opens several times from May to July to show off its collection of more than 100 cultivars of *Papaver orientale*.

Owned by Roy & Sandy Worth
Number of gardeners 2 part-time
Size 1ha (2½ acres)
NCCPG National Collections *Papaver orientale*

White Windows

LONGPARISH, ANDOVER, SP11 6PB

Tel & Fax 01264 720222
Location In village centre, opposite village school.
Opening hours 2 pm – 6 pm; by appointment from April to September on Wednesdays. And on 18 & 19 April and 26 & 27 June for National Gardens Scheme.
Admission fee Adults £2; Children 50p.

White Windows is one of the best small modern plantsman's gardens on chalk, remarkable for the way Jane Sterndale-Bennett, past Chairman of the Hardy Plant Society, arranges her material. Layer upon layer, White Windows bulges with good plants, well grown and controlled, so that the balance is kept between sun and shade. Leaves and stems are as important as flowers, especially in the combinations and contrasts of colour – gold and yellow, blue and silver, and crimsons, pinks and purples. Much use is made of evergreens and variegated plants. White Windows is a garden which is always changing, not just through the seasons (which it does very well), but because Jane Sterndale-Bennett is forever reworking its arrangements, renewing its plants and re-adjusting the balances. Perhaps the most luxuriant chalk garden in Hampshire and all made since 1980.

Features a plantsman's garden; good herbaceous borders; euphorbias; pulmonarias; hardy geraniums; sedums.

Owned by Mrs J. Sterndale-Bennett
Number of gardeners owner only
Size 0.3ha (¾ acre)
NCCPG National Collections *Helleborus* (part)

HEREFORDSHIRE

There is, of course, no such county as Herefordshire – not any more. It was dissolved in 1974, when the old county was linked to its neighbour as 'Hereford & Worcester'. This was never a popular union, and Herefordshire people were always quick to point out that they retained their own identity and Lord Lieutenant. Herefordshire is now a District Council but, so distinct does it consider itself, that we list it as a county again. It is a pity that so few of its historic gardens are open to the public. Hergest Croft has by far the most important collection of trees, with a large number of 'record breakers' among them: Eastnor Castle also has some magnificent conifers, the largest of their kind in England. There are comparatively few top-class modern gardens – the Lance Hattatt Design Garden is a memorable exception (as is Sir Roy Strong's private garden at Much Birch) – and the county does not do conspicuously well for the National Gardens Scheme. Likewise, it has comparatively few National Collections and National Collection holders and no RHS Partner Colleges. But good nurseries exist – Kenchester Water Gardens and Rickard's Hardy Ferns are two of the best – and the extensive fruit orchards testify to the county's suitability for horticulture. The NCCPG group has worked with the Marcher Apple Network to identify old trees, propagate them and establish new orchards to preserve them.

Abbey Dore Court Garden

ABBEY DORE, HEREFORD, HR2 0AD

Tel & Fax 01981 240419
Location 3 miles west of A465, midway between Hereford & Abergavenny.
Opening hours 11 am – 5.30 pm; daily (except Mondays, Wednesdays & Fridays) but open for Bank Holidays; 27 March to 3 October.
Admission fee Adults £3; Children 50p.

This is a splendid plant-lover's garden on a difficult site, with fine borders leading down to the ferny river walk and a meadow planted with interesting trees. Mrs Ward says her 'rambling garden' has 'stopped getting any bigger', but the truth is that the garden grows, changes and improves with every visit and she has just taken in another acre of field – bamboos, trees, shrubs and more perennials than ever: very exciting.

Features good herbaceous borders; handsome wellingtonias; ferns; hellebores; good nursery.

Owned by Mrs Charis Ward
Number of gardeners 1
Size 2.4ha (6 acres)

The Bannut

BRINGSTY, BROMYARD, WR6 5TA

Tel & Fax 01885 482206
Website www.bannut.co.uk
Location On the A44, 2½ miles east of Bromyard.
Opening hours 2 pm – 5 pm; Wednesdays,
Saturdays, Sundays & Bank Holidays; April to
September.
Admission fee Adults £2.50; Children £1.

Unlike many plantsman's gardens, the plants
at The Bannut have been used to great
decorative effect. The best example is the
knot garden made from the contrasting leaf
colours of different heathers, though the
Everetts are fond of all heathers and grow a
large number (over 10,000) in the summer
heather garden. They are, however,
interested in all types of plants and how to
display them in the garden. The beds and
borders are planted for colour harmonies
and contrasts, mainly of herbaceous plants
near the house, but with more shrubs
towards the little copse where cowslips
flower in spring. Near the house are a
formal yellow-and-white garden and an
'arbour garden' in silver, pink and blue. An
old paddock is now planted with
rhododendrons, azaleas, camellias and
pieris, plus hydrangeas for late-summer
interest. All has been achieved since 1984.
Recent additions include a laburnum and
clematis walk and a 'secret' garden, with
water features and a willow house. The
standard of maintenance throughout is
excellent.

Features over 300 different heathers;
colour-themed plantings; island beds
of shrubs and herbaceous plants; knot
garden; cowslips; tea-room; tea-garden.

Owned by Maurice & Daphne Everett
Number of gardeners owners, plus part-time help
Size 1ha (2½ acres)

Berrington Hall

LEOMINSTER, HR6 0DW

Tel 01568 615721 **Fax** 01568 613263
Website www.nationaltrust.org.uk
Location On A49, 3 miles north of Leominster.
Opening hours 12 noon – 5 pm (4.30 pm in
October); Saturday – Wednesday, plus Good Friday;
5 April to 31 October. Plus weekends only from 6
March to 4 April and 1 November to 14 December.
Admission fee £3.20.

This majestic park is classic Capability
Brown. The National Trust has laid out a
one-mile parkland walk which takes in the
best vantage points and shows you how the
landscape would have looked when young.
The pleasure gardens around the house are
Victorian – laurel walks and an avenue of
golden yews. In the old walled garden, a
comprehensive collection of Hereford
Pomona is supplemented by old pear
varieties, quinces and medlars.

Features fruit; classic parkland; apples
& pears; National Trust shop; licensed
restaurant for lunch & teas.

Owned by The National Trust
Number of gardeners 2
Size 4.6ha (11½ acres)
English Heritage Grade II*

Bryan's Ground

LETCHMOOR LANE, STAPLETON,
PRESTEIGNE, LD8 2LP

Tel 01544 260001 **Fax** 01544 260015
Website www.hortus.co.uk
Location On minor road between Stapleton &
Kinsham.
Opening hours 2 pm – 5 pm; Sundays & Mondays;
28 March to 30 August.
Admission fee Adults £3.50; Children £1.

A young garden: incredibly, the owners moved here as recently as November 1993. They have made wonderfully good use of the inherited structure (yew hedges and mature trees around the 1912 Arts & Crafts house) and filled it with good plants. Developments include a belvedere, a mirror pool, a 60-ft canal and a young four-acre arboretum. Full of original ideas, Bryan's Ground is already an influential garden. David Wheeler is the editor of the elegant gardening quarterly *Hortus*, of which Simon Dorrell is the art editor.

Features good modern design; refreshments.

Owned by David Wheeler & Simon Dorrell
Number of gardeners 1 part-time
Size 2.8ha (7 acres)

Eastnor Castle

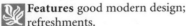

EASTNOR, LEDBURY, HR8 1RL

Tel 01531 633160 **Fax** 01531 631776
Website www.eastnorcastle.com
Location 2 miles east of Ledbury on A438 Tewkesbury road.
Opening hours 11 am – 5 pm; Sundays & Bank Holiday Mondays; 11 April to 3 October. Also daily except Saturdays in July & August.
Admission fee Adults £4.50; OAPs £4; Children £3.

Eastnor is all about trees. The arboretum planted by Lord Somers from 1852 to 1883 is now mature, and full of champion specimens. Many are rare, including a tall American beech (*Fagus grandifolia*) and an enormous red hickory (*Carya ovalis*). It is however the conifers which dominate the setting for the neo-Norman castle, largely because they were planted so thickly and in such great numbers. Miles Hadfield wrote

that Eastnor was 'embowered by vast conifers – plantations which spill out into the surrounding hills and fields'. Quite apart from the many hundreds of cedars, the record-breaking specimens include the Shensi fir (*Abies chensiensis*), the purple-coned fir (*Picea purpurea*) from south-east China, and *Pinus hartwegii* from Mexico. The rest of the garden is less interesting, but tree-lovers will find Eastnor a real treat.

Features mature conifers; fine collection of trees; spring bulbs; tallest deodar *Cedrus deodara* (38m.) in the British Isles, plus eleven more record trees; souvenirs and gift shop; lunches & teas.

Owned by James Hervey-Bathurst
Number of gardeners 2
Size 16ha (40 acres)
English Heritage Grade II*

The Lance Hattatt Design Garden

WEOBLEY, HR4 8RN

Tel & Fax 01544 318468
Location 1 mile from Weobley: off Wormsley road, signed Ledgemoor & second right, first house on left.
Opening hours 10 am – 5 pm; Wednesdays; April to October.
Admission fee Adults £3.75. Unsuitable for children.

The Lance Hattatt Design Garden used to be known as Arrow Cottage, a name which Lance Hattatt felt to be misleading: he specialises in 'contemporary garden design in the best English tradition' and believes that the new name is more appropriate. The garden is a good example of a modern design where a series of gardens in different styles exhibits a fair measure of plantsmanship. But there is still a problem of naming: though all are to some extent explained, it may be difficult for visitors to see the connection between the names and the gardens. Akademia, Luxor, Andrassy, Indigo Yard and Easter Island are just some of them. It should be said, however, that all are maintained to the highest standard. Moreover, the keen plantsman will find *Iris confusa* 'Martyn Rix' flourishing outside, and pots of *Agapanthus africanus* along the rill in summer. Few such gardens combine plantsmanship and artistry so well.

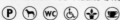**Features** good herbaceous borders; stream; wildflower orchard; fifty-metre yew-enclosed rill; good plants throughout; old roses; refreshments.

Owned by Jane & Lance Hattatt
Number of gardeners 1½
Size 0.8ha (2 acres)

Hergest Croft Gardens

KINGTON, HR5 3EG

Tel 01544 230160 **Fax** 01544 232031
Website www.hergest.co.uk
Location Signed from A44.
Opening hours 12.30 pm – 5.30 pm (noon – 6 pm in May & June); daily; 3 April to 31 October.
Admission fee Adults £4.50; Children free.

(P) (🐕) (WC) (🚹) (🌳) (☕)

Hergest Croft is an extremely important woodland garden and arboretum around a whopping Edwardian house. It has over 4,000 rare trees and shrubs, but there seems no end to the garden's marvels: huge conifers, magnificent birches, scores of interesting oaks, many acres of billowing rhododendrons – Hergest Croft is one of the best rhododendron gardens in Britain. But it is also worth visiting for its double herbaceous borders, alpine collections, roses, autumn gentians and kitchen garden, all on a scale that most of us have forgotten.

Features fine collection of trees; rhododendrons; tallest *Cercidiphyllum japonicum* (25m.) in the British Isles, among some 50 record trees; home-made teas.

Owned by W.L. Banks
Number of gardeners 6
Size 22ha (56 acres)
NCCPG National Collections *Acer*; *Betula*; *Zelkova*
English Heritage Grade II*

How Caple Court

HOW CAPLE, HEREFORD, HR1 4SX

Tel 01989 740626 **Fax** 01989 740611
Location Signed on B4224 & A449 junction.
Opening hours 10 am – 5 pm; daily; mid-March to mid-October.
Admission fee Adults £2.50; Children free.

(P) (🐕) (WC) (☕)

Spectacular formal gardens laid out about 100 years ago (some Italianate, others more Arts & Crafts), and now undergoing restoration. Pergolas, loggias, dramatic terraces and *giardini segreti* with stunning views across a lushly wooded valley. How Caple is a garden of national importance, but little known even locally.

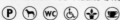**Features** mature conifers; Italian terraces surrounded by restored pergola; old roses; topiary; woodland gardens; tea-room.

Owned by Mr & Mrs Roger Lee
Number of gardeners 1
Size 4.4ha (11 acres)

Kenchester Water Gardens

CHURCH ROAD, LYDE, HEREFORD, HR1 3AB

Tel 01432 270981 **Fax** 01432 342243
Location On A49, 1 mile north of Hereford.

Opening hours 9 am – 6 pm (5.30 pm from October to March); daily; all year. 10.30 am – 4.30 pm on Sundays. Closed Christmas Day.
Admission fee Free.

The gardens and the nursery at Kenchester are equally important for anyone interested in water-plants. The range of plants grown and offered for sale is excellent, and includes nearly 210 cultivars of *Nymphaea*, of which they have a National Collection. The gardens have pools and ponds over a large area – well worth a longish visit. This is a dynamic nursery which is getting bigger and better all the time.

Features water plants and water gardens; light lunches & teas.

Owned by Mr & Mrs M.R. Edwards
Number of gardeners 2
Size 2.4ha (6 acres)
NCCPG National Collections *Nymphaea*

Kingstone Cottage Plants

WESTON UNDER PENYARD, ROSS-ON-WYE, HR9 7PH

Tel 01989 565267
Location Off A40, north of Weston under Penyard, on the road to Rudhall.
Opening hours 10 am – 5 pm; Sunday – Friday; 7 May to 6 July. And by appointment.
Admission fee Adults £2 for National Gardens Scheme.

The main feature of this garden is its National Collection of old *Dianthus* cultivars, some 140 cultivars which flower in early summer. This is the place to see such rarities as *D.* 'Fenbow Nutmeg Clove' and *D.* 'Cranborne Seedling'. Mr & Mrs Hughes also sell plants which they have propagated

from their collection – the best way to promote a wider interest in old cultivars and guarantee their future survival. But there is much more to see as well as the pinks – a sunken terrace garden, large pond and grotto.

Features ponds; grotto; summerhouse; pinks.

Owned by Michael & Sophie Hughes
Number of gardeners 2
Size 0.8ha (2 acres)
NCCPG National Collections *Dianthus*

Lakeside

GAINES ROAD, WHITBOURNE, WORCESTER, WR6 5RD

Tel 01886 821119
Location 9 miles west of Worcester off A44 at County boundary sign.
Opening hours Parties of 10+ by appointment only between April & September.
Admission fee Adults £2.50; Children free.

These six acres were dramatically planted by Chris Philip, who founded *The RHS Plant Finder*. Tender plants flourish against the old kitchen garden walls. Daffodils bred by Michael Jefferson-Brown run down to the lake, where clean-limbed alders stretch gothically heavenwards. Throughout the garden are good plants, used well: Lakeside is an inspiration to new gardeners, and a place from which all can learn.

Features woodland garden; small maturing pinetum; unusual plants; good herbaceous borders; ferns; hollies; heathers; lake; bog garden; teas.

Owned by Denys Gueroult
Number of gardeners 1 part-time
Size 2.4ha (6 acres)

The Picton Garden

OLD COURT NURSERIES, WALWYN
ROAD, COLWALL, MALVERN,
WR13 6QE

Tel 01684 540416 **Fax** 01684 565314
Website www.autumnasters.co.uk
Location 3 miles west of Great Malvern; 5 miles
east of Ledbury on B4218.
Opening hours 11 am – 5 pm; Wednesday –
Sunday; August. And daily from 1 September to 17
October. Thereafter by prior appointment only.
Admission fee Adults £2.50 for NGS.

The Picton Garden at Old Court Nurseries
holds the National Collection of
Michaelmas daisies (*Aster*). This is also the
nurseries' speciality: the extensive collection
is fully described in Paul Picton's excellent
book *Gardener's Guide to Growing Asters*
(1999). When the Michaelmas daisies are in
flower, the banks of colour, graded for
height, recall the grandest of Edwardian
gardens and the Picton Garden becomes
one of the great showpieces of English
horticulture. The new 'Jubilee Border' of
Aster nova-belgii cultivars was planted in
2002 and is now in its prime. But there are
also many other interesting perennials and
cottagey plants here, some arranged in
'prairie-style' plantings.

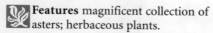

Features magnificent collection of
asters; herbaceous plants.

Owned by Paul & Meriel Picton
Number of gardeners 2
Size 0.6ha (1½ acres)
NCCPG National Collections *Aster* (autumn-
flowering)

Queen's Wood Arboretum & Country Park

DINMORE HILL, LEOMINSTER,
HR6 0PY

Tel 01568 798320 **Fax** 01568 798329
Location Midway between Leominster & Hereford
on A49.
Opening hours 9 am – dusk; daily; all year.
Admission fee Free.

A vigorous young arboretum, first planted
in 1953 with public amenity in mind.
Wonderful for walking, whatever the season,
and well run in a friendly, efficient manner
so that visitors get the most from it. The
rangers say that spring and autumn are the
best time for colour, but there are lots of
early purple orchids and spotted orchids in
summer too.

Features a fine collection of trees,
including mature conifers; bluebells;
wood anemones; gift shop; light meals from
9 am to 5 pm.

Owned by Hereford Council
Number of gardeners 4
Size 24ha (60 acres)

Rushfields of Ledbury

Ross Road, Ledbury, HR8 2LP

Tel 01531 632004 **Fax** 01531 633454
Website www.rushfields.co.uk
Location ½ mile south-west of Ledbury off A449,
behind the Leadon House Hotel.
Opening hours 10 am – 5 pm; Monday – Saturday;
& by appointment. Close at 3 pm from November to
February.
Admission fee Free.

Rushfields specialise in 'choice garden plants',
most of them herbaceous. They are
particularly good for hostas, and for
hellebores. Other specialities include
geraniums, euphorbias, penstemons and
monardas, but the nursery is a good place to
see and buy a wide range of well-chosen
herbaceous plants. More plants may be seen
in a large undercover area. Rushfields are
consistent gold medal winners at RHS shows.

Features hostas.

Owned by Miss J. Nicholls

Whitfield

Wormbridge, HR2 9BA

Tel 01981 570727 **Fax** 01981 570641
Location 8 miles south-west of Hereford on A465.
Opening hours 2 pm – 5 pm; 4 April & 6 June; for
NGS. And parties by appointment.
Admission fee Adults £2.50; Children free.

Whitfield has magnificent trees, most of
them planted by the Clives over the last 200
years. *Zelkova serrata*, a weeping oak, and a
ginkgo planted as early as 1778 are some of
the highlights, but there is nothing to beat
the grove of 20 or so *Sequoia sempervirens*
now pushing 150ft (46m) in height.

Features topiary; mature conifers; fine
collection of trees; huge grove of
redwoods; tallest dwarf alder *Alnus nitida*
and durmast oak *Quercus petraea* in the
British Isles.

Owned by Mr & Mrs Edward Clive
Number of gardeners 1 full-time, 2 part-time
Size 5.2ha (13 acres)
English Heritage Grade II

HERTFORDSHIRE

Hertfordshire has two great historic gardens (Hatfield House and St Paul's Walden Bury) which are open to the public, and a couple of lesser ones (Ashridge and Knebworth) but few of the others admit visitors. Nor does Hertfordshire have as many good modern gardens as its proximity to London might suggest. It is greatly to be regretted that the Gardens of the Rose are being sold by the Royal National Rose Society – the result of years of bad management and poor financial control – and may (or may not) be re-made next year in a more modern style on a nearby site. The only garden with really good herbaceous plantings in Hertfordshire is Benington Lordship. There is a sprinkling of fine trees at such gardens as Bayfordbury (sometimes open for the National Gardens Scheme) and Aldenham – both relics of keen gardening owners in the past – but no old-established arboretum or pinetum of special merit. The National Gardens Scheme can muster only about two-thirds of the number of gardens which open for charity in such a county as Northamptonshire and there are only six National Collections in the county. But Hertfordshire has some good nurseries and a large number of excellent garden centres. Nevertheless, it remains difficult to explain why a county so close to London should not be endowed with horticultural wealth on anything like the scale of Surrey or Kent.

Aylett Nurseries Ltd

NORTH ORBITAL ROAD, LONDON COLNEY, ST ALBANS, AL2 1DH

Tel 01727 822255 **Fax** 01727 823024
Website www.aylettnurseries.co.uk
Location On A414, on left-hand side when driving towards Hatfield.
Opening hours 8.30 am – 5.30 pm; Monday – Friday. 8.30 am – 5 pm; Saturdays. 9 am – 5 pm; Bank Holidays. 10.30 am – 4.30 pm; Sundays.
Admission fee Free.

This huge (and very busy) general garden centre has a prime trading position with a vast range of plants and every imaginable sundry. It also offers a design service and delivery. But Ayletts also has a speciality – its award-winning dahlias which have been a feature of RHS shows for many years. The growing fields are a mile or so from the nursery and well worth a visit in late summer or early autumn. All the different classes of dahlia hybrids are represented in both quantity and quality.

 Features gift shop; coffee shop.

Owned by The Aylett family
Size 2.8ha (7 acres)

Beale Arboretum

WEST LODGE PARK HOTEL,
COCKFOSTERS ROAD, HADLEY WOOD,
EN4 0PY

Tel 020 8216 3905 **Fax** 020 8449 9916
Website www.bealeshotels.co.uk
Location A111 one mile south of M25 Jct 24.
Opening hours 2 pm – 5 pm; Monday – Friday;
April to October. Plus: 16 May (2 pm – 5 pm) & 17
October (1 pm – 4 pm) for National Gardens
Scheme.
Admission fee £2.50.

The Beale Arboretum has been developed
since 1963 by adding to the original plantings
around the house. Young trees are planted
among much older specimens – Victorian
cedars and redwoods – with a view to the
overall effect. A grassy glade runs down from
the hotel terrace to a classical cupola at the
bottom, inviting exploration. There are fine
collections of oaks, hornbeams, liquidambars
and nyssas, as well as buddlejas, elaeagnus and
rhododendrons. The arboretum is maintained
to a high standard, primarily as a facility for
hotel guests. It is an excellent example of what
can be achieved by an enthusiastic individual.

Features eight-acre arboretum; mature
conifers; a fine collection of young
trees; 200-year-old *Arbutus unedo*;
refreshments in hotel.

Owned by Beales Hotels
Number of gardeners 2
Size 8ha (20 acres)
NCCPG National Collections *Carpinus betulus*
cvs; *Elaeagnus*

Benington Lordship

BENINGTON, STEVENAGE, SG2 7BS

Tel 01438 869668 **Fax** 01438 869622
Website www.beningtonlordship.co.uk

Location Off A602 Stevenage to Hertford, in
Benington village.
Opening hours 12 noon – 4 pm; daily; 7 – 22
February for snowdrops. Spring & Summer Bank
Holiday weekends: 2 pm – 5 pm on Sundays & 12
noon – 5 pm on Bank Holiday Mondays.
Herbaceous borders week: 2 pm – 5 pm, daily, 28
June to 4 July. And on request, all year (please
telephone).
Admission fee Adults £3.50; Children free. RHS
members free in February.

Benington Lordship is a Georgian house
with an Edwardian add-on, a mock Norman
gateway and the ruins of a real Norman
castle in the grounds. The extensive gardens
have been revived and replanted in recent
years without destroying the older features:
a Pulhamite folly, an Edwardian rock garden
and a sense of spacious parkland. But the
highlight of a visit today is the stupendous
double herbaceous border that Mrs Bott has
planted in gentle pastel shades: the best we
know.

Features roses (ancient & modern);
rock garden; very good herbaceous
borders; heather garden; cowslip bank;
water features (& kingfishers); kitchen
garden.

Owned by C.H.A. Bott
Number of gardeners 1
Size 2.8ha (7 acres)
English Heritage Grade II

Hopleys

HIGH STREET, MUCH HADHAM,
SG10 6BU

Tel 01279 842509 **Fax** 01279 843784
Website www.hopleys.co.uk
Location 50 yards north of The Bull pub.
Opening hours 9 am (2 pm on Sundays) – 5 pm;
daily except Tuesdays. Closed in January, February,
November & December.

Hatfield House

HATFIELD, AL9 5NQ

Tel 01707 287010 **Fax** 01707 287033
Website www.hatfield-house.co.uk
Location Off A1(M) Jct 4.
Opening hours 11 am – 5.30 pm; daily; 10 April to 30 September. East Gardens open only on Fridays.
Admission fee Park & gardens: Adults £4.50, but £6.50 on Fridays. RHS members free (except Fridays and special event days).

The gardens at Hatfield are mainly late 19th- and 20th-century. An 1890s parterre called the East Gardens is the outstanding feature: in 1977 The Dowager Marchioness of Salisbury enclosed it on either side with avenues of evergreen oaks – they are grown on two-metre stems and clipped like lollipops – and replanted the formal beds. Two years later she started on the Knot Garden, an historical recreation in front of the Old Palace. The designs are extracted from traditional English patterns in such herbaries as Parkinson's. Four central beds surround a small pool: the corners of the beds are marked by pyramids of box. Three are knots; the fourth is a gravel maze, to remind us that Hatfield already had a maze when Queen Elizabeth I visited it. The Elizabethan fruit garden is represented by pomegranates which are put out in the summer, another link to the earliest gardens at Hatfield. The planting is true to the period too: every plant is one that would have been introduced to England before 1620. They include clove carnations, ancient roses and a collection of historical tulips given by the *Hortus Bulborum* in Holland. The Dowager has tried to re-make the gardens as they might have been, and bring them back into sympathy with the great unchanging house. 'It is my dream' she wrote 'that one day they will become again a place of fancies and conceits, where not only pleasure and peace can be found but a measure of surprise and mystery'.

Features good herbaceous borders; knot gardens and good topiary; physic garden; organic kitchen garden (whole garden organically managed); souvenirs and gift shop; licensed restaurant, coffee shop, snacks & hot lunches.

Owned by The Marquess of Salisbury
Number of gardeners 6
Size 16.8ha (42 acres)
English Heritage Grade I

Admission fee Donation. Coaches £1.50 per person.

Hopleys has a fine four-acre garden with some excellent plants (some notable conifers and an ash-tree said to be the fourth largest in the UK), but the nursery is its principal draw. It offers an extensive choice of hardy shrubs and perennials, with many half-hardy plants too – being particularly strong on diascias, osteospermums, penstemons and salvias. Since its foundation in 1968, the nursery has been responsible for numerous introductions: the most famous are *Lavatera* 'Barnsley' and *Potentilla fruticosa* 'Red Ace'. The tradition continues with its new *Abelia* x *grandiflora* 'Hopleys'. The website is excellent – very comprehensive and informative.

Features self-service refreshments.

Owned by Aubrey Barker
Number of gardeners ½
Size 1.6ha (4 acres)

Knebworth House

KNEBWORTH, STEVENAGE, SG3 6PY

Tel 01438 812661 **Fax** 01438 811908
Website www.knebworthhouse.com
Location Off A1(M) Jct 7.
Opening hours 11 am – 5.30 pm; daily; 3 to 18 April, 29 May to 6 June; 3 July to 31 August. Plus weekends & Bank Holidays from 27 March to 26 September.
Admission fee Adults, Concessions & Children all £6.50.

Most of the garden was laid out by Lutyens, who married a daughter of the house. It has been well restored in recent years, with Jekyll plantings where appropriate. These include some inventive and harmonious colour-themed gardens and a herb garden made from Jekyll's original plans. In the park are fine Victorian conifers and handsome avenues of lime and horse-chestnut.

**Features** rose garden with herbaceous borders; sunken lawn; gold garden; wilderness; maze; ponds; herb garden; licensed tea-room.

Owned by The Hon. Henry Lytton Cobbold
Number of gardeners 4
Size 10ha (25 acres)
English Heritage Grade II*

St Paul's Walden Bury

WHITWELL, HITCHIN, SG4 8BP

Tel 01438 871218 **Fax** 01438 871229
Location B651 5 miles south of Hitchin.
Opening hours 2 pm – 7 pm; 11 April & 16 May. Also 2 pm – 6 pm, followed by lakeside concert, on 4 July. And groups by arrangement.
Admission fee Adults £3; Children 50p. Groups £6 per person.

St Paul's Walden Bury is highly important as a unique example of the French 18th-century style – hedged *allées* forming a *patte d'oie* lead into the woodland towards temples, statues and pools. The present owner and his father (the Queen Mother's brother and a past President of the Royal Horticultural Society) added rhododendrons, camellias, maples and magnolias (plus much more besides) into parts of the woodland. Other areas are dedicated to shrub roses and mixed herbaceous borders: there are many small-scale gardens within the overall design. It is therefore a garden that appeals to historians, plantsmen and artists alike.

Features woodland garden; formal French landscape; rhododendrons; teas & home-made cakes.

Owned by Simon Bowes Lyon
Size 24ha (60 acres)
English Heritage Grade I

The Van Hage Garden Company

GREAT AMWELL, WARE, SG12 9RP

Tel 01920 870811 **Fax** 01920 871861
Location On A1170.
Opening hours 9 am – 6 pm; Monday – Saturday.
10.30 am – 4.30 pm; Sundays. Opens at 9.30 am on Mondays.

This long-established and award-winning garden centre is particularly strong on house plants, specimen plants, hardy plants and bedding. Van Hage are also seed merchants: they sell their own flower and vegetable seed, including the record-breaking carrot 'Flak'. They have two other garden centres, one at Chenies near Rickmansworth and the other at Bragbury End on the south-east edge of Stevenage.

Owned by Mr & Mrs Van Hage

ISLE OF WIGHT

The Isle of Wight ('the Island' to its residents) may be small and deficient in wealth-creating industries, but it has two exceptional gardens: the 19th-century royal palace of Osborne which overlooks the Solent on the northern shores of the island, and the modern botanic garden at Ventnor on the sunny southern side. The two gardens have an unusual link: the head gardener at Osborne is married to the head gardener at Ventnor. The Isle of Wight also has some fine plantsman's gardens (most notably John Harrison's at North Court), an active Historic Gardens Trust and NCCPG group, several National Collections and some good nurseries. In addition to those listed below, there is a magnificent choice of daylilies available from A la Carte Daylilies (Little Hermitage, St Catherine's Down, Ventnor PO38 2PU – by appointment only), including many of the new American hybrids: the nursery has two National Collections of *Hemerocallis*, large flowered cultivars which have received awards since 1960, and miniature and small-flowered cultivars. Another National Collection is held by Springbank Nurseries (Winford Road, Newchurch, Sandown PO36 0JX), whose nerines have won several awards at RHS shows in recent years and extend to over 600 cultivars.

Barton Manor

WHIPPINGHAM, EAST COWES, PO32 6LB

Tel 01983 280676 **Fax** 01983 293923
Location Next to Osborne House on East Cowes Road (A3021).
Opening hours 10 am – 5 pm; 6 June, 4 July, 1 August, 5 September, for charity.
Admission fee Adults £3; Children £1.

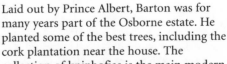

Laid out by Prince Albert, Barton was for many years part of the Osborne estate. He planted some of the best trees, including the cork plantation near the house. The collection of kniphofias is the main modern attraction for garden-visitors: many are available by mail order.

Features woodland garden; roses (mainly modern); good herbaceous borders; rhododendrons; gift shop.

Owned by R. Stigwood
Size 10.3ha (26 acres)
NCCPG National Collections *Kniphofia*

Deacon's Nursery

MOOR VIEW, GODSHILL, PO38 3HW

Tel 01983 840750/522243 **Fax** 01983 523575
Location Moor View is next to school, down School Crescent.
Opening hours 8 am – 4 pm (2 pm on Saturdays); Monday – Friday; all year.

Deacon's was established in 1966 and is now one of the leading fruit-tree nurseries in England, with tree- and soft fruit of every size and variety, including 'family' trees. The very comprehensive list has over 600 different cultivars, including 300 apples: many are not listed elsewhere – including such regional specialities as 'Devonshire Crimson Queen' and 'Welsh Russet'. All rootstocks are of virus-free origin. They mail anywhere in UK, and abroad.

Owned by Brian & Grahame Deacon
Size 6.7ha (17 acres)

Mottistone Manor

MOTTISTONE, NEWPORT, PO30 4ED

Tel 01983 741302
Website www.nationaltrust.org.uk
Location On B3399 west of Brighstone.
Opening hours 11 am – 5.30 pm on Tuesdays & Wednesdays; 2 pm – 5.30 pm on Sundays & Bank Holiday Mondays; 28 March to 31 October.
Admission fee Adults £2.90; Children £1.40.

Mottistone has a cleverly designed modern garden on a difficult site – steep and narrow. Much has been terraced and enclosed to allow a rose garden and good herbaceous borders. Most of the rest is given to a wide variety of fruit trees, trained to make avenues and underplanted with vegetables or spring bulbs. It is a model for this type of planting, and made long before the current fashion for ornamental *potagers*.

Features roses (mainly modern); fruit; mature conifers; good herbaceous borders; bluebells; irises; teas.

Owned by The National Trust
Number of gardeners 2
Size 2.4ha (6 acres)

North Court

SHORWELL, PO30 3JG

Tel 01983 740415 **Fax** 01983 821257
Website www.northcourt.info
Location 4 miles south-west of Newport, off B3323.
Opening hours For National Gardens Scheme on 30 May, 19 June & by appointment.
Admission fee Adults £2.50.

The Harrison family which owns the substantial 17th-century North Court inherited fine grounds with some magnificent trees and a clear stream at the bottom. John Harrison has extensively replanted it with a plantsman's enthusiasm and a special interest in tender exotica. It is now best private garden on 'the island'.

Features woodland garden; sub-tropical plants; roses (ancient & modern); plantsman's collection of plants; fruit; good herbaceous borders; large plane trees; B & B for garden-lovers; refreshments.

Owned by Mr & Mrs John Harrison
Number of gardeners 2 part-time
Size 6ha (15 acres)

Nunwell House

BRADING, RYDE, PO36 0JQ

Tel 01983 407240
Location Signed off A3055, 1 mile to the west of Brading.
Opening hours 1 pm – 5 pm; 30 & 31 May; then Monday – Wednesday from 5 July to 8 September.
Admission fee Gardens only: £2.50.

The garden at Nunwell, with its peaceful views across the Solent, dates back to about 1600. The walled garden was built about 100 years later and still has its original paths, flanked by excellent double herbaceous borders. Vernon Russell-Smith planted a small arboretum about 30 years ago. The present owners have added some highly attractive garden ornaments and have restored the fabric and the plantings after some years of neglect. The mass of 'Frensham' roses and the long stone steps lined with lavender are two of the more striking features. Work continues.

 Features roses (old-fashioned and modern); a plantsman's collection of plants; herbs; a fine collection of trees; statuary; 50m border of 'Frensham' roses.

Owned by Colonel & Mrs J.A. Aylmer
Number of gardeners owners, plus ½
Size 2.4ha (6 acres)
English Heritage Grade II

Osborne House

EAST COWES, PO32 6JY

Tel 01983 200022 **Fax** 01983 281380
Website www.english-heritage.org.uk
Location Follow the brown tourist signs.
Opening hours Not available as we went to press. 2003 times were: 10 am – 6 pm (5 pm in October); daily; April to October.
Admission fee Garden only: Adults £4.50; Concessions £3.40; Children £2.30. (2003 prices).

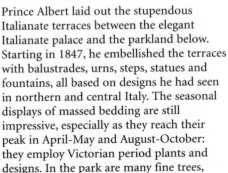

Prince Albert laid out the stupendous Italianate terraces between the elegant Italianate palace and the parkland below. Starting in 1847, he embellished the terraces with balustrades, urns, steps, statues and fountains, all based on designs he had seen in northern and central Italy. The seasonal displays of massed bedding are still impressive, especially as they reach their peak in April-May and August-October: they employ Victorian period plants and designs. In the park are many fine trees,

including stately cedars, cork oaks and holm oaks. The walled kitchen garden has recently been restored to use: English Heritage has repaired the wall and the old glasshouses, reinstated the original paths, started to train fruit trees against the walls (including 'Lane's Prince Albert' apples), and filled the beds with annual and perennial flowers for cutting. Heritage vegetables and fruit are grown organically at the royal children's gardens surrounding Swiss Cottage.

 Features Italianate terraces; working walled garden – cut flowers & fruit; Victorian pleasure gardens; English Heritage shop; tea-room.

Owned by English Heritage
Number of gardeners 9
Size 20ha (50 acres)
English Heritage Grade II*

Ventnor Botanic Garden

UNDERCLIFF DRIVE, VENTNOR, PO38 1UL

Tel 01983 855397 **Fax** 01983 856756
Website www.botanic.co.uk
Location 1½ miles west of Ventnor on A3055.
Opening hours Dawn – dusk; daily; all year. Show-house & plant sales open daily 10 am – 5 pm (but week-end only in winter, and closing at 4 pm). Visitor Centre open 10 am – 6 pm (4 pm in winter and only at weekends).
Admission fee Garden: free. Small charge to visit Show-house. Car-parking charges.

Originally an offshoot of Hilliers Nursery, the Ventnor Botanic Garden is devoted to exotic plants. It is not strictly a *botanic* garden, but it has a remarkable collection. Many of the plants – perhaps most – are from the southern hemisphere but flourish in the unique microclimate of the 'Undercliff':

widdringtonias from Zimbabwe and Tasmanian olearias, for instance, as well as astelias, *Sophora microphylla* and *Griselinia lucida* from New Zealand. *Geranium maderense* has naturalised on the sunny slopes and so has an amazing colony of 4m *Echium pininana*. Elsewhere are such Mediterranean natives as acanthus, cistus and *Coronilla valentina*, and a remarkable area called the Palm Garden, where stately foliage-plants like yuccas, cordylines, phormiums and beschornerias are underplanted with watsonias, cannas and kniphofias. Almost destroyed by the gales of 1987 and 1990, the collections were rapidly re-made and the garden now looks wonderfully vigorous again. 2001 saw some extensive re-landscaping of the Mediterranean garden. The energetic head gardener has a splendid eye for planting. A magnificent new visitor centre opened recently: it offers the venue for exhibitions and a programme of events as well as a restaurant for visitors. The nursery sells some very interesting and often tender plants which are surplus to the garden's own requirements. Most are seed-raised and come from all around the world wherever there is a Mediterranean-type climate.

Features sub-tropical plants; plantsman's collection of plants; good herbaceous borders; palms; olives; bananas; medicinal herbs from all over the world; largest collection of New Zealand plants in UK; new nursery specialising in rare plants from the garden; cafeteria & bar with snacks, tea/coffee, lunches.

Owned by Isle of Wight Council
Number of gardeners 8
Size 8.7ha (22 acres)

KENT

Kent is thick with good gardens and nurseries: the Garden of England has the oldest market gardens in the country. These were developed in the 16th century to supply fresh fruit and vegetables to the fast-growing population of London: the men of Kent filled their barges up with the capital's night soil on the return journey and applied this bounty to their orchards. Kent has long been a rich county, not only because of its soil and climate, but also because many Londoners have traditionally spent the fortunes they made in the City on the acquisition of houses and gardens there. The exceptional number of arboreta and record-sized trees in Kent testifies to its long tradition of ornamental gardening. Not only does it have an exceptional number of important historic gardens, but all six of those which are rated Grade I by English Heritage are open regularly to the public – Godington, Hever, Knole, Penshurst, Scotney and Sissinghurst. Many of the other graded gardens are also open throughout the summer – among them are Chartwell, Emmetts, Goodnestone, Leeds Castle, Mount Ephraim, Port Lympne, and Walmer Castle. Kent's historic gardens are supplemented by fine modern ones with important horticultural collections: the national pinetum at Bedgebury, for example, and the stupendous fruit collections at Brogdale. The gardens at Yalding and Broadview are important examples respectively of organic gardening, and a teaching garden. The National Gardens Scheme thrives in Kent. Gardens and gardening flourish in every town and village: a great number of good garden centres and nurseries exist to satisfy the demand for plants. The nurseries include some of the leading specialists in their field: Brenda Hyatt, for example, has won many awards over the years for her auriculas, while Downderry Nursery (another regular at RHS shows in season) has National Collections of lavender and rosemary. The RHS runs lectures at Cabbages & Kings and, in particular, at Hadlow College, which is one of its Partner Colleges.

Bedgebury National Pinetum

PARK LANE, GOUDHURST,
CRANBROOK, TN17 2SL

Tel 01580 211044 **Fax** 01580 212423
Website www.bedgeburypinetum.org.uk
Location 1 mile east of A21 at Flimwell on B2079.
Opening hours 10 am – 5 pm (4 pm in winter);
daily; all year.
Admission fee Adults £3.50; OAPs £3; Children
£1.50. RHS members free.

Bedgebury Pinetum is the national conifer
collection: the International Dendrological
Research Institute considers it the best conifer
collection in the world. It was founded as a
joint venture between the Forestry
Commission and the Royal Botanic Gardens
at Kew: the first plants for the pinetum were
raised at Kew in 1921 and planted out at
Bedgebury four years later. The collection
boasts some 330 different species and more
than 2,000 cultivars growing in landscaped
woodland around a series of lakes and
streams. But Bedgebury is not just for conifer
lovers. The woodland garden is also well
known for its deciduous trees: it has fine
collections of oaks and maples, azaleas and
rhododendrons. A new Japanese glade was
added in 1996. Bedgebury is also good for its
autumn colour and one of the best places we
know for a winter walk. The extensive new
plantings are promising.

Features mature conifers;
rhododendrons; fungi; new Japanese
maple glade; 18 record tree species,
including two broadleaves; shop & visitor
centre; tea-room.

Owned by Forestry Commission
Number of gardeners 6
Size 130ha (320 acres)

NCCPG National Collections *Chamaecyparis
lawsoniana* cvs.; *Juniperus*; *Taxus*;
Thuja; x *Cupressocyparis*
English Heritage Grade II*

Beech Court Gardens

CANTERBURY ROAD, CHALLOCK,
ASHFORD, TN25 4DJ

Tel 01233 740735 **Fax** 01233 740842
Website www.beechcourtgardens.co.uk
Location On A252 1 mile west of Challock (left-
hand side).
Opening hours 10.30 am – 5.30 pm; Monday –
Friday; 20 March to 2 November. Plus 12 noon –
6 pm on Saturdays & Sundays.
Admission fee Adults £4; OAPs £3.50; Wheelchair-
bound £2; Children £1.

Beech Court is a fine woodland garden,
very enjoyable to visit and explore at every
season. It was mainly laid out in 1947,
though parts have some much older trees
and the property dates back to mediaeval
times. There is lots to discover along its
paths and glades at every season –
hydrangeas, azaleas, maples, magnolias,
shrub roses, viburnums, climbing roses and
magnificent rhododendrons. Nearer the
house are expansive lawns (rather bumpy –
visitors must be careful), pools, and well-
planted, fluid island beds.

Features plants for sale; lunches &
teas.

Owned by Mr & Mrs Vyvyan Harmsworth
Number of gardeners 3 part-time
Size 4ha (10 acres)

Belmont Park

BELMONT, THROWLEY, FAVERSHAM,
ME13 0HH

Tel 01795 890202 **Fax** 01795 840042
Website www.belmont-house.org
Location Signed from A251 at Badlesmere.
Opening hours 10 am – 6 pm; Saturday –
Thursday; April to September.
Admission fee Garden: Adults £2.75; Children £1.

Quiet parkland and the relics of a 200-year old arboretum surround this handsome Samuel Wyatt house. The pleasure gardens include an ancient rock garden and a walled garden with herbaceous borders and a 7-metre tree of *Ilex aquifolium* 'Ferox Argentea'. The Coronation Avenue was planted in 1937: a dead-straight, 300-yard pathway, lined with immaculately clipped yew hedges and leading to a gothic flint folly. The old kitchen garden was prettily re-made for the millennium by Arabella Lennox-Boyd. Pergolas hung with apples, pears, roses and vines lead to the central pool and flower garden. Further afield are metal arbours dressed with golden hop. The standard of maintenance everywhere is extremely high.

Features rock garden; shell grotto; rhododendrons; pinetum; teas.

Owned by The Harris (Belmont) Charity
Number of gardeners 4
Size 16ha (40 acres)
English Heritage Grade II

Broadview Gardens

HADLOW, TONBRIDGE, TN11 0AL

Tel 01732 853211 **Fax** 01732 853207
Location Signed from A26, 3 miles north-east of Tonbridge.
Opening hours 10 am – 5 pm; daily; all year.

Admission fee Adults £2; Children free. RHS members free in September & October.

These new gardens attached to Hadlow College include a series of model designs and plantings which are intended to help students to learn the skills of garden design and horticulture. They are, of course, extremely interesting and inspiring for ordinary visitors: they include a sub-tropical garden, a low-maintenance garden, long herbaceous borders, a Japanese garden and a cottage garden. The college also has a good garden centre. There is a substantial programme of RHS special events at Hadlow during 2004: details from 020 7821 3408.

Owned by Hadlow College
Size 3.2ha (8 acres)
NCCPG National Collections *Anemone* (Japanese); *Helleborus*

Brogdale

BROGDALE ROAD, FAVERSHAM,
ME13 8XZ

Tel 01795 535286 **Fax** 01795 531710
Website www.brogdale.org.uk
Location 1 mile south-west of Faversham.
Opening hours 10 am – 5 pm; daily; 29 March to 31 October. 9.30 am – 4.30 pm; daily; winter. Closed over Christmas period.
Admission fee Adults £4; OAPs £3.50; Children £3. RHS members free from Easter to November, except at special events.

Brogdale describes itself as 'a living museum' and claims to have the largest collection of fruit cultivars in the world: more than 2,300 apples, 550 pears and 360 plums. There are demonstrations, exhibitions, workshops and events throughout the year. Fruit from the collections is sold, and scion wood supplied.

Features hardy fruit of every kind – the biggest collection in Europe; excellent shop with rare fruit varieties for sale in season; light lunches & teas.

Owned by Brogdale Horticultural Trust
Size 64ha (160 acres)
NCCPG National Collections *Corylus* (cobnuts & filberts); *Malus* (apples, ornamental cvs. & cider apples); *Prunus* (cherries); *Prunus* (plums); *Pyrus*; *Ribes grossularia* (gooseberries); *Ribes nigrum* (blackcurrants); *Ribes sativum* (currants other than blackcurrants); *Vitis vinifera* (grapes)

Chartwell

WESTERHAM, TN16 1PS

Tel 01732 868381 **Fax** 01732 868193
Website www.nationaltrust.org.uk/chartwell
Location A25 to Westerham then signed from B2026.
Opening hours 11 am – 5 pm; Wednesday – Sunday & Bank Holiday Mondays (plus Tuesdays in July & August); 20 March to 7 November.
Admission fee House & Gardens: Adults £7; Children £3.50.

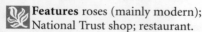

Sir Winston Churchill lived here from 1924 on and laid out the spacious and extensive gardens in a slightly old-fashioned style. One of the rose gardens has the cultivar 'Winston Churchill' but every part has a deep sense of history and all is maintained to a very high standard. The Trust has started to restore the garden to a closer representation of the way it was in Churchill's time.

 Features roses (mainly modern); National Trust shop; restaurant.

Owned by The National Trust
Number of gardeners 5
Size 33ha (82 acres)
English Heritage Grade II*

Church Hill Cottage Gardens

CHARING HEATH, ASHFORD, TN27 0BU

Tel & Fax 01233 712522
Location Church Hill is between the Red Lion pub and the church.
Opening hours 10 am – 5 pm; Tuesday – Sunday & Bank Holidays; March to September.
Admission fee £2.

This is a true cottage garden nursery, owned by enthusiastic plantsmen. It specialises in hardy herbaceous perennials, but there are many dianthus, alpines, hostas, violas, ferns and shrubs to choose from too. The garden has six distinct areas and some island beds but they are unified by the profusion of cottage plants, bulbs, alpine and herbaceous plantings in each of them. Ornamental trees like birches give added structure, and there is a pretty woodland area with yet more interesting plantings. Its year-round interest makes this a good garden to visit whatever the season.

 Features cottage garden plants; good borders.

Owned by Mr & Mrs M. Metianu
Number of gardeners 2
Size 0.6ha (1½ acres)

Copton Ash Gardens

105 ASHFORD ROAD, FAVERSHAM, ME13 8XW

Tel 01795 535919
Location On A251, opposite M2 eastbound exit.
Opening hours 2 pm – 6 pm; Tuesday – Sundays. And by appointment.
Admission fee Free to nursery visitors.

This is a first-rate plantsman's garden, attached to a nursery specialising in real rarities. Started in 1978, the garden now has over 3,000 different plants growing in 1½ acres – the fruit of Tim Ingram's constant quest for new things to try out. His interests are omnivorous, with unusual plants from every corner of the globe and endless different micro-habitats within the garden. Recent developments include extensive plantings of small bulbs like snowdrops, cyclamen and crocus (species only – no hybrids) and the best woodland perennials, especially hellebores, erythroniums and trilliums. Seldom have so many good plants been grown in such a small area. Visitors are especially welcome early in spring when the garden starts to wake up, but there is much of interest at every season. It is a garden to explore slowly. The nursery is excellent, offering the best of these rarities, and with a catalogue that is based on Tim Ingram's own observations, not the recycled nursery-speak of others. A paradise for plantsman.

Features important collection of dry-land plants of every kind.

Owned by Tim & Gillian Ingram
Number of gardeners 1½
Size 0.6ha (1½ acres)

Doddington Place Gardens

SITTINGBOURNE, ME9 0BB

Tel & Fax 01795 886101
Location Follow brown tourist signs from A2.
Opening hours 2 pm – 5 pm; Sundays & Bank Holiday Mondays; 11 April to 27 June. Plus 1, 29 & 30 August, and 19 September. Open at 11 am on Bank Holiday Mondays.
Admission fee Adults £3.50; Children 75p.

The house and garden both date back to the 1870s: Markham Nesfield had a hand in the original formal gardens. The handsome *Sequoiadendron giganteum* and billowing yew hedges are also 19th-century, but this is a garden to which every generation has added something. From the Edwardian era dates the rock garden of local stone: cyclamen have naturalised all through it. The woodland garden was developed in the 1960s on a small outcrop of greensand: rhododendrons, camellias, styrax, eucryphias and maples flourish here as nowhere nearby. More recent are a paved rose garden (*very* pretty), an avenue of *Sorbus aucuparia* 'Beissneri' planted for its winter bark, and excellent colour borders (red and white). And the present owners are adding architectural features and new plantings with great verve.

Features woodland gardens (4 acres); magnificent lumpy yew hedges; fine old wellingtonias; rhododendrons & azaleas.

Owned by Mr & Mrs R. Oldfield
Number of gardeners 1, plus 2 part-time
Size 4ha (10 acres)
English Heritage Grade II

Downderry Nursery

PILLAR BOX LANE, HADLOW, TONBRIDGE, TN11 9SW

Tel 01732 810081 **Fax** 01732 811398
Website www.downderry-nursery.co.uk
Location Follow Tourist signs off A26 north-east of Hadlow.
Opening hours 10 am – 5 pm; daily except Mondays; May to October.
Admission fee Free. Tours (including distillation demonstration) available at £5 per adult.

This nursery in an old walled garden has the widest imaginable list of lavender and rosemary cultivars. Almost all the species are here, including the most unusual ones, and a wide number of hybrids and selections, some of them bred or chosen by the owner Dr Charlesworth himself. His exhibits at the major RHS summer shows have been a source of inspiration to many gardeners, and hurried them to visit his nursery, where his display garden has come together very well. Customers speak well of the quality of his plants. He has now started to distil lavender oils and sell the products. There will be a special 'Lavender Weekend' on 26 & 27 June 2004, when an admission price of £2 will include free tours and light refreshments.

 Features lavender & rosemary.

Owned by Dr Simon J. Charlesworth
Size 0.4ha (1 acre)
NCCPG National Collections *Lavandula*; *Rosmarinus*

East Northdown Farm Nurseries

MARGATE, CT9 3TS

Tel 01843 862060 **Fax** 01843 860206
Website www.botanyplants.co.uk
Location On east fringes of town, along George Hill Road (the B2052) between Cliftonville & Kingsgate.
Opening hours 9 am – 5 pm; daily; all year, except Easter Sunday & Christmas week. Opens at 10 am on Sundays & Bank Holidays.
Admission fee Free.

East Northdown Farm Nursery specialises in plants that will tolerate chalk soil, low rainfall and drying sea winds. There are many Mediterranean species, but the emphasis is always upon their toughness in cultivation. The farmhouse garden is worth a visit in its own right – many rare plants grown in a charming and traditional setting.

 Features self-service teas & snacks.

Owned by William & Louise Friend
Number of gardeners owners only
Size 0.25ha (⅔ acre)

Edenbridge House

MAIN ROAD, EDENBRIDGE, TN8 6SJ

Tel 01732 862122 **Fax** 01732 867385
Location On B2026, 1½ miles north of Edenbridge, near Marlpit Hill.
Opening hours 2 pm – 6 pm; 18 & 25 April, 9 May, 13 June (Hardy Plant Society plant fair), 11 & 18 July, & 19 September. Plus 1 pm – 5 pm on 12 May & 15 September, & 6 pm – 9 pm on 16 June. Plus 2 pm – 5 pm; Tuesdays & Thursdays; April to September. And groups by appointment.
Admission fee Adults £2.50; Children 25p.

This 1930s garden has been renewed and replanted by the present owner as a series of garden rooms to offer something of interest at every season. The spacious terraces are home to a rich mix of tender plants, many of them put out in pots for the summer months. A stream with bog plants along its edges runs down to a small pool. In the kitchen garden is a fine greenhouse and small collection of ornamental trees, as well as apples and an appetising vegetable garden.

Features plantsman's garden; roses; herbaceous plants; orchard; gravel garden; teas (not on Tuesdays or Thursdays).

Owned by Mrs M.T. Lloyd
Size 2ha (5 acres)

Emmetts Garden

IDE HILL, SEVENOAKS, TN14 6AY

Tel 01732 750367 **Fax** 01732 750490
Website www.nationaltrust.org.uk/emmetts
Location Between Sundridge & Ide Hill off B2042.
Opening hours 11 am – 5 pm (last admission 4.15 pm); Wednesday – Sunday & Bank Holiday Mondays; 20 March to 27 June. Then Wednesdays, Saturdays, Sundays & Bank Holidays from 30 June to 31 October.
Admission fee Adults £4; Children £1.

A stiff walk up (or buggy ride) from the car-park brings you to this windswept hilltop garden, laid out in Edwardian times and maintained on a slim budget. The formal Italianate rose garden is pretty in July, but better still is the informal woodland garden laid out with trees and shrubs in the William Robinson style. Good in the autumn, but perhaps best in bluebell time.

Features rock garden; bluebells; Italianate rose garden; rare trees and shrubs; autumn colour; azaleas; tea-room.

Owned by The National Trust
Number of gardeners 2
Size 7ha (17½ acres)
English Heritage Grade II

Godinton Park

ASHFORD, TN23 3BP

Tel 01233 620773 **Fax** 01233 647351
Website www.godinton-house-gardens.co.uk
Location A20 to Charing, then follow brown signs.
Opening hours 2 pm – 5.30 pm; Thursday – Monday; 20 March to 3 October. House opens on 9 April.
Admission fee Gardens only: Adults £3; Children free. Honesty box.

Godinton is the prettiest house in Kent, a Jacobean mansion reworked in the 1920s by Sir Reginald Blomfield who advised on the spacious gardens for over 20 years. The charming Italian garden is his: statues, loggia, summerhouse, Persian rill, marble colonnade and Italian cypresses. The magnificent yew hedge dates from his first plantings in the 1900s: Dutch gables have been cut along its top to match the architecture of the house. Elsewhere are a sunken pool fringed with elegant weeping willows, a formal old-fashioned rose garden, herbaceous borders, sweeping lawns, a stupendous 18th-century park and a topiary garden with a statue of Pan at the centre. The trees include a pair of *Prunus* 'Taihaku' (one of them reputed to be the largest in the country) and a vast plane tree. The wild garden is a carpet of daffodils and fritillaries in spring. In the kitchen garden are rows of fruit, vegetables and cut-flowers, and a border with rare cultivars planted by members of the Delphinium Society. Every part has recently been restored and is very well maintained, to an unusually high standard.

Features topiary; formal Italianate garden; redesigned rose garden; teas.

Owned by The Godinton House Preservation Trust
Number of gardeners 4
Size 5ha (12½ acres)
English Heritage Grade I

Goodnestone Park

WINGHAM, CANTERBURY, CT3 1PL

Tel & Fax 01304 840107
Website www.goodnestoneparkgardens.co.uk
Location Follow brown tourist signs from B2046.
Opening hours 11 am – 5 pm; Mondays, Wednesday – Friday; 22 March to 1 October. Plus 12 noon – 6 pm on Sundays from 28 March to 26 September.

Admission fee Adults £3.50; OAPs £3; Children (under 12) 50p; Disabled in wheelchairs £1; Group (20+) £3; Guided Group £5.50. RHS members free in April, May & September.

Goodnestone is a handsome Palladian building. Jane Austen's brother married a daughter of the house: she will have known the fine chestnut avenue dating from about 1800 and the 18th-century parkland beyond. Later came the formal 19th-century terraces around the house, a 1920s woodland garden (best in spring when the rhododendrons and camellias are in flower) and the sloping cricket ground below the house. Very recent are a gravel garden on the edge of the wood, and a formal parterre on one of the terraces. The walled garden is quite exceptional. Actually there are three walled gardens, one after another, each of about one acre and enclosed by beautiful, worn old bricks. A long, broad, grass walk runs right down the middle and connects them to one another, with the flint tower of the parish church as a focal point beyond. Drifts of shrub roses, peonies, penstemons, clematis and herbaceous plants fill the borders, stuffed with interesting plants and arranged to create pretty colour plantings. Here, above all, you see the passionate plantsmanship which has imbued the present owners since they first started to garden here nearly 50 years ago.

Features woodland garden; topiary; snowdrops; roses (mainly old-fashioned); good herbaceous borders; teas.

Owned by Lord & Lady FitzWalter
Number of gardeners 2 full-time, 2 part-time
Size 5.6ha (14 acres)
English Heritage Grade II*

Great Comp

St Mary's Platt, Borough Green, Sevenoaks, TN15 8QS

Tel 01732 886154
Website www.greatcomp.co.uk
Location 2 miles east of Borough Green: take B2016 off A20.
Opening hours 11 am – 5.30 pm; daily; April to October.
Admission fee Adults £4; Children £1.

Great Comp is a monument to the energy and enthusiasm of Eric Cameron who has built up the garden over the last 40 years. The plant content is of considerable horticultural interest and includes some 30 magnolia cultivars and a good range of rhododendrons, conifers, heathers and herbaceous plants: over 3,000 different plants in all. But the most interesting thing about the garden is the way in which large areas have been planted for minimum maintenance. There is much to learn and admire here. Dysons Nurseries, best known for their salvias, are also based within the grounds.

Features woodland garden; plantsman's collection of plants; good herbaceous borders; ground cover; dwarf conifers; salvias; gifts, plants and souvenirs; refreshments.

Owned by Great Comp Charitable Trust
Number of gardeners 3
Size 2.8ha (7 acres)

Groombridge Place Gardens

Groombridge, Tunbridge Wells, TN3 9QG

Tel 01892 863999 **Fax** 01892 863996
Website www.groombridge.co.uk

Location On B2110, 4 miles south-west of Tunbridge Wells.
Opening hours 9.30 am – 6 pm; daily; 1 April to 5 November.
Admission fee Adults £8.50; OAPs £7.20; Children £7.

Groombridge has lots to offer: a drunken garden where the yews lean at tipsy angles, an oriental garden, a 'draughtsman's garden' and a chessboard garden. Ivan Hicks has been at work in the 'Enchanted Forest', where the gardens are said to be 'interactive'. Best of all are the brilliant colour plantings, among the best we know. But the entry price is high, and some may question whether the garden offers good value.

Features good colour plantings; gift shop; light lunches & teas.

Owned by Groombridge Asset Management Ltd.
Size 0.6ha (1½ acres) plus 80ha (200 acres) park & woods

Hever Castle

EDENBRIDGE, TN8 7NG

Tel 01732 865224 **Fax** 01732 866796
Website www.hevercastle.co.uk
Location 3 miles south-east of Edenbridge, signed from M25 Jct 5 & 6.
Opening hours 11 am – 5 pm (4 pm in winter); daily; March to November.
Admission fee Adults £7; OAPs £6; Children £4.60.

Hever is one of the most important Edwardian gardens in England. The pretty moated castle sits in a park of oaks and firs (underplanted with rhododendrons) with a yew maze and formal neo-Tudor garden to one side. The best part is a spectacular five-acre Italian garden where a long pergola (cool dripping fountains all along) leads past a series of exquisite Italian gardens, stuffed with outstanding sculptures, urns, sarcophagi and other loot brought by William Waldorf Astor from Rome in 1903; it finally bursts onto a theatrical terrace, known as the Piazza, and a 35-acre lake, hand-dug by 800 workmen in less than two years.

Features woodland garden; topiary; 3,000 roses (old-fashioned and modern, with some climbers too); rhododendrons & azaleas; snowdrops; crocus; daffodils; bluebells; tulips; dahlias; autumn colour; Christie's/HHA Garden of the Year in 1995; plant centre; shop; two restaurants.

Owned by Broadland Properties Ltd
Number of gardeners 10
Size 16ha (40 acres)
English Heritage Grade I

Hole Park

ROLVENDEN, CRANBROOK, TN17 4JB

Tel 01580 241386 **Fax** 01580 241882
Location Off B2086 between Rolvenden & Cranbrook.
Opening hours 2 pm – 6 pm; 21 March; 25 April; 2, 16 & 23 May; 13 & 27 June; 4 July (Hardy Plant Society summer plant fair); 10, 13 & 24 October. Plus Bank Holiday Mondays, Wednesdays & Thursdays from Easter to October. Guided tours & groups by appointment.
Admission fee Adults £3.50; Children 50p.

This great garden is far too little known. The drive runs under an avenue of horse chestnuts through classical parkland with wonderful views. The pleasure garden is Edwardian in origin, but has been revived and replanted by the present owner. Solid hedges and clipped specimens of yew are everywhere: backing the excellent herbaceous borders, around the waterlily pond and framing a croquet lawn with standard wisterias. The flowery woodlands have palm trees in the dell, surrounded by purple rhododendrons and orange azaleas. Daffodils abound in April and the millions of bluebells in the woodland walk never cease to astonish in early May. Autumn colours are good, too.

 Features good design and good plants; new millennium water garden; plant stall on Sundays; refreshments on special days, and for groups by arrangement.

Owned by David Barham
Number of gardeners 2
Size 6ha (15 acres)

Iden Croft Herbs

FRITTENDEN ROAD, STAPLEHURST, TN12 0DH

Tel 01580 891432 **Fax** 01580 892416
Website www.herbs-uk.com
Location Signed from A229, south of Staplehurst.
Opening hours 9 am – 5 pm; Monday – Saturday; all year. 11 am – 5 pm; Sundays & Bank Holidays; March to September only.
Admission fee Adults £2; Concessions £1.50; Children 50p.

This substantial nursery has been developed over the last 30 years and planted a series of demonstration gardens. These incorporate a 16th-century walled garden, originally attached to Staplehurst Manor. Other gardens include a cottage garden near the café, and a 'sensory garden' which shows how herbs may be arranged and appreciated for their scent, colour, shape, form and texture. The intention is to provide design and planting ideas for all visitors, whatever the size of their garden. Insects and birds are encouraged and the catalogue which the

nursery produces lists plants under both their Latin and common English names.

 Features herbs.

Owned by Philip Haynes
Number of gardeners 2
Size 0.6ha (1½ acres)
NCCPG National Collections *Mentha*; *Origanum*

Ightham Mote

IVY HATCH, SEVENOAKS, TN15 0NT

Tel 01732 810378 **Fax** 01732 811029
Website www.nationaltrust.org.uk/ighthammote
Location Signed from A25 in Ightham village.
Opening hours 10 am – 5.30 pm; daily except Tuesdays & Saturdays; 28 March to 7 November.
Admission fee Adults £6.50; Children £3.50.

Ightham Mote is a moated mediaeval manor in a wooded Kentish valley, with cottage-garden borders of pinks, old roses and lilies. These were re-made about 100 years ago in a dreamily English style. Fine lawns, natural springs orchards and cutting borders are some of the other features. In the woodland parts are thick rhododendrons and a substantial collection of hydrangeas and philadelphus.

 Features woodland garden; National Trust shop; restaurant.

Owned by The National Trust
Number of gardeners 3
Size 5.6ha (14 acres)
English Heritage Grade II

Keepers Nursery

GALLANTS COURT, EAST FARLEIGH,
MAIDSTONE, ME15 0LE

Tel 01622 726465 **Fax** 0870 705 2145
Website www.keepers-nursery.co.uk
Location At East Farleigh, 4 miles west of
Maidstone, on B2010.
Opening hours By appointment at all reasonable
times.

Less than 20 years old, Keepers is now the
leading fruit tree nursery in the UK. It offers
over 600 cultivars – apples, pears, plums and
cherries, as well as the more unusual fruits
like quince, medlars and mulberries. The
owners have an excellent on-line ordering
facility and a wide choice of rootstocks.
They claim – proudly and correctly – to
have made a significant contribution to the
conservation of old cultivars of fruit. More
than 100 of their apples are not available
from any other commercial source. Keepers
are planning a series of open days and
weekends in the autumn to see the fruit tree
collection; watch their website.

Owned by Hamid Habibi

Ladham House

LADHAM ROAD, GOUDHURST,
TN17 1DB

Tel 01580 212511
Location Left at Chequers Inn on Cranbrook road,
then 2nd right into Ladham Road.
Opening hours 2 pm – 5.30 pm; 4 April & 9 May.
And by appointment.
Admission fee Adults £3.50; Children (under 12) 50p.

Ladham was laid out by a botanist Master of
the Rolls in the mid-19th century, and has
been enthusiastically restored and updated
in recent years. There is a good mixture of

new planting and old: the latter include the
deep red form of *Magnolia campbellii* which
has been named 'Betty Jessel' and is now
available commercially.

Features woodland garden; good
herbaceous borders; fine collection of
trees; magnolias; teas.

Owned by C.G. Johnson
Number of gardeners 2
Size 4ha (10 acres)

Leeds Castle

MAIDSTONE, ME17 1PL

Tel 01622 765400 **Fax** 01622 735616
Website www.leeds-castle.com
Location Jct 8 off the M20.
Opening hours 10 am – 5 pm, March to October;
10 am – 3 pm, November to February. Closed on 28
June, 5 July, 8 November & 25 December)
Admission fee Castle, park & gardens: Adults £12;
OAPs & Students £10.50; Children £8.50 in July &
August. £1 off these prices from March to June and
September to October. And a further £1.50 off in
winter.

More a romantic castle than a garden, Leeds
is best seen across the lake (the 'Great Water')
which Russell Page created in the 1930s;
unfortunately, visitors do not have access to
this viewpoint. Page also designed and
planted the Culpeper Garden, which takes its
name partly from Sir Thomas Colepeper,
who bought the castle in 1632, and partly
from Nicholas Culpeper, the 17th-century
herbalist. It could be said that the Culpeper
Garden does not show the 20th century's
greatest garden designer at his best: informal
plantings of old garden flowers – roses, pinks,
lavender, poppies and lupins. Here too is the
National Collection of bergamot (*Monarda*)
cultivars. The latest development is the 'Lady
Baillie Garden', a series of sheltered terraces

between the Culpeper Garden and the lake. In this part of the garden the planting is more Mediterranean in character. The nearby maze, planted in 1988, is fun to visit: it resembles a topiary castle with towers and bastions and, when you get to its centre, you find the entrance to an underground grotto. There is also a new (2003) turf maze. The 'wood garden' is planted with rhododendrons and azaleas and underplanted with daffodils and anemones and there are further rhododendrons to the west of the moat. The greenhouses, built in 1927, include a fuchsia display and a peach house. Leeds is run by a high profile charitable trust with a big advertising budget, which may help to explain the high entry charges. Are they worth it for someone who is principally interested in gardens and plants? The answer – paradoxically – is yes, provided you also visit the castle and some of the many other attractions here. The owners say you need at least three hours to experience and enjoy them properly.

 **Features** woodland garden; roses (mainly old-fashioned); herbs; good herbaceous borders; vineyard; plant centre; refreshments in the 17th-century tithe barn.

Owned by Leeds Castle Foundation
Number of gardeners 17
Size 5ha (12½ acres), plus 200 ha (500 acres) of parkland
NCCPG National Collections *Monarda*.
English Heritage Grade II*

Madrona Nursery

PLUCKLEY ROAD, BETHERSDEN, TN26 3DD

Tel 01233 820100 **Fax** 01233 820091
Location Half way between Bethersden village & Pluckley railway station.
Opening hours 10 am – 5 pm; Saturday – Tuesday; mid-March to end October.

This is a first-rate general nursery, with a good choice of unusual cultivars across the range. Trees and shrubs are perhaps its main speciality – it is particularly strong on hydrangeas, *Aesculus* and unusual conifers like *Podocarpus macrophyllus* and several forms of *Sequoiadendron giganteum* – but Madrona also offers a fine choice of herbaceous perennials. All are well-grown and well-displayed: a thoroughly satisfying nursery to visit.

Marle Place Gardens

BRENCHLEY, TONBRIDGE, TN12 7HS

Tel 01892 722304 **Fax** 01892 724099
Website www.marleplace.co.uk
Location Follow tourist signs from Brenchley.
Opening hours 10 am – 5 pm; daily; 1 April to 3 October. And by appointment.
Admission fee Adults £4; Concessions £3.50.

The gardens around the Jacobean house are mainly formal. They were imaginatively designed and planted in the 1930s and have been well preserved and improved by the present owners since the early 1960s. The sunken garden, laid out with scented plants, is particularly charming. The Edwardian kitchen garden has been redesigned with exotic planters and the Victorian greenhouse (recently restored) holds a collection of over 200 orchids. Recent additions include some unusual sculptures, a 'mosaic terrace', a nut plat and a bog garden. The wilder parts are full of natural flowers, especially alliums. And all around are orchards of Kentish apples and pears.

 **Features** good herbaceous borders; some unusual plants; a Victorian gazebo; an Edwardian rock-garden; tea, coffee & cake.

Owned by Mrs Lindel Williams
Number of gardeners 1
Size 6ha (15 acres)

Mount Ephraim

HERNHILL, FAVERSHAM, ME13 9TX

Tel 01227 751496 Fax 01227 750940
Website www.mountephraimgardens.co.uk
Location Brown signs from A2 & A299.
Opening hours 1 pm – 6 pm; Wednesdays,
Thursdays, Saturdays, Sundays & Bank Holidays;
Easter to 30 September. Open at 11 am on Bank
Holiday weekends.
Admission fee Adults £3.50; Children £1.

Mount Ephraim is a handsome Edwardian
garden, in a spacious position surrounded
by orchards of apples and pears. The very
substantial rock-garden, with pools of water
and Japanese influences, was laid out by
Waterers in about 1910. The formal garden
has a series of terraces with yew topiary in
combinations of gold and green. Beyond are
a lake, a stream, good conifers and
rhododendron woods. The park trees
include a venerable, gnarled *Robinia
pseudoacacia* on the lawn in front of house.
Behind the house is a magnificent topiary
garden, with geometric shapes, animals,
birds and Great War regimental badges.
Below is the millennium rose garden, pretty
with old and David Austin roses. Everything
has been restored and brought to life again
in recent years, with some good new
plantings.

Features rock garden; topiary; small
shop; plants for sale; teas.

Owned by Mrs Lesley Dawes
Number of gardeners 2½
Size 4ha (10 acres)
English Heritage Grade II

Penshurst Place

PENSHURST, TONBRIDGE, TN11 8DG

Tel 01892 870307 Fax 01892 879866
Website www.penshurstplace.com
Location Follow brown tourist signs from A21
Hildenborough exit.
Opening hours 10.30 am – 6 pm, Saturday &
Sunday, 6 to 21 March; then daily, 27 March to 31
October.
Admission fee Gardens only: Adult £5.50; OAPs
£5; Children £4.50. RHS members free in April,
September & October.

This is an historic garden of great
importance: it has substantial genuine
Tudor remains. Nevertheless, much of what
we see now was developed in the mid-19th
century as a re-creation of the ideal
Elizabethan garden, divided into small self-
contained garden rooms each with its own
style and character. They have been well
restored and developed in recent years. A
vast Italianate parterre dominates the
immediate pleasure garden: it is planted
with *Rosa* 'Surrey' – another is planted as a
Union Jack. There are borders by Lanning
Roper and John Codrington, a 100m bed of
peonies, and a garden for the blind, bought
off the peg at the Chelsea Flower Show in
1994. One impressive statistic: the garden
has over one mile of yew hedging.

Features roses (mainly modern &
climbers); daffodils; good herbaceous
borders; formal Italian garden; spring bulbs;
plant centre; tea-room.

Owned by Viscount De L'Isle
Number of gardeners 6
Size 4.4ha (11 acres)
English Heritage Grade I

Port Lympne

LYMPNE, HYTHE, CT21 4PD

Tel 01303 264647 **Fax** 01303 264944
Website www.howletts.com
Location Exit 11 on M20 & follow brown tourist signs.
Opening hours 10 am – 5 pm in summer; 10 am –
3.30 pm in winter; daily except 25 December.
Admission fee Adults £11.95; OAPs & Children £8.95.

More than a zoo, Port Lympne is a stylish and
luxurious house, with a seriously important
20th-century garden. It was laid out by Philip
Tilden for Sir Philip Sassoon in 1911 on the
steepest of slopes above Romney Marshes and
worked on by Russell Page in the 1950s. The
modern approach is nothing if not dramatic
– an absolutely straight 100m walk lined with
hydrangeas which brings you suddenly to the
top of the stupendous long stone staircase
known as the Trojan stairs. Around the front
door is a forecourt with 16 statues acquired
from the sale at Stowe, in Buckinghamshire,
in 1921; castellations in the yew hedges give
views to the south. The slopes are terraced
into five levels and include a vineyard and
'figyard'. The chess board garden – oblong
rather than square – has squares of grass
contrasted with beds for bulbs and annual
displays: it is matched by a 'striped' garden on
the other side of the main terrace. Down one
side are the Long Borders, planted as mixtures
of shrubs and perennials, and leading to the
magnolia walk, the bowling green, the rose
terrace, the dahlia terrace and the herbaceous
border. Standards of maintenance remain
high: a good garden for grandparents who
want to see something more than animals.

Features topiary; good herbaceous
borders; bedding out; dahlias; shop;
restaurant.

Owned by The John Aspinall Foundationm
Number of gardeners 9
Size 6.2ha (15½ acres)

Riverhill House Gardens

SEVENOAKS, TN15 0RR

Tel 01732 452557 **Fax** 01732 458802
Location 2 miles south of Sevenoaks on A225.
Opening hours 12 noon – 6 pm; Wednesdays &
Sundays, plus Bank Holiday weekends; 31 March to
13 June.
Admission fee Garden only: Adults £3; Children
50p. House open by appointment to groups.

Riverhill is a handsome Queen Anne house
with grand views over the Weald: the garden
suffered badly in the Great Storm of 1987.
In the middle of the 19th century it
belonged to John Rogers the botanist, who
planted many of the surviving conifers and
specimen trees. The vast billowing
rhododendrons include original
introductions by Hooker and Fortune.
Rogers's descendants made the rose walk.

Features rhododendrons & azaleas;
mature conifers; bluebells; tallest
Magnolia x *soulangeana* (13m.) in the
British Isles; small gift shop; home-made
teas.

Owned by The Rogers Family
Number of gardeners 1
Size 3.2ha (8 acres)
English Heritage Grade II

Rock Farm

GIBBS HILL, NETTLESTEAD,
MAIDSTONE, ME18 5HT

Tel & Fax 01622 812244
Location 1 mile south of Wateringbury, up Gibbs Hill.
Opening hours 11 am – 5 pm; 19 & 22 May; 9, 12,
16, 19, 23, 26 & 30 June; 3, 7 & 10 July. And private
visits by appointment.
Admission fee Adults £3; Children free.

Rock Farm is a plantsman's garden, made over many years by a (now retired) nurserywoman on difficult, alkaline soil. There are natural springs and ponds, a bog garden, iris beds, interesting trees and shrubs, and a spectacular herbaceous border designed to be at its best in high summer. All is maintained to a very high standard.

Owned by Mrs S.E. Corfe
Number of gardeners owner only
Size 1ha (2.5 acres)

Rosewood Daylilies

70 DEANSWAY AVENUE, STURRY, CANTERBURY, CT2 0NN

Tel 01227 711071
Location Off to the right of Herne Bay Road, the main road leading north out of Sturry.
Opening hours By appointment. Special Open Day for NCCPG on 21 July (2 pm – 5 pm).
Admission fee Free.

Here is a splendid place to see more than 700 different daylilies, especially those bred and introduced since 1970. These include many of the hundreds of modern American hybrids: the owners trial new cultivars and then offer the best for sale. The nursery's list grows every year: a lot of cultivars with an RHS Award of Garden Merit have recently been added, as have many new spider forms and other specialities. It also offers a range of companion plants: agapanthus (80 cvs), crocosmias (30 cvs), and hardy geraniums.

 Features *Hemerocallis; Agapanthus.*

Owned by Chris Searle
NCCPG National Collections *Hemerocallis* cvs. post-1970

Scotney Castle Garden

LAMBERHURST, TUNBRIDGE WELLS, TN3 8JN

Tel 01892 891081 **Fax** 01892 890110
Website www.nationaltrust.org.uk/scotneycastle
Location On A21, south of Lamberhurst.
Opening hours 11 am – 6 pm; Wednesday – Sunday & Bank Holiday Mondays; 22 March to 31 October.
Admission fee Adults £4.40; Children £2.20.

The house (not open to the public) was designed by Salvin in the late 1830s: the quarry where they extracted the stone for building it is now a sheltered woodland dell. During the 19th century, many specimen trees were added to the parkland – cypresses, cedars and wellingtonias: those that survived the gales of 1987 still give structure to the gardens in their maturity. But the slopes between the house and the moated and abandoned castle at the bottom are now covered with ornamental trees and shrubs planted by Christopher Hussey in the 1950s – among them are many rhododendrons, azaleas, hydrangeas, kalmias and maples. The ruined castle is now the focus of the whole picturesque composition and the way it has been richly draped in wisteria, clematis, honeysuckles and roses is both romantic and photogenic. Among the ruins are a herb garden and a cottage garden designed by Lanning Roper in about 1970. The views of the castle as you meander round the edge of the moat are little short of miraculous.

Features woodland garden; plantsman's collection of plants; rhododendrons; azaleas; water lilies; wisteria; good autumn colour; plantings in ruins of fourteenth-century castle; shop.

Owned by The National Trust
Number of gardeners 4
Size 8ha (20 acres)
English Heritage Grade I

Sissinghurst Castle Garden

SISSINGHURST, CRANBROOK, TN17 2AB

Tel 01580 710700 **Fax** 01580 710702
Website www.nationaltrust.org.uk/sissinghurst
Location 1 mile east of Sissinghurst village, ½ mile off A262. Cross-country footpath from village.
Opening hours 11 am – 6.30 pm; Friday – Tuesday; 22 March to 2 November. Opens at 10 am on Saturdays, Sundays and Bank Holidays.
Admission fee Adults £7; Children £3.50.

So important, influential and well-known is Sissinghurst that it comes as a shock to realise that Harold Nicolson and Vita Sackville-West began to make the garden there as recently as 1930. Her writings made it famous right from the beginning so that it is possible to trace the history of such features as the white garden in her many books still in print. Harold Nicolson was a careful designer who understood the importance of line and measure: he was very much a classicist in taste. Vita Sackville-West was a romantic, exuberant, poetic plantswoman. It was the combination of these two complementary talents that made the garden a source of wonder and inspiration. Sissinghurst is now part of every English gardener's education, and one to which it is important to return time and again. The garden is always changing and developing. It was the Nicolsons' intention that the garden should continue to develop after they gave it to the National Trust, and this principle – that the garden must be kept up to date with new plants – is inherent in the way that it has been managed. The design is unaltered and unalterable, and the plantings continue to be governed by the Gertrude Jekyll principles of which Sissinghurst is a supremely beautiful interpretation. But the plants are always changing and Sissinghurst therefore remains an influential plantsman's garden too.

Features influential 20th-century garden; roses (mainly old-fashioned); plantsman's collection of plants; herbs; good herbaceous borders; National Trust gift shop; self-service restaurant.

Owned by The National Trust
Number of gardeners 8
Size 2.2ha (5½ acres)
English Heritage Grade I

Squerryes Court

WESTERHAM, TN16 1SJ

Tel 01959 562345 **Fax** 01959 565949
Website www.squerryes.co.uk
Location ½ mile from A25, signed from Westerham.
Opening hours 12 noon – 5.30 pm; Wednesdays, Thursdays, Sundays & Bank Holiday Mondays; April to September. For NGS on 11 July & 5 September.
Admission fee Garden only: Adults £3.40; OAPs £2.90; Children £1.70.

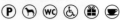

The gardens have been excellently restored with advice from Tom Wright since 1987, guided by a Badeslade plan of the original garden made in 1719, before they were landscaped later in the century. The main feature is a formal garden behind the house, where box-edged beds are filled with santolina, lavender and sage, alongside the beautifully planted Edwardian borders. The outline of the old formal garden is still apparent in the terracing and paths, and new borders have been added for year-round interest. The modern design and planting are inevitably a compromise, but Squerryes is place of great beauty and variety. Beyond the formal gardens is a woodland garden planted with rhododendrons and azaleas, and the whole is surrounded by an 18th-century park.

Features parterres; topiary; roses (mainly old-fashioned); herbaceous borders; formal design; gazebo; dovecote; woodland walks; lake; small shop in house; teas & light refreshments.

Owned by J. & A. Warde
Number of gardeners 1, plus 2 part-time
Size 10ha (25 acres)
English Heritage Grade II

Starborough Nursery

STARBOROUGH ROAD, MARSH GREEN, EDENBRIDGE, TN8 5RB

Tel 01732 865614 **Fax** 01732 862166
Location On B2028 Edenbridge to Lingfield Road.
Opening hours 9.30 am – 4 pm; daily, except Wednesdays & Sundays. Closed in January, July & August.

Starborough has for long been an important nursery for its wide range of trees and shrubs and, since it took over G. Reuthe Ltd, in the 1990s, of rhododendrons and azaleas too. Its list of liquidambars, cornus, camellias and magnolias is particularly good.

Owned by Mr & Mrs C.B. Tomlin

Stoneacre

OTHAM, MAIDSTONE, ME15 8RS

Tel 01622 862871 **Fax** 01622 862157
Website www.nationaltrust.org.uk
Location 1 mile south of A20; north end of Otham village.
Opening hours 2 pm – 6 pm; Wednesdays, Saturdays & Bank Holiday Mondays; 20 March to 13 October.
Admission fee Adults £2.60; Children £1.30.

Stoneacre is particularly interesting because the tenant until 2000 was Rosemary Alexander, Principal of the English Gardening School at the Chelsea Physic Garden. It was where she worked out her ideas and showed her students how the principles of design and planting look 'on the ground'. The new tenants have come to gardening from the fashion world and have made considerable alterations to the planting. They have incorporated their passion for strong shape and dark subtle colouring. The back courtyard has an unusual collection of plants and flowers grouped around the doors. The old potager has been transformed into an intimate red rose garden. It is still one of the most exciting new gardens in southern England, and in perfect harmony with the Tudorised house.

 Features spring bulbs; autumn colour; strong design.

Owned by The National Trust
Number of gardeners 2

Tile Barn Nursery

STANDEN STREET, IDEN GREEN, BENENDEN, TN17 4LB

Tel & Fax 01580 240221
Website www.tilebarn-cyclamen.co.uk
Location 2 miles south of Benenden; turn left at crossroads in Iden Green.
Opening hours 9 am – 5 pm, Wednesday – Saturday.

This is a splendid garden-nursery devoted to one genus – *Cyclamen*. Cyclamen are everywhere: they have spread through the lawns and into the drive, as well as under the shelter trees, shrubs and hedges. In the glasshouses are rows and rows of every imaginable hardy species and cultivar of cyclamen of different ages, all pot-grown and all of flowering size – a wonderful sight from August to April. Visitors will also find pots of some other unusual bulbs species, particularly the smaller, daintier colchicums, crocus, fritillarias, snowflakes and narcissus.

Owned by Peter & Liz Moore

Walmer Castle & Gardens

KINGSDOWN ROAD, WALMER, DEAL, CT14 7LJ

Tel 01304 364288 **Fax** 01304 364826
Location Follow brown tourist signs.
Opening hours 10 am – 6 pm (5 pm in October, & 4 pm from November to March). Daily from March to October; Wednesday – Sunday in November & March; weekends only in January & February. Closed 1 January & 24-26 December.
Admission fee Adults £5.50; Concessions £4.10; Children £2.80. (2003 prices).

The gardens at Walmer Castle are well worth a visit, partly for their horticultural interest and partly for their many historical associations – William Pitt, the Duke of Wellington and Winston Churchill were all Wardens of the Cinque Ports. The castle looks onto the Broad Walk, 100m long, on either side of a wide path backed by massive mature yew hedges (3m tall and 2m wide), and lined with fine herbaceous borders. Beyond are a croquet lawn, magnificent 19th-century terraces, and Penelope Hobhouse's new Queen Elizabeth the Queen Mother's Garden. To the north of the Broad Walk is the Kitchen Garden – an enclosed orchard with espaliered fruit trees, a cutting garden and glasshouses. Further away are drifts of daffodils, a lawnful of specimen trees planted by famous visitors from the 19th century onwards, a wildflower

meadow, a thickly wooded quarry and a holm oak avenue planted in 1866.

Features magnificent old yew hedges; new garden by Penelope Hobhouse; English Heritage shop; tea-room.

Owned by English Heritage
Number of gardeners 4
Size 3.2ha (8 acres)
English Heritage Grade II

Waystrode Manor

SPODE LANE, COWDEN, TN8 7HW

Tel 01342 850695
Location In village.
Opening hours 1.30 pm – 5 pm on 12 May, 23 June & 7 July. 2 pm – 5 pm on 23 May, 13 & 20 June. NCCPG Plant Sale 11 am – 5 pm on 2 May.
Admission fee Adults £3; Children 50p.

The garden at Waystrode Manor has been developed over the last 35 years. You approach it along an avenue of pink horse-chestnuts, but the garden has a good collection of plants and is laid out in the cottage style. Highlights include a bog garden, an old-fashioned rose garden, a white garden, irises, geraniums, ornamental trees and tender plants put out for the summer.

Features good borders; interesting plants; small shop; plant stall; teas & cakes.

Owned by Mrs Jill Wright
Number of gardeners 2
Size 3.2ha (8 acres)

Yalding Organic Gardens

YALDING, MAIDSTONE, ME18 6EX

Tel & Fax 01622 814650
Website www.hdra.org.uk
Location On B2162, ½ mile south of village.
Opening hours 10 am – 5 pm; Wednesday –
Sunday; May to September. Also weekends in April
& October & all Bank Holidays.
Admission fee Adults £3; Children free. RHS
members free.

Yalding has a series of 14 historically
themed gardens run organically by the
HDRA. They include an apothecary's
garden in the 13th-century style, a late-
19th-century artisan's garden and a post-
war allotment: all very stylish and
educational. Others show the influence of
William Cobbett and Gertrude Jekyll
through the centuries. There is a central
hop-pole pergola – a good example of how
design features should come out of their
surrounding landscape. A recent addition is
tall wooden henge. The HDRA sets out to
inspire, to educate and to give pleasure –
and succeeds.

Features gardens through the ages –
modern reconstructions; café open
from mid-morning to tea-time

Owned by Henry Doubleday Research Association
Number of gardeners 4
Size 2ha (5 acres)

LANCASHIRE, MERSEYSIDE & GREATER MANCHESTER

There are few historic gardens in this industrial corner of the north-west, but several public parks whose importance is both historical and contemporary: Sefton Park in Liverpool was designed by Edouard André, Birkenhead Park by Sir Joseph Paxton, and Heaton Park in Manchester by William Emes. The public gardens at the seaside resorts of Blackpool and Southport are famous for their summer displays. Few private gardens are open to the public, though the National Gardens Scheme has in several villages managed to persuade a cluster of gardens to open simultaneously and make up a good afternoon's visiting. Myerscough College near Preston is a RHS Partner College, with lectures and workshops all through the year. It also has a National Collection of *Eryngium* and is hoping for provisional acceptance for its collection of *Aesculus* (horse chestnut) species and cultivars, of which it holds around 60. There is a handful of other National Collections in the three counties, but this is not a corner of England with any established interest in plants apart, perhaps, from alpines: Reginald Kaye at Carnforth and Holden Clough near Clitheroe are both long-established nurseries specialising in plants for cold climates. The new garden of the Lennox-Boyds at Gresgarth is a rising star.

Catforth Garden

CHERRY TREE LODGE, ROOTS LANE, CATFORTH, PRESTON, PR4 0JB

Tel 01772 690561
Location At Blackleach end of Catforth, by the Lancaster Canal.

Opening hours 3 to 5 days a week from 1 May to 14 July; please telephone for exact times & dates.
Admission fee Adults £2; Children 50p.

This plantsman's garden was started in 1983. Trees and shrubs give it structure, often embellished by climbing roses and clematis. Within this background are plants of every kind – perennials, ferns, bulbs and grasses – planted to give year-round colour. Rock gardens, bog gardens, ponds, woodland and island beds support a wide variety of plants. The rhododendrons, azaleas and camellias are especially fine. The collection of hardy geraniums is the most extensive we know – 450 species and cultivars.

Owned by Judith & Tony Bradshaw
Number of gardeners 2
Size 0.4ha (1 acre)
NCCPG National Collections *Geranium*

Croxteth Hall & Country Park

CROXTETH HALL LANE, LIVERPOOL, L12 0HB

Tel 0151 228 5311 **Fax** 0151 228 2817
Website www.croxteth.co.uk
Location Muirhead Avenue East.
Opening hours 10.30 am – 5 pm; daily; Easter to September.
Admission fee Adults £1.25; OAPs & Children 75p for walled garden (subject to review). Grounds free.

(P) (WC) (&) (🌱) (🎁) (☕)

Very much a public amenity, Croxteth Hall has a fine woodland trail along the River Alt, but the main interest for gardeners is the Victorian walled garden. This aims to show visitors what they can achieve at home. There are lines of trained fruit trees, growing either against the walls or free-standing, a large vegetable garden (lots of varieties grown from the HDRA), an area for soft fruit, a herb garden, and a mushroom house – to remind people how mushrooms were once cultivated in grand gardens. These are interplanted with more ornamental features – a bedding display, a rose garden, some herbaceous borders and

the collection of fuchsias. There are also working greenhouses and some beehives, which add to the garden's interest.

**Features** herbs; plants under glass; fruit; good herbaceous borders; current holder of Sandford Award; shop; cafeteria.

Owned by City of Liverpool
Number of gardeners 5
Size 1.5ha (3¾ acres) walled garden
NCCPG National Collections *Fuchsia* (hardy)
English Heritage Grade II

Dunham Massey

ALTRINCHAM, WA14 4SJ

Tel 0161 941 1025 **Fax** 0161 929 7508
Website www.nationaltrust.org.uk
Location 3 miles south-west of Altrincham off A56, well signed (Dunham Massey Hall & Park).
Opening hours 11 am – 5.30 pm (4.30 from 24 October); daily; 27 March to 3 November.
Admission fee Gardens only: Adults £4; Children £2. Car park £4.

(P) (WC) (&) (🌱) (🎁) (☕)

Dunham Massey's 250 acres include an ancient deer park, a mediaeval moat made into a lake in the 18th century, an Elizabethan mount, an 18th-century orangery, a pump house and some early landscape avenues. Serpentine paths lead between borders thickly planted for texture and colour. The bog garden and moss garden take advantage of the unusual opportunities of the site. The woodlands are planted with Professor Pratt's azaleas, cardiocrinums, meconopsis, and more than 60 different hydrangeas. There are more unusual trees in the extensive lawns. The result is a potent cross-section of historical and modern styles with a solid core of Victorian excellence, while the standard of maintenance is one of the highest in any National Trust garden.

Features topiary; hydrangeas; skimmias; Edwardian parterre; garden shop; large restaurant.

Owned by The National Trust
Number of gardeners 5
Size 10ha (25 acres) of garden & 90ha park
English Heritage Grade II*

Fletcher Moss Botanical Gardens

MILL GATE LANE, DIDSBURY, M20 8SD

Tel 0161 434 1877
Location In East Didsbury, off A5145.
Opening hours 8 am (9 am at weekends & Bank Holidays) – dusk; daily; all year.
Admission fee Free.

Fletcher Moss is a model municipal botanic garden, beautifully maintained but open free to the public. In the rock garden, which is substantially constructed on three levels with a pool at the bottom, is a rich collection of alpine plants, small conifers, maples and aquatics. The woodland areas have excellent autumn colour, but are almost as good in spring.

 Features rock garden; mature conifers; bulbs; heathers; rhododendrons; cafeteria.

Owned by Manchester City Council
Size 5ha (12½ acres)

Hoghton Tower

HOGHTON, PRESTON, PR5 0SH

Tel 01254 852986 **Fax** 01254 852109
Location A675 midway between Preston & Blackburn.
Opening hours 11 am – 4 pm; Monday – Thursday; July to September. 1 pm – 5 pm;

Sundays; July to September. Also Bank Holiday Mondays from Easter to August.
Admission fee Adults £2; Children (under 5) free.

A series of spacious courtyards and walled gardens surround this fierce castellated house which is approached up a long avenue. Its garden is not among the greatest, but the setting is impressive and there are fine spring walks in the rhododendron woods below.

 Features good herbaceous borders; rhododendrons & azaleas; gift shop; tea-room.

Owned by Hoghton Tower Preservation Trust
English Heritage Grade II

Holden Clough Nursery

HOLDEN, BOLTON BY BOWLAND, CLITHEROE, BB7 4PF

Tel & Fax 01200 447615
Location 8 miles north-east of Clitheroe, off A59.
Opening hours 9 am – 5 pm; Monday – Saturday: all year. Plus 1.30 pm – 5 pm on certain Sundays in April & May. Other times by appointment.
Admission fee Free.

This long-established working nursery (founded in 1927) has a large range of interesting alpines, perennials, crocosmias, dwarf conifers, shrubs, ferns, grasses and foliage plants. It is well-known at shows, all over the country. One of its best introductions is the hardy and vigorous hybrid *Iris* 'Holden Clough'. Another, now available once again, is the rare and beautiful *Astilbe* 'Holden Clough'.

Owned by Peter Foley
Size 0.8ha (2 acres0

Gresgarth Hall

CATON, LANCASTER, LA2 9NB

Tel 01524 771838 Fax 01524 771281
Location ½ mile south of Caton.
Opening hours 11 am – 5 pm; 18 April, 9 May, 13 June, 11 July, 8 August & 12 September.
Admission fee Adults £4; Children free.

Mark and Arabella Lennox-Boyd bought Gresgarth Hall near Lancaster in 1982. Arabella is a distinguished garden designer, with a wonderful eye for structure, line and colour. The main formal gardens lie to the side of the house – terraces elegantly laid out with octagonal platforms, angled staircases and neat box edgings. Much of the planting here are white: *Daphne mezereum* 'Album', philadelphus, santolina and variegated hollies clipped as four-sided pyramids. *Clematis* 'Duchess of Edinburgh' and *C.* 'Henryi' grow against the retaining wall. Here and throughout the garden are magnificent hellebores, all the best modern cultivars from Helen Ballard, Elizabeth Strangman and Will McLewin in Cheshire. The surrounding borders are all in yellow and orange: rudbeckias, *Euphorbia dulcis* 'Chameleon', and annual sunflowers. The main herbaceous border is in pastel shades, and designed to flower from April to October – ending with a splendid show of Michaelmas daisies. The terraces run down to the lake, which the Lennox-Boyds have tripled in size. The damp border on its far side has glorious blue meconopsis, candelabra primulas in vast drifts, gunneras for late summer effect and both species of *Lysichiton*. A handsome bridge crosses the river to a long woodland garden which stretches along the valley bottom for about 400 metres. Springs are everywhere, and a great variety of soils which, together with the steep banks of the valley, make for an infinite number of microhabitats. The dominant species is English oak but there are also remnants of a Victorian planting of sequoias and wellingtonias. The principal underplanting is of winter-flowering witch-hazels – *Hamamelis* 'Pallida', *H.* 'Diane' and many new cultivars. The hillside across the river is laid out with an extensive collection of young rhododendrons and azaleas. The Lennox-Boyds have also planted a large number of *Magnolia stellata* forms and hybrids, an avenue of filberts and cobs along the outside of the walled garden and a substantial group of the different cultivars of lilac. Microhabitats support some surprisingly tender plants. *Embothrium coccineum*, *Drimys lanceolata* and *Olearia scillonensis* all grow out in the open: so does the sweet-scented *Daphne bholua*, which seeds around. Among the rarest plants are a fine *Emmenopterys henryi*, micropropagated by Kew. Lilies also flourish, particularly the tall white *Cardiocrinum yunnanense*. But it is above all the energy and the scale of the Lennox-Boyds' endeavours which create the greatest impression. They have successfully combined good design, thorough plantsmanship and fine eye for decoration in a uniquely romantic natural setting. There can be no doubt that Gresgarth is one of the greatest gardens of our times.

Features good design; colour plantings; rhododendrons; plant sales; teas & cakes.

Owned by The Hon. Sir Mark & Lady Lennox-Boyd
Number of gardeners 4
Size 5ha (12 acres)

Leighton Hall

CARNFORTH, LA5 9ST

Tel 01524 734474 **Fax** 01524 720357
Website www.leightonhall.co.uk
Location Signed from A6 junction with M6.
Opening hours 2 pm – 5 pm; daily except
Saturday & Monday; May to September. Open at
12.30 am in August. Rare Plant Fair on 1 August.
Admission fee Adults £5; OAPs £4.50.

The handsome semi-castellated house at
Leighton is set in lush parkland with the
Lakeland fells as a backdrop: the Victorian
conservatory to the side of the house has just
been restored. The main garden features are
in the 19th-century walled garden, whose
formal paths contrast with the exuberant
informality of the planting. Here are
herbaceous borders, a herb garden, fruit
trees, a vegetable plot and masses of climbing
roses – as well as the unusual gravel maze.

 Features roses (mainly old-fashioned);
herbs; fruit; good herbaceous borders;
'caterpillar' maze; gift shop; tea-room.

Owned by R.G. Reynolds
Number of gardeners 1½
Size 2ha (5 acres)

Rufford Old Hall

RUFFORD, ORMSKIRK, L40 1SG

Tel 01704 821254 **Fax** 01704 823823
Website www.nationaltrust.org.uk
Location 7 miles north of Ormskirk on A59.
Opening hours 11 am – 5.30 pm; Saturday –
Wednesday; 3 April to 27 October.
Admission fee Garden only: Adults £2.50;
Children £1.

   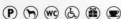

One of the National Trust's most successful
re-creations, the gardens are laid out in the

Victorian style around a remarkable 15th-
century timber-framed house.

 Features roses (mainly old-fashioned);
rhododendrons & azaleas; good
herbaceous borders; National Trust shop;
lunches & teas.

Owned by The National Trust
Number of gardeners 1
Size 5.6ha (14 acres)

Speke Hall

THE WALK, LIVERPOOL, L24 1XD

Tel 0151 427 7231 **Fax** 0151 427 9860
Website www.nationaltrust.org.uk
Location 1 mile off A561, surrounded by Liverpool
Airport.
Opening hours 11 am – 5.30 pm (4 pm from mid-
October to March); Tuesday – Sunday, plus Bank
Holiday Mondays; all year. Closed 1 January, 24-26
& 31 December.
Admission fee Adults £3; Children £1.50.

Speke is an oasis among the concrete deserts
of Merseyside's suburbs. At its heart is a
substantial half-timbered house, dating back
to the 14th century and surrounded by a
moat, now dry. The garden is mainly
modern, a sympathetic restoration of the
one which a rich Liverpool merchant made
in the mid-19th century. On the south lawn,
three Victorian island beds have recently
been re-made. The nearby rose-garden was
planted in 1984 with shrubs and
Floribundas. All around are rhododendrons,
daffodils and bluebells in spring.

Features roses; spring bulbs; summer
borders; stream garden; tea-room.

Owned by The National Trust
Number of gardeners 3
Size 7ha (17½ acres)
English Heritage Grade II

LEICESTERSHIRE

One of the reasons why there are so few historic gardens in Leicestershire (no Grade I and only two Grade II* gardens) is that much of the county was open and unenclosed until the latter half of the 18th century. Even today, it is not as rich in interesting gardens as its neighbours, Northamptonshire and Warwickshire. However the National Gardens Scheme offers a respectable number of gardens to visit in its Yellow Book, and the first-rate gardens at Wartnaby and Long Close, show just how much can be grown by an adventurous plantsman – so does the excellent University of Leicester Botanic Garden. Leicestershire has some good garden centres, and a handful of first-rate specialist nurseries. Brooksby Melton College is a RHS Partner College with a fine teaching garden and collection of plants. It also has two National Collections: *Liriope* and *Ophiopogon*. Contrary to local belief, there is no such county as Rutland: it was dissolved in 1974 and absorbed into Leicestershire until eventually it re-emerged as a unitary authority. We include its gardens here for convenience.

Barnsdale Gardens

THE AVENUE, EXTON, OAKHAM, LE15 8AH

Tel 01572 813200 **Fax** 01572 813346
Website www.barnsdalegardens.co.uk
Location The Avenue is on the south west edge of Exton.
Opening hours 9 am – 5 pm (7 pm June to August); daily; March to October. 10 am – 4 pm; daily; November to February. Last entry 2 hours before closure. Closed on 23 & 25 December.
Admission fee Adults £5; Groups £4; Children free. RHS members free.

Barnsdale was famous for 20 years as Geoff Hamilton's *BBC Gardener's World* garden. Within it are 37 smaller individual gardens and garden features, laid out and maintained with the same intention – to encourage people to make the most of their opportunities as garden-owners. The gardens are of every kind. Some have descriptive names like the Tranquil Garden and the Town Paradise: others are more specific like the Plantsman's Garden, the Fruit Orchard, the Rose Garden, the Stream and Bog Garden. But for many visitors the most interesting are those which match their own particular circumstances and inspire them to become better gardeners – the Cottage Gardens, the Small Town Garden, the Ornamental Kitchen Garden and the Allotment Garden. All are maintained to the highest standard and continue to educate, delight and inspire. The attached specialist nursery sells over 1,800 different plants, many of them rare and unusual. Owned and run by Geoff Hamilton's son and daughter-in-law, its policy is to offer the widest possible choice of good plants to its customers.

Features gift shop; nursery; licensed coffee shop.

Owned by Sue & Nick Hamilton
Number of gardeners 6
Size 3.2ha (8 acres)

Belvoir Castle

BELVOIR, GRANTHAM, NG32 1PD

Tel 01476 870262 **Fax** 01476 870443
Website www.belvoircastle.com
Location 6 miles west of Grantham.
Opening hours 11 am – 5 pm; daily; Easter to 30 September. Then Sundays only in October.
Admission fee Castle & gardens: Adults £7.25; OAPs £6.75; Children £4.75. RHS members free.

Belvoir has formal gardens along the Victorian terraces beneath the castle, and a Broad Walk overlooking the newly restored 19th-century rose garden. Some way off is a hedged enclosure with seven statues by Caius Cibber and an Art Park. The Spring Garden, a pretty woodland garden, has recently been restored to its early 19th-century form and is open by appointment to groups at any time of the year.

Features woodland garden; roses (mainly modern); tallest bird cherry *Prunus avium* (28m.) and yew tree *Taxus baccata* (29m.) in the British Isles; gift shop; refreshments: lunches and teas; picnic site.

Owned by The Duke of Rutland
Number of gardeners 4
English Heritage Grade II

Goscote Nurseries Ltd

SYSTON ROAD, COSSINGTON, LE7 4UZ

Tel 01509 812121 **Fax** 01509 814231
Website www.goscote.co.uk
Location 5 miles north of Leicester, on B5328.
Opening hours 9 am – 5 pm; Monday – Saturday. 10 am – 5 pm; Sundays. Closes at 4.30 pm in winter and between Christmas & New Year.
Admission fee Free.

Goscote has a wide range of reasonably-priced plants of all types – more than 1,500 different kinds are propagated on site. They offer an extensive collection of trees and shrubs, including acers, azaleas, clematis, conifers and rhododendrons, many of them rare or unusual but suitable to the cold Midlands. Plants can also be seen in the show gardens, laid out as island beds and borders, with a rock-garden, a water-garden and a new (2003) 20-metre pergola. The website is helpful and comprehensive.

Features mature show gardens.

Owned by Derek Cox & Frank-James Toone
Size 0.3ha (¾ acre)

The Herb Nursery

THISTLETON, OAKHAM, LE15 7RE

Tel 01572 767658 **Fax** 01572 768021
Location In the middle of the village.
Opening hours 9 am – 6 pm (or dusk); daily; closed from Christmas to New Year.

This family-run nursery lists nearly 500 herbs and wildflower plants, with a special emphasis upon lavender, mint and thyme. The range of scented-leaf pelargoniums is particularly good (80+ cultivars), and there is a extensive range of cottage garden plants. Local gardeners speak well of it. The demonstration beds and borders around the nursery are a bonus. Ask to see the new knot garden.

Owned by Peter & Christine Bench

Kayes Garden Nursery

1700 MELTON ROAD, REARSBY, LEICESTER, LE7 4YR

Tel 01664 424578
Location On A607, north-east of Leicester.
Opening hours 10 am – 5 pm (but 12 noon on Sundays); Tuesday – Sunday; March to October. By appointment from November to February.
Admission fee Garden £2; Nursery free.

This popular nursery has an excellent, mature display garden, densely planted with a wide range of interesting plants. It also opens for the National Gardens Scheme. The nursery's specialities are hardy herbaceous plants, grasses, aquatics and climbers. Hazel Kaye has a plantsman's eye for quality, and the list includes many of the best forms of a wide range of plants.

 Features eryngiums; tradescantias; teas.

Owned by Hazel Kaye
Number of gardeners 2
Size 0.6ha (1½ acres)
NCCPG National Collections *Tradescantia* Andersoniana Group

Long Close

MAIN STREET, WOODHOUSE EAVES, LOUGHBOROUGH, LE12 8RZ

Tel 01509 890616 (daytime)
Website www.longclose.org.uk
Location 4 miles south of Loughborough.

Opening hours 9.30 am – 5.30 pm; Monday – Saturday; March to July and again in autumn. Groups also welcome at other times by appointment. For NGS: 2 pm – 5.30 pm on 4 April (plant fair), 2 pm – 6 pm on 30 May (plants for sale) and 11 am – 4.30 pm on 28 September (plants for sale).
Admission fee Adults £3; Children 50p. Tickets from Pene Crafts Gift Shop, opposite (open 9.30 am – 1 pm and 2 pm – 5.30 pm). Groups & Sundays pay at garden.

This is a plantsman's garden, made over many years and now magnificently mature. Some of the plants might be thought too tender for so far north: it has been called 'a Cornish garden in Leicestershire'. The entrance courtyard has *Crinum* x *powellii* 'Album', *Sophora tetraptera* and *Clematis armandii*. You go round the side of the house and suddenly a spacious series of terraced gardens opens out below you, lined by clouds of rhododendrons and venerable conifers. The terraced lawns lead to a fine woodland garden, underplanted with bulbs, magnolias, camellias and massed rhododendrons and azaleas. Elsewhere are good herbaceous plantings, a thicket of *Prunus tenella*, penstemons (quite a collection), a box-edged *potager*, a very handsome, bulging, pendulous ash *Fraxinus excelsior* 'Pendula', aged wisterias, *Azara microphylla* 6 metres tall, Italian cypresses *Cupressus sempervirens* Stricta Group, a stream and pond thickly planted with both species of *Lysichiton*, and *Lathraea clandestina* spreading upon the roots of an old poplar. Soaring above are huge English oaks, and arborescent hawthorns (*Crataegus monogyna*) as much as 20 metres high. The whole garden is run organically.

 Features woodland garden; rhododendrons; azaleas; spring bulbs; penstemons; plants for sale, especially penstemons; tea & coffee; teas on Sundays.

Owned by John Oakland & Pene Johnson
Size 2ha (5 acres) plus 3-acre meadow

University of Leicester Botanic Garden

BEAUMONT HALL, STOUGHTON DRIVE, OADBY, LE2 2NA

Tel 0116 271 7725
Location 3 miles south of Leicester on A6 London Road opposite Racecourse: visitor entrance at The Knoll, Glebe Road.
Opening hours 10 am – 4 pm; Monday – Friday; all year. Plus Saturdays & Sundays from 16 March to 10 November. Closed 1 January, 25 & 26 December. Special Open Days: 11 am – 4 pm; 4 & 25 July, and 5 September.
Admission fee Free, but charge for special events.

(P) (WC) (&) (+)

The University of Leicester Botanic Garden moved to its present site in 1947. It fills the grounds surrounding four houses, which were built early in the 20th century and are now used as student residences. The four (once separate) gardens have been merged into a single entity, the University Botanic Garden with some 16 acres. They now support a wide variety of plants from historic trees to an 1980s ecological meadow. A pretty Edwardian pergola draped with roses, a well-planted rock-garden and a splendid display of hardy fuchsias from the National Collection all add to its interest. In 1997 the garden opened an out-station at Knighton, known as the Attenborough Arboretum. Though its plantings are still few and the trees very young, it is designed to display the native tree flora of England in an historical sequence of arrival dates – ending with beech (*Fagus sylvatica*) after the last ice age.

 Features rock garden; rhododendrons & azaleas; plants under glass; mature conifers; cacti; succulents; heathers; fuchsias.

Owned by The University of Leicester
Number of gardeners 5
Size 6.4ha (16 acres)
NCCPG National Collections *Aubrieta*; *Chamaecyparis lawsoniana*; *Fuchsia*; *Skimmia*

Warren Hills Cottage

WARREN HILLS ROAD, COALVILLE, LE67 4UY

Tel 01530 812350
Location On B587 near the schools on the Copt Oak to Whitwick road.
Opening hours 12 noon – 5 pm; 11, 24 & 25 April; 2, 3, 23, 29 & 30 May; 11 July (plant fair); 22 August; 19 September. And by appointment; groups welcome.
Admission fee Adults £1.50; Children 50p.

(P) (WC) (&) (+) (⊂)

This young garden is attached to a small nursery specialising in hardy plants, many of them unusual. The owners describe it as 'a plantaholic's garden', planted to provide year-round interest. The main feature is the collection of over 55 different astrantias, each growing in its own labelled bed. Other features hellebores, bulbs and early perennials underscoring the rhododendrons. There have been extensive new plantings recently. A garden to watch.

Features astrantias; campanulas; penstemons; salvias; cream teas on open days.

Owned by Mr & Mrs G. Waters
Number of gardeners 3 part-time
Size 0.8ha (2 acres)
NCCPG National Collections *Astrantia*

Wartnaby Gardens

WARTNABY, MELTON MOWBRAY,
LE14 3HY

Tel 01664 822549 **Fax** 01664 822231
Website
http://wartnabygardenlabels.co.uk/garden.htm
Location 3 miles north of Melton Mowbray on
A606. Left at A6 Kettley then 1 mile.
Opening hours 9.30 am – 12.30 pm; Tuesdays;
April to July. Plus 11 am – 4 pm; 25 April (Plant
Sale) & 20 June (Plant Fair) & parties by
appointment.
Admission fee Adults £2.50; Children free. RHS
members free on Tuesdays.

Wartnaby is the garden of someone who
loves roses and is prepared to make them
one of the principal elements of her garden
design: the result is one of the best modern
examples of how to grow roses in mixed
borders. Even in the so-called rose garden,
the roses do not dominate: they are
interplanted instead with other shrubs, like
ceanothus, hebes and tree peonies, and
underplanted with geraniums and bulbs.
Foliage, shapes, colours and textures take
over when the roses are not in flower. The
long central path in the substantial kitchen
garden is flanked by massed plantings of
hybrid musks, including 'Felicia', 'Prosperity'
and 'Pink Prosperity', underplanted with the
grey-leaved *Stachys byzantina* and *Lychnis
flos-jovis*, and edged with lavender and box.
Wartnaby is a garden of enormous interest
and charm.

Features roses (mainly old-fashioned)
used in mixed borders; fruit; fine
collection of trees; colour borders; many
new features; refreshments available.

Owned by Lady King
Size 2ha (5 acres)

Whatton House

LONG WHATTON, LOUGHBOROUGH,
LE12 5BG

Tel 01509 842225 **Fax** 01509 842268
Location 3 miles from Jct 24, Kegworth A6
towards Hathern.
Opening hours 11 am – 4 pm; Monday – Friday;
March to September. Plus 2 pm – 6 pm; 4 April, 23
May & 27 June, for NGS and 10 am – 5 pm on 3
May & 30 August for plant fairs. Groups welcome by
arrangement.
Admission fee Adults £2.50; Children free.

The garden at Whatton was started in 1880,
and many of the older features date from
about 1900 but there has been much
replanting over the years, especially recently.
A rose garden, a fine herbaceous border and
some magnificent specimen trees are among
the attractions. It is particularly interesting
in spring when the bulbs and flowering
shrubs are in full display.

Features roses (ancient & modern);
good herbaceous borders; arboretum;
climbing plants; bark temple; canyon
garden; bulbs; refreshments on NGS day.

Owned by Lord Crawshaw
Number of gardeners 1
Size 6ha (15 acres)
English Heritage Grade II

LINCOLNSHIRE

Lincolnshire, with which we include what was for a while south Humberside, has long been known for its horticultural industry based on bulb-growing, and it still has a high number of producers, both wholesale and retail. The show-garden at Springfields, together with its trade fairs and flower-parades, is one of the great attractions of Lincolnshire in spring, now open again after re-development. The county has its fair share of important historic gardens: Belton House and Grimsthorpe Castle are both open to the public, though the third Grade I garden at Brocklesby Park (Capability Brown, Humphry Repton, and Reginald Blomfield all worked there) remains strictly private. The National Gardens Scheme has a fair number of gardens opening for charity and the county is blessed with several specialist nurseries of national importance. In addition to the alpine experts Pottertons Nursery (formerly Potterton and Martin) near Caistor, there are two nurseries with significant National Collections – the fuchsia enthusiast Kathleen Muncaster on the north-west outskirts of Gainsborough and the auricula specialists Martin Nest Nurseries to the east of the same town. RHS members have free access for much of the year to Normanby Hall Country Park, one of the most interesting restoration projects on the East Coast of England.

Baytree Nurseries

HIGH ROAD, WESTON, SPALDING, PE12 6JU

Tel 01406 370242 **Fax** 01406 372829
Website www.baytree-gardencentre.com
Location 1½ miles east of Spalding, on A151.
Opening hours 9 am – 6 pm; summer. 9 am – 5 pm; winter. Closed for Easter Day, Christmas Day & Boxing Day.

Baytree won the Garden Centre of Excellence Award some years ago: in 2000 it also won the growers' Retailer of the Year Award. Its six hectares include a pets and aquatic department, a leisure complex devoted to selling garden furniture and an owl centre. But it also aims to carry the largest selection of bulbs available at retail level anywhere in the country and a very large stock of plants, many of them grown on-site. Roses are a speciality: Baytree lists over 300 cultivars including some which it has bred and introduced itself.

Features self-service, licensed restaurant.

Owned by Reinhard Biehler
Size 6.2ha (15½ acres)

Belton House

GRANTHAM, NG32 2LS

Tel 01476 566116 **Fax** 01476 579071
Website www.nationaltrust.org.uk
Location 3 miles north-east of Grantham on the A607.
Opening hours 11 am – 5.30 pm; Wednesday – Sunday plus Bank Holiday Mondays; 31 March to 31 October. Opens at 10.30 am in August. Closes at 4.30 pm on 17 July. 12 noon – 4 pm on Saturdays & Sundays from 6 November to 19 December.
Admission fee Adults £6.50; Children £3.

Grandeur and amenity go hand in hand at Belton. There are 1,000 acres of wooded deer park, a Wyattville orangery, a Dutch garden and an Italian garden with statues and parterres. But the adventure playground and other facilities make it popular with all ages.

Features woodland garden; topiary; snowdrops; daffodils; bluebells; good herbaceous borders; biggest sugar maple *Acer saccharum* in the British Isles; gift shop; lunches, teas, licensed restaurant.

Owned by The National Trust
Number of gardeners 4
Size 14ha (35 acres)
English Heritage Grade I

Doddington Hall

DODDINGTON, LINCOLN, LN6 4RU

Tel 01522 694308 **Fax** 01522 685259
Website www.doddingtonhall.free-online.co.uk
Location Signed off the A46 Lincoln bypass.
Opening hours Not available as we went to press. 2003 times were: Wednesdays, Sundays & Bank Holiday Mondays; May to September.
Admission fee Garden only: £3.50; Children £1.75. (2003 prices).

Doddington is a ravishing Elizabethan house around which successive generations have made a successful Tudor-style garden. The owners keep it simple and open at the front, but in the walled garden (thickly and richly planted) are Edwardian knots and parterres, a modern herb garden and pleached hornbeams. Wonderfully harmonious and strongly recommended in early summer.

Features good herbaceous borders; long succession of spring bulbs; irises; peonies; box-edged parterres, topiary; tea-shop.

Owned by Antony Jarvis
Number of gardeners 2
Size 2.4ha (6 acres)
English Heritage Grade II*

Easton Walled Gardens

EASTON, GRANTHAM, NG33 5AP

Tel 01476 530063 **Fax** 01476 550116
Website www.eastonwalledgardens.co.uk
Location Between A1 & B6403, 2 miles north of Colsterworth.
Opening hours 11 am – 3 pm; daily; 14 to 22 February for snowdrops. Then 10 am – 5 pm; Wednesdays; 31 March to 29 September.
Admission fee Adults £3; Children free. Coaches by appointment only.

Easton has a spectacular display of snowdrops in late winter, and the garden is always open for a week or ten days when they are at their peak. But there is even more to see at other times of the year, because the whole garden is undergoing a substantial restoration and reinterpretation by its young, enthusiastic owners. Easton Hall, the house, was pulled down in 1948 and the garden abandoned. Now – starting in 2002 – the avenues have been cleared, stonework restored and new planting schemes devised. Do not expect an instant garden, but visit Easton now as it emerges from 50 years of neglect, and then return to measure the progress. Work continues.

 Features plants for sale; gift shop.

Owned by Sir Fred & Lady Cholmeley
Number of gardeners 3
Size 4.8ha (12 acres)
English Heritage Grade II

Grimsthorpe Castle

GRIMSTHORPE, BOURNE, PE10 0LY

Tel 01778 591205 **Fax** 01778 591259
Website www.grimsthorpe.co.uk
Location On A151, 4 miles north-west of Bourne.
Opening hours 11 am – 6 pm; Thursdays, Sundays & Bank Holiday Mondays; April to September. Plus daily in August except Friday & Saturday.
Admission fee Adults £3; Concessions £2.50; Children £2.

Much is happening at Grimsthorpe. Recent researches have unearthed traces of the Stephen Switzer garden design from about 1700 and shown that it was probably a local engineer called John Grundy who designed the lake in 1771, not Capability Brown. Yew hedges have been planted to enclose the Victorian Italian garden, which is stylishly maintained with summer bedding among the topiary, urns and sculptures. The most interesting horticultural feature is a formal vegetable garden, made in the 1960s before the craze for *potagers*, right below the Italian garden. But new developments are planned for the near future.

 Features topiary; roses (mainly modern); fine collection of trees; shop; tea-room (licensed).

Owned by Grimsthorpe & Drummond Castle Trust Ltd
Number of gardeners 4
Size 10.7ha (27 acres)
English Heritage Grade I

Gunby Hall

GUNBY, SPILSBY, PE23 5SS

Tel 01909 486411 **Fax** 01909 486377
Website www.nationaltrust.org.uk
Location 2½ miles north-west of Burgh-le-Marsh.
Opening hours 2 pm – 6 pm; Wednesdays (plus Thursdays for garden only); 31 March to 30 September.
Admission fee Garden only: Adults £2.80.

Rich herbaceous borders, an arched apple walk, shrub roses, herbs and traditional English vegetables are planted in the exquisite walled garden.

 Features roses (mainly old-fashioned); herbs; fruit; good herbaceous borders.

Owned by The National Trust
Number of gardeners 2, plus volunteers
Size 2.8ha (7 acres)
English Heritage Grade II

Hall Farm & Nursery

HARPSWELL, GAINSBOROUGH, DN21 5UU

Tel 01427 668412 **Fax** 01427 667478
Website www.hall-farm.co.uk/nursery
Location On A361, 7 miles east of Gainsborough.
Opening hours 10 am – 5 pm (or dusk, if earlier); daily; all year. Phone first in winter. For National Gardens Scheme: 10 am – 5.30 pm on 5 September.
Admission fee Adults £2.50; Children 50p on National Gardens Scheme day; otherwise a charity donation is requested.

This garden is intensely planted and beautifully maintained as an adjunct to the nursery, and for the owners' pleasure. There are plants of every kind – trees, shrubs, bulbs and herbaceous plants – and over 100 different roses. The National Gardens Scheme day (always on the first Sunday in September) is a 'free seed collection' day.

Features roses (mainly old-fashioned) in a newly made rose garden; plantsman's collection of plants; good herbaceous borders; sunken garden; good nursery next door.

Owned by Pam & Mark Tatam
Size 0.6ha (1½ acres)

Hippopottering Nursery

ORCHARD HOUSE, BRACKENHILL ROAD, EAST LOUND, HAXEY, DONCASTER, DN9 2LR

Tel 07979 764677
Website www.hippopottering.com
Location Off A161 at Haxey on Owston Ferry road to East Lound.
Opening hours By appointment.

Hippopottering Nursery – the name has its origins in a family joke – are specialists in Japanese maples. They offer everything from selected colourful seedlings and bonsai material to mature specimens. Cultivars are selected from their collection of over 120; they also sell rootstocks. Look out for them also at Chelsea and other RHS shows.

Features maples.

Owned by Margaret & Patricia Gibbons
Size 0.4ha (1 acre)

Kathleen Muncaster Fuchsias

18 FIELD LANE, MORTON, GAINSBOROUGH, DN21 3BY

Tel 01427 612329
Website www.kathleenmuncasterfuchsias.co.uk
Location North-west of Gainsborough: Field Lane is off the minor road to Walkerith.
Opening hours 10 am – 5 pm; Thursday to Tuesday; from February to mid-June. Phone first at other times.

This is the nursery of a fuchsia specialist who began as an amateur and now has a National Collection of hardy cultivars and one of the largest nurseries in the country which specialises in the genus. The hardy fuchsias can be seen in the garden, together with the stock plants: almost all the glasshouses may also be visited. The list is impressive, though not all the cultivars in the collection are propagated regularly – ask if they have a cutting available. They introduce new fuchsias every year: there are five introductions for 2004, including a new hardy cultivar called 'John Green'.

Owned by Kathleen Muncaster
NCCPG National Collections *Fuchsia* (hardy)

Martin Nest Nurseries

GRANGE COTTAGE, HEMSWELL, GAINSBOROUGH, DN21 5UP

Tel 01427 668369 **Fax** 01427 668080
Location 6 miles east of Gainsborough on A631.
Opening hours 10 am – 4 pm; daily; all year. By appointment only at weekends from November to January.

Martin Nest Nurseries are wholesalers and retailers with a good business-like range of

tough pot-grown hardy alpine plants. Primulas and auriculas are their speciality: some of their cultivars are unique to them. Visitors may be shown the National Collection of *Primula auricula* cultivars on request.

Owned by Joe Shardlow
NCCPG National Collections *Primula auricula*

Normanby Hall Country Park

NORMANBY, SCUNTHORPE, DN15 9HU

Tel 01724 720588 **Fax** 01724 721248
Website www.northlincs.gov.uk/northlincs/
leisure/heritage/
Location 3 miles north of Scunthorpe.
Opening hours 10.30 am – 5 pm (4.30 in winter) daily; all year. Closed 1 January, 25 & 26 December.
Admission fee Adults £4; Children £2. RHS members free.

The Victorian Walled Garden (actually built in 1817, before Queen Victoria was even born) has been restored and planted – with help from the National Lottery – as a living museum of 19th-century horticulture. Old varieties of fruit and vegetables are grown organically. The glasshouses have recently been rebuilt to house peaches and other fruit. Ferns and exotic ornamentals fill a display house. New in 2002 was a bog garden along the base of the ha-ha (125m long) and a Christmas garden of hollies, ivies, hellebores and ferns. Now they are developing a Victorian woodland garden. Four RHS special events will take place during 2004: details from 020 7821 3408.

Features fruit & vegetables are a special feature; herbaceous borders, woodland walks and parkland outside; deer park; shop; new nursery; refreshments.

Owned by North Lincolnshire Council
Number of gardeners 4
Size 0.4ha (1 acre), plus 120ha (300 acres) parkland.

Pottertons Nursery

MOORTOWN ROAD, NETTLETON, CAISTOR, LN7 6HX

Tel 01472 851714 **Fax** 01472 852580
Website www.pottertons.co.uk
Location 20 miles north-east of Lincoln, on B1205: leave A46 at Nettleton.
Opening hours 9 am – 4.30 pm; daily.
Admission fee Free.

This alpine, bulb and rock plant specialist (formerly known as Potterton & Martin) has an interesting and extensive range of plants for sale, running from the easy to the unusual. All are propagated on-site, and most can be seen in the extensive display garden. The rock garden has a stream course, waterfalls and pools: elsewhere are raised beds, troughs, woodland and peat beds. The nursery holds many Chelsea gold medals, and has won the RHS Farrer Trophy (best alpine display) on several occasions. Satisfied customers praise not only the nursery's wide choice of plants, but also its cultivation skills and reasonable pricing policy.

Features large rock garden.

Owned by Robert & Jackie Potterton
Number of gardeners 3 part-time
Size 2ha (5 acres)

LONDON

London gardeners are much more fortunate than they would have you believe. They have a micro-climate which enables them to grow plants that are tender anywhere except in the mildest corners of the south-west, and they enjoy a good choice of suitably stylish plants from garden centres and other outlets within the city itself. Some of the world's greatest gardens are within a short journey: among them are the Chelsea Physic Garden, Chiswick House, the Royal Botanic Gardens at Kew, Richmond Park and Syon Park. The Royal Parks Agency manages the inner-city green spaces like Hyde Park and Regent's Park with immense horticultural skill: almost all the parks contain acres of well-kept grass and trees of record size. London is of course the seat of the Royal Horticultural Society, whose Chelsea Flower Show is traditionally regarded as the start of the London summer season. The Hampton Court Palace Flower show in July is, if possible, even more of a Londoners' show, while the regular London shows at the RHS's own halls in Westminster are attended by thousands of London gardeners keen to see plants and buy them. Nowhere has so many lectures and other educational garden events as London does. The RHS's Partner College at Capel Manor has a long programme of lectures, demonstrations and workshops throughout the year. Many of the specialist plant societies have their shows and administrative offices in London, too: if you want to see plants as diverse as orchids, carnations, vegetables, daffodils or camellias, London is the place to do so. The National Gardens Scheme thrives there; the Museum of Garden History is based there – just across the river from the Houses of Parliament; the Association of Gardens Trusts has its office in London and so does the Institute of Horticulture. The London Historic Parks & Gardens Trust is one of the country's most successful conservation societies. The greater part of the RHS's Lindley Library – Britain's largest collection of horticultural books and primary sources about gardening – is based in London and now housed in spacious purpose-built accommodation at 80 Vincent Square. Perhaps the only thing that a Londoner cannot do is to garden on a large scale. That apart, there is no better place to be a garden-lover.

Cannizaro Park

WEST SIDE COMMON, WIMBLEDON,
SW19 4UE

Tel 020 8545 3657
Location West side of Wimbledon Common.
Opening hours 8 am – sunset, Monday – Friday;
9 am – sunset, Saturday, Sunday & Bank Holidays;
all year.
Admission fee Free.

Cannizaro is well-known among
connoisseurs for its azaleas, planted about 40
years ago and a magnificent spectacle when
in full flower. It is one of the best woodland
gardens of its type in the country and
especially beautiful when the underplantings
of bulbs are in flower. There are some fine
specimen trees, including birches, horse
chestnuts and the tall sassafras.

Features woodland garden; mature
conifers; azaleas; magnolias; several
Sassafras albidum 15m or more; some
refreshments at summer weekends.

Owned by London Borough of Merton
Size 15.5ha (39 acres)
English Heritage Grade II*

Capel Manor

BULLSMOOR LANE, ENFIELD, EN1 4RQ

Tel 020 8366 4442 **Fax** 01992 717544
Website www.capel.ac.uk
Location A10 by Jct 25 on M25.
Opening hours 10 am – 6 pm (or dusk if sooner);
daily; March to October. Weekdays only from
November to February.
Admission fee £5 Adults; £4 OAPs; £2 Children.

There are three main areas at this high-
profile demonstration garden attached to a
horticultural college 'where the City meets
the Countryside'. First there is the National
Gardening Centre, where dozens of small
model gardens are designed and planted to
give people state-of-the-art ideas for their
own gardens. Second, there are the trial
grounds run by *Gardening Which?*, where
this influential monthly magazine carries out
all its trials and experiments, long-term and
seasonal. Third, there is the series of themed
gardens laid out for students to learn from: a
walled garden, a herb garden, a knot garden,
a disabled person's garden, a shade garden,
an Italianate holly maze, a pergola, a
Japanese garden, alpine beds and some
historical recreations. The latest additions
are a 'Diana, Princess of Wales Garden' and a
'H.M. The Queen Mother Garden', featuring
some of the favourite plants of the two royal
ladies. Whatever your interests and whatever
the time of the year, Capel Manor is a garden
which educates and delights. And it is
brilliant for new ideas, especially for small
gardens. There is a substantial programme of
RHS workshops, lectures and garden walks
at Capel Manor during 2004: details from
020 7821 3408.

Features vegetables & fruit; topiary;
plantsman's collection of plants; herbs;
plants under glass; daffodils; good herbaceous
borders; fine collection of trees; alpine plants;
roses of every kind; small shop; restaurant.

Owned by Capel Manor Corporation
Number of gardeners 8
Size 12ha (30 acres)
NCCPG National Collections *Achillea; Sarcococca*

Chelsea Physic Garden

66 ROYAL HOSPITAL ROAD, SW3 4HS

Tel 020 7352 5646 **Fax** 020 7376 3910
Website www.chelseaphysicgarden.co.uk
Location Entrance in Royal Hospital Road, towards
the Chelsea Embankment end, on Swan Walk on
public days.

Opening hours 12 noon – 5 pm, Wednesdays;
2 pm – 6 pm, Sundays; 2 April to 26 October. Plus
12 noon – 5 pm on 24 to 28 May for Chelsea Flower
Show.
Admission fee Adults £5; Children £3.

This oasis of peace between Royal Hospital
Road and the Chelsea Embankment started
life in 1673 as a pharmacological collection,
and has kept its original design – hence the
word 'Physic' in its name. But it also has the
oldest rock garden in Europe, the largest
olive tree in Britain, extensive botanical
order beds, a vast number of rare and
interesting plants, including the long-
flowering form of *Rosa chinensis* known as
'Crimson Bengal'. An historical walk
emphasises the importance of the garden
through the ages by drawing attention to the
number of plants first introduced to Britain
by the garden and its curators.

Features herbs; plants under glass;
good herbaceous borders; eighteenth-
century rock garden; large olive tree
growing outside; light refreshments.

Owned by Chelsea Physic Garden Company
Number of gardeners 5
Size 1.6ha (4 acres)
English Heritage Grade I

Chiswick House

BURLINGTON LANE, CHISWICK, W4 2RP

Tel 020 8742 1225
Location South-west London on A4 & A316.
Opening hours 8 am – dusk; daily; all year.
Admission fee Free.

Laid out by Bridgeman and Kent for Lord
Burlington, Chiswick is the best baroque
garden in southern England, and the
exquisite house is pure Palladian. The
bachelor Duke of Devonshire added an

Italian renaissance garden early in the 19th
century, and a Camellia House with slate
benches and huge bushes, mainly of old
Japonica hybrids. But it is the lay-out and
buildings which are so exceptional: the Ionic
temple, the Inigo Jones gateway, the obelisk
and the statues. Forget the dogs and the
joggers – almost all free-entry gardens have a
municipal heart – but explore the *pattes d'oie*,
allées and ilex groves of the main garden on a
hot July morning and you might be doing a
Grand Tour of Italy 250 years ago.

Features plants under glass; camellias;
parterres; summer bedding; luxuriant
evergreens; refreshments.

Owned by London Borough of Hounslow
Number of gardeners 5
Size 16ha (40 acres)
English Heritage Grade I

Clifton Nurseries

5A CLIFTON VILLAS, LITTLE VENICE,
W9 2PH

Tel 020 7289 6851 **Fax** 020 7286 4215
Website www.clifton.co.uk
Location In Little Venice, 100 yds from Warwick
Avenue.
Opening hours 8.30 am – 6 pm; Monday –
Saturday: 10.30 am – 4.30 pm; Sundays: March to
September. 8.30 am – 5.30 pm; Monday – Saturday:
10 am – 4 pm; Sundays: October to February.

Clifton Nurseries were founded in 1854 and
are now the capital's oldest garden centre.
They have become one of the smartest and
most stylish sources of good plants and
designer sundries for Londoners. They
concentrate on supplying town gardens with
containers, statuary, climbers and shrubs in
specimen sizes, indoor and conservatory
plants. Topiary is one of their specialities: so
are mature plants for instant gratification.

Down House

LUXTED ROAD, DOWNE, ORPINGTON,
BR6 7JT

Tel 01689 859119
Location In Downe, on left side of Luxted Road.
Opening hours 10 am – 6 pm; Wednesday –
Sunday, plus Bank Holiday Mondays; all year.
Closes at 5 pm in October, and 4 pm in November &
December.
Admission fee Adults £6; Concessions £4.50;
Children £3.

Charles Darwin's house and garden have been
restored as they were in the great scientist's
lifetime. It is a thoughtful, practical, middle-
class garden with none of the extravagances
of 'great' gardens. The borders, orchards and
kitchen gardens are just as they were in the
1860s: there are orchids and carnivorous
plants in the greenhouse and grassland fungi
in the lawns. Visitors can also explore the
'sandwalk' where Darwin thought through his
ideas as he paced along.

 Features Charles Darwin's garden; gift
shop; tea-room.

Eltham Palace

COURT YARD, ELTHAM, SE9 5QE

Tel 0208 294 2548 **Fax** 0208 294 2621
Location Follow English Heritage signs.
Opening hours Not available as we went to press.
Admission fee Adults £4.50 (garden only).

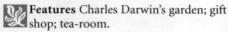

The ramparts and moat of the old royal
palace give structure to the modern garden.
There are fine rose gardens, herbaceous
borders, rock gardens and shade borders
dating from the 1930s, but restored recently.
Also from the pre-war period are several

huge specimens of *Ligustrum lucidum*.
Perhaps the best modern planting is the
110-metre South Moat border by Isabelle
van Groeningen, which won the English
Heritage competition as a reinterpretation
of the 1930s style.

 Features historic royal palace; unusual
1930s garden; modern prairie-style
garden; tea-shop.

Owned by English Heritage
Number of gardeners 3, plus volunteers
Size 8ha (20 acres)
English Heritage Grade II*

Fenton House

WINDMILL HILL, HAMPSTEAD,
NW3 6RT

Tel & Fax 020 7435 3471
Website www.nationaltrust.org.uk
Location Entrances in Hampstead Grove near
Hampstead Underground station.
Opening hours 2 pm – 5 pm; Saturdays &
Sundays; 6 to 28 March. Then 2 pm – 5 pm;
Wednesday – Sunday plus Bank Holiday Mondays;
7 April – 31 October. Opens at 11 am on Saturdays,
Sundays & Bank Holiday Mondays.
Admission fee Adults £4.60; Children £2.30.

Fenton House has a country garden in
Hampstead, with neat, terraced gardens near
the house, and a rather more informal
design at the bottom. It is not outstandingly
flowerful, but the hedges are good, plants
are firmly trained, and there is something to
see throughout the year: definitely worth
knowing, and very popular with visitors.

Features roses (mainly old-fashioned);
herbs; good herbaceous borders;
restored Edwardian garden.

Owned by The National Trust

Fulham Palace Garden Centre

BISHOPS AVENUE, FULHAM, SW6 6EE

Tel 020 7736 2640 **Fax** 020 7371 8468
Website www.fulhamgardencentre.com
Location Corner of Fulham Palace Road & Bishops Avenue.
Opening hours 9.30 am – 5.30 pm, Monday – Thursday; 9.30 am – 6 pm, Friday – Saturday; 10 am – 5 pm, Sundays. Shuts earlier in winter months.

Fulham Palace Garden Centre has everything for the town gardener, including specimen-sized plants, topiary and a good range of containers. The general range includes herbs, vegetables, fruit trees, herbaceous plants, climbers, ferns, grasses, olives, figs and oranges. The nursery will deliver seven days a week in London and further afield. It is owned by Fairbridge, the charity which arranges training for inner-city youth. The Fairbridge Garden Society, based at the Fulham Palace Garden Centre, runs a lively programme of lectures, demonstrations, and garden visits at home and abroad. For details ring 020 7736 2640 or see the website.

Features excellent general garden centre.

Ham House

HAM, RICHMOND, TW10 7RS

Tel 020 8940 1950 **Fax** 020 8332 6903
Website www.nationaltrust.org.uk
Location On River Thames, signed from A307.
Opening hours 11 am – 6 pm (or dusk, if earlier); Saturday – Wednesday; all year except 1 January & 25/26 December.
Admission fee Adults £3; Children £1.50.

Ham is a modern re-creation of the original 17th-century garden. It is not a literal copy, but more of a free-handed re-interpretation. The best part is a grand series of hornbeam enclosures with white summerhouses and seats, known as the Wilderness. The borders are all planted, so far as possible, in the 17th-century style. There are plans to re-develop the kitchen garden in front of the orangery to contrast its 17th-century design and plantings with the better-known 19th-century ones that are commonly seen elsewhere.

Features formal gardens in 17th-century style; roses (mainly modern & climbers); herbs; fruit; parterres; holm oak avenue; National Trust shop; tea-room open 15 February to 2 November.

Owned by The National Trust
Number of gardeners 4
Size 8ha (20 acres)
English Heritage Grade II*

Isabella Plantation

RICHMOND PARK, RICHMOND, TW10 5HS

Tel 020 8948 3209 **Fax** 020 8332 2730
Website www.royalparks.gov.uk
Location Richmond Park.
Opening hours Dawn – dusk; daily; all year.
Admission fee Free.

The Isabella Plantation in Richmond Park is at last getting the recognition it deserves: these 42 acres of rhododendrons and azaleas under a mature deciduous canopy are one of the finest woodland gardens in the country. They are probably best visited in late April and May, when the azaleas are accompanied by lush streamside plantings of candelabra primulas, ferns and hostas. And it all gets better still: the new bog

Hampton Court Palace

KT8 9AU

Tel 0870 752 7777
Website www.hrp.org.uk
Location North side of Kingston bridge over the Thames on A308 junction with A309.
Opening hours King's Privy Garden: 9.30 am – 5.30 pm (4 pm from October to March). Opens at 10.15 am on Mondays. Maze open 10 am – 5.45 pm (4.15 pm from October to March). Others gardens open daily from dawn to dusk.
Admission fee Privy Garden: Adults £3; Children £2. Maze: Adults £3.50; Children £2.50.

  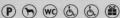

William III was responsible for the main features at Hampton Court today. His Privy Garden has been reconstructed as it was in 1702 and remains the outstanding example of a successful historic restoration from the 1990s. Even the planting is accurate – roses, fritillaries and other flowering plants chosen and cultivated exactly as they would have been 300 years ago. Note how widely spaced they are in their slightly raised beds, an exact copy of horticultural practices of the time. Next to the vast Privy Garden is the Pond Garden, a sunken formal garden with magnificent displays of bedding – tulips in spring and tender perennials in summer. Nearby is the Great Vine – actually 'Black Hamburgh' – planted in 1768 on the advice of Capability Brown: it is the world's oldest known vine and produces, on average, 300 kilos of grapes every year. To one side of the Privy Garden lies the great formal East Garden. Its central feature is the Long Water which cuts right through the deer park: the Hampton Court Palace Flower Show (organised by the Royal Horticultural Society) takes place astride its banks on 6-11 July (tickets from 0870 906 3791). The garden at the palace end of the long water was laid out as a parterre by William III with 12 marble fountains: Queen Anne added the semi-circular canals in 1710. On the other side of the palace are the wilderness gardens, extending over a considerable area, and a mass of naturalised daffodils in spring. Here too is the famous Hampton Court Maze, which covers about one third of an acre and has yew hedges totalling nearly half a mile. Other areas in the Wilderness also have considerable horticultural interest, including the rose garden, a herbaceous garden, and walls covered with climbing plants. Hampton Court is large and you need several hours to appreciate all the gardens, their different styles and what they offer. The website is excellent – educational and helpful.

Features topiary; roses (ancient & modern); herbs; fruit trees; good herbaceous borders; the famous maze; laburnum walk; knot gardens; the Great Vine; the Wilderness; shop.

Owned by Historic Royal Palaces
Number of gardeners 40
Size 24ha (60 acres) of formal gardens & 240ha (600 acres) of deer park
NCCPG National Collections *Heliotropium*
English Heritage Grade I

garden (opened in 2000) has been such a success that it was extended in 2002.

 Features woodland garden; rhododendrons & azaleas; camellias and magnolias; good ornamental trees; primulas.

Owned by The Royal Parks Agency
Number of gardeners 5
Size 17.2ha (42 acres)
NCCPG National Collections *Rhododendron* (Kurume azaleas, the Wilson 50)
English Heritage Grade I

Kenwood

HAMPSTEAD LANE, NW3 7JR

Tel 020 8348 1286
Website www.english-heritage.org.uk
Location North side of Hampstead Heath, off B519.
Opening hours 8 am to dusk (8.30 pm if sooner); daily; all year.
Admission fee Free.

Parts of this superb 18th-century parkland around two glittering lakes have recently been restored to Repton's original designs. There are splendid plantings of rhododendrons, fine azaleas, a mature *Davidia involucrata* and wonderful landscaped views to London and Westminster. Work continues.

 Features woodland garden; good herbaceous borders; fine collection of trees; restaurant; café.

Owned by English Heritage (Iveagh Bequest)
Number of gardeners 5
Size 43ha (108 acres)
English Heritage Grade II*

Museum of Garden History

LAMBETH PALACE ROAD, SE1 7LB

Tel 020 7401 8865 **Fax** 020 7401 8869
Website www.museumgardenhistory.org
Location Between Lambeth Bridge & Lambeth Palace.
Opening hours 10.30 am – 5 pm; daily; early February to mid-December
Admission fee £2.50 voluntary admission charge (£2 concessions).

The garden is small, and complements the Museum's fascinating collections and excellent exhibitions. Nevertheless it is neatly designed and planted – with a fair degree of historical correctness – as a 17th-century knot garden, using plants associated with the Tradescant period. A garden for contemplation. But the events, exhibitions, lectures and courses are well worth knowing about: the Museum is undergoing major redevelopment with the aim of becoming a first-class information resource about the history of gardening in Britain.

 Features 17th-century plants; good exhibitions; historic tool collection; books, cards and gifts; light refreshments.

Owned by Museum of Garden History
Number of gardeners 8 part-time volunteers

Myddelton House

BULLS CROSS, ENFIELD, EN2 9HG

Tel 01992 702200 **Fax** 01992 650714
Website www.enfield.gov.uk/tourism/myddel.htm
Location Off A10 onto Bullsmoor Lane: signed at Bulls Cross. Or train to Turkey Street Station.
Opening hours 10 am – 4.30 pm (3 pm from October to March); weekdays except Christmas Holidays; all year. Plus 12 noon – 4 pm; Sundays &

Bank Holiday Mondays; 11 April to 31 October. And 12 noon – 4 pm for NGS on 29 February, 30 May & 25 July.

Admission fee Adults £2.30; Concessions £1.70.

Holy ground for plantsmen with a sense of history, E.A. Bowles's garden was abandoned for 30 years: Lee Valley Regional Park Authority has started to restore it. Thousands of naturalised bulbs have survived: snowdrops, crocus and narcissi in spring, and cyclamen, colchicums and sternbergias in autumn. The large wisteria planted in 1903 has also survived, while the rose garden has been replanted with varieties that Bowles grew. The iris borders are spectacular in May but it is true to say that, as with all plantsman's gardens, there is much to see throughout the year. A current project is to restore the Lunatic Asylum, Bowles's collection of freak plants like the double-flowered (but non-berrying) blackberry *Rubus ulmifolius* 'Bellidiflorus'. The RHS thought so highly of this part of the garden that, even in the cash-strapped 1950s, it propagated the plants and created its own Lunatic Asylum corner at Wisley. And the Lee Valley Regional Park Authority has just re-acquired the kitchen garden and has plans to restore it too. There is a friends' group called the E.A. Bowles of Myddelton House Society which has an active programme of events: details from Mr A Pettitt, 2(A) Plough Hill, Cuffley, Potters Bar, Hertfordshire EN6 4DR or from *michaelkingdom@aol.com*

Features snowdrops; roses (mainly old-fashioned & climbers); plantsman's collection of plants; daffodils; good herbaceous borders; fine collection of trees.

Owned by Lee Valley Regional Park Authority
Number of gardeners 3
Size 2.4ha (6 acres)
NCCPG National Collections *Iris*
English Heritage Grade II

Osterley Park

JERSEY ROAD, ISLEWORTH, TW7 4RB

Tel 020 8232 5050 **Fax** 020 8232 5080
Website www.nationaltrust.org.uk
Location 5 miles west of central London on A4.
Opening hours 9 am – 7.30 pm (or dusk, if earlier); daily; all year.
Admission fee Park & pleasure grounds free.

Osterley is a classical 18th-century landscape with a fine semi-circular conservatory by Robert Adam and some good trees – especially cedars and oaks. Other highlights include the Chinese Pavilion and the Temple of Pan, but the greatest horticultural interest comes from large specimens of *Magnolia grandiflora* against the stable block wall.

Features woodland garden; herbs; fruit; fine rare oaks; autumn colour; tallest variegated chestnut *Castanea sativa* 'Albomarginata' (16m.) in the British Isles; National Trust shop; tea-room.

Owned by The National Trust
English Heritage Grade II*

The Palm Centre

HAM NURSERY, HAM STREET, HAM, RICHMOND, TW10 7HA

Tel 020 8255 6191 **Fax** 020 8255 6192
Website www.thepalmcentre.co.uk
Location Near Ham House, on right hand side of Ham Street opposite Riverside Drive.
Opening hours 9 am – 5 pm (or dusk, if earlier); daily; all year.
Admission fee Free.

The Palm Centre, close to Ham House, is a five-acre nursery with half-an-acre of glass. It specialises in hardy exotic plants, especially palms, bamboos, tree ferns, cycads, yuccas, cordylines, Mediterranean plants and grasses. It lists over 300 species. There are planted-out areas which display hardy palms and some impressive mature trees to admire. Customers are encouraged to browse.

Owned by Martin Gibbons
Size 2ha (5 acres)

Queen Mary's Gardens

INNER CIRCLE, REGENT'S PARK, NW1 4NR

Tel 020 7486 7905
Location In the middle of Regent's Park.
Opening hours Dawn – dusk; daily; all year.
Admission fee Free.

Queen Mary's Gardens are contained within Regent's Park's Inner Circle. Originally a display garden for the Royal Botanic Society (a 19th-century rival to the Royal Horticultural Society; Robert Marnock and William Robinson both worked there), the Japanese garden, the lake and the mound made from the excavations all date from the 1850s. The horticultural interest comes from the excellent herbaceous borders, tender bedding plants, displays of annuals and spring bulbs. Above all, Queen Mary's Gardens are known for their rose gardens, where large beds are planted each with just one cultivar – mainly modern Hybrid Teas and Floribundas, though there are English roses and old-fashioned ones too, often in mixed borders. At one end is a circular catenary of climbing and rambling roses around yet more beds of bright modern roses: a spectacular sight in early June – roses flower earlier in the London parks than anywhere else in England, and are worth a visit at any time after about the middle of May.

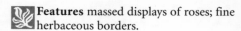**Features** massed displays of roses; fine herbaceous borders.

Owned by Royal Parks Agency

Syon Park

BRENTFORD, TW8 8JF

Tel 020 8560 0883 2 **Fax** 020 8568 0936
Website www.syonpark.co.uk
Location Between Brentford & Isleworth, north bank of Thames.
Opening hours 10.30 am – 5.30 pm, or sunset if earlier; daily except 25 & 26 December; all year.
Admission fee Adults £3.75; Concessions £2.50.

Syon is a wonderful mixture of 18th-century landscape, 19th-century horticultural seriousness, 20th-century plantsmanship and 21st-century theme park. The Great Conservatory was designed by Charles Fowler in the 1820s; the formal terraces followed in the 1830s. But one of the nicest details about Syon is the way the water meadows along the banks of the Thames are still grazed by cows: it creates a unique rural prospect so close to the heart of London. There are fine trees too, the relic of a botanical collection dating back to the 1820s: some, including four species of oak, are record-breakers.

Features spectacular Great Conservatory; woodland garden; mature conifers; good herbaceous borders; fine collection of trees; cacti; ferns; tallest *Catalpa ovata* (22m.) in the British Isles (and fourteen further record trees); Wyevale Garden Centre on site; shop; café.

Owned by The Duke of Northumberland
Number of gardeners 7
Size 16ha (40 acres)
English Heritage Grade I

Royal Botanic Gardens, Kew

KEW, RICHMOND, TW9 3AB

Tel 020 8332 5655
Website www.kew.org
Location Kew Green (parking), tube to Kew
Gardens Underground Station, or train from
Waterloo to Kew Bridge.
Opening hours 9.30 am – 6.30 pm (7.30 pm at
weekends), but closes at 5.30 pm from 9 February
to 26 March and 6 pm from 6 September to
25 October, & at 4.15 pm from 26 October to
8 February 2004; daily; all year except 24 &
25 December.
Admission fee Adults £7.50; Concessions £5.50;
Children free. Subject to review.

Kew Gardens are enormous – the guide book advises people to allow a whole day for their visit – and have one of the largest collections of plants in the world. The emphasis is upon species rather than garden cultivars, but there is an immense amount for gardeners to see and admire and – of course – to learn from. There are seasonal features like the winter garden and historic areas like the Queen's garden behind Kew Palace which was designed in the 1960s as a reconstructed 17th-century garden. Nor should the famous pagoda and Japanese landscape gardens be forgotten. There are also many horticulturally themed gardens. The azalea garden divides azaleas into 12 distinct horticultural groups, e.g. the Ghent hybrids and the Knap Hill hybrids, and arranges them all systematically in historic order. The bamboo garden has over 120 cultivars arranged to maximise the contrast between their forms and leaf shapes. The berberis dell is a unique feature with a comprehensive collection of berberis and mahonia – the tallest is a five-metre specimen of *Berberis lycoides*. Kew has one of the best bluebell woods in the London area, behind Queen Charlotte's cottage. The grass garden has over 550 species and is being added to continuously: although the scientific purpose is to display the diversity and importance of grasses, the garden is arranged ornamentally. The holly walk was laid out in 1874 by Sir Joseph Hooker: the original specimens are therefore over 130 years old and as high as 30m. The collection has over 600 hollies. The juniper collection is the largest in Europe. The lilac garden ('Go down to Kew in lilac time') was renovated in 1993 and has over 100 specimens in ten separate beds. The rhododendron dell (700 plants) includes some unique Kew hybrids as well as hardy species. The rose garden was created in 1923 and is very popular in high summer: it has roses of all types and an area which illustrates the history of roses in cultivation. There is also a rose pergola running through the order beds, which were originally designed as a living library of flowering plants systematically arranged for students of botany. The pinetum has an important collection of conifers and there are many record breakers among the deciduous species at Kew too. The rock garden was rebuilt in the 1980s to include more micro-habitats. It has over 2,500 different plants roughly arranged in geographical areas, e.g. the mountains of Europe, the Mediterranean and Patagonia. The glasshouses also contain a vast collection of plants. The Palm House was built in the 1840s to house tropical trees and shrubs – these include coconuts, bananas, bread-fruit, mangoes and paw-paws. The Princess of Wales Conservatory opened in 1987 and has ten distinct climatic zones ranging from arid to moist tropical: here are such plants as ginger, pineapple and orchids. The Temperate House is set out geographically:

among its most striking plants are proteas from South Africa. In the hot and humid waterlily house are tropical *Nymphaea* and *Victoria cruziana*, as well as such economic plants as rice and lemon grass. The alpine house was opened in 1981 and its systems of refrigeration and ventilation enable Kew to grow plants which would not otherwise survive the damp, mild climate of England, but it will probably be shut for most of 2004. Other glasshouses to visit include the Evolution House, which tells the story of plant evolution over the last 3,500 million years and the unique filmy fern house. There are twice-daily hour-long guided tours which leave from the Guides' Desk, just inside the Victoria Gate Visitors Centre, at 11 am and 2 pm (no extra fee payable). Kew has every imaginable facility for visits by schools, groups, tourists and students of botany. In summer it also has very good bedding-out schemes, but the garden is somewhat bedevilled by Canada geese, which foul the grass, and by aircraft noise.

Features woodland garden; sub-tropical plants; snowdrops; roses of every kind; rock garden; plantsman's collection of plants; herbs; plants under glass; fruit; mature conifers; good herbaceous borders; fine collection of trees; alpine plants; heather gardens; 138 record trees – more than any other garden in the British Isles – including 38 different oaks (*Quercus spp.*); gift & book shop; three restaurants; café.

Owned by Trustees of the Royal Botanic Gardens
Number of gardeners 150
Size 121ha (302 acres)
English Heritage Grade I

NORFOLK

Norfolk has a large number of important historic gardens. Only a few are open to the public, but they include Blickling, Felbrigg, Holkham, Sheringham and the royal gardens at Sandringham – an impressive list. The garden with the finest collection of trees is Ryston Hall, but it is not open to the public. The same is true of Talbot Manor, which was planted from about 1950 onwards by the late Maurice Mason with advice from Sir Harold Hillier. Nevertheless, the National Gardens Scheme does fairly well in Norfolk and the county also has a good number of first-rate nurseries: Peter Beales Roses, Norfolk Lavender, P.W. Plants, Reads Nursery at Hales Hall Gardens and the Romantic Garden Nursery are all of national importance. There are 11 National Collections in the county, including a collection of *Elaeagnus* which is spread among several members of the Norfolk Group of the NCCPG. The Royal Horticultural Society has good links with Norfolk: Easton College near Norwich is a RHS Partner College and there are RHS events at Thorncroft Clematis nursery, while Sandringham House, Fairhaven Woodland & Water Garden and East Ruston Old Vicarage are RHS Free Access gardens. Many people consider that East Ruston Old Vicarage is the most important new garden to have been made in the UK during the last few years. And there is no doubt that both the Dell Garden and Foggy Bottom (now jointly known as Bressingham Gardens) at Bressingham continue to be immensely influential: the Bloom family at Bressingham was largely responsible for the enormous renewal of interest in herbaceous plants from about 1970 onwards.

African Violet & Garden Centre

STATION ROAD, TERRINGTON ST CLEMENT, KING'S LYNN, PE34 4PL

Tel 01553 828374 **Fax** 01553 828376
Website www.africanvioletcentre.ltd.uk
Location 3 miles west of King's Lynn, on A17.
Opening hours 9 am – 5 pm; daily; all year. Opens at 10 am on Sundays. Closed for New Year's Day, Christmas Day & Boxing Day.

Admission fee Free.

This nursery built its reputation on African violets, and its Chelsea exhibits have been memorable. It offers 140+ cultivars and one of the largest collections of *Saintpaulia* species in the UK.

 Features African violets; house-plants; gift shop; café.

Owned by Paul Crake & Mark Leach

Blickling Hall

BLICKLING, NORWICH, NR11 6NF

Tel 01263 738030 **Fax** 01263 731660
Website www.nationaltrust.org.uk
Location 1½ mile north-west of Aylsham on B1354.
Opening hours 10.15 am – 5.15 pm; Wednesday –
Sunday & Bank Holiday Mondays; 20 March to
31 October. Plus Tuesdays in August. 11 am – 4 pm;
Thursday – Sunday; 4 November to 19 December.
Admission fee Adults £4; Children £2.

Blickling is the garden with everything: a
Jacobean mansion, handsomely symmetrical;
an early landscape lay-out (the Doric Temple
was built in about 1735); a pretty orangery by
Samuel Wyatt; a large mid-19th century
parterre, later simplified, with fine yew hedges
and topiary; and 1930s herbaceous plantings
by Norah Lindsay (her masterpiece). The
spring bulbs are magnificent, and there are
sheets of bluebells in the woods, but Blickling
is a garden to visit at all seasons.

Features woodland garden;
rhododendrons & azaleas; good
herbaceous borders; bluebells; herbaceous
borders at peak July/August; National Trust
shop; plant sales in season; restaurant.

Owned by The National Trust
Number of gardeners 5, plus volunteers
Size 20ha (50 acres)
English Heritage Grade II*

Bradenham Hall

BRADENHAM, THETFORD, IP25 7QR

Tel 01362 687243/687279 **Fax** 01362 687669
Website www.bradenhamhall.co.uk
Location West of East Dereham, north of
Bradenham.
Opening hours 2 pm – 5.30 pm; 2nd & 4th
Sundays of month; April to September. Groups at
other times by appointment.
Admission fee Adults £4; Children free.

This is an exceptional plant-lover's garden
for all seasons, made over the last 40 years
in a windy, open position at the top of what
passes in Norfolk for a hill. The first thing
you notice is that the house (early
Georgian) and garden walls are covered
with unusual shrubs, climbers and fruit. The
flower gardens are formally designed and
richly planted within beautiful yew hedges:
formal rose gardens, a paved garden, and
herbaceous and shrub borders. The
arboretum has a remarkable collection of
trees – more than 800 different species and
forms, many of them rare or very rare. All
are labelled. The walled kitchen gardens are
traditionally managed, with vegetables, cut
flowers, mixed borders, and two glasshouses.
In spring, the parkland and arboretum are
filled with daffodils – massed plantings of
more than 90 carefully chosen and graded
cultivars. A delight and an education.

Features roses (mainly old-fashioned);
plantsman's collection of plants;
daffodils; good herbaceous borders; fine
collection of trees; tea-room.

Owned by Chris & Panda Allhusen
Number of gardeners 3
Size 8.3ha (21 acres)

Chanticleer

DEREHAM ROAD, OVINGTON,
WATTON, THETFORD, IP25 6SA

Tel 01953 881194
Location On A1075, 2 miles from Watton on the
Dereham road.
Opening hours 10 am – 4 pm; 12 & 13 June, 7 & 8
August. And groups by appointment.
Admission fee Adults £2; OAPs £1.50; Children free.

Bressingham Gardens

BRESSINGHAM, DISS, IP22 2AB

Tel 01379 688585 **Fax** 01379 688490
Website www.bressinghamgardens.com
Location On A1066, 3 miles west of Diss.
Opening hours 12.30 am – 4.30 pm; Wednesday –
Sunday, plus Bank Holidays; April to October.
Admission fee Not available as we went to press.

Bressingham Gardens combines two gardens made by the Bloom family which were until recently open at different times – Alan Bloom's Dell Garden, and Adrian Bloom's Foggy Bottom. There is no better place to learn about herbaceous plants – what they look like, how they grow and how to place them, than the Dell. This is a six-acre complex of about 50 island beds, which act as a trial ground and conservation resource for the herbaceous and alpine plants (over 5,000 of them) for which Alan Bloom is famous. The new Summer Garden was designed by Adrian Bloom to provide a new and more dramatic entrance to the garden. It has a stunning display of *Crocosmia* and *Miscanthus* cultivars interplanted with other perennials. The Blooms are keen to emphasise that the Dell Garden is not a museum piece but a carefully tended collection of perennials, developing and growing all the time. The same is true of Foggy Bottom, which Adrian Bloom started planting in about 1975 as a garden for year-round seasonal colour and interest. Its centrepiece was his unique collection of conifers, collected from all over the world and tested for English conditions. They were, for many years, the dominant plants in the garden, and he used them to show off the innumerable contrasts of form, colour, texture and shape between different cultivars. Then he began to use them in other plant combinations – with ornamental grasses, perennials and shrubs –

chosen to give a succession of colour, texture and other interest throughout the year. Recently he overhauled the conifer bed and renamed it the 'All Seasons' bed. Some conifers were moved to other parts of the garden: others were heavily pruned. Some overgrown specimens were removed completely to make way for new planting schemes of shrubs, heathers, ornamental grasses and new young conifers. These new plantings are surrounded by an amphitheatre of mature beds. Adrian Bloom has also added a new woodland glade where shade- and moisture-loving plants surround a large pond. The net result is that both parts of Bressingham Gardens continue to be an inspirational source of ideas for the smaller garden.

Features superb herbaceous borders; some alpine plants; beautiful plantings; island beds; plantsman's collection of plants; mature dwarf conifers; refreshments in adjoining plant centre.

Owned by Alan & Adrian Bloom
Number of gardeners 4
Size 4.8ha (12 acres)

Chanticleer is a former 1830s public house, converted to a private dwelling in the 1950s and since extended. The present owners have lived and gardened there for 20 years, originally in just under two acres, but then with three further acres for a small flock of Jacob sheep, Vietnamese pot-bellied pigs, goats, geese, chickens and ducks. The main garden includes a kitchen garden, green-houses, orchard, herb garden and a large wildlife garden with a pond: all are managed organically. Great emphasis is placed on working with nature: the wildlife garden is frequented by birds, insects and small mammals, including breeding water voles. Most native shrubs and trees are represented, as are many wildflowers – including two species of orchids, which have colonised parts of the wildlife area. A small willow plantation supplies materials for hurdle-making. There are demonstrations of how to make compost (including the use of wormeries and liquid compost) during both open weekends.

 Features organic garden of great interest; refreshments.

Owned by Mr & Mrs T. Rands
Number of gardeners owners only
Size 2ha (5 acres)

Corpusty Mill Garden

THE MILL HOUSE, CORPUSTY, NORWICH, NR11 6QB

Tel 01263 587223
Location In middle of village on B1149.
Opening hours Groups by appointment.
Admission fee Adults £5.

Corpusty Mill has been made and developed by Roger Last and his late brother John since the 1965. It is highly architectural in design, and each section is full of ornament. There are many garden buildings or follies,

including a vast flint wall with the heads of Roman emperors, a Gothic arch and window, a grotto (with four chambers), a ruined tower, a classical pavilion and stainless steel spire. The planting is knowledgeable, varied and controlled. Most visitors come away quite amazed by the beauty and ingenuity of what they have seen.

 Features stylish design.

Owned by Roger Last
Number of gardeners owners only
Size 1.6ha (4 acres)

East Lode

NURSERY LANE, HOCKWOLD, THETFORD, IP26 4ND

Tel 01842 827096
Location Down Church Lane in Hockwold, left at iron seat, then first house on right.
Opening hours By arrangement.
Admission fee Adults £2.

This half-acre cottage garden is absolutely full of interest – shrubs, roses, clematis, and many unusual plants – all put together in the cottage style. Mrs Mansey fills it with colour throughout the year: many hellebores in spring, roses and clematis in summer, evergreens and silvers for autumn and winter, and tremendous underplantings of bulbs. There is a small pond, a greenhouse, some scree beds and a conservatory. It is also intended to be a haven for bees, birds and butterflies.

 Features plantsman's garden with many unusual plants; cottagey mix.

Owned by Mrs P. Mansey
Number of gardeners 1
Size 0.2ha (½ acre)

East Ruston Old Vicarage

EAST RUSTON, NORWICH, NR12 9HN

Tel 01692 650432 **Fax** 01692 651246
Website www.e-ruston-oldvicaragegardens.co.uk
Location Turn off A149 near Stalham – signed
Walcott, Bacton, Happisburgh. Left at T-junction.
On right after 2 miles, next to East Ruston church.
Opening hours 2 pm – 5.30 pm; Wednesdays,
Fridays, Saturdays, Sundays & Bank Holidays;
28 March to 30 October.
Admission fee Adults £4; Children £1. RHS
members free in September & October.

This fine modern garden has been conceived on the grand scale. The owners, Graham Robeson and Alan Gray, combine the rare qualities of superb architectural design and exceptional plantsmanship. The house was built by a Surrey architect in 1913 in the Arts and Crafts style, which is uncommon in Norfolk. When the owners started to make their garden in 1988, it sat in an empty field. It was then that they planted the shelter belts, almost all tough evergreens. One of the most exciting things about the garden is to see so many tender exotics growing happily outside – literally thousands of them – which would not have been possible without the shelter belts. This is helped by the garden's location close to the North Sea with its maritime influence. The garden has been designed as a series of 'rooms', getting larger the further you move from the house. There are fine views borrowed from the landscape on two local churches and a whimsical porthole view of Happisburgh lighthouse. The 20 acres feature superb long borders abundantly and richly planted, a box parterre annually bedded out with unusual and original plant combinations, a gravelled forecourt with large groups of *Aeonium* 'Zwartkop' and various echeverias, a sunken garden containing many varieties including a large group of *Lobelia tupa*, and the newly relocated and much extended exotic garden with fabulously bold plantings of palms, bananas, shrubby salvias and many tender exotics which are propagated on the premises. Much thought has gone into the design and preparation of beds for plants. The Mediterranean garden, for example, faces south and has a lot of brickwork and paving to preserve the warmth which plants need to survive through the winter. The beds are heavily mulched with gravel, and the result is that many plants survive which are typical of the Mediterranean *maquis*, the Californian chaparral and Australasia – clouds of yellow Australian mimosa, a very dark blue rosemary from the Mediterranean and *Beschorneria yuccoides* from Mexico. Even more impressive is the newly planted desert wash, made from over 300 tons of flints of varying sizes and covering an acre. It is intended to imitate the Arizona desert where the only rainfall is one of tumultuous thunderstorms every year. The plantings include some great specimens of palm trees, *Trithrinax campestris* from Argentina and *Brahea armata*, the Mexican blue palm, plus many agaves and aloes, some of which were grown from imported seed by the owners. East Ruston also has a pretty no-nonsense vegetable garden, a cutting garden, woodland walks, wildflower meadows, a walled garden and a spectacular corn field, brimming with field poppies, cornflowers and corn marigold. Four RHS special events will take place during 2004: details from 020 7821 3408.

Features a young garden on a large scale; architectural plants; tea-room.

Owned by Graham Robeson & Alan Gray
Size 8ha (20 acres), perhaps a little more

Fairhaven Woodland & Water Garden

SCHOOL ROAD, SOUTH WALSHAM, NORWICH, NR13 6DZ

Tel & Fax 01603 270449
Website www.norfolkbroads.com/fairhaven
Location Follow the brown signs off the A47 on to the B1140.
Opening hours 10 am – 5 pm; daily; all year except 25 December. Closes 9 pm on Wednesdays & Thursdays from May to August.
Admission fee Adults £4; OAPs £3.50; Children £1.50. RHS members free from February to April & in October.

This is a vast woodland garden of naturalised rhododendrons under a canopy of ancient oaks – one vast pollarded specimen known as the King Oak is estimated to be 950 years old. In 1946, Lord Fairhaven laid two fairly narrow paths straight across a section of boggy land where sheets of candelabra primulas flourish in alder woodland. On the drier ground he planted masses of rhododendrons and azaleas among the naturalised *R. ponticum*. The garden is at its loveliest throughout May and June, when the rhododendrons and candelabras are reflected in the still waters of the dykes and private Broad. It is a bit short on follow-up later in the year, though there are effective plantings of hydrangeas, hostas, *Osmunda regalis*, ligularias and gunneras. The snowdrops too are good in February, and the lysichitons in March and April. The garden is managed organically. Many people are more interested in the wildlife and the Broad than the garden, so that even in high season the horticultural visitor may be almost alone in the woodland garden.

Features woodland garden; bluebells; snowdrops; rhododendrons; lilies; candelabra primulas; shop; excellent plant sales area; tea-room.

Owned by Fairhaven Garden Trust
Number of gardeners 3
Size 36ha (90 acres)

Felbrigg Hall

FELBRIGG, NORWICH, NR11 8PR

Tel 01263 837444 **Fax** 01263 837032
Website www.nationaltrust.org.uk
Location Entrance off B1436, signed from A148 & A140.
Opening hours 11 am – 5 pm; Saturday – Wednesday; 23 March to 3 November.
Admission fee Adults £2.60; Children £1.

There are fine trees in the park, but the best bit of Felbrigg is the walled kitchen garden, oriented on a large brick dovecote flanked by Victorian vineries. Fruit trees are trained against the walls (figs, pears, plums) and the garden laid to neatly-grown vegetables with herbaceous borders, ribbon borders and a hot border enclosed by box-edged gravel paths.

Features fruit; good herbaceous borders; National Trust shop; restaurant & tea-room.

Owned by The National Trust
Number of gardeners 3, plus 1 trainee
Size 2.4ha (6 acres)
NCCPG National Collections *Colchicum*
English Heritage Grade II*

Elsing Hall

ELSING, DEREHAM, NR20 3DX

Tel & Fax 01362 637224
Location B1110 to North Tuddenham, then follow
signs.
Opening hours 2 pm – 6 pm; Sundays; June to
September; & by appointment for groups. 20 June
for NGS.
Admission fee Adults £3; Children free.

David and Shirley Cargill bought Elsing
Hall in 1984 and started to plant roses:
their taste is both catholic and voracious.
On the terracing in front of the house are
cultivars as distinct as the shrub rose
'Centenaire de Lourdes' (a great favourite in
France, but all too seldom seen in England),
the lanky purple moss-rose 'William Lobb',
pink 'Fimbriata' whose petals are fringed
like a carnation's, the sumptuous 'Ardoisée
de Lyon', and dainty white 'Katharina
Zeimet'. Now the Cargills grow more than
500 different roses, and the number rises
annually. They have a relaxed approach to
the demands of maintenance, since most
roses flourish on benign neglect and go on
flowering year after year with little or no
attention. The Cargills understand that
there are better ways of passing your time as
a gardener than following the conventional
routines of spraying, pruning and training.
There is no better place than Elsing Hall to
enjoy the wild romantic way of growing
roses. This is liberation gardening. Giant
hogweeds seed around the front door, their
outsize stateliness quite appropriate to the
scale of the gabled hall. The huge grey
thistle *Onopordum nervosum* self-seeds in
the lawn below and is spared by the mower.
But Elsing Hall is much more than a rose
garden. The Cargills are enthusiastic
plantsmen: their garden is a celebration of
the sheer variety of the plant kingdom.
Alongside the moat are bamboos, *Caltha*
polypetala, a patch of *Matteuccia*
struthiopteris under a huge weeping ash,
skunk cabbages, *Ligularia dentata*
'Desdemona', *Gunnera manicata* and *G.*
tinctoria too: all are vigorous plants, lush
growers, nudging each other for space.
Some of their more recent additions – the
garden is expanding all the time – include
an avenue of ginkgos, a collection of
willows, a small arboretum of trees chosen
for their coloured bark, a formal garden
with 64 yew pyramids and an old church
steeple in the middle, a lime tunnel, and an
autumn garden inspired by Piet Oudolf's
use of autumn colour in his garden in
Holland. Their latest project is a small
'theatre garden' with arches of variegated
holly.

Features roses (mainly old-fashioned);
fruit; fine collection of trees; kitchen
garden; otters.

Owned by Mr & Mrs D.H. Cargill
Number of gardeners 1

Hales Hall Gardens & Reads Nursery

HALES HALL, LODDON, NR14 6QW

Tel 01508 548395 **Fax** 01508 548040
Website www.readsnursery.co.uk
Location Off A146, 1 mile south of Loddon.
Opening hours 10 am – 5 pm (4 pm in winter);
Monday – Saturday; all year. Plus 11 am – 4 pm on
Sundays from April to October.
Admission fee Garden £1.50; Nursery free.

This important and long-established family
nursery specialises in citrus fruit-trees and
conservatory plants. Its extensive list of
Citrus cultivars is based upon the centuries-
old collection made by Rivers of
Sawbridgeworth. Rivers were famous fruit-
breeders in the 19th century, and their citrus
trees supplied the scions needed to start the
California fruit industry. Reads acquired
their stock when Rivers closed in 1983. They
also grow and sell over 70 different grape
cultivars, including many more English-
raised vines than any other nursery: this is
the place to find such Victorian delicacies as
'Lady Downe's Seedling' and 'Mrs Pince's
Black Muscat'. Their list of figs is equally
extensive, and unparalleled among UK
nurserymen: 'Goutte d'Or', 'Malcolm's
Giant' and 'White Ischia' are among their
specialities. But they also stock a large
number of proper traditional conservatory
plants – abutilons, bougainvilleas,
brugmansias, gardenias, jasmines,
passionflowers, sparmannias and hundreds
more. In the adjoining two-acre garden are
the moated remains of a mediaeval hall,
planted with topiary, a 'potted' fruit
orchard, a *potager*, a vegetable garden and a
plantsman's collection of shrubs, herbaceous
plants and bulbs.

Features conservatory plants; fruit;
teas by arrangement for groups.

Owned by The Read Family
Number of gardeners 1
Size 0.8ha (2 acres)
NCCPG National Collections *Citrus*; *Ficus*; *Vitis
vinifera* (grapes)

Hoecroft Plants

SEVERALS GRANGE, HOLT ROAD,
WOOD NORTON, DEREHAM, NR20 5BL

Tel & Fax 01362 684206
Website www.hoecroft.co.uk
Location 2 miles north of Guist on B1110 (not in
West Norton village).
Opening hours 10 am – 4 pm; Thursday – Sunday;
April to September. On 15 August for NGS.

Hoecroft is a small but well-known
specialist nursery which began by
concentrating upon variegated and coloured
foliage plants. These range from the smallest
alpines to large shrubs. Perhaps more
prominent now is its list of ornamental
grasses, rushes, sedges and bamboos: it
offers over 250 different cultivars, which
may be seen in the attached display garden.

Features grasses; mixed borders.

Owned by Jane Lister

Holkham Hall

HOLKHAM, WELLS-NEXT-THE-SEA,
NR23 1AB

Tel 01328 710227 **Fax** 01328 711707
Website www.holkham.co.uk
Location Off A149, 2 miles west of Wells.
Opening hours 1 pm – 5 pm; daily, except
Saturdays, Sundays & Bank Holiday Mondays; 24
May to 29 September. Park open from 9 am; every
day except Christmas Day.
Admission fee Park free.

Holkham is a big landscape garden, worked on by Kent, Brown and Repton. Formal terraces were added in the 1850s. The garden centre known as Holkham Nursery Gardens is in the 18th-century walled garden and has several demonstration gardens (including areas for herbs, roses and perennials) along with a recently restored fig house. The website is excellent.

 Features gift shop; garden centre; refreshments.

Owned by The Earl of Leicester
Number of gardeners 3
English Heritage Grade I

Hoveton Hall

WROXHAM, NORWICH, NR12 8RJ

Tel 01603 782798 **Fax** 01603 784564
Location 9 miles from Norwich: brown tourist signs from A1151.
Opening hours 11 am to 5.30 pm; Wednesdays, Fridays, Sundays & Bank Holiday Mondays; Easter to 22 September. Also open on Thursdays in May.
Admission fee Adults £3.75; Wheelchair-bound £2; Children £1.

The gardens are laid out around a series of streams, with beautiful waterside plantings, gunneras and candelabra primulas. Rhododendrons and azaleas fill the woodland gardens. Daffodils are a spring feature, and the hydrangeas are impressive later in the year. The walled garden, built as late as 1936, is set out for growing fruit and vegetables in the traditional way, with fine herbaceous borders too. There is a herb garden, a knot garden and a moon-gate in the shape of a spider's web.

 Features rhododendrons & azaleas; daffodils; good herbaceous borders; water garden; light lunches & teas.

Owned by Mr & Mrs Andrew Buxton
Number of gardeners 3
Size 6ha (15 acres)

Lynford Arboretum

MUNFORD, THETFORD, IP26 5HW

Tel 01842 810271
Location Turn right off A1065 just north of Munford.
Opening hours Dawn – dusk; daily; all year.
Admission fee Free.

The Lynford Arboretum was started in 1947 by students at the Forester Training School who at that time occupied nearby Lynford Hall. They planted about 100 species of conifers and broadleaves, some in forestry plots but mostly as individual specimens within the parkland and policies surrounding the house. The soil is thin and sandy, but some of those original plantings are already handsome specimens, including a *Nothofagus obliqua* and a *Pinus banksiana* each 20m tall. Rather simply maintained by the Forestry Commission, the arboretum has considerable potential for development. Lynford Hall is now an hotel: the extensive formal garden (rather gone back) was laid out by William Burn in the 1860s and was famous for its bedding until 1914. Beyond is a curving lake. Rather surprisingly, the Forestry Commission does not permit dogs in the arboretum.

 Features trees, deciduous & evergreen.

Owned by Forestry Agency

Mannington Gardens

MANNINGTON HALL, NORWICH,
NR11 7BB

Tel 01263 584175 **Fax** 01263 761214
Website www.manningtongardens.co.uk
Location Signed from B1149 at Saxthorpe.
Opening hours 12 noon – 5 pm; Sundays; May –
September. And 11 am – 5 pm; Wednesday –
Friday; June – August.
Admission fee Adults £3; Concessions £2.50;
Children free.

The gardens at Mannington embrace a
moated house, the ruins of Mannington
church, two lakes (recently landscaped), a
scented garden, an arboretum of native
trees, genuine wildflower meadows and
handsome herbaceous borders. But the best
part is the Heritage Rose Garden, made in
association with Peter Beales, where
thousands of old-fashioned roses are
planted to illustrate the history of roses in
cultivation. The developments are
represented by beds which display roses
according to their periods, from the 15th
century up to today. New last year (2003)
was a Sensory Garden, whose plants
stimulate sight, sound, touch and hearing.

Features roses (mainly old-fashioned
& climbers); natural surroundings;
colour borders; lakes; wildflowers; roses for
sale; light refreshments, teas.

Owned by Lord Walpole
Number of gardeners 3½
Size 8ha (20 acres)
English Heritage Grade II

Oxburgh Hall

OXBOROUGH, KING'S LYNN, PE33 9PS

Tel 01366 328258 **Fax** 01366 328066
Website www.nationaltrust.org.uk
Location 7 miles south-west of Swaffham on Stoke
Ferry road.
Opening hours 11 am – 4 pm; Saturdays &
Sundays; 3 January to 14 March and 13 November to
19 December. 11 am – 5.30 pm; Saturday –
Wednesday; 20 March to 7 November. Daily in August.
Admission fee Adults £2.90; Children £1.45.

The baroque 19th-century parterre has been
replanted by the National Trust with such
herbs as rue and cineraria making
permanent companions for annuals and
bedding plants. Good fruit trees in the
walled garden, especially medlars and
quinces. Not a great garden, but a good one.

Features roses (mainly modern); good
herbaceous borders; French-style
parterre; trained fruit trees; woodland
walks; vegetable garden; gift shop; licensed
restaurant.

Owned by The National Trust
Number of gardeners 2, plus volunteers
Size 6.2ha (15½ acres)
English Heritage Grade II

P.W. Plants

SUNNYSIDE, HEATH ROAD,
KENNINGHALL, NR16 2DS

Tel & Fax 01953 888212
Website www.hardybamboo.com
Location South-west of Norwich, between
Kenninghall & North Lopham.
Opening hours 9 am – 5 pm; Fridays; all year. Plus
the last Saturday of the month.
Admission fee Free.

This enterprising nursery offers a wide range of plants chosen for their general garden-worthiness, interesting foliage and shape. It is perhaps best known for its bamboos, which have won the nursery many medals at RHS shows, but P.W. Plants also stock grasses, shrubs, perennials and climbers. Most can be seen growing in the display gardens.

 Features bamboos.

Owned by Paul Whittaker
Number of gardeners 1
Size 0.6ha (1½ acres)

Peter Beales Roses

LONDON ROAD, ATTLEBOROUGH, NR17 1AY

Tel 01953 454707 **Fax** 01953 456845
Website www.classicroses.co.uk
Location 2 miles south of Attleborough: leave A11 at Breckland Lodge. Follow Tourist Board signs.
Opening hours 9 am – 5 pm (4 pm in January); Monday – Saturday. 10 am – 4 pm; Sundays & Bank Holidays.
Admission fee Free.

There is a small display garden attached to this well-known rose nursery and latest reports say that it is well maintained. A good range of older and classic roses is offered for sale, both at the nursery and from its mail-order catalogue and website, which list over 1,300 species and cultivars, many not available elsewhere in the United Kingdom.

 Features roses (mainly old-fashioned); garden sundries & gift shop; licensed bistro.

Owned by Peter Beales
Number of gardeners 2
Size 1ha (2½ acres)
NCCPG National Collections *Rosa* (species)

Plantation Garden

4 EARLHAM ROAD, NORWICH, NR2 3DB

Tel 01603 455223/621868 **Fax** 01603 631166
Website www.plantationgarden.co.uk
Location Between The Beeches Hotel and the Roman Catholic Cathedral.
Opening hours 9 am – 6 pm (or dusk, if earlier); daily; all year. On 28 March & 12 September for NGS. Summer Fête on 18 July.
Admission fee Adults £2; Children free. Honesty box when unattended. On the three special days: Adults £3; Children £1.

The Plantation Garden was made in an abandoned chalk quarry by Henry Trevor, a successful Norwich businessman, between around 1856 until his death in 1897. In the ensuing years the garden passed through various hands until, in 1980, it was totally overgrown, abandoned and forgotten. In that year it was re-discovered and the Plantation Garden Preservation Trust formed to save and restore the garden. The area, nearly 3 acres in all, contains many features including woodland walkways, flower beds, lawns, a gothic fountain, Italianate terrace, 'Mediaeval' terrace wall, rustic bridge and a new reconstruction of the original thatched summerhouse. There are many unique aspects to this very idiosyncratic garden making it a haven of peace and tranquillity – a refuge from the hurly-burly of modern life and a glimpse into a bygone age. Sir Roy Strong is patron of the Trust and points out that the garden is 'something of a rarity, for in most cases it is usually only the grandest of gardens which survive from earlier periods'. The original house, designed by Edward Boardman for Henry Trevor, is now part of Beeches Hotel.

Features historic Victorian suburban garden undergoing restoration; tea & cakes on Sunday afternoons, May to September.

Owned by The Plantation Garden Preservation Trust
Number of gardeners 1 part-time, plus volunteers
Size 1.2ha (3 acres) approx.
English Heritage Grade II

Raveningham Hall Gardens

RAVENINGHAM, NORWICH, NR14 6NS

Tel 01508 548480 **Fax** 01508 548958
Website www.raveningham.com
Location Signed off A146 at Hales.
Opening hours 2 pm – 5 pm; 11 & 12 April; 2, 3, 30 & 31 May; 13 & 14 June; 29 & 30 August.
Admission fee Adults £2.50; OAPs £2; Children free.

The house at Raveningham is partly Georgian and partly 20th-century: the 14th-century church of St Andrew near the house is an integral part of the landscape. Both are set in a splendid 18th-century park and enhanced by 19th-century tree plantings. Despite all this history, the main attraction now is the modern plantings. These were largely the work of Priscilla, Lady Bacon, who collected rare plants and arranged them beautifully in areas like the long herbaceous border. She was also a keen dendrologist and planted the young arboretum. In the working walled garden (very pretty) is a recently restored Victorian glasshouse. Outside the walled garden are an orchard and herb garden. A new lake has been made in the park, and there are contemporary sculptures by the present owner's wife throughout.

Features roses (mainly modern); good herbaceous borders; fine collection of trees; splendid eighteenth-century walled garden and Victorian glasshouses.

Owned by Sir Nicholas Bacon Bt.
Number of gardeners 3
Size 2ha (5 acres)
English Heritage Grade II

The Romantic Garden Nursery

SWANNINGTON, NORWICH, NR9 5NW

Tel 01603 261488 **Fax** 01603 864231
Website www.romantic-garden-nursery.co.uk
Location 7 miles north-west of Norwich.
Opening hours 10 am – 5 pm; Wednesdays, Fridays, Saturdays & Bank Holidays.
Admission fee Free.

The Romantic Garden Nursery sells topiary: ornamental standards, bobbles and pyramids in *Cupressus* and *Ilex*, as well as box in animal and other shapes. It is a specialist nursery holding one of the largest selections of topiary and ornamental standards in the country. It offers topiary packages too – these include a layout together with the necessary plants – and a range of wire frames for growing and shaping your own topiary. Also available are large specimens of conservatory plants and a 'plant hire' service, borrowing topiary and specimen plants for special occasions.

Owned by John Powles

Sandringham House

SANDRINGHAM, KING'S LYNN, PE35 6EN

Tel 01553 772675 **Fax** 01485 541571
Website www.sandringhamestate.co.uk
Location Signed from A148.
Opening hours 10.30 am – 5 pm (4 pm in October); daily; 10 April to 23 July & 1 August to 31 October.
Admission fee Adults £4.50; OAPs £3.50; Children £2.50. RHS members free.

The best of the royal gardens. The woodland and lakes are rich with ornamental plantings. The splendid herbaceous borders were designed by Eric Savill and the North Garden by Geoffrey Jellicoe, but it is the scale of it all that most impresses, and the grandeur too.

 Features good herbaceous borders; rhododendrons; azaleas; maples; hydrangeas; gift shop; restaurant & tearooms.

Owned by H.M. The Queen
Number of gardeners 8
Size 24ha (60 acres)
English Heritage Grade II*

Sheringham Park

SHERINGHAM, NR26 8TB

Tel & Fax 01263 823778
Website www.nationaltrust.org.uk
Location Junction of A148 & B1157.
Opening hours Dawn – dusk; daily; all year.
Admission fee Cars £2.80.

This is one of the best Repton landscapes to have survived the last 200 years, but it was also fleshed out with a great 20th-century collection of rhododendrons. The elegant classical temple was built in 1975 to a design by Repton. Recent clearing and replanting have opened up the rhododendron woods very successfully.

Features woodland garden; mature conifers; rhododendrons; refreshments.

Owned by The National Trust
Number of gardeners 1
Size 20ha (50 acres)
English Heritage Grade II*

Stow Hall

STOW BARDOLPH, KING'S LYNN, PE34 3HU

Tel 01366 383194
Location 2 miles north of Downham Market, off A10.
Opening hours 2 pm – 5 pm; 20 June. And by appointment.
Admission fee Adults £3; Children free.

Although the Hares have lived here for 450 years, the gardens at Stow Hall are largely modern. Little remains of earlier gardens except for their outline and the magnificent, mature trees. These include London plane trees, cedars of Lebanon and vast beeches. The outbuildings, stables and walled gardens are covered in climbing roses and tender plants like *Azara microphylla*. There is a working kitchen garden, and a young collection of old apple cultivars. Old-fashioned roses are everywhere.

Features roses; kitchen garden; plant stall; home-made teas.

Owned by Lady Rose Hare
Number of gardeners 1½
Size 8ha (20 acres)

Thorncroft Clematis Nursery

THE LINGS, REYMERSTON, NORWICH, NR9 4QG

Tel 01953 850407 **Fax** 01953 851788
Website www.thorncroft.co.uk
Location Between Dereham & Wymondham on B1135.
Opening hours 10 am – 4 pm; Tuesday – Saturday; March to October. Plus Bank Holiday Mondays.
Admission fee Free.

(P) (WC) (&) (♨)

This family-run specialist nursery began as a hobby and has now developed into a substantial business. In the display garden attached to the nursery, the owners have set out some of the many ways that clematis may be grown – in borders and island beds, over shrub roses, through ornamental trees and in containers. There is also a formal sunken garden with clipped box hedges and classical obelisks (covered by yet more clematis, and roses). The nursery does not stock all clematis cultivars, but prefers to list those it regards as best, selected for such qualities as their length of flowering, colour, form, quantity of bloom, strength of growth and so on. These amount to some 300+ cultivars, including many new introductions from around the world. It will be hosting two RHS special events during 2004: details from 020 7821 3408.

Owned by Ruth & Jonathan Gooch

NORTHAMPTONSHIRE

Despite its industrial importance and its proximity to London, Northamptonshire is still a county of large estates. Three of the four Grade I historic gardens are open to the public (Althorp, Boughton House and Castle Ashby), while the fourth (Drayton) is occasionally open to groups from organisations like the Garden History Society. Althorp and Boughton also have good arboreta, each with a few champion trees. The National Gardens Scheme does well in Northamptonshire: it is particularly successful in persuading groups of gardens, as many as eight or nine in a village, to open together on the same day. It is therefore something of a paradox that there appear to be comparatively few nurseries in the county and only two National Collections. On the other hand, its RHS Free Access garden – Cottesbrooke – is a modern classic, an historic landscape with a really good horticultural garden inserted into it.

Althorp

ALTHORP, NORTHAMPTON, NN7 4HQ

Tel 01604 770107 **Fax** 01604 770042
Website www.althorp.com
Location Signed from M1, Jct 16.
Opening hours Not yet available.
Admission fee Adults £10.50; OAPs £8.50; Children £5.50 for tickets bought in advance from 0870 167 9000. Adults £11.50; OAPs £9.50; Children £5.50 on the gate. (2003 prices).

Althorp is interesting more for its ex-royal associations than as a great garden. However, it is said to be undergoing some improvement under the direction of Dan Pearson. The 19th-century formal gardens are impressive and the traditional parkland deeply pastoral. In the 19th-century arboretum are some fine mature trees, including a record-breaking Santa Lucia fir (*Abies bracteata*) over 30m high.

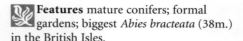

Features mature conifers; formal gardens; biggest *Abies bracteata* (38m.) in the British Isles.

Owned by Earl Spencer
English Heritage Grade I

Boughton House

KETTERING, NN14 1BJ

Tel 01536 515731 **Fax** 01536 417255
Website www.boughtonhouse.org.uk
Location A43, three miles north of Kettering, signed through Geddington.
Opening hours 1 pm – 5 pm; Saturday – Thursday; 1 May to 1 September. Plus Fridays in August.
Admission fee Adults £1.50; OAPs & Children £1.

Boughton has a seriously important landscaped park (350 acres – 140ha) dating from the early 18th century. The lay-out is intact, and some of the plantings too – one of the lime avenues was planted in 1715. The original landscaping features have been purposefully restored over the last 20 years or so: rides, avenues, *allées*, lakes, canals and prospects. There is little of horticultural interest, but the sense of history is strongly felt.

 Features roses (mainly modern); good herbaceous borders; good website; current holder of Sandford Award; shop; plant centre in walled kitchen garden; tearooms (weekends only; daily in August).

Owned by The Duke & Duchess of Buccleuch & The Living Landscape Trust
Number of gardeners 5
Size 8ha (20 acres) garden; 150ha park
English Heritage Grade I

Canons Ashby House

DAVENTRY, NN11 3SD

Tel 01327 861900 **Fax** 01327 861909
Website www.nationaltrust.org.uk
Location Signed from A5 & A422.
Opening hours 11 am – 5.30 pm (4.30 pm in October & November); Saturday – Wednesday; 22 March to 3 November. Plus 11 am – 3 pm; Saturdays & Sundays; 6 November to 19 December.
Admission fee Adults £2 (garden only).

Canons Ashby is a rare survivor among gardens. The Drydens, who owned it, never really took to the landscape movement. The early 18th-century lay-out is intact and has been carefully restored by the National Trust. The terraces below the house (*very* pretty) are planted with clipped Portugal laurel (*Prunus lusitanica*) and period fruit trees. A place to contemplate old Tory values.

 Features topiary; fruit; good herbaceous borders; light lunches & teas.

Owned by The National Trust
Number of gardeners 2
Size 1.4ha (3½ acres)
English Heritage Grade II*

Castle Ashby Gardens

CASTLE ASHBY, NORTHAMPTON, NN7 1LQ

Tel & Fax 01604 696187
Website www.castleashby.co.uk
Location Off A428 between Northampton & Bedford.
Opening hours 10 am – dusk; daily; all year. Closes at 4.30 pm from October to March.
Admission fee Adults £2.50; OAPs & Children £1.50.

Much thought and money has recently been spent on restoring the gardens at Castle Ashby. The Italian formal gardens were among the first to be renewed, and the arboretum has been restocked. There are stylish terraces, an orangery and greenhouses built by Sir Matthew Digby Wyatt in the 1860s but perhaps the best thing about Castle Ashby is the park – 200 acres of it, designed by Capability Brown.

 Features topiary; fine collection of trees; gift shops; refreshments.

Owned by Marquess of Northampton
Number of gardeners 5
Size 8ha (20 acres)
English Heritage Grade I

Coton Manor

GUILSBOROUGH, NN6 8RQ

Tel 01604 740219 Fax 01604 740838
Website www.cotonmanor.co.uk
Location Signed from A5199 (formerly A50) & A428.
Opening hours 12 noon – 5.30 pm; Tuesday –
Saturday & Bank Holiday weekends; April to
September. Plus Sundays in April & May.
Admission fee Adults £4; OAPs £3.50; Children £2.

The Pasley-Tylers have lived at Coton since
the 1920s, and every generation has left its
mark upon the garden. Among the best
features are a rose garden, a herb garden, a
woodland garden, colour plantings
(including a wonderful crimson and pink
border), a Mediterranean bank, a five-acre
bluebell wood, an apple orchard with 80
English cultivars, and a wildflower meadow.
Water is everywhere: pools, streams and
ponds support hostas, primulas and the
black-and-yellow flowers of *Kirengeshoma
palmata*. There are surprises too: one might
suppose that the sweet-scented
Trachelospermum asiaticum and long-
flowering *Fremontodendron californicum*
were too tender for Northamptonshire, but
they both grow against the walls of the
house. Recent plantings include a herb
garden and a rose garden with pink 'Mary
Rose' and white 'Winchester Cathedral'. The
whole garden comes together nicely because
the plants are chosen for their overall
contribution as well as their intrinsic merits.
The standard of maintenance is excellent,
while the presence of a few ornamental
birds adds quite another dimension to a
visit.

Features roses (mainly old cultivars);
good herbaceous borders; bluebells;
waterfowl; lots of pots; good garden
nursery; home produce & gifts; excellent
small nursery; light lunches & teas.

Owned by Ian Pasley-Tyler
Number of gardeners 3
Size 4ha (10 acres)

Cottesbrooke Hall

NORTHAMPTON, NN6 8PF

Tel 01604 505808 Fax 01604 505619
Website www.cottesbrookehall.co.uk
Location 10 miles north of Northampton.
Opening hours 2 pm – 5.30 pm; Thursdays; 8 May
to 30 September. Plus Wednesdays in May & June,
3 & 31 May & 30 August.
Admission fee Garden only: Adults £4; Children
£2. RHS members free.

Cottesbrooke is the garden with everything: a
two-mile drive, majestic parkland, a classical
bridge, a fabulously pretty house, an 18th-
century park, lakes, waterfalls, bluebell
woods, rhododendrons, acres of daffodils, 27
cultivars of naturalised snowdrops, half-a-
dozen garden rooms, Scheemaker's statues
from Stowe, an armillary garden, pergolas,
allées, 300-year old cedars, new developments
every year, immaculate maintenance, plants
a-plenty, and the signatures of Geoffrey
Jellicoe and Sylvia Crowe among the
designers who have helped to develop it. And
free entry for RHS members.

Features roses (mainly old-fashioned);
good herbaceous borders; exceptionally
harmonious design; thoughtful plantings;
water gardens; wild gardens; HHA/Christie's
Garden of the Year in 2000; tea/coffee, cold
drinks & home-made cakes.

Owned by Mr & Mrs A. R. Macdonald-Buchanan
Number of gardeners 6
English Heritage Grade II

Holdenby House Gardens

HOLDENBY, NORTHAMPTON, NN6 8DJ

Tel 01604 770074 **Fax** 01604 770962
Website www.holdenby.com
Location 6 miles north-west of Northampton, off A5199 or A428.
Opening hours 1 pm – 5 pm; Sunday – Friday; July & August. Plus Sundays & Bank Holiday Mondays from April to September. Closes at 6 pm on Bank Holiday Sundays & Mondays.
Admission fee Adults £4.50; OAPs £4; Children £3. A small supplement may be payable for Special Events.

The outlines of the garden at Holdenby are Elizabethan: a bowling alley, some parterres and terraces which were built in 1580 to impress Queen Elizabeth on one of her progresses through England. They explain why Holdenby is so highly regarded as an historical garden. What we see now is modern and pretty. The Elizabethan-style garden was planted by Rosemary Verey, using only those plants which were available in 1580. Rupert Golby planted the 'fragrant border' and there is a charming 'silver border' made to display the owners' ever-growing collection of silver- and grey-leaved plants.

Features roses (mainly old-fashioned); herbs; good herbaceous borders; Elizabethan-style garden; fragrant and silver borders; kitchen garden; current holder of Sandford Award; souvenirs and crafts for sale; tea-room in original Victorian kitchen.

Owned by Mr & Mrs James Lowther
Number of gardeners 2
Size 6ha (15 acres)
English Heritage Grade II*

Kelmarsh Hall

NORTHAMPTON, NN6 9LU

Tel 01604 686543 **Fax** 01604 686437
Website www.kelmarsh.com
Location On A508 at crossroads in Kelmarsh.
Opening hours 2 pm – 5 pm; Monday – Thursday, plus Sundays & Bank Holiday Mondays; 11 April to 30 September.
Admission fee Adults £3.50; Concessions £3; Children £2.

Kelmarsh is a handsome Palladian house: it looks out over a formal terrace to formalised parkland, designed by Geoffrey Jellicoe in 1936. The view extends across a meadow lined with horse chestnuts to a lake before wilder, open semi-parkland carries the eye to the horizon. Most of the horticultural interest is off to the side, around the outside of a triangular walled garden. First come lumpy box hedges, pleached limes and a pretty sunken garden, designed as a quincunx and planted with white and scented flowers. Further on, *Tropaeolum speciosum* clambers through the hedges which flank a sequence of narrow, intimate beds, designed by Nancy Lancaster with help from Norah Lindsay. Some of the yew hedges have been breached by cutting the yew trees back to the trunks and letting them grow into curious hump-backed shapes – a very effective and unique feature of the garden. At the furthest extremity, the narrow path bursts out into a fan-shaped old-fashioned rose garden, recently re-made, with a splendid view of the parish church across parkland. On the way back (outside the walled garden again) is the long border, another Lancaster-Lindsay collaboration, which is currently being restored and replanted. This is a fine garden, which will be interesting to watch as it develops in years to come. A Heritage Lottery grant has funded the restoration of the vinery and back sheds, which means that the walled garden with its cut flower borders is now fully accessible.

 Features spring bulbs; old hedges; lots of recent restoration; teas.

Owned by The Kelmarsh Trust
Number of gardeners 3
Size 5.6ha (14 acres)

The Menagerie

NEWPORT PAGNELL ROAD, HORTON, NN7 2BX

Tel & Fax 01604 870957
Location One mile south of Horton on the B526.
Opening hours 2 pm – 5 pm; Mondays & Thursdays; May to September. Plus 2 pm – 6 pm on the last Sunday of those months.
Admission fee Adults £3.50; Children £1.50.

This folly, built in 1750 for the 2nd Earl of Halifax by Thomas Wright of Durham, stands above Grade II listed parkland. Derelict until 1975 – it was originally intended as a dining house with an attached zoo – it was completely restored by the architectural historian Gervase Jackson-Stops. The garden was conceived and laid out in the 1980s in a goosefoot pattern, with a central lime avenue leading to a spiral mount and obelisk, and two hornbeam-lined *allées* leading to restored 18th-century pools with fountains. The two thatched arbours are recent, one triangular and gothic, the other round and classical (now used as a chapel). Orpheus plays to the animals in the shell grotto beneath the house. The rose garden was designed by Vernon Russell-Smith and the exotic bog garden was by Jinny Blom in the spirit of Ian Kirby's original design. This is currently being expanded to reach the new 500 sq.m walled garden with its opulent central fountain. The plantings are bold and romantic. The nursery was designed by Charles Morris.

 Features good modern design; inventive garden follies; pretty plantings.

Owned by Alexander Myers
Number of gardeners 2
Size 1.6ha (4 acres)

Old Rectory

SUDBOROUGH, NN14 3BX

Tel 01832 733247 **Fax** 01832 733832
Website www.oldrectorygardens.co.uk
Location A14, exit 12. In village centre, by church, off A6116.
Opening hours 10 am to 4 pm; Tuesdays; April to September. Plus Saturdays at Easter & Spring Bank Holiday weekends. Groups welcome at other times by appointment.
Admission fee Adults £3.50; Children free.

This immaculately maintained modern garden has been made around a handsome Georgian rectory with a bit of advice from Rosemary Verey and Rupert Golby. In front of the house, on the edge of the lawn, is a handsome and ancient *Robinia pseudoacacia*: everything else is fairly recent and extremely well grown. The garden is thickly and thoughtfully planted so that every season is rich in interest. Few of the plants are rare, but all are well chosen – some for their flowers, some for their foliage and others because they look good in mixed groups. Roses are much in evidence throughout the garden and in a dedicated rose garden. The best feature is an extensive and very pretty *potager*, which has an infinite number of beds edged in *Ilex crenata* (a good replacement for diseased box) and fairly narrow brick paths between them. Clematis and roses cover the framework of a tunnel: they are joined, in season, by ornamental gourds which are encouraged to grow up the same structure. The fruit trees are trained in many different ways and good use is made of flowers in pots to ensure that the *potager* has colour at all seasons.

 Features roses (ancient & modern); herbs; fruit; good herbaceous borders; handsome new *potager*; tea, coffee & biscuits.

Owned by Mr & Mrs A.P. Huntington
Number of gardeners 2
Size 1.2ha (3 acres)

Rockingham Castle

MARKET HARBOROUGH, LE16 8TH

Tel 01586 770240 **Fax** 01586 771692
Website www.rockinghamcastle.com
Location 2 miles north of Corby on A6003.
Opening hours 12 noon – 5 pm; Sundays & Bank Holiday Mondays; April to September. Plus Tuesdays & Thursdays in July & August.
Admission fee £4.50.

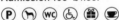

Rockingham has centuries of garden history in its layout: the park was landscaped in the 18th century but goes back to the 13th century as a deer park. The formal circular rose garden on the site of the old keep was added in the 19th century: it is surrounded by a billowing yew hedge 400 years old. The wild garden in a ravine was replanted 20 years ago as a mini-arboretum: all the modern plantings are very effective.

 Features roses (mainly old-fashioned); good herbaceous borders; fine collection of trees; gift shop; tea-room.

Owned by James Saunders Watson
Number of gardeners 3
Size 5ha (12½ acres)
English Heritage Grade II*

Sulgrave Manor

SULGRAVE, BANBURY, OX17 2SD

Tel 01295 760205 **Fax** 01295 768056
Website www.sulgravemanor.org.uk
Location 7 miles from Banbury.
Opening hours 2 pm – 5.30 pm; 1 April to 31 October. Closed Mondays & Fridays except Bank Holidays.
Admission fee Adults £5; Children £2.50. But Adults £6.50; Children £3.25 for special events.

There are two reasons for visiting Sulgrave. The first is that it belonged to George Washington's family or, at least, to his ancestors. This places the Great American firmly among the English minor gentry. The second is that, after the estate was underwritten by the Colonial Dames in 1924, Sir Reginald Blomfield was called in to design a period garden. In his day, Blomfield was one of England's foremost architect-designers, and the garden he made for Sulgrave is formally laid out in a simple, 17th-century style, to complement the old house. The plantings are suitably olde worlde. The Herb Society moved its headquarters to Sulgrave in 2001 and has planted work a herb garden which is full of interest but rather spoils the spirit of the place.

 Features herbs; tea-room.

Owned by Sulgrave Manor Board
Number of gardeners 2
Size 2ha (5 acres)
English Heritage Grade II

NORTHUMBERLAND AND TYNE & WEAR

Northumberland and Tyne & Wear are two sides of the same historical phenomenon: men made their fortunes in Newcastle or Sunderland, both now in Tyne & Wear, and then moved out to build houses and plant gardens in Northumberland. Belsay, Cragside and Lindisfarne all owe their gardens to this social pattern. Belsay is a Grade I garden: the only other one in Northumberland is Alnwick, where the Duchess of Northumberland is building a spectacular new water garden. The greatest 19th-century garden in Northumberland is Cragside, which now has a collection of champion conifers. There are record-breakers too at Alnwick, and a good arboretum at Howick, where many new plantings have also been made in recent years. The National Gardens Scheme does not have a large portfolio of gardens in Northumberland and Tyne & Wear, but there are several first-rate nurseries in the two counties, including Halls of Heddon, Herterton House and Hexham Herbs. The real interests of ordinary gardeners in Northumberland and Tyne & Wear are quite different: alpines and leeks. Both the Alpine Garden Society and the Scottish Rock Garden Club are well supported here, while the National Pot Leek Society could be described as a uniquely Geordie success story.

The Alnwick Garden

DENWICK LANE, ALNWICK, NE66 1YU

Tel 01665 511350 **Fax** 01665 511351
Website www.alnwickgarden.com
Location Signed in Alnwick & from A1.
Opening hours 10 am – 5 pm (later in summer); daily; all year. Closed Christmas Day.
Admission fee Adults £4; Concessions £3.75; Children free.

The Duchess of Northumberland is the driving force behind this imaginative new garden, and the gifted Jacques Wirtz is its designer. First open to the public in 2001, it is a continuing project, but the main feature is already impressive – a grand water cascade flanked by hornbeam tunnels and ending in fountains. At the top, you enter the Ornamental Garden, a place of box-lined paths, pleached apples, old roses and mixed plantings, as dreamily English as the cascade is exotic. The new Rose Garden has pergolas, climbers, shrub roses and mixed plantings – very beautiful. More new developments are planned for 2004.

Features grand cascade; new gardens; shop; garden café.

Owned by Alnwick Garden Enterprises
Number of gardeners 7
Size 16ha (40 acres) including 4.8ha (12 acres) of walled garden

Bede's World Herb Garden

BEDE'S WORLD, CHURCH BANK, JARROW, NE32 3DY

Tel 0191 489 2106 **Fax** 0191 428 2361
Website www.bedesworld.co.uk
Location Signed from A185 & A19.
Opening hours 10.30 am – 5 .30 pm; daily; all year. Opens 12 noon on Sundays. Closes 4.30 pm from November to March.
Admission fee Garden only: free.

Bede's World is an educational experience: one of its main parts is an 'Anglo-Saxon farm' with a vegetable garden where early cultivars of vegetables are grown. But there is also a herb garden, based on a plan of the 9th-century original at St Gall in Switzerland, where culinary, aromatic and medicinal herbs are grown. It is a small part of an ambitious enterprise which seeks to impart a feeling for the Anglo-Saxon world.

 Features herbs; shop for herbal products; lunches & light refreshments.

Owned by Jarrow 700 AD Ltd

Belsay Hall

BELSAY, NEWCASTLE-UPON-TYNE, NE20 0DX

Tel 01661 881636 **Fax** 01661 881043
Website www.english-heritage.org.uk

Location At Belsay on A696 Ponteland to Jedburgh road.
Opening hours 10 am – 6 pm (5 pm in October & 4 pm from November to March); daily except 1 January & 24 – 26 December.
Admission fee Adults £4.50; Concessions £3.40; Children £2.30. (2003 prices).

The wildly Picturesque gardens at Belsay were created by Sir Charles Monck in the 19th century around his new Greek Revival house. The outstanding feature is 11 acres (4.4ha) of disused quarry with a sequence of gloomy chasms, corridors and pinnacles, which house all manner of exotic and rare plants. Rhododendron species flower here from November to August, climbers scramble 10m up the quarry faces, spring bulbs carpet the meadow and modern underplantings like lilies flower from May to September. The ravines create a microclimate which allows such plants as *Trachycarpus* palms and eucryphias to flourish in a cold upland site: Belsay is of great interest to plantsmen. The house is very austere – inspired by ancient Athens – but underpinned by fine formal terraces where the gardeners arrange magnificent displays of bedding. Down the valley are splendid woods planted with two acres of hardy hybrid rhododendrons – not open to the public, but a magnificent sight from the terraces. Elsewhere are fine weed-free lawns (one is for croquet), intensive modern herbaceous plantings, a magnolia terrace, a recently restored rose border, tall heathers, brooding conifers (some of the earliest Douglas firs in England) and the stately ruins of Belsay Castle. The standard of maintenance is superb.

 **Features** snowdrops; rhododendrons & azaleas (species & hardy hybrids); formal terraces; winter garden; unique quarry garden; gift shop; refreshments in summer.

Bide-a-Wee Cottage

STANTON, NETHERWITTON, MORPETH, NE65 8PR

Tel & Fax 01670 772262
Location 7 miles north-west of Morpeth.
Opening hours 1.30 pm – 5 pm; Wednesdays &
Saturdays; 24 April to 28 August. Parties by
arrangement at other times.
Admission fee £2. RHS members free.

The situation of the garden at Bide-a-Wee
Cottage is extraordinary: most of the
garden is hidden in a disused quarry on the
edge of a 500ft (160m) ridge. The unusual
site means that there are enormous
variations within its two acres – variations
of aspect, topography, soil-type and
moisture. Over the last 20 years, Mark
Robson has seized on this natural diversity
to plant a remarkably wide spectrum of
plants. In the wet, shaded quarry bottom, by
the ponds, are swathes of primulas,
rodgersias, ostrich ferns, sensitive ferns and
gunneras. Away from the water, on the
north-facing slopes of the quarry and in the
shade of trees, are meconopsis,
rhododendrons and gentians. Quite a
different type of plant grows on the south-
facing slopes: abutilons, agapanthus,
eremurus and eryngiums for example.
Throughout the garden, the natural rock
walls are contrasted with hedges and
complemented by evergreens – conifers,
rhododendrons and grasses. Then more
ephemeral perennials and wildflowers are
woven into the design, as are the more
unusual plants that are the hallmark of a
plantsman. Robson describes his garden as
'bold perennial plantings linked with a
network of winding paths and steps, all
associated with dramatic changes of level'.
These are designed to create views across the
garden or down onto lower levels, as well as
into the countryside beyond. To the east,
above the quarry, drifts of late-flowering
perennials (including lythrum, eupatorium
and helianthus) melt into the half-acre
wildflower meadow that is also home to the
beehives. Then the garden opens out and
blends into the rough landscape of
Northumberland – tough grassland grazed
by sheep.

Features rock garden; plantsman's
collection of plants; excellent nursery
selling plants from garden.

Owned by Mark Robson
Size 0.8ha (2 acres)
NCCPG National Collections *Centaurea*

Owned by Managed by English Heritage on behalf of the Belsay Trust
Number of gardeners 4, plus 1 trainee
Size 16ha (40 acres)
NCCPG National Collections *Iris spuria*
English Heritage Grade I

Birkheads Cottage Garden Nursery

BIRKHEADS LANE, CAUSEY ARCH, SUNNISIDE, NEWCASTLE-UPON-TYNE, NE16 5EL

Tel 07778 447920 **Fax** 01207 232262
Website www.birkheadsnursery.co.uk
Location Follow brown sign on A6076 between Sunniside & Stanley.
Opening hours 10 am – 5 pm; daily; March to October. And by appointment at other times and seasons. Guided walks at 2 pm on the first Tuesday of the month (booking essential).
Admission fee Garden £1. Nursery free.

This nursery offers a varied and informed selection of alpines, perennials and shrubs: the owner is a garden designer with a passion for plants. There are over 4,500 different plants growing in the adjoining garden: this is an remarkable number by any standards. Other features in the garden include a formal topiary garden made in the 19th century, a gravel garden with herbaceous beds, some rock gardens, a wildlife pond and wildflower garden, a mini arboretum, a spring garden and a grass garden.

Features a plantsman's garden attached to a plantsman's nursery; tea & coffee.

Owned by Christine Liddle
Number of gardeners 3
Size 1.2ha (3 acres)

Chesters Walled Garden

CHOLLERFORD, HEXHAM, NE46 4BQ

Tel 01434 681483
Website www.chesterswalledgarden.co.uk
Location 6 miles north of Hexham, off B6318 near Chollerford.
Opening hours 10 am – 5 pm; daily; April to October. Telephone for winter opening times.
Admission fee Adults £2; Children (under 10) free.

This energetic and successful garden-nursery is strategically placed near the fort at Chesters. The original name of the nursery was 'Hexham Herbs'. Now the garden is a tourist attraction in its own right, and the nursery better than ever. The herb collection is remarkable (over 900 cultivars) and the design within a two-acre brick-walled garden is charming. Dye plants, a Mediterranean garden, an astilbe bed and a knot garden are just some of the features. In addition to their National Collections of *Origanum* and *Thymus*, the nursery has a very good collection of mint cultivars. The garden has over 3,000 different plant cultivars growing in it, and the owner aims to propagate and sell them all in rotation, which means that if they do not have something just at the moment, you should be able to buy it from them in the future.

Features thyme bank; roses (mainly old-fashioned); herbs; 'Roman' garden; grass garden; wildlife ponds; nursery attached; gift & produce shop.

Owned by Mrs S. White
Size 0.8ha (2 acres)
NCCPG National Collections *Origanum*; *Thymus*

Cragside

ROTHBURY, MORPETH, NE65 7PX

Tel 01669 620333 **Fax** 01699 620066
Website www.nationaltrust.org.uk
Location 15 miles north-west of Morpeth off A697 & B6341.
Opening hours Not available as we went to press. In 2003, the gardens were open 10.30 am – 7 pm (last admissions 5 pm). Tuesday – Sunday & Bank Holiday Mondays; April to October. Plus 11 am – 4 pm; Wednesday-Sunday; November & December.
Admission fee Adults £4.80; Children £2.40. (2003 prices)

There are two gardens at Cragside. The newly-acquired Italianate formal garden has splendid carpet bedding, ferneries and a fruit house with rotating pots. Even more impressive are the rhododendron woods – hundreds and hundreds of acres of 19th-century hybrids, plus trusty *R. ponticum* and *R. luteum*, breathtaking in late May.

Features roses (mainly old-fashioned); rock garden; fruit; mature conifers; massive rock garden; tallest *Abies nordmanniana* (50m.), *Cupressus nootkatensis* (33m.) and *Picea glauca* (28m.) in the British Isles; National Trust shop; refreshments.

Owned by The National Trust
Number of gardeners 4
English Heritage Grade II*

The Garden Station

LANGLEY-ON-TYNE, HEXHAM, NE47 5LA

Tel 01434 684391
Website www.thegardenstation.co.uk
Location On the B6295, at Langley. Look for yellow signs.
Opening hours 10 am – 5 pm; daily, except Mondays; May to August.
Admission fee Free; donation welcome.

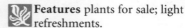

A small centre for gardening and art courses, The Garden Station is a very attractive restored Victorian railway station in a sheltered, tranquil woodland garden. Following along the old track under stone arched bridges, the garden extends into a newly planted walk, planted with foxgloves, *Meconopsis*, hostas, ferns and primulas. Three RHS special events will take place during 2004: details from 020 7821 3408.

Features plants for sale; light refreshments.

Owned by Jane Torday
Number of gardeners 2 part-time

Halls of Heddon

WEST HEDDON NURSERIES, HEDDON ON THE WALL, NEWCASTLE-UPON-TYNE, NE15 0JS

Tel 01661 852445
Website www.hallsofheddon.co.uk
Location 1 mile north-west of Heddon, off the B6318.
Opening hours 9 am – 5 pm, Monday – Saturday; 10 am – 5 pm, Sundays.
Admission fee Free.

Halls produced their first dahlia and chrysanthemum catalogue in 1931: now they offer cultivars for many purposes, including showing, cutting, garden display and greenhouse cultivation. Their extensive list includes many cultivars which are unique to them – not offered by any other nursery. Their magnificent show fields are open from September until the plants are cut down by the frosts: they have over 10,000 plants on display. The garden centre carries a general range.

Number of gardeners 4
Size 0.4ha (1 acre)

Herterton House Gardens & Nursery

HARTINGTON, CAMBO, NE61 4BN

Tel 01670 774278
Location 2 miles north of Cambo (B6342).
Opening hours 1.30 pm – 5.30 pm; daily except Tuesdays & Thursdays; April to September. For National Gardens Scheme on 17 June, 15 July & 5 August.
Admission fee Adults £2.50; Children £1.

This excellent plantsman's garden is (rather unusually) firmly designed and meticulously planted. It is also attached to a small nursery – so firmly attached, in fact, that it is difficult to say whether this is a garden with a nursery or a nursery with a garden. The knot garden is famous, and much photographed, full of herbs and pharmacological plants. More impressive still are the herbaceous plantings, all weaving through each other in beautifully co-ordinated colours. In the gazebo at the top are photographs showing how the garden has developed, expanded, grown up and intensified over the years: a most inspirational display. The Lawleys added a new parterre to the 'fancy garden' in 2001: there are further plans for the future.

Features plantsman's collection of plants; small formal garden; physic garden; flower garden; fancy garden with a gazebo; nursery garden; first-class nursery attached.

Owned by Mr & Mrs Frank Lawley
Number of gardeners 2
Size 0.4ha (1 acre)

Howick Hall

ALNWICK, NE66 3LB

Tel & Fax 01665 577285
Location Off B1399 between Longhoughton & Craster.
Opening hours 1 pm – 6 pm; daily; April to October.
Admission fee Adults £3; OAPs £2; Children free.

Rather an un-Northumbrian garden, because its closeness to the sea makes possible the cultivation of such tender plants as *Carpenteria* and *Ceanothus*. Formal terraces below the house are well planted, but the great joy of the garden at Howick is a small woodland which has acid soil. This was planted in the 1930s with a fine collection of rhododendrons and camellias: other plants are still being added. The result looks more west coast than east.

Features roses (mainly old-fashioned); rhododendrons & azaleas; plantsman's collection of plants; mature conifers; spring bulbs; eucryphias; much new planting; champion *Magnolia wilsonii*; tea-room.

Owned by Howick Trustees Ltd
Number of gardeners 5
English Heritage Grade II

Kirkley Hall Gardens

PONTELAND, NE20 0AQ

Tel 01670 841200 **Fax** 01661 860047
Location Signed in Ponteland.
Opening hours 10 am – 5 pm; daily; all year. Closes at 3 pm from October to March.
Admission fee Free.

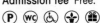

The three-acre, Victorian, walled garden at Kirkley Hall is one of the best in the north of England in which to learn how to garden.

The emphasis is on plants – their selection, cultivation and enjoyment. Along the front of the house are formal gardens with colourful containers in the modern style, and traditional bedding-out: a rising star among gardens.

 Features woodland garden; plantsman's collection of plants; plants under glass; fruit; mature conifers; good herbaceous borders; plant centre.

Owned by Northumberland College at Kirkley Hall
Number of gardeners 3
Size 4ha (10 acres)
NCCPG National Collections *Fagus*

The Longframlington Centre for Plants

SWARLAND ROAD, LONGFRAMLINGTON, MORPETH, NE65 8BE

Tel & Fax 01665 570382
Website www.longframlingtongardens.co.uk
Location ½ mile east of Longframlington along the B6345.
Opening hours 8.30 am – 5 pm (or dusk); daily; all year. Closed Christmas to New Year. Evenings by appointment.
Admission fee Adults £3. Nursery free.

This is a young garden (started in 1998), with lots of ambition. Hazel Huddleston is planting an arboretum for year-round interest to run it alongside her (equally young) plant centre and nursery – which she describes as 'probably the best in the north of England'. Her hope is that Longframlington will become 'a garden of national distinction' as well as 'a garden for today and the future'. The main problem at this stage is to acquire sufficient shelter on the green-field site to allow ornamentals to grow and establish well. The nursery is said to offer over 2,500 different plants, all of them suitable for the cold Northumbrian climate.

 Features young nursery; new garden; coffee shop.

Owned by Hazel Huddleston
Size 5ha (12½ acres)

Seaton Delaval Hall

SEATON SLUICE, WHITLEY BAY, NE26 4QR

Tel 0191 237 1493
Location ½ mile from coast between Whitley Bay & Blyth.
Opening hours 2 pm – 6 pm; Wednesdays & Sundays; June to September. Plus Bank Holidays in May.
Admission fee Adults £4; OAPs £3; Children £1.

Ⓟ ⓦⓒ

The garden is modern: one of Jim Russell's earliest works, it dates from 1948. Parterres and topiary of yew and box are used to enclose old-fashioned roses, handsome ornaments and a fountain: a fair match for the sumptuous house – Vanbrugh's masterpiece. The horticultural interest comes from a fine weeping ash, good plantings of rhododendrons and azaleas, and a laburnum walk.

Features rhododendrons & azaleas; laburnum tunnel; ice house; roses.

Owned by Lord Hastings
Number of gardeners 2
Size 0.8ha (2 acres)
English Heritage Grade II*

St Luke's Cottage

NORTH ROAD, WOOLEY, HEXHAM, NE46 1TN

Tel 01434 673445
Location 3 miles south of Hexham (A69); 3 miles east of A68.
Opening hours By appointment.
Admission fee Donation to Multiple Sclerosis Society.

Alan Furness is a long-standing stalwart of the Alpine Garden Society, that most august of specialist horticultural societies. His garden in a cool valley in southern Northumberland illustrates the enormous opportunities for growing alpine plants which such a situation offers. Within his garden is a wide range of specially constructed habitats to suit an equally wide range of plants: a large limestone scree, and one for acid-loving plants; several high humus beds and meadow beds; a tufa rock bed; a pond, a bog and several damp areas; and four alpine houses. Celmisias (species and garden hybrids), primulas, saxifrages, gentians and pulsatillas are especially well represented, but the whole garden is both a revelation and an inspiration.

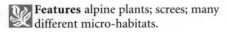**Features** alpine plants; screes; many different micro-habitats.

Owned by Alan Furness
Size 0.3ha (¾ acre)
NCCPG National Collections *Celmisia*

Wallington

CAMBO, MORPETH, NE61 4AR

Tel 01670 773600   **Fax** 01670 774420
Website www.nationaltrust.org.uk
Location 6 miles north-west of Belsay (A696).
Opening hours Not available as we went to press. 2003 times were: 10 am – 7 pm; daily; all year. Closes at 6 pm in October & 4 pm between November and March. Grounds open daily in daylight hours.
Admission fee Adults £4.30; Children £2.15. (2003 prices).

There are three reasons to visit Wallington. First, because Capability Brown was born in nearby Kirkharle. Second, to gawp at the ancient tree-like specimen of *Fuchsia* 'Rose of Castile' in the conservatory. Third, to admire the modern mixed borders (*very* Graham Stuart Thomas) in the long, irregular, walled garden, in a sheltered valley far from the house. Worth the journey for any of them, but prepare for a longish walk to the walled garden.

Features woodland garden; roses (mainly old-fashioned & climbers); rhododendrons & azaleas; plants under glass; daffodils; good herbaceous borders; tallest *Sorbus discolor* (7m.) in the British Isles; shop; restaurant.

Owned by The National Trust
Number of gardeners 5
NCCPG National Collections *Sambucus*
English Heritage Grade II*

NOTTINGHAMSHIRE

For a county of such historic importance, Nottinghamshire has comparatively few historic gardens. Clumber Park has lost the house that was once at its centre, and Newstead Abbey has long lost its most famous owner, Lord Byron. Nevertheless there are some interesting 19th-century gardens in Nottinghamshire, including the curious little arboretum at Papplewick Pumping Station. One of the best civic parks in England is the Nottingham Arboretum, 8ha (20 acres) in extent, which opened in 1852: the architect Sir Joseph Paxton and the nurseryman Samuel Curtis both advised the founders. Nowadays there are few nurseries of national importance in the county. Nevertheless, the *RHS Plant Finder* had its origins in the list of nurseries prepared by the Nottingham Group of the Hardy Plant Society in the 1970s and early 1980s. The county also has some 12 National Collections. The National Gardens Scheme lists a fair number of gardens of all sizes which open in Nottinghamshire for charity: the RHS Free Access garden at Felley Priory is one of exceptional interest and beauty, and a good example of what can be achieved on an unpromising site in only a few years. One further sight should not be missed – the incredible hulk of the Major Oak, also known as Robin Hood's Oak, in Sherwood Forest.

Clumber Park

WORKSOP, S80 3AZ

Tel 01909 476592/544917 **Fax** 01909 500721
Website www.nationaltrust.org.uk
Location Off A614 Nottingham Road, 4 miles south of Worksop.
Opening hours Park: dawn to dusk; every day; all year, but closed on 10 July, 21 August & 25 December. Walled garden: 10 am – 5.30 pm on Monday – Friday & 10 – 6 pm on Saturdays, Sundays & Bank Holidays; 28 March to 30 October.
Admission fee Walled garden: Adults £1. Cars £3.80; pedestrians, cyclists & coaches free.

Clumber has over 3,800 acres of thickly wooded parkland with a Gothic chapel, classical bridge, temples, an avenue of cedars, a heroic double avenue of limes and masses of rhododendrons. There are good conservatories and a garden tools exhibition in the old walled garden. The main glasshouse range, at 150m, is the longest owned by the National Trust. But the scale of everything at Clumber is enormous: very impressive.

Features woodland garden; autumn colour; vineries; old rhubarb cultivars; superb trees; tallest *Ilex aquifolium* 'Laurifolia' (20m.) in the British Isles; National Trust shop; restaurant.

Felley Priory

UNDERWOOD, NG16 5FL

Tel 01773 810230 **Fax** 01773 580440
Location ½ mile west of M1 Jct 27, on A608.
Opening hours 9 am – 12.30 pm; Tuesdays,
Wednesdays & Fridays; all year. Plus 9 am – 4 pm;
2nd & 4th Wednesday of every month; March to
October. And 11 am – 4 pm; every 3rd Sunday of
month; March to October. 11 am – 4 pm on 11 April
for National Gardens Scheme. NCCPG plants fairs
12 noon – 4 pm; 6 June & 3 October. Parties
welcome, by appointment.
Admission fee Adults £2.50; Children free. RHS
members free.

Parts of the house at Felley Priory – a
wonderful brick and dark red sandstone
building – date back to 1150. One link with
the 16th century is a venerable pear-tree
which grows against the house: the Royal
Horticultural Society has identified it as
'Jargonelle', an ancient cultivar well-known
before 1600. Major & Mrs Chaworth-
Musters started work on the garden in 1976
and were, from the start, adventurous
gardeners, willing to try plants which might
be considered doubtfully hardy at 600ft
(180m) so far inland. The results are
astonishing. Against the garden walls are
Buddleja colvilei, nandinas, eucryphias,
several hebes and *Drimys winteri*: elsewhere
in the garden are *Podocarpus salignus* and
Correa backhouseana. Felley Priory is an
excellent garden for plants, with a very large
number of interesting ones in flower at
every season – enough to start a nursery
where everything is propagated from the
garden. Shrubs are a major interest, and
Felley has good collections of magnolias,
cornus, hydrangeas, *Paeonia suffruticosa* and
viburnums. Bulbs are planted in great
numbers: as well as snowdrops and
cyclamen there are massive displays of
daffodils in spring. The handsome yew
hedges are little more than 20 years old, yet
they fill the garden with their bulk: some
have been turned into objects of topiary,
with curvy tops and bobbles. In the rose
garden is a good display of well-grown old-
fashioned roses: there are about 90 different
cultivars, some imported directly from
French nurseries. The rarities include a
pink-and-white form of *Rosa multiflora*
which was collected in Korea by Jamie
Compton. The mediaeval garden harks back
to the original priory which was lost at the
time of the Reformation: it is planted with
plants that were known in the 15th century
– among them are lilies, roses, violas,
columbines, irises, tulips and *Phillyrea
latifolia*. Everything at Felley is charming,
stylish well-trained and well-grown. New
plants arrive constantly from all the best
nurseries: the garden gets better all the time.

Features old-fashioned rose-gardens;
good herbaceous borders; knot
gardens, two pergolas and thousands of
daffodils; new pleached hedge of *Crataegus
tanacetifolia*; unusual trees and shrubs;
nursery attached; tea-room.

Owned by The Hon. Mrs Chaworth-Musters
Size 1ha (2½ acres)

Owned by The National Trust
Number of gardeners 3½, plus seasonal help
Size 10ha (25 acres) of gardens in 1,500ha (3,800 acres) of park
English Heritage Grade I

Hodsock Priory

BLYTH, WORKSOP, S81 0TY

Tel 01909 591204 **Fax** 01909 591578
Website www.snowdrops.co.uk
Location Signed off the B6045 between Blyth & Worksop.
Opening hours 10 am – 4 pm; daily; 31 January to 7 March.
Admission fee Adults £3.50; Children 50p.

The gardens at Hodsock are unique in February when visitors can see a remarkable winter feature – snowdrops. There are thousands and thousands of them: they planted another 250,000 to celebrate the millennium alone and attracted more than 30,000 visitors last year. The Buchanans have also been planting ferns and lots of winter-flowering plants: *Cyclamen coum*, sarcococcas, daphnes and loniceras.

Features aconites; hellebores; hepaticas; winter-flowering plants of all kinds; large *Catalpa* (Indian bean tree); tea-room.

Owned by Sir Andrew & Lady Buchanan
Number of gardeners 1 full-time, 3 part-time
Size 2ha (5 acres) plus woodland

Holme Pierrepont Hall

HOLME PIERREPONT, NOTTINGHAM, NG12 2LD

Tel & Fax 0115 933 2371
Location 3 miles east of Trent Bridge.
Opening hours 2 pm – 5.30 pm; Easter & Spring Bank Holiday Mondays; Thursdays in June; Wednesdays & Thursdays in July; Tuesday – Thursday in August. Summer Bank Holiday Sunday & Monday.
Admission fee House & gardens £4; Gardens £2.

The house at Holme Pierrepont is both beautiful and historic. The main attraction of the garden is a large courtyard garden, designed in 1875, whose box parterre is filled with modern plantings. But there are fine recent additions too: an old rose collection, splendid herbaceous borders and interesting fruit trees. The rare English tulip *Tulipa sylvestris* grows wild in a remote part of the estate.

Features roses (mainly old-fashioned); formal gardens; teas in the long gallery.

Owned by Mr & Mrs Robin Brackenbury
English Heritage Grade II

Mill Hill Plants

MILL HILL HOUSE, ELSTON LANE, EAST STOKE, NEWARK, NG23 5QJ

Tel 01636 525460
Website http://come.to/mill.hill.plants&garden
Location 5 miles south-west of Newark. Leave A46 at East Stoke, for Elston; ½ mile down, on right.
Opening hours 11 am – 5 pm; by appointment; April to October. 3 & 31 May for NGS.
Admission fee Garden: £2. Nursery free.

The garden is generously planted for year-round interest with hardy and half-hardy perennials, annuals and shrubs. Wildlife is encouraged. A good range of hardy perennials is normally available.

Features good nursery.

Owned by Mr & Mrs R.J. Gregory
Size 0.2ha (½ acre)
NCCPG National Collections *Berberis*

Naturescape

LAPWING MEADOWS, COACH GAP
LANE, LANGAR, NG13 9HP

Tel 01949 860592 **Fax** 01949 869047
Website www.naturescape.co.uk
Location Signed off A46 & A52.
Opening hours 11 am – 5.30 pm; daily; April to
September.
Admission fee Free.

  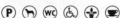

Naturescape is a significant nursery,
specialising in British wild plants. These
include wildflowers, bulbs, native shrubs
and trees, pond and marsh species and
cottage-garden favourites: many are
available both as plants and as seeds.
Meadows, hedges, ponds, woodland edges
and wetlands are supplemented by cottage
gardens and such features as a bee garden.

Features wildflowers; native plants;
tea-room.

Owned by Mr & Mrs B. Scarborough
Number of gardeners 2½
Size 18ha (45 acres)

Newstead Abbey

NEWSTEAD ABBEY PARK,
RAVENSHEAD, NG15 8NA

Tel 01623 455900 **Fax** 01623 455904
Website www.newsteadabbey.org.uk
Location 4 miles south of Mansfield on A60; 12
miles north of Nottingham.
Opening hours 9 am – dusk; daily; all year except
the last Friday in November & Christmas Day.
Admission fee Adults £2.50; Concessions £1.50.
(Adults £2 from October to March).

Chiefly of interest for being the debt-ridden
estate which Lord Byron the poet inherited
and had to sell, Newstead has a good

modern garden. Features include a Spanish
garden, a tropical garden, an iris garden, a
rose garden, a heather garden, fern garden,
ponds and lakes. Best are the Japanese
garden and the substantial rockery. The
Council has restored and extensively
replanted it as a public amenity: lots of
cheerful roses and summer bedding.

Features rock garden; herbs; Japanese
garden; water features; shop; restaurant
& refreshments.

Owned by Nottingham City Council
Number of gardeners 5
Size 120ha (300 acres) of parkland
English Heritage Grade I

Salley Gardens

SIMKINS FARM, ADBOLTON LANE,
WEST BRIDGFORD, NG2 5AS

Tel 0115 923 3878 or 07811 7039
Location Just off the A52 from Nottingham to
Grantham.
Opening hours 9 am – 5 pm; Sunday –
Wednesday; April to September. And by
appointment.
Admission fee Free.

Salley Gardens is a nursery which
concentrates upon plants that are especially
beneficial to mankind: all are organically
grown. They include dye and beverage
plants, and culinary and aromatic herbs and
spices. The main emphasis however is on
plants with medicinal properties. Three
major herbal traditions are represented:
North American, European, and Traditional
Chinese Medicine. Plants used in
homoeopathy, ayurveda, and conventional
medicine are also listed. Last year (2003)
saw an expanded section of culinary herbs,
including some 30 different types of basil.

Owned by Richard Lewin

OXFORDSHIRE

Oxfordshire is one of the best counties for keen gardeners. The natives may grumble about the cold, wet, heavy, clay soils of the Thames Valley, but they have some of the finest English gardens, ancient and modern, to show what those soils can do for them. There are no less than nine Grade I historic gardens in the county, and all are open to the public. Both the Oxford Botanic Garden and its country offshoot the Harcourt Arboretum at Nuneham Courtenay have seriously important plant collections, laid out to attract the ordinary garden-owner. It is in these two collections, too, that many of the county's record-breaking trees grow. Several 20th-century gardens were also laid out on a grand scale, including Sutton Courtenay, Buscot, Garsington, Waterperry and Pusey – the latter, alas, no longer open to the public. The county also has a host of good small gardens: it has long been a matter for pride that Oxfordshire should have more gardens open for the National Gardens Scheme and raise more money for its charities than any other English county (over 180 last year). Nevertheless it has only a handful of National Collections and comparatively few first-rate nurseries – Mattocks Roses, now part of the Notcutt chain, is perhaps the best known. It is as if Oxford were relying for its horticultural reputation more upon its past achievements than its present – rather like its university, some would say. Nevertheless it was at Oxford University that the Garden History Society was born, thanks to the energy and acumen of Mavis Batey. And the many college gardens which open to the public are another of the city's gifts to garden-lovers: Robin Lane-Fox looks after the Fellows' garden at New College. The Royal Horticultural Society has arranged free access for its members, albeit for only one month of the year, to a great teaching garden – Waterperry.

Blenheim Palace

WOODSTOCK, OXFORD, OX20 1PX

Tel 01993 811091 **Fax** 01993 813527
Website www.blenheimpalace.com
Location 8 miles north of Oxford.

Opening hours 10.30 am – 5.30 pm or dusk if earlier (last entry 4.45 pm); daily; 14 March to 31 October.
Admission fee Park, gardens & maze: Adults £6; OAPs £4; Children £2. RHS members free in September and October.

Blenheim is the grandest of grand gardens. Vanbrugh, Bridgeman, Hawksmoor and Wise worked here: the grand bridge, the triumphal arch and the column of victory all date from the 1720s. The huge park (2,000 acre – 800ha) was landscaped by Capability Brown. Achille Duchêne designed the formal gardens in the 1920s: the water terraces centre on a Bernini fountain and took five years to build. The Italian garden focuses on the neo-classical mermaid fountain and is decked with orange trees in summer. There is a pretty Victorian rose garden and, further away from the house, a maze and a lavender garden. The Secret Garden, made by the 10th Duke in the Japanese style, has been restored and is due to be opened for the first time this spring. The arboretum has some interesting trees, including four fine upright incense cedars (*Calocedrus decurrens*): in 1908, Winston Churchill proposed to his wife here.

Features formal gardens; new maze; current holder of Sandford Award; good shops; one restaurant & two self-service cafés.

Owned by The Duke of Marlborough
Number of gardeners 6
Size 40ha (100 acres)
English Heritage Grade I

Brook Cottage

WELL LANE, ALKERTON, BANBURY, OX15 6NL

Tel 01295 670303/670590 **Fax** 01295 730362
Location 6 miles north-west of Banbury, ½ mile off A422.
Opening hours 9 am – 6 pm; Monday – Friday; Easter Monday to 31 October. Groups, evening & weekend visits by appointment.
Admission fee Adults £4; OAPs £3; Children free.

This first-rate plantsman's garden has been made by the present owner and her husband since 1964 on four acres of sloping pasture. The good plants are moreover displayed with a fine sense of colour and form. Parts of the garden are winding and cottagey; parts more spacious and open. Beautiful flowering trees in spring are followed by opulent old roses in summer and rich autumn colour. A recent addition is a border of blue and white agapanthus interspersed with kniphofias in shades of lemon and lime. The yellow border is backed by a hedge of copper beech, while the white border is brought to life by a dark hedge of yew. The diversity of planting is supplemented by tender perennials displayed in numerous ornamental containers. All the wooden furniture has been designed and hand-made to complement the character of the different areas. There is much to study and enjoy here.

Features plantsman's collection of plants; roses (over 200, mainly species & shrubs); good herbaceous borders (colour co-ordinated); 50 different clematis; gravel & water gardens; plants for sale; DIY tea and coffee; refreshments for groups by arrangement.

Owned by Mrs D.M. Hodges
Number of gardeners 1, plus some part-time help
Size 1.6ha (4 acres)

Broughton Castle

BANBURY, OX15 5EB

Tel 01295 722547 **Fax** 01295 276070
Website www.broughtoncastle.demon.co.uk
Location 2½ miles west of Banbury on the B4035.
Opening hours 2 pm – 5 pm; Wednesdays & Sundays; 1 May to 14 September. Plus: Thursdays in July & August; Bank Holiday Sundays & Bank Holiday Mondays (including Easter).

Buscot Park

FARINGDON, SN7 8BU

Tel 01367 240786 **Fax** 01367 241794
Website www.faringdon-coll.com
Location On A417 west of Faringdon.
Opening hours Garden only: 2 pm – 6 pm;
Monday – Friday; April to September. And Saturdays
& Sundays on 2nd & 4th weekends from April to
September. Plus all weekends in May.
Admission fee Adults £4; Children £2.

There are three fairly distinct gardens at Buscot. You enter through the newest – a series of colour plantings and horticultural features created by the National Trust over the last 20 years. Here is the 'Parents' Walk', a lush double herbaceous border designed by Peter Coats in the 1980s: it uses a lot of yellow foliage and contrasts it with purple, to create a sense of lightness and brightness even on the dullest of days. Next to it is the old kitchen garden which Tim Rees turned into a 'four seasons' garden in the early 1990s: each of the quadrants has plantings to represent one of the four seasons. It also has prettily trained fruit trees, vegetables used as climbing plants and gooseberries grown as standards. You climb out of the walled garden, up a steep staircase lined with yews, and walk past the front of the house on your way to the second of the gardens: a perfect *patte d'oie*, focused on the archway which leads into the service courtyard – it is pleasant to think that Lord Faringdon (who commissioned it in the 1890s) and his family used to go in and out of the kitchens on their way to the garden. The temptation is to explore all three avenues of the *patte d'oie* at once, but they are linked by cross-paths which run between further gardens cut out of the woodland: these include a circular sunken garden furnished in summer with orange- and lemon-trees in pots, and a pretty white-and-

green garden which is known as the 'swinging garden' because of the swinging seats which surround it. But the third and best-known garden at Buscot is Harold Peto's water-garden, which dates from the 1900s and stretches down over hundreds of yards in a series of steps and then along a long, narrow, straight canal punctuated towards the end by a chunky Italianate bridge until it bursts out into the view of the lake at the bottom. The canal – little more than a rill really, and narrow enough to jump over in places – is framed first by Irish yews and then by clipped box hedges. It has an amazing dynamism and strength of design which makes it an entirely self-contained garden. The only downside to a visit is that the lake is actually the furthest point of the garden, and there is then no other way out except to re-trace your steps across the park and through the modern gardens. But Peter Coats's borders look even better as you approach them again from outside the walled gardens. And a word of warning: Buscot is a big garden, so allow lots of time for your visit.

Features topiary; roses (mainly old-fashioned); fruit; good herbaceous borders; tallest *Pinus nigra* var. *cebennensis* (32m.) in the British Isles; light refreshments.

Owned by The National Trust
English Heritage Grade II*

Admission fee Castle & gardens: Adults £5.50; OAPs & Students £4.50; Children £2.50.

The garden at Broughton Castle dates back to the 19th century: the neat formal garden with roses and lavender (best seen from the house) was designed by Lady Algernon Gordon-Lennox in the 1890s. The modern garden was established in 1970 with advice from Lanning Roper. It has two pretty colour-themed mixed borders – blue-yellow-white and pink-and-silver – both at their best towards the end of June when the roses are in full flower. The plants play second fiddle to the stupendous setting – the castle, the moat and the spacious parkland beyond.

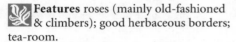**Features** roses (mainly old-fashioned & climbers); good herbaceous borders; tea-room.

Owned by Lord Saye
Number of gardeners 1
Size 0.8ha (2 acres)
English Heritage Grade II*

Garsington Manor

GARSINGTON, OXFORD, OX44 9DH

Location East of the B480 Oxford-Watlington road.
Opening hours 2 pm – 6 pm; 3 May & 26 September. And for opera festival.
Admission fee Adults £3; Children free.

The gardens at Garsington were laid out in the Italian style about 100 years ago by Philip & Ottoline Morrell. The parterre has square beds and Irish yews at the corners; the Italian garden has an large ornamental pool enclosed by yew hedges and set about with statues; beyond, is a wild garden, with shrubs, a stream and pond. They make an incomparable setting for the summer opera season.

Features Italianate gardens; modern plantings; teas.

Owned by Mr & Mrs L.V. Ingrams
Number of gardeners 3
Size 1.6ha (4 acres)
English Heritage Grade II*

Greenways

40 OSLER ROAD, HEADINGTON, OXFORD, OX3 9BJ

Tel 01865 767680 (after dark) **Fax** 01865 767922
Location Osler Road is off London Road, within Ring road.
Opening hours 2 pm – 6 pm; 16 May; 11 July; 8 August. And groups by appointment.
Admission fee Adults £2.50; Children free.

This garden is totally different. The Cootes have emphasised the Provençal looks of the house by planting a rich Mediterranean garden – glittering evergreens, terracotta pots, old oil jars, gravel, parterres – with an exuberance of tender plants including olives, brugmansias, yuccas, oleanders, palms, acanthus and *Albizia julibrissin*. It revelled in the hot summer of 2003 and should be outstanding in 2004 – quite the most stylish small garden in England, and intensively maintained to the highest standard.

Features beautiful modern Italianate garden; sub-tropical plants; plantsman's collection of plants; good herbaceous borders; painted obelisks; long view to monumental classical vase.

Owned by Mr & Mrs N.H.N. Coote
Number of gardeners owners only
Size 0.3ha (¾ acre)

Harcourt Arboretum

NUNEHAM COURTENAY, OX44 9PQ

Tel 01865 343501 **Fax** 01865 341828
Website www.botanic-garden.ox.ac.uk
Location On A4074, just south of village of
Nuneham Courtenay.
Opening hours 10 am – 5 pm; daily; May to
November. 10 am – 4.30 pm; Monday – Friday;
December to April. Closed over the Easter weekend
& 22 December – 4 January 2003.
Admission fee Free: £2 for car park.

Though it belongs to the University of
Oxford Botanic Garden, Harcourt
Arboretum is best regarded as a stand-alone
woodland garden with a distinct history and
character. It has been developed since 1950
around a nucleus of magnificent American
conifers planted about 1840 in a corner of
the Nuneham Courtenay estate. The new
plantings include 'plants from high places'
(geographically arranged), conservation
areas, an extensive glade of ornamental
maples, and fine modern features like
collections of *Nothofagus*, magnolias and
camellias. The labelling is fairly good and
there are useful information boards in front
of specimens of particular interest. It is
perhaps best visited in May, when the
mature oak woodland which surrounds the
conifers is filled with vast oceans of
bluebells.

Features woodland garden;
rhododendrons & azaleas; mature
conifers; camellias; fine collection of trees;
bluebells.

Owned by University of Oxford
Number of gardeners 3
Size 32ha (80 acres)

Kelmscott Manor

KELMSCOTT, LECHLADE, GL7 3HJ

Tel 01367 252486 **Fax** 01367 253754
Website www.kelmscottmanor.co.uk
Location Signed from B4449 & A4095.
Opening hours 11 am – 1 pm & 2 pm – 5 pm;
Wednesdays; April to September. Plus 2 pm – 5 pm
on the 3rd Saturday of the month in April, May, June
& September & 1st & 3rd Saturdays in July &
August.
Admission fee Adults £8.50; Students £4.25.
Gardens only: Adults £2; Children free.

Kelmscott Manor was the summer home of
William Morris, an unspoilt Tudor
farmhouse on the banks of the Thames. The
surrounding countryside, river and garden
were inspirational to Morris's designs and
writings. Work on restoring the garden
started in 1996 and the result is something
that Morris would recognise being typical of
the 1890s, with rustic fencing, herbaceous
borders edged with box and an orchard and
pergola. The planting reflects the rich
botanical content of his designs – wild
tulips (*T. sylvestris*) and fritillaries (*F.
meleagris*) grow thickly under the original
mulberry tree. Elsewhere are crocuses,
aconites and snowdrops, followed by roses,
hollyhocks, cottage annuals, poppies, pinks
and China asters. Morris's original topiary
dragon 'Fafnir' is currently being restored
and the standard rose bushes flanking the
garden path featured in his most famous
book *News from Nowhere*.

Features gift shop; licensed restaurant
for coffee, lunches & teas.

Owned by The Society of Antiquaries of London
Number of gardeners 1 part-time
Size 1.3ha (3¼ acres)
English Heritage Grade II

Lime Close

35 HENLEY'S LANE, DRAYTON,
ABINGDON, OX14 4HU

Tel 07831 861463
Location Off main road through Drayton.
Opening hours 2 pm – 5.30 pm; 18 April & 6 June.
And groups by prior appointment.
Admission fee Adults £2.50; Children 50p.

This modern garden has been much praised,
and deservedly, for its wide range of plants
and the way in which they are grouped. As
well as rare trees, shrubs, alpines, perennials
and bulbs, it can boast a recently-planted
shade border, a pond, a pergola, some
unusual topiary, an ornamental kitchen
garden, a herb garden designed by
Rosemary Verey and a wonderful selection
of raised beds and troughs planted by the
owner's aunt Miss C. Christie-Miller. A new
cottage garden is in the making.

Features good mixed borders; unusual
plants; cream teas.

Owned by M-C. de Laubarède
Size 1.2ha (3 acres)

Le Manoir aux Quat'Saisons

CHURCH ROAD, GREAT MILTON,
OXFORD, OX44 7PD

Tel 01844 278881 **Fax** 01844 278847
Website www.manoir.com
Location Signed in village.
Opening hours All year; patrons only.
Admission fee Free to patrons.

Raymond Blanc insists that the gardens at Le
Manoir aux Quat'Saisons are 'very much a
part of the le Manoir experience and are as
important as the cuisine'. Features include a
Japanese water garden and a 17th-century
pond, but the soul of the garden is a two-
acre kitchen garden. It is organically run,
and registered with the Soil Association. The
herb garden grows about 120 different herbs,
alongside some 90 different vegetables. There
will be RHS special events at Le Manoir aux
Quat'Saisons during 2004: for details, please
contact the restaurant directly.

Features famous restaurant.

Owned by Raymond Blanc
Number of gardeners 6
Size 11ha (27 acres)

Mattocks Roses

NUNEHAM COURTENAY, OXFORD,
OX44 9PY

Tel 08457 585652 **Fax** 01865 343166
Website www.mattocks.co.uk
Location On B4015, Roundabout Golden Ball
(A4074).
Opening hours 9 am – 5.30 pm (5 pm in winter);
Monday – Saturday. 11 am – 5 pm; Sundays.
Admission fee Free.

This is one of the oldest nurseries in
England, founded in 1875 and now part of
the Notcutts group. Mattocks have been
particularly successful in promoting their
'County' series of ground-cover roses, though
most of them were actually raised in
Germany and Denmark. They offer a large
choice of all kinds of roses, and on-line
ordering too. One of their specialities, bred by
John Mattock and introduced in 1973, is the
yellow repeat-flowering climber 'Dreaming
Spires'. The new rose garden, opened in 2001,
is now in its prime: it contains many of the
roses in the list. There will be a Rose
Celebration weekend on 26 & 27 June 2004.

Old Rectory

FARNBOROUGH, WANTAGE, OX12 8NX

Tel 01488 638298
Location In Farnborough village, opposite church.
Opening hours 2 pm – 5.30 pm; 18 April, 9 May & 20 June. And by written appointment (£5, which includes tea, coffee & cakes).
Admission fee Adults £2 for National Gardens Scheme.

This excellent garden has been made by the owners on a high, cold, windy site since 1965. Lots of hedges and thick planting were the keys to survival, but the effect now is of shelter and luxuriance. There are splendid double herbaceous borders, clever colour plantings, a collection of small-flowered clematis, a kitchen garden, a *boule* garden and an expanding arboretum (150+ trees so far).

Features roses (mainly old-fashioned & climbers); good herbaceous borders.

Owned by Mr & Mrs Michael Todhunter
Number of gardeners 1½
Size 2.4ha (6 acres)

Oxford Botanic Garden

ROSE LANE, OXFORD, OX1 4AZ

Tel 01865 286690 **Fax** 01865 286693
Website www.botanic-garden.ox.ac.uk
Location East end of High Street next to river, opposite Magdalen College tower.
Opening hours 9 am – 5 pm (4.30 pm from October to February); daily; all year except Good Friday & Christmas Day. Glasshouses open 10 am – 4 pm. Late night openings to 8 pm on Thursdays from June to August.
Admission fee £2.50 from March to September. Donation box at other times.

This is the oldest botanic garden in England, first laid out in 1621: the handsome gateways were added a few years later. It has kept its original rectangular design and many of the statues and garden ornaments. It also has a calm that is far from the bustle outside and has proved a refuge for generations of undergraduates. There are good and representative collections of almost every type of plant, including a grass garden, ferns, carnivorous plants, a water garden, fernery, orangery and several conservatories. Everything is well-labelled, of course, and designed not only as an aesthetically pleasing living collection of plants for the university botanists but, much more generally, as an educational resource. In recent years the area outside the walled garden has been developed as a garden to inspire gardeners: here are a new water garden, rock garden, herbaceous border and autumn border. The palm house was re-designed in 2000 so that visiting schoolchildren could enjoy 'the ultimate rainforest experience'. The garden is very good on education, and its website is brilliant.

Features roses (mainly old-fashioned); rock garden; herbs; plants under glass; systematic beds; huge service tree; *Victoria amazonica*.

Owned by University of Oxford
Number of gardeners 8
Size 1.8ha (4½ acres)
NCCPG National Collections *Euphorbia*
English Heritage Grade I

Rousham House

STEEPLE ASTON, BICESTER, OX6 3QX

Tel & Fax 01869 347110
Website www.rousham.org
Location A4260 then off the B4030.
Opening hours 10 am – 4.30 pm; daily; all year.
Admission fee Adults £3. No Children under 15.

Rousham is the most perfect surviving example of William Kent's landscaping: *Kentissimo*, according to Horace Walpole. The main axis brings you to Scheemakers's statue of a lion devouring a horse, high above the infant River Cherwell. Follow the correct circuit: the serpentine landscape lies away to the side. Here are Venus's Vale, the Cold Bath and Townsend's Building, from which a lime walk will lead you to the Praeneste. Rousham is an Arcadian experience. The pretty herbaceous border in the walled garden and the modern rose garden by the dovecote seem almost an irrelevance.

Features early eighteenth-century landscape; important sculptures & garden buildings.

Owned by C. Cottrell-Dormer
Number of gardeners 4
Size 10ha (25 acres)
English Heritage Grade I

Stansfield

49 HIGH STREET, STANFORD-IN-THE-VALE, SN7 8NQ

Tel 01367 710340
Location Off A417 opposite Vale garage.
Opening hours 10 am – 4 pm; first Tuesday of month; April to September. And by appointment, including evenings. Garden clubs especially welcome.
Admission fee Adults £1.50; Children free.

Stansfield is a modern plantsman's garden, and a fascinating model of what an enthusiastic collector and cultivator of plants can achieve in a few years. Over 2,000 different plants grow in just over one acre. The special features include troughs, screes, open borders and endless micro-habitats.

Features plantsman's collection of plants; good herbaceous borders; Mediterranean garden.

Owned by Mr & Mrs D. Keeble
Number of gardeners owners only

Stonor

HENLEY-ON-THAMES, RG9 6HF

Tel 01491 638587 **Fax** 01491 639348
Website www.stonor.com
Location On B480 , 5 miles north of Henley-on-Thames.
Opening hours 1 pm – 5.30 pm; Sundays & Bank Holiday Mondays from April to September; Wednesdays from July to September.
Admission fee £3.50.

Stonor fills a hillside and can all be seen from the road below: classical parkland (with a deer park, too), the Elizabethan house, lawns, terraces, a 17th-century walled garden, and finally the wood with wonderful views at the top. Nothing appears to have changed for 200 years: the effect is miraculous.

Features roses (mainly old-fashioned); rock garden; daffodils; tea-room.

Owned by Lord Camoys
Number of gardeners 1
English Heritage Grade I

Waterperry Gardens

WHEATLEY, OXFORD, OX33 1JZ

Tel 01844 339226 **Fax** 01844 339883
Website www.waterperrygardens.co.uk
Location Jct 8 or 8a on M40, well signed locally.
Opening hours 9 am – 5 pm; daily; all year except 17-20 July and Christmas/New Year period.
Admission fee April to October: Adults £3.75;

OAPs £3.25; Children £2.25. November to March: all £1.75. RHS members free in September.

The gardens at Waterperry are extensive, well-maintained and full of interesting plants. Much has been re-designed and replanted in recent years, with some fine formal features and pleasing plant combinations. The glasshouse in the walled garden is notable for a large Seville orange tree and there is a small gravel garden. The Virgin's Walk is a good place to study shade loving plants, but the main feature of this area is a long classical herbaceous border brilliantly colourful from late May until October. The Mary Rose Garden, enclosed by yew hedges, illustrates both modern and older roses, and the formal garden is particularly neatly designed and colourful, with a small knot garden, herb border and wisteria tunnel. Nearby are some interesting ways of training apples and roses, but the main part of the garden is the extensive shrub borders, alpine beds and flower borders. Waterperry offers much to enjoy and learn from at every season.

Features roses; rock garden; herbs; good herbaceous borders; apple orchards; irises; home produce, stoneware, books; excellent plant centre; tea-shop; wine licence.

Owned by School of Economic Science
Number of gardeners 3½
Size 2.8ha (7 acres)
NCCPG National Collections *Saxifraga*

Westwell Manor

BURFORD, OX18 4JT

Location 2 miles from A40, west of Burford roundabout.
Opening hours 2 pm – 6.30 pm; 6 June. And by prior appointment for serious horticultural groups of more than 20.
Admission fee Adults £3; Children 50p.

Westwell is a large and peaceful Cotswold garden with several distinct 'rooms'. The features include rills, a water garden, herbaceous borders, an orchard, a lavender meadow, lots of hazel and willow fencing, a vegetable garden, a moonlight garden and a clematis wall.

Features topiary; roses (mainly old-fashioned); good herbaceous borders; water.

Owned by Mr & Mrs T.H. Gibson
Number of gardeners 2
Size 2.8ha (7 acres)

SHROPSHIRE

Shropshire has the reputation of being a remote and quasi-feudal county. It is certainly true that very few of its historic gardens are ever open to the public. Hawkstone is the most notable exception, but this – the county's only Grade I garden – is now in multiple occupation: nevertheless its principal parts are still highly visitable and also have the best collection of trees, mainly conifers, in Shropshire. Among 20th-century gardens, Hodnet Hall is of national importance, and a sizeable achievement by modern standards. Three further recent gardens are also outstanding each in its own way – Burford House, the David Austin rose gardens and Wollerton Old Hall. Wollerton is a RHS Free Access garden, though the concession does not apply in the peak months of summer. There are 18 National Collections in Shropshire; and the National Gardens Scheme is well supported, mainly by gardens which are large or medium-sized.

Attingham Park

SHREWSBURY, SY4 4TP

Tel 01743 708123 **Fax** 01743 708155
Website www.nationaltrust.org.uk
Location 5 miles south-east of Shrewsbury on B4380.
Opening hours 10 am – 8 pm (5 pm from November to February); Friday – Tuesday; 19 March to 2 November. Weekends only at other times.
Admission fee Adults £2.70; Children £1.35.

No garden to speak of, but the classical late 18th-century parkland round the vast Georgian house is a joy to walk around at any time of the year.

Features rhododendrons & azaleas; daffodils; newly restored orangery; National Trust shop; light lunches & teas.

Owned by The National Trust
Number of gardeners 2

Size 20ha (50 acres)
English Heritage Grade II*

Benthall Hall

BROSELEY, TF12 5RX

Tel & Fax 01952 882159
Website www.nationaltrust.org.uk
Location 1 mile north-west of Broseley (B4375).
Opening hours 1.30 pm – 5.30 pm; Tuesdays, Wednesdays & Bank Holiday Sundays & Mondays; 6 April to 30 September. Plus all Sundays from July to September.
Admission fee Adults £2.40; Children £1.20.

The smallish garden has been well restored with a Graham Stuart Thomas rose garden. Home of the 19th-century botanist George Maw. His Mediterranean collection is still the backbone of the garden – crocus naturalised everywhere.

Features roses (mainly old-fashioned); herbs; good herbaceous borders; spring bulbs.

Owned by The National Trust
Number of gardeners 1
Size 1.2ha (3 acres)

Burford House Gardens

TENBURY WELLS, WR15 8HQ

Tel 01584 810777 **Fax** 01584 810673
Location A456 between Tenbury Wells & Ludlow.
Opening hours 9 am – 6 pm (gardens close at dusk if earlier); daily; all year. Closed 25 & 26 December.
Admission fee Adults £3.95; Children £1; Groups (20+) £3.

This glamorous seven-acre garden, made to complement a stylish Georgian house, is now beautiful and mature. The fluid design is enhanced by interesting plants, imaginatively used and comprehensively labelled. There are good roses and herbaceous borders, and a magnificent series of water gardens, but Burford means *Clematis* – over 350 varieties – cleverly trained, grown and displayed among shrubs and in the new Clematis Maze near the coach house. Charles Chesshire has renewed and reordered much of the planting, and the results are excellent. There are new developments on the other side of the river, too: bulbs and wildflower plantings in particular.

Features clematis; roses (mainly old-fashioned & climbers); plantsman's collection of plants; mature conifers; good herbaceous borders; *Rosa* 'Treasure Trove'; new wildflower garden; new collection of bamboos; café bar with morning coffee, home-made cakes, lunches, teas.

Owned by Burford Garden Company
Number of gardeners 4
Size 2.8ha (7 acres)
NCCPG National Collections Clematis

David Austin Roses

BOWLING GREEN LANE, ALBRIGHTON, WOLVERHAMPTON, WV7 3HB

Tel 01902 376376 **Fax** 01902 372142
Website www.davidaustinroses.com
Location Signed in Albrighton.
Opening hours 9 am – 5 pm; daily; all year except 25 December to 2 January. Open for National Gardens Scheme on last Sunday in June.
Admission fee Free.

David Austin has developed an entirely new strain of 'English' roses which combine the shape and scent of old-fashioned roses with the colours, health and floriferousness of modern types. The display gardens adjoining his nursery are impressive: five different sections, each extensive and thickly planted with old-fashioned roses and his own hybrids – over 700 different cultivars of English roses, 19th-century roses, shrub roses, climbers, ramblers and species, as well as some modern Hybrid Teas and Floribundas. In late June and early July it is a place of magic beauty. The garden is maintained to an extremely high standard: all the roses look happy and healthy, and flower profusely. Sculptures by David Austin's wife add a further dimension to a visit. Several new roses are introduced every year at Chelsea. Groups are sometimes allowed to see the breeding houses and trial grounds. There are five RHS special events planned at David Austin Roses during 2004: details from 020 7821 3408.

Features roses of every kind, especially 'English' roses; important rose nursery & plant centre; restaurant & light refreshments.

Owned by David Austin
Number of gardeners 1
Size 0.8ha (2 acres)
NCCPG National Collections *Rosa* (Austin 'English' cultivars)

The Dower House

MORVILLE HALL, MORVILLE,
BRIDGNORTH, WV16 5NB

Tel & Fax 01746 714407
Location At junction of A458 & B4368, 3 miles from Bridgnorth.
Opening hours 2 pm – 6 pm; Wednesdays, Sundays & Bank Holiday Mondays; April to September.
Admission fee Adults £3; Children 50p.

Dr Swift is a distinguished garden-writer with a special gift for putting our gardening practices in an historical context. Her own garden is both beautiful and instructive. The aim is to tell the story of English gardening in a series of gardens which represent the styles and aspirations of different historical periods. The oldest feature, in spirit, is a turf maze, followed by a mediaeval cloister garden. Then come the Elizabethan-style knot garden, a 17th-century 'plat', a William-and-Mary canal garden and so on, up to a stupendous Victorian rose border. And Dr Swift is a dedicated conservationist, not just of historical style, but also of old garden cultivars of everything from roses to apples and vegetables. The Dower House is therefore of great interest both to modern plantsman and to lovers of things ancient.

Features plants from garden for sale; home-made teas.

Owned by Dr Katherine Swift, as tenant of the National Trust
Number of gardeners owner, plus part-time help
Size 0.6ha (1½ acres)

Dudmaston

QUATT, BRIDGNORTH, WV15 6QN

Tel 01746 780866 **Fax** 01746 780744
Website www.nationaltrust.org.uk
Location 4 miles south-east of Bridgnorth on A442.
Opening hours 12 noon – 6 pm; Sunday – Wednesday; 4 April to 29 September.
Admission fee Adults £4.50; Children £2.20.

Dudmaston has a fine collection of trees and shrubs, put together by several generations of keen plantsmen in the 19th and 20th centuries. Rhododendrons form the background: there are many magnolias, cherries, kalmias, maples and roses, underplanted with daffodils and primroses, which makes this a particularly fine garden in spring. But there is also a natural rock-garden made of the local red sandstone. Elsewhere are a bog garden and a good herbaceous border, recently replanted.

Features rhododendrons & azaleas; fine trees; sculptures; shop; plant sales; tea-room.

Owned by The National Trust
Number of gardeners 2
Size 3.2ha (8 acres)
English Heritage Grade II

Hall Farm Nursery

VICARAGE LANE, KINNERLEY,
OSWESTRY, SY10 8DH

Tel & Fax 01691 682135
Website www.hallfarmnursery.co.uk
Location 2 miles from A5, between Shrewsbury & Oswestry.
Opening hours 10 am – 5 pm; Tuesday – Saturday; 2 March to 9 October.
Admission fee Free.

Hall Farm Nursery carries a good range of fashionable herbaceous perennials, including a great number of geraniums and ornamental grasses. Pulmonarias, hostas, astrantias, bog plants, sempervivums and aeoniums are other specialities. All its plants are grown and propagated on site: requests for cultural advice are therefore welcome. The display borders around the nursery are attractive and well maintained. Four RHS special events will take place at Hall Farm Nursery during 2004: details from 020 7821 3408. the nursery won three gold medals at RHS shows in 2003.

 Features herbaceous plants; ornamental; grasses.

Owned by Christine & Nick Ffoulkes Jones

Hawkstone Historic Park & Follies

WESTON UNDER REDCASTLE, SHREWSBURY, SY4 5UY

Tel 01939 200611 **Fax** 01939 200311
Location Off the A49 between Shrewsbury & Whitchurch.
Opening hours Not available as we went to press.
Admission fee Adults £5.50; OAPs £4.50; Children £3. (2003).

Sir Rowland Hill began landscaping Hawkstone in the 1750s, but most of what remains was initiated by his elder son Sir Richard and completed by his grandson, another Sir Rowland Hill, best known for inventing the postage stamp. It is a fine example of the 'sublime' movement, which sought to create contrasts of emotion in the natural landscape. Hawkstone has deep ravines and gloomy chasms, accompanied by dizzying pinnacles, soaring sandstone rocks, and ornamental follies which fill the whole estate, once more than 700 acres in extent. It is the contrasts which make this landscape unique: the mosses, ferns, and dampness of its dark gullies turn suddenly into dramatic cliffs, tunnels, crags and bridges, while the peaks of the precipitous outcrops offer views across 13 counties. But allow lots of time for your visit – the owner recommends at least three hours.

 Features a remarkable series of landscaped follies; some good trees.

Owned by M.C. Boler
English Heritage Grade I

Hillview Hardy Plants

WORFIELD, BRIDGNORTH, WV15 5NT

Tel & Fax 01746 716454
Website www.hillviewhardyplants.com
Location Between Worfield & Albrighton, off B4176.
Opening hours 9 am – 5 pm, Monday – Saturday, March to mid-October. And by appointment.
Admission fee Free.

This is a good nursery for hardy herbaceous perennials. Its range of primulas and auriculas, aquilegias and South African plants is especially noteworthy. Guided tours of the nursery can be arranged for groups. Four RHS special events will take place at Hillview Hardy Plants during 2004: details from 020 7821 3408.

Owned by John & Ingrid Millington
Number of gardeners 3½
Size 0.4ha (1 acre)

Hodnet Hall Gardens

HODNET, MARKET DRAYTON, TF9 3NN

Tel 01630 685786 **Fax** 01630 685853
Location Near junction of A53 & A442.
Opening hours 12 noon – 5 pm; Tuesday – Sunday

& Bank Holiday Mondays; April to September.
Admission fee Adults £3.50; OAPs £3; Children £1.50.

In the 1950s, *The RHS Journal* (forerunner of *The Garden*) described Hodnet as a 'small modern garden'. Now it has more than 60 acres of woodland garden around a chain of ornamental pools. The woodlands are planted with exotic trees like magnolias, maples and davidias against a background of native oaks, sycamores, limes and beech-trees. Underneath are rhododendrons, azaleas, camellias, prunus and berberis, themselves underplanted when they flower in spring with a wide variety of herbaceous plants, especially hostas, primulas, daffodils and bluebells. The spacious mixed borders near the house are particularly interesting in July, when they are complemented by the beds of old-fashioned roses and modern floribundas. But Hodnet is a garden for everyone and every season – good in late summer too, when the hydrangeas and astilbes flower. Allow lots of time for a thorough visit to one of the greatest 20th-century gardens.

Features woodland garden; roses (mainly old-fashioned); good herbaceous borders; camellias; primulas; rhododendrons; HHA/Christie's Garden of the Year in 1985; gift shop; 17th-century tea-rooms.

Owned by A.E.H. Heber-Percy
Number of gardeners 4
Size 24+ha (60+ acres)
English Heritage Grade II

Jessamine Cottage

KENLEY, SHREWSBURY, SY5 6NS

Tel 01694 771279
Location Signed from B4371.
Opening hours 2 pm – 6 pm; Fridays, Sundays &

Bank Holiday Mondays; 31 May to 30 August.
Admission fee Adults £3; Children 50p.

This is a very new garden, made from an open paddock since 1999: the owners seek to combine good plants, fluid design, and all-season interest. Features include a small parterre, a wildflower meadow, a stream and pond, island beds (main herbaceous) and young shrub borders. Worth visiting now, and returning to see how it grows up.

**Features** good plants; fluid design; plants for sale; home-made teas.

Owned by Leon & Pamela Wheeler
Number of gardeners 2
Size 1.2ha (3 acres)

Lingen Nursery and Gardens

LINGEN, BUCKNELL, SY7 0DY

Tel & Fax 01544 267720
Website www.lingennursery.co.uk
Location Follow brown tourist signs from the A4113 & A4362, north-east of Presteigne.
Opening hours 10 am – 5 pm; Thursday – Monday; Easter to September. Nursery opens from February to October.
Admission fee Garden £2.50. Nursery free.

Lingen was started in 1979, and is celebrating its silver jubilee this year. It has become one of the best-known specialist nurseries for unusual alpine and herbaceous plants. In addition to their two National Collections, the owners have put together notable collections of auriculas and penstemons (both alpine and herbaceous) and have a number of interesting aquilegias and irises too. But it is true to say that you will not visit Lingen without seeing a plant that you have never seen before. The gardens are worth a visit in their own right: one acre is intensively planted with a rock garden and cottage garden, supplemented by an alpine house and raised beds. Two further acres are under development to create a bog garden, further herbaceous borders, a scree and a rock outcrop.

 Features auriculas; penstemons; tearoom.

Owned by Kim & Maggie Davis
Size garden 1.2ha (3 acres); nursery 0.4ha (1 acre)
NCCPG National Collections *Iris sibirica*; *Campanula*

Lower Hall

WORFIELD, BRIDGNORTH, WV15 5LH

Tel 01746 716607 **Fax** 01746 716325
Location In centre of village of Worfield.
Opening hours 13 June for NGS. And by appointment. Groups welcome.
Admission fee Adults £3.50; Children free.

Lanning Roper helped to get this splendid garden going in the 1960s. It bestrides the River Worfe and every part has a distinct character. There are lush streamside plantings (some replanted in 2002-2003), infinite colour schemes, and a woodland area at the bottom. These contrast with formal designs, straight brick paths, a pergola and more colour themes in the old walled garden. It is one of the best gardens to be made since World War II, still evolving and neatly kept.

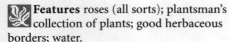 **Features** roses (all sorts); plantsman's collection of plants; good herbaceous borders; water.

Owned by C.F. Dumbell
Number of gardeners 1
Size 1.7ha (4¼ acres)

Preen Manor

CHURCH PREEN, CHURCH STRETTON, SY6 7LQ

Tel 01694 771207
Location Signed from B4371 Much Wenlock/Church Stretton.
Opening hours 2 pm – 6 pm; 2 May, 10 & 24 June; 15 & 29 July; 3 October (4.30 pm Harvest Thanksgiving). And parties by appointment in June & July.
Admission fee Adults £3.50; Children 50p.

Preen has a stylish new garden with some original ideas to complement the historic old site. These include a chess garden, a collection of plants in handsome old pots, a pebble garden, a fern garden and that symbol of the 1990s – a gravel garden. Down in the woodland garden are rhododendrons and candelabra primulas. And it gets better every year.

 Features woodland garden; fruit; fern garden; home-made teas.

Owned by Mrs Philip Trevor-Jones
Number of gardeners 2½
Size 2.4ha (6 acres), plus woodland

Ruthall Manor

DITTON PRIORS, BRIDGNORTH, WV16 6TN

Tel 01746 712608
Location Take Weston road from church then 2nd left.
Opening hours For National Gardens Scheme.

This one-acre plantsman's garden, some 250m (800ft) up, has been made over the last 20 years. It has good trees, rare shrubs, lots of groundcover, and a pretty pool with aquatics and marginals.

Features plantsman's collection of plants.

Owned by Mr & Mrs G.T. Clarke

Swallow Hayes

RECTORY ROAD, ALBRIGHTON,
WOLVERHAMPTON, WV7 3EP

Tel 01902 372624 **Fax** 01902 373151
Location M54, Jct 3, then A41 towards
Wolverhampton & first right after garden centre.
Opening hours 2 pm – 5 pm on 30 May. And by
appointment.
Admission fee Adults £3; Children 10p. £3.50 per
head for groups, to include light refreshments.

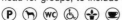

Swallow Hayes is a plantswoman's garden
(3,000 plants) entirely made since 1968 and
a model of its kind, where groundcover
helps to minimise labour and maximise
enjoyment. The garden started life as a
stock-ground and trial-ground for the
owner's wholesale nursery. Mrs Edwards has
more than 100 different cultivars of
Geranium in a garden which is packed with
different micro-habitats, each of them
themed and exploited as fully as possible.
There is much to see and enjoy at every
season. The garden is open every January for
about a week to view the National Collection
of winter-flowering witch-hazels *Hamamelis*
of which there are over 50 cultivars. Please
telephone for January 2005 dates.

Features rock garden; herbs; fruit;
mature conifers; good herbaceous
borders; ferns; geraniums; trees & shrubs;
teas on open day.

Owned by Mrs P. Edwards
Number of gardeners owner, plus some very part-
time help
Size 0.8ha (2 acres)
NCCPG National Collections *Hamamelis*; *Lupinus*
(Russell strains)

Wollerton Old Hall

WOLLERTON, MARKET DRAYTON,
TF9 3NA

Tel 01630 685760 **Fax** 01630 685583
Website www.wollertonoldhallgarden.com
Location Follow brown tourist signs from A53 in
Hodnet or A53/A41 junction.
Opening hours 12 noon – 5 pm; Fridays, Sundays
& Bank Holidays; 18 April to 30 August. Plus
Sundays in September.
Admission fee Adults £4; Children £1. RHS
members free in April, May & September.

Started in 1984, this outstanding garden
creation seeks to combine horticultural
excellence with unrestrained planting of
perennials, careful colour design with strong
contrasts, and intimacy with bold design
structure. As the site is centuries old, the
dominant theme is of linear formality but
this gradually gives way to total informality
where the garden meets the Shropshire
countryside.

Features plantsman's collection of
plants; good herbaceous borders;
deciduous euonymus; salvias; clematis;
shrub roses; crocosmias; lunches & teas.

Owned by Lesley Jenkins
Number of gardeners 2
Size 1.2ha (3 acres)

SOMERSET

Like its neighbour Devon, Somerset is rich in both gardens and nurseries: it is a county where gardeners are well served. Four of its five Grade I historic gardens – Dunster, East Lambrook, Hestercombe and Montacute – are regularly open to the public. Somerset also has an exceptional number of good small and medium-sized gardens, often made by the present owners – as witness the large number (in quite a small county) which open in aid of the National Gardens Scheme. Somerset is famous for its mild climate – warm and wet – and the rich soils which are put to cider and dairying: they also induce good growth in gardens. It has long been recognised that along the coast – at Porlock and Cannington, for example – plants flourish which would not survive in any but the mildest parts of Devon and Cornwall. Nevertheless the county has no arboreta of note and few trees which are thought to be among the tallest or largest of their kind. Somerset has many nurseries and among them are several of national or international importance: Avon Bulbs and Broadleigh Gardens for bulbs, Kelways for peonies, Mallet Court for rare trees, P.M.A. Plants for Japanese maples, Thornleigh for fruit trees.

Somerset also has a large number (over 20) of National Collections, which is always a good indicator of the general level of interest in gardening. And it has long been well served by the county horticultural college at Cannington, which is one of the leading centres in all England for the teaching of amenity horticulture. Cannington is also a RHS Partner College, with a programme of public lectures, demonstrations and workshops all through the year.

The American Museum

CLAVERTON MANOR, BATH, BA2 7BD

Tel 01225 460503 **Fax** 01225 469160
Website www.americanmuseum.org
Location Off A36 south of Bath.
Opening hours 12 noon – 6 pm; daily, except Mondays; 20 March to 31 October.
Admission fee Adults £4; Children £2.50. Private tours by prior arrangement.

The 15 enchanting acres of garden at Claverton Manor were created by two artistic Americans, Dallas Pratt and John Judkyn, from about 1960 onwards. They bought the handsome classical house, built in 1820, to hold their collection of early American domestic arts and artefacts: the American Museum is now the largest of its kind outside the USA and well worth a visit.

The house has a stunning situation with wide views across to the west-facing slopes of the Avon valley, yet sheltered and screened from all but the prettiest eye-catchers on the other side. Tea is served on the terrace in front of the house, next to the little Colonial herb garden ('Colonial' = pre-1778). Sloping lawns lead to the Mount Vernon garden, a box-edged re-creation of George Washington's own original. The first enclosure has beds of old roses: the main section is a herbaceous garden. Despite a little historical latitude with the choice of 18th-century plants, it is all very neat and instructive, and prettily enclosed by white picket fencing. Also of horticultural interest is a young arboretum which opened in 1985 on the slopes below. This celebration of hardy American trees and shrubs adds up to a fine, well-labelled collection, and includes (among many other rarities) *Alnus rhombifolia*, *Salix mackenziana* and *Philadelphus insignis*. Also worth discovering are a ferny dell at the bottom of the arboretum and a collection of American apple cultivars, with such names as 'Smokehouse' and 'Sheep's Nose'. The American Museum is a well-endowed foundation and its gardens are very well maintained, which adds enormously to the pleasure of a visit, though rabbits are a problem.

 Features topiary; roses (mainly old-fashioned); herbs; fruit; good herbaceous borders; fine collection of trees; book shop, herb shop and country store; light lunches at weekends; tea, coffee and American cookies.

Owned by Trustees of the American Museum in Britain
Number of gardeners 4
Size 6ha (15 acres)
English Heritage Grade II

Ammerdown Park

KILMERSDON, RADSTOCK, BATH, BA3 5SH

Tel 01761 432227 **Fax** 01761 433094
Location West of Terry Hill crossroads: A362/A366.
Opening hours 11 am – 5 pm; 12 April, 3 & 31 May, 30 August.
Admission fee Adults £3; £2 OAPs; Children free.

Ammerdown's lay-out is Lutyens at his most ingenious. The lie of the land precludes right angles, but long straight views cover up the irregularities. It has some nice plants, particularly trees, but the design is everything and there are good spring bulbs. A restoration plan has recently got under way.

 Features major Lutyens garden; good design; refreshments.

Owned by The Hon. Andrew Jolliffe
Number of gardeners 3
Size 6ha (15 acres)
English Heritage Grade II*

Avon Bulbs

BURNT HOUSE FARM, MID-LAMBROOK, SOUTH PETHERTON, TA13 5HE

Tel & Fax 01460 242177
Website www.avonbulbs.co.uk
Location Turn south, down 'no through road', halfway between West Lambrook & East Lambrook.
Opening hours 9 am – 4.30 pm; Thursday – Saturday; mid-February to end March & mid-September to end October.
Admission fee Free.

Avon Bulbs offers an impressive variety of bulbs (and close relatives) of all sizes, types and seasons – mainly by mail order. The nursery is well-run and the plants are beautifully grown. It is well worth a visit early in the year to see the wide range of its stock, including much which is not listed in the catalogue. The opening hours are limited because of the seasonal nature of the business and the nursery's show commitments. It is a good idea to check with them before visiting.

Features hardy bulbs of every kind.

Owned by Chris Ireland-Jones
Number of gardeners 4
Size 1.2ha (3 acres)

Barrington Court

BARRINGTON, ILMINSTER, TA19 0NQ

Tel 01460 241938 **Fax** 01460 243133
Website www.nationaltrust.org.uk
Location In Barrington village.
Opening hours 11 am – 5.30 pm; Thursday – Tuesday; April to September. 11 am – 4.30 pm; Thursday – Sunday; March & October.
Admission fee Adults £5.50; Children £2.50.

There is still an Edwardian opulence about Barrington. Massive plantings of irises, lilies and rich dark dahlias. And good design detail too: the patterns of the brick paving are a study in themselves.

Features roses (mainly old-fashioned); fruit; fine collection of trees; shop; tea-room; licensed restaurant.

Owned by The National Trust
Number of gardeners 3, plus 1 trainee
Size 4ha (10 acres)
English Heritage Grade II*

Bath Botanic Gardens

ROYAL VICTORIA PARK, BATH, BA1 2NQ

Tel 01225 448433 **Fax** 01225 480072
Location West of city centre by Upper Bristol Road.
Opening hours 9 am – dusk; daily; all year except Christmas Day.
Admission fee Free.

Bath's Botanic Gardens were founded in 1887, extended in 1926 and again in 1987. It has nine acres of trees, shrubs, borders, limestone-loving plants and scented walks. It has never been attached to a university or institute, so it is more of a horticultural collection than a botanic garden, and public amenity is its main function. The central feature is a rocky pool designed in the Japanese style, surrounded by venerable not-so-dwarf maples. Standards are high, maintenance is good, and the seasonal highlights of bulbs, bedding and herbaceous plants are among the best. The excellent guidebook is a model of visitor-friendliness.

Features rock garden; autumn colour; fine bedding displays; good *Scilla* collection; tallest tree of heaven *Ailanthus altissima* (31m.) and tallest hornbeam *Carpinus betulus* (27m.) in England (and eleven other record trees).

Owned by Bath & North East Somerset Council
Number of gardeners 4
Size 3.8ha (9½ acres)
English Heritage Grade II

Blackmore & Langdon

STANTON NURSERIES, PENSFORD,
BRISTOL, BS39 4JL

Tel 01275 332300 **Fax** 01275 331207
Website www.blackmore-langdon.com
Location 8 miles south of Bristol on B3130,
between A37 Wells road & A38.
Opening hours 9 am – 5 pm; Monday – Friday. 10
am – 4 pm; Saturdays & Sundays.

This family business was started in 1901 and
is still run by the founder's grandchildren.
Blackmore & Langdon has a long tradition
of breeding and growing showy border
plants – huge begonias and tall delphiniums,
in particular. The nursery's immaculately
grown flowers have been a feature of RHS
Flowers Shows – and especially the Chelsea
Flower Show – for many years. What is not
so well known is that the nursery also
produces phlox, aquilegias and polyanthus.
All its plants are grown on site. The begonias
and delphiniums fill a 0.4ha (1-acre)
glasshouse; there are also delphiniums in
flower in the field from the end of May until
September. There will be two RHS special
events at Blackmore & Langdon during
2004: details from 020 7821 3408.

Features delphiniums; begonias.

Owned by The Langdon family

Broadleigh Gardens

BISHOPS HULL, TAUNTON, TA4 1AE

Tel 01823 286231 **Fax** 01823 232464
Website www.broadleighbulbs.co.uk
Location At Barr, 1½ miles north-west of Bishops
Hull.
Opening hours 9 am – 4 pm; Monday – Friday.
Viewing & collection of pre-booked orders.
Admission fee £1 charity donation.

This nursery, with strong RHS connections,
is best known for its small bulbs, though it
now grows almost as many foliage and
woodland perennials. Look out for the
agapanthus, crocosmias, snowdrops, the
many miniature narcissus and species tulips,
and Broadleigh's own Pacific Coast hybrid
irises. The nursery and three-acre display
garden are open for viewing.

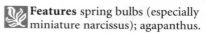**Features** spring bulbs (especially
miniature narcissus); agapanthus.

Owned by Christine Skelmersdale
Number of gardeners 4
Size 2ha (5 acres)
NCCPG National Collections Narcissus
(miniature)

Cannington College Heritage Garden

CANNINGTON, BRIDGWATER, TA5 2LS

Tel 01278 655000 **Fax** 01278 655055
Website www.cannington.ac.uk
Location 3 miles west of Bridgwater on A39.
Opening hours 9 am – 5 pm; daily; 12 April to
October.
Admission fee £1. Guided tours £25 per tour (by
arrangement).

Cannington can claim to have one of the
largest collections of rare and unusual
plants in the south-west of England. This
makes it highly attractive to all plantsmen
and gardeners, whatever their particular
interest. Within a mediaeval walled garden
next to Cannington Court are areas devoted
to a Winter Garden, an Australasian garden,
a Bible-themed garden, a kitchen garden
and the 'Tiffany Blue' garden which won a
gold medal at Chelsea. The garden has a
good number of different Wisteria cultivars

on its old buildings. There will be a very large number of RHS special events at Cannington during 2004: details from 020 7821 3408.

 Features plantsman's collection of plants; good herbaceous borders.

Owned by Cannington College
Size 1ha (2½ acres)

Cleeve Nursery

CLEEVE, BRISTOL, BS49 4PW

Tel 01934 832134 **Fax** 01934 876498
Website www.cleevenursery.co.uk
Location On A370 between Bristol & Weston-super-Mare.
Opening hours 9 am -6 pm (5 pm in winter); Monday – Saturday; all year. Plus 10 am – 5 pm on Sundays & Bank Holidays. Closed 25 December to 1 January.
Admission fee Free.

This is a well-regarded garden centre with a wide range of plants of all sorts for sale. There will be a RHS special event here during 2004: details from 020 7821 3408.

 Features garden centre; coffee shop.

Owned by Alan & Felicity Down

Cothay Manor

GREENHAM, WELLINGTON, TA21 0JR

Tel 01823 672283 **Fax** 01823 672345
Location Off A38, 1½ miles from Greenham.
Opening hours 2 pm – 6 pm; Wednesdays, Thursdays, Sundays & Bank Holiday Mondays; May to September. Group (21+) by appointment throughout the season.
Admission fee £4.

Cothay is an exciting old/new garden on either side of the River Tone. The seven acres of formal gardens designed in the 1920s by Reggie Cooper (a friend of Lawrence Johnston, and Harold & Vita too) have now been completely replanted, room by room, colour by colour, since the Robbs came here in 1993. Cothay makes a model study of how a garden can be rejuvenated. It is now in the prime of life, brimming with vigour. The avenue of mop-headed acacias (*Robinia pseudoacacia* 'Umbraculifera'), nearly 100m long, looks stunning underplanted with nepeta and a thousand white tulips. New for 2004 are a Mount, planted with wild flowers and bulbs, and a lake.

 Features stylish 1920s design; good plants; cream teas.

Owned by Mr & Mrs Alastair Robb
Number of gardeners 1½
Size 2.8ha (7 acres); plus 2ha (5 acres) of new trees
English Heritage Grade II*

Crowe Hall

WIDCOMBE HILL, BATH, BA2 6AR

Tel 01225 310322
Location Off A36 up Widcombe Hill.
Opening hours 2 pm – 6 pm; 4 April, 9 May, 6 June, 11 July & by appointment.
Admission fee Adults £3; Children £1.

Crowe Hall is a most extraordinary and exciting garden. It looks straight out at the Capability Brown landscape at Prior Park, and 'borrows' it. Mown grass paths have been cut through the meadows above the house to create an ever-changing view of the park and Palladian bridge. Below the house is an Italianate terrace, which leads to a ferny rock garden (real rocky outcrops here) and down into a semi-woodland garden. Recent developments include a 'Sauce' garden, in memory of Lady Barratt (a former owner), a 'Hercules' garden and the 'Teazle' garden with a cascade, pool and pergola in memory of a much-loved dog.

 Features roses (mainly old-fashioned); fine greenhouse & grotto; teas.

Owned by John Barratt
Number of gardeners 2
Size 4.4ha (11 acres)
English Heritage Grade II

Dunster Castle

MINEHEAD, TA24 6SL

Tel 01643 821314 **Fax** 01643 823000
Website www.nationaltrust.org.uk
Location 3 miles south-east of Minehead on A39.
Opening hours 11 am – 4 pm; daily; January to 19 March, & 24 October to 31 December. 10 am – 5 pm; daily; 20 March to 23 October. Closed 25 & 26 December.
Admission fee Adults £3.70; Children £1.60.

Dunster is a Victorian woodland on a steep slope, terraced in places and planted with tender exotica – mimosa, *Beschorneria* and a 150-year-old lemon tree in an unheated conservatory.

 Features *Arbutus* grove; woodland garden; sub-tropical plants; National Trust shop; tea-room at Dunster Mill.

Owned by The National Trust
Number of gardeners 4
Size 6.7ha (17 acres)
NCCPG National Collections *Arbutus*
English Heritage Grade I

East Lambrook Manor

EAST LAMBROOK, SOUTH PETHERTON, TA13 5HL

Tel 01460 240328 **Fax** 01460 242344
Website www.eastlambrook.com
Location Signed from A303 at South Petherton.
Opening hours 10 am – 5 pm; daily; February to October. Plus special openings for National Gardens Scheme.
Admission fee Adults £3.95; OAPs £3.50; Children & Students £1 (subject to review).

East Lambrook is the archetypal cottage garden, made by Margery Fish, the popular gardening writer, and charmingly restored in recent years. Margery Fish was an important influence in British gardening in the 1950s and 1960s. She learnt about gardening not from books but from her own observations, so that she developed her own unselfconscious style of gardening. As a journalist, she knew how to communicate, and her books about the garden she made at East Lambrook have been very influential. The new owners are continuing the work of restoration begun in the 1980s, and have updated the plantings while respecting the original spirit. They have returned Margery Fish's nursery to its original site, made a special bed for the National Collection of hardy geraniums and restored the malthouse. They also run RHS courses for gardeners all through the year.

 Features Margery Fish's garden; plantsman's collection of plants; good herbaceous borders; 150 different snowdrops; hellebores; euphorbias; geraniums; cottage garden plants; lunches & teas from Easter to end of September.

Owned by Marianne & Robert Williams
Number of gardeners 1½
Size 0.8ha (2 acres)
NCCPG National Collections *Geranium*
English Heritage Grade I

Elworthy Cottage Plants

ELWORTHY COTTAGE, ELWORTHY,
LYDEARD ST LAWRENCE, TAUNTON,
TA4 3PX

Tel 01984 656427
Website www.elworthy-cottage.co.uk
Location 10 miles north-west of Taunton, on
B3188 in Elworthy village centre.
Opening hours 10 am – 4 pm, Wednesday –
Friday, mid-March to the end of June. Then
Thursdays only from July to September. And by
appointment.
Admission fee £1.50.

Elworthy offers a pleasant selection of
perennials and cottage garden plants,
including quite a number which are
uncommon or hard-to-find, as well as old
favourites. The nursery is strong on
geraniums (over 200), clematis (over 100),
pulmonarias (over 50), as well as violas,
crocosmias and grasses. Some of the plants
the nursery offers are not available from any
other source. It has also introduced a
number of new plants, including *Geranium*
x *oxonianum* 'Elworthy Misty' and *G.*
'Elworthy Eyecatcher'. Most of the plants
can be seen growing in the display garden,
which is neatly laid out with island beds and
themed colours for year-round interest but
also to blend into the surrounding
countryside (Exmoor National Park) and to
encourage wildlife. Recent additions include
a hedge of native species and a wildflower
bank, a rockery and gravel area for shade-
tolerant plants, a formal *potager*, and a new
orange-and-yellow border for autumn.

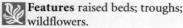**Features** raised beds; troughs;
wildflowers.

Owned by Mike & Jenny Spiller
Number of gardeners owners only
Size 0.4ha (1 acre)

Gaulden Manor

TOLLAND, LYDEARD ST LAWRENCE,
TA4 3PN

Tel 01984 667213
Location 1 mile east of Tolland church, off B3224.
Opening hours 2 pm – 5 pm; Thursdays, Sundays
& Bank Holidays; June to August. And groups by
appointment at other times.
Admission fee £3.25.

Gaulden is a modern garden, well designed
and well planted. It has a series of small
garden rooms, each devoted to a different
theme (roses, herbs etc.) which makes it
seem much larger than it really is and a
pleasure to explore. The stream garden –
very pretty – is below the monks' pond, its
sides planted with candelabra primulas,
ferns and gunneras.

**Features** woodland garden; roses
(ancient & modern); herbs; good
herbaceous borders; scent gardens; secret
garden; book & gift shop.

Owned by James Starkie
Number of gardeners 2
Size 0.8ha (2 acres)

Greencombe Gardens

PORLOCK, TA24 8NU

Tel 01643 862363
Location ½ mile west of Porlock on left of road to
Porlock Weir.
Opening hours 2 pm – 6 pm; Saturday –
Wednesday; April to July & again in autumn
Admission fee Adults £4.50; Children (under 16) £1.

Greencombe is an organic showpiece of
international renown. The garden stretches
across a sheltered hillside which looks up to
the tree-covered slopes of Exmoor behind

and down across ancient fields to Porlock Bay and an uninterrupted view of the sea. It is a woodland garden, long and narrow, with a rich underplanting of ornamental plants beneath an outstanding canopy of oaks, hollies, conifers and sweet chestnuts. Camellias, rhododendrons, azaleas, maples, lilies, roses, clematis, and hydrangeas are in turn underplanted with many ferns and the garden's four National Collections: *Erythronium*, which are small mountain-lilies; *Vaccinium*, which the curator Joan Loraine calls 'whortleberries worldwide'; *Gaultheria*, which she refers to as 'whortleberries for bears'; and *Polystichum*, the 'thumbs-up' fern. The garden is completely organic, with compost heaps and leaf mould pits on show, and a riot of birds, butterflies and lesser insects. But, above all, like all good plantsman's gardens, Greencombe is full of rare plants and has lots to interest the visitor at every time of the year.

Features woodland garden; plantsman's collection of plants; good herbaceous borders; organically run; tea.

Owned by Greencombe Garden Trust
Number of gardeners 2 part-time
Size 1.4ha (3½ acres)
NCCPG National Collections *Erythronium*; *Gaultheria*; *Polystichum*; *Vaccinium*

Hadspen Garden

CASTLE CARY, BA7 7NG

Tel & Fax 01749 813707
Website www.hadspengarden.co.uk
Location 2 miles east of Castle Cary on A371. New access off A359.
Opening hours 10 am – 5 pm; Thursday – Sunday & Bank Holiday Mondays; March to September.
Admission fee Adults £4; Children 50p.

Ⓟ ⓦⓒ 🅿 🌱 🎁 ☕

Part garden, part nursery specialising in colour-plantings and unusual plants. Little remains of Penelope Hobhouse's first garden: the Popes have re-made it in the modern idiom, using a wide range of rare plants to create decorative effects. Most visitors speak highly of it. The Popes' book on using colour in the garden has now been reprinted as *Planting with Colour*. It is published by Conran Octopus and based on their work at Hadspen.

Features roses (mainly old-fashioned); plantsman's collection of plants; good herbaceous borders; Eric Smith's *Hosta* collection; tulips; excellent nursery; colour gardening; nursery; light lunches & teas.

Owned by N. & S. Pope
Number of gardeners 2½
Size 2ha (5 acres)
NCCPG National Collections *Rodgersia*

Hestercombe Gardens

CHEDDON FITZPAINE, TAUNTON, TA2 8LG

Tel 01823 413923 **Fax** 01823 413747
Website www.hestercombegardens.com
Location 4 miles north of Taunton.
Opening hours 10 am – 5 pm; daily; all year.
Admission fee Adults £5.20; OAPs £4.90; Children £1.30.

 Ⓟ 🅗 ⓦⓒ 🌱 🎁 ☕

Ignore the house – a Victorian mansion now used as Council offices – and look at the famously restored garden. Lutyens's hallmarks are everywhere: iris-choked rills, pergolas, seats, relieved staircases and pools where reflections twinkle on recessed apses. Gertrude Jekyll's planting is bold and simple, which adds to the vigour. The combination of Lutyens design and Jekyll plants is extremely photogenic: Hestercombe is a highly rewarding garden to learn about symmetry, balance and proportion. The secret landscape garden which Coplestone Warre Bampfylde laid out in the late 18th century re-opened in 1997: 40 acres of lakes, temples, combes and woodlands which have not been seen for over 100 years. Last year, the Heritage Lottery Fund agreed to a grant of £5.5m to be paid between 2003 and 2007. This will confirm Hestercombe as Somerset's most visited garden.

 Features good herbaceous borders; classical landscaping; Lutyens design & Jekyll planting; gift shop; plant sales (March to October); refreshments.

Owned by Hestercombe Gardens Trust
Number of gardeners 8
Size 20ha (50 acres)
English Heritage Grade I

Kelways Ltd

BARRYMORE FARM, LANGPORT, TA10 9EZ

Tel 01458 250521 **Fax** 01458 253351
Website www.kelways.co.uk
Location On B3153, just east of Langport.
Opening hours 9 am – 5 pm; Monday – Friday. 10 am – 5 pm on Saturdays and 10 am – 4 pm on Sundays.

Long famous for its peonies (500+ herbaceous and 35 tree peonies) , Kelways also has a large range of irises (700+), and an expanding range of perennials, shrubs and bedding plants. An orchid house displays and sells English-grown orchids.

 Features peonies; irises; orchids.

Owned by C. Johnson
NCCPG National Collections *Paeonia lactiflora*

Lower Severalls Gardens & Nursery

CREWKERNE, TA18 7NX

Tel 01460 73234 **Fax** 01460 76105
Website www.lowerseveralls.co.uk
Location 1½ miles north-east of Crewkerne. Signed from A30 & A352.
Opening hours 10 am – 5 pm; daily; 1 March to mid-October. Closed Thursdays & Sundays, but open 2 pm – 5 pm on Sundays in May & June.
Admission fee Adults £2.50.

Both the garden and nursery started in 1985. At first, the nursery specialised in herbs, of which it still has a wide range. However, there are also good selections of hardy geraniums, salvias and lots more besides. The garden is set in front of an 18th-century Ham-stone farmhouse: it has fine herbaceous borders, island beds, a living 'dogwood basket' and an area for bog plants known as 'the Wadi'.

 Features herbaceous borders; island beds; herbs; self-service tea.

Owned by Mary Pring
Number of gardeners 2
Size 1.2ha (3 acres)

Lytes Cary Manor

CHARLTON MACKRELL, SOMERTON, TA11 7HU

Tel & Fax 01458 224471
Website www.nationaltrust.org.uk
Location Near A303 junction with A372 & A37.
Opening hours 11 am – 5 pm; Mondays, Wednesdays, Fridays & Sundays; 5 April to 31 October.
Admission fee Adults £3; Children £1.

Lytes Cary has a neo-Elizabethan garden to go with the prettiest of manor houses: yew hedges, hornbeam walks, alleys and lawns, medlars, quinces and a simple Elizabethan flower border.

 Features topiary; good herbaceous borders.

Owned by The National Trust
Number of gardeners 1
English Heritage Grade II

Mallet Court Nursery

CURRY MALLET, TAUNTON, TA3 6SY

Tel & Fax 01823 481493
Website www.malletcourt.co.uk
Location In the centre of Curry Mallet.
Opening hours 10 am – 4 pm; Mondays to Fridays. Plus special Open Days in April and October. Weekends by appointment.
Admission fee Free.

This is a wonderful specialist tree nursery with an excellent list of unusual trees. Its displays at RHS flower shows, including Chelsea and Hampton Court, have been a delight and a revelation over many years now. Many of the species it sells are offered by no other nursery anywhere in the world. It is particularly good for *Quercus* and *Acer*, and strong on species from China and Korea, but the nursery's list is full of species of every imaginable genus of rare trees. Every dendrophile in Britain knows of it and buys from it: the array of plants to be seen at the nursery is itself an education. Three RHS special events will take place at Mallet Court during 2004: details from 020 7821 3408.

Owned by J.G.S. Harris & Mrs P.M.E. Mallet-Harris

Meadows Nursery

5 RECTORY COTTAGES, SELWOOD STREET, MELLS, FROME, BA11 3PN

Tel 01373 813025 **Fax** 01373 812268
Location In centre of village.
Opening hours 10 am – 6 pm; Wednesday – Sunday; February to October.
Admission fee Free.

Meadows Nursery has a pretty, cottage-style garden, well maintained and boosted by putting out some spectacular succulents and other glasshouse plants in summer. The nursery specialises in perennials and has a particularly good line in hostas. Both make very good use of a confined space. There are plans for an extension.

 Features good nursery.

Owned by Sue Lees & Eddie Wheatley
Number of gardeners owners
Size 0.2ha (½ acre)

Mill Cottage Plants

HENLEY MILL, WOOKEY, BA5 1AW

Tel 01749 676966
Location 2 miles from Wells, off A371. Left into Henley Lane, then 50 yards on left.
Opening hours Nursery: 10 am – 5.30 pm, Wednesdays, March to September. Garden also open by appointment.
Admission fee Garden £1.50; Nursery free.

The nursery grows a selection of unusual perennials, including a wide range of geraniums, hellebores, oriental poppies, dieramas, ferns and grasses. It also has a good line in rare hydrangea cultivars. The garden is well worth seeing, though it is best to ask if you can see it in advance of your visit. It includes a sunny formal garden, a shaded 'folly' garden; kitchen garden, 'hot red' borders, and a late summer bed (mainly grasses and perennials). Groups are especially welcome.

Features beautiful waterside setting; hardy perennials.

Owned by Peter & Sally Gregson
Number of gardeners 2½
Size 1ha (2½ acres)

Milton Lodge

OLD BRISTOL ROAD, WELLS, BA5 3AQ

Tel 01749 672168
Location Old Bristol road off of A39.
Opening hours 2 pm – 5 pm; Tuesdays, Wednesdays, Sundays & Bank Holidays; Easter to 31 October.
Admission fee Adults £2.50; Children (under 14) free. Groups by arrangement.

This impressive Edwardian garden is terraced down a hillside against a backdrop of Wells Cathedral. Most of the plantings are modern, and look good against the walls and bulky yew hedges. In a combe, across the main road, is an eight-acre 19th-century arboretum. Both parts are full of interesting plants, excellently maintained and constantly improving, with considerable new planting in recent years.

Features roses (mainly modern); good herbaceous borders; fine collection of trees; teas on Sundays (May to August); tallest *Populus alba* (20m.) in the British Isles.

Owned by D.C. Tudway Quilter
Size 1.6ha (4 acres)
English Heritage Grade II

Montacute House

MONTACUTE, YEOVIL, TA15 6XP

Tel 01935 823289 **Fax** 01935 826921
Website www.nationaltrust.org.uk
Location In Montacute village, 4 miles west of Yeovil.
Opening hours 11 am – 6 pm (dusk if earlier); daily except Tuesday; 19 March to 31 October. Then 11 am – 4 pm; Wednesday – Sunday; 3 November to 25 March 2005.
Admission fee Adults £3.70; Children £1.70. Reduced rates in winter.

The sunken gardens at Montacute are a perfect foil for the amazing Elizabethan mansion and beautifully maintained. They cannot be beaten for the sense of English renaissance grandeur they impart. The National Trust has recently had the courage to replant the borders not as they were originally planned by Vita Sackville-West, nor as subsequently laid out by Graham Thomas in pretty pastel shades, but using the brilliant colours devised by Phyllis Reiss of nearby Tintinhull in the 1950s. The vivid colours of 'Frensham' roses, purple berberis and late-summer dahlias are the ideal complement to the Ham-stone house.

Features good herbaceous borders; exquisite gazebos; shop; light lunches & teas, licensed restaurant.

Owned by The National Trust
Number of gardeners 4
Size 5ha (12½ acres), plus 10.2ha (26 acres) parkland
English Heritage Grade I

P.M.A. Plant Specialities

JUNKER'S NURSERY LTD., LOWER MEAD, WEST HATCH, TAUNTON, TA3 5RN

Tel 01823 480774 Fax 01823 481046
Location West Hatch is 4 miles south of Taunton.
Opening hours By appointment only.
Admission fee Free.

P.M.A. has some interesting container-grown trees and shrubs. It is particularly strong on Japanese and snakebark acers, daphnes, magnolias and the ornamental tree *Cornus*. Some plants are available in larger sizes for instant impact. The display borders are particularly instructive – new areas are planted and developed every year – and visitors also have free access to the stock plants.

Owned by Nick & Karan Junker
Number of gardeners owners only
Size 1.2ha (3 acres)

Prior Park

RALPH ALLEN DRIVE, BATH, BA2 5AH

Tel & Fax 01225 833422
Website www.nationaltrust.org.uk
Location 1½ miles south of Bath city centre.
Opening hours 11 am – 5.30 pm (or dusk, if earlier); Wednesday – Monday; 1 February to 29 November. 11 am – dusk; Friday – Sunday; 3 December – 31 January 2005.
Admission fee Adults £4.10; Children £2.

The classical landscape at Prior Park was laid out between 1734 and 1764 by a property developer called Ralph Allen, who was a friend of Pope and Burlington. Pope advised extensively on the original lay-out and buildings before Capability Brown gave them a make-over in the early 1760s. The park is no more than 28 acres, stretching from the extremely handsome Palladian house (not National Trust) at the top of the steep valley to the Palladian bridge right at the bottom, which is the focus of the entire landscape. It is reached by a rugged and sometimes slippery path through the woods on either side, quite unfitted for wheelchairs and buggies and only suitable for the sure-footed and confident. There is nothing of horticultural interest, but some fine trees – mainly beech, with some yew, sycamore and seedling ashes – underplanted with ferns and laurels. Nevertheless it is hard to imagine a more elegant landscape than this one, which uses the busy and fashionable city of Bath as its background. Photographers may wish to visit it early in the afternoon, when the sun shines on the Palladian bridge. There is one snag, however: the Trust can offer no on-site parking. Badgerline runs buses (Nos. 2 & 4) from the Grand Parade or Dorchester Street, every 20 minutes on weekdays and half-hourly from Dorchester Street on Sundays.

Features Palladian bridge; handsome parkland.

Owned by The National Trust
Number of gardeners 3, plus volunteers
Size 11.1ha (28 acres)
English Heritage Grade I

Scotts Nurseries (Merriott) Ltd

MERRIOTT, TA16 5PL

Tel 01460 72306 Fax 01460 77433
Location 2 miles north of Crewkerne between the A30 & the A303.
Opening hours 8 am – 5 pm; Monday – Friday. 9 am – 5 pm; Saturdays. 10.30 am – 4.30 pm; Sundays.
Admission fee Free.

Scotts of Merriott is a first-rate, long-established and respected nursery-cum-garden centre, offering a very wide range of field- and container-grown plants. It is particularly strong on old-fashioned roses, ornamental trees, top fruit and shrubs.

Sherborne Garden

PEAR TREE HOUSE, LITTON, BA3 4PP

Tel 01761 241220
Location On B3114, ½ mile west of Litton village, 7 miles north of Wells.
Opening hours 11 am – 6 pm; Mondays; June to September. Plus 6 June & 11 July for NGS.
Admission fee Adults £2.50; Children free. Groups welcome by appointment.

This plantsman's garden started in a modest enough way in 1964 but now extends to more than six acres. It is very thickly planted, yet it also seems to sit very well in the countryside. The owners are particularly interested in trees and plant them in groups for comparison: hence the 'prickly wood' (of hollies), the pinetum and an acer glade, as well as some 50 different oaks. But there are also good herbaceous plantings and bulbs, a fine collection of *Rosa* species, hemerocallis (200) and ferns (200), which makes it an excellent garden to dawdle in and learn from.

Features woodland garden; roses (ancient & modern, plus many species); plantsman's collection of plants; small pinetum; collection of hollies (180 varieties) and hardy ferns (250 varieties); 29 different waterlilies; tea/coffee.

Owned by Mr & Mrs John Southwell
Number of gardeners owners, with part-time help.
Size 2.4ha (6 acres)

Tintinhull House

TINTINHULL, YEOVIL, BA22 8PZ

Tel 01935 822545 **Fax** 01935 826357
Website www.nationaltrust.org.uk
Location In Tintinhull village, 5 miles north-west of Yeovil.
Opening hours 12 noon – 6 pm; Wednesdays – Sunday; 24 March to 30 September.
Admission fee Adults £4.20; Children £2.10.

This small garden – less than two acres – is the most famous example of a Jekyll-style garden on a small scale. It combines great design with a wide range of plants and the most skilful use of colour combinations in planting them. The garden looks larger than it really is because it has been divided into a sequence of small rooms of different size, all of them hedged or walled. Perhaps the most famous part is the largest, around a formal rectangular pool in front of a pillared summerhouse. The borders on either side are in complete contrast to each other: one is made in the bright bold colours of scarlet, yellow, orange and white, while the other is dominated by pastel pinks, mauves, blues and pale yellows. Yet they are also mirror images of each other because each uses grey-leaved plants and striking leaf shapes as well as colour. No garden employs such a wide palette of plants so rigorously as elements of design. There has been much cutting back, clearing, renewal and replanting recently.

Features topiary; roses (mainly old-fashioned); good herbaceous borders; colour borders; kitchen garden; light refreshments.

Owned by The National Trust
Number of gardeners 2
Size 0.8ha (2 acres)
English Heritage Grade II

Wayford Manor

CREWKERNE, TA18 8QG

Tel 01460 73253 **Fax** 01460 76365
Location 3 miles south-west of Crewkerne off A30 or B3165.
Opening hours 11 April; 2, 3 & 23 May; 13 June. For NGS. And parties by appointment.
Admission fee Adults £2; Children 50p.

Wayford is one of the best gardens designed by Harold Peto: terraces and courtyards, pools and arbours, balustrades and staircases, Tuscan and Byzantine. Down in the wild garden is an extensive collection of mature acers and magnolias, as well as many rhododendrons, bog plants and daffodils. The whole garden is being restored by the enthusiastic and knowledgeable owners. In 2000, they reinstated the pergola with stone Tuscan columns as Peto originally designed it.

Features good herbaceous borders; rhododendrons; spring bulbs; maples; tallest *Photinia davidiana* (13m.) in the British Isles; plants for sale; teas.

Owned by Mr & Mrs R.L. Goffe
Number of gardeners 1
Size 1.6ha (4 acres)
English Heritage Grade II

STAFFORDSHIRE

Staffordshire has three historic gardens to which English Heritage has accorded Grade I status: Alton Towers, Biddulph Grange and Shugborough. All are open to the public. The county is not, however, a magnet for garden-visitors with horticultural interests. The Dorothy Clive Garden is the only really first-rate garden in Staffordshire to have come out of the 20th century. There are only two National Collections and the National Garden Scheme has comparatively little success within the county. Why this should be remains a puzzle: the county is fairly wealthy, its soils are fertile, and its climate is not too subject to extremes. Staffordshire's historic gardens trust is however very active and its historic gardens are well-visited – Shugborough, Weston and Trentham have all enjoyed long traditions of popular participation in their public programmes events. There are few arboreta of note and practically no record-sized trees anywhere in the county. But Ashwood Nurseries, on the borders of West Midlands, is a place of international standing.

Alton Towers

ALTON, STOKE-ON-TRENT,
ST10 4DB

Tel 0870 5204060 **Fax** 01538 704092
Website www.altontowers.com
Location Signed for miles around.
Opening hours 9.30 am – 5/6/7 pm depending on season; daily; 27 March to 31 October.
Admission fee Tickets vary in cost according to season but are always fairly expensive: Alton offers much more than gardens to visit.

  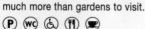

Alton has 300 acres of dotty and exuberant display, best seen from the sky-ride. The gardens are by and large detached from the razzmatazz of the theme park. There are splendid Victorian conifers and gaudy bedding, magnificently done. The highlights include a Swiss Cottage, a Roman bridge, a Chinese pagoda, a flag tower, and a corkscrew fountain. It is seriously important to garden historians and excellent entertainment still – but not for contemplative souls. Best in term time.

Features woodland garden; roses (mainly modern); rock garden; mature conifers; good herbaceous borders; many restaurants.

Owned by Tussauds Group
Size 120ha (300 acres)
English Heritage Grade I

Ashwood Nurseries Ltd

ASHWOOD LOWER LANE,
KINGSWINFORD, DY6 0AE

Tel 01384 401996 **Fax** 01308 401108
Website www.ashwood-nurseries.co.uk
Location 2 miles west of Kingswinford, near A449.
Opening hours 9 am – 6 pm; Monday – Saturday.
9.30 am – 6 pm; Sundays. All year, except 25 & 26
December.
Admission fee Free.

Ashwood is a rising star among nurseries.
The owners have the happy knack of
anticipating trends in horticultural fashion:
they then put a lot of thought into
developing new plants and, thus, new
markets. They began in the 1970s with
lewisias, crossing and selecting them until
they could offer a remarkable range of
colours. In 1996 they were awarded a gold
medal for their lewisias at the Chelsea
Flower Show, their first ever exhibit at the
Royal Horticultural Society's most
prestigious show. Next they began to breed
hellebores – strains of *H. orientalis* in
particular. The Ashwood hybrids are
remarkable for their purity of colour, vigour
and form – but, above all, for the new
developments that they have brought to the
genus: doubles, anemone-centred and
upright forms. Now they are turning their
attention to hybrids of *H. niger*. More
recent, but no less promising, has been their
involvement with hardy cyclamen, auriculas,
and hepaticas. Hepaticas are extremely
fashionable in Japan, where rare cultivars
may cost the equivalent of several hundred
pounds, and there is clearly money to be
made from developing this genus yet
further. Above all, Ashwood means quality:
the exhibits the nursery brings to RHS
Flower Shows are beautifully grown. A visit
to their nursery is strongly recommended.
Six very interesting RHS special events are
planned here for 2004; details from 020
7821 3408.

Features hellebores; cyclamen;
lewisias; hepaticas; auriculas; gift shop;
tea-room.

Owned by John Massey
Size 2ha (5 acres)
NCCPG National Collections *Lewisia*

Biddulph Grange

BIDDULPH, STOKE-ON-TRENT, ST8 7SD

Tel 01782 517999 **Fax** 01782 510624
Website www.nationaltrust.org.uk
Location ½ mile north of Biddulph, 3½ miles south-
east of Congleton.
Opening hours 12 noon – 5.30 pm; Wednesday –
Sunday & Bank Holiday Mondays (closed Good
Friday); 21 & 22 March, then 27 March to 31
October. Also 11 am – 3 pm; Saturdays & Sundays;
1 November to 19 December.
Admission fee Adults £4.80; Children £2.40 (but
less from 1 November to 21 December).

The garden at Biddulph was made in the
middle of the 19th century by James
Bateman – an important amateur garden
designer, plantsman and writer. His wife
Maria and their friend Edward Coke also
had a hand in it. Their garden has dozens of
different microclimates, compartments,
follies and whimsies: it is, in fact, the earliest
example of a garden being divided into a
series of smaller rooms, each designed and
planted to a different theme. Some are so
original and inventive that they still strike us
as frankly rather wacky – the Dragon
Parterre, for example, which is dominated
by a golden cow, or the stumpery where
carefully excavated and inverted tree stumps
and roots form a framework for trailing
ivies and other plants. One of the more
eccentric novelties is the 'upside-down tree'

replanted with its roots in the air between the Rhododendron Ground and the Lime Avenue. Others are the Egyptian courtyard with its own pyramid, a bowling green and quoits ground, the Chinese garden (surprisingly large and beautiful, with a joss house, temple and section of the Great Wall) and the ferny Scottish glen. Elsewhere are areas devoted to collections of plants – a wellingtonia avenue, a pinetum and the dahlia walk. The estate suffered years of neglect when the house (fairly ugly, mid-Victorian and neo-Jacobean) was used as a hospital but the National Trust has restored it energetically and many of the quirkier features are as good as ever again. The trees survived best: some of the conifers are very large handsome specimens in the prime of middle age now.

Features Victorian garden with many different styles & rooms; excellent plants & plantings; mature conifers; mosaic parterre; gift shop; tea-room.

Owned by The National Trust
Number of gardeners 5, plus 2 part-time
Size 6ha (15 acres)
English Heritage Grade I

Dorothy Clive Garden

WILLOUGHBRIDGE, MARKET DRAYTON, TF9 4EU

Tel 01630 647237 **Fax** 01630 647902
Website www.dorothyclivegarden.co.uk
Location A51, midway between Nantwich & Stone.
Opening hours 10 am – 5.30 pm; daily; April to October.
Admission fee Adults £3.80; OAPs & Groups (20+) £3.30; Children £1 (under 11 free). RHS members free in July & August.

Meticulously maintained and still expanding, this garden was begun in 1940 but seems ageless. It was made on an unpromising site, a cold windy hilltop, but advice on plants and planting came from Frank Knight, then director of Wisley. The lay-out is informal, yet full of incidents, each with a distinct character: they include a superb woodland garden, an alpine scree, a damp garden, a conifer collection and spectacular summer flower borders. The Dorothy Clive Garden is best perhaps in May, when the woodland quarry is brilliant with rhododendrons, but the scree (replanted in 1998) and rock garden (reflected in the pond) are hard to beat at any season. And, since it has many well-grown but unusual plants of all kinds, there is always much to see whatever the season.

Features woodland garden; mature conifers; camellias; good herbaceous borders; heather; cyclamen; tea-room with beverages & home-baked food.

Owned by Willoughbridge Garden Trust
Number of gardeners 3
Size 3.2ha (8 acres)

Moseley Old Hall

MOSELEY OLD HALL LANE, FORDHOUSES, WV10 7HY

Tel & Fax 01902 782808
Website www.nationaltrust.org.uk
Location South of M54 between A449 & A460.
Opening hours 12 noon – 5 pm (but 11 am to 5 pm on Bank Holiday Mondays); Wednesdays, Saturdays, Sundays, Bank Holiday Mondays & the following Tuesdays; 20 March to 31 October. 1 pm – 4 pm; Sundays; 7 November to 19 December.
Admission fee Adults £4.40.

This is a modern reconstruction of a 17th-century town garden: neat box parterres, a nut walk and an arched pergola hung with clematis and vines. The plantings are all of a period, including the fruit trees: quietly inspirational.

Features topiary; snowdrops; herbs; current holder of Sandford Award; gift shop; tea-room.

Owned by The National Trust
Number of gardeners 2 part-time
Size 0.4ha (1 acre)

Oulton House

OULTON, STONE, ST15 8UR

Tel 01785 813556 **Fax** 01785 816141
Location From Stone take Oulton Road & turn left after Oulton sign. 3rd driveway on right. Steep, winding drive; house at top of hill.
Opening hours By appointment, February to July.
Admission fee Adults £2; Children 75p.

This three-acre garden has been made by Mrs Fairbairn over many years, essentially for private enjoyment not for public display. It is full of good plants – roses, rhododendrons, geraniums and clematis – arranged in colour groupings. The snowdrops and hellebores are especially good early in the year, followed by more spring bulbs and a field of daffodils.

Features snowdrops; roses (mainly old-fashioned); rock garden; plants under glass; good herbaceous borders; hellebores; spring bulbs; plants for sale sometimes; teas.

Owned by Mr & Mrs W.A. Fairbairn
Number of gardeners owners, plus part-time help
Size 1.4ha (3½ acres)

Shugborough Hall

MILFORD, STAFFORD, ST17 0XB

Tel 01889 881388 **Fax** 01889 881323
Website www.staffordshire.gov.uk/shugborough
Location Signed from Jct 13 M6.
Opening hours 11 am – 5 pm; Tuesday-Sunday & Bank Holiday Mondays; 27 March to 26 September, plus first four Sundays in October, and parties by appointment. Last admissions 4.15 pm. Times may vary: please ring to check.
Admission fee Parkland: Vehicles £2.

This classical and neo-classical landscape has Chinese additions; a handsome William Andrews Nesfield terrace dominated by dumplings of clipped golden yew; 50 oaks in the new arboretum; and a rose garden restored by Graham Stuart Thomas. All very popular with the locals.

Features woodland garden; roses (mainly old-fashioned); good herbaceous borders; formal terraces with rhododendrons; current holder of Sandford Award; garden centre; lunches, snacks, tea & evening dinners.

Owned by The National Trust
Number of gardeners 4
Size 4ha (10 acres)
English Heritage Grade I

Trentham Gardens

STONE ROAD, STOKE-ON-TRENT, ST4 8AX

Tel 01782 657341
Location Signed from M6.
Opening hours 10 am – 4 pm; daily; all year. Garden may close for redevelopment.
Admission fee Not yet known.

The Trentham estate is currently undergoing development, part of which will involve restoring the important Victorian formal gardens, park, lakes and woods. It is expected that some of the gardens will be open this spring (2004), but would-be visitors are advised to telephone before making their visit.

Features important Italianate formal gardens; summer bedding; café in summer.

Owned by Trentham Leisure Ltd.
English Heritage Grade II*

Weston Park

WESTON-UNDER-LIZARD, SHIFNAL, TF11 8LE

Tel 01952 852100 **Fax** 01952 850430
Website www.weston-park.com
Location Off the A5 to Telford.
Opening hours 11 am – 7 pm (last admissions 5 pm); 10-18 and 24-25 April; Saturdays, Sundays & Bank Holidays in May; 1-6, 12-13, 19-20 & 26-27 June; 3-30 July; 1-18 & 26-31 August; 1-5 September.
Admission fee Adults £3; OAPs £2.50; Children £2.

Weston has a fine 18th-century landscape (Capability Brown worked there) and a 19th-century Italianate parterre, a temple of Diana, a grotto called Pendrill's Cave, and a handsome orangery by James Paine. It is not of major horticultural interest, but the rose walk and rhododendrons are worth seeing. It is perhaps best for its fine collection of trees, some of them record-breakers, and the collection of *Nothofagus* planted by the late Lord Bradford.

Features fine collection of trees; landscaped park; rhododendrons; gift shop; restaurant.

Owned by The Weston Park Foundation
Number of gardeners 3
English Heritage Grade II*

SUFFOLK

Suffolk has comparatively few historic gardens of national importance but, such as they are, they are of great interest to the garden-lover. Both Helmingham and Shrubland are rated as Grade I gardens, while Euston, Ickworth and Somerleyton are all Grade II*. There is a particularly fine collection of trees at East Bergholt Place, which has a good nursery attached. Suffolk is a rich county but was, until recently, rather cut off from London and its markets, which may help in part to explain why it has so many good nurseries. Notcutts is one of the largest quality nurseries in the country, with a long and distinguished history of plant introductions and exhibits at RHS flower shows. The leading seedsmen Thompson & Morgan have been at Ipswich for over 100 years: their trial grounds may also be visited in season. But it is the sheer number of good small modern nurseries which is so surprising: we list Goldbrook, Mills Farm, Park Green and Rougham Hall among others – but Gardiner's Hall Plants at Braiseworth (over 3,000 different plants) and North Green Snowdrops (sent 'in the green') are also worth knowing. Suffolk has many good modern gardens like Wyken Hall and others which we do not list, including the Blakenham Woodland Garden at Little Blakenham (made by the late Lord Blakenham, Treasurer of the RHS). The National Garden Scheme does well in the county and there is an active historic gardens trust too. The NCCPG is represented by about a dozen National Collections, including some horticulturally important genera like lilacs (*Syringa*), delphiniums and fuchsias. Otley College near Ipswich is a RHS Partner College, with lectures, workshops and garden walks throughout the year: further details from 020 7821 3408.

East Bergholt Place

EAST BERGHOLT, CO7 6UP

Tel & Fax 01206 299224
Location 2 miles east of A12, on B1070, ENE of East Bergholt.
Opening hours 10 am – 5 pm; daily; March to October.
Admission fee Adults £2.50; Children free.

East Bergholt has a wonderful woodland garden planted by Charles Eley, the present owner's great-grandfather, at the start of the 20th century. It is the home of *Malus* x *purpurea* 'Eleyi' and has been called a 'Cornish Garden in Suffolk'. Unfortunately, there are still parts which are not open to the public. Of greatest interest is a collection of trees known as the 'Swale', around a gentle valley with a small brook running down the middle. Many of the older trees and shrubs were grown from original collections by George Forrest: others represent modern plantings and re-plantings. The collection is well-labelled and well-maintained – a fine place to see a wide range of trees and shrubs. Good specimens include a very handsome variegated cherry-laurel *Prunus laurocerasus* 'Castlewellan' 5m high, a magnificent *Quercus castaneifolia* and a fine three-stemmed *Davidia involucrata* var. *vilmoriniana*. Some are record-breakers, including a *Lithocarpus densiflorus* 12m tall. The valley is sheltered by hedges of holly and yew and a mature collection of hardy rhododendrons. And it is good for insects and wildlife too. Restoration and replanting continue. The much-praised nursery in the walled garden has a good general stock, much of it bought in.

Features topiary; rhododendrons & azaleas; camellias; fine collection of trees; specialist plant centre in walled garden.

Owned by Mr & Mrs Rupert Eley
Number of gardeners 1
Size 6ha (15 acres)

Euston Hall

EUSTON, THETFORD,
IP24 2QP

Tel 01842 766366 **Fax** 01842 766764
Website www.eustonhall.co.uk
Location On A1088 3 miles south of Thetford & 12 miles north of Bury St Edmunds.
Opening hours 2.30 pm – 5 pm; Thursdays; 17 June to 16 September, plus 27 June, 18 July & 5 September. NCCPG Plant Sale on 30 May.
Admission fee £2.

The classical 18th-century landscaping at Euston is very beautiful. William Kent made the serpentine lake, though it was later modified by Capability Brown. Kent also built the elegant banqueting house. There are avenues of beech and lime, and clumps, spinneys and belts of mature trees. The formal terraces by the house lead to herbaceous borders and rose gardens. It all adds up to a most satisfying composition where horticulture plays second fiddle to landscaping.

Features roses (mainly old-fashioned); William Kent temple and summerhouse; new 'Monet' bridge on lake; river walk & watermill; craft shop; home-made teas.

Owned by The Duke of Grafton
Number of gardeners 2
Size 28ha (70 acres)
English Heritage Grade II*

Goldbrook Plants

HOXNE, EYE, IP21 5AN

Tel & Fax 01379 668770
Location On south-east edge of Hoxne.
Opening hours 10 am – 5 pm; Thursday – Sunday; April to September. Saturdays & Sundays only; October to March. Other days by appointment. Closed January & around Chelsea & Hampton Court Shows.

Goldbrook's exhibits at Chelsea and other RHS flower shows have won them much praise – and an impressive run of gold medals. Their collection of hostas is quite exceptional – over 1,000 cultivars, of which a great many are available from no other nursery. The same is true of their hemerocallis. Look out for their American introductions too – many of the hemerocallis bear the prefix 'Siloam' (e.g. *H.* 'Siloam Fairy Tale') – while the hostas they have raised themselves are often prefixed by 'Goldbrook'.

 Features hostas; hemerocallis.

Owned by Sandra Bond

Harveys Garden Plants

BRADFIELD ST GEORGE, BURY ST EDMUNDS, IP30 0AY

Tel & Fax 01284 386777
Website www.harveysgardenplants.co.uk
Location On the left of the Rougham Road out of the village.
Opening hours 9.30 am – 5 pm; Thursday – Saturday; 15 January to 30 June and 1 September to 31 October. Closes at 1 pm on Saturdays.
Admission fee Free.

Harveys Garden Plants is a small family-run nursery in Suffolk, UK, growing an extensive range of hardy herbaceous plants. They specialise in unusual perennials, especially those not commonly found in garden centres. Their specialities include hellebores, heleniums and shade-loving woodland plants. They have now started to develop their own strain of up-facing hellebores which they call the Bradfield hybrids. Six RHS special events will take place during 2004: details from 020 7821 3408.

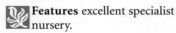 **Features** excellent specialist nursery.

Haughley Park

STOWMARKET, IP14 3JY

Tel 01359 240701 **Fax** 01359 240546
Website www.haughleyparkbarn.co.uk
Location Signed from A14.
Opening hours 2 pm – 5.30 pm; Tuesdays; May to September, plus 25 April & 2 May for bluebells.
Admission fee Adults £3; Children free.

Haughley has a Jacobean mansion with well-kept modern flower gardens and fine trees (especially a magnolia, probably *Magnolia denudata*, 8m high and 11m across). In the walled garden are vegetables, trained fruit trees, a rose arbour and other ornamental features. But the acres of lily-of-the-valley and bluebells in the woodland garden are worth the journey no matter how far. There is a choice of three woodland walks, from one-and-a-half to two-and-a-half miles long: the camellias are good in May and the rhododendrons in June. In the West Woods, the owners have been carrying out an interesting experiment since the great gale of 1987. This arises from the different way in which each part was subsequently managed. Some areas were undamaged and remain 'natural'; one area of damaged woodland has been left in place to recover naturally; one area had the stumps left in place to shoot as coppice timber and several areas were cleared and replanted between 1992 and 1996.

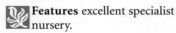 **Features** woodland garden; rhododendrons & azaleas; good herbaceous borders; bluebells; lily-of-the-valley; 1,000-year-old oak with 9.15m girth.

Owned by Robert Williams
Number of gardeners 3½
Size 3.2ha (8 acres), plus 105ha (265 acres) of park & woods.

Helmingham Hall

STOWMARKET, IP14 6EF

Tel 01473 890363 **Fax** 01473 890776
Website www.helmingham.com
Location 9 miles north of Ipswich on B1077.
Opening hours 2 pm – 6 pm; Sundays; 2 May to
12 September; plus individuals & groups on
Wednesday afternoons by prior arrangement.
Admission fee Adults £4; Children £2.

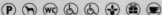

A visit to Helmingham is a step back into history, to a time of ancient certainties, order and peace. The Tollemaches have lived here since 1487. The house is a moated manor, half-timbered when built in 1480, but given a cladding of bricks and tiles in the 18th century. It is set in the most spacious 400-acre deer-park, loosely studded with vast centennial oaks grown to their full spread. Helmingham's formal garden lies beyond the moat to the south of the house. It is surrounded by 60 hybrid musks, lightly pruned and allowed to billow out, to fill the beds. The entire garden, about 100m long, is edged with 'Hidcote' lavender, underplanted with variegated London pride, and complemented by *Campanula lactiflora*, alstroemerias, foxgloves and peonies. This is gardening on a large scale, and makes its impact through simplicity and repetition: it is immensely grand. Beyond the formal garden is the walled garden proper, built of brick in 1745. On either side of the central grassy path runs a broad and stately double herbaceous border perhaps 120m long. Climbing roses are tied to straining wires all along its back: they include 'Guinée', 'Long John Silver', and *Rosa multiflora* var. *cathayensis*. The roses are underplanted with herbaceous plantings chosen to blend with the soft colours of the roses: pinks, blues, mauves, whites and the palest of creamy-yellows. Not until the main rose-flowering has finished in mid-August do yellows, bronzes, oranges and reds come to the fore. A spring border runs the whole way along one of the outer walls of the walled garden and is planted mainly with irises, tulips and peonies, backed by more climbing roses, vines, clematis, chaenomeles, ceanothus and myrtle from Queen Victoria's wedding posy. Nearer the house is a new series of knot gardens planted in 1982, which look as if they have been here for hundreds of years. The knots include the Tollemaches' heraldic device, a fret or interlacing pattern of bands, which has been made to interweave by pruning the strips of box at different levels. It leads to another rose garden: albas and species roses, centifolias and mosses, a large choice of gallicas and so on, underplanted with spring bulbs, white foxgloves, *Campanula persicifolia*, *Alchemilla mollis*, purple violas and geraniums. One reason why the garden is so successful is that the roses and their companion plantings all fall within a narrow colour range: it is a discipline from which every garden-owner can learn. But everything here is carefully thought through and controlled: you see this firmness too in the immaculately edged lawns and weedless borders. Everywhere at Helmingham, order prevails over anarchy.

Features roses (mainly old-fashioned); good herbaceous borders; deer park; moat; fine walled garden; good parterres and knots; shop; tea-room.

Owned by Lord Tollemache
English Heritage Grade I

Ickworth

HORRINGER, BURY ST EDMUNDS,
IP29 5QE

Tel 01284 735270 **Fax** 01284 735175
Website www.nationaltrust.org.uk/ickworth
Location 3 miles south-west of Bury St Edmunds.
Opening hours 10 am – 5 pm (4 pm in winter);
daily; all year except Christmas period. Closed at
weekends from 1 November to 22 December.
Admission fee Adults £2.95; Children 85p.

Ickworth is an extraordinary garden for an
extraordinary house: both were influenced
by Italy. The main borders follow the curves
of the house. There are also an Italian garden
with Mediterranean plants and long vistas in
the park. Capability Brown had a hand in it.
Please note that parts may be closed off from
time to time for essential work.

Features autumn colour; Italian
garden; Victorian 'stumpery'; display of
lemon trees in orangery; tallest *Quercus
pubescens* (29m.) in the British Isles;
National Trust shop; large licensed
restaurant, self-service.

Owned by The National Trust
Number of gardeners 5, plus a trainee
Size 28ha (70 acres)
NCCPG National Collections *Buxus*
English Heritage Grade II*

Mills Farm Plants and Gardens

NORWICH ROAD, MENDLESHAM,
IP14 5NQ

Tel & Fax 01449 766425
Website www.millsfarmplants.co.uk
Location On A140 just south of Mendlesham
village turning.
Opening hours 9 am – 5.30 pm; Wednesday –
Sunday, plus Bank Holiday Mondays; all year.
Closed all January, February & December.
Admission fee Free.

Mills Farm specialises in *Dianthus* (new and
old hybrids, species and rock garden types)
and roses: there is a list for each genus. The
roses are mostly old-fashioned varieties, in a
well-chosen selection – about 100 different
cultivars. They also list about 500 herbaceous
perennials out of a total of 1,100 at any time.
The owners claim to have one of the widest
commercial collections of pinks (*Dianthus*) in
the UK. They also breed their own and have
introduced quite a number of *Dianthus*
cultivars with the prefix 'Mendlesham',
including 'Mendlesham Frilly', 'Mendlesham
Glow' and 'Mendlesham Maid'. The garden is
well worth visiting in its own right – designed
entirely for the owners' pleasure as a formal
and restrained place for contemplation, with
a limited colour palette and the sound of
falling water. It is surrounded by yew hedges
and planted so that something is in flower
throughout the year. Everything has good,
strong foliage, too. The owners have recently
added a demonstration bed for dianthus,
planted with all the cultivars they grow. Three
RHS special events will take place during
2004: details from 020 7821 3408.

Features dianthus.

Owned by Dr & Mrs P.L. Russell

Notcutts Nurseries

IPSWICH ROAD, WOODBRIDGE,
IP12 4AF

Tel 01394 383344 **Fax** 01394 445440
Website www.notcutts.co.uk
Location On the Ipswich Road.
Opening hours 9 am – 6 pm; Monday – Saturday.
10.30 am – 4.30 pm; Sundays.
Admission fee Free.

Notcutts are large wholesale nurseries with a garden centre chain and branches in Ardleigh, Bagshot, Booker, Cambridge, Cranleigh, Maidstone, Norwich, Oxford (Mattocks roses), Peterborough, Solihull, St Albans, Staines and Tunbridge Wells. Woodbridge is their HQ. The company as a whole is strongest on flowering shrubs and trees and their large, beautifully colour-co-ordinated displays of these at the Chelsea Flower Show have been a source of wonder and praise for many years. But they offer every type of plant in all their branches and the quality of their stock is first class. They list over 3,000 different plants. Staff are also extremely helpful and knowledgeable. It is difficult for even the most experienced gardener not to come away from a visit to a branch of Notcutts without several new additions to his garden. There will be an open weekend for the National Collection of *Hibiscus syriacus* cultivars over the August Bank Holiday, 28-30 August 2004.

 Features flowering trees & shrubs; rhododendrons; hibiscus; large restaurant.

Owned by Notcutts Ltd.
NCCPG National Collections *Hibiscus syiacus* cvs.

Park Green Nurseries

WETHERINGSETT, STOWMARKET, IP14 5QH

Tel 01728 860139 **Fax** 01728 861277
Website www.parkgreen.co.uk
Location 6 miles north-east of Stowmarket.
Opening hours 10 am – 4 pm; Monday – Friday; 1 March to 24 September. Plus 10 am – 1 pm on Saturdays in same period.
Admission fee Free.

This excellent nursery specialises in ornamental grasses and other hardy perennial plants, but its most important line is hostas. It stocks over 200 different cultivars and introduces new ones every year. Recent home-raised releases include *Hosta* 'Delia', *H.* 'Knave's Green', *H.* 'Sarah Kennedy', *H.* 'Gay Search' and *H.* 'Royal Golden Jubilee'. Park Green Nurseries will host a RHS special event on 24 June 2004: details from 020 7821 3408.

Owned by Richard & Mary Ford

Rougham Hall Nurseries

A14 ROUGHAM, BURY ST EDMUNDS, IP30 9LZ

Tel 0800 970 7516 **Fax** 01359 271149
Website www.roughamhallnurseries.co.uk
Location Off the west-bound carriageway of the A14.
Opening hours 10 am – 4 pm; daily; March to October.

Rougham Hall Nurseries – always very popular when they come to RHS flower shows – are breeders, introducers and growers of an extensive and interesting range of perennials. Their selection of asters is particularly good, as is their list of delphiniums, of which they have a National Collection. Their other National Collection is of gooseberries: they have by far the most extensive list anywhere in the world. The whole history of this most highly prized of dessert fruits is contained within the hundreds of cultivars which they list. The range is always increasing, too: it is worthwhile enquiring if they do not appear to have one that you are looking for. They will be hosting four RHS special events during 2004: details from 020 7821 3408.

Owned by K. Harbutt
NCCPG National Collections *Delphinium*; *Ribes grossularia* (gooseberries)

Shrubland Park Gardens

CODDENHAM, IPSWICH, IP6 9QQ

Tel 01473 830221 **Fax** 01473 832202
Website www.shrublandpark.co.uk
Location Between Claydon & Coddenham: come by A14 or A140.
Opening hours 2 pm – 5 pm; Sundays & Bank Holiday Mondays; 4 April to 12 September.
Admission fee Adults £3; OAPs & Children £2. Subject to review.

Ⓟ ⓦⓒ

This grand Victorian garden was designed by Charles Barry and has been famous ever since for the spectacular Italianate staircase which connects the terrace around the house with the formal gardens below. William Robinson later helped with the planting, both around the formal garden and in the park and woodland gardens beyond. Much restoration and recovery has been completed in recent years: Shrubland is getting better and better.

 Features spectacular garden architecture; woodland garden; roses (mainly modern); good herbaceous borders; box maze; Swiss chálet.

Owned by Lord de Saumarez
Number of gardeners 5
Size 16ha (40 acres)
English Heritage Grade I

Somerleyton Hall

SOMERLEYTON, LOWESTOFT, NR32 5QQ

Tel 01502 730224 **Fax** 01502 732143
Website www.somerleyton.co.uk
Location 4 miles north-west of Lowestoft on B1074.
Opening hours 11 am – 5.30 pm; Thursdays, Sundays & Bank Holidays, plus Tuesdays & Wednesdays in July & August; 4 April to 31 October.
Admission fee Adults £6.20; OAPs £5.80; Children £3.20.

Somerleyton is a splendid place to visit: there is much for the garden- and plant-lover to see and enjoy. In front of the house (palatial, Victorian) is an extremely grand formal garden. William Andrews Nesfield laid out the terraces and the yew maze, which was planted in 1846: it is not too difficult to get to the centre – less than 400m from the entrance, provided you make no mistakes on the way. The gardens are full of topiary and good statuary, including a great equatorial sundial, encircled by signs of the Zodiac. Near the house are quantities of roses, herbaceous borders and seasonal bedding. Further afield are large plantings of rhododendrons and azaleas. Though none is actually a record-breaker, Somerleyton has some very fine specimen trees, including a giant redwood (*Sequoiadendron giganteum*), *Eucalyptus gunnii*, Monterey pine (*Pinus radiata*), Atlas cedar (*Cedrus atlantica*) and a particularly good maidenhair tree (*Ginkgo biloba*). There has been much replanting since the hurricane of 1987 and the new plantings are already making quite an impact. The walled garden was once the kitchen garden but is now planted with flowers: on the walls are many different climbers including roses, clematis, figs, climbing hydrangeas and such wall-shrubs as *Hoheria sexstylosa*. The glasshouses and peach-cases were designed by Sir Joseph Paxton, architect of the Crystal Palace with his characteristic ridge-and-furrow roofs. They are now planted with tender ornamentals like Meyer's lemon, abutilons, *Cassia* (*Senna*)*corymbosa* and the sweetly-scented *Dregea sinensis*. An old boiler house has a collection of old garden equipment in it. Other good features include an elegant, long, metal pergola with lots of different wisterias and a young avenue of lime trees along the driveway, planted in 1981. The whole estate is well-kept and well-run for visitors' enjoyment.

Features roses (mainly modern); plants under glass; maze; new bamboo bed; fine statues; magnificent trees; pergola; formal garden; walled garden; souvenir gift shop; tea-room for light lunches & teas.

Owned by The Hon. Hugh Crossley
Number of gardeners 4½
Size 5ha (12½ acres)
English Heritage Grade II*

White Hall Plants

SOUTHOLT ROAD, WORLINGWORTH, IP13 7HW

Tel 01728 628490 **Fax** 01728 628160
Location Brown signs on A1120 from Earl Soham.
Opening hours 10 am – 5 pm; daily, except Wednesday; March to October.
Admission fee Free.

There are stock beds and sale displays for over 2,000 different plants in this excellent nursery. There are good numbers of heucheras, ligularias, hostas, dicentras, grasses, salvias, penstemons, lilies, hellebores, foxgloves, cardamines and epimediums – and much else besides.

Features excellent plantsman's nursery.

Owned by Charles Walker
Number of gardeners 3
Size 1.2ha (3 acres)

Wyken Hall

STANTON, BURY ST EDMUNDS, IP31 2DW

Tel 01359 250287 **Fax** 01359 253420
Location 9 miles north-east from Bury St Edmunds; follow brown signs from A143 at Ixworth to Wyken Vineyards.
Opening hours 2 pm – 6 pm; Sunday – Friday; 1 April to 1 October. Plus 8 June for National Gardens Scheme.
Admission fee Adults £3; OAPs £2.50; Children free.

The garden at Wyken is ingeniously designed: a series of old-style gardens to complement the Elizabethan house. These include a knot garden, a herb garden, a traditional English kitchen garden, wildflower meadows, a nuttery and a copper beech maze. All are in scale with the house and the farmland around. Stylish and well maintained, this is one of the best modern private gardens in the country. The restaurant features in the *Good Food Guide* and is a Michelin *Bib Gourmand*. The 'Giant Stride' (a sort of revolving maypole) was added to commemorate the millennium.

Features woodland garden; roses (ancient & modern); plantsman's collection of plants; herbs; fruit; good shrubs; good herbaceous borders; award-winning seven-acre vineyard; country store shop; lunches & teas at excellent Vineyard Restaurant.

Owned by Sir Kenneth & Lady Carlisle
Number of gardeners 2
Size 1.6ha (4 acres)

SURREY

A Martian could be excused for thinking that Surrey was the centre of the horticultural universe. It is the county with everything that gardeners could ever want. Its six Grade I gardens include two very important landscapes – Claremont and Painshill – and two highly influential 20th-century gardens – Munstead Wood and the Savill Garden. Because of its closeness to London, it has become a very rich county during the last 100 years, which means that people have the time and money to garden on a large scale. The National Gardens Scheme does extremely well in Surrey, with a large number of medium-sized gardens opening for charity, as well as a handful of intensely cultivated smaller gardens. It is the county where the National Gardens Scheme has its headquarters. Surrey has many of the country's best known nurseries – the light soils being poor for agriculture but excellent for growing plants: the floral mile along the A30 is a famous landmark, where some of the trees and shrubs in the old Waterer nurseries have grown to exceptional size. There are good trees too – and many record-breakers – at Winkworth Arboretum, the Savill Garden and the RHS Garden Wisley. Surrey still has a large number of first-class nurseries: we include the important Knap Hill Nursery, Millais Nurseries and the newer star Toobees Exotics. There are other nurseries which we do not have space to list but which are well worth visiting – Secretts near Godalming, Lincluden at Bisley and Pantiles at Chertsey for example. The Surrey Gardens Trust and the Surrey group of the NCCPG are both very active in the county: the NCCPG has its base at Wisley. There are some 34 National Collections in Surrey, including seven at Wisley and nine at the Savill Garden. And of course the Royal Horticultural Society's own flagship garden at Wisley dominates every aspect of gardens and gardening in the county: as many as 20% of the society's members live in Surrey.

Cadenza

BUTTERFLY WALK, WARLINGHAM, CR6 9JA

Tel 01883 623565
Location M25 Jct 6; north up A22 for 4 miles; fourth exit at large roundabout; uphill & turn right.

Opening hours By appointment only.
Admission fee Free.

This is the private garden of keen plantsmen. Their special interest is small bulbs, and they have one of England's most interesting collections of hardy cyclamen. Frames and greenhouses extend the range of what is grown. An education and an inspiration.

 Features cyclamen; fritillaries; bulbs.

Owned by Mr & Mrs Ronald Frank
Number of gardeners part-time help
Size 0.3ha (¾ acre)

Clandon Park

WEST CLANDON, GUILDFORD, GU4 7RQ

Tel 01483 222482 **Fax** 01483 223479
Website www.nationaltrust.org.uk/clandonpark
Location Off the A247 at West Clandon.
Opening hours 11 am – 5 pm; Tuesdays – Thursdays, plus Sundays; 28 March to 31 October.
Admission fee House & Garden: Adult £6; Children £3. No garden-only prices.

Capability Brown's magnificent mature beeches are now underplanted with sombre Victorian shrubberies and slabs of comfrey, bergenias and *Geranium macrorrhizum* – the apotheosis of National Trust groundcover. There is a modern pastiche of a Dutch garden at the east end of the grounds but the daffodils in spring are breathtaking. Unfortunately the National Trust no longer sells garden-only tickets, and £6 is expensive for what the garden offers.

 Features parterres; grotto; Dutch garden; Maori meeting-house; Clandon Park Garden Centre is nearby; restaurant.

Owned by The National Trust
Number of gardeners 1
Size 3.8ha (9½ acres)
English Heritage Grade II

Claremont Landscape Garden

PORTSMOUTH ROAD, ESHER, KT10 9JG

Tel 01372 467806 **Fax** 01372 464394
Website www.nationaltrust.org.uk/claremont
Location On southern edge of town (A307).
Opening hours 10 am – 6 pm (but dusk from November to March & 7 pm or sunset if earlier on Saturdays, Sundays & Bank Holiday Mondays from April to October); daily, all year, but closed on Mondays from November to March. Closed on 25 December and major events days in July.
Admission fee Adults £4; Children £2.

This vast historic landscape – now much reduced – was worked over by Vanbrugh, Bridgeman, Kent and Capability Brown and has been energetically restored in recent years. The elegant green theatre is best seen flanked by spreading cedars from across the dark lake. Very popular locally, it is apt to get crowded at summer weekends.

 Features laurel lawns; tallest service tree *Sorbus domestica* (23m.) in the British Isles, and two further record trees; shop; tea-room.

Owned by The National Trust
Number of gardeners 3, plus volunteers
Size 19.6ha (49 acres)
English Heritage Grade I

Hannah Peschar Sculpture Garden

BLACK AND WHITE COTTAGE, STANDON LANE, OCKLEY, RH5 5QR

Tel 01306 627269 **Fax** 01306 627662
Website www.hannahpescharsculpture.com
Location Turn off A29 down Cathill Lane, left at T junction, over bridge & entrance is 400 yards on right.

Opening hours 11 am – 6 pm; Fridays & Saturdays. 2 pm – 5 pm; Sundays & Bank Holidays. May to October. And by appointment.
Admission fee Adults £8; Concessions £6; Children £5.

The lush water-gardens and woodlands surrounding a black-and-white cottage are the setting for this remarkable and ever-changing collection of contemporary British sculpture. The water-garden has been revamped by Anthony Paul with lots of architectural plants. There are pools and a stream, and surprisingly few flowers – the structure of the background is more important for sculpture than any transient colour. Nevertheless, an earlier owner was the distinguished horticulturist Dick Trotter, Mr Bowles's 'nephew Dick' and sometime Treasurer of the RHS.

Features sculptures; water; glass.

Owned by Hannah Peschar
Number of gardeners 2 part-time
Size 4ha (10 acres)

Hatchlands Park

EAST CLANDON, GUILDFORD, GU4 7RT

Tel 01483 222482 **Fax** 01483 223176
Website www.nationaltrust.org.uk/hatchlands
Location Off A246 Guildford to Leatherhead.
Opening hours 2 pm – 5.30 pm; Tuesday – Thursday, Sundays & Bank Holiday Mondays; April to October. Also Fridays in August. Park walks in Repton Park open daily 11 am – 6 pm from April to October.
Admission fee House & Garden: Adult £6; Children £3. No garden-only prices. Park walks: Adults £2.50; Children £1.25.

Apart from the Jekyll garden (roses, lupins, box and columbines) Hatchlands is an 18th-century landscape with parkland. But the garden buildings are charming and the National Trust has made good progress with restoration and replanting. Unfortunately the National Trust no longer sells garden-only tickets, and £6 is expensive for what the garden offers.

Features woodland garden; National Trust shop; restaurant.

Owned by The National Trust
Number of gardeners 2
Size 180ha (450 acres) of parkland

Herons Bonsai Ltd

WIRE MILL LANE, NEWCHAPEL, LINGFIELD, RH7 6HJ

Tel 01342 832657
Website www.herons.co.uk
Location Turn left off the A22, ½ mile south of junction with B2028.
Opening hours 9.30 am – 5.30 pm; Monday-Saturday. 10.30 am – 4.30 pm on Sundays. Closes at dusk in winter months.
Admission fee £1 donation to charity. Nursery free.

This bonsai nursery has a string of gold medals behind it from Chelsea Flower Shows. As well as trees for indoors and outdoors, there are pots, tools and accessories (retail and wholesale). The Chans are recognised experts and donated the bonsai collection and Japanese garden at RHS Garden Wisley. They run bonsai classes and offer Japanese garden design. The whole nursery is landscaped in the Japanese style, with several examples of different types of Japanese gardens.

Owned by Peter & Dawn Chan
Number of gardeners 3
Size 3ha (7½ acres)

Hydon Nurseries

CLOCK BARN LANE, HYDON HEATH, GODALMING, GU8 4AZ

Tel 01483 860252 **Fax** 01483 419937
Location 2 miles east of A3, Milford exit. Near Cheshire Home.
Opening hours 8.30 am – 5 pm (4 pm in winter), Monday – Friday. Plus Saturdays 9.30 am – 12.45 pm (5 pm from 1 March to 15 June and from late September to October). Sundays by appointment. Closed for lunch 12.45 pm – 2 pm. Conducted tours for small groups by prior appointment.
Admission fee Free. Parties by arrangement.

These rhododendron and azalea specialists have an extensive range of all classes, including some tender species and their own hybrids (*Rhododendron yakushimanum* and others). They have a comprehensive stock of evergreen azaleas, including 36 of the Wilson Kurume azaleas. They also sell companion trees and shrubs, especially camellias (another speciality – 100+ cultivars). The nursery extends over 25 acres: among the many fine trees are five large trees of the dark pink form of *Magnolia campbellii* and fine mature specimens of *Nothofagus dombeyi* and *N. antarctica*, as well as the two record-breakers. Visitors are particularly welcome to see the magnolias in early spring; the gardens are at their best between mid-March and June and there is an annual sale of plants during March.

 Features rhododendrons & azaleas; tallest *Eucalyptus pauciflora* subsp. *niphophila* and *Sorbus* 'Joseph Rock' in the British Isles.

Number of gardeners 5
Size 10ha (25 acres)

Knap Hill Nursery Ltd

BARRS LANE, KNAPHILL, WOKING, GU21 2JW

Tel 01483 481214 **Fax** 01483 797261
Location 2½ miles west of Woking, off A322.
Opening hours 9 am – 5 pm; Monday – Friday. Closed on bank holidays.

This large and famous rhododendron nursery is also one of England's oldest, founded over 200 years ago: members of the Slocock family have been hybridising rhododendrons for several generations and their nursery covers more than 200 acres. Their extensive list includes hybrids, dwarf, semi-dwarf and *R. yakushimanum* hybrids, as well as deciduous and evergreen azaleas. The display area has about 600 different cultivars: not all are listed at any one time. Over the years, the nursery has won 28 gold medals at the Chelsea Flower Show and was awarded the Rothschild Cup in 1997 and 1999.

 **Features** rhododendrons; azaleas.

Loseley Park

GUILDFORD, GU3 1HS

Tel 01483 304440 **Fax** 01483 302036
Website www.loseley-park.com
Location Off B3000 at Compton, south of Guildford.
Opening hours 11 am – 5 pm; Wednesday – Sunday; 5 May to 30 September. Plus Bank Holiday Mondays in May & August.
Admission fee Adults £3; OAPs £2.50; Children £1.50. RHS members free in May & September.

The walled garden attached to this fine Elizabethan house has recently been re-made and re-planted in the Jekyll style, with 1,000 old-fashioned roses framed by long, low, box hedges. The herb garden is divided into six sections, respectively devoted to culinary, medicinal, ornamental, dye plants, cosmetic plants and an area of native wildflowers to attract wildlife. The fiery fruit and flower garden comes into its own in July and August, while the moat walk's borders make for a quiet amble at any season. The peaceful fountain garden is filled with plants of a cream, white and silver theme. The cut-flower and vegetable garden (re-vamped in 2003) is also good.

 Features roses (mainly old-fashioned); herbs; fruit; lakeside walk; gift shop; courtyard tea-room; restaurant.

Owned by Michael More-Molyneux
Number of gardeners 3
Size 1ha (2½ acres)

Millais Nurseries

CROSSWATER FARM, CROSSWATER LANE, CHURT, FARNHAM, GU10 2JN

Tel 01252 792698 **Fax** 01252 792526
Website www.rhododendrons.co.uk
Location In Crosswater Lane, ½ mile north of Churt village.
Opening hours Nursery: 10 am – 1 pm & 2 pm – 5 pm; Monday – Friday. Also Saturdays in spring & autumn. And daily in May. Garden: late April to early June.
Admission fee Garden £2.50; Nursery free.

This important and dynamic rhododendron and azalea nursery has an extensive range of species and hybrids, including some new Himalayan species, late-flowering cultivars chosen to avoid the frost, large-leaved species for sheltered gardens, scented deciduous azaleas, *R. yakushimanum* hybrids for the smaller garden, dwarf cultivars for the rock garden and Maddenia

series rhododendrons for the conservatory. The six-acre garden (ponds, stream and companion plantings) has an extensive collection of new magnolias and acers. There is also a trials garden where hundreds of new cultivars from around the world are labelled and tested.

 Features rhododendrons; sorbus; tea & coffee.

Owned by The Millais family
Size 2.4ha (6 acres)

Munstead Wood

HEATH LANE, BUSBRIDGE, GODALMING, GU7 1UN

Tel 01483 417867 **Fax** 01483 425041
Location 1 mile south of Godalming on B2130: turn along Heath Lane. Parking in field 300 yards along on left.
Opening hours 2 pm – 6 pm; 18 April, 23 May & 13 June.
Admission fee Adults £3; OAPs £1.50; Children free.

  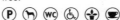

Munstead Wood is important for being Gertrude Jekyll's own garden. Here she worked out the principles she expounded in her best-known books *Wood and Garden* (1899) and *Colour in the Flower Garden* (1908). Her garden has now been split into several smaller holdings each in separate ownership, but the main parts are still attached to the house which Lutyens designed in 1896. The wood garden is fairly intact: the views up and down its main path to and from the lawn in front of the house seem just as they were a hundred years ago: birches underplanted mainly with rhododendrons and azaleas. Closer to the house is a block of borders full of good plantings – herbaceous plants, in particular. The nut walk and its nearby borders have recently been replanted: the Clarks have spent many years restoring the garden – and the results are admirable.

Features woodland garden; roses (mainly old-fashioned); sunken rock garden; good herbaceous borders; rhododendrons & azaleas; spring garden; cream teas.

Owned by Sir Robert & Lady Clark
Number of gardeners 2
Size 4ha (10 acres)
English Heritage Grade I

Painshill Park

PORTSMOUTH ROAD, COBHAM, KT11 1JE

Tel 01932 868113 **Fax** 01932 868001
Website www.painshill.co.uk
Location Signed from M25 Jct 10 & A3.
Opening hours 10.30 am – 6 pm (last tickets 4.30 pm); Tuesday – Sunday & Bank Holiday Mondays; March to October. 11 am – 4 pm (last tickets 3 pm) Tuesday – Thursday, Saturdays & Sundays; November to February. Closed 25 December.
Admission fee Adults £6; Concessions £5.25; Children (under 16) £3.50.

(P) (WC) (&) (🍵)

Charles Hamilton was the plantsman, painter and designer who created Painshill between 1738 and 1773, when he finally went bankrupt. His lasting achievement was to transform a barren heathland into ornamental pleasure grounds and parkland of dramatic beauty. A fourteen-acre lake is at the centre of the design: it offers a focus for the garden's most famous features, the white gothic temple and the grotto, which is approached across a 'Chinese' bridge. Hamilton sought to provoke the greatest variety of moods: other features included a ruined abbey and a Turkish tent. Hamilton was a pioneer of the naturalistic landscape

style, and very influential, but never a rich man: he leased Painshill from the Crown and had little to spend, which makes his achievement all the more remarkable. He was also a great plantsman, importing many new species from North America for his shrubberies. After 1948 the garden fell into dereliction. Over the past 20 years it has been meticulously restored (for which it won a Europa Nostra award) and the Painshill Trust has made enormous progress in raising the substantial funds needed. The Heritage Lottery Fund is a major supporter and grant-aided the new Visitor and Education Centre.

Features 'American' garden; grotto; Turkish tent; tallest *Juniperus virginiana* (26m.) in the British Isles; new (2002) visitor centre & licensed restaurant.

Owned by Painshill Park Trust
Number of gardeners 6
Size 63ha (158 acres)
English Heritage Grade I

Pantiles Plant & Garden Centre

ALMNERS ROAD, LYNE, CHERTSEY, KT16 0BJ

Tel 01932 872195 **Fax** 01923 874030
Website www.pantiles-nurseries.co.uk
Location 5 mins from M25 Jct 11.
Opening hours 9 am – 6 pm (5 pm in winter); Monday – Saturday; all year. Plus 11 am – 5 pm on Sundays (10 am – 4 pm in winter).
Admission fee Free.

(P) (🌱) (🍵)

The nursery specialises in outsize container-grown specimens up to eight metres high. It is popular with professionals and impatient amateurs alike – anyone, in fact, in search of that instant air of maturity which a large and well-grown tree can bring. The range of specimen trees is very impressive, and includes tree ferns like *Dicksonia antarctica* as well as large specimens of yew and box, cloud-pruned in the Japanese style.

 **Features** large plants; bonsai; aquatics; coffee shop.

Owned by Brendan Gallagher & Tony Winder
Size 4.4ha (11 acres)

Polesden Lacey

GREAT BOOKHAM, DORKING, RH5 6BD

Tel 01372 452048 **Fax** 01372 452023
Website www.nationaltrust.org.uk/polesdenlacey
Location Off A246 between Leatherhead & Guildford.
Opening hours 11 am – 6 pm (or dusk, if earlier); daily; all year.
Admission fee Adults £5; Children £2.50.

Ⓟ ⓦⓒ ♿ ✿ 🎁 ☕

Polesden Lacy is best for the long terraced walk, laid out by Sheridan, and the return through an Edwardian-style rose garden whose pergolas drip with ramblers. The park is good and there are fine views and walks around the estate.

Features snowdrops; roses of every kind; good herbaceous borders; lavender garden; large National Trust shop; self-service tea-room.

Owned by The National Trust
Number of gardeners 6, plus 1 trainee
Size 12ha (30 acres), plus landscaped park
English Heritage Grade II*

Ramster

CHIDDINGFOLD, GU8 4SN

Tel 01428 654167 **Fax** 01428 658345
Website www.ramstergardens.co.uk
Location 1½ miles south of Chiddingfold on A283.
Opening hours 11 am – 5 pm; daily; 24 April to 27 June. Parties by appointment at other times.
Admission fee Adults £4; Children free.

Ⓟ 🐕 ⓦⓒ ♿ ✿ ☕

Ramster was first laid out in 1890, with help from a local nursery, Gauntletts of Chiddingfold, who were known for their interest in flowering shrubs and especially for Japanese plants and planting. From this original influence date the ornamental stone lanterns, the large plantings of bamboos, and the avenue of *Acer palmatum* var. *dissectum* seedlings, now over 100 years old. In 1922 the property was bought by Miranda Gunn's grandparents Sir Henry and Lady Norman. Lady Norman was a keen gardener, the sister of the second Lord Aberconway, who was President of the RHS. She had been brought up at Bodnant, where she imbibed the family's great love of rhododendrons: many of the plants at Ramster came from Bodnant, and some of the rhododendrons and azaleas are her own hybrids. Ramster is an important garden for rhododendrons and, in the part known as Ant Wood, the Gunns have been building up a comprehensive collection of the old Hardy Hybrids – over 200 plants. But the garden is full of other projects and developments: the bog garden has come together very quickly since it was planted in 1998, and there is a new Millennium Garden. The garden is maintained in such a way as to allow meadow grasses, wildflowers and orchids to flourish and flower later in the year, but Ramster is essentially a garden for spring and early summer.

RHS Garden Wisley

WOKING, GU23 6QB

Tel 01483 224234 **Fax** 01483 211750
Website www.rhs.org.uk
Location M25 Jct 10. Follow brown tourist signs.
Opening hours 10 am (but 9 am at weekends) to 6 pm; daily; all year except Christmas Day. Closes at 4.30 pm from November to February. Last admissions one hour before closing.
Admission fee Adults £7; Children £2. Discounts for groups (pre-booked 21 days) – ring 01483 212307. RHS members (plus one guest) free.

Wisley is the most important horticultural demonstration garden in Europe – perhaps in the world. It has many incidents of great intrinsic value – the vast Pulhamite rock garden which fills an entire hillside, for example – but its true worth lies in its comprehensiveness: everything that a gardener could possibly want to see and learn from is here within its 240 acres. The only problem is its very size: Wisley is not a garden you could ever hope to get round properly in just a day, let alone a few hours. It is somewhere to explore over many visits at different times of the year, until the lay-out and the principal features become familiar and you learn where you should go to see what is good and instructive at the time of your visit.

This year (2004), the Royal Horticultural Society is celebrating the bicentenary of its foundation. Last year marked the centenary of the Royal Horticultural Society at Wisley. It was in 1903 that Sir Thomas Hanbury bought the Wisley estate and gave it to the Society for 'the encouragement and improvement of the science and practice of horticulture in all its branches.' When the Society moved its experimental garden from Chiswick, Wisley was in a remote part of Surrey with no public transport to serve it. The move would not have been possible without the invention of the motor car: 6,000 Fellows (as members were then called) visited it during its first 12 months. Now more than 700,000 visitors come to the garden every year. Wisley was unashamedly a trials garden where the Society practised the perfect cultivation of every type of plant that could be grown in the British Isles from alpines to hothouse orchids, whether in the open ground or in artificial conditions. This was backed up – then, as now – by an important system of trials which grew, tested, examined and made awards to flowers, fruit and vegetables. Those trials remain one of the garden's most important activities. Wisley was, above all, conceived as a scientific garden: to this day, the main building which dominates the formal garden near the entrance is known as the laboratory and contains scientific and administrative offices.

Sir Simon Hornby, president of the RHS until 2001, describes Wisley as 'a garden to delight, instruct and inspire.' His assertion is true at every time of the year. For many visitors the pulling power of Wisley is greatest in the short, dark days of winter. That is the time when such plants as cyclamen and narcissi fill the alpine pan house: there is always colour and interest here because suitable pots are brought from the growing-frames and plunged into its sandy benches specifically to maintain the display through every week of the year. In the landscaped alpine house, too, there is much of interest even in deep mid-winter. The main glasshouses certainly come into their own in winter. The display range has three sections – cool, warm and hot. Each is landscaped and supports a large number of plants growing in the soil that are suitable for greenhouses and conservatories at home.

Sometimes the seasonal display is augmented by pots brought from the growing areas behind and placed on the benches: 'Charm' and 'Cascade' chrysanthemums in November, for example. There are many other houses open to visitors: the orchid collections and the cacti house are among the most popular.

Wisley really begins to come into its own in spring. The alpine meadow is the best of its kind anywhere in Britain: from about the middle of March onwards, for at least four weeks, it is completely carpeted with hoop-petticoat narcissi (forms of *N. bulbocodium*). Clearly the conditions and the regime of cultivation suit them, because the narcissi continue to spread and increase every year. In September, the same meadows are thick with autumn-flowering crocus. Beyond them is the Pulhamite rock garden, constructed in 1911-12 which is probably the finest in Britain. It does not provide the variety of habitats which more modern rock gardens offer, but it is a majestic and beautiful construction. It covers the whole hillside from the 'monocot border' (full of such plants as agapanthus, daylilies, amaryllis, nerines and kniphofias – best in late summer) at the top to the stream at the bottom of the valley, whose margins are thick with such plants as *Lobelia cardinalis* and lysichitons. Beyond is an area of light woodland where magnolias and tall rhododendrons give shelter to such woodlanders as meconopsis, hellebores and snowdrops and huge patches of candelabra primulas.

By late spring, one of the best areas is Battleston Hill, the highest point in the gardens, where winding paths take you through a beautifully laid out woodland garden underplanted with rhododendrons, azaleas, magnolias and camellias. Crocuses in late winter, lilies in high summer and colchicums in autumn extend the season so that this is always an area of colour and interest. Here, and throughout the garden, are many unusual rare and interesting plants which add so much to the horticultural quality of Wisley. Also on Battleston Hill is a 'Mediterranean' garden where an extensive collection of plants with a reputation for tenderness shows what can be grown successfully on light, well-drained soil when trees provide shelter and frost rolls away downhill.

Wisley has a fine collection of roses, from such rare and tender species as the plant of *R. gigantea* on the wall of the Laboratory to the massed ranks of modern roses which fill the beds around the Bowes-Lyon pavilion and in behind the mixed borders. Wisley is, in short, one of the best places in Britain to see roses of every sort, including some which are rare elsewhere in English gardens open to the public. The mixed borders also come into their own from midsummer onwards: there are two of them, and they face each other on either side of the broad, grass ride which leads up to Battleston Hill. These borders are 130m long, backed by beech hedges and have a light framework of shrubs as a background for deep plantings of all the traditional perennials of the English herbaceous border. In contrast to the mixed borders are the new Piet Oudolf borders. Planted in 2001, the borders were designed by the Dutch plantsman Piet Oudolf, who has used the modern style of perennial planting. The borders, 147m long and 11m wide, are planted with over 16,000 perennials and grasses. The RHS says that the plants are chosen for their movement and colour and planted in diagonal 'rivers' across the borders, which gives a feel of walking in a meadow. It will be interesting to see how they develop in the future.

Wisley has many other areas dedicated to the cultivation and display of particular plants. The pinetum is one example – an under-visited area of stately conifers, some of them record-breakers and all of them interesting at every season. The heather garden in Howard's Field is another dedicated garden, a National Collection with probably the best collection of heathers in England. The fruit fields too are a part of the garden that far too few venture into: over 1,400 cultivars of top, bush and soft fruit are grown here, including more than 670 apple cultivars. The Society has been associated with the cultivation of fruit ever since its foundation in 1804, and displays of Wisley fruit have long been a feature of RHS London shows.

Wisley has its formal gardens too. These centre upon the long rectangular canal in front of the Laboratory and the walled gardens beyond. Designed by Geoffrey Jellicoe and Lanning Roper, the canal is a formal setting for waterlilies while the walled enclosures have spectacular summer and winter bedding displays. Rare and tender climbers cover their walls. Formal in a different sense are the model gardens which seem to grow and develop every year. The first were model fruit gardens, which showed people how to grow a great variety of fruit (and grow it well) in a small area. Nearby are model vegetable gardens, now supplemented by many ornamental model gardens, which serve the same function – to show visitors what may be achieved in their own gardens. Each is full of design ideas on a realisable scale, reflecting changing styles and new techniques. A new Town Garden reflects the mood of today's urban gardeners. There have been other new developments in this area recently – part of the garden's rolling programme of development – including a country garden by Penelope Hobhouse, and the loan of some fine garden sculpture on Battleston Hill. New for the millennium was the renovation of the Walled Garden (west) to create a plantsman's corner filled with a mixture of hardy and tender plants.

For many people, one of the most fascinating areas is the main Trials area in Portsmouth Field – over the brow of Battleston Hill and down towards the furthest boundary with the old Portsmouth road. This is where the Royal Horticultural Society runs most of its trials (more than 50 every year, some temporary and some permanent) of a very wide selection of annuals, perennials, shrubs, bulbs, fruit and vegetables. Trials of woody plants take place nearby at Deers Farm. The permanent trials are conducted (among others) with border carnations, chrysanthemums, daffodils, dahlias, daylilies, delphiniums, garden pinks, irises and sweet peas. These trials continue from year to year with periodic replanting, at which time additions and removals are made. They are of exceptional interest to visitors, and often of remarkable beauty too. There can be few horticultural experiences more exciting than to walk through the massed ranks of thickly planted delphiniums or sweet peas that tower over you in July or August.

Wisley is always changing. Four new features have recently been developed. First, the new Herb Garden, designed by Lucy and Francis Huntington. It is based on a circular theme, with a main path allowing free movement around and through the garden. The central area has the more conventional herbs, with other less well-known herbs and cottage plants separated from them by a low hedge. Outside the path are three areas displaying a range of cosmetic, apothecary and medicinal herbs. There are also cottage-style plantings, insect-repellent herbs and a collection of North American herbs. The centrepiece is a David Harber armillary sphere sundial. Second, is the Golden Jubilee Rose Garden, to celebrate the Golden Jubilee of the Society's patron. The new Rose Garden has been designed to display a collection of modern roses, including Hybrid Tea, Floribunda, English and Modern Shrub roses, Climbers, Ramblers,

Groundcover and Patio roses. Most of these have been introduced commercially over the last 20 years, and provide an opportunity to see some of the latest cultivars. The modern circular design leads the visitor through roses and companion plantings of herbaceous perennials and bulbs. Innovative 'spiral twist' metal pergolas provide support for a collection of climbers and ramblers, creating a vertical element and illustrating the cultivation techniques of 'bending rose stems' to encourage flowering lower down on the stems. Spiral twist posts connected together by horizontal stainless steel wires run parallel to a central grass pathway, and provide support for a collection of fragrant hybrid musk roses. There is a central paved area for visitor seating and displays of roses in containers. Third, a recent addition to the range of glasshouses is a Victorian-style greenhouse donated by Alitex Ltd. It measures 3m by 5m and has a porch-style entrance. The house protects a range of frost-tender plants. The area around the greenhouse has also been landscaped with raised beds and large planters for seasonal and permanent plantings to provide a sub-tropical atmosphere. Fourth, the Container Garden, whose hard landscaping has recently been updated using terracotta paving to act as a backdrop to display a range of assorted containers with a mixture of annuals, perennials and foliage to create innovative displays. These are changed three times a year, in spring, summer and autumn, using many of the most recently introduced cultivars. All are available in the Wisley Plant Centre which is an exceptionally good source of rare and new plants.

An enormous number of events, shows, workshops, lectures, demonstrations and gardens walks take place at Wisley all through the year: for details see the Society's (excellent) website.

Features woodland garden; snowdrops; roses (ancient & modern); rock garden; plantsman's collection of plants; plants under glass; fruit; mature conifers; good herbaceous borders; fine collection of trees; heather garden; herb garden; horticultural trials; vegetable gardens; tallest *Ostrya virginiana* (15.5m.) in the British Isles, and 25 further record trees; marvellous book- and gift-shop; plant centre; restaurant & café.

Owned by The Royal Horticultural Society
Number of gardeners 79
Size 96ha (240 acres)
NCCPG National Collections *Calluna vulgaris*; *Crocus*; *Daboecia*; *Epimedium*; *Erica*; *Galanthus*; *Rheum* (culinary)
English Heritage Grade II*

Features mature woodland garden with rhododendrons, magnolias, camellias, azaleas; bluebells; largest *Euonymus europaeus* (6m.) in the British Isles; home-made teas in May & at weekends.

Owned by Mr & Mrs Paul Gunn
Number of gardeners 1
Size 10ha (25 acres)

Titsey Place

OXTED, RH8 0SD

Tel 01273 407056 **Fax** 01273 478995
Website www.titsey.com
Location Off the B269 north of Limpsfield.
Opening hours 1 pm – 5 pm; Easter Monday, then on Wednesdays, Sundays & Bank Holiday Mondays from 12 May to 29 September. NGS days: 19 June, 17 July, 21 August & 18 September.
Admission fee Adults £2.50; Children £1.

The historic garden at Titsey has been well restored with advice from Elizabeth Banks since it first opened to the public in 1993. The lay-out is gardenesque and most of the plantings date from the middle of the 19th century. The large triple-trunked horse chestnut (*Aesculus hippocastanum*) on the upper terrace dates from that time. The formal gardens are planted with roses (replanted in 2002) and herbaceous plants, while the old walled kitchen garden has been planted as an example of how fruit, vegetables and flowers were grown in Victorian times.

Features fine parkland.

Owned by The Trustees of the Titsey Place Foundation
Number of gardeners 5
Size 5ha (12½ acres)

Toobees Exotics

BLACKHORSE ROAD, WOKING, GU22 0QT

Tel 01483 797534 **Fax** 01483 751995
Website www.toobees-exotics.com
Location Off A324 between Woking & Brookwood.
Opening hours 10 am – 5 pm; Thursday – Sunday & Bank Holiday Mondays; 8 April to 26 September. And by appointment.

Toobees are well known to visitors to RHS London shows: they have a constant flow of new and rare succulents from Africa and Madagascar. These include species of euphorbia, pachypodium, carnivorous plants, air-plants, palms and cycads. Visitors are always welcome to inspect the propagation areas and the amazing display of large stock plants. The address for correspondence is 20 Inglewood, Woking, Surrey GU21 3HX.

Owned by Bob & Beryl Potter

Vale End

ALBURY, GUILDFORD, GU5 9BE

Tel & Fax 01483 202296
Website www.ngs.org.uk
Location 500 yards west of Albury on A248.
Opening hours 10 am – 5 pm; 9 & 10 May (together with two adjacent Waterloo Pond gardens). Plus 6 pm – 9 pm on 9 June, by itself. Groups by arrangement.
Admission fee Adults £3.50; Children free. £4 on 9 June.

Vale End is a traditional plantsman's garden, one of the best on Bagshot sand, where a love of plants has not been allowed to obscure either the design or the landscape beyond. It is walled around, and made on many levels, on a site that faces south-west: the owners have taken the opportunity to

Savill Garden

THE GREAT PARK, WINDSOR, SL4 2HT

Tel 01753 847518 **Fax** 01753 847536
Website www.savillgarden.co.uk
Location Off Wick Lane at Englefield Green, 3 miles west of Egham off the A30 & 5 miles from Windsor.
Opening hours 10 am – 6 pm (4 pm from November to February); daily except 25 & 26 December.
Admission fee Adults £5.50; OAPs £5; Children £2.50 in April & May. Less in other months.

This is quite simply the finest woodland garden in England, developed since 1932 on an undulating site framed by magnificent deciduous trees. There are, in fact, several gardens here, some formal and some informal, but all are seamlessly linked together. The woodlands contain unrivalled spring plantings with masses of camellias, rhododendrons, azaleas, maples and flowering dogwoods underplanted with subtle drifts of bulbs, ferns and herbaceous plants. Recent refurbishment of the bog garden has allowed the development of stunning associations of meconopsis, primulas, astilbes, hostas and wild narcissi. The primulas have just been replanted, and come in monospecific masses, from the earliest *P. rosea* and *P. denticulata* through to *P. florindae* in July and August. In high summer, the rose garden and tremendous set-piece double herbaceous borders are worth a long trip to see. The nearby gravel garden is one of England's oldest and largest: parts of it have recently been replanted with a fine display of drought-tolerant plants – many of them rare – and plants which benefit from the mulching effect of the gravel. Extensive and intelligent use is made of a wide range of summer perennials in the borders and in containers. The new Golden Jubilee Garden, opened by the Queen in 2002, has a formal structure, informal planting, and exquisite pastel shades. By late summer the woods are filled with hydrangeas, whose cool blues and whites are stunningly effective. Then the deciduous broad-leaved trees begin their autumn spectacle. From November to March the newly created winter beds display flowers, stems and berries in effective colour groupings. But there are many reasons to visit the Savill Garden at other times of the year – the drifts of *Narcissus bulbocodium* (second only in their splendour to the alpine meadow at Wisley) in March, for example, and the floods of lysichitons in April. The collections of maples, camellias, rhododendrons and azaleas are also exemplary. The raised beds, the cool greenhouse and the monocot border are each full of interest in due season. The guide book, the plant centre and the website are all alike excellent.

Features roses (mainly modern); camellias; fine collection of trees; mahonias; magnificent late summer borders; tallest silver birch *Betula pendula* (30m.) in the British Isles (& 13 other record trees); gift and plant shop; licensed restaurant.

Owned by Crown Estate
Number of gardeners 12
Size 14ha (35 acres)
NCCPG National Collections *Ilex*; *Magnolia*; *Mahonia*; *Pernettya*; *Rhododendron* (species & Glenn Dale azaleas); ferns; dwarf & slow-growing conifers
English Heritage Grade I

grow sun-loving and Mediterranean plants. Daphne Foulsham is a Vice-President (and a very successful ex-Chairman) of the National Gardens Scheme.

 Features plantsman's collection of plants; good herbaceous borders; roses (mainly old-fashioned); vegetables; fruit; herbs; refreshments.

Owned by Mr & Mrs John Foulsham
Size 0.4ha (1 acre)

Valley Gardens

GREAT PARK, WINDSOR, SL4 2HT

Tel 01753 847518 **Fax** 01753 847536
Location At Englefield Green, 5 miles from Windsor, off A30: follow signs for Savill Garden.
Opening hours 8 am – 7 pm (3.30 pm in winter); daily; all year.
Admission fee Cars £4 (£5.50 in April & May); occupants free.

This is a woodland garden on a royal scale. The Valley Garden has over 200 acres of plantings across a site of great natural beauty which falls in vast sweeps to the open expanse of Virginia Water. As in the Savill Garden, huge trees of oak, beech, sweet chestnut and Scots pine provide a magnificent framework and have been used with great sensitivity. The whole composition conveys the feeling of a flowering forest from some far-off corner of Asia. From March and April until the end of June, a succession of camellias, rhododendrons and azaleas provide an unbelievable kaleidoscope of colour, most notably in the Punch Bowl where a natural combe is filled with terrace upon terrace of brightly coloured Japanese Kurume azaleas. Giant magnolias garland themselves overhead with thousands of chalice-shaped blooms. A huge array of supporting trees, shrubs and perennials jostles for attention.

Enormous groups of hydrangeas provide late summer colour, from the white foaming flowers of *H. paniculata* to the blues and pale pinks of the lacecaps and mopheads. In autumn the hillsides light up in a spectacle unrivalled this side of the Appalachian Mountains. In the nearby heather garden an old gravel pit has been transformed into a horticultural wonder to rival the Punch Bowl: ostensibly dominated by heathers and dwarf conifers (there is a National Collection here), the garden contains unrivalled collections of exotic and native birches, whitebeams and rowans, wild roses, cotoneasters and cistus. Recent plantings have made extensive use of ornamental grasses to provide relief amongst the stolid conifers. On the next hillside is to be found the National Collection of *Rhododendron* species, brought here in the 1950s from the famous garden of Tower Court near Ascot. A sweeping valley also contains a pinetum of some note, carpeted by countless thousands of dwarf narcissi in March and April. All in all, a garden of the blue-stocking variety.

 Features outstanding collection of trees; hydrangeas; heathers; primulas; magnolias; rhododendrons & azaleas; refreshments at the Savill Garden.

Owned by Crown Estate
Number of gardeners 16
Size 87ha (220 acres)
NCCPG National Collections *Ilex*; *Magnolia*; *Mahonia*; *Pernettya*; *Rhododendron* (species & Glenn Dale azaleas); ferns; dwarf & slow-growing conifers

Vann

HAMBLEDON, GODALMING, GU8 4EF

Tel & Fax 01428 683413
Location 2 miles from Chiddingfold. Signs from A283 on NGS days.
Opening hours 10 am – 6 pm; daily; 21 to 28 March; 13 to 18 April; 3 to 9 May. And by appointment.

Admission fee Adults £3.50; Children 50p. Pre-booked groups welcome.

This high-profile Jekyll garden has been well restored and meticulously maintained by the present Caroes, the third generation to live here. Start with the old cottage garden at the back of the house and move along the Arts & Crafts pergola straight to the lake. This is the heart of the garden, from which several distinct gardens lead from one to the next and melt into the Surrey woods: among them, a yew walk (1909), island beds, mixed borders, the Jekyll water garden (1991), a woodland cherry walk, and a woodland garden under vast oaks leading to a hazel coppice. The plantings are dense and thoughtful.

Features woodland garden; good herbaceous borders; bluebells; fritillaries; wood anemones; teas on 21 March; other refreshments for groups by arrangement.

Owned by Mrs Martin Caroe
Number of gardeners ½
Size 2ha (5 acres)
English Heritage Grade II

The Vernon Geranium Nursery

CUDDINGTON WAY, CHEAM, SUTTON, SM2 7JB

Tel 020 8393 7616 **Fax** 020 8786 7437
Website www.geraniumsuk.com
Location South-west of Cheam.
Opening hours 9.30 am – 5.30 pm; Monday – Saturday. 10 am – 4 pm; Sundays. March to June.

As it names indicates, this is a specialist pelargonium nursery. The number of pelargonium cultivars here speaks for itself – over 1,100 doubles and semi-doubles,

Deacons, stellars, rosebuds, finger-flowered, fancy-leaved, speckled, uniques, dwarfs, miniatures, angels and regals – the list seems endless. Guided tours are given daily at 11 am and 2.30 pm between 19 and 27 June.

Features pelargoniums.

Winkworth Arboretum

HASCOMBE ROAD, GODALMING, GU8 4AD

Tel 01483 208477 **Fax** 01483 208252
Website www.nationaltrust.org.uk/winkwortharboretum
Location 2 miles south-east of Godalming, off B2130.
Opening hours All year; dawn – dusk. Groups *must* pre-book in writing.
Admission fee Adults £4; Children £2.

Winkworth is a true arboretum in the sense that it has a large collection of full-sized trees – as many taxa as possible – planted liberally over a large area. Many of the plantings are now in their prime. The red oaks (*Quercus coccinea*), tupelos *Nyssa sylvestris* and sweet gums *Liquidambar styraciflua* are quite spectacular in autumn.

Features woodland garden; fine collection of trees; bluebells; wood anemones; autumn colour; tallest *Acer davidii* (19m.) in the British Isles, and 5 further record trees; shop; tea-room.

Owned by The National Trust
Number of gardeners 3
Size 44ha (110 acres)
NCCPG National Collections *Sorbus* (Aria & Micromeles groups)

SUSSEX, EAST

The two historic gardens in East Sussex which English Heritage has rated Grade I could not be more different – Great Dixter and Sheffield Park. Yet they have one thing in common which is typical of East Sussex gardens generally – they are gardens whose historic features have been overlaid with plants. Few of the other historic gardens in the county are open to the public, but plant-lovers are almost spoiled for choice. Every corner of East Sussex seems to brim with good modern gardens – those like Pashley Manor and Merriments have been widely recognised for their beauty and invention – and good collections of trees, including those at Sheffield Park and Stanmer Park, near Brighton. The National Gardens Scheme does well in East Sussex, especially in the area around Crowborough where there are many medium-sized gardens to see. Nurseries, too, are good and fairly plentiful: some of the best are attached to gardens, like Great Dixter, or have a fine display garden attached to them, like Merriments. There are comparatively few National Collections: one of the most interesting is the collection of lilacs (*Syringa* cvs.) kept by the City of Brighton & Hove Parks Department.

Bateman's

BURWASH, ETCHINGHAM, TN19 7DS

Tel 01435 882302 **Fax** 01435 882811
Website www.nationaltrust.org.uk/batemans
Location Signed at west end of village.
Opening hours 11 am – 5 pm; Saturday – Wednesday; 3 April to 31 October.
Admission fee Adults £5.50; Children £2.70.

These ten acres on the banks of the River Dudwell were Rudyard Kipling's home from 1902 until his death in 1936. The garden is fun for children, because there is a working flour mill, but not spectacular for the knowledgeable gardener, except for the *Campsis grandiflora* on the house and the herbaceous borders designed by Graham Stuart Thomas.

Features roses (mainly old-fashioned); herbs; good herbaceous borders; Kipling pear arch; National Trust shop; tea-room.

Owned by The National Trust
Number of gardeners 2
Size 4ha (10 acres)
English Heritage Grade II

Bates Green Farm

TYE HILL ROAD, ARLINGTON, POLEGATE, BN26 6SH

Tel 01323 482039 **Fax** 01323 485151
Location 3 miles south-west of Hailsham.
Opening hours 11 am – 5 pm; 11 April, 13 June &

12 September for National Gardens Scheme. And by appointment.
Admission fee Adults £2.50; Children free.

Made by the present owners since the mid-1970s, the garden at Bates Green Farm has several different areas: a handsome rock garden, a shady garden, and wonderful mixed borders planted for year-round colour associations. New last year (2003) were a vegetable garden with raised beds and a monocot border.

Features woodland garden; good herbaceous borders; colour borders; bluebells; rockery; pond; light lunches & teas on NGS days.

Owned by Mr & Mrs J.R. McCutchan
Number of gardeners 1 part-time
Size 0.8ha (2 acres)

Cabbages & Kings Garden

WILDERNESS FARM, WILDERNESS LANE, HADLOW DOWN, TN22 4HU

Tel 01825 830552 **Fax** 01825 830736
Website www.ckings.co.uk
Location ½ mile south of A272.
Opening hours 10 – 25 July. Times not available as we went to press. Closed Mondays.
Admission fee Adults £4; Concessions £3.50. RHS members free from 18 to 21 July.

'Cabbages & Kings' (subtitled 'The Centre for Garden Design') is a good garden, conceived as a series of interlinking garden-rooms, terraces and incidents, lushly and vividly planted. The idea is to give visitors lots of ideas for their own gardens – how to transform them, how to create garden rooms, and how to design sitting areas, features and focal points. There will be two

RHS special events at 'Cabbages & Kings' during 2004: details from 020 7821 3408.

Features good modern design & planting; tea, coffee, home-made cakes.

Owned by Andrew & Ryl Nowell

Clinton Lodge

FLETCHING, UCKFIELD, TN22 3ST

Tel 01825 722952 **Fax** 01825 723967
Location In main village street.
Opening hours 2 pm – 5.30 pm; 6, 7, 18 & 25 June, 2 & 9 July & 20 August for NGS. And by appointment on weekdays.
Admission fee NGS days: Adults £4; Children £2. £5 for groups (minimum 25 people).

Clinton Lodge is a rising star among new gardens, designed round a handsome 17th-century house. There are formal gardens of different periods, starting with a 'mediaeval' *potager* and an Elizabethan-style herb garden with camomile paths and turf seats. The most successful parts are the pre-Raphaelite walk of lilies and pale roses, the Victorian-style herbaceous borders in soft pastel shades and very cheerful garden of old roses. A canal garden and an *allée* of fastigiate hornbeams were added in 2001, and a knot garden and 'shade glade' in 2003. The garden has recovered well from recent flood damage.

Features roses (mainly old-fashioned); herbs; good herbaceous borders; yew hedges; lime walks; *potager*; knot gardens; teas.

Owned by Mr & Mrs H.R. Collum
Number of gardeners 1½
Size 2.4ha (6 acres)

Great Dixter

Dixter Road, Northiam, TN31 6PH

Tel 01797 252878 **Fax** 01797 252879
Website www.greatdixter.co.uk
Location Off A28 at Northiam Post Office.
Opening hours 2 pm – 5 pm; Tuesday – Sunday; 1
April to 24 October, plus Bank Holiday Mondays.
Open at 11 am on the Sundays & Mondays of Bank
Holiday weekends.
Admission fee Adults £5; Children £1.50.

Christopher Lloyd's father Nathaniel bought Great Dixter in 1910: Lutyens did a conversion job on the house and laid out part of the gardens. Most of the brickwork, yew hedges, steps, walls, doorways and arts-and-crafts details date back to the original design – contemporary with Hidcote and earlier than Sissinghurst. The topiary was Nathaniel Lloyd's contribution – he wrote a book about it. But the main reason for the garden's pre-eminent reputation is the decades of horticultural skill which Christopher Lloyd himself has put into its planting. He is a knowledgeable plantsman who once taught horticulture at Wye College and has a remarkable eye for combining plants in harmonious groupings throughout the year. His books – especially the compilation of articles from *Country Life* published as *The Well-Tempered Garden* – have been popular and influential, so that the Lloyd style of planting and maintaining a garden is probably more widely copied now than any other. The heart of the garden is the Long Border, about 65m long and 4½m yards deep, which has become a showcase and trial ground for his experiments. It is a series of compositions loosely strung together with a wide variety of weaving colours, heights and textures but unified as much by good foliage as by flowers. Every section of it teaches you something new that could be made to work in your own garden. One of Lloyd's strengths is his fondness for change – his desire to refine and improve his garden all the time. He was one of the first garden-owners to use lots of annuals and tender perennials to extend the summer season right through into autumn. He shocked the country's rosarians by replacing his parents' collection of old-fashioned roses with a late-summer explosion of dahlias, cannas and exotic foliage. And nobody has practised the gentle, patient art of long-term meadow-gardening so successfully as Christopher Lloyd: indeed, he has written so eloquently and prolifically about the principles and practices of meadow gardening that, even if he had never penned a word on any other aspect of ornamental horticulture, he would be established as a great apostle of this charming and relaxed art form which he sometimes refers to as 'tapestry gardening'. Visiting Great Dixter should be a compulsory part of every gardener's ongoing education.

Features topiary; sub-tropical plants; plantsman's collection of plants; good herbaceous borders; meadow garden; colour schemes; gift shop.

Owned by Christopher Lloyd & Olivia Eller
Number of gardeners 5
Size 2ha (5 acres)
English Heritage Grade I

Marchants Hardy Plants

2 MARCHANTS COTTAGES, RIPE
ROAD, LAUGHTON, BN8 6AJ

Tel & Fax 01323 811737
Location ½ mile east of Laughton; take right turn signed to Ripe.
Opening hours April to mid-October.
Admission fee Free.

This acclaimed young garden, at its peak in late summer, is attached to a nursery with an excellent selection of herbaceous plants and grasses. Their introductions include *Lithodora diffusa* 'Star' and *Sedum* 'Purple Emperor'.

Features herbaceous plants; grasses; good nursery.

Owned by Graham Gough & Lucy Goffin
Number of gardeners 1
Size 0.4ha (1 acre)

Merriments Gardens

HAWKHURST ROAD, HURST GREEN,
TN19 7RA

Tel 01580 860666 **Fax** 01580 860324
Website www.merriments.co.uk
Location On A229.
Opening hours 10 am – 5 pm; daily; 1 April to mid-October. Opens at 10.30 am on Sundays.
Admission fee Adults £3.50; Children £2.

The gardens at this nursery are young – started in 1991 on a bare clay field – but the tail is already wagging the dog. Four remarkable acres of imaginative design and striking planting are kept meticulously tidy. The planting has been chosen so that each area blends seamlessly into the next and

creates a satisfying and harmonious whole. The deep sweeping borders are designed and planted to combine colour, form and texture in endlessly imaginative planting schemes. The features include foliage borders, two ponds, a border for spring, several borders designed to peak in summer and autumn, a blue garden – and dozens more. Recent developments include a dry area which has been transformed into a Mediterranean-inspired scree garden and a waterlogged area which has been turned into a bog garden and planted with moisture-loving plants. New for 2004 will be a redevelopment of the formal gardens, and improvements to the wheelchair access. The nursery is excellent.

Features plantsman's collection of plants; good herbaceous borders; brilliant modern design; tropical border; first-rate nursery attached; garden café.

Owned by David & Peggy Weeks
Number of gardeners 3
Size 1.6ha (4 acres)

Michelham Priory

UPPER DICKER, HAILSHAM, BN27 3QS

Tel 01323 844224 **Fax** 01323 844030
Website www.sussexpast.co.uk
Location Signed from A22 & A27.
Opening hours 10.30 am – 4 pm; Tuesday – Sunday; March & October. 10.30 am – 5 pm; Tuesday – Sunday; April – July & September; 10.30 am – 5.30 pm; daily; August.
Admission fee Adults £5.20; OAPs £4.50; Children £2.70; Disabled £2.60.

The old Augustinian priory has an Elizabethan barn, a blacksmith shop, a rope museum, a working watermill and England's largest mediaeval water-filled moat. Within the garden are several distinct areas, including a physic garden and cloister garden, with mediaeval plantings (faithful, if a little dull), some very good borders, a bog garden, a kitchen garden and several wildflower areas. It all makes for an enjoyable visit, highly educational for children and interesting for parents too.

 **Features** herbs; mature conifers; good herbaceous borders; sculpture trail; dovecote gift shop; licensed restaurant & tea-room.

Owned by The Sussex Archaeological Society & Sussex Past
Number of gardeners 2, plus volunteers
Size 2.8ha (7 acres)

Moorlands

FRIARS GATE, CROWBOROUGH, TN6 1XF

Tel 01892 652474
Location 2 miles north of Crowborough, off B2188.
Opening hours 11 am – 5 pm; Wednesdays; April to September. Plus 2 pm – 6 pm on 27 June for NGS.
Admission fee Adults £3; Children free.

The garden at Moorlands was begun by Dr Smith's parents in 1929: Dr Smith took over in 1974, made a lake and ponds, and planted a lot of woodland and bog-loving plants. The garden now combines mature trees with modern herbaceous plantings. By the house, on a sloping site, is a long herbaceous border. This leads to the main stream, red with iron ore but clean enough for trout and protected enough for kingfishers. It is spring-fed, full of waterfalls, and planted with grasses and bamboos. Moorlands is a plantsman's garden of fine trees, rhododendrons and collectors' shrubs, underplanted with bog plants as well as wildflowers such as native daffodils (*Narcissus pseudonarcissus*) and orchids. It

was closed in 2003 for substantial repairs, but is now looking better than ever.

 Features good plants for plantsmen; Japanese anemones; teas on NGS open day.

Owned by Dr & Mrs Steven Smith
Number of gardeners 3 part-time
Size 1.6ha (4 acres)

Paradise Park

AVIS ROAD, NEWHAVEN, BN9 0DH

Tel 01273 512123 **Fax** 01273 616005
Website www.paradisepark.co.uk
Location Signed from A26 & A259.
Opening hours 10 am – 6 pm; daily; all year except 25 & 26 December.
Admission fee Adults £5.99; OAPs & Children £4.99.

Part of a leisure complex attached to a garden centre, the most interesting features are a tropical house and a cactus house, each landscaped with handsome plant collections chosen for display. There are some imaginative garden designs – Caribbean, seaside, desert and oriental, for example. It is a haven in winter, and the outside gardens are a pleasure to explore in summer, full of contrasting designs and splendid water features. They contain a Sussex History trail – beautiful models of important historic buildings in the county, each in a different setting. Other attractions include a hemerocallis collection, a fuchsia border and an alpine rock garden.

 **Features** plants under glass; hydroponic demonstration area; *Streptocarpus* collection; plant centre; large coffee-shop.

Owned by Jonathan Tate
Number of gardeners 3
Size 1ha (2½ acres) of garden and 0.1ha (½ acre) under glass

Pashley Manor Gardens

TICEHURST, TN5 7HE

Tel 01580 200888 **Fax** 01580 200102
Website www.pashleymanorgardens.com
Location On B2099 between A21 & Ticehurst village.
Opening hours 11 am – 5 pm; Tuesday – Thursday, Saturday & Bank Holiday Mondays; 6 April to 30 September.
Admission fee Adults £6; OAPs & Children £5.50.

Pashley Manor is a new/old garden, made or re-made in the Victorian style over the last ten years or so with advice from the brilliant Anthony du Gard Pasley. The original structure came from fine old trees, fountains, springs and large ponds or small lakes. The modern plantings have added gentle shapes, spacious expanses, harmonious colours and solid plantings. There is a sumptuous series of new enclosed gardens where colour-gardening is practised to brilliant effect. And it gets better every year.

Features roses (mainly old-fashioned & climbers); mature conifers; Victorian shrubberies; hydrangeas; irises; HHA/Christie's Garden of the Year in 1999; fresh produce for sale; lunches & teas.

Owned by James & Angela Sellick
Number of gardeners 5
Size 5ha (12½ acres)

Rotherview Nursery with Coghurst Camellias

IVY HOUSE LANE, THREE OAKS, HASTINGS, TN35 4NP

Tel 01424 756228 **Fax** 01424 428944
Location Follow brown tourist signs to Coghurst Hall Holiday Village (next door).
Opening hours Not available as we went to press. 2003 times were: 9 am – 5 pm; daily; March to October. 10 am – 4 pm; daily; November to February.
Admission fee Free.

Rotherview Nursery with Coghurst Camellias is an inter-nursery hybrid – two specialist nurseries recently combined on one site. Rotherview produces a wide range of alpines and perennials (especially hardy ferns) whilst Coghurst has a list of over 200 camellias, including the autumn-flowering *C. sasanqua* cultivars. Both nurseries have been regular exhibitors at RHS Flower Shows. The list of camellias is being expanded and the garden is already much improved, with raised beds for Rotherview's alpines and an area of trough gardens, as well as a camellia walk.

Sheffield Park Garden

UCKFIELD, TN22 3QX

Tel 01825 790231 **Fax** 01825 791264
Website www.nationaltrust.org.uk/sheffieldpark
Location Between East Grinstead & Lewes on A275.
Opening hours 10.30 am – 6 pm; Tuesday – Sunday plus Bank Holidays; 2 March to 23 December. Closes at 4 pm from 2 November.
Admission fee Adults £5.20; Children £2.60 RHS members free.

Sheffield Park is a beautiful 120-acre garden around five lakes. These were laid out in the 18th century by Capability Brown and Humphry Repton. The result is landscaping on the grandest of scales, though the lakes now reflect the 20th-century plantings of exotics. Carpeted with daffodils and bluebells in spring, its rhododendrons, azaleas and stream garden are spectacular in early summer. In autumn, the garden is ablaze with wonderful leaf colours, and long beds of gentians. But the collection of rare trees and shrubs makes it a fascinating visit at any time of year and the National Trust has just started on the first phase of a major restoration project which will involve planting 9,000 trees and shrubs between 2003 and 2008.

Features mature conifers; fine collection of trees; bluebells; daffodils; kalmias; autumn crocuses; rhododendrons; tallest *Nyssa sylvatica* (21m.) in the British Isles, plus two other record trees; National Trust shop.

Owned by The National Trust
Number of gardeners 5
Size 48ha (120 acres)
NCCPG National Collections *Rhododendron* (Ghent azaleas)
English Heritage Grade I

Standen

EAST GRINSTEAD, RH19 4NE

Tel 01342 323029 **Fax** 01342 316424
Website www.nationaltrust.org.uk/standen
Location 2 miles south of East Grinstead, signed from B2110.
Opening hours 11 am – 6 pm; Wednesday – Sunday & Bank Holidays; 27 March to 31 October. 11 am – 3 pm; Friday – Sunday; 5 November to 19 December.
Admission fee Adults £3.20; Children £1.60.

This Edwardian garden has magnificent views across the Medway valley. A series of enclosed gardens around the house gives way to woodland slopes and an old quarry furnished with ferns and azaleas. Parts are rather overgrown (and are being restored) but there is much to trigger the imagination here – not least, how the National Trust achieves so much with only one full-time and one part-time gardener.

Features roses (mainly Rugosas & old-fashioned); rock garden; mature conifers; good herbaceous borders; rhododendrons; azaleas; woodland shrubs; National Trust shop; restaurant.

Owned by The National Trust
Number of gardeners 1½
Size 5ha (12½ acres)

SUSSEX, WEST

West Sussex is even better endowed with fine gardens and interesting nurseries than East Sussex. All five Grade I gardens are open to the public – Goodwood, Leonardslee, Parham, Petworth House and Stansted Park – though only Leonardslee and Parham are of great horticultural interest. However there is also a glut of Grade II* gardens open to the public, and all of them chiefly of importance for their plant collections – Borde Hill, Cowdray, Gravetye, Highdown, Nymans, High Beeches, Wakehurst and West Dean. These are matched by a great number of good medium-sized gardens which open for the National Gardens Scheme and a large number of good nurseries and garden centres. Architectural Plants, Coghurst Camellias (now part of Rotherview Nursery), Croftway and Ingwersens are all nurseries of national or international status and often seen at RHS Flower Shows. The NCCPG has a good number of National Collections in the county. Borde Hill and Nymans offer free access to RHS members, though Borde Hill extends this privilege only in the quiet months. The old county horticultural society at Brinsbury, now part of Chichester College, is a RHS Partner College with a series of public lectures, demonstrations and workshops throughout the year: details from 020 7821 3408.

Architectural Plants

COOKS FARM, NUTHURST, HORSHAM, RH13 6LH

Tel 01403 891772 **Fax** 01403 891056
Website www.architecturalplants.com
Location 3 miles south of Horsham, behind the Black Horse pub in Nuthurst.
Opening hours 9 am – 5 pm; Monday – Saturday.
Admission fee Free.

Somewhat out of the ordinary, Architectural Plants specialises in exotic-looking, evergreen foliage plants, often with architectural or sculptural shapes. 'Architectural' means that the plants themselves have their own architecture – strong, sometimes spectacular, shapes which bring a distinctive year-round presence to a garden. Examples include eucalyptus, bamboos, hardy palms, hardy bananas and evergreen magnolias. Larger specimens are available for immediate impact. The display area around the nursery is stylishly laid out and a pleasure to visit in its own right. The nursery also has a branch at Lidsey Road, Woodgate, near Chichester (open 10 am – 4 pm, Sunday to Friday): it has phillyreas, arbutus and many rare trees, plus seaside exotics, but no display garden.

Features architectural plants; large specimens.

Owned by Angus White
Size 1.2ha (3 acres)

Borde Hill Garden

BALCOMBE ROAD, HAYWARDS HEATH,
RH16 1XP

Tel 01444 450326 **Fax** 01444 440427
Website www.bordehill.co.uk
Location 1½ miles north of Haywards Heath.
Opening hours 10 am – 6 pm (or dusk); daily; all year.
Admission fee Adults £6; OAPs £5; Children £3.50. Reductions in winter. RHS members free in January, February, November & December.

This important woodland garden has been significantly developed and improved in recent years. It was originally planted in the early 1900s with exotic trees and a large collection of rhododendron species grown from such introducers as Forrest and Kingdon Ward. Some of those trees are record-breakers, including a rare Chinese tulip tree (*Liriodendron chinense*) now 19m tall, a Greek beech (*Fagus orientalis*) of the same height, and a splendid *Magnolia campbellii* now 22m high. The garden has recently been substantially re-developed for the recreation market and is all the better for the new capital. The gardens surrounding the house are divided into 'rooms'. These include the Garden of Allah with a new wildlife pool; a ring of Knap Hill azaleas backed by rhododendrons from Farrer and Cox's expedition to Burma and China in 1919; the newly-restored Victorian greenhouses, one of which is a peach house and another devoted to South African plants (including nerines); a small Mediterranean garden designed by Robin Williams; a rose garden planted with 450 David Austin roses; the Italian garden and two dells with *Trachycarpus* palms.

Features woodland garden; plantsman's collection of plants; fine collection of trees; rhododendrons; azaleas; magnolias; plants from original seed; 48 different record trees, one of the largest collections in the British Isles; gift shop; plant centre; tea-room & restaurant.

Owned by Borde Hill Garden Ltd
Number of gardeners 5
Size 4.4ha (11 acres) of formal gardens, plus 16ha (40 acres) of woodland and 150 acres of parkland
English Heritage Grade II*

Champs Hill

COLDWALTHAM, PULBOROUGH,
RH20 1LY

Tel 01789 831868 **Fax** 01789 831536
Location West of Coldwaltham, on road to Fittleworth (Waltham Park Road).
Opening hours 2 pm – 5 pm on 14 & 21 March; 9 & 16 May; and 8 & 15 August.
Admission fee Adults £2.50; Children free.

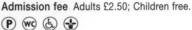

This garden has been developed around three disused sand-quarries since 1960. The woodlands are full of beautiful rhododendrons and azaleas, but the most striking feature is the collection of heathers – over 300 cultivars – interplanted with dwarf conifers. The garden also has some interesting sculptures, and stupendous views.

Features heathers; rhododendrons & azaleas.

Owned by Mr & Mrs David Bowerman
Size 10.7ha (27 acres), including woodland

Coombland Gardens & Nursery

CONEYHURST, BILLINGSHURST,
RH14 9DY

Tel 01403 741727 **Fax** 01403 741079
Website www.coombland.co.uk
Location Turn right off A272 Billingshurst-

Coneyhurst road; then ½ mile along West Chiltington Lane on right.
Opening hours Nursery: 2 pm – 4 pm; Monday – Friday; March to November. Garden open for NGS from 10 am (2 pm on Wednesdays) to 5 pm; 5, 26 & 31 May, 7, 11, 14, 21 & 25 June;.
Admission fee Adults £2.50; Children free.

The garden at Coombland was started in 1981 to display the owners' love of old roses and geraniums. Graham Stuart Thomas helped with the design. It now has some fine plant collections, including violas, peonies and lilies, as well as areas of woodland garden. The nursery specialises in hardy geraniums. There will be four RHS special events at Coombland during 2004: details from 020 7821 3408.

Features specialist nursery.

Owned by Neville Lee (gardens) & David Browne (nursery)
Number of gardeners owners only
Size 2.4ha (6 acres)
NCCPG National Collections Geranium (cvs)

Cowdray Park

MIDHURST, GU29 0AY

Tel 01730 812461 **Fax** 01730 812122
Location South of A272, 1 mile east of Midhurst.
Opening hours For NGS on 16 May. There will also be an autumn opening for local charities.
Admission fee Adults £3; Children £1.

Cowdray is seldom open, but worth a long journey to see the ornate house and its contemporary (100-year-old) collection of trees, particularly conifers – don't miss the avenue of wellingtonias up at the top. Some are now record-breakers, and the sweeps of rhododendrons and azaleas, especially the hardy hybrids down 'the dell', are on the grand scale too. There are also two lakes, waterfalls, wildflower areas and a lot of new planting.

**Features** 300-year-old Lebanon cedar; wellingtonia avenue; rhododendrons; grapes & fruit in the glasshouses; valley garden; tallest *Abies concolor* f. *violacea* (28m.) and *Chamaecyparis pisifera* (29m.) in the UK; refreshments.

Owned by Viscount & Viscountess Cowdray
Size 10ha (25 acres)
English Heritage Grade II*

Denmans

FONTWELL, ARUNDEL, BN18 0SU

Tel 01243 542808 **Fax** 01243 544064
Website www.denmans-garden.co.uk
Location Off A29 or A27, near Fontwell racecourse.
Opening hours 9 am – 5 pm; daily; March to October. Or by appointment.
Admission fee Adults £3.50; OAPs £3; Children (4-16) £1.95.

This modern garden is a showpiece for John Brookes's ideas and commitment to easy care. He uses foliage, gravel mulches, contrasts of form, coloured stems, winter bark and plants as elements of design. The garden's design is so fluid that you feel carried along by its momentum and, of course, it is a brilliant source of ideas for your own garden. The plant centre opens daily (9 am – 5 pm) from February to Christmas, and the café (11 am – 5 pm) from April to September.

Features excellent modern design; gravel and grass; roses (mainly old-fashioned); herbs; good herbaceous borders; spring bulbs; shop; garden centre; lunches & teas.

Size 1.6ha (4 acres)

Floraldene

FINDON ROAD, WORTHING,
BN14 0BW

Tel 01903 261231
Location West side on Findon Road, next to
Durrington Cemetery, opposite Mayfield Close.
Parking in Mayfield Close.
Opening hours 2 pm – 5.30 pm; 30 March & 31
August. And by appointment.

This garden, started in the early 1950s, is
particularly good for heathers – hundreds of
different cultivars grown in a small garden
by a true devotee. Amazingly, the garden is
on chalk, and also supports some dwarf
rhododendrons, camellias and azaleas. New
in 2003 was a small collection of bud-
blooming callunas.

Features heathers; free teas.

Owned by John Tucker
Number of gardeners owner only
Size 0.2ha (½ acre)

Gravetye Manor Hotel

EAST GRINSTEAD, RH19 4LJ

Tel 01342 810567 **Fax** 01342 810080
Location 4 miles south-west of East Grinstead.
Opening hours Hotel & restaurant guests only; all
year. The perimeter path is open to the public free of
charge from 10 am to 5 pm on Tuesdays & Fridays.

Gravetye is William Robinson's own garden,
very influential about 100 years ago, and
scrupulously maintained by Peter Herbert as
it was in its prime. It was here that
Robinson put into practice the natural style
of gardening which he promoted so
vigorously in his magazines and books.
Robinson's own original woodland garden
has many of the trees he planted – fine
davidias and nyssas, for example. And the
meadows below the house are planted with
naturalised bulbs in the style that Robinson
made popular through his writings.
Gravetye is still a garden to learn from: there
is much to admire and copy.

Features William Robinson's
woodland garden; topiary; roses
(mainly old-fashioned); plantsman's
collection of plants; good herbaceous
borders; fine collection of trees; alpine
meadow; gazebo.

Owned by Peter Herbert
Number of gardeners 4
Size 12ha (30 acres)
English Heritage Grade II*

High Beeches

HANDCROSS, RH17 6HQ

Tel 01444 400589 **Fax** 01444 401543
Website www.highbeeches.com
Location South of B2110, 1 mile east of M23 at
Handcross.
Opening hours 1 pm – 5 pm; daily, except
Wednesdays; 1 April to 31 October. Closed on
Saturdays in July & August.
Admission fee Adults £5. Reductions for groups of
30+. Coaches by appointment.

One of the best (and most magical) of the
famous Sussex woodland gardens, High
Beeches was originally laid out by Colonel
Giles Loder, a cousin of the Loders of
Wakehurst. In 1966 it was acquired by Anne
and Edward Boscawen, who have devoted
many years to its maintenance and
improvement. Now it is now managed by a
non-profit-making charitable trust. The
original woodland has been thinned and
underplanted with exotics, many of them
rare. Some are trees like nyssas, magnolias,

Tetracentron sinense and davidias; others are shrubs – there is a 'Loderi Walk' planted with *Rhododendron* x *loderi* cultivars. A valley of ponds and woodland glades is beautifully planted with splendid rhododendrons, azaleas and camellias for spring, and swathes of native bluebells. The garden has wonderful autumn colours too, and a policy of letting good plants naturalise – cowslips, wild orchids, willow gentians and *Primula helodoxa*. The clock in the Clock Tower (now the restaurant) was installed to commemorate Colonel Loder's Derby winner, Spion Cop.

Features woodland garden; plantsman's collection of plants; mature conifers; fine collection of trees; rhododendrons; five-acre natural wildflower meadow; tallest *Stewartia monodelpha* (11m.) in the British Isles; restaurant open from noon; pretty tea garden.

Owned by High Beeches Gardens Conservation Trust
Number of gardeners 2
Size 10ha (25 acres)
NCCPG National Collections *Stewartia*
English Heritage Grade II*

Highdown

LITTLEHAMPTON ROAD, GORING-BY-SEA, BN12 6PE

Tel 01903 239999 ext 1112 **Fax** 01903 821384
Location Signed from A259.
Opening hours 10 am – 6 pm (4.30 pm in February, March, October & November, & 4 pm in January & December); daily (but not weekends from October to March); all year.
Admission fee Free – donations welcome.

This is the most famous garden to be made on chalk, and one of the best. It was actually laid out in a disused chalk quarry and on the surrounding, south-facing downland. Its

maker, Sir Frederick Stern, was determined to try anything that might grow in these unusual conditions. Eighty years on, the results are some handsome trees, vigorous roses, and long-forgotten peony hybrids. The gardens are designed on a large grid and planted mainly as mixed borders. Mediterranean plants do especially well: hellebores, tulips, daffodils and anemones have naturalised over large areas. Stern was a fine plantsman and scholar, and wrote the classic book *A Chalk Garden* as a memoir of his gardening experiences. He was also a distinguished plant breeder: Highdown has given us two very fine roses in *Rosa* 'Highdownensis' and 'Wedding Day'. The garden is now well maintained by Worthing Borough Council and a pleasure to visit at any season, but perhaps especially in spring.

Features woodland garden; roses (mainly old-fashioned); rock garden; plantsman's collection of plants; mature conifers; good herbaceous borders; fine collection of trees; tallest specimen of *Carpinus turczaninowii* in the UK, a handsome tree; refreshments from March to September.

Owned by Worthing Borough Council
Number of gardeners 4
Size 4ha (10 acres)
NCCPG National Collections plants introduced by Sir Frederick Stern
English Heritage Grade II*

Holly Gate Cactus Nursery

BILLINGSHURST ROAD, ASHINGTON, RH20 3BB

Tel 01903 892930
Website www.hollygatecactus.co.uk
Location ½ mile from Ashington, on B2133 to Billingshurst.

Opening hours 9 am – 5 pm; daily. Closed 25 – 26 December.
Admission fee Adults £2; OAPs & Children £1.50.

Holly Gate specialises in cacti and succulents. It carries over 50,000 plants of all types in stock and sells them both retail and wholesale. Many are also planted in the cactus garden, which has some fine specimens and a wide range of taxa – fascinating for the *cognoscenti* and an eye-opener for the uninitiated, whatever the weather.

 Features cacti; succulents.

Owned by T.M. Hewitt
Number of gardeners 2
Size 930 sq.m. (10,000 sq.ft.)

W.E.Th. Ingwersen Ltd

BIRCH FARM NURSERY, GRAVETYE, EAST GRINSTEAD, RH19 4LE

Tel 01342 810236
Website www.ingwersen.co.uk
Location 4 miles south-west of East Grinstead.
Opening hours 9 am – 1 pm & 1.30 pm – 4 pm; daily, except Sundays & Bank Holidays; March to September. Weekdays only from October to February. Closed for 2 weeks at Christmas.
Admission fee Free

This was the first alpine nursery in the south of England: when it started in March 1927, Mr Ingwersen was a tenant of William Robinson at nearby Gravetye Manor. The company's exhibits at RHS Flower Shows have been a source of much praise. It still has one of the best collections in the country of traditional alpines, especially European primulas, sempervivums and autumn-flowering gentians, but it is also a good place to find less common rock plants, the smaller

perennials, dwarf shrubs and conifers. There are many raised beds and troughs to see at the nursery (which is in a most beautiful setting): one can spend a long and very happy time here looking at alpines and browsing through possible purchases.

 Features rock plants; troughs; lots of small plants for interested plantsmen.

Owned by Paul Ingwersen

Nymans

HANDCROSS, HAYWARDS HEATH, RH17 6EB

Tel 01444 400321 **Fax** 01444 400253
Website www.nationaltrust.org.uk/nymans
Location Handcross, off the main road on B2114.
Opening hours 11 am – 6 pm; Wednesday – Sunday, plus Bank Holiday Mondays; 18 February to 31 October. 11 am – 4 pm; Saturdays & Sundays; 1 November to February 2005. Closed 25 & 26 December.
Admission fee Adults £6.50; Children £3.25. Reductions in winter. RHS members free.

The garden at Nymans was made in the early years of the 20th century by Leonard Messel, and his head gardener James Comber. Although it is now owned by the National Trust, there is still a substantial input from latter-day members of the Messel family. Nymans is a stupendous plantsman's garden with a wonderful collection of plants of every type which have been marshalled with a fair degree of artistry and made to fit within a strong overall design. It is one of the best gardens of the Sussex Weald, and one which retains much of the distinctive style dictated by its historic collection of shrubs and trees. There are opulent yellow-and-blue herbaceous borders in the walled garden, a pioneering collection of old roses, a stupendous

Leonardslee Lakes & Gardens

LOWER BEEDING, HORSHAM, RH13 6PP

Tel 01403 891212 **Fax** 01403 891305
Website www.leonardslee.com
Location 4 miles south-west of Handcross at
junction of B2110 & A281.
Opening hours 9.30 am – 6 pm; daily; April to
October.
Admission fee Adults £6 (but, in May, £7 on week-
days and £8 at weekends); Children £4 at all times.

Leonardslee is a plantsman's garden on an
enormous scale. It was begun in 1801
and enlarged from 1889 by Sir Edmund
Loder – and still belongs to his descendants.
It is important historically as one of the
earliest examples of a collection of rare
plants in a designed setting – a series of
woodland valleys with panoramic views on
the edge of the Wealden Forest. The gardens
are beautiful when they first open in April
with magnificent magnolias and camellias.
Autumn colour is another feature: from the
middle of September onwards maples,
azaleas, liquidambars, carryas and nyssas
produce one of the finest arrays of autumn
colour in England. But Leonardslee is
famous above all for its rhododendrons and
azaleas which line the many miles of paths
up and down the hillsides and around the
seven lakes. Sheets of bluebells accompany
their main flowering in May, while the
banks of the lakes and streams are densely
planted with candelabra primulas,
lysichitons and gunneras. There are many
other fascinating features: magnificent
conifers; large plantings of modern
Rhododendron yakushimanum hybrids;
several original plants of *Rhododendron* x
loderi hybrids; a large area naturalised by
Scilla liliohyacinthus; rare shrubs like *Ilex
dipyrena*; a European cork oak (*Quercus
suber*) and the Amur cork oak
(*Phellodendron amurense*); a magnificent

Pulhamite rock garden about 100 years old,
which has a very striking clump of the
hardy Chusan palm (*Trachycarpus fortunei*
and a fine form of *T. fortunei* var. *surculosa*
*an*d a bright mixture of evergreen azaleas;
and a truly beautiful valley on the other side
of the main lake which is filled from top to
bottom with a flood of sweet-scented yellow
azaleas *Rhododendron luteum*. The garden is
very large – allow lots of time – and the
labelling sparse.

Features rock garden; plantsman's
collection of plants; mature conifers;
new Millennium plantings (100 oak species;
100 maple species; many flowering *Cornus*);
bonsai; tallest fossil tree *Metasequoia
glyptostroboides* (28m.) and *Magnolia
campbellii* (27m.) in the British Isles, and 5
further champion trees; gift shop; licensed
restaurant & café.

Owned by The Loder family
Number of gardeners 7
Size 100ha (250 acres)
English Heritage Grade I

wisteria pergola and vast collections of magnolias and camellias. Further afield, the woodland and wild garden have a great collection of rare trees and shrubs. Nymans suffered very severely from the Great Storm of 1987, but has since made a brilliant recovery and many would say now that the garden looks better than ever.

Features woodland garden; topiary; roses (mainly old-fashioned); plantsman's collection of plants; good herbaceous borders; fine collection of trees; eight different record-breaking trees; shop; plant centre open daily 11 am – 6 pm; licensed restaurant.

Owned by The National Trust
Number of gardeners 7
Size 12ha (30 acres)
English Heritage Grade II*

Parham

PARHAM HOUSE, PULBOROUGH, RH20 4HS

Tel 01903 742021 **Fax** 01903 746557
Website www.parhaminsussex.co.uk
Location On A283 midway between Pulborough & Storrington.
Opening hours 12 noon – 6 pm; Wednesdays, Thursdays, Sundays & Bank Holiday Mondays; Easter to September. Plus Tuesdays & Fridays in August.
Admission fee Gardens only: Adults £4.50; Children £1.

Parham is an ethereal English garden for the loveliest of Elizabethan manor houses. In the deer park are a landscaped lake and a cricket ground. The fun for garden-lovers is in the old walled garden: four acres of lush borders, colour plantings in yellow, blue and mauve, old and new fruit trees, and all maintained to the highest standard. The aim

is to achieve 'Edwardian opulence...without being too purist'. There are striking colour combinations too within the vegetable garden, while extensive cutting borders supply material for the arrangements of cut flowers for which the house is famous. The voluminous conservatory has a splendid display of fuchsias and old-fashioned pelargonium cultivars.

Features roses (mainly old-fashioned); trained fruit; good herbaceous borders; organic kitchen garden; HHA/Christie's Garden of the Year in 1990; shop; light lunches & teas.

Owned by Parham Park Trust
Number of gardeners 4½, plus volunteers
Size 4.4ha (11 acres)
English Heritage Grade I

Petworth House

PETWORTH, GU28 0AE

Tel 01798 342207 **Fax** 01798 342963
Website www.nationaltrust.org.uk/petworth
Location At Petworth, well signed.
Opening hours Garden: 11 am – 6 pm; Saturday – Wednesday; 27 March to 31 October. Plus some dates in March (ring for details) for spring bulbs. Plus Good Friday. Park: 8 am – dusk; daily; all year (but closes at 12 noon for concerts on 3 & 4 July).
Admission fee Garden ('Pleasure grounds'): Adults £1.50; Children free. Park free.

One of the best Capability Brown landscapes in England sweeps right up to the windows of Petworth House. The National Trust has added acres of bright azaleas to the woodland garden. Both park and garden have enjoyed a renaissance since the damage caused by the great storms of 1987. The Pleasure Ground is one of the most historically interesting parts of Petworth: the layout dates back to

Elizabethan times. Winding pathways lead through shrubberies, punctuated by unexpected vistas and areas for quiet contemplation.

Features Capability Brown landscape; woodland garden; good herbaceous borders; deer park; one million daffodils; shop; restaurant.

Owned by The National Trust
Number of gardeners 4
Size 12ha (30 acres) of pleasure grounds; 280-ha (700-acre) park.
English Heritage Grade I

Wakehurst Place

ARDINGLY, HAYWARDS HEATH, RH17 6TN

Tel 01444 894066 **Fax** 01444 894069
Website www.kew.org
Location On B2028 between Turners Hill & Ardingly.
Opening hours 10 am – 7 pm (6 pm in March, 5 pm in February & October, & 4 pm from November to January); daily except 24 & 25 December; all year.
Admission fee Adults £7; OAPs £5; Children free. Subject to review. Free to National Trust members.

Wakehurst Place, now managed by the Royal Botanic Gardens at Kew as a country outlier, has a long horticultural history. Most of the planting, however, began after Gerald Loder bought the estate in 1903 and began to introduce exotic trees and shrubs – a development which continued throughout the mid-20th century under the next owner Sir Henry Price. The planting suffered badly in the great storm of 1987 but the survivors include many rare trees including the King William pine (*Athrotaxis selaginoides*). Among the record-breaking trees which survived the gales are *Cornus nuttallii* and

Torreya nucifera both 17m high, *Carya tomentosa* at 27m, and two cultivars of *Chamaecyparis lawsoniana* – 'President Roosevelt' at 15m and 'Winston Churchill' slightly shorter at 13m. A recent addition has been the 'iris dell', planted with authentic Japanese cultivars of water iris (*Iris ensata*), against a brilliant background of Kurume azaleas – Wakehurst has significant connections with Japan. The water garden is surrounded by sheets of blue meconopsis and the giant Himalayan *Cardiocrinum giganteum*. Wakehurst also has its botanic collections, including a Monocot border – wonderful ginger plants (*Hedychium*) in autumn – and specimen beds with especially comprehensive collections of hypericums, hydrangeas and agapanthus. Many parts of the woodland garden are underplanted with rhododendrons, which are at their best in April and May. Wakehurst has also benefited from major funding by the Millennium Commission, which has enabled it to develop the world's largest seed bank: it aims to collect and conserve some ten per cent of the world's flora – 24,000 species – by the year 2010.

Features ornamental woodland garden; roses (mainly old-fashioned & climbers); rhododendrons & azaleas; plantsman's collection of plants; daffodils; camellias; fine collection of trees; alpine plants; bluebells; Asian heath garden; pinetum; cardiocrinums; good autumn colour; *Iris ensata* dell; water garden; tallest *Ostrya japonica* (15m.) in the British Isles, plus 25 further tree records; gift shop; plant sales (March to October); light refreshments & restaurant.

Owned by RBG Kew, on lease from National Trust
Number of gardeners 40
Size 127ha (316 acres)
NCCPG National Collections Betula; Hypericum; Nothofagus; Skimmia
English Heritage Grade II*

West Dean Gardens

WEST DEAN, CHICHESTER, PO18 0QZ

Tel 01243 818210 **Fax** 01243 811342
Website www.westdean.org.uk
Location 6 miles north of Chichester on A286.
Opening hours 11 am – 5 pm; daily; March to
October. Opens at 10.30 am from May to
September.
Admission fee Adults £5.50; OAPs £5; Children
£2.50.

Laid out in the 1890s and 1900s, West Dean
has now been extensively restored. Harold
Peto's 100m pergola has been replanted with
roses. Much of the damage to the 20ha St
Roche's arboretum caused by the 1987 storm
has been made good. The great range of
glasshouses in the walled garden has been
repaired and the garden itself planted as a
working kitchen garden which is now the
crowning glory of West Dean. A huge variety
of plants – from peaches to peppers,
cucumbers to coleus, aubergines to orchids –
grow in the 16 glasshouses and frames. Out
of doors are orderly rows of cabbage, carrots,
lettuce and beetroot, alongside herbaceous
borders in rich red, oranges and yellows. No
space is wasted: the kitchen garden has over
200 different apples, pears and plums. No
private garden has so many beautifully
grown fruit and vegetables. Beyond the
walled garden (2½ acres in size) are 35 acres
of ornamental gardens, the St Roche's
arboretum and 240 acres of landscaped
park. Herbaceous borders and annual
bedding schemes have been reinstated, rustic
summer houses rebuilt and the arboretum
taken in hand. The redevelopment of the
spring garden, including the 1820s rustic
thatched summerhouse with its moss- and
heather-lined interior and its floor of
knapped flints and horses' molars is now
complete. Further plantings for the wild
garden are planned for 2004.

Features plants under glass; museum of
old lawn mowers; long pergola with roses
& clematis; tallest *Cupressus goveniana* (22m.)
and *Ailanthus vilmoriniana* (26m.) in UK;
amazing kitchen garden; licensed restaurant.

Owned by The Edward James Foundation
Number of gardeners 9
Size 36ha (90 acres) in all
NCCPG National Collections *Aesculus*;
Liriodendron
English Heritage Grade II*

Yew Tree Cottage

BANKTON HILL, CRAWLEY DOWN, CRAWLEY, RH10 3EB

Tel 01342 714633
Location Opposite Grange Farm on B2028.
Opening hours By appointment from May to
September.
Admission fee Adults £1.50; OAPs £1.

This miraculous small garden (about one-
third of an acre) has been designed, planted
and maintained by the nonagenarian owner
over many years. For much of the 1980s and
1990s, there was no better example of the
cottage-garden style. It won infinite plaudits
for its display of plants, including a *BBC
Gardener's World* interview with Gay Search
in 1998. Then, in 1999, Mrs Hudson decided
to replace it with a gravel-and-grasses
garden inspired by Piet Oudolf. The latest
change is to replant some of the herbaceous
borders with gravel and shrubs: 'less is
more' is Mrs Hudson's verdict.

Features good herbaceous borders;
cottage garden style; colour borders;
ornamental grass garden; refreshments for
small parties.

Owned by Mrs K. Hudson
Number of gardeners 1
Size 0.15ha (one-third of an acre)

WARWICKSHIRE

Warwickshire has for centuries been a prosperous county: it has the rich clay soils, the country estates and the gardens to prove it. Many of its historic gardens are open to the public throughout the season, including such top attractions as Arbury Hall, Charlecote Park, Farnborough Hall, Packwood House, Upton House and Warwick Castle. The National Gardens Scheme is very successful in persuading the owners of modern gardens to open them to the public, especially by grouping several together within a village. Warwickshire has many first-rate garden centres and a few top-class specialist nurseries too – notably Fibrex Nurseries, who specialise in pelargoniums, ivies, hardy ferns and hellebores. Fibrex also has two of the county's National Collections. The Henry Doubleday Research Association, the organic gardening organisation, has its headquarters at Ryton near Coventry: it offers free access to RHS members throughout the year.

Arbury Hall

NUNEATON, CV10 7PT

Tel 024 7638 2804 **Fax** 024 7664 1147
Location 3 miles south-west of Nuneaton off the B4102.
Opening hours 2 pm – 6 pm; Bank Holiday Sundays & Mondays; Easter Sunday to September.
Admission fee Adults £4.50; Children £3.

Arbury is more important historically than horticulturally: Sanderson Miller was involved in some 18th-century improvements and there is a wonderfully landscaped sequence of canals and lakes. During the 19th century, many good trees were planted, now in the full-grown beauty of their maturity: purple beeches and a golden sycamore for example. Then there are bluebell woods, pollarded limes, a large rose garden, a walled garden and a huge wisteria. Nothing is outstanding in itself, but the ensemble is an oasis of peace on the edge of industrial Daventry and worth the journey from far away.

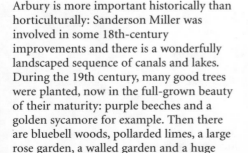 **Features** woodland garden; roses (mainly modern); rhododendrons & azaleas; daffodils; bluebells; gift & crafts shop; tea-room.

Owned by Viscount Daventry
Number of gardeners 4
English Heritage Grade II*

Baddesley Clinton

KNOWLE, SOLIHULL, B93 0DQ

Tel 01564 783294 **Fax** 01564 782706
Website www.nationaltrust.org.uk
Location 1 mile west of A4141.
Opening hours 12 noon – 5.30 pm; Wednesday – Sunday; 3 March to 12 December. Also open on Bank Holiday Mondays. Closes at 5 pm in March, April, October & 1-2 November; closes at 4.30 pm

from 10 November to 12 December.
Admission fee Adults £3.10; Children £1.55.

The walled garden at Baddesley Clinton has fine mixed plantings, including a good collection of shrub roses, herbaceous plants, herbs and annuals. One of the Victorian lean-to glasshouses has recently been restored. In front of the house (an ancient manor house) is a formal courtyard garden. Further away are woodland walks, a lake and wildflower meadows.

Features formal courtyard garden; walled garden; shop; plant sales; restaurant.

Owned by The National Trust
Number of gardeners 2
Size 4.4ha (11 acres)
English Heritage Grade II

Charlecote Park

WELLESBOURNE, WARWICK, CV35 9ER

Tel 01789 470277 **Fax** 01789 470544
Website www.nationaltrust.org.uk
Location Signed from A429.
Opening hours 11 am – 6 pm; Friday – Tuesday; 8 March to 2 November. Also 11 am – 4 pm on Saturdays & Sundays from 8 November to 20 December.
Admission fee Adults £3; Children £1.50.

Fine cedars and a Capability Brown park are the main claims to Charlecote's fame, but the young William Shakespeare is reputed to have poached deer from the park, so the National Trust has planted a border with plants mentioned in his works. Recent additions include a parterre, a large herbaceous border, a sensory garden and 'green court' garden designed by the tenant, Sir Edmund Fairfax-Lucy.

Features topiary; parterre; mature conifers; deer park; orangery; National Trust shop; restaurant.

Owned by The National Trust
Number of gardeners 2
Size 1.6ha (4 acres)
English Heritage Grade II*

Coughton Court

ALCESTER, B49 5JA

Tel 01789 400777 **Fax** 01789 765544
Website www.coughtoncourt.co.uk
Location 2 miles north of Alcester on A435.
Opening hours 11 am – 5.30 pm; Wednesday – Sunday; April to September. Plus Tuesdays in July & August. Plus Saturdays & Sundays only in March & October. Closed 9 April & 26 June, but open on 12 & 13 April, 3 & 4 May, 31 May & 1 June, and 30 & 31 August.
Admission fee Adults £5.50; Children £2.75. RHS members free. Parking 75p per car.

The garden at Coughton has all been made since 1992, designed by Christina Williams, the owner's daughter. An Elizabethan-style knot garden fills the courtyard, and extensive new plantings beyond lead the eye out to the distant landscape. There is a rose labyrinth in the walled garden and a herb garden, as well as an orchard planted with local varieties of fruit. The bog garden, planted in 1997, has come together well. New this year (2004) is a fruit and vegetable garden.

Features interesting historic gardens (new) around the house (old); pretty plants and plantings; gift shop & plant centre; restaurant/café.

Owned by Mrs Clare Throckmorton & the National Trust
Number of gardeners 4
Size 10ha (25 acres)

Farnborough Hall

BANBURY, OX17 1DU

Tel 01295 690002
Website www.nationaltrust.org.uk
Location Off A423, 6 miles north of Banbury.
Opening hours 2 pm – 6 pm; Wednesdays &
Saturdays; April to September. Also 4 & 5 May.
Terrace walk also open on Wednesdays &
Saturdays, by prior appointment.
Admission fee Grounds £1.75; Terrace Walk £1.
Prices subject to review.

Farnborough Hall is Sanderson Millar's
masterpiece – a broad grass walk leads
gently uphill for ½ mile to an obelisk erected
in 1751. On the way up are an Ionic temple
and the Oval Pavilion, both hemmed in by
vegetation now. Below the house lies a
pretty series of landscaped lakes. No flowers,
but a sense of space and peace: only the
distant roar of the M40 takes the edge off
the sense of awe. The National Trust
suggests taking the woodland walk back –
pretty wild flowers in spring and a
hexagonal game-larder.

Features historic landscape.

Owned by The National Trust
English Heritage Grade I

Fibrex Nurseries Ltd

HONEYBOURNE ROAD, PEBWORTH,
STRATFORD-UPON-AVON, CV37 8XP

Tel 01789 720788 **Fax** 01789 721162
Website www.fibrex.co.uk
Location South-east edge of village, on road to
Honeybourne.
Opening hours 10.30 am – 4 pm; Monday –
Friday; all year. Plus weekends (12 noon – 5 pm)
from March to July. Closed for last two weeks of
December & first week of January. Also closed on
Easter Sunday and August Bank Holiday Monday.
Admission fee Free.

Fibrex is a family nursery, built up over
more than 40 years and a regular prize-
winner at RHS Flower Shows. It has four
specialities – pelargoniums, ivies, hardy
ferns and hellebores – and holds National
Collections in two of them. The National
Collection of pelargoniums has over 2,000
different species and cultivars and claims to
be the largest in the world. The National
Collection of ivies (*Hedera*) has over 300
different species and cultivars. The ferns are
planted out in the show garden in a natural
manner using mature plants: the hellebores
too are planted out for viewing when they
are in flower. A RHS special event will take
place at Fibrex on 12 May 2004: details from
020 7821 3408.

Features pelargoniums; ivies; hardy
ferns; hellebores.

NCCPG National Collections *Hedera*; *Pelargonium*

The Hiller Garden

DUNNINGTON HEATH FARM,
DUNNINGTON, ALCESTER, B49 5PD

Tel 01789 490991 **Fax** 01789 490439
Location On B4088 near Ragley Hall, 2 miles south
of Alcester.
Opening hours 10 am – 5 pm (4 pm in winter);
daily; all year. Nursery open from April to November.
Admission fee Free.

This is an unusually fine display garden,
with colour and interest all the year round.
The rose garden has roses from mediaeval
times through to the latest David Austin
English roses. The nursery specialises in old
roses and perennial plants, of which it has a
wide range.

Features gift shop; garden centre; tea-room & light lunches.

Owned by Richard Beach
Number of gardeners 1½
Size 0.8ha (2 acres)

The Mill Garden

55 MILL STREET, WARWICK,
CV34 4HB

Tel 01926 492877
Location Off A425, beside the old castle gate, at the bottom of Mill Street.
Opening hours 9 am – 6 pm; daily; early April to late October.
Admission fee Adults £1; Children free.

No garden has such an idyllic setting, on the banks of the Avon at the foot of Warwick castle: the views in all directions are superb. The garden is planted in the cottage style and seems much larger than its half acre: it burgeons with plants, and the use of annuals to supplement the varied permanent planting enables it to have colour and form, contrasts and harmonies, at every season. This garden was made by Arthur Measures over a long period: it remains open in his memory.

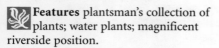**Features** plantsman's collection of plants; water plants; magnificent riverside position.

Owned by D.G. & J. Measures
Number of gardeners owners & part-time help
Size 0.2ha (½ acre)

Packwood House

GROVE ROAD, LAPWORTH, SOLIHULL,
B94 6AT

Tel 01564 783294 **Fax** 01564 782706
Website www.nationaltrust.org.uk
Location 2 miles east of Hockley Heath: signed from A3400.
Opening hours 11 am – 5.30 pm; Wednesday – Sunday, plus Bank Holiday Mondays; 3 March to 7 November. Closes at 4.30 pm in March, April, October & November.
Admission fee Garden only: Adults £2.80; Children £1.40.

Long famous for its topiary, Packwood also has magnificent herbaceous borders which make a visit in July or August particularly rewarding.

Features National Trust shop; plants for sale.

Owned by The National Trust
Number of gardeners 3½
Size 2.8ha (7 acres)
English Heritage Grade I

Ryton Organic Gardens

COVENTRY, CV8 3LG

Tel 024 7630 3517 **Fax** 024 7663 9229
Website www.hdra.org.uk
Location 5 miles south-east of Coventry off A45.
Opening hours 9 am – 5 pm; daily; all year except Christmas week.
Admission fee Adults £3.95; Children £1.50. RHS members free.

Ryton is the UK centre of excellence for organic gardening. It is very well laid out and landscaped, with 35 different small gardens, all highly instructive. The gardens include herb gardens, rose gardens, fruit and vegetable displays plus wildlife and conservation areas. A new development is the area called the Vegetable Kingdom, which tells the history of British vegetables. The website is good.

Features organic gardens; considerable educational interest; shop with gardening products, books, food, wine & gifts; organic whole-food restaurant.

Owned by Henry Doubleday Research Association
Number of gardeners 7
Size 4ha (10 acres)

Upton House

BANBURY, OX15 6HT

Tel 01295 670266 **Fax** 01295 671144
Website www.nationaltrust.org.uk
Location A422, 7 miles north-west of Banbury & 12 miles south-east of Stratford-upon-Avon.
Opening hours 12 noon – 5 pm; Saturday – Wednesday, plus Good Friday; 3 April to 31 October. Opens at 11 am on Saturdays, Sundays & Bank Holidays. Then from 12 noon to 4 pm on Saturdays & Sundays only from 6 November to 19 December.
Admission fee Adults £3.50; Children £2.

Upton House is set off by a flat and spacious expanse of grass; only when you reach the far side of this immense lawn do the real gardens appear, tumbling down the terraced hillside to the pool at the bottom. The structure is early 1700s: the gardens are 1930s – Kitty Lloyd-Jones's masterpiece. It is dominated by a sloping kitchen garden, reached by flights of Italianate stairs. There are also small formal gardens, one with standard *Hibiscus syriacus* 'Bluebird' underplanted with eryngiums, and another planted with roses. One way back runs through good herbaceous borders – simply planted, but effective. The best area for

interesting plants is the bog garden, with fine cercidiphyllums, gunneras, magnolias and an *Acer carpinifolium* leaning low over another pool. Be prepared for quite a long walk from the car-park – and be careful on the slopes in wet weather.

Features good herbaceous borders; bog garden; National Trust shop; licensed restaurant.

Owned by The National Trust
Number of gardeners 5, plus 2 students
Size 14ha (35 acres)
NCCPG National Collections *Aster*
English Heritage Grade II*

Warwick Castle

WARWICK, CV34 4QU

Tel 01926 495421 **Fax** 01926 401692
Website www.warwick-castle.co.uk
Location In town centre.
Opening hours 10 am – 6 pm (5 pm from October to March); daily; all year except 25 December.
Admission fee Adults £13.50; OAPs £9.75; Children £8. Slightly less on weekdays and out-of-season. Ticket price includes entry to Castle (no 'garden only' price).

This classic 18th-century landscape looks good after some recent restoration, as do the late 19th-century formal garden and a re-created Victorian rose garden (both by Robert Marnock), and the Backhouse rock garden.

Features topiary; roses (mainly old-fashioned); rhododendrons & azaleas; mature conifers; Capability Brown landscape; handsome conservatory; shop; refreshments.

Owned by Tussauds Group
Number of gardeners 3
Size 23ha (58 acres)
English Heritage Grade I

WEST MIDLANDS

As an administrative entity, West Midlands was a short-lived county: created in 1974 from parts of Warwickshire and Staffordshire: it is now entirely split up into unitary authorities. Its historic gardens are few, but they include what is left of the poet Shenstone's The Leasowes, together with the Birmingham Botanical Gardens and Castle Bromwich Hall. The latter are both highly visitable and highly visited – excellent gardens, deservedly popular still. Being such an urban county, West Midlands is short on old estates, landscaped parks and arboreta, but full of large villa-gardens like the one in Edgbaston which became the University of Birmingham Botanic Garden. This is the area too where the National Gardens Scheme does best. The biggest RHS event in the Midlands takes place at the NEC from 16 to 20 June 2004: *BBC Gardener's World Live* is very different from such shows as Chelsea and Hampton Court, though the great draw is the enormously long floral marquee which the Royal Horticultural Society runs with great aplomb. The county, though small, also has a surprisingly large number of National Collections, including two, (*Ceanothus* and *Rudbeckia*), held by Dudley Borough Council.

Birmingham Botanical Gardens & Glasshouses

WESTBOURNE ROAD, EDGBASTON, BIRMINGHAM, B15 3TR

Tel 0121 454 1860 **Fax** 0121 454 7835
Website www.birminghambotanicalgardens.org.uk
Location Follow brown tourist signs in Edgbaston.
Opening hours 9 am (10 am on Sundays) – 7 pm, or dusk if earlier; daily; all year except Christmas Day.
Admission fee Adults £5.70 (£6 on summer Sundays); Concessions £3.30.

Part botanic garden, part public park, wholly delightful, the Birmingham Botanical Gardens & Glasshouses can boast an historic lay-out (John Claudius Loudon), rare trees and shrubs, gardens for rhododendrons, roses, herbs and alpines, and four glasshouses (tropical, subtropical, Mediterranean and arid) as well as a good restaurant, brilliant standards of maintenance and a brass band playing on Sunday afternoons in summer. The plant highlights are innumerable, but include water hyacinths (the weed that is choking the Nile), rice plants, papyrus plants, coffee and sugar, bananas and pineapples, many cycads, insectivorous plants, 'living stones', *Paulownia tomentosa*, good herbaceous plants (phlox, euphorbias, geraniums, delphiniums) and the National Collection of Bonsai housed in a secure courtyard.

Features roses (ancient & modern); rock garden; plantsman's collection of plants; plants under glass; fruit; mature conifers; good herbaceous borders; alpine yard; bonsai; three 'historic' gardens – Roman, Mediaeval & Tudor; gift shop; restaurant & light refreshments.

Owned by Birmingham Botanical & Horticultural Society
Number of gardeners 10, plus students
Size 6ha (15 acres)
NCCPG National Collections Bonsai
English Heritage Grade II*

Castle Bromwich Hall Gardens

CHESTER ROAD, CASTLE BROMWICH, B36 9BT

Tel & Fax 0121 749 4100
Website www.cbhgt.colebridge.net
Location 5 miles from city centre just off B4114.
Opening hours 1.30 pm – 4 30 pm; Tuesday – Thursday. 2 pm – 6 pm; Saturdays, Sundays & Bank Holiday Mondays. 1 April to 31 October.
Admission fee Adults £3.50; Concessions £2.50; Children £1.50.

The garden at Castle Bromwich Hall is garden archaeology at work – educational, instructive and highly enjoyable. The gardens at Castle Bromwich are being restored as they were in about 1700 by a privately funded trust. For many years they were neglected, lost beneath a tangled mass of vegetation. Work began in 1985 and has been very successful: the result is both beautiful, inspiring and educational. The gardens contain a large collection of unusual period plants, and a 19th-century holly maze. There is also a holly walk – a broad path lined with variegated hollies. At its end, the elegant Summer House looks

across to an early orangery known as the Green House. Nearby is the formal vegetable garden, laid out to the design of Batty Langley's *New Principles of Gardening* (1728). Many historic vegetables and herbs are grown, along with unusual varieties like the black 'Congo' potato and white carrot. Fruit trees are formally trained – apples, pears, apricots, figs and cherries. The Upper and Lower Wildernesses have grown to maturity, with period underplanting. The North Garden has recently been restored to the design shown in Henry Beighton's Prospect of 1726, its parterre outlined with yew, mown grass and gravel.

 Features walled gardens; historic vegetables, fruit and herbs; holly maze; gift shop; courtyard coffee shop.

Owned by Castle Bromwich Hall Gardens Trust
Number of gardeners 3, plus volunteers
Size 4ha (10 acres)
English Heritage Grade II*

University of Birmingham Botanic Garden at Winterbourne

58 EDGBASTON PARK ROAD, EDGBASTON, B15 2RT

Tel 0121 414 4944 **Fax** 0121 414 5619
Website www.botanic.bham.ac.uk
Location Off A38 Bristol Road, ½ mile.
Opening hours 11 am – 4 pm; Monday – Friday; all year. Plus 1 pm – 5 pm on Sundays from May to July. Closed Bank Holidays, Easter & Christmas holidays.
Admission fee Adults £2.

This was originally a private garden, belonging to one of Birmingham's great-

and-good families: it was given to the university in 1944 but still has the 'feel' of a private garden – one with an exceptional collection of plants. The rhododendrons and naturalised bulbs are very pretty: even the roses, chosen to illustrate their history in cultivation, fit well into an ornamental garden. Perhaps the most interesting plants are the collection of alpines in troughs, in the sandstone rockery and in the scree beds. There are some geographic beds which put together plants that combine naturally in the wild, but everything else about the garden is horticultural, rather than botanic. The garden went back a little during the 1980s and early 1990s, but is now being restored and redeveloped most effectively. It is a charming place to spend a couple of hours at almost any time of the year.

Features roses of every kind; a good collection of plants of every kind.

Owned by University of Birmingham
Number of gardeners 3
Size 2.4ha (6 acres)
NCCPG National Collections *Anthemis*; *Rosa* (History of European roses)

Wightwick Manor

WIGHTWICK, WOLVERHAMPTON, WV6 8EE

Tel 01902 761400 **Fax** 01902 764663
Website www.nationaltrust.org.uk
Location 3 miles west of Wolverhampton on A454.
Opening hours 11 am – 6 pm on Wednesdays, Thursdays, Saturdays & Bank Holidays; 1 March to 24 December.
Admission fee Adults £3; Children free.

Wightwick is a substantial Victorian garden, designed by Alfred Parsons and Thomas Mawson. It has topiary, a rose arbour, avenues of Irish yews and a Poets' Corner where all the plants were taken as cuttings from the gardens of literary men – Keats, Tennyson and Dickens among them.

Features topiary; roses (mainly old-fashioned & climbers); rock garden; good herbaceous borders; current holder of Sandford Award; shop; tea-room.

Owned by The National Trust
Number of gardeners 3, plus 6 volunteers
Size 6.7ha (17 acres)

WILTSHIRE

Wiltshire is the county that people travel through on their way to somewhere else. For gardeners, this is a mistake. Unlike so many counties whose great Grade I historic gardens are often rather dull, Wiltshire's are all supremely beautiful – Bowood, Iford, Longleat, Stourhead and Wilton. All are open to the public, as are many of the other graded gardens. Wiltshire also has a number of very good plantsman's gardens – notably Broadleas and Home Covert near Devizes, and the Old Vicarage at nearby Edington. It has some fine arboreta: tree-enthusiasts should also try to see the record-breaking multi-stemmed specimen of *Zelkova carpinifolia* at Wardour Castle – 35m high when last officially measured in 1977. The National Gardens Scheme does well in the county, particularly among the owners of medium-sized and large gardens. The Wiltshire Gardens Trust is active in conservation and also represents the NCCPG in the county: there is a sprinkling of National Collections among its members. Wiltshire does not, however, do so well for nurseries: perhaps only the Botanic Nursery at Atworth can be said to have a national profile. Geoffrey Jellicoe's masterpiece at Shute House, Donhead St Mary, has recently been open to groups by prior appointment. It is worth noting that, contrary to widespread belief, both Shute House and Larmer Tree Gardens are actually in Wiltshire, not in Dorset.

The Abbey House

MARKET CROSS, MALMESBURY, SN16 9AS

Tel 01666 822212 **Fax** 01666 822782
Website www.abbeyhousegardens.co.uk
Location In town centre, behind abbey. Public car-parks nearby.
Opening hours 11 am – 6 pm; daily; 21 March to 21 October.
Admission fee Adults £5; Concessions £4.75; Children £2.

This remarkable five-acre garden has all been made by the Pollards since 1995. They planted 2,000 different roses to celebrate the millennium, and 2,000 different herb cultivars. Other features include an arcaded fruit walk, a knot garden, huge herbaceous borders, a striking laburnum tunnel and a formal garden. But it is the design and planting which are so distinctive: bold, varied and inspirational. The woodland garden running down to the river is home to more than 40,000 spring bulbs. At the bottom are fish ponds, a 6m waterfall (a recent addition), heather banks and a fernery. Alan Titchmarsh came here for *BBC Gardeners World* in June 2002. His verdict: 'the Wow factor is here in abundance!'.

Features plantsman's collection of plants; herbaceous borders; roses of every kind; good design; colour contrasts; refreshments.

Owned by Ian Pollard
Number of gardeners 3
Size 2ha (5 acres)

Avebury Manor Garden

AVEBURY, MARLBOROUGH, SN8 1RF

Tel 01672 539250 **Fax** 01672 538038
Website www.nationaltrust.org.uk
Location In the village, well signed.
Opening hours 11 am – 5.30 pm; daily except Wednesdays & Thursdays; 4 April to 31 October. Open Bank Holiday Mondays.
Admission fee Adults £2.90; Children £1.40.

The National Trust is continuing the work of restoration at this great Edwardian garden and the 'garden rooms' are being revived and replanted: the results are well worth another visit.

Features topiary; roses (mainly old-fashioned); good herbaceous borders; double lavender walk; shop just outside the garden; National Trust restaurant in village.

Owned by The National Trust
Number of gardeners 2
Size 2.4ha (6 acres)

Bolehyde Manor

ALLINGTON, CHIPPENHAM, SN14 6LW

Tel 01249 652105 **Fax** 01249 659296
Location 2 miles west of Chippenham.
Opening hours 2.30 pm – 6 pm; 20 June. And by appointment.
Admission fee Adults £3; Children 50p.

This charming house is surrounded by outbuildings and walls of old Cotswold stone, which form the background to a series of enclosed gardens. Each is very prettily designed and planted in the modern style – using plants for their contrasts and combinations of flower, shape, colour and form. The gardens seem to brim over with flowers and an abundance of beauty. If only it were open more often.

Features roses (mainly old-fashioned); pretty *potager*; good herbaceous borders; climbing roses.

Owned by Earl & Countess Cairns
Number of gardeners 1
Size 1.2ha (3 acres)

The Botanic Nursery

COTTLES LANE, ATWORTH, MELKSHAM, SN12 8NU

Tel 07850 328756 **Fax** 01225 700953
Website www.botanicnursery.com
Location Next to grounds of Stonar School, just outside Atworth on road to South Wraxall.
Opening hours 10 am – 5 pm; Fridays & Saturdays; March to November. And by appointment.
Admission fee Free.

The Botanic Nursery built its reputation on growing lime-tolerant plants, but has become better known as a plantsman's nursery, where a long browse will winkle out all sorts of rarities. It is best known at RHS Flower Shows for its spectacular displays of foxgloves (*Digitalis*) from its National Collection, though it also has very good collections of unusual shrubs, eryngiums and dieramas. The one-acre display garden (mainly trees and shrubs) is well worth a visit, too. There will be four

RHS special events at The Botanic Nursery during 2004: details from 020 7821 3408.

Features 2,000 different plants, many rare, all lime-tolerant.

Owned by Terence & Mary Baker
Number of gardeners 1
Size 0.8ha (2 acres)
NCCPG National Collections *Digitalis*

Bowood House & Gardens

CALNE, SN11 0LZ

Tel 01249 812102 **Fax** 01249 821757
Website www.bowood.org
Location Off A4 in Derry Hill village between Calne & Chippenham.
Opening hours 11 am – 6 pm; daily; 1 April to 2 November. Separate charge of £3.60 for rhododendron walks, open from mid April to early June (telephone for exact dates, which depend upon the flowering season).
Admission fee Adults £6.40; OAPs £5.30; Children (under 15) £4.10; Children (2-4 yrs) £3.25.

Beautifully maintained and welcoming, Bowood has something from every period of English garden history. Capability Brown made the lake and planted many of the trees and lawns which give such a beautiful setting to the house. Charles Hamilton added the famous cascade below the lake in the picturesque style. There is an important 19th-century pinetum and laid out on pre-Linnaean principles – geographically – with oceans of grass to separate the continents. It is not just a collection of magnificent conifers, but contains many rare and beautiful deciduous trees too, including the tallest specimen of the cut-leaved horse-chestnut (*Aesculus hippocastanum* 'Laciniata') in the British Isles. By the house are handsome Italianate formal gardens

designed by Smirke and Kennedy in the 19th century and recently replanted by Lady Mary Keen. Up in the woods in a separate part of the estate, and entered directly from the A342, is a magnificent display of modern rhododendrons around the beautiful Robert Adam mausoleum. The oceans of bluebells which surround these rhododendron drives is one of the finest in the south of England. Be sure to miss the reclining nude above the formal gardens.

**Features** lake; 100-acre Capability Brown landscaped parkland; famous old arboretum; topiary; mature conifers; modern borders; rhododendrons, azaleas & bluebells (separate garden); tallest *Thuya occidentalis* 'Wareana' in the UK; gift shop; coffee shop; buffet lunches & afternoon teas in licensed restaurant.

Owned by The Marquis of Lansdowne
Number of gardeners 4
Size 80ha (200 acres) of grounds
English Heritage Grade I

Broadleas

DEVIZES, SN10 5JQ

Tel 01380 722035
Location 1 mile south of Devizes.
Opening hours 2 pm – 6 pm; Wednesdays, Thursdays & Sundays; April to October.
Admission fee Adults £4; Children £1. Groups (10+) £3.50.

Lady Anne Cowdray started to make this garden – now owned by a charitable trust – in 1947. Since then it has grown into a very fine plantsman's garden, with lots of different kinds of plant but an especially good collection of ornamental trees and shrubs. Broadleas has a rose garden, a grey border, a rock garden and a 'secret' garden, all near the Regency house. But the main attraction is the Dell, a greensand combe that stretches down to the valley below, its sides just stuffed with good things. At the top are two tall magnolias, thought to be *M. sargentiana* var. *robusta* and the very rare cultivar known as 'Multipetal'. Pass between them, and past a very tall paulownia, and you come into a world of rare trees, vast magnolias, sheets of *Primula whitei* and cyclamen. And Broadleas has two characteristics common to all good plantsman's gardens: it is worth visiting at any time of the year and it gets better all the time. The nursery sells surplus plants propagated from the garden.

Features a plantsman's collection of plants; woodland garden; roses (ancient & modern); good herbaceous borders; fine ornamental trees; excellent small nursery for rare plants; teas on summer Sundays.

Owned by Broadleas Gardens Charitable Trust
Number of gardeners 2½
Size 3.6ha (9 acres)
English Heritage Grade II

Conock Manor

DEVIZES, SN10 3QQ

Tel 01380 840227
Location 5 miles south-east of Devizes off A342.
Opening hours For NGS, and by appointment.
Admission fee Adults £2.50; Children free.

Beautiful parkland surrounds this covetable Georgian house. Behind the copper-domed stables, an elegant shrub walk meanders past *Sorbus*, maples and magnolias. Some of the trees which have been planted in recent years are already making a good show. A recent addition is a Persian garden – brickwork in stylised script with water runnels and small fountains.

Features *Cottages orneés*; fine trees and mixed borders; good *Sorbus* and *Eucalyptus*; woodland walk; cream teas.

Owned by Mrs Bonar Sykes
Number of gardeners 1 part-time
Size 0.8ha (2 acres), plus parkland
English Heritage Grade II

Corsham Court

CORSHAM, SN13 0BZ

Tel & Fax 01249 701610
Website www.corsham-court.co.uk
Location Signed from A4 Bath to Chippenham.
Opening hours 2 pm – 5.30 pm; Tuesday – Thursday, plus Saturdays, Sundays & Bank Holiday Mondays; 20 March to 30 September. Plus 2 pm – 4.30 pm; Saturdays & Sundays; 1 January to 19 March & October to December.
Admission fee Adults £2; OAPs £1.50; Children £1. RHS members & wheelchair-users free.

Corsham is a major 18th-century landscape garden, one of the few where both Capability Brown and Humphry Repton worked. Then the flower garden was developed in the middle of the 19th century: box-edged borders and a pretty fountain, all kept up with some good modern planting. An 18-acre (7ha) arboretum was planted in the 1980s: there are plans to landscape it and enlarge its collections.

Features fine trees; designed by Capability Brown and Humphry Repton; young arboretum; magnolias; amazing oriental plane *Platanus orientalis* whose sweeping limbs have rooted over a huge area

Owned by James Methuen-Campbell
Number of gardeners 4
English Heritage Grade II*

The Courts Garden

HOLT, TROWBRIDGE, BA14 6RR

Tel & Fax 01225 782340
Website www.nationaltrust.org.uk
Location In the middle of Holt village, 2½ miles east of Bradford-on-Avon.
Opening hours 11 am – 5.30 pm; Thursday – Tuesday; 27 March to 17 October.
Admission fee Adults £4.50; Children £2.25.

Holt Court (as it used to be called) is a 1920s masterpiece in the Hidcote style. It has rich colour plantings in a series of garden rooms and excellent plants, beautifully used. It is also well maintained by the Head Gardener, who came from Sissinghurst.

Features plantsman's collection of plants; good herbaceous borders; fine collection of trees.

Owned by The National Trust
Number of gardeners 2
Size 10ha (25 acres)
English Heritage Grade II

Heale House Garden

MIDDLE WOODFORD, SALISBURY, SP4 6NT

Tel 01722 782504
Location Signed off the western Woodford valley road, & from A345 & A360.
Opening hours 10 am – 5 pm; daily; all year. Closed on Mondays, except Bank Holidays.
Admission fee Adults £3.75; Children £1.50.

Many would agree that Heale is the prettiest garden in southern England. It sits at the bottom of a broad, chalk valley, with the River Avon and its leats flowing through.

The house is Carolean, with substantial additions so sympathetically designed by Detmar Blow that it is difficult to know which parts belong to the original house. Harold Peto laid out the garden: you see his handiwork in the formal gardens which run up towards the south along an avenue of *Robinia pseudoacacia* 'Umbraculifera' (recent replacements for the original laburnums). There are formal pools, terraces, balustrades and Italianate garden architecture on the way. Alongside the river are more balustrading, old rambling roses and a lawn which is richly planted with hybrid musk roses and herbaceous plants. On an island in the river is a Japanese garden, laid out in 1901 and much altered by the sheer growth of the original Japanese maples: however, the scarlet lacquered bridge and the neat tea-house seem almost new. Perhaps the best part of the garden is the old kitchen garden, surrounded by cob walls and designed around topiary and pergolas. Here, over 30 years from the mid-1960s onwards, Lady Anne Rasch developed a wonderful series of mixed borders, exuberantly planted with roses, clematis and herbaceous plants which is one of the best examples of the genre in England. But the garden and its excellent nursery are open all through the year, and there is always something to see, including swarms of cyclamen in autumn, and woodlands full of snowdrops and aconites in winter.

Features roses (mainly old-fashioned); good herbaceous borders; Japanese gardens; good plant associations; first Christie's/HHA Garden of the Year in 1984; plant centre; garden & gift shop; tea & coffee shop.

Owned by Mr & Mrs Guy Rasch
Number of gardeners 2, plus owners
Size 3.2ha (8 acres)
English Heritage Grade II*

Home Covert Garden & Arboretum

ROUNDWAY, DEVIZES, SN10 2JA

Tel 01380 723407
Location 1 mile north of Devizes in Roundway Village.
Opening hours 11 am – 5.30 pm; 16 May & 11 July. Groups welcome at any time by appointment, **Admission fee** Adults £3; Children free.

Home Covert is one of the most influential and largest plantsman's gardens in England. The knowledge and taste of the owners – together with their generosity towards visitors – have made it a cult garden among *cognoscenti* and learner-gardeners alike. The Phillips describe it as 'a botanical madhouse': it would be truer to call it a horticultural treasure-house. Every type of plant is grown but, above all, rare trees: *Cercis racemosa*, for example, and hundreds of plants – perhaps thousands – grown from seeds collected by such friends as Roy Lancaster, Martyn Rix and Maurice Foster. An older generation of plantsman is also commemorated here – Maurice Mason, Norman Haddon and Margery Fish, for example. Home Covert is a large garden, informally laid out within natural oak woodland, and it needs a long time to see round. Down in the bog garden are collections of willows and alders, naturalised *Lathraea clandestina* and swathes of candelabra primulas. Near the house is an enormous lawn, completely free of weeds, with a view for miles down the Avon valley. Raised beds, a rock garden, shade borders, protected beds for tender plants, swarms of erythroniums, fat clumps of lilies, old-fashioned roses and wild species – there seems no end to the number and variety of what is grown here.

Features woodland garden; plantsman's plants of every kind; teas.

Owned by Mr & Mrs John Phillips
Number of gardeners owners only, plus one day a week of help
Size 13ha (33 acres)

Iford Manor

BRADFORD-ON-AVON, BA15 2BA

Tel 01225 863146 **Fax** 01225 852364
Website www.ifordmanor.co.uk
Location 7 miles south-east of Bath, signed from A36 & Bradford-on-Avon.
Opening hours 2 pm – 5 pm; Sundays & Easter Monday; April & October. Plus Tuesday – Thursday, Saturdays, Sundays & Bank Holiday Mondays from May to September.
Admission fee Adults £4; OAPs & Children (over 10) £3.50. Children under 10 free on weekdays but not admitted at weekends.

Harold Peto's own Italianate garden on a steep wooded hillside is meticulously maintained and a delight to visit. Peto was a fashionable architect with a passion for classical Italian architecture and landscaping. When he returned from working in France and Italy, he bought Iford to house his collections of statues and architectural marbles. He planted phillyreas, Italian cypresses and other Mediterranean species and laid out the garden as a series of formal terraces on the steep hillside behind the house. The architectural highlights include a Romanesque cloister, an octagonal gazebo, and a gloriously colonnaded terrace. Every detail is wonderfully photogenic, especially when contrasted with wisterias, roses or well-chosen acanthus. The woodland garden is worth exploring (it hides a recently restored Japanese garden) and there is much of horticultural interest too at Iford, notably a meadow of naturalised martagon lilies.

Features Harold Peto's own garden; opulent Edwardian design; Italian cypresses and handsome *Phillyrea*; martagon lilies; cyclamen; roses; teas on Bank Holidays and weekends from May to August.

Owned by Mrs E. Cartwright-Hignett
Number of gardeners 3
Size 0.6ha (1½ acres) plus 5ha (12 acres) of woodland
English Heritage Grade I

Lacock Abbey

LACOCK, CHIPPENHAM, SN15 2LG

Tel 01249 730141 **Fax** 01249 730501
Website www.nationaltrust.org.uk
Location 3 miles south of Chippenham, east of A350.
Opening hours 11 am – 5.30 pm; daily; 1 March to 31 October. Closed on Good Friday.
Admission fee Adults £4.40; Children £2.20.

The National Trust has recently recreated the 'botanic garden' planted by Lacock's most famous past owner, William Fox Talbot, the 'inventor' of photography. It was he who planted many of the mature trees in the park, including the London plane (*Platanus* x *hispanica*), swamp cypress (*Taxodium distichum*) and walnut (*Juglans nigra*).

 Features snowdrops; crocus; parkland.

Owned by The National Trust
Number of gardeners 1
Size 4.4ha (11 acres)

Landford Trees

LANDFORD LODGE, LANDFORD, SALISBURY, SP5 2EH

Tel 01794 390808 **Fax** 01794 390037
Website www.landfordtrees.co.uk
Location By junction of A36 & B3079.

Opening hours By appointment for groups at weekends. Visitors to nursery at all times.
Admission fee Free.

This is an excellent tree nursery, with over 600 lines to sell. These include 40 different acers, 20 birches, 15 crataegus, 10 beech, 50 *Malus*, 40 *Prunus*, 50 *Sorbus* and 30 different pines. There will be an RHS special event at Landford Trees on 20 May 2004: details from 020 7821 3408.

 Features well-known tree nursery.

Owned by Christopher Pilkington
Size 12ha (30 acres)

Larmer Tree Gardens

TOLLARD ROYAL, SALISBURY, SP5 5PT

Tel 01725 516228 **Fax** 01725 516449
Website www.larmertreegardens.co.uk
Location Follow brown signs from A354 or B3081.
Opening hours 11 am – 5 pm; Sunday – Thursday; all year. Closed 7 to 21 July, plus December. Closed in Sundays in February, March & November.
Admission fee Adults £3.75; OAPs £3; Children £2.50.

The Larmer Tree Gardens were laid out by General Augustus Pitt-Rivers as a public amenity. He put up a series of eccentric garden buildings around a spacious lawn of perhaps two acres: they include the Singing Theatre, the Indian Room, the Roman Temple and the Lower Indian Building in the Nepalese style, brought here in 1880 after the Colonial Exhibition in London. In the 1880s and 1890s, trainloads of East Enders were brought there by the philanthropic owner for a jolly cultural day in the country. His descendants have entirely restored the gardens since about 1990 and added some modern horticultural features. The best of these is a series of artificial pools in an artificial dell, surrounded by multi-coloured hydrangeas. All is set in light oak woodland with splendid thickets of cherry laurel. It is not a garden of the highest horticultural interest, though there are some venerable eucryphias, crinodendrons and stewartias. It is however spaciously laid out and very enjoyable to visit.

Features hydrangeas; woodland gardens; remarkable series of follies; tea room on Sundays in season.

Owned by W. Gronow-Davies & Trustees
Number of gardeners 2
Size 4.4ha (11 acres)
English Heritage Grade II

Longleat House

WARMINSTER, BA12 7NW

Tel 01985 844400 **Fax** 01985 844885
Website www.longleat.co.uk
Location Off A362 Warminster to Frome road.
Opening hours 10 am – 4.30 pm; daily. Telephone for confirmation. Closed 25 December.
Admission fee Grounds & gardens: Adults £3; OAPs & Children £2.

Longleat has a classic 18th-century landscape by Capability Brown, a home park of 900 acres best seen from Heaven's Gate and a grand Victorian garden reworked by Russell Page in the 1930s. Capability Brown's landscape has been carefully managed and replanted over many years, so that it keeps its intended form. The Victorian garden between the house and the elegant conservatory built by Wyatville in the 1820s is now a very beautiful rose garden. The plantings of ornamental trees and rhododendrons woodlands have been thickened and updated with many new introductions. In short, Lord Bath (like his

father before him) has conserved the best of Longleat and reinvigorated the rest. Worth another visit.

Features woodland garden; topiary; rhododendrons & azaleas; fine collection of trees; orangery; rose garden planted as a 'love labyrinth'; sun maze & lunar labyrinth; shops; cafeterias & restaurants.

Owned by 7th Marquess of Bath
Number of gardeners 8
English Heritage Grade I

The Mead Nursery

BROKERSWOOD, WESTBURY, BA13 4EG

Tel 01373 859990
Location Off A36 or A361, between Rudge & Brokerswood Country Park.
Opening hours 9 am – 5 pm, Wednesday – Saturday, & Bank Holiday Mondays; 12 noon – 5 pm, Sundays, 1 February to 10 October. 12 noon – 5 pm on 15 August for NGS.
Admission fee Adults £2.50 & Children £2 (tea & cake included) on 15 August. Otherwise free.

The Mead Nursery specialises in alpine plants (including varieties suitable for trough plantings), pot-grown bulbs and herbaceous perennials. All plants are grown in peat-free compost. The display garden is excellent: raised alpine beds, a sink garden, a bog bed, a small wildlife pond, a new Mediterranean raised bed, and herbaceous borders planted with colour combinations in mind.

Features perennials; alpines; bulbs; all plants grown on site; pretty demonstration garden.

Owned by Stephen & Emma Lewis-Dale
Size 0.3ha (¾ acre)

Old Vicarage

EDINGTON, WESTBURY, BA13 4QF

Tel & Fax 01380 830512
Location On B3098 in Edington village.
Opening hours 2 pm – 6 pm; 13 June.
Admission fee Adults £2.50; Children free.

John d'Arcy bought the Old Vicarage in 1982: it is now one of the best examples of a plantsman's garden in southern England. The site offers a surprising range of mini-habitats, and d'Arcy took advantage of their potential to grow the widest possible number of plants. The features now include a sunken garden, a shady pergola, an avenue of fastigiate hornbeams *Carpinus betulus* 'Fastigiata', a gravel garden where *Morina afghanica* and *Ptilostemon afer* seed around, hot walls, raised beds, peat beds and shady beds – all blended with the rest of the garden so that no feature dominates any part of it. d'Arcy's great skill is as a cultivator: the fact that there is so much colour and interest at every time of the year proves that good plantsmanship can produce effects to challenge the most carefully designed and planted of gardens. Trees are underplanted with shrubs, which are underscored in turn by herbaceous plants and bulbs, several different plants being placed together to give a succession of interest throughout the year. d'Arcy's special interests include mahonias, cyclamen, nerines and hollies. He is also well known as a plant collector. *Corydalis flexuosa* came from Sichuan in 1989; several new species of *Dierama* came from South Africa, together with such new species of *Geranium* as *G. harveyi* and *G. pulchrum*. All are still here, together with the living holotype of *Salvia darcyi*.

Features plantsman's plants – a collector's collection; herbaceous borders; alpine plants; shade plants; gravel garden; small arboretum.

Owned by John d'Arcy
Number of gardeners 1
Size 1ha (2½ acres)
NCCPG National Collections Oenothera

Pound Hill House

WEST KINGTON, CHIPPENHAM, SN14 7JG

Tel 01249 783880 **Fax** 01249 782953
Website www.poundhillplants.co.uk
Location Follow signs from A420 between 'The Shoe' & Marshfield (Nettleton & West Kington turning).
Opening hours 2 pm – 5 pm; daily; April to October. On 20 June for NGS and on 4 & 25 September for local charities.
Admission fee Adults £3.50; Children free. RHS members free from July to October.

The garden has been laid out and planted since 1988 by Barbara and Philip Stockitt, with advice from their daughter, garden-designer Bunny Guinness, a Chelsea gold medal-winner. They supplemented the Cotswold dry-stone walls with hedges of yew and box to make a series of neat rooms, in scale with the substantial Cotswold farmhouse. Barbara is a nurserywoman, the owner of the highly successful Barbara Austin Perennials Ltd. at West Kington Nurseries and, incidentally, a sister of David Austin the rose-breeder. You approach the garden through an excellent small retail nursery which is beautifully laid out with a most inviting selection of plants, especially topiary and architectural plants, and well-integrated into the overall design. Inside the garden proper you encounter first a neat, formal kitchen garden, full of interesting vegetables, and a small old rose garden where the polyanthas 'The Fairy' and 'Little White Pet' are grown as standards. The main part of the garden lies behind the house, most enjoyably laid out with structure given by box edging, yew cones and architectural plants at key points in the design. The plantings offer a stylish selection of plants, including many of the best modern cultivars, thickly planted and very well grown. Two particularly good features are a short avenue of Spanish chestnuts clipped to keep the trees small and the leaves large, and another of *Betula jacquemontii* entirely underplanted on both sides by white pulmonarias, black tulips and alliums – very striking in spring. But this excellent two-acre showcase-garden is interesting throughout the year.

Features roses (ancient & modern); fruit; alpine plants; walled area for topiary & specimen plants; adjacent to West Kington Nurseries Plant Centre; lunches; refreshments.

Owned by Mr & Mrs Philip Stockitt
Number of gardeners 1
Size 0.8ha (2 acres)

Sharcott Manor

PEWSEY, SN9 5PA

Tel 01672 563485
Location Off A345, one mile south-west of Pewsey.
Opening hours 11 am – 5 pm; first Wednesday of every month; April to October. Plus two Sundays for NGS. And by appointment.
Admission fee Adults £3; Children free.

This extensive modern garden has been quite transformed over the last 25 years into a densely planted plantsman's paradise. There is much to see as you move gently between the garden rooms near the house and out into the spacious lawns and woodland garden. There are harmonies and contrasts to please the most colour-conscious, while the dark shady lake at the bottom is a haven of romantic broodiness. New (in 2003) is an

avenue of *Pyrus calleryana* 'Chanticleer'. Sharcott is an excellent garden which deserves to be better known.

Features plantsman's collection of plants; good herbaceous borders; woodland and stream gardens; good plant sales area, all propagated from garden; home-made teas.

Owned by Captain & Mrs David Armytage
Number of gardeners 2 part-time
Size 2.4ha (6 acres)

Stourhead

STOURTON, BA12 6QD

Tel 01747 841152 **Fax** 01747 842005
Website www.nationaltrust.org.uk
Location 3 miles north-west of Mere, signed off the A303/B3092.
Opening hours 9 am – 7 pm, or dusk if earlier; daily; all year.
Admission fee Adults £5.40; Children £3. Reductions in winter.

Whatever the weather or season, Stourhead conveys a sense of majesty and harmony. Try it early on a May morning, when the air is sweet with azaleas. Or scuff the fallen leaves in late November. Think of it 200 years ago, without the rhododendrons or exotic trees, when all the beech trees were interplanted with spruces and the colours came all from shades of green. Ponder the 18th-century aesthetic, which esteemed tones and shades more highly than colours, and follow the iconographic tour inspired (they say) by Virgil. Spot the change from classical to gothic, from Pope to Walpole, and wonder at the National Trust's ability to maintain it so well with only six gardeners.

Features snowdrops; rhododendrons & azaleas; mature conifers; fine collection of trees; good autumn colour;

tallest tulip tree *Liriodendron tulipifera* (37m.) in the British Isles, and seven other record tree species; shop & plant centre; restaurant.

Owned by The National Trust
Number of gardeners 6
Size 40ha (100 acres)
English Heritage Grade I

Stourton House Flower Garden

STOURTON, WARMINSTER, BA12 6QF

Tel 01747 840417
Location Next to Stourhead, 2 miles north of A303 at Mere.
Opening hours 11 am – 6 pm; Wednesdays, Thursdays, Sundays & Bank Holiday Mondays; April to November. Groups at other times by appointment.
Admission fee Adults £3; Children 50p.

This five-acre garden next to Stourhead is famous for its dried flowers, thanks to the energy and personality of Elizabeth Bullivant. It also has a strong, natural design and some beautiful plant combinations. The baroque curves to the Leylandii hedges are completely original. Stourton is also a garden with a tremendous number of different and unusual plants (of all sorts) and some particular favourites – hence the enormous collection of hydrangeas, the split-corona daffodils, the *Magnolia campbellii*, the Kiwi fruit and the plantings of rhododendrons, azaleas and camellias. Mrs Bullivant has also been successful in plant competitions at RHS shows, bringing up a great variety of plants to show to a wider audience. But Stourton is not a garden for show – rather, it is a romantic, well-loved private garden with a sideline in dried flowers. It is very good at all seasons –

and especially in early autumn when it is frankly stunning.

Features good herbaceous borders; Victorian greenhouse; elegantly curving hedges of Leylandii; 270 different hydrangeas; delphiniums; hosts of daffodils, in innumerable shapes, sizes and colours; plants & dried flowers for sale all year; home-made teas; light lunches; creamy cakes.

Owned by Mrs Anthony Bullivant
Number of gardeners 1½
Size 2ha (5 acres)

Westdale Nurseries

HOLT ROAD, BRADFORD ON AVON, BA15 1TS

Tel & Fax 01225 863258
Location 1 mile east of Bradford town centre; left-hand side.
Opening hours 9 am – 6 pm (10 am – 5 pm from October to March, and 10 am – 4 pm on Sundays); daily; all year except Christmas.

Westdale has made quite an impact at RHS Flower Shows in recent years with its wonderful displays of bougainvilleas. It lists over 200 different cultivars, which are available in different sizes. All can be seen growing in their extensive glasshouses outside Bradford on Avon. But their range of other conservatory plants is very wide, and they are enthusiastic plantsmen, willing to try any plant which may have value as an ornament to the conservatory or greenhouse. Well worth a visit.

Features bougainvilleas; conservatory plants.

Owned by C.W. & P.A. Clarke
Number of gardeners 3
Size 0.4ha (1 acre) of glass

Wilton House

WILTON, SALISBURY, SP2 0BJ

Tel 01722 746720 **Fax** 01722 744447
Website www.wiltonhouse.com
Location In village, 3 miles west of Salisbury by A36.
Opening hours 10.30 am – 5.30 pm; daily; 2 April
– 31 October.
Admission fee Adults £4.50; Children £3.50.

Wilton has a sublime 18th-century park around its classical Inigo Jones house, which is famous for its paintings. It is this stupendous parkland setting above the river Nadder which is the chief delight of visiting the gardens at Wilton. There are comparatively few horticultural excitements, though the house has pleasant mixed borders along one of its sides and a stylish modern garden, rather formal, in the entrance court designed by Lady Tollemache. On the edge of the park are a pretty new garden of old-fashioned roses and an oriental water garden: opinions are divided as to the merits of the new millennium water feature.

Features roses; handsome cedars; famous Palladian bridge; magnificent golden-leaved oak; self-service restaurant.

Owned by Earl of Pembroke/Wilton House Trust
Number of gardeners 4
Size 8.3ha (21 acres)
English Heritage Grade I

Wiltshire College Lackham

LACOCK, CHIPPENHAM, SN15 2NY

Tel 01249 466800 **Fax** 01249 444474
Website www.wiltscoll.ac.uk
Location 3 miles south of Chippenham on A350.
Opening hours 10 am – 5 pm; Sundays & Bank Holiday Mondays; Easter Sunday to 31 August. Plus Tuesday-Thursday in August.
Admission fee Adults £2; Concessions £1.50; Children free.

Lackham is among the best of the old county college gardens and now better known, following its appearance on TV gardening programme like 'Roots & Shoots' and 'Gardeners To Be'. A major extension was opened in 1996 – an Italian-style garden, an historic rose garden, a sensory garden, herbaceous borders and illustrations of English gardens over each of the last four centuries. The heart of Lackham is its walled garden of flowers, ornamentals, herbs, fruit and vegetables, beautifully laid out to educate and delight. In one of the glasshouses is the champion plant of *Citrus medica* which grew the largest citron (over 10lbs) ever seen in Britain (according to the Guinness Book of Records). The grounds are good for an exploration too, especially in bluebell time: there has been a lot of attractive companion planting for the National Collection of poplars.

Features plantsman's collection of plants; herbs; fruit & vegetables; plants under glass; daffodils; good herbaceous borders; fine collection of trees; alpine plants; bluebells; roses of every kind; sensory garden; laurel maze; woodland walk; souvenirs for sale; refreshments.

Owned by Wiltshire College Lackham
Number of gardeners 4, plus students
Size 8ha (20 acres)
NCCPG National Collections *Populus*

WORCESTERSHIRE

Worcestershire has been reconstituted not as a county (which it was until 1974) but as a District Council. But such is the feeling of distinct identity that we have treated it in this book as a legal county again: the same applies to Herefordshire, to which it was yoked for 25 years. Worcestershire a lot going for it: a flourishing National Gardens Scheme, the site of the only dedicated horticultural college in England at Pershore (a RHS Partner College), the headquarters of the Alpine Garden Society, ten National Collection holders, and two of the most popular gardening shows in the country – the Spring Gardening Show (7-9 May 2004) and the Autumn Garden & Country Show (25-26 September 2004), both at the Three Counties Showground at Malvern. Worcestershire also has some excellent specialist nurseries, including Cotswold Garden Flowers, Old Court Nurseries and Stone House Cottage Garden. Though few of its historic parks and gardens are open to the public, they include that great plantsman's garden Spetchley Park (substantially re-made by a great-nephew of Miss Ellen Willmott) and Witley Court (now undergoing extensive renovation by English Heritage).

Arley Arboretum

ARLEY, BEWDLEY, DY12 1XG

Tel 01299 861368
Website www.arley-arboretum.org.uk
Location Brown signs from A442.
Opening hours 10 am – 5 pm; Wednesday – Friday, Sundays and Bank Holiday Mondays; April to October.
Admission fee Adults £3; Children £1.

This beautiful arboretum first opened to the public in 2002. It was first planted in the 1820s (very early for arboreta) and has been continuously expanded and replanted since. There are very fine Crimean pines *Pinus nigra* var. *caramanica*, one of which is the tallest in the United Kingdom. In all there are over 300 different taxa. Within the arboretum is a walled garden with a formal Italian garden and fine herbaceous borders, quite a contrast to the awesome trees outside.

Features tea & biscuits.

Owned by R.D. Turner Charitable Trust
Number of gardeners 3
Size 14ha (35 acres)

Bodenham Arboretum

WOLVERLEY, KIDDERMINSTER, DY11 5SY

Tel 01562 852444 **Fax** 01562 852777
Website www.bodenham-arboretum.co.uk
Location B4189 or B4190 to Wolverley village and follow the brown signs.

Opening hours 11 am – 5 pm or dusk; daily; all year. Restaurant closed at weekends in January & February.
Admission fee Adults £4; Children £1.50. RHS members free in May, June & October.

Bodenham Arboretum has more than 2,700 different trees and shrubs in a total of 156 acres, containing eleven pools and four miles of footpaths. In May and early June, the rhododendrons, azaleas and laburnum tunnel are spectacular but, like all arboreta, there is much to enjoy in all seasons. Two RHS special events will take place during 2004: details from 020 7821 3408.

 Features light refreshments & lunches.

Size 62ha (156 acres)

Cotswold Garden Flowers

SANDS LANE, BADSEY, EVESHAM, WR11 5EZ

Tel 01386 422829 **Fax** 01386 49844
Website www.cgf.net
Location On south-east edge of village.
Opening hours 9 am – 5.30 pm; Monday – Friday. 10 am – 5.30 pm; Saturday – Sunday. Other times by appointment. Closed at weekends from mid-October to March.
Admission fee Free.

Don't be put off by the bumpy driveway – the nursery is right at the end of Sands Lane – Cotswold Garden Flowers is a treasure-house of rare plants: over 8,000 different cultivars are grown in the display garden. Actually the garden is no more than the nursery's stock beds, but quite spectacular, because the owner has a knack for seeking out and introducing plants which are highly 'garden-worthy'. The catalogue is both amusing and informative, but it is nothing compared to the joy of visiting the nursery and having the opportunity to see so many well-grown, new and interesting plants.

Owned by Bob Brown
NCCPG National Collections *Lysimachia*

Eastgrove Cottage Garden

SANKYNS GREEN, SHRAWLEY, LITTLE WITLEY, WORCESTER, WR6 6LQ

Tel 01299 896389
Website www.eastgrove.co.uk
Location On road between Great Witley (on A443) & Shrawley (on B4196).
Opening hours 2 pm – 5 pm; Thursday – Sunday, plus Bank Holiday Mondays; 8 April to 31 July and 2 September to 16 October.
Admission fee Adults £3. RHS members free.

Eastgrove is a very pretty, 17th-century, half-timbered, black-and-white cottage in a beautiful country setting. It has an equally pretty cottage garden that has been entirely made by the Skinners since they bought the near-derelict property in 1970. The scale is small, but the quality and variety of the plantings are stunning. There is a developing collection of trees, a raised bed (known as the 'Great Wall of China') and, above all, thickly planted herbaceous plants. The design and planting of the borders is carefully thought through, with curving borders and several enclosed rooms. The 'secret garden' concentrates on mauves, pinks, silvers and crimsons. Although perhaps best in high summer, the garden is good enough to visit at any time of the year and beautifully maintained. The nursery propagates only plants from the garden and has a list of over 1,000 different varieties.

Specialities include aquilegias, hardy chrysanthemums, dianthus, heleniums, irises, peonies, rosemary, salvias and violas.

**Features** cottage garden; rose arches; plantsman's plants; herbaceous borders; wall plantings; pots & containers; attached to good small nursery.

Owned by Malcolm & Carol Skinner
Number of gardeners owners only
Size 0.6ha (1½ acres)

The Manor House

BIRLINGHAM, PERSHORE, WR10 3AF

Tel 01386 750005 **Fax** 01386 751288
Location At south-east end of Birlingham.
Opening hours 11 am – 5 pm; 12 June (for NGS) and 13 June (Plant Fair).
Admission fee Adults £2.50; Children free. £3.50 on 13 June.

(P) (WC) (&) (⚲) (☕)

The garden was first set out in the late 1780s: relics of these original plantings include giant box hedges and a very fine *Phillyrea*, as well as the ha-ha which allows the eye an unhindered sweep to the River Avon and the magnificent views of Bredon Hill. Jane Williams-Thomas has replanted the garden with a designer's eye, making terraces and using hedges to create enclosed intimate areas. One important element of the design has been the use of many benches to encourage repose and create a peaceful atmosphere. Roses are a particular love – the garden has over 100 different cultivars – and they are interplanted with silver plants and perennials that will respond to the dry, warm site. The white garden is particularly successful: it has brick paths surrounded by yew hedges and the lush, romantic planting which characterises the whole garden. Rare plants are used in unusual combinations to bring out contrasts and harmonies of form

and colour. The garden is a member of the Quiet Garden Trust. The owners are hoping to move later this year, so this may be the last chance to see a remarkable garden.

Features plantsman's collection of plants; good herbaceous borders; walled garden; white garden; teas.

Owned by Mr & Mrs David Williams-Thomas
Number of gardeners owners, plus part-time help
Size 0.7ha (1¾ acres)

Overbury Court

TEWKESBURY, G20 7NP

Tel 01386 725111 **Fax** 01386 725678
Location 5 miles north-east of Tewkesbury.
Opening hours By appointment.
Admission fee Adults £2.50. Minimum charge for groups £15.

(P) (🐕) (&)

A peaceful and expansive garden laid out around the large, handsome, Georgian house, with a view of the Parish church worked in. Geoffrey Jellicoe, Aubrey Waterfield and Russell Page all worked on the design and planting: the result is a garden of exceptional harmony.

Features topiary; landscaped park; daffodils.

Owned by Mr & Mrs Bruce Bossom
Number of gardeners 2

Pershore College

PERSHORE, WR10 3JP

Tel 01386 554609 **Fax** 01386 556528
Website www.pershore.ac.uk
Location Signed in village.
Opening hours 10 am – 4.30 pm; daily; all year.
Admission fee Free.

Pershore College specialises in horticultural education. Within its grounds are a 15-ha fruit and vegetable production unit, an 8-ha nursery stock and specialist plant unit, and a garden centre. The garden centre sells a selection of College-grown trees and shrubs including plants from the National Collection of penstemons, alpines, herbaceous plants, climbers, roses, houseplants and fruit trees and bushes in season. It is open daily from 9 am – 5 pm (10.30 pm – 4.30 pm on Sundays – 4 pm in winter). The College also has show gardens designed and maintained by the Hardy Plant Society and the Alpine Garden Society. Both are full of interesting plants and ideas for design and cultivation. The RHS Centre at Pershore was established in 1989 to offer a variety of courses, lectures and workshops on all aspects of horticulture for both members and non-members in the Central Region. The list of RHS Events at Pershore for 2004 is extremely impressive – totalling more 60 demonstrations, lectures, garden walks, workshops and special events.

Size 54ha (135 acres)
NCCPG National Collections Penstemon; Philadelphus

Spetchley Park

WORCESTER, WR5 1RS

Tel 01905 345224 **Fax** 01453 511915
Website www.spetchleygardens.co.uk
Location 2 miles east of Worcester on A422.
Opening hours 11 am – 6 pm; Tuesday – Friday & Bank Holiday Mondays, (plus 2 pm – 6 pm on Sundays); April to September. Last admissions 4 pm.
Admission fee Adults £4; Children £2.

In a classic English landscaped park, three generations of Berkeleys have created one of the best plantsman's gardens in the Midlands. Ellen Willmott was the owner's great aunt and many of the most exciting trees and shrubs date from her time – a gnarled specimen of the laciniate walnut (*Juglans nigra* 'Laciniata'), for example. In the Fountain Gardens, *Tulipa sprengeri* has seeded and naturalised over a large area. Other spring flowers include peonies, columbines and masses of bulbs. In summer, there are hundreds of different roses – old-fashioned roses, tea roses, David Austin roses, floribunda roses – every type of rose is here. Martagon lilies have naturalised in large quantities. The conservatory is crammed with unusual plants. The planting continues: everywhere in the garden are new designs, new plants and new combinations. A whole new garden has been planted to commemorate the millennium, with tunnels of *Cercis canadensis* 'Forest Pansy' and *Robinia hispida* 'Macrophylla'. Because of its scale and variety, this garden offers something to everyone, but most especially to the plantsman.

Features many good plants of every kind for plantsmen; roses (ancient & modern); rhododendrons & azaleas; daffodils; good herbaceous borders; fine trees; a deer park; good new plantings in the kitchen garden; naturalised lilies; teas & refreshments.

Owned by R.J. Berkeley
Number of gardeners 4
Size 12ha (30 acres)
English Heritage Grade II*

Stone House Cottage Garden

STONE, KIDDERMINSTER, DY10 4BG

Tel 01562 69902 **Fax** 01562 69960
Website www.shcn.co.uk
Location In village, 2 miles from Kidderminster on A448.
Opening hours 10 am – 5.30 pm; Wednesday – Saturday; March to September. And by appointment between October & March.
Admission fee Adults £2.50; Children free. RHS members free.

This is the garden of a famous nursery, which it matches for the range of beautiful and unusual plants it offers. The owners are compulsive plantsmen and, as the garden is small, they have to move plants around or replace them altogether to make room for new arrivals. This means that the garden is constantly developing and improving – especially since much thought is given to the way each plant will associate with its neighbours. Around the walls is an eccentric collection of follies built as towers, which makes this garden quite unique.

Features plantsman's plants; herbs; good herbaceous borders; alpine plants; unusual climbing plants; roses (mainly old-fashioned & climbers); excellent nursery attached.

Owned by James & Louisa Arbuthnott
Number of gardeners 1
Size 0.3ha (¾ acre)

The Walled Garden

6 ROSE TERRACE, WORCESTER, WR5 1BU

Tel & Fax 01905 354629
Location Off Fort Royal Hill (which is off A44); ½ mile from Cathedral.
Opening hours 12 noon – 5 pm; 29 May, 12 & 26 June & 31 July.
Admission fee Adults £2; Children 50p.

This all-organic private garden has an integrated mixture of flowers, fruits and herbs. The owners have reclaimed the walled garden, dating from Victorian times, and planted a series of areas for studying and demonstrating organic gardening techniques and the uses of herbs.

Features herb gardens.

Owned by William & Julia Scott
Number of gardeners owners only
Size 0.3ha (¾ acre)

Webbs of Wychbold

WYCHBOLD, DROITWICH SPA, WR9 0DG

Tel 01527 860000 **Fax** 01527 861284
Website www.webbsofwychbold.co.uk
Location 1 mile from M5, Jct 5: follow brown tourist signs.
Opening hours 9 am – 6 pm; Monday – Friday (8 pm spring- Christmas). 9 am – 6 pm; Saturdays & Bank Holidays. 10.30 am – 4.30 pm; Sundays. Closed Easter Sunday, 25 & 26 December.

Webbs are a major garden centre, a regional heavyweight with several trade awards for excellence. They have an extremely large stock of plants of every kind, as well as a wide range of in-house retail opportunities of interest to gardeners and non-gardeners alike. They have a reputation as plant-introducers too: *Diascia fetcaniensis* 'Daydream' and *Dianthus* 'Tickled Pink' are two of their plant introductions. Their display gardens (over an acre of them) include a herb garden, a series of patio gardens and a sequence of other model lay-outs called the Riverside Gardens, where Noel Kingsbury has recently been working on the plantings.

Features model gardens; award-winning garden centre; gift shop; restaurant.

Size 20ha (50 acres)
NCCPG National Collections *Potentilla fruticosa* cvs.

Witley Court

GREAT WITLEY, WR6 7JT

Tel 01299 896636
Website www.english-heritage.org.uk
Location 10 miles north of Worcester on A443.
Opening hours Not available as we went to press. 2003 times were: 10 am – 6 pm (5 pm in October); daily; April to October. 9 am – 4 pm; Wednesday – Sunday; November to March.
Admission fee Adults £4; Concessions £3; Children £2. (2003 times).

The gardens at Witley Court are undergoing extensive restoration and are increasingly in good condition, thanks to English Heritage. You enter through the rhododendron woods, planted mainly with hardy hybrids under a canopy of American conifers. At the bottom of the valley, below the cascade which runs from the lake, is an Elizabeth Frink statue – one of eight sculptures in the woods. More interesting, though, is the spectacular ruined mansion and the immense formal gardens behind. They are one of William Andrews Nesfield's masterpieces, built on a monumental scale by the first Earl of Dudley: English Heritage has begun to restore them and to add some new contemporary gardens too. The sheer size of the roofless conservatory and the fountains is remarkable: a place to fantasise about life among the plutocrats 100 years ago.

Features Victorian formal garden; rhododendron woodlands; sculpture; café.

Owned by English Heritage
Number of gardeners 2
Size 16ha (40 acres)
English Heritage Grade II*

YORKSHIRE, EAST RIDING OF

Since the demise of much-disliked Humberside, the East Riding has been reconstituted as an administrative area. Many of the Yorkshire's gardening institutions are organised on an all-Yorkshire basis: thus, for example, the Yorkshire Gardens Trust and the Yorkshire Group of the NCCPG are county-wide societies. Sledmere House is the outstanding historic garden in East Yorkshire, though Burton Constable is also well-known for its Capability Brown landscape garden. There are comparatively few good modern gardens in East Yorkshire, apart from the charming water-gardens at Burnby, where a National Collection of waterlilies (*Nymphaea*) is displayed in a beautifully landscaped site. There are four further National Collections in East Yorkshire, including a collection of *Crataegus laevigata* and *C. monogyna* cultivars at the University of Hull's garden at Cottingham – a botanic garden which has lost the botany department that was once the reason for its existence. There is a sprinkling of gardens that open for the National Gardens Scheme in East Yorkshire, which has its own county organiser. There are few nurseries of national repute: one which is not listed below is Swanland Nurseries, which has a good collection of *Pelargonium* cultivars – over 800 of them. Burnby Hall and Burton Agnes offer free entry to RHS members – both very enjoyable gardens to visit – and the garden at Bishop Burton College is a stunner.

Bishop Burton Botanic Garden

BISHOP BURTON COLLEGE, BEVERLEY, HU17 8QG

Tel 01964 553000 **Fax** 01964 553101
Location In Bishop Burton: entrance off village green.
Opening hours 9 am – 5 pm; Monday to Friday; all year.
Admission fee Free.

Bishop Burton is a college where horticulture is taught, so this is not so much a botanic garden as a demonstration garden to teach students about plants – and a very good one, too. There are areas for fruit, vegetables and herbs, fine herbaceous borders supplemented by annuals and bedding, hot colour borders, a heather collection, dwarf conifers, rose beds and show gardens, some of them designed by students. The glasshouses include a cactus house and tropical house. Outside, in the park, is a 19th-century landscape with good wellingtonias, cedars and a cucumber tree (*Magnolia acuminata*).

 Features a good collection of plants; fine trees in park; café open in term-time.

Owned by Bishop Burton College
Number of gardeners 4, plus students
Size 0.8ha (2 acres) walled garden, plus park

Burnby Hall Gardens

POCKLINGTON, YO42 2QF

Tel 01759 302068 **Fax** 01759 388272
Website www.burnbyhallgardens.co.uk
Location Off A1079 13 miles east of York.
Opening hours 10 am – 6 pm; daily; 29 March to 28 September.
Admission fee Adults £3; OAPs £2.50; Children £1.50. RHS members free.

Burnby Hall is famed for its waterlilies, planted by Amos Perry in the 1930 and now totalling over 100 different cultivars. They are grown in two long, landscaped lakes. But there is much more to Burnby: a large, walled Victorian garden, a rock garden, a woodland walk, heather beds, a 'secret garden', seasonal bedding and a good collection of conifers all contribute to its visitor-friendly air. Follow the tarmac path around the lakes: Burnby is a grand place for a promenade, especially when a brass band is playing on Sunday afternoons in summer.

 Features waterlilies; rock garden; mature conifers; plants for sale; café; gift shop.

Owned by Stewarts Trust
Number of gardeners 3
Size 3.2ha (8 acres)
NCCPG National Collections *Nymphaea*

Burton Agnes Hall Gardens

BURTON AGNES, DRIFFIELD, YO25 0ND

Tel 01262 490324 **Fax** 01262 490513
Location On A166 Driffield-Bridlington road.
Opening hours 11 am – 5 pm; daily; April to October.
Admission fee Adults £2.60; OAPs £2.35; Children £1.20. RHS members free. House extra.

The old walled garden has been re-designed in a neo-Elizabethan style (to complement the nearby house) and cut up into numerous, thickly planted gardens with narrow paths and changes of level. As well as a *potager* and herb garden it has such unconventional features as life-size games boards for chess, draughts and snakes-and-ladders, a jungle garden and a maze with a riddle. Rather more conventional are the colour-schemed gardens and sumptuous plantings of shrub roses, clematis and herbaceous plants. There are also some enjoyable horticultural surprises, including cordylines and *Echium pininana* growing outside, and lots of furcraeas put out in pots for the summer.

 Features good modern plantings; inventive design; café & ice-cream parlour.

Owned by Burton Agnes Hall Preservation Trust Ltd
Number of gardeners 3½
NCCPG National Collections *Campanula*

Burton Constable

SKIRLAUGH, HULL, HU11 4LN

Tel 01964 562400 **Fax** 01964 563229
Website www.burtonconstable.com
Location Via Hull, A165 Bridlington road, then
B1238 to Sproatley – follow brown tourist signs.
Opening hours 12.30 pm – 5 pm (last admission 4
pm); Saturday – Thursday; Easter Sunday to 31
October.
Admission fee Grounds only: Adults £1; Children
50p.

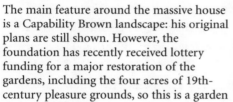

The main feature around the massive house
is a Capability Brown landscape: his original
plans are still shown. However, the
foundation has recently received lottery
funding for a major restoration of the
gardens, including the four acres of 19th-
century pleasure grounds, so this is a garden
to watch in future.

Features woodland garden; fine 18th-
century orangery; Victorian parterre;
shop; light snacks.

Owned by Burton Constable Foundation
Number of gardeners 3
English Heritage Grade II

Sledmere House

SLEDMERE, DRIFFIELD, YO25 3XG

Tel 01377 236637 **Fax** 01377 236500
Location Off A166 between York & Bridlington.
Opening hours 11 am – 4.30 pm; daily except
Mondays & Saturdays; Easter weekend, then from 2
May to 19 September.
Admission fee Adults £3; Children £1.

Sledmere has a classical Capability Brown
landscape: his originals plans can be seen in
the museum. An Italianate formal garden
was added in 1911, with Greek and Roman
busts swathed in climbing roses. In recent
years, Sledmere has enjoyed extensive
replanting in the 18th-century walled
garden: a new rose and clematis arcade;
young roses and fruit trees on the walls; a
dedicated rose garden; a Mediterranean
border. And it gets better every year as the
head gardener – who is a genius – restores,
improves, takes more borders in hand and
adds more plants. There are fine purple
beeches in the park.

Features roses; Capability Brown
landscape; craft & gift shop; tea-terrace
& cafeteria.

Owned by Sir Tatton Sykes
Number of gardeners 3
English Heritage Grade I

YORKSHIRE, NORTH

North Yorkshire corresponds with the old North Riding of Yorkshire: it is a county of large estates and small market towns. Among its historic gardens are some of the grandest landscapes in England: Castle Howard, Duncombe Park and Studley Royal are all Grade I gardens. North Yorkshire also has three very important modern gardens – Harlow Carr, Newby Hall and Thorpe Perrow – each quite different in character but all horticultural heavyweights. Harlow Carr, for years the flagship the Northern Horticultural Society, joined the RHS's growing fleet of top gardens in 2001 and has now embarked on substantial redevelopment and improvement at the RHS's hands. The National Gardens Scheme does well in North Yorkshire and so does the NCCPG, which has over 20 National Collections in the county. The best nurseries are also in North Yorkshire, including R.V. Roger Ltd, which has a good line in exotic 'architectural' plants, and the *Pulmonaria* and rare plant specialist Stillingfleet Lodge Nurseries: Stillingfleet also has a good garden which RHS members can visit free. There are many others which offer free access to RHS members for all or part of their open season: Duncombe Park, Harewood House, Millgate House, Newby Hall, Parceval Hall, Ripley Castle and Thorp Perrow. The Royal Horticultural Society has a Partner College at Askham Bryan, the old county horticultural college: it has several events during the year – details from the School Secretary on 01904 772220.

Beningbrough Hall & Gardens

BENINGBROUGH, YORK, YO30 1DD

Tel 01904 470666 **Fax** 01904 470002
Website www.nationaltrust.org.uk
Location 8 miles north-west of York off the A19.
Opening hours 11 am – 5.30 pm; Saturday – Wednesday, plus Good Friday & Fridays in July & August; 27 March to 31 October.
Admission fee Adults £5; Children £2.50.

Beningbrough is approached by an avenue of limes through stately parkland. Apart from a gloomy Victorian shrubbery, the gardens are modern and pretty. Two small formal gardens, one with reds and oranges and the other with pastel shades, lie on either side of the early Georgian house. A sumptuous mixed border, graded from hot colours to cool, runs right to the gate of the walled kitchen garden.

Features fruit; good herbaceous borders; American garden; good conservatory on house; traditional Victorian

Castle Howard

YORK, YO6 7DA

Tel 01653 648333 **Fax** 01653 648501
Location 15 miles north-east of York, off A64.
Opening hours 10 am – 4.30 pm (last entry); daily;
14 February to 31 October.
Admission fee Adults £6.50; Concessions £6;
Children £4.50.

Be prepared to spend all day at Castle Howard: it is essential visiting both for plantsmen and for anyone with a sense of history. At every time of the year, there are really good walks through woodlands and formal gardens, along the terraces and beside the water, and views of the buildings and sculptures in the landscape. The heroic megapark was first laid out by the 3rd Earl of Carlisle in 1700. Vanbrugh filled the five axes with landscapings and important buildings: the south lake, the terraces, the statues and the waterfalls down to the new river are all his. Vanbrugh's masterpiece, built in 1724-6, is the Temple of the Four Winds. The Mausoleum was designed by Hawksmoor in 1728. In front of the house are the remains of a vast 19th-century parterre, whose centre point is the Atlas fountain built by William Andrews Nesfield in the 1850s. Within a walled garden is a series of grand 1980s rose gardens (slightly Surrey) designed by Jim Russell, with every type of rose from ancient to modern. Of more interest to gardeners and plantsmen is Ray Wood, where a fine and historic collection of rhododendrons and other ericaceous plants (all meticulously labelled) is destined to develop as one of the greatest woodland gardens in Europe. The rhododendrons and other plants of 20th-century plant hunters are here in abundance – collections by Forrest, Rock, Kingdon Ward, Ludlow and Sheriff are all here, as are more recent collections from Nepal, Bhutan, Japan, and China. Since 1999 the wood has been managed jointly by Castle Howard and the Royal Botanic Gardens at Kew: there is a small additional charge to visit it.

Features important buildings; impressive landscape; sculptures; woodland garden; roses (ancient & modern); good herbaceous borders; tallest elm *Ulmus glabra* (37m.) in British Isles; shop and plant centre; cafeteria.

Owned by Castle Howard Estates Ltd
Size 400ha (1,000 acres)
English Heritage Grade I

kitchen garden undergoing restoration; 'Lady Downe's Seedling' grape, raised at Beningbrough in 1835; vast Portuguese laurel *Prunus lusitanica*; National Trust gift shop; morning coffee; hot & cold lunches; afternoon teas.

Owned by The National Trust
Number of gardeners 4½, plus volunteers
Size 2.8ha (7 acres)
English Heritage Grade II

Duncombe Park

HELMSLEY, YO62 5EB

Tel 01439 770213 **Fax** 01439 771114
Website www.duncombepark.com
Location Off A170; signed from Helmsley.
Opening hours 11 am – 5.30 pm or dusk if earlier; Sunday – Thursday; 11 April – 24 October.
Admission fee Adults £3.50; OAPs £3; Children £1.75. RHS members free.

Christopher Hussey wrote that 'the grass terraces of Duncombe are unique, and perhaps the most spectacularly beautiful among English landscape conceptions of the 18th century'. They were probably completed between 1713 and 1730 to the designs of either Charles Bridgeman or Stephen Switzer, or both. A long, broad, grass terrace curves along the edge of a steep escarpment from an Ionic rotunda to the north. Woodland clothes the hillside: you see nothing until you reach the Doric temple at the southern end and look down to the ruins of Rievaulx Abbey. Hidden in more woodland is a small, classical conservatory fronting the ruins of a Victorian rose-garden. Duncombe has little or nothing of horticultural interest, but it can scarcely be bettered for Palladian grandeur.

Features stately 18th-century landscape; gift shop; licensed tea-room.

Owned by Lord Feversham
Number of gardeners 1
Size 14ha (35 acres), within 160ha (400 acres) of parkland
English Heritage Grade I

Fir Trees Pelargonium Nursery

FIR TREES COTTAGE, STOKESLEY, TS9 5LD

Tel & Fax 01642 713066
Website www.firtreespelargoniums.co.uk
Location South of Stokesley, by the junction of the A172 & B1365.
Opening hours 10 am – 4 pm; daily; all year. Closed at weekends between October & February.
Admission fee Free.

This family-run nursery specialises in pelargoniums, and stocks more than 370 cultivars. Visitors are free to wander around the nursery, including its stock and show plant areas and propagation unit. Its new releases this year (2004) include 'Quantock Piksi' , a striking delicate Angel cultivar with wine-red upper petals and white lower ones, and 'Fir Tress Nan', a ruby-red sport of 'Marchioness of Bute'. Two RHS special events will take place during 2004, on 11 August and 2 September: details from 020 7821 3408.

Owned by Helen Bainbridge
Number of gardeners 3
Size 0.4ha (1 acre) of glass

Helmsley Walled Garden

CLEVELAND WAY, HELMSLEY, YO62 5AH

Tel & Fax 01439 771427
Website www.helmsleywalledgarden.co.uk
Location Behind the castle. Park in Cleveland Way long-stay car-park.
Opening hours 10.30 am – 5 pm; daily; April to October.
Admission fee Adults £3; Concessions £2; Children free.

This was originally the walled kitchen garden of Duncombe Park; it is now run by a charitable trust devoted to horticultural therapy and received a £½m grant from the Heritage Lottery Fund in 2002. The award is principally for the restoration of the glasshouses, which should be completed during the course of this year (2004). Apart from its sheer size and splendour, the main features of horticultural interest in the walled garden are some 150 clematis cultivars, 52 different Yorkshire apples, 34 Victorian vines and a splendid Orchid House. The nursery has some interesting and unusual plants.

 Features rare plant nursery; restaurant.

Owned by Helmsley Walled Garden Ltd.
Number of gardeners 3
Size 2ha (5 acres)
English Heritage Grade I

Middlethorpe Hall

BISHOPTHORPE ROAD, YORK, YO23 2GB

Tel 01904 641241 **Fax** 01904 620176
Website www.middlethorpe.com
Location 1½ miles south of city centre, by York Racecourse.
Opening hours By appointment

Middlethorpe Hall is a William III country house close to the city, set in 8ha of its own gardens and parkland. After a period of neglect, the gardens have been carefully restored to their 18th century splendour and include ha-has, a white garden, a walled garden, a small lake and some beautiful specimen trees. Two RHS special events will take place during 2004: details from 020 7821 3408.

 Features renowned hotel.

Owned by Historic House Hotels Ltd.
Size 8ha (20 acres)

Millgate House

RICHMOND, DL10 4JN

Tel 01748 823571 **Fax** 01748 823571
Website www.millgatehouse.com
Location Bottom of Market Place; first house in Millgate on left.
Opening hours 10 am – 5 pm; daily; April to October. And by appointment on Sundays in February & March for snowdrops.
Admission fee Adults £1.50; Children free. RHS members free, except for charity days.

This is a walled garden in the middle of the town, and thus remarkably sheltered. Since starting work in the garden in 1980, the owners' aim has been to create structure, bulk, year-round interest and a sense of profusion. They have achieved this by re-designing the garden to suggest that it is much larger than it really is, and by planting only the best plants of every type. The most prominent are roses, clematis, hostas, snowdrops, hellebores, ferns and foliage shrubs. By 1995 the owners had won the National Garden Competition, against 3,200 other entries. The garden continues to improve: Professor David Stevens calls it 'a sophisticated study in both the manipulation of spatial concepts and [in] planting design'. It is immensely stylish, a model for all town gardens.

Owned by Tim Culkin & Austin Lynch
Number of gardeners owners only
Size 0.15ha (one-third of an acre)

Mount Grace Priory

OSMOTHERLEY, NORTHALLERTON, DL6 3JG

Tel 01609 883494 **Fax** 01609 883361
Website www.nationaltrust.org.uk
Location 12 miles north of Thirsk on A19.
Opening hours 10 am – 6 pm; daily; April to September. 10 am – 5 pm; daily; October. 10 am – 1 pm & 2 pm – 4 pm; Wednesday – Sunday; November to March.
Admission fee Adults £3.20; Concessions £2.40; Children £1.60.

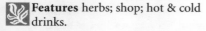

The herb garden, designed by Stephen Anderton in 1994, is of most interest to gardeners. It is a recreation of a 15th-century monastic garden. Around the house, the 1920s flower borders are being restored: there are terraces, acers, rhododendrons and azaleas. It is not a garden in which to dally, but an interesting add-on to the whole experience of a visit to the property.

**Features** herbs; shop; hot & cold drinks.

Owned by The National Trust (managed by English Heritage)
Number of gardeners 2
Size 5ha (12½ acres)

Newby Hall

RIPON, HG4 5AE

Tel 01423 322583 **Fax** 01423 324452
Website www.newbyhall.co.uk
Location Off B6265, 2 miles from A1 between Boroughbridge & Ripon.
Opening hours 11 am – 5.30 pm; Tuesday – Sunday & Bank Holiday Mondays; 1 April to 26 September.
Admission fee Adults £6.30; OAPs £5.30; Children £4.80. RHS members free.

Newby is the garden with everything: firm design, an endless variety of features, great plantsmanship and immaculate maintenance. Its axis is a bold, wide, double border stretching gently down to the River Ure. The National Collection of *Cornus* now extends to 32 species and 53 cultivars, planted to give colour, beauty and interest. Newby also has a large number of other rare trees and shrubs and a comprehensive collection of shrubby salvias, many of them collected in central and southern America by the owner's brother Dr James Compton. Newby is second only to Hidcote as an example of 20th-century gardening, but very much grander: visit it at any season and expect to spend all day there.

Features woodland garden; roses (mainly old-fashioned & climbers); rock garden; plantsman's collection of plants; daffodils; good herbaceous borders; HHA/Christie's Garden of the Year in 1986; tallest *Acer griseum* (15m.) in UK; adventure garden for children; shop and plant stall; licensed restaurant.

Owned by Richard Compton
Number of gardeners 7
Size 10ha (25 acres)
NCCPG National Collections *Cornus* (excluding *C. florida* cvs.)
English Heritage Grade II*

The Ornamental Grass & Plant Nursery

CHURCH FARM, WESTGATE,
RILLINGTON, MALTON, YO17 8LN

Tel 07913 327886 **Fax** 01944 758247
Website www.ornamentalgrass.co.uk
Location In middle of Rillington, on Malton Road.
Opening hours 9.30 am – 4.30 pm; Tuesday –
Sunday; Easter to 1 October. And by appointment.
Admission fee Free.

The Ornamental Grass nursery specialises in
hostas, ferns, bamboos, ornamental grasses
and unusual herbaceous plants suitable for
prairie-style plantings. There are display
gardens and specialist advice is available.
Three RHS special events will take place
during 2004 details from 020 7821 3408.

Features specialist nursery.

Parcevall Hall Gardens

SKYREHOLME, SKIPTON, BD23 6DE

Tel 01756 720311 **Fax** 01756 720441
Website www.parcevallhallgardens.co.uk
Location Off B6160 from Burnsall.
Opening hours 10 am – 6 pm; daily; April to
October; winter visits by appointment. NGS day
27 April.
Admission fee Adults £3.50; Children 50p. RHS
members free from May to August.

The gardens at Parcevall Hall have a
breathtaking architectural layout and views
of the Yorkshire dales. They were largely
designed and planted by Sir William Milner
in 1927 and benefit from a great variety of
soils (limestone and gritstone) which means
that rhododendrons and camellias grow
alongside limestone outcrops. It is
something of a plantsman's garden too: the
naturalised daffodils in the orchard include
'W.P. Milner' while the *Primula florindae*
given by Kingdon Ward has now naturalised
around the lily pond. Within the grounds
are 14 Stations of the Cross.

Features woodland garden; climbing
roses; rock garden; rhododendrons &
azaleas; water features; candelabra primulas;
tea-room.

Owned by Walsingham College (Yorkshire
Properties) Ltd
Number of gardeners 3
Size 6.4ha (16 acres)

Ripley Castle Gardens

RIPLEY, HARROGATE, HG3 3AY

Tel 01423 770152 **Fax** 01423 771745
Website www.ripleycastle.co.uk
Location 3½ miles north of Harrogate, off A61.
Opening hours 9 am – 5 pm (or dusk if earlier);
daily; all year.
Admission fee Adults £3.50; OAPs £3; Children
£2. RHS members free.

Ripley has a garden with something for
everyone: a 14th-century castle (restored);
temples; a landscape designed by Capability
Brown; a fine Regency conservatory; a
Victorian formal garden; evergreen
shrubberies (handsome yews); rare
vegetables from Henry Doubleday Research
Association in the traditional Victorian
walled garden; colour at every season; over
2,000 hyacinths in 40 varieties; woodland
walks; herbaceous borders; and hundreds of
thousands of bulbs – daffodils in hosts.

Features hyacinths; sub-tropical
plants; parkland; bluebells; gift shop
with plants, fruit and vegetables; castle tea-
room.

Owned by Sir Thomas Ingilby Bt.
Number of gardeners 4
NCCPG National Collections *Hyacinthus orientalis*
English Heritage Grade II

R.V. Roger Ltd

THE NURSERIES, PICKERING,
YO18 7HG

Tel 01751 472226 **Fax** 01751 476749
Website www.rvroger.co.uk
Location 1 mile south of Pickering, on A169.
Opening hours 9 am – 5 pm; Monday – Saturday.
1 pm – 5 pm; Sundays. All year.

R.V. Roger was founded in 1913. It is best-known for its excellent and extensive range of alpines, bulbs, conifers, perennials, roses, ornamental trees, hedging and shrubs. However, it also specialises in trained fruit trees – everything from espaliered apples to gooseberries grown as standards (it still lists 60 different apples and almost as many gooseberries). Excellence and variety remain the nursery's guiding principles.

Features trained fruit trees.

NCCPG National Collections *Erythronium*

Sleightholmedale Lodge

FADMOOR, KIRKBYMOORSIDE,
YO62 7JG

Tel 01751 431942 **Fax** 01751 430106
Location Signed from Fadmoor.
Opening hours For NGS, and by written appointment at any time.
Admission fee Adults £2.50; Children 50p.

This family garden – Mrs James is the third generation to garden here – is a plantsman's paradise right on the edge of the moors. The walled garden was built on a south-facing slope, which makes it possible to grow a wide range of plants that might not otherwise survive. As well as magnificent meconopsis and hardy herbaceous plants it has Mexican and Mediterranean rarities (a cistus walk, for example) which are a triumph for good cultivation and manipulation of the microclimate. The herbaceous borders are held together by repeating certain plants throughout: foxgloves, campanulas, martagon lilies, for example. Outside the walled garden is an orchard underplanted with snowdrops and narcissi. Up at the top is a hollyhock walk. And there are roses of every sort – hundreds of them, perhaps thousands.

Features roses (ancient & modern); plantsman's collection of plants; good herbaceous borders; teas in July.

Owned by Mrs R. James
Number of gardeners 1, plus 2 very part-time
Size 1.2ha (3 acres)

Stillingfleet Lodge Nurseries

STILLINGFLEET, YORK, YO19 6HP

Tel & Fax 01904 728506
Website www.stillingfleetlodgenurseries.co.uk
Location 6 miles south of York: turn opposite the church.
Opening hours 1 pm – 4 pm; Wednesdays & Sundays; May to September. Special 'Pulmonaria Open Day' on 18 April, 1.30 pm – 4.30 pm.
Admission fee Adults £2.50; Children 50p. RHS members free.

Stillingfleet is a series of small gardens surrounding a late 18th-century farmhouse. The emphasis is on a cottage garden style of planting, for ease of maintenance. Foliage is used to add interest and texture: the result is a sequence of sumptuous herbaceous borders – a living lesson in how to plant a garden. The collection of pulmonarias is fascinating: 13 species and over 150 cultivars flower over a long period. A wildflower walk leads to a pond planted for natural effect. The nursery has an excellent herbaceous list with a high proportion of unusual plants: the catalogue changes each year but is always good for geraniums and pulmonarias. Worth a long journey to visit.

 Features herbaceous plants; wildflower walk.

Owned by Vanessa Cook
Number of gardeners owner, plus a little part-time help
Size 0.6ha (1½ acres)
NCCPG National Collections *Pulmonaria*

Studley Royal

FOUNTAINS, RIPON, HG4 3DZ

Tel 01765 608888 **Fax** 01765 608889
Website www.nationaltrust.org.uk
Location 3 miles west of Ripon off B6265, via the Visitor Centre.
Opening hours 10 am – 4 pm (6 pm in summer) or dusk if sooner; daily; all year, except Fridays from November to January & 24 & 25 December. Closes at 3 pm on 12 & 19 July.
Admission fee Adults £5.50; Children £3.

Studley Royal is inextricably linked to Fountains Abbey: nothing can beat the surprise view of the ruined Cistercian abbey from Anne Boleyn's Seat. The most spectacular water garden in England was laid out in between 1716 and 1781 in the sheltered flat bottom of the River Skell. The abbey is at one end, the deer park at the other. The combination of the formal canal, moon pools, grotto springs, rustic bridge, sculptures and the Temple of Piety against a dark background of trees is a supreme example of 18th-century landscaping at its most individual.

**Features** topiary; snowdrops; World Heritage site; 400-acre deer park; water garden; biggest *Prunus avium* (bird cherry) in British Isles; National Trust visitor centre shop; tea-room.

Owned by The National Trust
Number of gardeners 9, plus volunteers
Size 60ha (150 acres)
English Heritage Grade I

Sutton Park

SUTTON-ON-THE-FOREST, YORK, YO6 1DP

Tel 01347 810249 **Fax** 01347 811251
Website www.statelyhome.co.uk
Location 8 miles north of York on B1363.
Opening hours 11 am – 5 pm; daily; 29 March to 29 September.
Admission fee Adults £3; OAPs £2; Children 50p.

Capability Brown was here in the 18th century, but the joy of Sutton is the formal garden laid out on three broad terraces below the house. It was designed by Percy Cane in the 1960s and planted by the late Nancie Sheffield with exquisite taste. It was one of the first to throw off the austerity of the post-war years and insist upon floral profusion and segregated colour schemes, though it looks a little dated nowadays – rather a period piece – and standards of maintenance are somewhat relaxed. In the grounds are a Georgian ice-house, a woodland walk, some fine Victorian conifers, and a tulip tree *Liriodendron tulipifera* planted by Prince George, later Duke of Kent, on 7 October 1933.

 Features influential formal gardens; plantsman's plants; good herbaceous borders; plants for sale occasionally; refreshments on Wednesdays to Sundays in summer.

Owned by Sir Reginald & Lady Sheffield
Number of gardeners 2½
Size 3.2ha (8 acres), plus parkland

Thorp Perrow Arboretum & Woodland Garden

BEDALE, DL8 2PR

Tel & Fax 01677 425323
Website www.thorpperrow.com
Location On the Bedale-Ripon road, 2 miles south of Bedale.
Opening hours Dawn to dusk; daily; all year.
Admission fee Adults £5.75; OAPs & Students £4.40; Children £2.95. RHS members free from Monday to Friday (excluding Bank Holidays).

Thorp Perrow is the most important arboretum in the north of England, with more than 20 record-breaking trees among the thousands planted since Sir Leonard Ropner started work in 1931. There was already a pinetum on the estate, planted by Lady Augusta Milbank in the 1840s and 1850s. Ropner surrounded it with his new plantings – over 1,000 different taxa still survive, to which his son Sir John has added at least another 300. There are handsome avenues to walk along, often lined with a single genus or species – red oaks, rowans, cherries or cypresses, for example. Many are thickly lined with daffodils in spring, as are the glades and bays where you can study a

particular collection like acers or hollies. The only downside to Thorp Perrow is that all the trees are identified only with a number, which you then have to look up in the catalogue of plantings. This minor irritation apart, Thorp Perrow is in every way an inspiring and enjoyable place to visit.

 Features the best collection of trees in northern England; daffodils; bluebells; new Millennium Glade; information centre; plant centre; licensed tea-room.

Owned by Sir John Ropner Bt.
Size 34ha (85 acres)
NCCPG National Collections *Fraxinus*; *Juglans*; *Laburnum*; *Tilia*
English Heritage Grade II

Valley Gardens

VALLEY DRIVE, HARROGATE

Tel 01423 500600 **Fax** 01423 556720
Website www.harrogate.gov.uk
Location Signed from town centre.
Opening hours Dawn – dusk; daily; all year.
Admission fee Free.

The Valley Gardens at Harrogate are a good example of plantsmanship in a public garden, first laid out between 1880 and 1900. The gardens have alpine rarities in spring, a romantic rhododendron dell, good roses, a fine dahlia display in late summer and good colour bedding.

 Features rock garden; herbaceous borders; bedding; small cafeteria.

Owned by Harrogate Borough Council
Size 6.7ha (17 acres)
English Heritage Grade II

Wytherstone House

POCKLEY, YO62 7TE

Tel 01439 770012 **Fax** 01439 770468
Location Far end of village (coming from A170) on left side.
Opening hours 1 pm – 5 pm; Wednesdays; 9 June to 25 August. Plus 23 May, 6 & 20 June, 18 July & 15 August for charity. And for parties by appointment at other times.
Admission fee Adults £2.50; Children £1.

There is a lot to see – and tender plants especially – in this remote garden, which has received a boost in recent years by the arrival of a plant-wise head gardener. In a sheltered area near the entrance are bananas, *Pinus montezumae*, trachycarpus, cordylines and phormiums. Rhododendrons thrive nearby in a specially made-up bed. Fremontodendrons and (remarkably) *Eucalyptus gunnii* have been trained against the south-facing side of the house. Around the house is a series of small, linked gardens with mixed borders, often backed by climbing roses, and good colour-schemed plantings. A garden made of old railway sleepers is terraced up with raised beds full of interesting plants – zauschnerias, succulents (put out for the summer), agapanthus and *Lobelia tupa*. Elsewhere are carpenterias, phlomis, crinums, *Melianthus major* and *Salvia greggii* and its hybrids, all apparently quite hardy in the free-draining, limestone soil. *Buddleja colvilei* is grown as a free-standing shrub. Further away from the house, a collection of trees around a pond promises to develop into a domestic arboretum. The nursery is excellent.

Features tender plants; good colour combinations; interesting nursery; teas on charity days.

Owned by Lady Clarissa Collin
Number of gardeners 2
Size 3.2ha (8 acres)

YORKSHIRE, SOUTH

The county of South Yorkshire was invented in 1974 and is, in effect, Greater Sheffield. Nevertheless it has a couple of good historic gardens which are open to the public – Wentworth Castle and Brodsworth Hall. The Sheffield Botanical Gardens too are of great horticultural interest, having been planted and maintained over many years as a garden of ornamental plants of every kind. Both the Sheffield Botanical Gardens and the gardens at Wentworth Castle have benefited from lottery funding in recent years and are very visitor-friendly as a result, though it is still possible to visit Wentworth only as part of a guided tour. The National Gardens Scheme has very few gardens opening for it in the county and, though it is well provided with garden centres, South Yorkshire has no specialist nurseries of national importance. There are several NCCPG National Collections – including two at Sheffield Botanical Gardens and three at Wentworth Castle.

Brodsworth Hall & Gardens

ENGLISH HERITAGE, BRODSWORTH, DONCASTER, DN5 7XJ

Tel 01302 722598 **Fax** 01302 337165
Location 6 miles north-west of Doncaster.
Opening hours 12 noon – 6 pm; Tuesday – Sunday & Bank Holiday Mondays; April to September. Then 11 am – 4 pm; weekends only.
Admission fee Garden only: Adults £3.50; OAPs £2.60; Children £1.80. Cheap rates in winter.

Brodsworth has proved a triumph for English Heritage – a splendid Victorian garden, unkempt for 50 years, but now spectacularly restored as first laid out in the 1860s. It offers Italianate terraces, statues and classical follies; a rose garden where the vigorous ramblers are trained on bizarre ironwork arcades and box-edged beds are filled with period roses; magnificent trees (especially cedars, pines and monkey puzzles); bright Victorian bedding in a huge formal garden; and lots of clipped evergreens – laurels, yews, laurels, aucubas and many more, even free-standing griselinias. Best of all, perhaps, are the hollies – hundreds and hundreds of them, planted to display their vast colour palette. The spring bulbs, too, are exceptional. Every part of the garden is well-maintained and a joy to visit at any time of the year.

Features good specimen conifers; Victorian spring & summer bedding; large fern collection; significant clipped evergreen shrubberies; statuary; shop; licensed restaurant.

Owned by English Heritage
Number of gardeners 6
Size 5.2ha (13 acres)
English Heritage Grade II*

Earth Centre

DENABY MAIN, DONCASTER,
DN12 4EA

Tel 01709 513933
Website www.earthcentre.org.uk
Location Opposite Conisbrough railway station.
Opening hours Not available as we went to press.
Admission fee Adults £5.

The Earth Centre is not so much a garden as an exploration of the themes of sustainability, biomass, conservation and biodiversity. Within the overall design are a herb garden, a bog garden and a dry garden, but these are not as important as the overall message which comes across in exhibitions, practical demonstrations and interactive trails – very educational, and brilliant for children.

Features sustainability demonstrations; plants in season; coffee shop & restaurant.

Size 8.7ha (22 acres)

Wentworth Castle Gardens

LOWE LANE, STAINBOROUGH,
BARNSLEY, S75 3ET

Tel 01226 776040 **Fax** 01226 776042
Website www.wentworthcastle.org
Location Signed 'Northern College'. 3 miles south of Barnsley; 2 miles from M1.
Opening hours Mainly by guided tours from mid-April to the end of August. Also open on selected Sunday afternoons from May to August. Annual open days 30 & 31 May. Details from 01226 776040 or website.
Admission fee Adults £2.50; Concessions £2 (£2.50 on 30 & 31 May); Children free. RHS members free, except 30 & 31 May.

Wentworth Castle has a major landscape garden, one of the earliest in England, which accounts for the amazing series of buildings in the grounds – among them are an Ionic rotunda, the gothic folly of Stainborough Castle, an obelisk to Queen Anne and another to Lady Mary Wortley-Montagu to commemorate her introduction of smallpox inoculation to England. The garden was then overlaid with a seriously important collection of hardy hybrid rhododendrons at the end of the 19th century. It was then that the handsome cast-iron conservatory was built: it was recently voted into third place by BBC Two's *Restoration* series. This has been the basis of its current development as an educational and cultural resource. A Heritage Lottery Fund grant of £10.3 million will allow extensive restoration of the pleasure grounds, parkland and landscape buildings to begin this year (2004). Wentworth Castle is twinned with the Kunming Academy of Sciences in China. There is only one problem about visiting it – you have to go with a guided tour.

Features historic landscape; woodland garden; newly excavated 19th-century rock garden; educational collection of rhododendrons.

Owned by Barnsley Metropolitan Borough Council
Number of gardeners 5
Size 16ha (40 acres)
NCCPG National Collections *Rhododendron* species; *Magnolia* species; *Camellia* x *williamsii*
English Heritage Grade I

YORKSHIRE, WEST

West Yorkshire corresponds to the old West Riding. It is a county of great contrasts, from the industrial and commercial cities of Bradford and Leeds to the wool towns of Huddersfield and Halifax, with a chunk of the Peak District in the south-west and some large agricultural estates in the north. The most important historic gardens are Bramham Park – a remarkable pre-landscape garden on a big scale – and the opulent Harewood House. But they are matched for sheer horticultural value by four gardens which all have an historic past but are now owned and managed by Leeds City Council as gardens for public recreation – Lotherton Hall, Temple Newsam, The Hollies, and the Canal Gardens & Tropical World in Roundhay Park. The NCCPG has no fewer than 11 National Collections in the care of the Leeds City Parks Department. There are rather few specialist nurseries of national standing in the county, though it is well served by garden centres.

8 Dunstarn Lane

ADEL, LEEDS, LS16 8EL

Tel 0113 267 3938
Location Off Long causeway, Adel.
Opening hours 2 pm – 7 pm; 4 July and by appointment.
Admission fee Adults £1.50; Children free.

The Wainwrights have grown delphiniums here for more than half a century. It is probably the finest and most extensive collection of delphiniums in private hands, with nearly seventy cultivars. They are interplanted with their traditional border companions – roses (mainly modern), phlox, dahlias, Michaelmas daisies and many unusual perennials.

Features roses; delphiniums; fine trees.

Owned by Mrs Richard Wainwright

Number of gardeners 1
Size 1.2ha (3 acres)

Bramham Park

WETHERBY, LS23 6ND

Tel 01937 846000 **Fax** 01937 846007
Website www.bramhampark.co.uk
Location 5 miles south of Wetherby on A1.
Opening hours 11.30 am – 4.30 pm; daily; April to September. Closed for horse trials from 7 to 14 June, Leeds Festival from 16 August to 4 September & occasionally for other events. Ring before visiting.
Admission fee Gardens only: Adults £4; OAPs £2; Children £2.

Bramham is a very important pre-landscape formal garden, laid out in the grand manner in the early 18th century. A long driveway winds through the woods, turns a corner, and suddenly reveals the magnificent Palladian house, framed by the most spacious of avenues. Behind the house are long, straight rides carved through dense woodland and edged with tall beech hedges, neatly cut. Focal points include loggias, statues, temples, an obelisk and a sequence of formal cascades running down to a square, lake-sized pond.. The parkland turf is speckled with cowslips and wild onions run amok in the woods, but the scale and complexity of the design have nothing to match them anywhere in the British Isles: Bramham is the finest French garden in England – awesome, uplifting and built to impress.

 Features very important pre-landscape park; daffodils.

Owned by George Lane Fox
Number of gardeners 3
Size 27ha (68 acres)
English Heritage Grade I

Golden Acre Park

OTLEY ROAD, BRAMHOPE, LEEDS, LS16 5NZ

Tel 0113 267 3729
Website www.leeds.gov.uk
Location 6 miles north-west of Leeds city centre on A660 Otley Road.
Opening hours Dawn – dusk; daily; all year.
Admission fee Free.

Golden Acre is part historic park, part botanic collection, part demonstration garden and part test ground for Fleuroselect and *Gardening Which?*. It began life in the 1930s as an amusement park, but the City Council decided after the war to develop it as a public garden with a strong botanical interest. Perhaps the best of the five impressive public gardens in Leeds, it is certainly the most popular.

 Features rock garden; large heather garden; new 'harmony' garden; herb garden; limestone rock garden; sandstone rock garden; arboretum; pinetum; display houses; rhododendrons & azaleas; cherry orchard; gifts/souvenirs; restaurant.

Owned by Leeds City Council
Size 54ha (135 acres)
NCCPG National Collections *Primula auricula*; *Syringa*

Harewood House

HAREWOOD, LEEDS, LS17 9LQ

Tel 0113 218 1010 **Fax** 0113 218 1002
Website www.harewood.org
Location Between Leeds & Harrogate on A61.
Opening hours 10 am – 6 pm; daily; 11 February to 31 October, then Saturdays & Sundays until 12 December.
Admission fee Grounds: Adults £7.25; OAPs £6.25; Children £4.50. RHS members free from 26 March to 25 June, excluding weekends & Bank Holidays.

Capability Brown was the first famous landscaper to work at Harewood for the super-rich Lascelles family: he was followed by Humphry Repton, John Claudius Loudon and Sir Charles Barry. The latter came in the 1840s, to build the stupendous Italianate terrace whose grand parterre and ornate fountains are the perfect link between the house and the landscaped park. Bedding out is practised here on a large scale – very impressive – and ensures colour throughout the year. The border below the parterre is planted with bold foliage plants – yuccas, phormiums, irises, artichokes, peonies, eriobotryas, bananas, callistemons and acanthus. Around the lake at the bottom are hundreds of rhododendrons, unusual shrubs and bulbs, particularly daffodils. The waterfall at the lake head feeds a picturesque rock-garden where primulas, astilbes, hostas and gunneras grow rampantly in the damp. The rose garden at the end of the lakeside walk is an extra delight in early summer. The large, traditional walled garden displays a wide selection of vegetables and economic crops from around the world: Harewood is a registered Seed Library garden.

 Features formal terraces; good bedding; woodland garden; rhododendrons; current holder of Sandford Award; two shops; licensed café selling light lunches.

Owned by Harewood House Trust Ltd.
Number of gardeners 12
Size 56ha (140 acres)
English Heritage Grade I

The Hollies Park

Weetwood Lane, Leeds, LS16 5NZ

Tel 0113 278 2030 **Fax** 0113 247 8277
Website www.leeds.gov.uk
Location 3 miles north of city off A660.
Opening hours Dawn – dusk; daily; all year.
Admission fee Free.

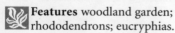

This public park is made in a plantsman's garden, and is well run by a hard-pressed and enthusiastic team. Visitors wishing to see the National Collections are advised to make a prior appointment.

Features woodland garden; rhododendrons; eucryphias.

Owned by Leeds City Council
Size 37ha (93 acres)
NCCPG National Collections *Deutzia*; *Hemerocallis* (Coe hybrids); *Hosta* (large-leaved); *Philadelphus*; *Syringa*

Land Farm Gardens

Colden, Hebden Bridge, Halifax, HX7 7PJ

Tel 01422 842260
Location On right, 2 miles from Hebden Bridge on Colden road.
Opening hours 10 am – 5 pm; Saturdays, Sundays & Bank Holiday Mondays; May to August.
Admission fee Adults £3. Guided parties £5 per head, including refreshments.

This is a pioneering plantsman's garden, high in the Pennines and facing north. The range of plants that can successfully be grown in such an unpromising situation is an eye-opener – lots of hardy rhododendrons, shrubs, trees and alpines. There is also a good collection of sculpture, with more pieces arriving all the time.

Features garden created by owners on green field site; good conifers and herbaceous borders; new woodland garden (2 acres); *Meconopsis*; *Tropaeolum*; art gallery.

Owned by John Williams
Size 1.6ha (4 acres)

Lotherton Hall

Aberford, Leeds, LS25 3EB

Tel 0113 281 3259 **Fax** 0113 281 3068
Website www.leeds.gov.uk/lothertonhall
Location Off A1, ½ mile east on B1217.
Opening hours 8 am – 8 pm or dusk, if earlier; daily; all year.
Admission fee Garden free, but charges for parking.

This showpiece garden was laid out about 1885-1915 by a friend of Ellen Willmott. It was given to the Council in 1968 and has been well restored in recent years. It offers gazebos, walks, yew hedging, rose gardens, and a lily pond recently replanted with period varieties. The rock garden known as the Dell is especially good. The formal garden is laid out with gravel paths and lots of bedding. Lotherton is a garden that is on the move again, with a woodland trail recently added for disabled users. It is extremely popular – over ½ million visitors a year.

 **Features** Edwardian plantswoman's garden; roses (mainly modern); good trees; fine hedges; mature layout; shop; cafeteria.

Owned by Leeds City Council
Number of gardeners 2
Size 4ha (10 acres)
English Heritage Grade II

Roundway Park & Tropical World

ROUNDHAY PARK, PRINCES AVENUE, LEEDS, LS8 2ER

Tel 0113 266 1850 **Fax** 0113 237 0077
Website www.leeds.gov.uk
Location 3 miles north-west of city centre, off A6120 ring road.
Opening hours Open 10 am all year. Close at 4 pm in January & December; 5 pm in February & November; 6 pm in March & October; 7 pm in April & September; 8 pm from May to August.
Admission fee Tropical World: Adults £3; Children £2. Gardens free.

Ⓟ 🐕 ⓦⓒ ♿ 🎁 ☕

Tropical World's glasshouses contain South American rain forest plants, bromeliads, hoyas, cacti and a butterfly house. It is said to have the largest collection of tropical plants outside Kew. It is in any event a wonderful retreat from a Yorkshire winter and a triumph of municipal horticultural excellence. Roundhay Park has a £6.1m

project to preserve and enhance the gardens which has received support from the Heritage Lottery Fund. Tropical World is visited by over 1,000,000 people every year. The gardens outside have fine herbaceous and mixed borders, and splendid formal bedding schemes, including a clock surrounded by carpet bedding and two further raised carpet beds. Nearby is a re-interpretation of Monet's garden at Giverny and another of the Alhambra Gardens in Granada, complete with fountains. Add in two lakes and extensive woodland walks in the park and you have a most enjoyable place to visit at any time of the year.

 **Features** sub-tropical plants; roses (mainly modern); plants under glass; good carpet bedding; orchids; desert house; souvenirs; cafeteria by lakeside.

Owned by Leeds City Council
Number of gardeners 40
Size 240ha (600 acres)
English Heritage Grade II

Temple Newsam Park

LEEDS, LS15 0AD

Tel 0113 264 5535
Website www.leeds.gov.uk
Location 3 miles south-east of city, off A63 Selby Road.
Opening hours Dawn – dusk; daily; all year.
Admission fee Free. Admission charge to house.

Ⓟ 🐕 ⓦⓒ ♿ 🌳 🎁 ☕

This prodigious house on a windy bluff, surrounded by 1,500 acres of parkland, has been a 'green lung' for Leeds since 1923. Somewhat dilapidated in the past, the garden is now improved by some recent plantings. These include a spring garden full of bulbs; the Italian garden with formal flower beds; box, yew and beech hedges; pleached laburnum walks; and a clipped hornbeam

RHS Garden Harlow Carr

CRAG LANE, BECKWITHSHAW, HARROGATE, HG3 1QB

Tel 01423 565418 **Fax** 01423 530663
Website www.rhs.org.uk
Location Crag Lane is off Otley Road (B6162),
1½ miles from Harrogate centre.
Opening hours 9.30 am – 6 pm, or dusk if earlier;
daily; all year.
Admission fee Adults £5; OAPs £4.50; Children
(6-16 years) £1; Children (under 6) free. RHS
members (plus one guest) free.

For more than 50 years, Harlow Carr has set itself the challenge of educating, inspiring and delighting northern gardeners. The garden was opened in 1950, by the Northern Horticultural Society, as a trial ground for assessing the suitability of various plants for growing in northern climates. Trials continue to be a central purpose of the gardens today. The gardens are comprehensive and spectacular. One of the highlights is the famous Streamside Garden – possibly one of the longest in the country – a breathtaking sight from spring onwards. From June the streamside is bursting with the vivid colours of the famous Harlow Carr hybrid candelabra primulas, along with blue Himalayan poppies, astilbes and hostas. The woodland and arboretum (with a wildflower meadow) are home not only to a wide range of shrubs and trees, but also to a profusion of wildlife, from insects to birds, squirrels, stoat and roe deer. The ornamental gardens include scented, foliage, herb, grasses and winter gardens, alpine display houses, stone sink gardens, heathers and a rhododendron collection. Several NCCPG National Plant Collections are held at Harlow Carr: there are more than 140 cultivars of *Rheum* (rhubarb) (viewing by appointment only), two fern collections (*Dryopteris* and *Polypodium*) and a collection of fuchsias

(Section Quelusia) which is jointly maintained with members of the British Fuchsia Society. New features appear every year: look out for the new kitchen garden and fruit garden, the re-designed and replanted herb garden, and the new border which mixes herbaceous plants with ornamental grasses. The new lake is a memorial to H.M. Queen Elizabeth The Queen Mother, Patron of the RHS for 65 years. Seven new historical gardens have been constructed to commemorate the RHS bicentenary in 2004; they will be the centrepiece of a seven-part BBC television series during this year. Each garden represents a different phase in gardening history: circa 1804, the 1850s, the end of the 19th century, a garden in the style of Gertrude Jekyll, a modern garden from the Festival of Britain (1951), a scene from the 1970s and finally a contemporary garden by Diarmuid Gavin. The Royal Horticultural Society also ensures that Harlow Carr is an important centre for horticultural learning, with an extensive list of events and courses all through the year for amateurs and professionals alike.

Features fruit; vegetables; herbs; daffodils; fine collection of trees; heathers and alpines; good autumn colour; gift shop; large bookshop; plant centre; licensed café.

Owned by The Royal Horticultural Society
Number of gardeners 15
Size 23ha (58 acres)
NCCPG National Collections *Dryopteris*; *Fuchsia* section Quelusia; *Polypodium*; *Rheum*

stilt hedge. A fine rhododendron and azalea walk runs down to the lakes. Nearby is an arboretum and a bog garden. Further on still, the old walled kitchen garden is planted with roses and wide herbaceous borders. The long conservatory has a fine display of flowering plants, ivies and cacti: its back wall (1788) still has the flues which were used to keep it warm with hot air.

Features spacious parkland; roses (ancient & modern); good herbaceous borders; rhododendrons; visitor centre & gift shop; tea-room open daily from 10.30 am.

Owned by Leeds City Council
NCCPG National Collections *Aster*; *Chrysanthemum* (Charms & Cascade); *Delphinium*; *Phlox paniculata*; *Solenostemon*
English Heritage Grade II

York Gate

BACK CHURCH LANE, ADEL, LEEDS, LS16 8DW

Tel 0113 267 8240
Website www.perennial.org.uk
Location 2½ miles south-east of Bramhope and ½ mile east of A660, behind Adel Church.
Opening hours 2 pm – 5 pm; Thursdays, Sundays & Bank Holiday Mondays; April to September. Plus Thursday evenings (6.30 pm – 9 pm) in July. And by appointment.

Admission fee Adults £3 (more for private visits); Children free.

This one-acre masterpiece – a modern cult garden – was made by the Spencer family between 1951 and 1994. It is of equal interest to the designer and the plantsman. Its marvels include shrub and herbaceous borders, an arbour, a miniature pinetum, a dell with stream, a folly, a nut walk, a peony bed, a fern border, the famous herb garden, a pretty summerhouse, an alley, a white and silver garden, a kitchen garden, and a pavement maze. This masterpiece of tight design, invention, colour sense and sheer creative opportunism is now in the care of Perennial, the new name for the Gardeners' Royal Benevolent Society .

Features brilliant design; plantsman's collection of plants; famous herb garden; endless inventive details; plants for sale sometimes; tea & biscuits, June to September (& BH weekends).

Owned by Perennial – Gardeners' Royal Benevolent Society
Number of gardeners 1, plus part-timers & volunteers
Size 0.4ha (1 acre)

GARDENS
OF
SCOTLAND

Scottish gardens are very variable – this is a factor of their soil and climate. All along the west coast, from Dumfries & Galloway up to Ullapool and beyond, are fine, subtropical woodland gardens, where one can enjoy acres of large-leaved rhododendrons and eucalyptus trees and all manner of curiosities like *Myosotidium hortensia*, which would not be hardy in any but the most favoured parts of England. There is no better place to go visiting gardens in May or June – provided the weather is kind. There are comparatively few good gardens in inland Scotland. Historically, the big estates were (and still are) in remote places where the land is unsuitable for agriculture and, in consequence, their gardens tend to be few and disappointing. In the Borders, for example, there are several estates along the valleys of Tweed and the Teviot whose gardens are open to the public: all have collections of 19th-century conifers underplanted with hardy hybrid rhododendrons or common *R. ponticum*, but little else in the way of horticultural interest. On the East Coast, however, there are once again many worthy gardens, above all the superb botanic garden at Edinburgh, which (like all botanic gardens nowadays) is laid out to please visitors, and other good botanic gardens at Dundee, St Andrews and Aberdeen. There are interesting gardens too near Edinburgh (especially Malleny at Balerno) and on Deeside (Crathes, Kildrummy and Drum).

Trees flourish in much of Scotland – especially those North American conifers for which the cool, damp west coast provides perfect growing conditions: many of the tallest pines, firs and spruces in Britain are in Scotland. The largest collection of record-breaking trees is at the Royal Botanic Gardens in Edinburgh, which has 45.

We have listed the gardens to visit in Scotland under the old 1974 regions, rather than the historic counties or the plethora of more recent local councils. The regions divide the country into areas of acceptable size for the purpose of this book, though there is a preponderance of gardens in the old region of Strathclyde – as indeed there still is in Argyll & Bute. If readers can suggest a better way than the old regions to list gardens, we would be pleased to hear from them. Scotland's Garden Scheme divides the country into areas which are even more confusing – 'Etterick & Lauderdale', for example, and 'Lochaber, Badenoch & Strathspey'. The 1974 regions do at least have the advantage of having been administrative areas until very recently.

Scotland has many great historic gardens. The basis of the protection they enjoy is the *Inventory of Gardens & Designed Landscapes in Scotland* which was published in 1987. The Inventory listed 275 sites, which are graded in a more specific way than the gardens on the English register, for example, according to the value of their horticultural content or historic importance. Historic Scotland has recently begun to extend the Inventory.

Nobody has done more to acquire, save, restore and redevelop Scotland's great gardens than the National Trust for Scotland. Its portfolio of properties includes many of the best historic and horticultural gardens in the country: Branklyn, Brodick, Crathes, Culzean and Inverewe are gardens of international renown. It has now taken the splendid garden at Crarae into its care. The Royal Botanic Garden at Edinburgh too has developed four of the finest gardens anywhere in the world – Dawyck, Logan, Benmore (Younger Botanic Garden) and its own incomparable garden in north Edinburgh.

Members of the Royal Horticultural Society have free access for at least some months of the year to a fine list of Scottish gardens from Dunrobin Castle in the north to Harmony Garden in the Borders. More may be added during the course of the year: see the Society's website www.rhs.org.uk for the latest news. Scotland also has its own Yellow Book called *The Gardens of Scotland*, available from Scotland's Gardens Scheme, 31 Castle Terrace, Edinburgh EH1 2EL. It lists over 350 gardens throughout Scotland and, like its English equivalent, is the essential starting point for choosing more gardens to visit than this book recommends.

Scotland is well served by garden centres, especially by such chains as Dobbies in the Lowlands, which now has branches in northern England too. Scotland has some excellent specialist nurseries too: Jack Drake is Britain's premier alpine nursery; nobody has bred more or better new rhododendrons than Peter Cox at Glendoick; and Cally in Dumfries & Galloway has a great reputation for rare plants. However, it is fair to say that there are fewer nurseries *per capita* in

Scotland as a whole than in England.

Scotland also has its own rather basic horticultural structure: these include, for example, such societies as the Scottish Rock Garden Club, the Scottish Rhododendron Society, the Royal Caledonian Horticultural Society and the Scottish Orchid Society. All are excellent organisations and some, like the Scottish Rock Garden Club and the Scottish Rhododendron Society, are substantial societies with good programmes of events and publications of record. Scotland also has a number of horticultural training colleges, notably Threave and the Scottish Agricultural College at Auchincruive, both of them RHS Partner Colleges.

BORDERS

Abbotsford

MELROSE, TD6 9BQ

Tel 01896 752043 **Fax** 01896 752916
Location On B6360, 2 miles west of Melrose.
Opening hours 9.30 am – 5 pm (but 2 pm – 5 pm
on Sundays in March, April, May & October); daily;
17 March to 31 October.
Admission fee Adults £4.50; Children £2.2510.

Sir Walter Scott laid out the gardens at
Abbotsford in the 1820s: he designed the
formal Court garden by the house and
planted the surrounding woodlands. The
walled garden centres on a handsome
orangery, with roses, fruit trees and
herbaceous borders planted for late summer
effect.

Features fine walled garden; orangery;
topiary; herbaceous borders; gift shop;
self-service tea-room.

Owned by Dame Jean Maxwell-Scott DCVO
Number of gardeners 2
Size 0.4ha (1 acre)

Dawyck Botanic Garden

STOBO, EH45 9JU

Tel 01721 760254 **Fax** 01721 760214
Website www.rbge.org.uk
Location 8 miles south-west of Peebles on B712.
Opening hours 10 am – 6 pm; daily; 14 February
to 16 November. Closes at 4 pm in February &
November, and at 5 pm in March & October.
Admission fee Adults £3.50; Concessions £3;
Children £1.

Dawyck is a woodland garden, run as a
regional garden of the Royal Botanic
Garden Edinburgh. It is very different from
Edinburgh's other outliers: its 60 acres are
high in the hills where the climate is more
continental than temperate. The trees for
which the garden is famous were first
planted in the 1830s: the owners subscribed
to the great plant-hunting expeditions of
the day, including those of David Douglas.
This explains the many fine North
American conifers in the garden. In the
early 20th century, the owners received
plants from the early Chinese collections of
E.H. Wilson. The gardens are also famous
for their rhododendrons, berberis and
cotoneasters and – of course – the Dawyck
beech, an upright, fastigiate form of the
common beech, first found in the policies in
the mid-19th century.

Features good herbaceous borders;
meconopsis; Chinese conifers; Dawyck
beech; Douglas fir from original seed; tallest
Abies mariesii (21m.) in the British Isles, and
12 further record trees; gift shop; light
refreshments.

Owned by Royal Botanic Garden Edinburgh
Size 24ha (60 acres)

Edrom Nurseries

COLDINGHAM, EYEMOUTH,
TD14 5TZ

Tel 01890 771386 **Fax** 01890 771387
Website www.edromnurseries.co.uk
Location A1107, 5 minutes from A1.
Opening hours 9 am – 5.30 pm; daily; March
to October.
Admission fee Free.

This nursery specialises in alpine primulas, arisaemas, trilliums, gentians and meconopsis. The list of these three genera is particularly comprehensive, and includes many forms that are not available elsewhere. As with the other alpines it lists, many are new to commerce or grown under collectors' numbers.

Owned by T. Hunt & C. Davis
Number of gardeners 2
Size 0.2ha (½ acre)

Floors Castle

KELSO, TD5 7SF

Tel 01573 223333 **Fax** 01573 226056
Website www.floorscastle.com
Location Signed in Kelso.
Opening hours 10 am – 4.30 pm; daily; 3 April to 31 October. RHS members free.
Admission fee Adults £3; OAPs £1.50.

Floors has handsome traditional herbaceous borders in the walled garden and the castle is impressively sited in its parkland. But change and restoration continue too: a new two-acre parterre in front of the castle is surmounted by a ducal coronet, while the 'star plantation' was entirely replanted with azaleas and rhododendrons in 1998. There are some good trees in the park, including a holm oak (*Quercus ilex*) and a Dawyck beech (*Fagus sylvatica* 'Fastigiata'), and a venerable holly on the spot where King James II of Scotland was blown up while besieging Roxburgh Castle in 1460.

Features good borders; garden centre in walled garden; coffee shop, licensed restaurant & gift shop.

Owned by The Duke of Roxburghe
Number of gardeners 5

Harmony Garden

ST MARY'S ROAD, MELROSE, TD6 9LJ

Tel 01721 722502
Website www.nts.org.uk
Location In Melrose, opposite the abbey.
Opening hours 10 am – 5 pm; daily; 9 to 12 April, and 1 June to 30 September. Sundays 1 pm – 5 pm.
Admission fee Adults £2; Concessions £1. RHS members free.

'Harmony' takes its name from the Jamaican pimento plantation where its original builder James Waugh made his fortune. It is a modest, quiet walled garden with lawns, herbaceous and mixed borders, vegetable and fruit areas, and a rich display of spring bulbs. The views of Melrose Abbey and the Eildon Hills are a bonus.

Owned by The National Trust for Scotland
Number of gardeners 1
Size 0.8ha (2 acres)

Kailzie Gardens

KAILZIE, PEEBLES, EH45 9HT

Tel & Fax 01721 720007
Location On B7062 2 miles east of Peebles.
Opening hours 11 am – 5.30 pm; daily; all year.
Admission fee Adults £3; Children £1 (but £2.50 & 75p respectively from mid-March to 1 June, and £2 & 50p from November to mid-March).

Kailzie has been revived over the last 20 years. The large walled garden has a mixture of flowers and produce: a laburnum alley, a rose garden and double herbaceous borders are some of the attractions. There are meconopsis and primulas in the rhododendron woodland walks outside.

Features woodland garden; snowdrops; daffodils; shop; restaurant & teas.

Owned by Angela, Lady Buchan-Hepburn
Number of gardeners 3
Size 8ha (20 acres)

Lilliesleaf Nursery

GARDEN COTTAGE, LINTHILL,
LILLIESLEAF, TD6 9HU

Tel & Fax 01835 870415
Location On B6359 between Midlem & Lilliesleaf.
Opening hours 10 am – 5 pm, Monday – Saturday;
10 am – 4 pm, Sundays. November to March, phone first.
Admission fee Free.

This nursery, in a pretty position on the bank of the river Ale, has a general plant range, with an emphasis on perennials and hard-to-find plants of every kind. It is particularly good for epimediums, and offers a number of hybrids listed by no other nursery. The demonstration garden is also worth seeing: attractive mixed borders in a walled garden.

Owned by Teyl de Bordes
Number of gardeners 2
Size 0.4ha (1 acre)
NCCPG National Collections *Epimedium*

Manderston

DUNS, TD11 3PP

Tel 01361 883450 **Fax** 01361 882010
Website www.manderston.co.uk
Location On A6105 2 miles east of Duns.
Opening hours 2 pm – dusk; Sundays & Thursdays; mid-May to September, plus 31 May & 30 August. Parties at any time by appointment.
Admission fee Gardens only: Adults £3.50; Children £1.50.

The house is Edwardian, built in classical neo-Georgian style, and was the location for Channel 4's *The Edwardian Country House*. Below it are four expansive terraces with rich planting around clipped yews and hollies and fountains on the upper terrace. Below is a small lake with an ornamental boathouse and an 18th-century Chinese-style bridge. On the other side of the lake are the woodland gardens with a large collection of unusual species of trees and shrubs: the extensive collection of rhododendrons and azaleas dates back 100 years. This woodland garden is criss-crossed with numerous paths so that visitors can see all parts of it. On the north side of the house, after crossing wide lawns set about with mature trees, visitors reach the formal garden and herbaceous borders, both at their best in summer.

Features woodland garden with rhododendrons & azaleas; mature conifers; good herbaceous borders; good bedding out on the formal terraces; tea-room.

Owned by Lord Palmer
Number of gardeners 2
Size 22ha (56 acres)

Mellerstain

GORDON, TD3 6LG

Tel 01573 410225 **Fax** 01573 410636
Website www.mellerstain.com
Location 1 mile west of A6089 Kelso – Edinburgh road.
Opening hours 11.30 pm – 5.30 pm; daily, except Tuesdays & Saturdays; 9 to 12 April then 1 May to 30 September. Plus weekends in October.
Admission fee £3.

The house has extensive views south to the Cheviots: it was built by the Adams (father and son) between 1725 and 1778. It is set off by Sir Reginald Blomfield's formal garden, balustraded and terraced, but now rather covered by lichen. The garden is planted with floribunda roses and lavender. Beneath it runs the landscaped park, also laid out by William and Robert Adam, sauntering down to a lake. The whole picture is uncompromisingly grand.

 Features topiary; roses (mainly modern); Italian terraced garden by Sir Reginald Blomfield; licensed restaurant.

Owned by Mellerstain Trust
Number of gardeners 1
Size 1.8ha (4½ acres)

Mertoun Gardens

ST BOSWELLS, MELROSE, TD6 0EA

Tel 01835 823236 **Fax** 01835 822474
Location B6404, 2 miles north-east of St Boswells.
Opening hours 2 pm – 6 pm; Saturdays, Sundays & Public Holiday Mondays; April to September.
Admission fee Adults £2; OAPs £1.50; Children 50p.

Ⓟ ⓌⒸ ♿

Mertoun is the home of the Duke & Duchess of Sutherland, on the banks of the Tweed, with rolling lawns, herbaceous borders and azaleas. Its gardens are best known for their immaculately maintained, traditional, three-acre kitchen garden in which is situated Old Mertoun House. Here is a great variety of fruit trees, vegetables, flowers and a range of heated greenhouses and cold frames. Nearby is a circular dovecot dated 1567 and thought to be the oldest in the county. Mertoun also has a young arboretum, established since 1975, with a good selection of conifers and hardwoods, most of which have grown away very well. For many years now, the Dukes have grown a strain of pea which is said to

have come from one found by Lord Carnarvon in the tomb of Tutenkhamen.

 **Features** vegetables; herbs; plants under glass; daffodils; good herbaceous borders.

Owned by Mertoun Gardens Trust
Number of gardeners 3
Size 10.3ha (26 acres)

Monteviot House Gardens

JEDBURGH, TD8 6UQ

Tel 01835 830380/830704 **Fax** 01835 830288
Location Off A68 north of Jedburgh & B6400 to Nisbet.
Opening hours 12 noon – 5 pm; daily; April to October.
Admission fee Adults £2.50 (under review); Children free.

Ⓟ 🐕 ⓌⒸ ♿ ♿ 🌳 ☕

The gardens at Monteviot lie along a dramatic slope of the Teviot valley. The box-hedged herb garden and terrace along the front of the house have a breathtaking view of the river below. The sheltered terraced rose garden is Victorian: the river garden at the bottom was originally designed in the 1930s by Percy Cane. Italianate in inspiration, this sheltered garden slopes down between curved borders of herbaceous plants, shrubs, bulbs and roses, to a broad stone landing stage above the waters of the Teviot itself. In the nearby water garden, fed by a natural spring, three islands are linked by elegant curved wooden bridges. Here are bog plants and bamboos. The dramatic impact of the garden as a whole is heightened by the contrast between formal and the informal and by the way that the planting leads seamlessly through the different parts. The trees in the arboretum are exceptional: recent clearing has displayed them in their glory. *Fagus sylvatica* 'Riversii' is 30m high.

 Features fine collection of trees; water garden; Victorian rose garden; refreshments for pre-booked groups.

Number of gardeners 3

Priorwood Garden

MELROSE, TD6 9PX

Tel 01896 822493 **Fax** 01896 823181
Website www.nts.org.uk
Location Next to Melrose Abbey.
Opening hours 12 noon – 5 pm; daily; 9 to 12 April and 1 May to 24 December. Opens at 10 am in July & August and at 1 pm on Sundays.
Admission fee Adults £2; Concessions £1.50. Honesty box.

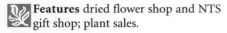

Priorwood is best known for its shop, which was recently extended and improved. Everything in the garden is geared towards dried flowers. The plants are chosen because they are suitable for drying, but they are also very colourful. Courses on drying flowers are also held here. In the orchard is a collection of historic apple cultivars, all organically grown.

 Features dried flower shop and NTS gift shop; plant sales.

Owned by The National Trust for Scotland
Number of gardeners 1

Traquair House

INNERLEITHEN, EH44 6PW

Tel 01896 830323 **Fax** 01896 830639
Website www.traquair.co.uk
Location Signed from Innerleithen.
Opening hours 12 noon – 5 pm; daily; 3 April to 31 October. 11 am – 4 pm in October.
Admission fee Grounds only: Adults £2.50; Children £1.25.

The main attraction is a large maze, planted in 1980 of beech and Leyland cypress. The house is a Catholic time-warp, said to be the oldest inhabited and most romantic house in Scotland. The Bear Gates in the park, once the main entrance to the estate, have been closed ever since Bonnie Prince Charlie passed through them for the last time in 1746.

 Features woodland garden; roses (mainly old-fashioned); good herbaceous borders; gift shop; restaurant serving lunch & tea; Traquair ale.

Owned by Mrs Maxwell Stuart
Number of gardeners 1
Size 12ha (30 acres)

Dumfries & Galloway

Broughton House Gardens

12 HIGH STREET, KIRKCUDBRIGHT, DG6 4JX

Tel & Fax 01557 330437
Location Signed in centre of Kirkcudbright.
Opening hours 11 am – 5 pm; daily; April to September. Plus 11 am – 4 pm in February & March and from 1 to 20 October.
Admission fee Donations.

E.A. Hornel the artist laid out the Japanese-style garden in the 1900s: it is the best known part of the garden here and featured in many of his portraits. Most of the rest is a 'Scottish' garden with a fine position above the River Dee. The house contains many of Hornel's works and an extensive collection of Scottish books. It will be closed for repair during 2004 and there may also be restrictions on access to the garden.

Owned by National Trust for Scotland
Number of gardeners 1
Size 0.8ha (2 acres)

Cally Gardens

GATEHOUSE OF FLEET, CASTLE DOUGLAS, DG7 2DJ

Tel none **Fax** 01557 815029
Website www.callygardens.co.uk
Location 12 miles west of Castle Douglas, on Gatehouse road off A75.

Opening hours 10 am – 5.30 pm; Saturdays & Sundays; plus 2 pm – 5.30 pm from Tuesday to Friday. Easter Sunday to 26 September.
Admission fee Adults £1.50; Children free.

Cally is a nursery for the horticultural *avant-garde*. It specialises in new and rare perennials, including some from wild-collected and botanic garden seed. Many are culled from a collection of over 3,500 plants, which makes it one of the most interesting in Scotland – the owner, Michael Wickenden, has an excellent eye for quality. The walled garden has 30 large borders where all these novelties and rarities can be seen growing. It is particularly good in September but it is also spectacular in early June, when 1,000 *Meconopsis betonicifolia* and 1,000 *M. x sheldonii* come into flower. The list of what is for sale changes by as much as half each year.

Owned by Michael Wickenden
Number of gardeners 2, plus students
Size 1.2ha (3 acres)

Craigieburn Classic Plants

BY MOFFAT, DG10 9LF

Tel 01683 221250
Location 2½ miles east of Moffat, on A708. On the left, beyond Craiglochan signs.
Opening hours 11 am – 6 pm; Friday to Sunday; Easter to mid-October. Other times by prior arrangement.
Admission fee Adults £2; Children (under 12) free.

Castle Kennedy Garden

Stair Estates, Rephad, Stranraer, DG9 8BX

Tel 01776 702024 **Fax** 01776 706248
Website www.castlekennedygardens.co.uk
Location 5 miles east of Stranraer on A75.
Opening hours 10 am – 5 pm; daily; April to
September.
Admission fee Adults £4; OAPs £3; Children £1.

Castle Kennedy is a ruined keep, destroyed in the first half of the 18th century when the bedding which was being aired for the return of the master, the 2nd Earl of Stair, caught fire. Its imposing bulk overlooks the walled garden, which is a riot of herbaceous colour in the summer, with gnarled old apple trees heavy with lichen in its midst, and some interesting tender shrubs, including bottle-brushes (*Callistemon* species) against its walls. The main horticultural interest lies outside, although the romantic planting continues. The 2nd Earl was a military man, and bequeathed to the garden its highly original structure of dashing rides, ridges and earthworks which represent battle encampments. They were made by the Royal Scots Greys and the Inniskilling Fusiliers when they should have been occupied suppressing religious dissent in the area. The extensive gardens now occupy an isthmus bounded by two lochs, with the ruined castle at one end, and its 19th-century replacement Lochinch Castle at the other – the place where *Buddleja* 'Lochinch' originated. There is a two-acre round pond, from which an ancient, slightly decrepit avenue of monkey puzzle trees leads off. These trees, *Araucaria araucana*, were grown from original seed sent from Chile: elsewhere are plants garnered by Stair forbears who subscribed to the collecting expeditions of Sir Joseph Hooker (*Rhododendron arboreum* for example). The

gardens generally are well stocked with rhododendrons, at their best in April and May. Later in the season, in an area known as the dancing green, a semi-circle of crimson *Embothrium coccineum* (June) is interplanted with flower-decked *Eucryphia* x *nymansensis* (August). There are more conventional flower borders in the area beside Lochinch Castle. In gardens as old as these, time has started to take its toll, but restoration and replanting is underway. The gardens recommend visitors to follow one of four graded walks to get the most out of their visit. For the energetic, this is a marvellous place just to wander at will.

Features woodland garden; good herbaceous borders; rhododendrons; embothriums; eucryphias; monkey puzzle avenue; tallest *Pittosporum tenuifolium* (17m.) in the British Isles, tallest *Rhododendron arboreum* (16m.) and three other record-breaking trees; plant centre; tea-room.

Owned by Lochinch Heritage Estate
Size 30ha (75 acres)

Craigieburn continues to develop and improve every year. The Wheatcrofts have close links with Nepal, and Himalayan plants – including many found by Janet – flourish in the mild, damp climate. The long (75m) herbaceous borders are now fully planted but, as in all good gardens, the Wheatcrofts are always in the process of changing, moving and adding to the contents. Craigieburn is particularly good for *Meconopsis*, of which they used to have a National Collection, and *Primula*. The mild climate means that *Lobelia tupa* grows to 2.5m and *Impatiens tinctoria* flourishes voluptuously. 'Meconopsis Month' from 20 May to 20 June is perhaps the peak time to visit, but there is always lots of interest to the plantsman. The nursery sells plants grown from the garden.

Features meconopsis; woodland plants; Himalayan plants.

Owned by Janet & Andrew Wheatcroft
Number of gardeners 2
Size 3.2ha (8 acres)

Elizabeth MacGregor

ELLENBANK, TONGLAND ROAD, KIRKCUDBRIGHT, DG6 4UU

Tel & Fax 01557 330620
Location On A711, 1 mile north of Kirkcudbright.
Opening hours 10 am – 5 pm; Mondays, Fridays & Saturdays; 23 April to 4 October.
Admission fee Free.

Violas – over 100 of them – are the speciality at this excellent nursery: some are not available from any other source. They are complemented by a lively selection of 500 other perennials for cottage gardens and mixed-border planting. The walled garden is worth a visit in its own right.

Features violas; perennials.

Owned by Elizabeth & Alasdair MacGregor
Size 0.2ha (½ acre), plus 0.6ha (1½ acres) stock beds & trials

Galloway House Gardens

GARLIESTON, NEWTON STEWART, DG8 8HF

Tel & Fax 01988 600680
Website www.garlieston.net/gardens
Location Off B7004 at Garlieston.
Opening hours 9 am – 5 pm; daily; March to October.
Admission fee £1.

Galloway House is where Neil McEacharn learnt to garden, before moving to Lake Maggiore to create the great gardens of Villa Taranto. A vast *Davidia involucrata* dates from his ownership, as do many of the tender trees and shrubs which he planted to take advantage of the mild maritime climate – eucryphias, for example. The fine conifers date back to the Earls of Galloway in the 19th century, while most of the *Rhododendron* species were planted after the war. The garden is still undergoing restoration, but is already a great pleasure to visit, especially in late spring.

Features snowdrops; rhododendrons & azaleas; daffodils; camellias; bluebells; camellia house; extensive new plantings.

Owned by Galloway House Gardens Trust
Number of gardeners 1
Size 26ha (65 acres)

Glenwhan Garden

DUNRAGIT, BY STRANRAER, DG9 8PH

Tel 01581 400222 **Fax** 01581 440397
Website www.glenwhangardens.co.uk
Location 1 mile off A75 at Dunragit Village. Follow brown tourist signs.
Opening hours 10 am – 5 pm; daily; April to September. And by appointment.
Admission fee Adults £3.50; OAPs £3; Children £1. RHS members free from August to October.

Glenwhan is a plantsman's garden which has been created since 1979 by its present owners, starting from moorland, bog and scrub. Ambitious in scale, the heart of the garden is a pair of lochans or bog lakes. Above them rises a series of roped terraces, planted with heathers, azaleas, small conifers, golden elders, hardy fuchsias and massed Rugosa roses. A small folly stands at the peak. In prospect, the whole design is beautifully composed and tranquil. From the folly there are extensive views across the garden to Luce Bay and the Mull of Galloway beyond. Tessa Knott's first plantings (in 1980) were a sturdy shelter belt of small trees, including native Scots pines, English oaks and mountain ashes. Now maturing very well, there are occasional glimpses through these lichen-stained ancients to the gorse scrub and bog which surround the garden. The shelter belt is a transitional feature: it is a refinement of the more primitive vegetation beyond the perimeter fence, and it introduces planting themes which are then developed within the garden, in the form, for example, of collections of choicer *Sorbus* and *Quercus* species (including *Q*. x *bushii* and *Q. dentata*). Pools have been cut out of the blackest peat to make an attractive sequence of grassy water gardens, planted with primula and meconopsis cultivars. Glenwhan is very much a plantsman's

garden, but Tessa Knott also uses plants to create effects, and she has capitalised upon the lie of the land to produce different habitats. The new plantings include large-leaved rhododendron species (*R. fictolacteum* for example), and some interesting southern hemisphere plants, including eucalyptus and olearias around the summerhouse, embothriums, eucryphias, callistemons and dicksonias. Another highlight is the dappled woodland walk with yet more new planting. Indeed many parts of this garden are 'work in progress' which will be worth returning to see again as they mature. New last year (2003) were an extension to the water gardens and a fine collection of hydrangeas.

Features woodland garden; roses (mainly old-fashioned); plantsman's collection of plants; bluebells; cistus; camellias; primulas; bog plants; trees and shrubs; many new *Rhododendron* species from collected seed; shop; nursery with interesting plants; licensed garden restaurant.

Owned by Mr & Mrs William Knott
Number of gardeners 2
Size 5ha (12½ acres)

Logan Botanic Garden

PORT LOGAN, STRANRAER, DG9 9ND

Tel 01776 860231 **Fax** 01776 860333
Website www.rbge.org.uk
Location 14 miles south of Stranraer on B7065.
Opening hours 10 am - 6 pm; daily; March to
October. Closes at 5 pm in March & October.
Admission fee Adults £3.50; Concessions £3;
Children £1; Family £8.

This extraordinarily exotic garden, started by the McDouall family in the 19th century, is now part of the Royal Botanic Garden Edinburgh. Logan's sheltered aspect and proximity to the warming waters of the Atlantic enable a wide range of tender and southern hemisphere plants to be grown out of doors. The bedding out of thousands of half-hardy perennials makes the garden a blaze of colour on bright sunny days. In the walled garden, overlooked by the slender remains of Castle Balzieland, there is a fine collection of established tree ferns (*Dicksonia antarctica*). They are underplanted with the smaller fern, *Blechnum chilense*, which creates an impression of lush fertility, as if the dicksonias have seeded themselves everywhere. The formal lily pond is partly framed by a diagonal avenue of cabbage palms (*Cordyline australis*) 10m high. Around the pond are waving wands of *Dierama pulcherrimum* and *Kniphofia*, and the air glints with dragonflies in summer. Among the trees which flower in the sheltered walls are a tall *Metrosideros umbellatus* and the flame tree, *Embothrium coccineum*. Also flowering freely here, as it does in other gardens in south-west Scotland, is *Eucryphia* x *nymansensis* 'Nymansay'. Beyond the brilliance of the walled garden, and past an avenue of Chusan palms (*Trachycarpus fortunei*), lies Logan's woodland garden. Some of its

pleasures are more hidden than others, but a spectacular specimen of *Magnolia campbellii* 'Charles Raffill' stands on the edge, in flower in April, and decked with swollen red pods by August. Look out in particular for plants from the southern hemisphere, including *Leptospermum lanigerum*, *Crinodendron hookerianum*, and the Chatham Island daisy bush, *Olearia semidentata* (syn. *O.* 'Henry Travers'). Do not miss the gunnera bog either, where this giant rhubarb-like plant grows so tall and thick that you can lose yourself under its prickly, slightly sinister canopy. In the Discovery Centre there are reference books, computers and microscopes which the visitor can use, perhaps to learn more about the Maddenia section of the genus *Rhododendron*, in which the garden specialises. Visitors can borrow innovative free audio guides, which are keyed to numbers marked on labels throughout the gardens. It is slightly surreal to see your fellow visitors wandering around clasping these futuristic wands, but the guide is informative and chatty.

Features sub-tropical plants; good herbaceous borders; tree ferns; cardiocrinums; gunnera; cordylines; trachycarpus palms; tender perennials (diascias, fuchsias, salvias); eucalyptus; shop selling books, gifts and local crafts; light meals & refreshments.

Owned by Royal Botanic Garden Edinburgh
Size 12ha (30 acres)

Threave Garden

CASTLE DOUGLAS, DG7 1RX

Tel 01556 502575 **Fax** 01556 502683
Website www.nts.org.uk
Location Off A75, 1 mile west of Castle Douglas.
Opening hours 9.30 am – sunset; daily; all year.
Walled garden & glasshouses close at 5 pm.
Admission fee Adults £5; Concessions £3.75. RHS
members free in April, May, September & October.

Threave is a teaching garden with a very
wide range of attractions – something to
interest every gardener, in fact. It has been
developed since 1960 with the needs of
students at the School of Horticulture,
garden-owners and tourists all in mind.
There are over 200 daffodil cultivars to
admire in spring; roses and colourful
herbaceous borders in summer; and good
autumn colour. A new Victorian-style
conservatory has recently been built in the
walled garden.

Features tallest *Alnus rubra* (23m.) in
the British Isles, and two other record
trees shop; plant centre; restaurant & snacks.

Owned by The National Trust for Scotland
Number of gardeners 2, plus 3 instructors
Size 26ha (65 acres)

Woodfall Gardens

GLASSERTON, WHITHORN, NEWTON
STEWART, DG8 8LY

Tel 01988 500692 **Fax** 01988 500080
Website www.woodfall-gardens.co.uk
Location By Gosserton Church, 2 miles south of
Whithorn.
Opening hours Thursdays 10 am – 5.30 pm;
Sundays 2 pm – 5.30 pm; 16 May to 19 September.
Admission fee Adults £2; Concessions £1.50;
Children free.

After the big house at Glasserton was
demolished in 1948, the large walled garden
was abandoned. The Roberts have brought
it to life again over the last ten years as a
private garden. A small area is devoted to
raising and selling box and yew for topiary,
parterres and knots. The rest is a garden of
great interest at all seasons, with a winter
garden, a rose garden, a grasses garden and a
fern garden, as well as colourful mixed
borders and a productive *potager*.

Features topiary plants; *Parthenocissus*;
plant sales area.

Owned by Lesley & David Roberts
Number of gardeners owners, plus 1 part-time
Size 1.2ha (3 acres)

FIFE

Cambo Gardens

KINGSBARNS, ST ANDREWS, KY16 8QD

Tel 01333 450054 **Fax** 01333 450987
Website www.camboestate.com
Location On A917 between Kingsbarns & Crail.
Opening hours 10 am – dusk; daily; all year.
Guided tours by arrangement.
Admission fee Adults £3; Children free.

Cambo's large romantic Victorian walled garden is built around the Cambo Burn, a most unusual feature which gives the garden its unique character. The burn is lined with willows, traversed by elegant wrought-iron bridges, and incorporates a waterfall. The atmosphere is informal, with plantings of herbaceous perennials (many of them unusual) in the natural style. There are also masses of spring bulbs, a lilac walk (26 cultivars), rambler roses, and fine herbaceous borders for summer and autumn. The garden also has an ornamental *potager* which supplies fruit and vegetables to the handsome Victorian house. Outside are 70 acres of woodland walks leading down to the sea, spectacular in early spring when carpeted with aconites, snowflakes and snowdrops (they are hoping to be awarded a National Collection of *Galanthus*) and again when the meadows are purple with colchicums.

Features roses (mainly old-fashioned); daffodils; snowflakes; aconites; colchicum meadows; autumn colour; plants for sale.

Owned by Mr & Mrs T.P.N. Erskine
Number of gardeners 3
Size 1ha (2½ acres), plus 28ha (70 acres) woodland

Falkland Palace

FALKLAND, CUPAR, KY15 7BU

Tel 01337 857397 **Fax** 01337 857980
Website www.nts.org.uk
Location On A912, 11 miles north of Kirkcaldy. 10 miles from M90, Jct 8.
Opening hours 10 am – 6 pm; daily; March to October. Sundays 1 pm – 5 pm.
Admission fee Adults £3.50; Concessions £2.60.

The palace at Falkland is old: it dates from the first half of the 16th century. Today's flower garden was built in 1952 by Percy Cane. The pastiche of a Scottish renaissance garden has a herb garden in the Jacobean style, an astrolabe walk and formal parterres prettily planted in pastel colours.

Features gift shop; plant centre.

Owned by The National Trust for Scotland
Number of gardeners 2
Size 4.4ha (11 acres)

Hill of Tarvit

CUPAR, KY15 5PB

Tel & Fax 01334 653127
Website www.nts.org.uk
Location Off A916, 2½ miles south of Cupar.
Opening hours 9.30 am – sunset; daily; all year.
Admission fee Adults £2; Concessions £1 in honesty box. RHS members free.

Both house and garden at Hill of Tarvit were designed by Lorimer. The formal garden is not so well planted and maintained as it used to be, but the Trust has begun to restore and replant the borders on the top terrace in an Edwardian style.

 Features plants for sale; tea-room in house (open in summer).

Owned by The National Trust for Scotland
Number of gardeners 2
Size 8ha (20 acres)

Kellie Castle

PITTENWEEN, KY10 2RF

Tel 01333 720271 **Fax** 01333 720736
Website www.nts.org.uk
Location On B9171, 3 miles north-west of Pittenween.
Opening hours 9.30 am – sunset; daily; all year.
Admission fee Adults £2.

Kellie Castle was Sir Robert Lorimer's own family house: it was he who initiated the reconstruction of the garden in its present form. The walled garden is no more than one acre in extent, but strong lines and thick planting create a sense of both space and enclosure. Much of the planting is a modern re-interpretation of Lorimer's original design: later family members have made alterations and additions. The organic walled garden contains a fine collection of old-fashioned roses, fruit trees and herbaceous plants: there are displays in the summerhouse about the history of the walled garden. The yew hedges are threaded with scarlet *Tropaeolum speciosum*.

 **Features** extended collection of historic vegetables; gift shop; tea-room.

Owned by The National Trust for Scotland
Number of gardeners 2
Size 6.4ha (16 acres)

St Andrews Botanic Garden

THE CANONGATE, ST ANDREWS, KY16 8RT

Tel 01334 477178 **Fax** 01334 476452
Website www.st-andrews-botanic.org
Location A915, Largo Road, then entrance in The Canongate.
Opening hours 10 am – 7 pm (4 pm October – April); daily; all year.
Admission fee Adults £2; OAPs & Children £1. RHS members free.

The botanic garden at St Andrews is currently undergoing much improvement. The garden's main asset, the peat, rock and water complex (crag, scree, moraine, alpine meadow and bog) is being repaired and replanted. Work on the cactus house has been completed, a new alpine house is now open, and the orchid house re-opened recently. There is also a tropical house and a house for Maddenia rhododendrons. The garden caters particularly well for children and is interesting to visit at every season.

Features woodland garden; rock garden; rhododendrons & azaleas; plants under glass; fine collection of trees; peat beds; ferns; heath garden; order beds; herbaceous borders.

Owned by St Andrews University, but managed by Fife Council.
Number of gardeners 5
Size 7.2ha (18 acres)

GRAMPIAN

Blackhills

BY ELGIN, MORAY, IV30 3QU

Tel 01343 842223 **Fax** 01343 843136
Website www.blackhills.co.uk
Location 1 mile south of Lhanbryde, near Elgin on the B9103.
Opening hours 12 noon – 6 pm; 16 & 23 May. And by appointment.
Admission fee Adults £1.50; Children free.

Blackhills is a magnificent collection of rhododendrons in two steep-sided glacial valleys: these possess a microclimate which allows many plants to grow that are normally considered too tender for the north-east coast of Scotland. The rhododendrons were planted throughout the 20th century by successive generations of the Christie family, along with many other Himalayan and Chinese plants, in a woodland garden which is now fully mature. There are about 360 different rhododendron species growing at Blackhills, all of wild origin: most were collected in the Himalayas, some came from North America, Central Asia and Northern Europe. The garden now contains one of the finest and most extensive private collections of species rhododendrons in the world. Some of the species self-seed.

Features rhododendrons.

Owned by T.S. Christie
Number of gardeners 1
Size 20ha (50 acres)

Brodie Castle

BRODIE, FORRES, MORAY, IV36 2TE

Tel 01309 641371 **Fax** 01309 641600
Website www.nts.org.uk
Location Signed from A96. 4½ miles west of Forres.
Opening hours Grounds: 9.30 am – sunset; daily; all year.
Admission fee £1 in honesty box.

Brodie Castle came to the National Trust for Scotland in 1980. It sits in a landscaped park and there are rhododendrons in the woodland policies, but Brodie is famous, above all, for its daffodils. Many were bred here at the turn of the 19th century and the Trust has tried assiduously to identify, propagate and distribute them more widely. They are a glorious sight when they bloom in the lawns around the baronial battlements.

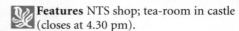**Features** NTS shop; tea-room in castle (closes at 4.30 pm).

Owned by The National Trust for Scotland
Number of gardeners 6, plus 2 part-time
Size 32ha (80 acres)
NCCPG National Collections Narcissus

Crathes Castle

BANCHORY, AB31 5QJ

Tel 01330 844525 **Fax** 01330 844797
Website www.nts.org.uk
Location On A93, 15 miles west of Aberdeen.
Opening hours 9 am – sunset; daily; all year.
Admission fee Adults £7; Concessions £5.25.

Crathes is famous for its walled garden, which started as a kitchen garden and was later developed as a flower garden, both before World War I and in the 1920s and 1930s. It is divided into eight distinct gardens, each with its own character. These include a white border, a yellow enclosure known as the Golden Garden, a misty blue garden, and a dreamy high summer border with pastel shades for long Highland evenings. The garden is intensively planted to give colour all the year round. Some of the topiary yew hedges date back to 1702.

 Features current holder of Sandford Award; tallest *Zelkova* x *verschaffeltii* in the British Isles, and four further tree records; NTS shop; plant centre; restaurant/café open most of the year.

Owned by The National Trust for Scotland
Number of gardeners 5
Size 1.5ha (3¾ acres)
NCCPG National Collections *Dianthus* (Malmaison carnations)

Cruickshank Botanic Garden

St Machar Drive, Aberdeen, AB24 3UU

Tel 01224 272704 **Fax** 01224 272703
Location Follow signs for Aberdeen University and/or Old Aberdeen. Entrance in The Chanonry, not St Machar Drive.
Opening hours 9 am – 4.30 pm; Monday – Friday; all year. Plus 2 pm – 5 pm; Saturdays & Sundays; May to September.
Admission fee Free.

(wc) (&)

Cruickshank Botanic Garden was founded in 1898 for the teaching and study of botany at the University of Aberdeen. Its 12 acres still have an educational element but also serve as an amenity for the wider public. Its

leading features include: a rock garden for alpine plants and bulbs, where wild orchids seed around; an arboretum, planted quite recently – in about 1970 – with natives, exotics and garden cultivars, many of them now semi-mature; collections of native plants, including all the endemic *Sorbus* species of the British Isles; and a rose garden which has been laid out to illustrate the history of the rose in cultivation. The garden is well-maintained and – like all botanic gardens – worth visiting at any time of the year. It is also supported by an enthusiastic Friends organisation. The latest development is a wildflower meadow.

 Features lots of plants; roses (mainly old-fashioned); rock garden; good herbaceous borders; fine collection of trees; stone troughs; peat beds; Scottish upland plants; *Meconopsis* x *sheldonii*.

Owned by Aberdeen University
Number of gardeners 3
Size 4.4ha (11 acres)

Drum Castle

Drumoak, Banchory, AB31 3EY

Tel 01330 811204 **Fax** 01330 811962
Website www.drum-castle.org.uk
Location Off A93, 10 miles west of Aberdeen.
Opening hours Grounds: 9.30 – sunset; daily; all year. Garden: 12.30 pm – 5.30 pm; daily; April to September. Garden opens at 10 am from June to August.
Admission fee Adults £2.50; Concessions £1.90.

The gardens at Drum are modern – begun in 1991 with the intention of providing an appropriate historic setting for the castle and a place where old Scottish roses could be grown. There is a knot garden planted with herbs in the style of the early 17th century and a formal garden with *allées* and topiary to represent the early 18th century. The Victorian-style garden has a decorative, rose-covered catenary and the sunken garden a collection of modern roses, shrubs and perennials

 Features shop; small tea-room.

Owned by The National Trust for Scotland
Number of gardeners 2
Size 8ha (20 acres)

Duthie Park

POLMUIR ROAD, ABERDEEN, AB11 7SL

Tel 01224 522984
Location By the river, in the Ferryhill area of Aberdeen.
Opening hours 9.30 am – dusk; daily; all year. Closed 1 January & 25 December.
Admission fee Free.

Duthie Park is one of Scotland's top tourist attractions: 350,000 people visit it every year – and it is free. The park was laid out in 1883, but substantially improved when David Welch was director in the 1970s and 1980s. Its main attraction in summer is the Rose Mountain, a massed display of bright modern roses, themselves quite a feature of Aberdeen's roadside landscaping. But the jewel in the crown is the Winter Gardens, a series of linked glasshouses with beautiful and instructive plant displays. They include the Bromeliad House, Cacti & Succulents hall, Victorian Corridor; Floral Hall, Corridor or Perfumes and Fern House.

Owned by Aberdeen City Council
Number of gardeners 9

Kildrummy Castle

KILDRUMMY, ALFORD, AB33 8RA

Tel 01975 571203/571277
Location On A97, off A944.
Opening hours 10 am – 5 pm; daily; April to October.
Admission fee Adults £2.50; Children free.

Kildrummy has a glen-garden, laid out about 100 years ago. The richly planted pools and ponds are complemented by a plantsman's collection on the hillside, and a large mature rock garden made from the natural sandstone. It is one of the most romantic gardens in Scotland.

 **Features** roses (mainly old-fashioned); plantsman's collection of plants; fine collection of trees; autumn colour; heathers; tea & coffee.

Owned by Kildrummy Castle Garden Trust
Number of gardeners 2½
Size 8ha (20 acres)

Leith Hall

KENNETHMONT, HUNTLY, AB54 4NQ

Tel 01464 831216 **Fax** 01464 831594
Website www.nts.org.uk
Location On B9002, 1 mile west of Kennethmont.
Opening hours 9.30 am – sunset; daily; all year.
Admission fee Adults £2.50; Concessions £1.90. RHS members free.

From this garden's historic past come two ponds and an ice house, but richly planted borders are the pride of Leith Hall today: they are full of colour all through the summer. Also impressive is the rock garden, restored and replanted by that most successful of societies, the Scottish Rock Garden Club. Leith gets better and better.

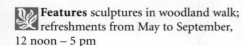 **Features** sculptures in woodland walk; refreshments from May to September, 12 noon – 5 pm

Owned by The National Trust for Scotland
Number of gardeners 2
Size 2.4ha (6 acres)

Pitmedden

ELLON, ABERDEEN, AB41 7PD

Tel 01651 842352 **Fax** 01651 843188
Website www.nts.org.uk
Location 1 mile west of Pitmedden on A920.
Opening hours 10 am – 5.30 pm; daily; May to September.
Admission fee Adults £5; Concessions £3.75; Children £1.

The spectacular formal garden at Pitmedden was meticulously created in the 1950s by the National Trust for Scotland, using 17th-century Scottish designs. Three of the four parterres came from patterns associated with Holyroodhouse: the fourth is an heraldic design based on the coat-of-arms of Sir Alexander Seton, who first laid out a garden here in 1675. The result has three miles of box hedging and uses 40,000 bedding plants every summer. It may not be completely authentic, but it certainly looks genuine enough, as well as being both impressive, satisfying and peaceful.

Features plants for sale; tea-room.

Owned by The National Trust for Scotland
Number of gardeners 5
Size 6ha (15 acres)

HIGHLAND

Abriachan Gardens

LOCH NESS SIDE, BY INVERNESS,
IV3 8LA

Tel & Fax 01463 861232
Website www.lochnessgarden.com
Location Just off the A82.
Opening hours 9 am – 7 pm (5 pm from October to March); daily; all year.
Admission fee Adults £2; OAPs £1; Children 20p. RHS members free from March to October.

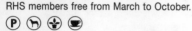

These unique gardens on the shores of Loch Ness wind their way through the native hazel and oak woodland and offer spectacular views down the Great Glen. Many choice plants are grown here: their specialities are hardy perennials and shrubs. There are extensive garden walks among dry stone dykes and raised beds.

Features good modern garden; herbaceous plants; geraniums, helianthemums and Barnhaven primulas; hot drinks machine.

Owned by Mr & Mrs D. Davidson
Number of gardeners 2
Size 1.6ha (4 acres)

Allangrange

MUNLOCHY, BLACK ISLE, IV8 8NZ

Tel 0146 3811249 **Fax** 0146 3811407
Location Signed off A9, 5 miles north of Inverness.
Opening hours 2 pm – 5.30 pm; 2 May & 13 June; or by appointment.
Admission fee £2.

Colour gardening by Mrs Cameron, a botanical artist, has made this one of the loveliest summer gardens in the British Isles. The spring flowers are good, too. Prints of some of her drawings are also available.

Features woodland garden; roses (mainly old-fashioned); primulas; rhododendrons; colour borders; teas in house.

Owned by Major Allan Cameron
Number of gardeners 1
Size 1.2ha (3 acres)

Ardfearn Nursery

BUNCHREW, INVERNESS, IV3 8RH

Tel 01463 243250 **Fax** 01463 711713
Location On A862, 5 miles west of Inverness.
Opening hours 9 am – 5 pm; daily.

Alpines, ericaceous plants and shrubs and trees are produced at this intensive nursery in a lovely Highland farmstead. It is particularly good for plants from New Zealand and the Himalayas and, above all, for primulas. But the stock is always changing and expanding – especially of rare and unusual plants – which is what draws back both novices and the nursery's discriminating clientele year after year.

Owned by Messrs Jim & Alasdair Sutherland

Attadale Gardens

STRATHCARRON, WESTER ROSS,
IV54 8YX

Tel 01520 722217 or 722603 **Fax** 01520 722546
Website www.attadale.com
Location ON A890 between Strathcarron & South
Strome.
Opening hours 10 am – 5.30 pm; Monday –
Saturday; April to October. Coaches by prior
arrangement only.
Admission fee Adults £3; Children £1.

The gardens at Attadale were started in the
1890s: many rhododendrons, azaleas and
specimen trees date from that time. The
recent expansion of planting began in the
1980s, with over 2,000 trees and shrubs,
which are now underplanted with irises,
candelabra primulas, gunneras and
bamboos. The ponds and waterfalls are
spanned by bridges and richly planted with
marginals and waterlilies. In the fern
garden, backed by dripping black rocks, a
new geodesic dome (2003) houses an exotic
fern collection. There is also a Japanese
garden and a kitchen garden. The nursery
specialises in bog plants – among them,
meconopsis, primulas and rodgersias.

Features rhododendrons; meconopsis;
primulas; bog plants; nursery.

Owned by Mr & Mrs Ewen Macpherson
Number of gardeners 3½
Size 8ha (20 acres)

Auchgourish Gardens & Arboretum

STREET OF KINCARDINE, BY BOAT OF
GARTEN, PH24 3BY

Tel 01479 831464 **Fax** 01479 831672
Website www.falsyde.sol.co.uk

Location Brown signs from Aviemore & Inverness.
Opening hours 10 am – 5 pm; daily; March to
October. 11 am – 3 pm in winter.
Admission fee Adults £3.50; Children free.

Auchgourish is a new garden, designed as a
tourist attraction. It majors on a Japanese
garden, a series of oriental rock-gardens,
heather beds and collections of Scottish
plants, wild and cultivated.

Features Scottish native plants;
oriental gardens; surplus plants for
sale.

Owned by Iain Brodie of Falsyde
Number of gardeners 1
Size 4ha (10 acres)

Cawdor Castle

CAWDOR, NAIRN, IV12 5RD

Tel 01667 404401 **Fax** 01667 404674
Website www.cawdorcastle.com
Location Between Inverness & Nairn on B9090.
Opening hours 10 am – 5.30 pm; daily; 1 May to
10 October.
Admission fee £3.50. RHS members free in May,
June, September & October.

Cawdor Castle could claim to be the most
romantic castle in the Highlands – the 14th-
century home of the Thanes of Cawdor. It
has several gardens: the earliest dates from
the 16th century and has the maze. There is
also an 18th-century flower garden with
large herbaceous borders and roses and a
19th-century wild garden with a good
collection of rhododendrons and spring
bulbs as well as splendid trees. Recent
additions include a holly maze, a laburnum
walk and coloured planting schemes. Earth,
Purgatory and Paradise are somehow
represented in the new plantings, but they
are best enjoyed as colours and shapes. The

effect is neither cranky nor grand, just extremely charming. The Auchindoune garden, originally planted in the 1920s with plants brought back by Lord Cawdor from his expedition to the Himalayas with Frank Kingdon Ward, is being restored with almost all the plants they brought back from the Tsangpo Gorges: it open only by prior appointment.

 Features woodland garden; roses (mainly old-fashioned); fruit; good herbaceous borders; good late summer plantings; gift shop; licensed restaurant in castle.

Owned by The Dowager Countess Cawdor
Number of gardeners 4
Size 1.4ha (3½ acres)

Coiltie Garden

DIVACH, DRUMNADROCHIT, IV63 6XW

Tel 01456 450219
Location Take the small uphill road off the A82 Drumnadrochit to Divach for about 2 miles.
Opening hours 12 noon – 7 pm; daily; June & July.
Admission fee Adults £2; Children free.

There was little except a few old trees and a 30m waterfall when the Nelsons came to Coiltie in 1980 and took on the neglected and overgrown Victorian garden. They decided not to reconstruct it, but to lay a new informal one on the sloping site, and planted it with trees (100+), hedges, shrubs, climbers, herbaceous plants and lots of roses. Below is a steep ravine with ancient woodlands.

 Features roses; trees; mixed borders.

Owned by Mr & Mrs David Nelson
Number of gardeners 1
Size 1.6ha (4 acres)

Dunrobin Castle Gardens

GOLSPIE, SUTHERLAND, KW10 6SF

Tel 01408 633177 **Fax** 01408 634081
Website www.great-houses-scotland.co.uk
Location 1 mile north of Golspie on A9.
Opening hours Dawn to dusk; daily; all year round. Castle gardens: 10.30 am – 5.30 pm (4.30 pm in April, May & October); 1 April to 15 October. Last entry 30 minutes before closing.
Admission fee Castle & garden: Adults £6.60; OAPs £4.50, but subject to review. Reductions for groups. RHS members free. Gardens open free in winter.

The grand terraced gardens at Dunrobin were laid out in 1850 by Sir Charles Barry, architect of the Houses of Parliament. Their formal style, striding down to the Dornoch Forth, is appropriate to the French-style *château*. Three parterres surround the fountains, two bedded out traditionally and one planted with hardy geraniums and myosotis, underplanted with tulips and lilies. Recent restoration and replanting have produced a line of whitebeams, gunneras, new rhododendrons and three herbaceous borders. Another addition has been some 20 wooden pyramids planted with clematis and climbing roses – very pretty. It is good to see these old and important gardens on the up again. In summer the gardens are open for £2 a head from 5 pm to 8.30 pm in the evening.

 Features woodland garden; topiary; roses (mainly modern); good herbaceous borders; formal gardens; gift shop; tea-room in castle.

Owned by The Sutherland Trust
Number of gardeners 3
Size 2ha (5 acres)

The Hydroponicum

ACHILTIBUIE, ULLAPOOL, IV26 2YG

Tel 01854 622202 **Fax** 01854 622201
Location Signed off A835, 25 miles north of Ullapool.
Opening hours 10 am – 6 pm; daily; 29 March to
30 September. Guided tours on the hour (last one at
5 pm). Plus tours at 12 noon & 2 pm from Monday
to Friday in October. SGS open days on 16 May &
22 August.
Admission fee Adults £4.75; Concessions £3.50;
Children £2.75.

The Hydroponicum has three growing
houses, each individually heated and
featuring plants from different climatic zones.
Salads, herbs and tree fruits grow in the
'cottage garden' house. Tomatoes, citrus fruit
and olives fill the 'South of France' house.
And the 'Canary Island zone' is planted with
vines, figs, tamarillos and bananas. 'Planted'
is not quite the right word: hydroponics are
all about soilless cultivation – essential in
places like Saudi Arabia but a small miracle
here in the north-west of Scotland.

Features hydroponic culture; fruit
under glass; café.

Owned by Viscount Gough
Number of gardeners 2
Size 0.1ha (¼ acre) glasshouses & 0.8ha (2 acres)
grounds

Inverewe

POOLEWE, ROSS AND CROMARTY,
IV22 2LG

Tel 01445 781200 **Fax** 01445 781497
Website www.nts.org.uk
Location On A832, 6 miles north-east of Gairloch.
Opening hours 9.30 am – 9 pm; daily; all year.
Closes at 4 pm from November to March.
Admission fee Adults £7; Concessions £5.25;
Children £1.

Inverewe is one of the wonders of the
horticultural world, a subtropical garden in
the north-west Highlands. Its position on a
sheltered peninsular, warmed by the Gulf
Stream, explains the luxuriance of its
plantings. It is also the reason why, even so
far north, it has much to interest the
plantsman at every time of the year. The
garden owes its origins to Osgood
Mackenzie, who from 1862 to 1922 planted
windbreaks to protect more delicate exotics
within. Spectacular large-leaved Himalayan
rhododendrons, magnolias, eucalyptus, tree
ferns, palms and tender rarities are
underplanted with drifts of blue poppies
and candelabra primulas. Among Inverewe's
record trees are specimens of *Eucalyptus
cordata* and *Salix magnifica*, neither of
which would be fully hardy in the home
counties of England. Inverewe is
exceptionally well maintained, though
perhaps best on a sunny, dry day in May,
before the midges breed.

Features tallest *Eucalyptus cordata*
(30m.) in the British Isles, and three
further record trees; large shop; plant centre;
excellent new restaurant.

Owned by The National Trust for Scotland
Number of gardeners 8
Size 20ha (50 acres)
NCCPG National Collections *Olearia*;
Brachyglottis; *Rhododendron* (Barbatum, Glischra &
Maculifera sections)

Jack Drake

INSHRIACH ALPINE NURSERY,
AVIEMORE, INVERNESS-SHIRE,
PH22 1QS

Tel 01540 651287 **Fax** 01540 651656
Website www.drakesalpines.com
Location 4 miles south of Aviemore. Take B970 to
Inverdruie. Turn right, ½ mile after the Spey Bridge.

Opening hours 10 am – 5 pm; daily; March to October.
Admission fee Free. Donations welcome.

For more than 60 years this famous Highland nursery has been a Mecca for devotees of alpine and rock garden plants. It offers a large number of selected or collected forms. True alpines rub shoulders with herbaceous plants for wild and bog gardens. The nursery is laid out with demonstration gardens – screes, peat walls, wild gardens and bog gardens. A new woodland walk is under development.

Features Scotland's premier alpine nursery; primulas; meconopsis; gentians; heathers; tea-room.

Owned by John & Gunnbjørg Borrowman
Size 0.8ha (2 acres)

Leckmelm Arboretum

BY ULLAPOOL, IV23 2RH

Location 3 miles south of Ullapool on the A835.
Opening hours 10 am – 6 pm; daily; April to September.
Admission fee Adults £2; Children free.

The Leckmelm arboretum was laid out in the 1870s, and it is from those days that many of the finest rhododendron species and trees date – wellingtonias, cedars, monkey puzzles and a huge weeping beech (*Fagus sylvatica* 'Pendula'). Some of the trees are record-breakers, including an *Abies amabilis* 40m high, a good *Chamaecyparis lawsoniana* 'Wisselii', a *Thujopsis dolabrata* and a *Kalopanax pictus*, whose presence at such a northerly point may be explained by the mild climate. The Troughtons have taken advantage of the arboretum's position on the shores of Loch Broom to make new plantings in recent years: they have put in

such large-leaved rhododendrons as *R. sinogrande* and *R. macabeanum*, and even a selection of dicksonias and palms.

**Features** ancient trees; good rhododendrons.

Owned by Mr & Mrs Peter Troughton
Number of gardeners 1
Size 5ha (12½ acres)

Lochalsh Woodland Garden

BALMACARA, BY KYLE OF LOCHALSH, ROSS, IV40 8DN

Tel 01599 566325 **Fax** 01599 566359
Website www.nts.org.uk
Location On A87, 3 miles east of Kyle.
Opening hours 9 am – sunset; daily; all year.
Admission fee Adults £2; Concessions £1. Honesty box.

This woodland garden is becoming much better known, and deservedly. The structure is about 100 years old – tall pines, oaks and larches with ornamental underplantings started in the late 1960s. Rhododendrons from Euan Cox at Glendoick came first: newer plantings include collections of hardy ferns, bamboos, fuchsias, hydrangeas and Maddenia rhododendrons, as well as plants from Tasmania and New Zealand. The season of interest extends from early spring well into autumn.

Features plants for sale; shop.

Owned by The National Trust for Scotland
Number of gardeners 1
Size 5.2ha (13 acres)

The Castle of Mey

THURSO, CAITHNESS, KW14 8XH

Tel 01808 851473 **Fax** 01808 521466
Website www.castleofmey.org.uk
Location On A836 between Thurso & John
O'Groats.
Opening hours 11 am – 4.30 pm; Tuesday to
Saturday; 18 May to 29 July and 11 August to 30
September. And 2 pm – 5 pm on Sundays.
Admission fee Adults £7; Children £3.

The garden attached to Queen Elizabeth the
Queen Mother's summer home has been
open for the SGS for many years, but now it
is open almost continuously in season,
unless required by members of the royal
family. It was laid out in about 1820, and
protected by the Great Wall of Mey, 12ft
high. As well as a productive kitchen garden,
Mey has colour-graded borders with many
of the Queen's favourite plants.

Features flowers borders; kitchen
garden; plants & produce for sale.

Owned by The Queen Elizabeth Castle of Mey
Trust
Number of gardeners 3
Size 1.6ha (4 acres)

Tournaig House

POOLEWE, ACHNASHEEN, IV22 2LH

Tel 01445 781250
Location 1½ miles north of Inverewe.
Opening hours 26 May & 30 July, for SGS. And at
any reasonable time, by appointment.
Admission fee Adults £2; Children free. Please, no
groups.

Tournaig has magnificent woodland walks,
lined with rhododendrons and azaleas, and
views across Loch Ewe. But there are rare
shrubs, water gardens and fine herbaceous
plants too – including meconopsis,
candelabra primulas and lysichitons.

Features plants; teas on open days.

Owned by Lady Horlick
Number of gardeners 1

LOTHIAN

Binny Plants

ECCLESMACHAN ROAD, BROXBURN, EH52 6NL

Tel 01506 858931 **Fax** 01506 858155
Website www.binnyplants.co.uk
Location 2 miles north of Uphall on B8048.
Opening hours 10 am – 5 pm; daily; March to October. Phone first in winter months.
Admission fee Free.

This excellent nursery has an expanding range. It claims to have Scotland's largest range of ornamental grasses and a massive range of hardy ferns and other plants for the shady garden, as well as hundreds of perennials and shrubs. Its irises (100+ cultivars), peonies, euphorbias, geraniums, hostas and small shrubs are especially noteworthy. The catalogue has good, helpful plant descriptions, with some shrewd observations that give the reader confidence.

Owned by Billy Carruthers

Dalmeny House

ROSEBERY ESTATES, SOUTH QUEENSFERRY, EH30 9TQ

Tel 0131 331 1888 **Fax** 0131 331 1788
Website www.dalmeny.co.uk
Location B924 off A90.
Opening hours 2 pm – 5.30 pm; Sunday – Tuesday; July & August. And for SGS in snowdrop time.
Admission fee Grounds only: free.

The grounds at Dalmeny are extensive, and visitors are encouraged to see the valley walk with rhododendrons, wellingtonias and other conifers. But the estate concentrates upon the house and its remarkable collections rather than promoting the gardens and grounds.

 Features woodland garden; snowdrops; mature conifers; rhododendrons & azaleas; wellingtonias; refreshments.

Owned by The Earl of Rosebery

Inveresk Lodge

24 INVERESK VILLAGE, MUSSELBURGH, EH21 7TE

Tel 01721 722502
Website www.nts.org.uk
Location A6124 south of Musselburgh, 6 miles east of Edinburgh.
Opening hours 10 am – 6 pm; daily; all year.
Admission fee Adults £2; Concessions £1. Honesty box.

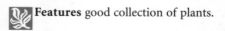

The modern plantings in this terraced, Victorian garden have much of horticultural interest. In the fine Edwardian conservatory are an aviary and some tree ferns. Elsewhere are good herbaceous borders and interesting climbing plants. Graham Stuart Thomas designed the rose borders.

Features good collection of plants.

Owned by The National Trust for Scotland
Number of gardeners 1
Size 5.2ha (13 acres)
NCCPG National Collections *Tropaeolum* species

Lauriston Castle

2A CRAMOND ROAD SOUTH,
DAVIDSONS MAINS, EDINBURGH,
EH4 5QD

Tel 0131 336 2060 **Fax** 0131 312 7165
Location 3 miles from city centre; take Queensferry
Road (A90) to Davidsons Mains.
Opening hours 8 am – dusk; daily; all year.
Admission fee Free.

Lauriston Castle has an historic 30-acre
garden but the main attraction is the new
Japanese garden, the largest in Britain, made
to celebrate the twinning of Kyoto
Prefecture with Edinburgh. Highlights
include a magnificent view across the Firth
of Forth, cherry trees in spring, and spring-
flowering bulbs.

Features Japanese garden.

Owned by Lauriston Castle Trust
Number of gardeners 2
Size 0.8ha (2 acres)

Malleny House Garden

BALERNO, EH14 7AF

Tel 0131 449 2283
Website www.nts.org.uk
Location In Balerno, south-west of Edinburgh, off
A70.
Opening hours 10 am – 6 pm (or dusk, if earlier);
daily; all year.
Admission fee Adults £2; Concessions £1.
Honesty box.

Malleny is one of the National Trust for
Scotland's best gardens, much praised for its
'personal' quality. The 19th-century shrub
roses are richly underplanted with
herbaceous plants which carry the display
through into the autumn: there is a sense of
opulence about the garden throughout the
summer and autumn. The magnificent
conservatory creates quite another
dimension, as do the huge cones of yew
topiary, relics of a 17th-century formal
garden. It is, above all, a very peaceful
garden – and far too little visited.

Owned by The National Trust for Scotland
Number of gardeners 1
Size 1.2ha (3 acres)
NCCPG National Collections *Rosa* (19th-century
shrubs)

Suntrap Garden

43 GOGARBANK, EDINBURGH,
EH12 9BY

Tel 0131 339 7283
Location 1 mile west of Edinburgh bypass,
between A8 & A71.
Opening hours 10 am – 6 pm (4 pm in winter);
daily; all year, but with limited facilities at weekends.
SGS Open day for 2004 is 23 May.
Admission fee Adults £1; Children free.

Suntrap has three acres of demonstration
gardens attached to Oatridge College: it is
one of the best places in Lothian to learn
how to be a better gardener. It has been
developed as a life-long learning centre,
with courses and events throughout the
year. The features include island beds, a rock
garden, a peat garden, sculptures, vegetable
plots, a sensory garden, annual borders –
and much more.

Features woodland garden; vegetables;
roses (mainly modern); plants under
glass; daffodils; good herbaceous borders;
alpine plants; 'Italian' garden; peat walls.

Owned by Oatridge College
Number of gardeners 2
Size 1.2ha (3 acres)

Royal Botanic Garden Edinburgh

20A INVERLEITH ROW, EDINBURGH, EH3 5LR

Tel 0131 552 7171 **Fax** 0131 248 2901
Website www.rbge.org.uk
Location 1 mile north of Princes Street.
Opening hours 10 am – 7 pm; daily; April to September. Closes at 6 pm in March & October, 4 pm from November to February. Closed 1 January & 25 December.
Admission fee Free. Admission charge at the glasshouses. Guided tours available (£3) at 11 am & 2 pm, daily from April to September.

The Royal Botanic Garden Edinburgh has an important amenity function for both tourists and local people, but is principally a collection of plants of scientific and educational importance. It is internationally renowned for its collection of plants from temperate and tropical regions around the world including: plants from the Himalaya and west China; the rhododendron collection – the best in the world; the collection of orchids from south-east Asia; alpines; and the flora of Arabia. So far as possible, these have been displayed within the gardens in a naturalistic setting which hints at their native habitats. The landscaping in the glasshouses is particularly good and recreates a whole series of different environments from arid deserts to humid tropics. It goes without saying that everything is extremely well labelled and the standard of maintenance is among the highest in any garden anywhere in the world. The members of staff are also invariably courteous and helpful. The rock garden is over two acres in extent and composed of many different micro-habitats, most of them helped by the naturally light sandy soil and low rainfall. More than 5,000 species (from areas as different as high mountains, the arctic regions and the Mediterranean) flourish in the mounds and gullies of sandstone and conglomerate alongside the stream and in the screes. The heath garden has recently been restored as a Scottish moorland complete with Landrover tracks. The arboretum has nearly 2,000 different trees, many of them seldom seen in cultivation – the sort that visitors consider attractive but are then disappointed to find unavailable commercially. There are also extensive areas dedicated to azaleas and to systematic demonstration gardens. A must for any visitor to Scotland.

Features woodland garden; sub-tropical plants; roses (ancient & modern); rock garden; rhododendrons & azaleas; herbs; plants under glass; mature conifers; good herbaceous borders; fine collection of trees; alpine plants; peat beds; 45 UK record-breaking trees, more than any other Scottish garden; shop; recently enlarged plant sales area; licensed café.

Owned by Board of Trustees
Size 31ha (77 acres)

STRATHCLYDE

Achamore Gardens

ISLE OF GIGHA, PA41 7AD

Tel 01583 505254 **Fax** 01583 505244
Website www.isle-of-gigha.co.uk
Location Take Gigha ferry from Tainloan (20 mins)
then easy walking for 1½ miles.
Opening hours Dawn – dusk; daily; all year.
Admission fee Adults £2; Children £1.

Achamore is one of the best rhododendron
gardens in the British Isles, and started as
recently as 1944. Despite such a short
existence (many rhododendron gardens date
well back into the 19th century) Achamore
has also had its fair share of ups and downs.
It was largely planted by Sir James Horlick,
with advice from Jim Russell. It has about
20 distinct areas cut out of the woodland
(overgrown with *R. ponticum*) but they all
have rhododendrons in common: their
names include the Loderi garden, Thomson
Garden and Macabeanum Wood. Camellias,
eucalyptus and nothofagus also grow well
here, as do many of the Surrey-type trees
recommended by Russell – flowering
cherries, sorbus and birches. And there are
good herbaceous plantings too, from
daffodils through to pulmonarias and
primulas.

Features woodland garden; sub-
tropical plants; rhododendrons;
azaleas; biggest *Larix gmelinii* in the
British Isles.

Owned by Isle of Gigha Heritage Trust
Number of gardeners 2
Size 16ha (40 acres)

Achnacloich

CONNEL, OBAN, PA37 1PR

Tel 01631 710221 **Fax** 01631 710796
Location On A85, 3 miles east of Connel.
Opening hours 10 am – 6 pm; daily; 3 April to 31
October.
Admission fee Adults £2; OAPs £1; Children free.

Achnacloich is a substantial woodland
garden, made in three stages. First there
were the Scots pine and European larch,
which have grown to great heights. Then
came the large-scale plantings of
rhododendrons, particularly the *triflora*
species which have begun to naturalise. The
latest stage has been the creation of a
plantsman's garden using the tender shrubs
and trees which flourish on the west coast
on Argyll. Some of the embothriums are
taller than the native oaks.

Features woodland garden;
rhododendrons & azaleas; good shrubs;
plants for sale.

Owned by Mrs J. Nelson
Number of gardeners 1
Size 14ha (35 acres)

An Cala

ISLE OF SEIL, PA34 4RF

Tel & Fax 01852 300237
Website www.gardens-of-argyll.co.uk
Location In village of Easdale.
Opening hours 10 am – 6 pm; daily; April to
October.
Admission fee Adults £2; Children free.

This sheltered garden on the wild west coast was designed by Thomas Mawson and planted by the actress Faith Celli: it still has a 1930s feel to it. There is a natural rock garden and several streams which have been dammed and planted with moisture-loving species. The result is a garden of great lushness with splendid views across the islets of the Inner Hebrides. A flock of Rupert Till wire-sculpted sheep complement the straying real ones outside the garden.

Features rock garden; wild garden; bog garden; waterfalls & streams.

Owned by Mrs T. Downie
Number of gardeners 1
Size 2ha (5 acres)

Ardchattan Priory

CONNEL, OBAN, PA37 1RQ

Tel 01796 481355 **Fax** 01796 481211
Website www.gardens-of-argyll.co.uk
Location 5 miles east of Connel Bridge, on the north shore of Loch Etive.
Opening hours 9 am – 6 pm; daily; April to October.
Admission fee Adults £2; Children free.

Daffodils, rock plants and azaleas are the main attraction in spring, but Ardchattan is also planted for high summer, with an emphasis on roses and herbaceous borders. The garden is good in late summer and autumn too: late-flowering *Eucryphia glutinosa* and *Hoheria lyallii* are complemented by fine leaf-colour from the *Sorbus* species and *Cornus kousa*.

Features roses (mainly old-fashioned); daffodils; good herbaceous borders; good collection of *Sorbus* species; huge *Hebe* bushes.

Owned by Mrs Sarah Troughton
Number of gardeners 1½
Size 1.6ha (4 acres)

Ardkinglas Woodland Garden

CAIRNDOW, PA26 8BH

Tel 01499 600261 **Fax** 01499 600241
Website www.ardkinglas.com
Location On A83 at Cairndow.
Opening hours Daylight hours; daily; all year.
Admission fee Adults £3; Children free.

Formerly known as Strone Gardens, Ardkinglas is famous for its magnificent conifers and its fine Lorimer house. As well as one of the tallest trees in Britain, it has the 'mightiest conifer in Europe', a specimen of *Abies alba* with a huge girth. The garden has been substantially improved by recent restoration and new plantings: these include a gazebo, an extension to the woodland garden itself and a new bridge across the River Kinglas to a 17th-century mill. Among the rhododendrons are many hybrids bred by Michael Noble, Lord Glenkinglas, when he was Secretary of State for Scotland. The nearby Tree Shop, run by the Ardkinglas Estate, is a nursery specialising in trees and shrubs – especially rhododendrons. It is open seven days a week and has a handsome list of unusual plants.

Features woodland garden; rhododendrons & azaleas; mature conifers; one of the tallest trees in Britain *Abies grandis* (63m.); the mightiest conifer in Europe *Abies alba*, and many other champion trees; excellent nursery.

Owned by Ardkinglas Estate
Number of gardeners 1
Size 10ha (25 acres)
NCCPG National Collections *Abies*; *Picea*

Ardtornish Garden

LOCHALINE, MORVERN BY OBAN,
PA34 5VZ

Tel 01967 421288 **Fax** 01967 421211
Location 2 miles north-east of Lochaline.
Opening hours 10 am – 5 pm; daily; April to
October.
Admission fee £3.

This is Faith Raven's other garden – see
Docwra's Manor in Cambridgeshire – and a
complete contrast: 28 acres of rocky hillside
full of rhododendron species and
Edwardian hybrids. Mrs Raven has actively
improved it with a great range of interesting
plants, including eucryphias, embothriums
and acers.

Features plantsman's collection of
plants; mature conifers; bluebells;
kitchen garden; gunnera; rhododendrons;
autumn colour.

Owned by Mrs John Raven
Number of gardeners 1
Size 11.1ha (28 acres)

Arduaine Garden

ARDUAINE, BY OBAN, ARGYLL,
PA34 4XQ

Tel & Fax 01852 200366
Website www.nts.org.uk
Location On A816 between Oban & Lochgilphead.
Opening hours 9.30 am – sunset; daily; all year.
Admission fee Adults £3.50; Concessions £2.60.

Arduaine is a luxuriant woodland garden in
a sheltered, south-facing situation at the
edge of the sea. Stout conifers and 12m
thickets of *Griselinia* protect the spectacular
rhododendrons which two nurserymen
planted in the 1970s. *Primula denticulata*

and *Narcissus cyclamineus* have naturalised
in grassy glades. *Cardiocrinum giganteum*
and *Myosotidium hortensia* grow vigorously.
There are several outsize and champion
trees, including *Eucryphia glutinosa,
Gevuina avellana, Trochodendron aralioides*
and the upright form of the tulip tree
known as *Liriodendron tulipifera*
'Fastigiatum'. Some of the giant
rhododendrons (*R. arboreum* subsp.
zeylanicum) are 100 years old: the plant of
R. griffithianum too must be one of the
largest in existence. But the sheer variety of
the plantings is an education, while the
whole garden is handsomely maintained.

 Features tallest *Nothofagus antarctica*
(26m.) in the British Isles and 6 further
records; reception centre Apr-Sept; no
refreshments in the garden, but Loch
Melfort Hotel is next door.

Owned by The National Trust for Scotland
Number of gardeners 3
Size 8ha (20 acres)

Barwinnock Herbs

BARRHILL, GIRVAN, KA26 0RB

Tel & Fax 01465 821338
Website www.barwinnock.com
Location Off B7207, 12 miles north-west of
Newton Stewart.
Opening hours 10 am – 5 pm; daily; 3 April to 3
October.
Admission fee free.

Although not far from such tourist
destinations as Galloway Forest Park,
Barwinnock Herbs is set among wonderfully
wild scenery, which forms a spectacular
backdrop to this beautifully laid out
nursery. Primarily a nursery which
specialises in organically-grown culinary,
medicinal and aromatic herbs, there is a

small garden too, in which these plants are prettily displayed. The plant yard itself is most attractive, with the pots arranged on rustic tables amidst a collection of agricultural bygones. There is a small rural museum attached, with some local produce and seed on sale and, for those who want to venture further afield, there are some enticing walks mapped out from the nursery. If you do not want to take your purchases with you, they are happy to post them for you.

Owned by Dave & Mon Holtom
Number of gardeners 1

Benmore Botanic Garden

DUNOON, PA23 8QU

Tel 01369 706261 **Fax** 01369 706369
Website www.rbge.org.uk
Location 7 miles north of Dunoon on A815.
Opening hours 10 am – 6 pm; daily; March to October. Closes at 5 pm in March & October.
Admission fee Adults £3.50; Concessions £3; Children £1; Family £8.

Benmore Botanic Garden has been a regional annexe of the Royal Botanic Garden Edinburgh since 1929, having been given to the nation a few years earlier by the brewer Harry Younger. The stupendous redwood avenue which greets the visitor at the entrance dates from 1863 and was the start of a systematic programme of planting conifers on the estate, into which the Youngers introduced ornamental trees and shrubs. The mild, wet climate makes possible the cultivation of tender plants from lower altitudes of the Sino-Himalaya, Bhutan, China and the New World. Benmore is a living textbook of the genus *Rhododendron*: over 350 species and sub-

species grow at Benmore, and hundreds of hybrids and cultivars. Their background is of conifers planted early in the 19th century, perhaps the best collection in Scotland. The conifers are at the heart of RBGE's conservation programme and have been supplemented by recent ecological plantings including a Bhutanese glade and a Chilean glade. But the whole garden is spacious, educational and beautifully maintained.

Features woodland garden; mature conifers; fine collection of trees; giant redwood avenue planted in 1863; rhododendrons; ferns; new Chilean plant collection; ten record-breaking trees, including *Nothofagus betuloides* at over 20m; gift shop; tea-room.

Owned by Board of Trustees/Royal Botanic Garden, Edinburgh
Size 52ha (130 acres)

Biggar Park

BIGGAR, ML12 6JS

Tel 01899 221085
Location ½ mile south-west of Biggar on A702: black iron gates & a lodge on the north side.
Opening hours By appointment for groups, May to August.
Admission fee Adults £2.50; Children 50p.

Biggar Park garden is a mixture of woodland (formal and informal), spacious lawns, and unusual trees, shrubs and rhododendrons. It is 225m above sea-level, so somewhat susceptible to late spring frosts. In the traditional working walled garden are fine herbaceous borders, vegetables, fruit-trees and a greenhouse. Shrub Roses are a special interest: there are good collections of both old and modern cultivars. The gardens also have a good collection of meconopsis. A small Japanese

Garden is in the process of development. Several ornamental ponds are landscaped into the garden.

Features herbaceous borders; spring bulbs, especially fritillaries; rhododendrons & azaleas; meconopsis; old roses; good collection of shrubs and trees.

Owned by Captain & Mrs David Barnes
Number of gardeners 1
Size 4ha (10 acres)

Brodick Castle

ISLE OF ARRAN, KA27 8HY

Tel 01770 302202 **Fax** 01770 302312
Website www.nts.org.uk
Location Ferry from Ardrossan to Brodick, follows signs.
Opening hours Park: 9.30 am – sunset; daily; all year. Walled garden 10 am – 4.30 pm (3.30 pm in October); daily; April to October.
Admission fee Adults £3.50; Concessions £2.60.

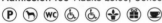

This lush rhododendron garden was begun by Molly, Duchess of Montrose, in 1923. The climate at Brodick is mild and wet: the sloping hillside is almost frost-free. Some of the Duchess's plantings are now record-breakers, including *Embothrium coccineum* at more than 20m, the seldom-seen *Euonymus tingens*, the wild form of *Leptospermum scoparium* more than 10m high, and the rare *Nothofagus nervosa* which is over 30m high. In the woodland are fine magnolias, camellias, crinodendrons and olearias too, but none of these plantings is a match for the rhododendrons, many of which were grown from collectors' seed. The work of collectors Forrest, Ludlow and Kingdon Ward are all represented here. The walled garden has a late Victorian layout, but the plantings take advantage of the mild climate. For those with longer to dally,

Brodick also has a fine park with further features including a restored ice-house.

Features tallest *Drimys winteri* (21m.) and *Embothrium coccineum* (20m.) in the British Isles (& three further records); NTS shop; plant centre; restaurant & tea-rooms.

Owned by The National Trust for Scotland
Number of gardeners 6, plus 2 part-time
Size 32ha (80 acres)
NCCPG National Collections *Rhododendron* (subsections Falconera, Grandia and Maddenia)

Colzium Walled Garden

OFF STIRLING ROAD, KILSYTH, GLASGOW, G65 0PY

Tel 01236 828150 **Fax** 01236 826322
Location Signed from Kilsyth on B803.
Opening hours 12 noon – 7 pm; daily; Easter to mid-September. 12 noon – 4 pm; Saturdays & Sundays; rest of year.
Admission fee Free.

Colzium Walled Garden is an up-and-coming young garden, which the Council has developed on an ancient site since 1976. A wide range of plants is grown within the protection of high walls, particularly conifers, rhododendrons and ornamental trees and shrubs of dwarf habit. They are intended to offer colour and interest throughout the year. The standards of maintenance and labelling are excellent.

Features snowdrops; over 100 different *Galanthus* cultivars.

Owned by North Lanarkshire Council
Number of gardeners 3
Size 0.2ha (½ acre)

Crarae Gardens

CRARAE, BY INVERARY, PA32 8YA

Tel & Fax 01546 886614
Location South of Inverary on A83.
Opening hours 9.30 am – sunset; daily; all year.
Admission fee Adults £3.50; Concessions £2.60;
Children £1.

Crarae was finally saved for the nation by the National Trust for Scotland, which took possession in April 2002. There are plans for extensive restoration to these fifty acres of romantic woodland, centred on a steep glen spanned by wooden bridges. The long narrow climb up the glen is a pilgrim's progress for plantsmen, past all manner of exotic plants displayed for effect, but especially large-leaved rhododendrons. Best in the morning, and in late May.

Features woodland garden; camellias; rhododendrons; autumn colour; tallest *Acer pensylvanicum* in the British Isles (and 12 further tree records); visitor centre open Apr-Sept; light refreshments.

Owned by The National Trust for Scotland
Number of gardeners 2½
Size 20ha (50 acres)
NCCPG National Collections *Nothofagus*

Culzean Castle & Country Park

MAYBOLE, AYRSHIRE, KA19 8LE

Tel 01655 884455 **Fax** 01655 884503
Website www.culzeancastle.net
Location Off A719, west of Maybole & South of Ayr.
Opening hours Park: 9.30 am – sunset; daily; all year.
Admission fee Adults £5; Concessions £3.75; Children £1.

Culzean is the flagship of the National Trust for Scotland, thoroughly restored and seriously open to the public (more than 400,000 visitors a year). The gardens are important and include a deer park, a ruined arch, a viaduct, an ice house, a beautiful gothic camellia house, gazebos, a pagoda and a vinery. The three areas of horticultural interest are the walled garden, the fountain court and 'Happy Valley', which is a woodland garden with fine specimen trees. Record-breakers include an upright Irish yew (*Taxus baccata* 'Fastigiata') at 20m, and the rare southern Japanese hemlock *Tsuga sieboldii* at 25m.

Features tallest Irish yew *Taxus baccata* 'Fastigiata' (20m.) in the British Isles (plus two further tree records); current holder of the Sandford Award; good shops; plant centre; restaurant; coffee shop.

Owned by The National Trust for Scotland
Number of gardeners 7, plus 4 groundsmen
Size 50ha (125 acres)

Finlaystone Country Estate

LANGBANK, PA14 6TJ

Tel 01475 540 285
Website www.finlaystone.co.uk
Location On A8, 10 mins west of Glasgow Airport.
Opening hours 10 am – 5 pm; daily; all year. SGS opening on 18 April, and plant sale 2 pm – 5 pm on 12 September.
Admission fee Adults £3; OAPs & Children £2.

Much of the garden at Finlaystone was laid out in 1900. The formal gardens date from this period: the walled garden, the knot garden and the sunken garden. All were set within a natural landscape of ornamental trees and shrubs. The sunken garden is enclosed within a yew hedge which was castellated by 'an enthusiastic family governess and a French aunt' in about 1918. But much of today's imaginative and beautiful garden is more recent, including the long, winding herbaceous border. The wooded areas are thick with azaleas, as well as rhododendrons, bluebells and snowdrops. Celtic themes have inspired the MacMillans to construct two new features. The Celtic paving has an intricate pattern set into grass, using a design in the Book of Kells. In the walled garden is a 'garden oasis' in the form of a Celtic cross with a pool at its centre but all enclosed by a circular brick pergola. There is also a garden of scented plants for blind visitors which is sometimes known as the 'Fragrant Garden' and on other occasions as the 'Smelly Garden'. The 'New Garden' dates from 1959: the banks of a burn are lined with *Darmera peltata*, spectacular in autumn. The rhododendrons and azaleas merge into the wilder woods on the far bank.

Features rhododendrons & azaleas; daffodils; bluebells; gift shop; good play areas; light meals, 11 am – 5 pm, April to September.

Owned by Arthur Macmillan
Number of gardeners 1, plus family members
Size 4ha (10 acres)

Geilston Garden

CARDROSS, DUMBARTON, G82 5HD

Tel 01389 849187 **Fax** 01389 849189
Location On A814, at western end of Cardross.
Opening hours 9.30 am – 5 pm; daily; April to October.
Admission fee Adults £2.50; Concessions £1.90. RHS members free.

(P) (WC) (&) (&)

Geilston is a nice example of the many small country houses, villas and estates which were put together by successful Glasgow industrialists along the banks of the Clyde. The garden retains a sense of being a private space in which the visitor is an invited guest. The many attractive features include a fruit and vegetable garden with a central 'dipping pond', a walled garden with traditional glasshouses and a burn which winds through the wooded glen.

Owned by The National Trust for Scotland
Number of gardeners 1
Size 2.8ha (7 acres)

Glasgow Botanic Garden

730 GREAT WESTERN ROAD, GLASGOW, G12 0UE

Tel 0141 334 2422 **Fax** 0141 339 6964
Location On A82, 2 miles from city centre.
Opening hours Grounds: 7 am – dusk; daily; all year. Glasshouses & Kibble Palace: 10 am – 4.45 pm (4.15 pm in winter); daily; all year.
Admission fee Free.

(&) (WC) (&) (&)

Most of the elements of the traditional botanic garden are here, including chronological beds, but the glory of Glasgow is its two glasshouses – the Kibble Palace and the Main Range. The Kibble Palace is now closed for complete restoration and will not open until 2006. The west wing of the Main Range will be closed for repair during 2004, but the tropical collections will still be open to visitors. There are interesting new gardens outside, too: a fine rose garden, a herb garden, vegetable beds and the long, scented border.

Features roses (ancient & modern); herbs; plants under glass; mature conifers; good herbaceous borders; fine collection of trees; beautiful glasshouse (the 'Kibble Palace').

Owned by Glasgow City Council
Number of gardeners 12, plus apprentices
Size 10.7ha (27 acres)
NCCPG National Collections *Begonia*; *Dendrobium*; *Dicksoniaceae*

Glenarn

RHU, HELENSBURGH, G84 8LL

Tel 01436 820493 **Fax** 0141 221 8450
Website www.gardens-of-argyll.co.uk
Location Turn up Pier Road at Rhu Marina, first right is Glenarn Road.
Opening hours Dawn to dusk; daily; 21 March to 21 September.
Admission fee Adults £3; OAPs & Children £1.50.

Glenarn's ten acres of woodland garden has at least one venerable old rhododendron dating from Joseph Hooker's Himalayan expedition (1849-51) and many species from the 1930s trips of Kingdon Ward and Ludlow & Sheriff. The garden owes its present outline to the Gibson family who owned it from 1927 to 1982, and many of their own rhododendron hybrids still flourish here, though there are plenty of magnolias, camellias, pieris, and other good plants too. *Magnolia campbellii* var. *mollicomata* is 12m tall, and *Magnolia sprengeri* var. *diva* has made 10m so far. Other plants which date back to the Gibson are the rare climbing gesneriad *Asterantha ovata* and the swarms of *Primula pulverulenta* which are such a splendid feature in early summer. The Thornleys took over in 1983 – both of them professional architects whose gardening was moulded by the formal gardens of Italy – but their commitment to the woodland nature of the garden is remarkable. They

have re-laid the steps, re-cut the paths, restored the vegetable garden and added a pond with a water chute. Work is still progressing in the rock garden, where the owners are excavating and restoring the quarry face. Meanwhile they have also propagated the unique plants, renewed the plantings, created spaces, and maintained the balance between individual specimens. It is a remarkable achievement and worth a visit at any season, though especially in spring. There will be a special opening on 2 May for Scotland's Gardens Scheme.

Features rock garden; plantsman's collection of plants; mature conifers; rhododendrons; embothriums; refreshments may be booked in advance for groups.

Owned by Mr & Mrs Michael Thornley
Number of gardeners owners only
Size 4ha (10 acres)

Greenbank Garden

FLENDERS ROAD, CLARKSTON, GLASGOW, G76 8RB

Tel 0141 616 5126
Website www.nts.org.uk
Location 1 mile along Mearns Road from Clarkston Toll, take 1st left.
Opening hours Garden: 9.30 am – sunset; daily; all year.
Admission fee Adults £3.50; Concessions £2.60; Children £1.

Greenbank is a demonstration garden: it was left to the National Trust for Scotland in 1976 on condition that it was developed as a teaching resource for people with small gardens. The walled garden has therefore been divided into a great number of sections which represent different interests and skills: a rock garden, fruit garden, dried flower plot, raised beds, winter garden, and so on.

 **Features** woodland garden; rock garden; fruit in the walled garden; good herbaceous borders; a garden for the disabled; roses of every kind; NTS gift shop; plant sales; tea-room.

Owned by The National Trust for Scotland
Number of gardeners 3
Size 1ha (2½ acres) walled garden; 6ha (15 acres) of policies
NCCPG National Collections *Bergenia*

Mount Stuart

ISLE OF BUTE, PA20 9LR

Tel 01700 503877 **Fax** 01700 505313
Website www.mountstuart.com
Location 5 miles south of Rothesay.
Opening hours 10 am – 6 pm; daily except Tuesdays & Thursdays; 1 May to 29 August. Plus Saturdays & Sundays in April & September.
Admission fee Adults £3.50; OAPs £3; Children £2. (2003 prices).

Mount Stuart has a vast and fascinating garden to accompany the sumptuous house. Its 300 acres include: a mature Victorian pinetum; a two-acre rock garden designed by Thomas Mawson and thickly planted with rare collected plants; a 'wee' garden of five acres, planted with tender exotics from Australia and New Zealand; and a kitchen garden re-designed by the late Lord Bute with help from Rosemary Verey. Add in the relics of an 18th-century landscape, a tropical greenhouse, acres of bluebells and established rhododendrons, and you have the measure of a long and fascinating visit.

 Features woodland garden; rhododendrons & azaleas; plants under glass; mature conifers; bluebells; important rock garden; tender plants; fine new visitor centre; restaurant & café.

Owned by The Mount Stuart Trust
Number of gardeners 8
Size 120ha (300 acres)

Torosay Castle & Gardens

CRAIGNURE, ISLE OF MULL, PA65 6AY

Tel 01680 812421 **Fax** 01680 812470
Location 1½ miles from Craignure on A849 to Iona.
Opening hours Gardens: 9 am – dusk; daily; all year.
Admission fee Adults £5; Concessions £4; Children £1.75. RHS members free from April to June.

The best feature of the gardens at Torosay is the Italian Statue Walk, lined with 19 figures by Antonio Bonazza. The formal terraces (attributed to Lorimer) are covered with rambling roses, other climbers and perennials. The oriental garden, bog garden, greenhouses and rock garden add to the sheer variety. The woodland garden is stuffed with interesting specimens: *Eucryphia*, *Embothrium* and *Crinodendron* among many Chilean plants, underplanted with old daffodil cultivars, meconopsis and primulas.

Features rock garden; water garden; *Eucalyptus* walk; new conservation plantings with conifers from Royal Botanic Garden at Edinburgh; eucalyptus walk; shop; tea-room (April – October) with light lunches.

Owned by Mr C. James
Number of gardeners 2½, plus 1 apprentice and seasonal extras
Size 5ha (12½ acres)

TAYSIDE

Bell's Cherrybank Centre

CHERRYBANK, PERTH, PH2 0PF

Tel 01738 472800 **Fax** 01738 472805
Location Just off A93 Glasgow Road, Perth, between Broxden roundabout & city centre.
Opening hours 10 am – 5 pm; daily; May to December. Plus 12 noon – 4 pm on Sundays. Closed on Mondays & Tuesdays from October to December.
Admission fee Adults £3.

These immaculately maintained show gardens make good use of water and incorporate some striking modern sculptures. They are best known for the collection of heaths and heathers, the most comprehensive in the British Isles with over 900 cultivars. The National Heather Collection is part of a proposal by Scotland's Garden Trust to create a 45-acre garden of national importance on adjacent land.

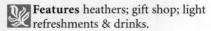**Features** heathers; gift shop; light refreshments & drinks.

Owned by Scotland's Garden Trust
Number of gardeners 2
Size 2.6ha (6½ acres)
NCCPG National Collections *Erica*

Blair Castle

BLAIR ATHOLL, PITLOCHRY, PH18 5TH

Tel 01796 481207 **Fax** 01796 481487
Website www.blair-castle.co.uk
Location Signed from A9.

Opening hours 9.30 am – 5 pm; daily; April to October.
Admission fee Adults £2; Children £1.

The landscaping around Blair Castle is some of Scotland's finest. The Hercules Garden was first laid out by the 2nd Duke of Atholl in 1744 and includes a formal water tank, 1 ha (2.5 acres) in extent, and extensive herbaceous borders. Nearby is Diana's Grove where axial paths and avenues radiate out from a statue of Diana. The fine conifers date from the 19th century and include the tallest Japanese Larch in the United Kingdom (44m).

Features shop; restaurant.

Owned by The Blair Charitable Trust
Number of gardeners 2
Size 3.8ha (9½ acres)

Bolfracks Garden

ABERFELDY, PH15 2EX

Tel 01887 820344 **Fax** 01887 829522
Website www.bolfracks.com
Location 2 miles west of Aberfeldy on A827.
Opening hours 10 am – 6 pm; daily; April to October.
Admission fee Adults £2.50; Children free.

Bolfracks is a plantsman's garden, unusual among Scottish gardens for having a good display of flowers throughout the year. There are rhododendrons and azaleas, of course, but they are principally dwarf species and hybrids, and joined by a large number of daphnes, phyllodoces, pieris, quinces and berberis. Midsummer sees the shrub roses, of which there is a good collection, with everything from Gallicas through to modern Shrub roses. But Bolfracks is particularly good for its herbaceous borders: the perennials make an effective display by June and continue through until autumn, when gentians, cyclamen and colchicums take over.

 Features herbaceous plants; roses; lots of plants at every season.

Owned by R.A. Price
Number of gardeners 1
Size 1.2ha (3 acres)

Branklyn Garden

116 DUNDEE ROAD, PERTH, PH2 7BB

Tel 01738 625535
Website www.nts.org.uk
Location Off Dundee Road, on eastern edge of Perth, ½ mile from Queen's Bridge.
Opening hours 10 am – 5 pm; Friday – Tuesday; April to September. Daily in May & June.
Admission fee Adults £5; Concessions £3.75; Children £1.

The apotheosis of Scottish rock gardening, Branklyn is a suburban garden absolutely crammed with rare plants growing in a series of artificial micro-habitats. This is a garden to go round slowly, looking at all the plants – small rhododendrons, alpines, herbaceous plants and peat-lovers. It was built up between 1922 and 1967 by John & Dorothy Renton, who bequeathed it to the National Trust for Scotland. This sort of garden depends for its success upon the understanding and plantsmanship of the gardeners who work in it, and the Trust has been fortunate with their employees at Branklyn since they took it on.

 Features small NTS gift shop; plant sales.

Owned by The National Trust for Scotland
Number of gardeners 2
Size 0.8ha (2 acres)
NCCPG National Collections Cassiope

Christie's Nursery

DOWNFIELD, WESTMUIR, KIRRIEMUIR, DD5 8LP

Tel & Fax 01575 572977
Website www.christiealpines.co.uk
Location On A926 1 mile west of Kirriemuir.
Opening hours 10 am – 5 pm; daily except Sundays & Tuesdays; March to October. Groups welcome on Sundays, by appointment.
Admission fee Free.

This alpine nursery has an impressive list, particularly strong on gentians, hardy orchids, meconopsis, corydalis and lewisias. The owners reckon to have about 1,000 different items in stock at any time, and about 2,000 growing in their pretty display garden.

 Features meconopsis; trilliums; lilies; new limestone scree (2002); refreshments by arrangement.

Owned by Ian & Ann Christie
Size 0.6ha (1½ acres)
NCCPG National Collections Gentiana

Cluny House

BY ABERFELDY, PERTHSHIRE, PH15 2JT

Tel 01887 820795
Location 3½ miles from Aberfeldy, on the Weem – Strathtay Road.
Opening hours 10 am – 6 pm; daily; March to October.

Admission fee Adults £3; Children under 16 free.
Season ticket £5.

Cluny is a plantsman's garden, largely
made in the 1950s by Mrs Mattingley's
father, who subscribed to the Ludlow and
Sherriff expeditions. Some older trees date
from the 19th century – notably two vast
wellingtonias – and the Mattingleys have
continued to develop the garden since
they took over in 1987. It is very much
a woodland garden, with a natural
appearance, except that the canopy is now
of rhododendrons, acers, sorbus, euonymus,
and birches. It has superb rhododendrons
and many other ornamental trees and
shrubs from the Himalayas and North
America, as well as an underplanting of
meconopsis, trilliums, gentians,
nomocharis, cardiocrinums, erythroniums,
lilies, arisaema and hellebores. But it is
memorable, above all, for primulas, of
which the Mattingleys used to have a
National Collection. The annual display
starts with the early-flowering petiolarid
species – P. whitei, P. tanneri, P. sonchifolia
and P. nana, for example. Then come sheets
of candelabra species: the first is yellow
P. chungensis, followed by purple
P. pulverulenta, the dark pink and white
forms of P. japonica, purple P. beesiana,
orange P. bulleyana, yellow P. sikkimensis
and yellow P. florindae – as well as naturally
occurring hybrids between them. Many
exotic species – and not just primulas –
seed and regenerate freely in the acid,
humus-rich soil. Cluny has lots to excite
the visitor throughout the season: bulbs in
April, followed by primulas in May-June,
lilies in July and excellent autumn interest.
The whole garden is hand-weeded and
chemical-free: promising seedlings are
thereby spotted and protected.

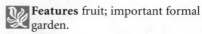Features plantsman's collection of
plants; fine collection of trees;
meconopsis; primulas; cardiocrinums;

wellingtonia (*Sequoiadendron giganteum*)
with the widest girth in the British Isles.

Owned by Mr J. & Mrs W. Mattingley
Size 2.4ha (6 acres)

Drummond Castle Gardens

MUTHILL, CRIEFF, PH7 4HZ

Tel 01764 681257 Fax 01764 681550
Website www.drummondcastlegardens.co.uk
Location South of Crieff on A822.
Opening hours 1 pm – 6 pm; daily; Easter
weekend, then from May to October.
Admission fee Adults £3.50; OAPs £2.50; Children
£1.50.

Drummond has probably the most
important formal garden in Scotland, laid
out in about 1830 as a St Andrew's cross,
with complex parterres filled since the 1950s
with roses, statues, clipped cones,
herbaceous plants, gravel and lots more
beside. The ongoing programme of
renovation has already restored much of the
garden to a very high standard. The result is
order, shape, structure, mass, profusion and
colour. There is also a copper beech planted
by Queen Victoria to commemorate her
visit in 1842. Parts of the film *Rob Roy* were
shot in the gardens.

Features fruit; important formal
garden.

Owned by Grimsthorpe & Drummond Castle Trust
Ltd
Number of gardeners 5
Size 6ha (15 acres)

Dundee Botanic Garden

RIVERSIDE DRIVE, DUNDEE, DD2 1QH

Tel 01382 647190 **Fax** 01382 640574
Website www.dundeebotanicgardens.co.uk
Location Signed from Riverside Drive (A85), near its junction with Perth Road.
Opening hours 10 am – 4.30 pm (3.30 pm from November to February); daily; all year. Closed 1 & 2 January, 25 & 26 December.
Admission fee Adults £2; OAPs & Children £1. RHS members free.

Dundee has a fine modern Botanic Garden which caters well for visitors: its gentle south-facing slopes are just above the banks of the River Tay. Founded in 1971, it can boast fine collections of conifers and broad-leaved trees, good shrubs, tropical and temperate glasshouses, a water garden and a herb garden. There is a whole series of native plant communities from montane to coastal habitats. These include a collection of *Sorbus* species native to Britain. These are also plant groupings which demonstrate adaptations for survival, such as drought resistance (the Mediterranean garden) and specialised pollination. Among the more surprising collections are *Nothofagus* species from South America and a large number of *Eucalyptus* trees from Australia.

Features sub-tropical plants; herbs; plants under glass; mature conifers; drought-resistant plants; carnivorous plants; shop; café.

Owned by University of Dundee
Number of gardeners 3
Size 9.2ha (23 acres)

Edzell Castle

EDZELL, ANGUS, DD9 7VE

Tel 01356 648631
Website www.historic-scotland.gov.uk
Location On B966 to Edzell Village, then signed for 1 mile.
Opening hours 9.30 am – 6.30 pm; April to September. 9 am – 4 pm; October to March. Closed on Thursdays after 12 noon, and all day on Friday. Not open until 2 pm on Sundays.
Admission fee Adults £3; OAPs £2.30; Children £1.

   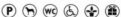

Edzell has a 1930s formal garden in the 17th-century style, designed to be seen from the ruined keep. It is shaped like a quincunx of sorts, with yew bobbles, box edging and roses in the beds. The four main segments have the motto of the Lindsey family *DUM SPIRO SPERO* ('While I breathe, I hope') cut round their edges in box. It is a garden of considerable historic importance as the only complete 'pleasaunce' in Scotland but, once you have seen the parterre, Edzell is not a garden to linger in.

Features topiary; bedding; formal garden; shop.

Owned by Historic Scotland
Number of gardeners 1
Size 0.4ha (1 acre)

Glendoick Gardens

GLENDOICK, PERTH, PH2 7NS

Tel 01738 860205 **Fax** 01738 860630
Website www.glendoick.com
Location A90 between Perth & Dundee.
Opening hours 10 am – 4 pm; Monday-Friday; 12 April to 11 June. Buy tickets at garden centre. Plus 2 pm – 5 pm; 2 & 16 May for SGS. And pre-booked parties of 20+ between mid-April and mid-June.
Admission fee Adults £3; Children free.

Everyone knows of the Glendoick nursery, but the garden is even more important. Started by Farrer's friend Euan Cox in the 1920s, it has one of the best collections of plants, especially rhododendron species, forms and hybrids, in the British Isles. The nursery propagates all its stock on site. Peter Cox has specialised in breeding low-growing rhododendrons for small gardens: his successes include such well-known cultivars as 'Curlew', 'Razorbill' and 'Egret', as well as evergreen azaleas like 'Panda'. He has also continued to hunt for plants in China, as his father did before him. His own son Kenneth has made ten expeditions to Tibet and Arunachal Pradesh. There is a good demonstration garden in the garden centre which is open all year. The website is very good indeed.

Features woodland garden; fine trees; plantsman's collection of plants; primulas; meconopsis; lilies; famous garden centre attached; restaurant.

Owned by Mr & Mrs Peter A. Cox & Kenneth Cox
Number of gardeners owners, with (very) part-time help
Size 4ha (10 acres), including nursery

House of Dun

MONTROSE, ANGUS, DD10 9LQ

Tel 01674 810264 **Fax** 01674 810722
Website www.nts.org.uk
Location On A395, halfway between Montrose & Brechin.
Opening hours 9.30 am – sunset; daily; all year.
Admission fee £1 in honesty box.

The first thing you notice at House of Dun, particularly in winter, is the magnificent line of mature wellingtonias, but there are sheets of spring bulbs, a Victorian rose garden for summer, a border of *Nerine bowdenii* over 100m long, and a collection of old fruit trees of interest in autumn. The walled garden (next to the house) has been restored as it might have been in the late 19th century and planted with cultivars that date back to the 1880s.

Features NTS shop; restaurant, open with house.

Owned by The National Trust for Scotland
Number of gardeners 1
Size 18ha (45 acres)

House of Pitmuies

GUTHRIE, BY FORFAR, ANGUS, DD8 2SN

Tel & Fax 01241 828245
Website www.pitmuies.com
Location Signed off A932 Forfar to Arbroath Road.
Opening hours 10 am – 5 pm; daily; April to October.
Admission fee Adults £2.50; Children free.

House of Pitmuies is one of the most beautiful modern gardens in Scotland, and still expanding. Laid out and planted in the Hidcote style, Pitmuies has wonderful shrub roses in mixed plantings, clever colour schemes, and innumerable different gardens within the garden: a delphinium border, cherry walk, an alpine meadow for wildflowers, rhododendrons glades, vast hollies, a superb *Acer griseum* and splendid trees inherited from Victorian times – and earlier, for there are 400-year-old Spanish chestnuts on the lawn. Enchanted and enchanting.

Features roses (ancient & modern); plants under glass; fruit; good herbaceous borders; alpine meadow; ferns;

colour schemes; tallest *Ilex aquifolium* 'Argenteomarginata' in the British Isles; home-raised plants & produce in season.

Owned by Mrs Farquhar Ogilvie
Number of gardeners 1, plus 1 groundsman
Size 10.3ha (26 acres)

Kinross House

KINROSS, KY13 8ET

Tel 01577 862900 **Fax** 01577 863372
Website www.kinrosshouse.com
Location Jct 6 from M90, into Kinross, right at mini-roundabout, first left.
Opening hours 10 am – 7 pm; daily; April to September.
Admission fee Adults £2; Children 50p.

Many consider Kinross the most beautiful house in Scotland, and its views across Loch Leven are extensive. It is approached along a magnificent avenue of lime trees. The elegant walled garden has herbaceous borders and roses and, above all, a 17th-century sense of proportion. It is one of the few Scottish gardens which are genuinely at their best in July and August. The website is excellent.

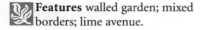**Features** walled garden; mixed borders; lime avenue.

Owned by James Montgomery
Number of gardeners 4
Size 4ha (10 acres) of walled garden

Scone Palace

PERTH, PH2 6BD

Tel 0845 126 1060 **Fax** 01738 552588
Website www.scone-palace.co.uk
Location Signed from A93, 1½ miles north of Perth.
Opening hours 9.30 am – 5 pm; daily; April to October.
Admission fee Gardens only: Adults £3.90; OAPs £2.80; Children £2. RHS members free.

  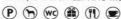

Scone is best known for its pinetum and for the Douglas firs (*Pseudotsuga menziesii*) grown from original seed sent back by their discoverer David Douglas, who was born on the estate here. Lord Mansfield has the largest private collection of orchids in the country. A selection is always on view in the state rooms.

Features established pinetum; woodland walks; rhododendrons & azaleas; daffodils; new 'Murray' maze; tallest *Tilia platyphyllos* (37m.) in the British Isles; handsome Douglas fir; and 3 other record trees; largest private collection of orchid hybrids in Britain; gift shop; restaurant in old kitchens; self-service coffee-shop.

Owned by The Earl of Mansfield
Number of gardeners 4
Size 40ha (100 acres)

GARDENS OF WALES

Most of the best-known gardens of Wales are close to the sea – as, indeed, are most of its larger centres of population. This gives the principality a reputation for being able to grow tender plants that would not be hardy – say – in Surrey. There is some truth in this, though no Welsh garden is truly sub-tropical in the way that Tresco and Inverewe are. The National Gardens Scheme offers gardens to visit in every part of Wales, and in respectable numbers. The Royal Horticultural Society has negotiated free access for its members, for some or all of the year, to some of the Principality's finest gardens, including Bodnant, the National Botanic Garden of Wales and Picton Castle. This book lists gardens in Wales under the old 1974 counties, rather than the historic counties or the present administrative units. The 1974 counties are a useful size for the purpose of this book, and their names are readily recognised.

Wales has many historic gardens, made mainly in the 18th and 19th centuries and usually in the styles that were fashionable in England at the time. The National Trust has played an important part in preserving and restoring some of the finest. Bodnant, Plas Newydd and Powis Castle are gardens of the utmost international importance. By and large, however, they share with other Welsh gardens the characteristic of having acquired their horticultural importance during the 20th century: the same is true of other classic Welsh gardens like Portmeirion and Dyffryn. Much of that horticultural input came from England and there was until quite recently a sense among some that gardening was a hobby either for very rich anglicised Welshmen or for the English who came to live in Wales. Despite its troubles, and although it cannot rival such major botanic gardens as Kew and Edinburgh, the new National Botanic Garden of Wales does give a new focus to Welsh horticulture.

Wales's historic gardens are well supported by the Welsh Historic Gardens Trust which has taken action to identify, evaluate and conserve the principality's heritage. Its declared aims are to initiate and assist in the conservation of gardens, parks and designed landscapes that are of historic, cultural and aesthetic importance in the Welsh heritage, and to alert public awareness to the decline in particular places. Comparatively few historic gardens in Wales are open to the public.

CADW, the Welsh Historic Monuments Commission in Cardiff, publishes a Register of Parks and Gardens of Special Historic Interest in Wales. This is the work of Elisabeth Whittle who wrote the standard modern work on the subject *The Historic Gardens of Wales* (HMSO, 1992). The Register is modelled on English Heritage's list for England and the criteria for selection and grading gardens are comparable.

The best collection of trees in Wales is at Bodnant, which has a large number of rarities and some 20 champions among them. There are good tree collections also at Dyffryn and Margam in Glamorgan. Wales has comparatively few top-class nurseries, and practically none in South Wales near Cardiff or Swansea. However, the outstanding examples elsewhere in the principality are among Britain's best. Celyn Vale has a unique list of Australasian trees; Dibleys Nurseries are the leading nursery for *Streptocarpus* and other house plants; and Crûg Farm Plants is a true plantsman's nursery which introduces more new collected plants into cultivation than any other in Britain.

The two principal horticultural colleges are at opposite ends of Wales. Both the Welsh College of Horticulture at Mold (Tel: 01352 841000) and Pencoed College at Bridgend (Tel: 01656 302600) are RHS Partner Colleges with a good number of public lectures and workshops throughout the year.

CLWYD

Aberconwy Nursery

GRAIG, GLAN CONWY, COLWYN BAY,
LL28 5TL

Tel 01492 580875
Location South of Glan Conwy, 2nd right off A470.
Turn right at top of hill: nursery is on the right.
Opening hours 10 am – 5 pm; Tuesday – Sunday;
February to October.

This nursery is best known as one of our
leading nurseries for alpine plants and a
steady introducer of new cultivars, especially
autumn-flowering gentians. But it also
offers unusual shrubs, and herbaceous and
woodland plants, including many dwarf
rhododendrons and small ericaceous plants.
Other specialities are cistus, primulas, small
ferns and hybrids of *Helleborus niger*.

Owned by Keith Lever

Bodrhyddan

RHUDDLAN, LL18 5SB

Tel 01745 590414 **Fax** 01745 590155
Location On A5151, midway between Dyserth &
Rhuddlan.
Opening hours 2 pm – 5.30 pm; Tuesdays &
Thursdays; June to September. And by
appointment.
Admission fee Adults £2; Children £1.

The house and garden at Bodrhyddan date
back to mediaeval times, but most of what
we see today was opulently laid out in the
1870s and restored in the 1980s. There is
also an avenue of Monterey pines (*Pinus
radiata*) dating from 1928. William Andrews
Nesfield designed the long parterre, which
was planted with vegetables when the present
Lord Langford returned from World War II,
but is now absolutely stunning with
seasonal bedding. The Pleasaunce was made
in the mid-1980s to recreate an earlier
woodland garden; it has extensive shrub
plantings around four ponds. It is good to see
such a distinguished garden on the up again.

 Features teas.

Owned by Lord Langford O.B.E., D.L.
Number of gardeners 2
Size 2.4ha (6 acres)

Celyn Vale Nurseries

ALLT-Y-CELYN, CARROG, CORWEN,
LL21 9LD

Tel & Fax 01490 430671
Website www.eucalyptus.co.uk
Location 3 miles east of Corwen, near A5.
Opening hours 9 am – 4 pm; Monday – Friday;
January to November.

Specialist growers of eucalyptus and acacias:
they use seed from high altitude specimens
to maximise hardiness and will advise also
on suitable species for coppicing, poor
drainage, alkaline soils, hedging, salt
tolerance and so on. They say that the
hardiest gum trees are *E. archeri*, *E. coccifera*,
E. pauciflora subsp. *debeuzevillei*,
E. pauciflora subsp. *niphophila*, *E. parvifolia*,
E. perriniana and *E. subcrenulata*.

Owned by Andrew McConnell

Bodnant Gardens

TAL-Y-CAFN, COLWYN BAY, LL28 5RE

Tel 01492 650460 **Fax** 01492 650448
Website www.bodnantgarden.co.uk
Location 8 miles south of Llandudno & Colwyn Bay
on A470. Entrance ½ mile along Eglwysbach Road.
Opening hours 10 am – 5 pm; daily; 13 March to
31 October.
Admission fee Adults £5.50; Children £2.75. RHS
members free.

Two Lords Aberconway, both past-Presidents of the Royal Horticultural Society, and three successive generations of the Puddle family, as Head Gardeners and Managers, have made Bodnant compulsory visiting. From its position above the valley of the River Conwy, Bodnant combines dramatic formal terraces with extensive woodland plantings on the grandest of scales. A deep herbaceous border, backing onto a high wall, is instantly striking, with mature, often tender climbers rampant above bold, warm plantings. Although this is North Wales, and the views from the lawns are across the valley to the Carneddau mountains and Snowdonia National Park, parts of the garden feel distinctly Italianate. Beside the house, two enormous cedars overshadow a formal lily pond, on the third of five terraces, where hydrangeas abound. A crisply shaved yew hedge curves above a mezzanine rose pergola, and there are specimens of *Magnolia grandiflora* everywhere. Below is a stately gazebo from the early 18th century, the Pin Mill, which looks across a flat pool to a grassy stage at the opposite end of its terrace, edged with cut cubes of topiary. Plantings of pencil-thin cypresses, and *Cistus* and *Potentilla* cultivars, help to create an intensely Mediterranean feel on clear summer days. Behind the Pin Mill, the mood changes, as the grassy valley fills with tall specimen trees, marching beside a fast flowing mill stream and a stern old mill. Along the stream there are hostas, bergenias and meconopsis. Some of the massive *Sequoiadendron* specimens bear planting plaques which show them to be in their second century. Winding back in an extended arc towards the house, there are gentler woodland plantings, with shrubbery borders, and smaller trees growing in grass. There is a magnificent collection of magnolias, rhododendrons and camellias. Other good plantings include *Viburnum* x *bodnantense*, hybrid camellias, huge rhododendrons, white wisterias, a vast *Arbutus* x *andrachnoides*, flaming embothriums and the famous laburnum tunnel. The garden is admirably maintained, and is popular with visitors, too. The walled plant centre (not National Trust) is strong on many of the tender climbers from the garden, and reasonably priced.

Features tallest Californian redwood *Sequoia sempervirens* (47m.) in the British Isles and 18 further record-breaking tree species – more than any other garden in Wales; plant centre; light lunches, teas, refreshments 11 am – 5 pm.

Owned by The National Trust
Number of gardeners 18
Size 32ha (80 acres)
NCCPG National Collections *Embothrium*; *Eucryphia*; *Magnolia* (spp.); *Rhododendron forrestii*

Chirk Castle

CHIRK, LL14 5AF

Tel 01691 777701 **Fax** 01691 774706
Website www.nationaltrust.org.uk
Location 1½ miles west of Chirk off A5.
Opening hours 11 am – 6 pm; Wednesday –
Sunday, plus Bank Holiday Mondays; 20 March to
31 October. Closes at 5 pm in October.
Admission fee Adults £3.80; Children £1.90.

Chirk has handsome 19th-century formal
gardens, one planted with roses and another
with billowing yew topiary. There is also a
good 1930s collection of trees and shrubs,
the relics of a garden by Norah Lindsay. The
National Trust has done much to provide
shelter from the wind, so that more tender
plants may be grown.

 Features shop; restaurant & tea-room.

Owned by The National Trust
Number of gardeners 4
Size 2.2ha (5½ acres)

Dibleys Nurseries

LLANELIDAN, RUTHIN, LL15 2LG

Tel 01978 790677 **Fax** 01978 790668
Website www.dibleys.com
Location 6 miles south of Ruthin: follow brown
tourist signs from A525.
Opening hours 10 am – 5 pm; daily; April to
September. Plus weekdays in March & October
Admission fee Garden £2; Glasshouses free.

Dibleys is the leading British nursery for
gesneriads – especially streptocarpus, of
which they have a comprehensive collection
of cultivars, from 'Constant Nymph' to the
latest modern hybrids like the ever-
blooming 'Crystal Ice'. They will be
introducing three new cultivars this year
(2004). They have made a great impact on
RHS Flower Shows in recent years, and won
15 consecutive gold medals at Chelsea.
Dibleys also have a long list of other
gesneriads like *Kohleria* and *Columnea*, and
a good line in foliage begonias. An excellent
nursery, in top form. The garden has a wide
range of trees and shrubs, and extensive
views over the Vale of Clwyd.

Owned by The Dibley family
Size 0.4ha (1 acre) glasshouses; 4ha (10 acres)
garden
NCCPG National Collections *Streptocarpus*

Erddig

WREXHAM, LL13 0YT

Tel 01978 355314 **Fax** 01978 313333
Website www.nationaltrust.org.uk
Location Signed from A483 & A525.
Opening hours 11 am – 6 pm; Saturday –
Wednesday; 20 March to 31 October. Opens at 10
am in July & August; closes at 5 pm in October.
Admission fee Gardens only: Adults £3.50;
Children £1.80.

More of a re-creation than a restoration,
Erddig today majors on domestic life in the
early 18th century. There are old-fashioned
fruit trees (an excellent collection of apples,
plums, pears and cherries, beautifully
trained), an avenue of pleached limes, and a
long canal to frame the house, but all are
slightly awed by the Victorian overlay –
avenues of monkey puzzles and
wellingtonias.

 Features restaurant, tea-room.

Owned by The National Trust
Number of gardeners 4
Size 5.2ha (13 acres)
NCCPG National Collections *Hedera*

DYFED

Aberglasney Gardens

LLANGATHEN, SA32 8QH

Tel & Fax 01558 668998
Website www.aberglasney.org
Location 4 miles west of Landeilo, signed from A40.
Opening hours 10 am – 6 pm; daily; April to
October. 10.30 am – 4 pm; daily; November to
March. Coaches by appointment only.
Admission fee Adults £5.50; OAPs £4.50; Children
£2.50.

Aberglasney has a garden that lay dormant
for about 400 years, until plans were made to
restore it in the style of the 16th and 17th
centuries. The structure remains fairly intact
from that time – including a cloister and a
(very rare) parapet walk – and reproduction
gardens have been inserted within that
framework. There are six gardens in all,
including three walled gardens. Hal
Moggridge and Penelope Hobhouse have
both been involved with the project: work
continues. The modern plantings include
meconopsis, primulas, trilliums and lilies.
The dense yew tunnel dates from about 1700.

Features important historic garden;
yew tunnel; pool garden; shop; café.

Owned by Aberglasney Restoration Trust
Number of gardeners 3
Size 3.6ha (9 acres)

Bro-Meigan Gardens

BONCATH, SA37 0JE

Tel 01239 841232
Location On B4332 between Boncath & Eglwyswrw.
Opening hours 11 am – 6 pm; Wednesday –
Monday; April to November.
Admission fee Adults £3; OAPs £2.75; Children free.

There are many gardens within the garden at
Bro-Meigan: a turf maze, a limetree avenue,
a cottage garden, a primrose patch, a herb
garden and an oriental garden. All have been
made since 1986 and are held together by
the owners' plantsmanship, which ensures
that there is always interest in every season.
Bro-Meigan is organically maintained.

Features tea-rooms.

Size 2.6ha (6½ acres)

Cae Hir

CRIBYN, LAMPETER, SA48 7NG

Tel & Fax 01570 470839
Location In village.
Opening hours 1 pm – 6 pm; daily except
Mondays (but open on Bank Holiday Mondays).
Closed in winter.
Admission fee Adults £2.50; OAPs £2; Children
50p.

This vigorous and expanding garden was
begun in 1985 and has already been featured
many times on television. Mr Akkermans'
energy and achievement are an inspiration.
He has taken six acres from the surrounding
meadows and made them into a series of
beautiful colour-conscious gardens. All
different types of plants are here: trees,
shrubs and herbaceous plants, often used in
original ways. Mr Akkermans is now
experimenting with half-hardy trees and

shrubs, allowing wildflowers to mix with cultivated ones in some parts of his immaculately tidy garden.

Features colour gardens; bonsai; mature ornamental trees; bog garden; light refreshments.

Owned by Wil Akkermans
Number of gardeners owner only
Size 2.6ha (6½ acres)

Colby Woodland Garden

AMROTH, NARBERTH, SA67 8PP

Tel 01834 811885
Website www.nationaltrust.org.uk
Location Signed from A477.
Opening hours 10 am – 5 pm; daily; 1 April to 31 October. Walled garden opens at 11 am.
Admission fee Adults £340; Children £1.70.

Colby is an attractive woodland garden, best in late spring and early summer when the rhododendrons and azaleas are in full flower. Among the 19th-century plantings are vast cryptomerias, clumps of *Embothrium coccineum* and a huge specimen of *Rhododendron falconeri* subsp. *eximium*, planted in 1883. In the walled garden, a rill runs down from the *trompe l'oeil* gazebo to a pool. There have been many new plantings recently throughout the garden.

Features shop; tea-room.

Owned by The National Trust
Number of gardeners 2
Size 11.1ha (28 acres)

Moorland Cottage Plants

RHYD-Y-GROES, BRYNBERIAN, CRYMYCH, SA41 3TT

Tel 01239 891363
Website www.moorlandcottageplants.co.uk
Location On B4329, 12 miles south-west of Cardigan & 7 miles west of Crymych.
Opening hours 10 am – 6 pm; daily, except Wednesday; mid-May to September. Nursery opens 1 March.
Admission fee Adults £1.50; Children free. For NGS.

This is a promising young nursery, attached to a charming display garden. It is high up in the Pembrokeshire Coast National Park, and surrounded by hills. Perennials are the main speciality, especially geraniums, campanulas, crocosmias, geums and potentillas. Grasses and groundcover plants are also offered in a wide variety. The garden is open and windy, though now more sheltered as the early plantings grow up; its areas include a grasses garden, a cottage garden and fine mixed borders.

Owned by Jennifer Matthews

The National Botanic Garden of Wales

MIDDLETON HALL, LLANARTHNE, CARMARTHEN, SA32 8HG

Tel 01558 668768 **Fax** 01558 668933
Website www.gardenofwales.org.uk
Location 7 miles east of Carmarthen, off A48.
Opening hours 10 am – 6 pm (or dusk, if earlier); daily, except Christmas Day.
Admission fee Adults £6.95; Concessions £5; Children £3.50. RHS members free in January & February. (Prices under review).

The landscaped park and gardens of the original 18th-century Middleton Hall estate are the setting for this new national botanic garden which opened to the public in 2000 amid great public acclamation. The Gardd Fotaneg Genedlaethol Cymru near Llanarthne in the Vale of Towy sees itself as the Welsh Kew, and will carry out research into conservation and biology. Near the entrance to the garden is a 'Welsh landscape' with native meadows and woodlands. Then comes the Broadwalk, 220m long, with a rill which runs down through a geological display of Welsh rocks. The garden's collection of herbaceous plants is planted along its edges, with narrow paths leading into the plantings to facilitate access. There is also a herb garden, named after the Physicians of Myddfai, with an ethnobotanical collection of native pharmacological Welsh plants. However, it is the Great Glasshouse which has received most of the adulation, and rightly so, because it is a stunning piece of architecture – the largest single-span glasshouse in the world. It concentrates upon the Mediterranean floras of the world – cheaper to maintain than tropical floras – including Chile, California, south-west Australia, South Africa, the Mediterranean basin and the Canary Isles. However, there is some uncertainty about the garden's future as we go to press; check before making a visit.

Features good glasshouses; herbaceous plants; herbs; shop; plant sales; café; restaurant.

Owned by Trustees of the NBG, Wales
Number of gardeners 12+
Size 40ha (100 acres)

Picton Castle

PICTON, HAVERFORDWEST, PEMBROKESHIRE, SA62 4AS

Tel & Fax 01437 751326
Website www.pictoncastle.co.uk
Location 4 miles east of Haverfordwest off A40.
Opening hours 10.30 am – 5 pm; Tuesday – Sunday & Bank Holiday Mondays; April to October.
Admission fee Adults £3.95; OAPs £3.75; Children £1.95. RHS members free from April to September.

This 13th-century castle has been the home of the Philipps family for some 400 years, and the 40 acres of grounds include fine collections of rhododendrons, azaleas, magnolias, camellias, myrtles, embothriums and eucryphias, some of which have been bred by the castle gardeners. Older specimens like a vast multi-trunked *Abies alba* have been joined by new plantings of recent introductions – *Taiwania cryptomerioides* and *Calocedrus formosana* among them. The climate is mild, and supports normally tender plants like *Pittosporum tobira* 'Variegatum' and *Vestia foetida*. The display is at its best in May to June: summer and autumn bring woodland walks among the massive oaks and giant redwoods. Recent additions include a fern walk and a collection of bamboos. The walled garden has a fish pond, an indoor fernery, rose beds, herbaceous borders and a fountain in the centre. Four RHS special events will take place at Picton during 2004: details from 020 7821 3408.

Features woodland garden; rhododendrons & azaleas; camellias; garden shop selling surplus garden produce; restaurant.

Owned by Picton Castle Trust
Number of gardeners 4, plus 2 part-time
Size 16ha (40 acres)

GLAMORGAN

Clyne Gardens

MILL LANE, BLACK PILL, SWANSEA,
SA3 5BD

Tel 01792 298637/401737 **Fax** 01792 297394
Website www.swansea.gov.uk/leisure/clyne.html
Location 3 miles west of Swansea on coast road.
Opening hours Dawn to dusk; daily; all year.
Admission fee Free. Pre-arranged tours at £1 a head.

Clyne is a stupendous woodland garden, the best in South Wales, well cared for by enthusiastic and knowledgeable staff. It is supreme as a magic rhododendron valley in May, but the range of rare and tender plants provides interest all year. Bluebells, lysichitons and gunneras are among its other features. It was planted between 1921 and 1952 by a local landowner called Algernon Walker-Heneage-Vivian, who subscribed to many of the Himalayan and Chinese plant-hunting expeditions of the day. The mild climate means that *R. fragrantissimum* grows happily outside, and there is a group of *R.* 'Loderi King George' 16m high. The car park is small, and tends to fill up early in the day. There are band concerts on Sunday afternoons in May and a plant sale on 18 May. Also worth visiting are the Swansea Botanical Gardens at Singleton Park.

Features woodland garden; rhododendrons & azaleas; good herbaceous borders; occasional light refreshments.

Owned by City & County of Swansea
Number of gardeners 5

Size 19.6ha (49 acres)
NCCPG National Collections *Pieris*; *Enkianthus*; *Rhododendron* (Triflora & Falconera subsections)

Dyffryn Botanic Garden

ST NICHOLAS, CARDIFF, CF5 6SU

Tel 029 2059 3328 **Fax** 029 2059 1966
Website www.dyffryngardens.org.uk
Location Jct 33 M4 on A48 then follow signs.
Opening hours 10 am – 6 pm; daily; all year.
Closes at 5 pm in October and 4 pm in winter. No facilities from November to March.
Admission fee Adults £3.50; OAPs & Children £2.50.

Dyffryn's sumptuous gardens were designed by Thomas Mawson for Reginald Cory around an Edwardian prodigy house. They are now being restored with a chunky £3.23m millennium grant. Originally intended partly for display – there is even a Roman garden with a temple and fountain – and partly for the Cory's own pleasure, Dyffryn has a huge collection of good plants built up in the early years of the 20th century. Watch it revive over the next year or so: the garden as a status symbol.

Features woodland garden; roses (mainly modern); rhododendrons & azaleas; good herbaceous borders; spring bulbs; summer bedding; tallest purple birch *Betula pendula* 'Purpurea' in the British Isles (and ten other record trees); plants sales area; tea-rooms; visitor centre.

Owned by Vale of Glamorgan Council
Size 22ha (55 acres)

Margam Park

Port Talbot, SA13 2TJ

Tel 01639 881635 **Fax** 01639 895897
Location Follow directions from M4 Jct 38.
Opening hours 10 am – 7 pm (5 pm in winter);
daily; all year.
Admission fee People free. Cars £2.

Margam is a popular country park with lots
to interest the garden historian and
plantsman: a wonderful range of
conservatories and glasshouses, including
the orangery for which Margam is famous,
big trees and rhododendrons (some grown
from Kingdon Ward's seed), and cheerful
bedding out. The orangery gardens (early
17th-century) have just been completely
restored, using some of the large grant
which the garden has received from the
European Regional Fund. Recent additions
include Tudor and monastic gardens and a
new pergola 410m (450 yards) long: further
work is promised. Margam is also the seat of
Fuchsia Research International, where
almost all the *Fuchsia* species are grown
under glass in a naturalistic landscape: it is
probably the largest collection in the world,
complete with humming-birds.

Features roses (mainly modern); fine
collection of trees; bedding out;
daffodils; rhododendrons; orangery; tallest
bay tree *Laurus nobilis* (21m.) in the British
Isles; gift shop; restaurant & light
refreshments.

Owned by Neath Port Talbot County Borough
Council
Number of gardeners 4
Size 24ha (60 acres)
NCCPG National Collections *Fuchsia*

Plantasia

Parc Tawe, Swansea, SA1 2AL

Tel 01792 298637/474555 **Fax** 01792 297394
Website
www.swansea.gov.uk/leisure/plantasia.html
Location Off main Eastern approach to Swansea.
Opening hours Not available as we went to press.
2003 times were: 10 am – 5 pm; Tuesdays –
Sundays & Bank Holidays; all year. Closed
1 January, 25 & 26 December.
Admission fee Adults £2.20; Concessions £1.50.
Subject to review.

Plantasia is a large glasshouse with three
climatic zones – arid, tropical, and rain
forest. Each is full with exotic plants –
palms, strelitzias, tree ferns, nepenthes, cacti
and such economic plants as coconuts and
pineapple. The authorities say that some of
the 5,000 plants represent species which are
actually extinct in the wild. It is the perfect
goal for a winter expedition, and not
expensive, but you may not enjoy the
insects, birds, monkeys and reptiles as much
as the flowers.

Features tropical & arid glasshouses;
good collection of exotic plants;
educational facilities; souvenirs; soft drinks.

Owned by City & County of Swansea
Number of gardeners 2
Size 0.4ha (1 acre)

GWENT

Penpergwm Lodge

ABERGAVENNY, NP7 9AS

Tel & Fax 01873 840208
Website www.penplants.com
Location 3 miles from Abergavenny on B4598, opposite King of Prussia pub.
Opening hours 2 pm – 6 pm; Thursday – Sunday; end of March to end of September.
Admission fee Adults £2.50; Children free.

Catriona Boyle has developed the garden at Penpergwm over the last 20 years, using some of the structure created when the house was built in Edwardian times – mature trees, open lawns, formal areas and old hedges. She has added two exuberant terraces, each planted to a colour theme and linked by a parterre and vine walk. The original vegetable garden has been re-designed and renamed a *potager*, with flowers, standard roses and vegetables. The result is both clever and satisfying – Mrs Boyle runs a well-regarded garden school. The nursery has lots of home-propagated plants, mostly unusual herbaceous plants, bulbs, climbers and shrubs, but also half-hardy perennials which extend the garden season. Specialities include *Aconitum*, euphorbias, cistus, philadelphus, clematis, loniceras, camassias, erythroniums, *Melianthus major* and salvias. The latest addition is a brick tower – a folly – at the corner of the *potager* overlooking the whole garden.

Features colour borders; good plants; nursery for unusual plants; teas on Saturdays & Sundays.

Owned by Mrs C. Boyle
Number of gardeners 1
Size 1.6ha (4 acres)

Tredegar House Country Park

NEWPORT, NP10 8YW

Tel 01633 815880 **Fax** 01633 815895
Location M4, Jct 28.
Opening hours Park open 9 am – dusk; daily; all year.
Admission fee Park & Garden free.

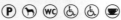

Tredegar is one of the great historic houses of south Wales, with a park and gardens to match. Much was lost to neglect in the mid-20th century, but the new owners have restored the walled formal gardens, the sunken garden and the orangery with parterres and espaliered fruit trees.

Features modern parterres; amenity parkland; refreshments in season.

Owned by Newport City Council
Number of gardeners 2
Size 8.7ha (22 acres)

Veddw House Garden

DEVAUDEN, NP16 6PH

Tel 01291 650836 **Fax** 01291 650948
Location Signed from the pub on the green at
Devauden.
Opening hours 2 pm – 5 pm; Sundays & Bank
Holiday Mondays; 30 May to 29 August. And by
appointment for parties.
Admission fee Adults £3.50; Children £1.50.

This is a young and expanding garden –
enjoyable to see now, and to watch as the
owners' ideas for its expansion develop. It is
also interesting because it is a low-budget
garden and the owners are happy to tell you
about their mistakes as well as their
successes. For example, the front garden was
at first planted as a careless, random 'cottage
garden': then they decided that it just
'looked a mess', so they added structural
elements like clipped box. On the other side
of the house is a crescent-shaped border
which is planted with pastel colours to
provide flowers from spring to autumn.
Much attention is given to colour planting
throughout the garden: pinks, mauves,
whites and purples in some parts, but reds,
oranges and yellows in the front garden.
Thoughts about what 'natural' and 'wild'
mean are explored in the 'Cornfield Garden'
where cornfield weeds and barley are grown
in formal beds. There is much variety
within its two acres, and good design and
many good plants too. The two-acre
woodland is also destined to become part of
the garden proper, but the owners say they
are finding it difficult to get the ornamental
underplantings established. All in all, a
garden of great charm – and promise.

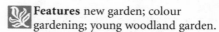 **Features** new garden; colour
gardening; young woodland garden.

Owned by Anne Wareham & Charles Hawes
Number of gardeners very part-time
Size 1.6ha (4 acres)

GWYNEDD

Bodysgallen Hall

LLANDUDNO, LL30 1RS

Tel 01492 584466 **Fax** 01492 582519
Website www.bodysgallen.com
Location On right, off A470 to Llandudno.
Opening hours Daily; all year.
Admission fee Open only to Hotel Guests.
Children over 8 welcome.

Bodysgallen Hall is a top hotel, and the
gardens live up to its high standards. They
include a knot garden divided into eight
segments, an extremely busy kitchen garden,
woodland walks, a little sunken garden with
a lily pond and a parterre with white
floribundas in the old walled garden. And it
is handy for Bodnant, too.

Features woodland garden; roses
(mainly old-fashioned); rock garden;
herbs; fruit; knot garden; parterres;
refreshments at hotel.

Owned by Historic House Hotels Ltd
Number of gardeners 4
Size 87ha (220 acres), including parkland

Cefn Bere

CAE DEINTUR, DOLGELLAU, LL40 2YS

Tel 01341 422768
Location At Cae Deintur, behind primary school, up
short steep hill, left half way up, 4th house.
Opening hours By appointment from early spring
to late autumn.
Admission fee Contribution to National Gardens
Scheme.

Cefn Bere is a plantsman's garden within a
disciplined design: the owners say that it
encapsulates their own development as
gardeners over the last 45 years. It has a
great variety of rare plants within a small
compass, especially alpines, perennials,
grasses, ferns and evergreens. And
wonderful views.

Features plantsman's collection of
plants; plants under glass; troughs;
roses (mainly old-fashioned); cuttings &
seeds available.

Owned by Mr & Mrs G.M. Thomas
Number of gardeners owners only
Size 0.08ha (one-fifth of an acre)

Crûg Farm Plants

GRIFFITH'S CROSSING, CAERNARFON, LL55 1TU

Tel & Fax 01248 670232
Website www.crug-farm.co.uk
Location 2 miles north-east of Caernarfon, off
A487, follow signs to Bethel.
Opening hours 10 am – 6 pm; Thursday – Sunday
& Bank Holidays; 28 February to 26 September.
Garden open for NGS on 11 April, 30 & 31 May,
18 July & 29 August.
Admission fee Nursery free. Garden £1.50 for
NGS.

Crûg Farm is unusual in specialising in
plants for shade: perennials, shrubs and
climbers. The range is extensive and
interesting. The selection of hardy
geraniums equals many specialists in the

genera. The owners' collecting expeditions to Korea, Sikkim, Japan, China, Vietnam, Laos, the Philippines and Taiwan are making an impact on the gardens of many discerning plantsmen: new-to-science names a-plenty. The display garden and private garden are worth seeing when they are open for the National Gardens Scheme.

Owned by Bleddyn & Sue Wynn-Jones
Number of gardeners 1
Size 1.2ha (3 acres)
NCCPG National Collections Coriaria; Paris

Penrhyn Castle

BANGOR, LL57 4HN

Tel 01248 353084 **Fax** 01248 371281
Website www.nationaltrust.org.uk
Location 2 miles east of Bangor on A5122, signed from A55 – A5 junction.
Opening hours 11 am – 5 pm; daily except Tuesday; 27 March to 31 October. Open at 10 am in July & August. Last admission 4.30 pm.
Admission fee Adults £5; Children £2.50.

A neo-Norman castle with a distant walled garden of parterres and terraces merging into the slopes of rhododendrons and camellias. There is much of dendrological interest (ancient conifers, holm oaks, champion eucryphias and naturalised arbutus trees) and a 'dinosaur landscape' of tree ferns, gunneras and aralias. The snowdrops are spectacular in February.

Features light lunches in licensed tea-room.

Owned by The National Trust
Number of gardeners 3
Size 19ha (47 acres)

Plas Brondanw Gardens

LLANFROTHEN, PANRHYNDEUDRAETH, LL48 6SW

Tel 01743 241181 **Fax** 01743 242300
Location On Croesor road off A4085.
Opening hours 9 am – 5 pm; daily; all year.
Admission fee Adult £3 (further Adults £2); Children free.

Plas Brondanw is the highly original and architectural Edwardian garden laid out by Sir Clough Williams-Ellis 17 years before he began Portmeirion, and now assiduously restored by his granddaughter Menna. It is one of the best-kept secrets in North Wales, full of slate stonework and such original design ideas as the arbour of four red-twigged limes. The garden rooms are inward looking and almost cottagey in their planting, but the mountain peaks are ever present.

Features Arts & Crafts garden; topiary; follies.

Owned by Trustees of the Second Portmeirion Foundation
Number of gardeners 2

Plas Newydd

LLANFAIRPWLL, ANGLESEY, LL61 6EQ

Tel 01248 714795 **Fax** 01248 713673
Website www.nationaltrust.org.uk
Location 2 miles south-west of Llanfairpwll on A4080.
Opening hours 11 am – 5.30 pm; Saturday – Wednesday; 27 March to 3 November.
Admission fee Adults £3; Children £1.50.

Plas Newydd has a grand collection of rhododendrons (plus azaleas, magnolias and acers) within a Repton landscape on a spectacular site above the Menai Straits. Its many other horticultural attractions include an avenue of *Chamaecyparis pisifera* 'Squarrosa' running down to the sea, an arboretum of Australian plants (lots of eucalyptus and nothofagus) and 'hot & cold' borders. The *Rhododendron montroseanum* is probably the largest in Britain. Late-flowering hybrids like 'Polar Bear' extend the season well into July. The fine Italianate garden below the house is 1930s, most surprising.

 Features National Trust shop; tea-room.

Owned by The National Trust
Number of gardeners 4
Size 12.3ha (31 acres)

Plas-yn-Rhiw

RHIW, PWLLHELI, LL53 8AB

Tel & Fax 01758 780219
Website www.nationaltrust.org.uk
Location 16 miles from Pwllheli. Turn off B4413 at Botwnnog and follows signs along lanes & through village.
Opening hours 12 noon – 5 pm; daily except Tuesday; 27 March to 1 October. Also on Saturdays & Sundays in October and 25-31 October. Closed on Wednesdays until 2 June.
Admission fee Adults £2; Children £1. £2 for snow-drops in February (telephone for exact times & dates).

This pretty garden is small and fairly formal: it is divided into a series of rooms which are hedged with cherry laurel and bay to protect them from the sea-gales. Box-edged parterres are filled with rambling roses and billowing cottage garden flowers. Tender trees and shrubs flourish in the mild coastal climate.

Owned by The National Trust
Number of gardeners 1, plus 1 trainee
Size 0.4ha (1 acre)

Portmeirion

PENRHYNDEUDRAETH, LL48 6ET

Tel 01766 770000 **Fax** 01766 771331
Website www.portmeirion-village.com
Location Between Penrhyndeudraeth & Porthmadog.
Opening hours 9.30 am – 5.30 pm; daily; all year.
Admission fee Adults £5.70; OAPs £4.60; Children £2.80. Subject to review.

Portmeirion is where the architect Sir Clough Williams-Ellis worked out his Italianate fantasies. The gardens are carved out of a rhododendron woodland but formal, with a mixture of Mediterranean plants and exotic palms, and full of architectural bric-a-brac of every period. Other attractions include tree ferns, gunneras, phormiums, ginkgos and holm oaks. Williams-Ellis bought up further estates in later years, by which he acquired the collection of rhododendrons and azaleas which is known as the Gwyllt gardens. *Rhododendron arboreum* has grown to enormous size and in parts of the garden is still impenetrable. The peak display comes in May: the mainstay of late summer and autumn is thousands of hydrangeas throughout the Portmeirion estate. One garden – almost at the furthest end of the estate and planted with a background of eucalyptus trees – is known as the 'ghost garden' because of the way the wind whistles in the leaves.

 Features woodland garden; sub-tropical plants; rhododendrons & azaleas; giant yuccas; exuberant summer bedding; tallest *Maytenus boaria* (18m.) in the British Isles; several shops; refreshments, and hotel.

Owned by Portmeirion Ltd
Number of gardeners 11
Size 28ha (70 acres)

POWYS

Ashford House

TALYBONT-ON-USK, BRECON, LD3 7YR

Tel 01874 676271
Location 1 mile east of Talybont along B4588.
Opening hours 2 pm – 6 pm; Tuesdays; April to September. And by appointment (please telephone).
Admission fee Adults £2.50; Children free.

There are two parts to the garden at Ashford: both have been made by the Andersons. First there is the walled garden, about an acre in extent, with raised beds (lots of alpines), and a plantsman's collection of plants of every kind in fine mixed borders. Then there is the woodland garden, which the Andersons have underplanted with suitable shrubs, especially rhododendrons, camellias and bulbs.

Features alpines; woodland with rhododendrons; tea, coffee & biscuits.

Owned by Mr & Mrs D.A. Anderson
Number of gardeners 1 part-time
Size 1.4ha (3½ acres)

The Dingle

WELSHPOOL, SY21 9JD

Tel 01938 555145 **Fax** 01938 555778
Location Left turn to Nurseries off A490 to Llanfyllin.
Opening hours 9 am – 5 pm; daily; all year except Christmas week. Closed on Tuesdays until 2 pm.
Admission fee Adults £2; Children free.

This steep garden attached to a successful nursery is essentially a plantsman's private garden. It is mainly made up of unusual trees and shrubs, but it has some herbaceous plantings too. The beds are put together with a carefully co-ordinated colour mixtures and designed to look good all through the year.

**Features** south-facing bank; pool; north-facing woodland garden; unusual trees & shrubs; first-rate nursery attached; light refreshments.

Owned by Roy Joseph
Number of gardeners 2
Size 1.6ha (4 acres)

Dolwen

CEFN COCH, LLANRHAEADR-YM-MOCHNANT, SY10 0BU

Tel & Fax 01691 780411
Location Right at Three Tuns Inn, ½ mile up narrow lane.
Opening hours 2 pm – 4.30 pm; Fridays, plus last Sunday of month; May to August. And by appointment. NGS days 6 June & 11 July.
Admission fee Adults £2.50; Children free.

This plantsman's garden on a steep site was energetically made by Mrs Denby in the 1980s: it continues to be open under the enthusiastic guidance of the new owners who have replanted some of the beds and added features of their own. The new prospect mount is a splendid example, though there are stupendous views in many parts of the garden. The beautiful plantings around three large ponds are fed by natural springs and connected by waterfalls. Dolwen remains one of the best modern gardens in Wales, of ever-growing interest.

 Features woodland garden; roses (mainly old-fashioned); plantsman's collection of plants; good herbaceous borders; water features; tea-room.

Owned by Bob Yarwood & Jeny Marriott
Number of gardeners 4 part-time
Size 1ha (2½ acres)

Glansevern Gardens

GLANSEVERN, BERRIEW, WELSHPOOL, SY21 8AH

Tel 01686 640200 **Fax** 01686 640829
Website www.glansevern.co.uk
Location On A483, 4 miles south-west of Welshpool.
Opening hours 12 noon – 6 pm; Fridays, Saturdays & Bank Holiday Mondays; May to September. And parties by appointment on any day of the week.
Admission fee Adults £3.50; OAPs £3; Children free.

The handsome Greek-revival house at Glansevern sits in a landscaped park (1802), complete with its lake, rhododendrons and splendid Victorian specimen trees. The 1840s rock garden incorporates a spooky grotto. The 'Smoker's Walk' runs down through woodland to the banks of the River Severn. But it is the modern planting which really distinguishes Glansevern: luxuriant primulas in the water-garden, island beds around the house and roses in one of the walled gardens. Another walled garden, exactly one acre in size, has also been re-designed and replanted recently.

 Features rock garden and grotto; roses (mainly modern); water garden; lake; good herbaceous borders; good trees; plants for sale; gallery tea-room.

Owned by Gerran & Meriel Thomas
Number of gardeners 3
Size 7.2ha (18 acres)

Powis Castle & Garden

WELSHPOOL, SY21 8RF

Tel 01938 551920 **Fax** 01938 554336
Website www.nationaltrust.org.uk
Location 1 mile south of Welshpool off the A483.
Opening hours 11 am – 6 pm; Thursday – Monday; 21 March to 31 October.
Admission fee Adults £5.80; Children £2.90.

The hanging terraces draped with bulky overgrown yews and exuberant summer bedding are famous. If you visit Powis in summer or early autumn, you will be completely distracted by the rare and tender plants on the walls – they include Banksian roses, hoherias and a hefty *Acca sellowiana* – and by the containers brilliantly planted with annuals and tender plants. At other times it is the structure which impresses: the 17th-century terraces, lead statues, planters and clipped yews. The views are always a big draw, but especially when the rhododendrons and azaleas are in flower on the ridge opposite the castle. There is much wonderfully rich colour planting and in early autumn the maples colour the lower slopes, as does an Edwardian garden of roses and hollyhocks in summer. The aspect is south-east, so Powis is best seen in the morning light: photographers please note.

 **Features** plant shop & gift shop; restaurant for light lunches & teas.

Owned by The National Trust
Number of gardeners 8
Size 9.6ha (24 acres)
NCCPG National Collections *Aralia*; *Laburnum*

GARDENS OF THE CHANNEL ISLANDS

Sausmarez Manor

ST MARTIN, GUERNSEY GY4 6SG

Tel 01481 235571 **Fax** 01481 235572
Location Well-signed, off main road between St Peter Port & St Martin.
Opening hours Daily; 1 March to 23 December.
Admission fee Adults £4; OAPs & Children 33.

The main attraction at Sausmarez is the extensive collection of sculptures of every sort displayed for sale in the grounds. Although there may be as many as 200 around at a time, they are never intrusive. There is a lot more to see in the garden, especially in the thick, woodland jungle around the lake – 50 different bamboos, 8 species of palm, young tree ferns, 320 camellias, giant echiums, tree fuchsias, hydrangeas, hedychiums, gunneras and *Geranium maderense*.

Features sculpture; tender plants; jungly woodland; café from Easter to October.

Owned by Peter de Sausmarez
Number of gardeners 1
Size 0.5ha (1.2 acres)

Judith Quérée's Garden

CREUX BAILLOT COTTAGE, LE CHEMIN DES GARENNES, ST. OUEN, JERSEY JE3 2FE

Tel & Fax 01534 482191
Location Directions given when booking made.
Opening hours Pre-booked guided tours only, at 11 am or 2 pm on Tuesdays, Wednesdays & Thursdays from May to September.
Admission fee £4, to include guided tour.

Judith Quérée started her garden in 1977: seldom have such good design and so many plants been used together so effectively. It has a true plantsman's collection of rarities – collections of tender salvias, clematis and bog plants for example – but cultivated with great skill and assembled with artistic sensibility. The design is full of decorative details, and structural innovation like the raised wooden walkway from which you view the bog garden. Every corner has something of interest at every season. Wildlife is respected, too. It is Jersey's most original modern garden: other gardeners on the island talk of it with nothing but reverence.

Features some unusual plants for sale.

Owned by Mrs Judith Quérée
Number of gardeners owner only

GARDENS OF NORTHERN IRELAND

Northern Ireland has some fine historic landscapes dating back to the 18th century: Florence Court in Co. Fermanagh and Castle Ward in Co. Down are two that we list. However, there is no doubt that the two best gardens in Northern Ireland are the 20th-century masterpieces – Mount Stewart and Rowallane. Both are in the care of the National Trust, which has maintained them as major tourist attractions. It is a pity that so few people from Britain know them at first hand. Given good weather, they are among the most enchanting and extensive gardens anywhere in the British Isles – and especially lovely in late spring.

Many trees and shrubs flourish in the mild, damp climate of Co. Down and Co. Antrim. The National Arboretum at Castlewellan has a very fine collection of mature tress: 34 of them are record-breakers. Nevertheless, it is fair to say that gardening and garden visiting are not such popular activities in Northern Ireland as on the mainland of the United Kingdom. Prices reflect this: the cost of admission to National Trust properties in Northern Ireland is substantially less than one would pay to visit a garden of equivalent quality in England.

The most comprehensive list of historic parks, gardens and demesnes in Northern Ireland was written by Belinda Jupp and published in 1992 as *The Heritage Gardens Survey*. The Northern Ireland Gardens Committee is keen to complete a more formal register.

The Ulster Gardens Scheme raises funds every year for work in National Trust gardens which would not otherwise be possible. The scheme is run by the Northern Ireland region of the National Trust at Rowallane. The gardens tend to be small and private ones made by the present owners: the Ulster Gardens Scheme also issues a second list of gardens which are open only for group visits by appointment.

Northern Ireland has a few gardening clubs and societies of its own: there is, for example, a Northern Ireland Daffodil Group and a Rose Society of Northern Ireland. Daffodils have for long been a Northern Irish speciality: Brian Duncan and Carncairn Daffodils are two of the world's leading breeders, and their owners follow in the footsteps of other great Ulster daffodil men like Sir Frank Harrison and Guy Wilson. Roses are very popular: the roses in the Sir Thomas & Lady Dixon Park in south Belfast are a great draw in summer and the Dickson rose nursery – now only wholesale – has been at Newtownards for over 100 years. Since the closure of the Slieve Donard nursery, there has been no outstanding plantsman's nursery in Northern Ireland, though Gary Dunlop at Ballyrogan comes close to it, and Patrick Ford at Seaforde is a particularly good source of rare trees and shrubs. There are eight National Collections in Northern Ireland, most of them held by corporate owners like the National Trust.

Northern Ireland's only horticultural college is Greenmount College of Agriculture & Horticulture in Antrim, which is a RHS Partner College and is running public lectures and demonstrations in 2004: details are available from the college on 028 9442 6661. RHS members also have free access to a number of gardens in Northern Ireland during the summer, most notably Benvarden Garden and Carnfunnock Country Park in Co. Antrim.

Annesley Gardens & Castlewellan National Arboretum

CASTLEWELLAN, CO. DOWN BT31 9BU

Tel 028 4377 8664 **Fax** 028 4377 1762
Website www.forestserviceni.gov.uk/arboretum.htm
Location 30 miles south of Belfast, 4 miles west of Newcastle.
Opening hours 9 am – dusk; daily; all year.
Admission fee £4 per car.

Castlewellan means trees: 18 oldest existing specimens in the British Isles, 34 champion trees of the British Isles, and 42 champion trees of Ireland. The heart of the collection is in a 12-acre walled garden, interplanted with rhododendrons and other shrubs. The central path has mixed borders at the top: dwarf rhododendrons are prominent even here. Much has been restored in recent years: the two fountains have been restored and lost views of the Mountains of Mourne opened up again. Labelling is good, both here and in the adjoining six-acre woodland garden, and the standard of maintenance high. There are plans to make the collections of *Podocarpus* and *Eucryphia* comprehensive. In the Forest Park is the newly planted 'Peace Maze', representing the journey to peace in Northern Ireland. It is said to be the longest and largest hedge-maze in the world.

Features woodland garden; mature conifers; fine collection of trees; autumn colours; embothriums; eucryphias; tallest *Chamaecyparis nootkatensis* 'Lutea' (22m.) in the British Isles, plus 33 other tree records; new 'fragrant garden' around a Lutyensesque tea house; light refreshments at peak times.

Owned by Dept. of Agriculture & Rural Development, Forest Service
Number of gardeners 4
Size 40ha (100 acres)

Benvarden Garden & Grounds

BENVARDEN, DERVOCK, BALLYMONEY BT53 6NN

Tel 028 2074 1331 **Fax** 028 2074 1955
Website www.benvarden.com
Location Follow the brown signs on B67 Coleraine-Ballycastle road.
Opening hours 12 noon – 5.30 pm; Tuesday – Sunday, plus Bank Holiday Mondays; June to September. And by appointment.
Admission fee Adults £3; Children free. RHS members free from June to August.

The main feature of the 0.8ha walled garden is a spectacular curved red brick wall, nearly 4m high, dating from approximately 1780. Around the walls are espalier-trained apples and pear trees. Other features include a splendid rose garden, several herbaceous borders, a new box parterre, and a fully working kitchen garden. There are also walks around a small lake planted with rhododendrons, azaleas, magnolias and fine trees. A splendid cast-iron bridge, 120ft long and built in 1870, spans the River Bush.

Features roses; herbaceous plants; kitchen garden; rhododendrons & azaleas; tea-room.

Owned by Mr & Mrs Hugh Montgomery
Number of gardeners 2
Size 2ha (5 acres)

Carnfunnock Country Park

DRAINS BAY, COAST ROAD, LARNE, CO. ANTRIM BT40 2QG

Tel 028 2827 0541 **Fax** 028 2827 0852
Website www.larne.gov.uk

Location On Antrim Coast Road (A2), 3½ miles north of Larne.
Opening hours 9 am – dusk; daily; all year. Closed 1 January & 25 December.
Admission fee Parking fees. Free for RHS members in July & August.

The walled garden is set within Carnfunnock Country Park on the Antrim Coast, an Area of Outstanding Natural Beauty. It was originally the cottage garden of the Cairndhu Estate owned and run by Sir Thomas & Lady Dixon. The gardens contain a wide collection of plants from all over the world and enjoy a microclimate which allows plants such as the bottle brush (*Callistemon*) and eucalyptus to flourish. The gardens also boast an amphitheatre, while one of the central features to the walled garden is a unique collection of sundials tracing the history of time. The park also has a hornbeam maze in the shape of Northern Ireland.

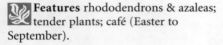**Features** rhododendrons & azaleas; tender plants; café (Easter to September).

Owned by Larne Borough Council
Number of gardeners 3
Size 190ha (473 acres)

Castle Ward

STRANGFORD, DOWNPATRICK, CO. DOWN BT30 7LS

Tel 028 4488 1204 **Fax** 028 4488 1729
Website www.ntni.org.uk
Location On A25, 7 miles from Downpatrick & 1½ miles from Strangford.
Opening hours 10 am – 4 pm (8 pm from May to September); daily; all year.
Admission fee Grounds free. Cars £3.

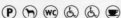

It is the position of the house at Castle Ward which makes it so special – set among rolling parkland with stupendous views across Strangford Lough – while the house itself intrigues the visitor by having one façade in the Georgian style and the other in Gothick. There are fine trees in the park, including embothriums and an avenue of ancient limes. In the walled garden are stately cordylines, dwarf palms, pittosporums and the rare *Mitraria coccinea*.

Features tea-room.

Owned by The National Trust
Number of gardeners 1, plus volunteers
Size 16ha (40 acres)

Florence Court

ENNISKILLEN, CO. FERMANAGH BT92 1DB

Tel 028 6634 8249 **Fax** 028 6634 8873
Website www.nationaltrust.org.uk
Location 8 miles south-west of Enniskillen.
Opening hours Grounds: 10 am – 8 pm (4 pm from October to April); daily; all year.
Admission fee £2.50 per car from March to September.

Florence Court has an 18th-century parkland, with stupendous views of Lough Erne and some magnificent trees. These include the original 'Irish Yew' (*Taxus baccata* 'Fastigiata') and many specimens of a beautiful form of weeping beech with a broad curving crown. The rhododendrons are, for the most part, huge ancient hybrids of *R. arboreum*, but there has been much new planting in recent years and the horticultural interest is now considerable.

Features National Trust shop; light lunches & teas, picnics welcome.

Owned by The National Trust
Number of gardeners 1, plus volunteers
Size 3.6ha (9 acres)

Mount Stewart

GREY ABBEY, NEWTOWNARDS, CO. DOWN BT22 2AD

Tel 028 4278 8387 **Fax** 028 4278 8569
Website www.nationaltrust.org.uk
Location East of Belfast on A20.
Opening hours Lakeside gardens & walks: 10 am – 8 pm; daily; all year. Formal gardens; 10 am – 8 pm; daily; April to September, at weekends only in March & October. Closes at 6 pm in April & October, and at 4 pm in winter.
Admission fee Adults £4.20; Children £2.20.

Mount Stewart is the greatest garden in Northern Ireland, arguably in all Ireland. There are two factors which have made this possible: the exceptionally mild climate which allows plants to thrive that would not survive in all but the mildest parts of the British Isles; and the willingness of the garden's principal maker, Edith, Marchioness of Londonderry, to spend money on a large scale on design, plants and staff. The formal garden in front of the house is grandly laid out with all manner of inventive details: best known are the stone carvings of animals known as the dodo terrace. Beyond the formal garden is a sunken Spanish garden and off to one side is the shamrock garden where a bed designed by Lady Londonderry to represent the Red Hand of Ulster has been surrounded in these more politically correct times by a green shamrock. The rare plants begin on the walls of the house itself: *Rosa gigantea* covers a large area and there are huge plants of *Ceanothus arboreus* 'Trewithen Blue'. Here too are the wonderfully flowing beds of the lily wood where exotic myrtles, pittosporums and phormiums are underplanted with primulas, cyclamen, narcissi and lilies, but here – as in every part of the garden – one is never far from amazing large-leaved rhododendrons, cordylines and tree ferns. Better still is the walk around the lake, where rhododendrons flood the woodlands: for many visitors in spring it is the highlight of a tour of Mount Stewart. The views across the lake are dominated by the mausoleum and the exceptional collection of rhododendrons is interplanted with rare shrubs like mimosas, clianthus, prostantheras, pittosporums and grevilleas. They are underplanted in places with meconopsis and candelabra primulas and, at one point, you catch a glimpse of a white stag in a glade. The outstanding area is the Jubilee Glade where plants in shades of red, white and blue provide colour all through the year. For design, variety, plants and plantings, Mount Stewart is a place of miracles. Allow lots of time for your visit.

Features souvenir shop; refreshments from 12.30 pm.

Owned by The National Trust
Number of gardeners 3, plus volunteers
Size 31ha (77 acres)
NCCPG National Collections *Phormium*; *Dianella*; *Libertia*

Rowallane Garden

SAINTFIELD, BALLYNAHINCH, CO. DOWN BT24 7LH

Tel 028 9751 0131 **Fax** 028 9751 1242
Website www.nationaltrust.org.uk
Location 1 mile south of Saintfield on A7.
Opening hours 10 am – 8 pm (4 pm between
October & April); daily; all year. Closed 24
December to 1 January.
Admission fee Adults £3.50; Children £1.50.
Subject to review.

The extensive gardens at Rowallane can be dated back to 1903, when Hugh Armytage Moore inherited the estate from his uncle John Moore. Uncle John had planted some of the larger trees – wellingtonias, beeches and rhododendrons – but everything else you see today dates from the 20th century. Hugh Armytage Moore was a great plantsman – not just a collector of horticultural curiosities, but a selector of good forms. As his appetite for plants grew, so the garden expanded into the little fields which pattern the estate. The seedlings grew and needed to be planted. The hedges and walls which surround these enclosures remain as the boundary features of each compartment, so that you still have the impression of walking from field to field although each is thickly planted with ornamental trees and shrubs. Moore subscribed to the plant collecting expeditions of E.H. Wilson and Frank Kingdon Ward. It is to those expeditions, that the vast collection of rhododendrons owes its origins. No garden can match it on a sunny day in April or May, as you amble from a glade of *R. augustinii* forms to a line of *R. macabeanum* or back through *R. yakushimanum* hybrids: the large-leaved species are particularly prominent. Because of the mild climate, many other good plants flourish here which are rare elsewhere – *Lomatia ferruginea*, *Grevillea rosmarinifolia*

and *Nothofagus cunninghamii*, for example. Other rarities include *Helwingia japonica* and *Cupressus duclouxiana*, the latter a record-breaking specimen. Rowallane has also given us some good garden hybrids (e.g. *Hypericum* 'Rowallane') and selected forms (e.g. *Viburnum plicatum* 'Rowallane'). Another notable feature is the rock garden – an outcrop of natural whinstone rock which actually has few plants growing in it, but many around the base of the boulders, including the striking candelabra primula 'Rowallane Rose'. And the walled garden too is a treasure-house of rare plants, including *Acca sellowiana* and the National Collection of *Penstemon* species, which gives colour long after the rhododendrons have faded. But it is still the rhododendrons and azaleas for which the garden is best remembered.

Features tallest *Cupressus duclouxiana* (14m.) in the British Isles and three other record trees; National Trust shop; new Information Centre; light refreshments 2 pm – 6 pm May to August & weekends in April & September.

Owned by The National Trust
Number of gardeners 3, plus volunteers
Size 20ha (50 acres)
NCCPG National Collections *Penstemon*

Guy Wilson Daffodil Garden

UNIVERSITY OF ULSTER, COLERAINE, CO. DERRY BT52 1SA

Tel 028 7044 4141
Location Signed from sports centre, or entry via Portstewart Road.
Opening hours Dawn – dusk; daily; all year. Peak flowering time is mid-March to mid-April.
Admission fee Free.

The name says it all – this is both a celebration of Guy Wilson as a daffodil breeder and a museum of his hybrids. Drifts of his cultivars, and others of Irish raising, sweep through the university gardens – more than 1,800 cultivars.

Features An exceptional collection of daffodils, best in second half of April.

Owned by University of Ulster at Coleraine
NCCPG National Collections *Narcissus*

Seaforde Gardens

SEAFORDE, DOWNPATRICK, CO. DOWN BT30 8PG

Tel 028 44 81 1225 Fax 028 44 81 1370
Website www.seafordegardens.com
Location Between Belfast & Newcastle.
Opening hours 10 am – 5 pm; Monday – Saturday. 1 pm – 6 pm; Sundays. Mid-March to late October. Please ring for winter times.
Admission fee Free.

Seaforde is a leading nursery for trees and shrubs, including Irish specialities (*Eucryphia* x *intermedia* 'Rostrevor') and tender taxa. The list now includes a growing number of rhododendrons grown from Patrick Forde's own collecting expeditions to Bhutan, Yunnan, Tibet and Vietnam. The gardens – open all year – are extensive and important: they have drifts of primulas, camassias and bluebells, as well as both pink forms of *Eucryphia lucida*. In the tropical butterfly house is a fascinating collection of tree-ferns.

Features rare trees; eucryphias; lots of interesting plants.

Owned by Patrick Forde
Number of gardeners 2
Size 2ha (5 acres)
NCCPG National Collections *Eucryphia*

GARDENS OF THE REPUBLIC OF IRELAND

Until quite recently, gardens were widely thought of in Ireland as part of the culture of the Anglo-Irish: real Irishmen possessed neither the resources nor the cultural points of reference to occupy themselves with horticulture. There was a grain of truth in this: one of the consequences of the troubles and the land reforms has been the disappearance of many of the historic gardens, parks and demesnes which accompanied the houses of the landed gentry. It is a problem of which the Irish are acutely aware and where such groups as the Irish Georgian Society have done much to change people's perceptions. The new wealth and confidence which Ireland has found within the European Union have helped to dispel the notion that gardens are yet another manifestation of British superiority: now they are seen as something which the Irish can seize upon and adapt to their own cultural styles, traditions, needs and conditions.

The old order is still there, of course. Most of the big gardens attached to big houses and open to the public date back to the 19th century – examples are Lismore, Derreen, Tullynally and Powerscourt. But a number were also made in the middle of the 20th century, often with English pounds (Birr and Malahide) or American dollars (Glenveagh and Mount Congreve). And the best modern gardens in Ireland have most certainly been made by Irishmen – one has only to think of Jim Reynolds's amazing combination of plantsmanship, artistry and style at Butterstream to wonder what further wonders we can expect from Irish horticulture in the years ahead. It is a matter for great concern that Jim Reynolds feels unable to open his garden again in 2004.

Irish gardens tend to be tagged on at the end of guidebooks to UK gardens. The truth is that they are one of the best reasons for visiting Ireland in the first place. This has been made clear from time to time by books that do not always receive the currency they deserve. Two recent titles with a heavy photographic input are *Guide to Irish Gardens* by Shirley Lanigan (The O'Brien Press, 2001) and *Glorious Gardens of Ireland* with pictures by Melanie Eclare (Kyle Cathie, 1999). The Irish Tourist Board (PO Box 273, Dublin 8) publishes a handsomely illustrated guide to *Great Houses, Castles & Gardens of Ireland*. In addition to some 80 of the best places in Eire, it lists about 20 Country House Hotels.

Ireland is well supplied with garden centres, but has few specialist nurseries. Good garden plants are more difficult to come by. Irish gardeners sometimes say that their best herbaceous plants tend to come from Britain and are then more widely distributed through an informal system of gifting. The NCCPG is represented by the Irish Garden Plant Society: there are only three National Collections in the country – *Garrya* and *Potentilla fruticosa* (cvs.) at National Botanic Gardens, Glasnevin, and *Olearia* in the care of Fingal County Council at Malahide Castle. It is also to be hoped that the new Irish interest in gardening will benefit the Royal Horticultural Society of Ireland, whose 'Royal' title hints at its ties to the United Kingdom but which has less than 2,000 members.

Garden restoration is a growth industry in Ireland today. During the last ten years the Heritage Service has helped to rescue the Lutyens gardens at Heywood in Co. Laois and taken over the administration of Fota. Private enterprise has come to the rescue of other gardens: Nicholas and Susan Mosse have made a grand job of restoring the romantic landscape garden at Kilfane in Co. Kilkenny while Benedictine nuns have started to restore the high Victorian gardens at Kylemore Abbey in Connemara. But perhaps the greatest measure of the popularity of gardening in Ireland today is the success of Helen Dillon as a garden-owner, horticultural guru and media star – a success which is very well deserved, for her Dublin garden is an inspiration and her ability to communicate by the written and spoken word is legendary.

Altamont Garden

ALTAMONT, TULLOW, CO. CARLOW

Tel 00 353 059 91 59444 **Fax** 00 353 059 91 59510
Website www.heritageireland.ie
Location Signed from N80 & N81.
Opening hours All year. Phone for opening times.
Admission fee Adults €2.75; OAPs €2; Children €1.25.

Altamont is a charming and romantic woodland garden, full of rare plants, together with lakes, islands, a bog garden and a shady glen. A new double herbaceous border, 75m long within the walled garden, was opened in 2000 with a plant sales area next to it. The woodland garden is a place of contemplation and wonder, and very old-world Irish.

Features woodland garden; rhododendrons & azaleas; cyclamen.

Owned by Dúchas, The Heritage Service
Number of gardeners 4
Size 16ha (40 acres)

Annes Grove Gardens

CASTLETOWNROCHE, MALLOW, CO. CORK

Tel & Fax 00 353 22 26145
Website www.annesgrovegardens.com
Location 1 mile north of Castletownroche on N72.
Opening hours 10 am – 5 pm, Monday – Saturday; 1 pm – 6 pm, Sundays; mid-March to 30 September.
Admission fee Adults €5; OAPs & Students €4; Children €2.

Annes Grove has long been famous for its 30-acre garden, begun in 1907: 'Robinsonian' is the word most often used to describe it. The walled garden is a flower garden, with a 17th-century mount and a Victorian gothic summer house on top. The river garden is lushly wild with lysichiton, gunnera and candelabra primulas around the pools. In the glen garden lies a wonderfully dense collection of rhododendrons and azaleas, many from Kingdon Ward's seed.

**Features** woodland garden; plantsman's collection of plants; good herbaceous borders; rhododendrons from wild seeds; rare trees; tallest *Azara microphylla* (11m) in the British Isles; lunches & teas by arrangement for groups.

Owned by Patrick Annesley
Number of gardeners 4
Size 12ha (30 acres)

Ardgillan Park

BALBRIGGAN, CO. DUBLIN

Tel 00 353 1 890 5629 **Fax** 00 353 1 890 5649
Location Off the coast road between Skerries & Balbriggan in Co. Dublin. Signed from N1/M1.
Opening hours 10 am – 5 pm; daily; all year.
Admission fee Adults £2.50; Children free. £3.50 on 13 June.

Ardgillan is a large country house with castellated embellishments, first built in 1738. The original gardens were almost lost, but restored by the Council and opened to the public as a Regional Park in 1985. To the west of the house are the formal rose gardens, where modern roses are planted in the traditional way with one cultivar per bed. Climbing roses on rope swags run down the central avenue. The Victorian conservatory at the end has also been restored: it was originally constructed at Malahide in the 1880s by the Scottish firm of McKenzie & Moncur. Nearby, the shrubby *Potentilla* collection is beautifully displayed for learning. The formal walled garden has been restored to its layout on the Ordnance Survey map of 1865. Four demonstration areas are devoted to herbs, vegetables, fruit (trained trees and soft fruit) and flowers. Along the walls are many interesting tender shrubs – crinodendrons, clianthus and huge echiums. But everywhere at Ardgillan you will find very high levels of horticultural interest and a good standard of maintenance.

 Features Roses (ancient & modern); potentillas (nearly 200 cultivars); walled garden; herb garden; *potager*; good herbaceous borders; ice house; 200-year-old yew walk; small garden museum; Victorian conservatory; refreshments.

Owned by Fingal County Council
Number of gardeners 1
Size 1.6ha (4 acres)
NCCPG National Collections *Potentilla*

Ardnamona

LOUGH ESKE, CO. DONEGAL

Tel 00 353 73 22650 **Fax** 00 353 73 22819
Website www.ardnamona.com
Location On Lough Eske, 5 miles north-east of Donegal.
Opening hours 10 am – 5 pm; daily; all year.
Admission fee Adults €5; Children free.

Ardnamona is masterpiece of huge arborescent rhododendrons, some as much as 20m high, like a Himalayan forest on the lower slopes of the Blue Stack mountains. A few date back to the introductions of Sir Joseph Hooker in the 1860s. Others were brought by Sir Arthur Wallace as seeds or cuttings from the imperial gardens in Peking and the palace gardens in Kathmandu. All are covered in moss and ferns that revel in the soft climate. Rocky outcrops add to the sense of awesome wilderness, but reclamation and replanting are well under way: the owners have made a big impact on the 40 acres of *Rhododendron ponticum*.

 Features woodland garden; mature conifers; ancient rhododendrons; bed & breakfast offered.

Owned by Mr & Mrs Kieran Clarke
Number of gardeners 1
Size 16ha (40 acres)

Ballymaloe Cookery School Garden

BALLYMALOE, SHANAGARRY, CO. CORK

Tel 00 353 21 4646785 **Fax** 00 353 21 4646909
Website www.cookingisfun.ie
Location Ballymaloe, signed from Castlemartyr & Shanagarry.
Opening hours 10 am – 6 pm; daily; 1 April to 1 October.
Admission fee Adults €5.50; OAPs €2.50; Children €2.

The garden attached to the famous Ballymaloe cookery school is full of unusual fruit, vegetables and herbs. Seldom is a functional garden so stylishly designed and planted, or so extensive. And it is organic.

Features vegetables; roses (mainly old-fashioned); fruit; good herbaceous borders; magnificent formal parterres for herbs; Celtic maze; shell house; garden shop.

Owned by Tim & Darina Allen
Number of gardeners 3
Size 1.2ha (3 acres)

Ballynacourty

BALLYSTEEN, CO. LIMERICK

Tel 00 353 61 396409 **Fax** 00 353 61 396733
Location 3 miles from Askeaton, on River
Shannon.
Opening hours By appointment.
Admission fee €5.

Ballynacourty is a fine modern family garden:
six densely planted acres won from open
farmland. It is interesting for its selection of
lime-tolerant trees and shrubs and to see how
a garden of this size may be maintained with
a minimum amount of help.

Features shrub roses (mainly old-
fashioned); herbaceous borders;
refreshments by arrangement.

Owned by George & Michelina Stacpoole
Number of gardeners 1 part-time
Size 2.4ha (6 acres)

Birr Castle Demesne

BIRR, CO. OFFALY

Tel 00 353 509 20336 **Fax** 00 353 509 21583
Website www.birrcastle.com
Location Rosse Row in Birr, Co. Offaly.
Opening hours 9 am – 6 pm or dusk; daily; all
year.
Admission fee Adults €8.50; OAPs €6.50;
Children €4.50.

The best garden in the Irish Midlands, Birr
has a huge collection of trees and shrubs, a
spacious river walk, a large park with wild
flowers, a reedy lake and a good woodland
garden. Many of the plants were grown
from original collectors' material: some were
collected in the wild by the owner's parents,
Michael and Anne Rosse. The best bit is the
formal garden designed by Anne Rosse in
1935 within the old walled garden. Here is a
cloister of arched hornbeams, a lilac avenue,
crinums, peonies, Irish yews, two rose
gardens (*Rosa roxburghii* 5m high), and the
tallest box hedges in the world,
extraordinarily slender. Good plants are
everywhere and the garden merits a long
visit, though parts are now somewhat
overrun by Irish melancholy and neglect.

Features roses (mainly old-fashioned);
plantsman's collection of plants; fine
collection of trees; *Paeonia* 'Anne Rosse';
Magnolia 'Anne Rosse'; tallest *Acer
monspessulanum* (15m.) and boxwood
Buxus sempervirens (12m.) in the British
Isles, plus 49 other record species; craft
shop; garden centre; café.

Owned by Earl of Rosse
Number of gardeners 5
Size 52ha (130 acres)

Coolcarrigan Gardens

COOLCARRIGAN, NAAS, CO. KILDARE

Tel 00 353 45 863512 **Fax** 00 353 45 863524
Location 12 miles north of Naas.
Opening hours By appointment only, from April to
October.
Admission fee €8.

This garden owes everything to a gale which
knocked the heart out of the established
plantings in 1974. Harold Hillier advised on
the replanting and the result is one of the
best modern collections of trees and shrubs
in Ireland – over 1,100 different species and
cultivars. The owners, keen plantsmen, have
added late summer borders and a rock
garden.

Features snowdrops; rock garden;
rhododendrons & azaleas; plantsman's
collection of shrubs & trees; daffodils;
bluebells; refreshments by arrangement.

Owned by Mr & Mrs Robert Wilson-Wright
Number of gardeners 1
Size 4ha (10 acres)

Curraghmore

PORTLAW, CO. WATERFORD

Tel 00 353 51 387102 **Fax** 00 353 51 387481
Location 14 miles west of Waterford: enter by
Portlaw gate.
Opening hours 2 pm – 5 pm; Thursdays & Bank
Holidays; Easter to mid October. Also (jointly with
House) 9 am – 1 pm; Monday – Friday; January,
May & June. Other times by prior appointment.
Admission fee Garden only €4; House €6.

Lord Waterford's family has lived at
Curraghmore since 1170, which is a long time
even by Irish standards. It has fine terraced
gardens with balustrades and an excellent
collection of trees and shrubs, dating mainly
from the 19th and early 20th centuries. The
outstanding feature is the Shell Grotto which
was built in 1754 by the heiress to the
property, Catherine Poer, Countess of Tyrone.
She personally decorated the interior walls
with shells which were collected from all
round the world. Curraghmore is a
magnificent estate which deserves to be
better known.

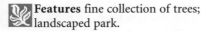**Features** fine collection of trees;
landscaped park.

Owned by The Marquess of Waterford

Derreen

LAURAGH, KILLARNEY, CO. KERRY

Tel 00 353 64 83588
Location 15 miles from Kenmare on the
Castletown Road.
Opening hours 10 am – 6 pm; daily; April to October.
Closed from Monday to Wednesday in August.

Admission fee Adults €5; Children €2.

Derreen is quite extraordinary. The rocky
outcrops come right to the front door, but
the fast lush growth of its trees and shrubs
is boundless. Tree ferns *Dicksonia antarctica*
and myrtles *Luma apiculata* have gone
native, and seed themselves everywhere.
Moss, lichen and ferns abound. Large-leaved
rhododendrons grow to great heights. It is a
place of wonder on a sunny day in late
April. Great for children, too.

Features woodland garden; sub-
tropical plants; tree ferns;
rhododendrons; tea-room.

Owned by Charlie Bigham
Number of gardeners 2
Size 24ha (60 acres)

The Dillon Garden

RANELAGH, DUBLIN 6, CO. DUBLIN

Tel 00 353 1 4971308 **Fax** 00 353 1 4971308
Website www.dillongarden.com
Location 45 Sandford Road.
Opening hours 2 pm – 6 pm; daily; March, July &
August. Plus Sundays only April to June, &
September. Groups by appointment.
Admission fee Adults €5.

This much acclaimed plantsman's garden
offers a fantastic range of rarities, from
snowdrops and hellebores in spring, to
tropaeolums in autumn. Unlike some
collectors' gardens, Helen Dillon's is
immaculately maintained, strictly planted
according to colour and beautifully designed
as a series of garden rooms. Then, in 2000,
she replaced the main lawn with a canal
with formal beds and small cascades set in
limestone paving. More changes took place
in 2003 when she took out the second lawn.

This must be the most intensively gardened garden in the British Isles – a source of constant admiration and inspiration.

Features plantsman's collection of plants; excellent design; good herbaceous borders.

Owned by Helen & Val Dillon
Number of gardeners 1
Size 0.2ha (½ acre)

Earlscliffe

BAILY, CO. DUBLIN

Tel 00 353 1 8322556 **Fax** 00 353 1 8323021
Website www.earlscliffe.com
Location At the end of Ceanchor Road, off the L86 on the south side of the Howth peninsular.
Opening hours By appointment for groups only.
Admission fee Prices on application.

(P) (🐦) (wc)

Dr & Mrs Robinson have developed Earlscliffe since 1969 as a low-maintenance garden devoted to rare and tender plants. The secret is the microclimate which the garden enjoys on a south-facing slope above the sea and, according to Dr Robinson, the complete absence of root damage due to the judicious use of herbicides. No plants are protected and the Robinsons have concentrated on woody plants to facilitate maintenance. It is a stupendous achievement. The range of plants which have succeeded is frankly staggering: among them are some 70 *Eucalyptus* species from Australia, *Juania australis* from the Juan Fernandez Islands, *Araucaria bidwillii* from Australia, *Cordyline baueri, Cyathea dealbata* and *Dacrycarpus dacrydioides* from New Zealand, *Protea* species from South Africa, *Itoa orientalis* from Vietnam and many *Puya* species from Chile. The Ryukyu Island banana *Musa basjoo* fruits most years. *Luma apiculata* and *Cordyline australis* are weeded

out in their hundreds. Other self-seeders include *Echium pininana, E. wildpretii* and *Euphorbia mellifera* from the Canary Islands, *Cyperus alternifolius* from Madagascar and *Erica lusitanica* from Iberia. The planting continues. And the website is excellent.

Features Australian and South African plants.

Owned by Dr & Mrs David Robinson
Number of gardeners owners only
Size 4.4ha (11 acres)

Fernhill

SANDYFORD, DUBLIN 18, CO. DUBLIN

Tel 00 353 1 295 6000
Website www.gardensireland.com/fernhill-gardens.html
Location 7 miles south of central Dublin on the Enniskerry Road, between Lambs Cross & Stepaside.
Opening hours 11 am – 5 pm (2 pm – 5 pm on Sundays & Bank Holidays); Tuesday – Sunday (& Bank Holidays); all year.
Admission fee Adults €5; OAPs €4; Children €2. RHS Members €4.

(P) (wc) (🌳)

This popular garden on the outskirts of Dublin has a good collection of rhododendrons and other woodland plants and some magnificent trees 150 years old. There are steep woodland walks, an enclosed 19th-century garden and an excellent nursery which now sells plants all the year round.

Features woodland garden; rock garden; good herbaceous borders; fine collection of trees; sculpture exhibitions; rhododendrons; new fern plantings.

Owned by Mrs Sally Walker
Number of gardeners 2
Size 16ha (40 acres)

Fota Arboretum & Garden

FOTA ESTATE, CARRIGTWOHILL, CO. CORK

Tel & Fax 00 353 21 4812728
Location 9 miles from Cork city, off Cobh road.
Opening hours 9 am (11 am on Sundays) – 6 pm (5 pm from November to March); daily; all year. Closed for Christmas holidays.
Admission fee Cars €2; pedestrians free.

Fota is famous above all for its trees, most of them planted by the Smith-Barry family towards the end of the 19th century. As well as a fine collection of Victorian conifers (huge redwoods and wellingtonias), the garden and arboretum are notable for the collection of flowering mimosas (*Acacia*), a beautiful *Styrax japonica*, a magnificent collection of mature magnolias, and a spectacular specimen of *Phoenix canariensis* which was planted out over 100 years ago. Some of the record-breaking trees have been lost in recent years but many of Fota's very rare trees still survive, including *Dacrycarpus dacrydioides* and *Phyllocladus tricomanoides*. The garden and arboretum were transferred to the State in 1996 and have since undergone much restoration, regeneration and improvement. New plants have been added, often as part of international conservation programmes. The old walled kitchen garden has been converted to a formal rose garden, with themed borders of monocots, shade-loving and South American plants, a large selection of climbers on the walls, and a collection of Irish-bred daffodils. The Victorian orangery was restored in 2000 and displays a fine collection of contemporary plants. The original formal gardens, known as the 'pleasure gardens' are presently undergoing restoration.

Features woodland garden; mature conifers; 160 Irish-bred daffodil cultivars.

Owned by Dúchas
Number of gardeners 5
Size 11ha (27 acres)

Gash Gardens

GASH, CASTLETOWN, PORTLAOISE, CO. LAOIS

Tel 00 353 502 32247
Location ½ mile from N7 at Castletown.
Opening hours 10 am – 5 pm; Monday – Saturday; May to September. And 2 pm on Sundays in May & June.
Admission fee €4. Group rates by appointment. Not suitable for children.

Nothing outside the garden gate suggests the length, extent or beauty of this extraordinary garden, tucked in along the edges of a dairy farm. It was initially laid out and developed by Noël Keenan in 1984 as a complement to his nursery business: his daughter Mary (who trained at UCD and taught at Glasnevin) is continuing to develop and maintain it. You open the high gates, and walk straight into a vast rock garden stuffed with interesting alpines and well-grown rhododendrons, where great artistry is shown in the choice and positioning of plants. Next comes a long narrow garden like a grassy glade with specimen trees and flowing island beds on either side, a bog garden with an island in the middle, foliage borders with phormiums, gunneras and brilliant contrasts of colour and shape, and a laburnum tunnel at the end. Every part is full of unusual plants and maintained to very high standard. Open a small gate beyond the laburnum tunnel, and a long narrow walk, sometimes in shade, sometimes in the open, runs down alongside a planted stream until finally you reach the River Nore right at the bottom. Here is a long, looped river walk, planted with poplars and larches, beautiful, simple and ingenious. The beauty, the ingenuity and the horticultural interest of the gardens at Gash are incomparable.

 Features herbaceous perennials; rock garden; rhododendrons; plantsman's collection of plants; nursery at entrance, open all year.

Owned by Mary Keenan
Number of gardeners owner, plus part-time
Size 1.6ha (4 acres)

Glenveagh Castle

CHURCHILL, LETTERKENNY, CO. DONEGAL

Tel 00 353 74 9137090 **Fax** 00 353 74 9137072
Location 14 miles north-west of Letterkenny on R251.
Opening hours 13 March to 7 November.
Admission fee Free. Shuttle bus to garden €2.

(P) (WC) (&) (&) (🍴)

Glenveagh was built for its view down the rocky slopes of Lough Veagh: nowhere in Ireland can boast such a contrast between the wild and rugged landscape of a National Park and its carefully nurtured gardens. Part of the gardens is known as the View Garden. Elsewhere is a series of outdoor rooms, each with a different character. The two-acre lawn in the Pleasure Grounds is fringed with rhododendron shrubberies, tree ferns and eucryphias, with massed underplantings of hostas, rodgersias and astilbes. Within the oak woods grow scented rhododendrons, rare trees and tender shrubs: Jim Russell advised on the planting. Paths lead to terraced enclosures furnished with Italian statuary and massive terracotta pots. The unusual shrubs are magnificent: tree-like griselinias and *Michelia doltsopa*,

for instance. The *Jardin Potager* is bounded by herbaceous borders and planted with heritage vegetables, Irish apple cultivars and the rare *Dahlia* 'Matt Armour'. Prepare for a long and fascinating visit.

 Features sub-tropical plants; roses (mainly old-fashioned); plantsman's collection of plants; plants under glass; fruit; good herbaceous borders; fine collection of trees; restaurant at visitor centre; tea-room at castle.

Owned by The Heritage Service
Number of gardeners 6
Size 11ha (27 acres)

Glin Castle

GLIN, CO. LIMERICK

Tel 00 353 68 34173 **Fax** 00 353 68 34364
Website www.glincastle.com
Location On N69, 32 miles west of Limerick.
Opening hours By appointment.
Admission fee Adults €7.

(P) (WC) (&) (&)

Simple formal gardens run down towards the park and merge with the surrounding woodland. The walled kitchen garden has recently received a make-over: cutting borders, herbs, herbaceous borders and such vegetables as sea-kale and asparagus. In the pleasure gardens are some fine ornamental trees – dogwoods, magnolias, cherries and parrotias, as well as rhododendrons and camellias. Taken with the Gothicised castle and its magnificent position on the Shannon estuary, Glin is a place of rare enchantment.

Features vegetables; sub-tropical plants; rhododendrons & azaleas; daffodils; camellias; bluebells.

Owned by Desmond Fitzgerald, Knight of Glin
Number of gardeners 2
Size 2ha (5 acres)

Hillside

ANNMOUNT, GLOUNTHANE, CO. CORK

Tel & Fax 00 353 21 4353119
Location From Cork, turn left at Glounthane Church, up hill, under bridge, 100 yards on right.
Opening hours By appointment between May & September.
Admission fee €5.

This is an intensely cultivated plantsman's garden in a setting of mature trees (beech and pines) and rhododendrons, azaleas, pieris and woodland plants. It burgeons with alpine plants in every part – stone troughs, a scree bed and gravel areas. It also won the 'Top Garden in Ireland' award in 1996 and 2000 for its all-season attractions. And it is forever changing and improving: this year (2004) sees a new gravel garden in old orchard.

Features rhododendrons & azaleas; plantsman's collection of plants; alpine plants; woodland plants.

Owned by Mrs Mary Byrne
Number of gardeners owner only
Size 1.6ha (4 acres)

Japanese Gardens & St Fiacra's Garden

TULLY, KILDARE TOWN, CO. KILDARE

Tel 00 353 45 521617 **Fax** 00 353 45 522964
Website www.irish-national-stud.ie
Location Signed in Kildare.
Opening hours 9.30 am – 6 pm; daily; 12 February to 12 November.
Admission fee €8.50 Adults; €6.50 OAPs; €4.50 Children.

The Japanese garden is a sequence which symbolises Man's journey through life. It was made for Lord Wavertree by Japanese gardeners in the early years of the 20th century and contains some handsome old bonsai and cloud-clipped trees. That said, the garden is planted and maintained in a very Irish style – especially pretty in late spring when the wisteria and water irises are in flower. The standard of maintenance is excellent. Elsewhere on the estate is a very substantial new garden, dedicated to St Fiacre the patron saint of gardeners, which provides a grand contrast. It has little of horticultural interest, but is very evocative of the Irish landscape as it developed in the 6th and 7th centuries. The unusual design, with its strange pseudo-outcrops of weathered limestone, has a strong spiritual quality which perfectly complements the oriental intellectualism of the Japanese garden.

**Features** famous Japanese garden; souvenir shop; light refreshments.

Owned by Irish National Stud
Number of gardeners 3
Size 1.6ha (4 acres) in all

John F. Kennedy Arboretum

NEW ROSS, CO. WEXFORD

Tel 00 353 51 388171 **Fax** 00 353 51 388172
Location 8 miles south of New Ross off R733.
Opening hours 10 am – 8 pm, May to August; 10 am – 6.30 pm, April & September; 10 am – 5 pm, October to March. Closed 9 April & 25 December.
Admission fee Adults €2.75; OAPs €2; Children & Students €1.25; Family €7.

This is a memorial arboretum founded in 1968 with financial help from Irish/American citizens on 623 acres near the Kennedy homestead. Thirty years on, the statistics are impressive: 4,500 types of trees and shrubs arranged taxonomically, and 200 plots by geographical distribution. All are meticulously labelled, and planted with artistry. There is one circuit for broadleaves and another for conifers, interwoven at times to improve the overall appearance of the collection. Special features include an 'ericaceous garden' with 500 different rhododendrons, and many varieties of azaleas and heathers. There is also a slow-growing conifer collection, a hedge collection, a display of groundcover plants and a selection of climbing plants on a series of stone and timber shelters. In summer a miniature railway runs through plantings that represent each continent.

Features mature conifers; fine collection of trees; eight different tree records for the British Isles; souvenirs; cafeteria for teas/refreshments in summer.

Owned by The Heritage Service
Number of gardeners 14
Size 252ha (623 acres)

Johnstown Castle Gardens

WEXFORD, CO. WEXFORD

Tel 00 353 53 42888 **Fax** 00 353 53 42213
Location 4 miles south-west of Wexford.
Opening hours 9 am – 5.30 pm; daily; all year except Christmas day.
Admission fee €4 car and passengers.

Johnstown Castle has 50 acres of ornamental grounds with good trees, tall cordylines, three lakes and the Irish Agricultural Museum. There is a section in the museum devoted to old lawnmowers and antique garden equipment.

Features woodland garden; mature conifers; walled gardens; ornamental

lakes; tallest *Cupressus macrocarpa* (40m.) in the British Isles; coffee shop with snacks, July and August only.

Owned by TEAGASC (Food & Agriculture Development Authority)
Number of gardeners 4
Size 20ha (50 acres)

Kilfane Glen & Waterfall

THOMASTOWN, CO. KILKENNY

Tel 00 353 56 24558 **Fax** 00 353 56 27491
Location Off N9, 2 miles north of Thomastown.
Opening hours 11 am – 6 pm; daily; July & August.
Admission fee Adults €5.50.

A romantic landscape garden laid out in the 1790s and vigorously restored by the present owners. Sit in the tiny *cottage ornée*, admire the exquisite form of the waterfall across the ravine, and dream of Rousseau.

Features woodland garden; bluebells; excellent modern art pieces; teas by arrangement.

Owned by Nicholas & Susan Mosse
Number of gardeners 2
Size 8ha (20 acres)

Lismore Castle

LISMORE, CO. WATERFORD

Tel 00 353 58 54424 **Fax** 00 353 58 54896
Website www.lismorecastle.com
Location Centre of Lismore.
Opening hours 1.45 pm – 4.45 pm; daily; 10 April to 3 October. Opens at 11 am in high season.
Admission fee Adults €5; Children €2.50.

Lismore is best for the castellated house: the gardens are interesting rather than exceptional, but there is a pretty grove of camellias and a double yew walk planted in 1707. The upper enclosure is even older, a Jacobean survivor. The herbaceous border aligned on the cathedral spire has recently been replanted to give colour throughout the summer. Visit the walled garden for some fine traditional kitchen gardening: the vinery was designed by Paxton – this is the Irish Chatsworth.

Features woodland garden; roses (mainly old-fashioned); magnolias; spring bulbs; interesting modern sculptures (including Anthony Gormley).

Owned by Lismore Estates
Number of gardeners 4
Size 2.8ha (7 acres)

Lodge Park Walled Garden

STRAFFAN, CO. KILDARE

Tel 00 353 1 628 8412 **Fax** 00 353 1 627 3477
Website www.steam-museum.ie
Location Follow sign to Steam Museum Straffan from Maynooth & Kill.
Opening hours 2.30 pm – 6 pm; Wednesday – Sunday, plus Bank Holidays; June to August. Visits in May & September by appointment.
Admission fee €7.50.

As it did in the 18th century, the walled garden at Lodge Park continues to produce fruit and vegetables with much more besides. The edible crops grow alongside an ever-increasing collection of lesser-known ornamental plants. Coloured borders of white, blue and yellow greet the visitor and a pink border begins the main walk of the garden, near a collection of peonies. Behind a new classical entrance, the original cold greenhouse allows semi-tender plants to be displayed. A more modern heated greenhouse gives protection for such plants as cymbidiums and brugmansias. The main walk of the garden is lined with box hedges, interrupted by topiary yews: behind the box lies a south-facing border of shrubs and perennials. In the centre is new area of lawn and wide flower borders, with vegetables planted decoratively behind. The main herbaceous border has a backdrop of roses and is spectacular in July. The rose garden includes a circular iron structure clad in climbing roses topped by a copper rosebud. The north-facing border allows for a collection of shade-loving plants, especially hellebores and pulmonarias.

Features roses; good herbaceous borders; gift shop at Museum; tea-room.

Owned by Mr & Mrs Robert Guinness
Number of gardeners 1
Size 0.8ha (2 acres)

Mount Usher Gardens

ASHFORD, CO. WICKLOW

Tel 00 353 404 40205 **Fax** 00 353 404 40116
Website www.mount-usher-gardens.com
Location Ashford, 30 miles south of Dublin on the N11.
Opening hours 10.30 am – 6 pm; daily; 5 March to 31 October.
Admission fee Adults €6; OAPs & Children €5. Guided tours for pre-booked groups available.

These twenty acres of garden have the River Vartry running through their middle: both sides of the river are crowded with unusual trees and shrubs – 5,000 different species and cultivars, some of them *very* rare. The self-sown *Pinus montezumae* are justly famous. There are good herbaceous plants too, and lilies in July. It is a truly remarkable plantsman's garden made in the Robinsonian style by four generations of Walpoles from 1868 to 1980 and extensively restored by the present owner.

Features woodland garden; sub-tropical plants; plantsman's collection of plants; mature conifers; fine trees; spring bulbs; pretty bridges across the river; tallest *Cornus capitata* (18m.) in the British Isles, plus 28 other record tree species; shopping courtyard; tea-room with home-baked food.

Owned by Mrs Madelaine Jay
Number of gardeners 5
Size 8ha (20 acres)

Muckross House & Gardens

MUCKROSS, KILLARNEY, CO. KERRY

Tel 00 353 64 31440 **Fax** 00 353 64 33926
Location 4 miles south of Killarney on N71.
Opening hours Dawn – dusk; daily; all year except one week at Christmas.
Admission fee Free.

Killarney National Park provides a most beautiful setting for the gardens and ancient parkland of Muckross House. The walled garden has just been restored: so has the range of Richardson greenhouses which re-opened in 2002. There are a young arboretum (now fully open to visitors) and some enormous old rhododendrons, but the woodland is of oak, yew, Scots pines and arbutus trees and, even more exciting for a garden-visitor, the rock garden is a natural one, of carboniferous limestone. Well maintained.

Features woodland garden; rock garden; mature conifers; fine collection of trees; rhododendrons; azaleas; greenhouse collection; extensive young

conifer plantings in arboretum; lunches, hot & cold snacks daily.

Owned by Dúchas, The Heritage Service
Size 6ha (15 acres), plus 10-ha (25-acre) arboretum

National Botanic Gardens

GLASNEVIN, DUBLIN 9, CO. DUBLIN

Tel 00 353 1 857 0909 **Fax** 00 353 1 836 0080
Location 3 miles north of City Centre between N1 & N2: exit from M 50 to City Centre at Jct X or Y.
Opening hours 9 am – 6 pm (10 am – 4.30 pm in winter); daily except 25 December. Open at 10 am on Sundays.
Admission fee Free.

Glasnevin was founded in 1795 to promote a scientific approach to the practice of agriculture: education remains a priority at the gardens which have a flourishing school of horticulture. The design of the botanic garden is classically Victorian, laid out as a beautiful public park in undulating ground on the south bank of the River Tolka: plants are comprehensively documented, labelled and classified. Notable trees include a magnificent Caucasian ironwood (*Zelkova carpinifolia*) near the new Herbarium building, good specimens of *Tetradium daniellii*, *Gymnocladus dioica* and *Davidia involucrata* and notable plants of a prostrate form of maidenhair tree (*Ginkgo biloba*) and the weeping Atlantic cedar (*Cedrus atlantica* 'Pendula'). Recent years have seen a dramatic programme of restoration and renewal. The elegant curvilinear range of glasshouses, built by Richard Turner between 1843 and 1868, has been magnificently restored. It has – among many tropical plants – a good collection of cycads. The cactus and fern houses – the borders around them are planted with arum lilies and white watsonias – each have extensive collections, including a 400-year-old tree fern presented by the Melbourne Botanic Garden in the 1890s. Now the restoration of the great palm house is under way. The gardens are a focal point for horticulture in Ireland and still fulfil the function of distributing new introductions among the gardens of Ireland. New education and visitor facilities have recently been added and it remains the finest collection of plants in Ireland. Allow a full day to do justice to the garden and its attractions.

Features large collection of trees including conifers; plant families collection; rock garden and alpine yard; rose garden; vegetable garden; native plants; arboretum; herbaceous borders; seasonal bedding and displays; serpentine pond and heather garden; four ranges of public glasshouses; tropical water lilies; succulents; tender conifers and cycads; Vireya rhododendrons; house plants; palms; orchids; tallest variegated Plane tree *Platanus* x *hispanica* 'Suttneri' (21m.) in the British Isles, plus 25 other tree records tea-rooms.

Owned by Office of Public Works
Number of gardeners 18
Size 20ha (50 acres)
NCCPG National Collections *Garrya*

National Garden Exhibition Centre

KILQUADE, KILPEDDER, CO. WICKLOW

Tel 00 353 1 2819890 **Fax** 00 353 1 2810359
Website www.clubi.ie/calumet
Location Signed from the N11, 7 miles south of Bray.
Opening hours 10 am (1 pm on Sundays) – 6 pm (dusk in winter); daily; all year.
Admission fee Adults €4.50; OAPs €3.50 Groups (10+) €4.

This is a permanent exhibition of contemporary style attached to a garden centre. It has 20 linked but distinct gardens: the Herb Garden; 'Oriental Reflections'; 'Shady Secrets'; the Contemplative Garden; the Celtic Garden; the 'Sensory Garden', and so on. Each was made by a different designer and construction team. New for 2004 is an innovative gothic-style garden. It all adds up to the best of modern Irish design for small gardens: a shop window for ideas on style, plants and materials.

Features model gardens; garden centre; restaurant.

Owned by Tim & Suzanne Wallis

Powerscourt Gardens

POWERSCOURT ESTATE, ENNISKERRY, CO. WICKLOW

Tel 00 353 1 204 6000 **Fax** 00 353 1 204 6900
Website www.powerscourt.ie/gardens
Location 12 miles south of Dublin off N11.
Opening hours 9.30 am – 5.30 pm (dusk in winter); daily except 25 & 26 December; all year.
Admission fee Gardens only: Adults €6; OAPs €5.50; Children €3.50.

Powerscourt is a wonderful mixture of awesome grandeur and sheer fun. It is also extremely well organised for visitors. The main Italianate garden, dominated by a stately 1860s staircase down to a lake, has Great Sugarloaf Mountain as an off-centre backdrop. It is lined with bedding plants, statues and urns (look out for the sulky cherubs). To one side is the Japanese garden – not strongly Japanese – but full of twists and hummocks. In the arboretum are many rare trees. Powerscourt is busy in summer, but you can escape into solitude along the avenue of monkey puzzles. The magnificent house is now open to visitors again.

Features woodland garden; mature conifers; fine collection of trees; much recent restoration, including the Bamberg gates, and a remodelling of the Japanese garden; tallest *Abies spectabilis* (32m.) in the British Isles, plus 10 other record tree specimens; garden centre; terrace café with lunches.

Owned by Powerscourt Estate
Number of gardeners 6
Size 19ha (47 acres)

Primrose Hill

PRIMROSE LANE, LUCAN, CO. DUBLIN

Tel 00 353 1 6280373
Location Lucan village, at top of Primrose Lane, through black iron gates.
Opening hours 2 pm – 6 pm; daily; February, then June to the beginning of August. And by appointment.
Admission fee Adults €4; Children €2.

(P) (WC) (garden)

Primrose Hill is a plantsman's garden, particularly interesting for its rare forms of herbaceous plants and its snowdrops. The planting continues, and includes a small arboretum, but this is a garden which gets better every year.

 Features snowdrops; plantsman's collection of plants; good herbaceous borders.

Owned by Robin Hall
Number of gardeners owner only
Size 2.4ha (6 acres)

Talbot Botanic Gardens

MALAHIDE CASTLE, MALAHIDE, CO. DUBLIN

Tel 00 353 1 8160014/8462456 **Fax** 00 353 1 8169910/8463620
Website www.fingalcoco.ie
Location 10 miles north of Dublin off R107 Malahide Road.
Opening hours 2 pm – 5 pm (or by appointment); daily; May to September. Groups only by arrangement.
Admission fee Adults €3.50; Groups €3. (2003 prices).

The Talbot Botanic Garden at Malahide Demesne was the work of Milo Talbot, a passionate amateur botanist with a particular interest in southern hemisphere plants, notably the flora of Tasmania and Chile. He built up a collection of 5,000 different taxa and, since the soil is limey, they are mostly calcicole plants. The gardens consist of an eighteen-acre woodland garden and a four-acre walled garden, divided into seven distinct areas which give the impression of a series of secret gardens each with its own particular range of plants. It is in this walled garden that the rarer and tender species will be found. There are seven small glasshouses including a Victorian Conservatory at the end of the central path – a prominent focal point. Each house is very different in its style and in its plantings. The smallest has a collection of *Primula auricula* cultivars, while the Victorian house has a collection of Australasian plants. There are extensive collections of escallonias, *Syringa*, philadelphus, nothofagus and pittosporum as well as the National Collection of *Olearia*. Malahide is best visited at 2 pm on Wednesday afternoons when guided tours are offered of the walled garden (not otherwise open).

Features woodland garden; plantsman's collection of plants; mature conifers; fine collection of trees; alpine plants; Tasmanian plants; restaurant.

Owned by Fingal County Council
Size 8.7ha (22 acres)
NCCPG National Collections *Olearia*

Tullynally Castle

CASTLEPOLLARD, CO. WESTMEATH

Tel 00 353 44 61159 **Fax** 00 353 44 61856
Website www.tullynallycastle.com
Location Signposted from Castlepollard. 12 miles from Mullingar.
Opening hours 2 pm – 6 pm; daily; June to August. Plus weekends & Bank Holidays in May.
Admission fee Adults €5; Children €2.

Tullynally has a romantic Loudonesque garden for a rambling Gothic Revival house.

Formal terraces overlook the park and lead to the woodland gardens, enriched with recent plantings of maples and magnolias. A fine avenue of Irish yews is the centrepiece of the walled garden: they are thought to be about 200 years old and thus among the oldest in existence. The owner Thomas Pakenham has now followed up his acclaimed *Meetings with Remarkable Trees*, some of whose photographs were taken at Tullynally, with *Remarkable Trees of the World* (Weidenfeld, 2002). And he has introduced some interesting exotics to Tullynally from his travels abroad.

 Features woodland garden; grotto; lake; new Chinese & Tibetan gardens; plants collected by owners; several largest beech trees *Fagus sylvatica* in the British Isles ; shop; tea-room.

Owned by Mr & Mrs Thomas Pakenham
Number of gardeners 2
Size 10ha (25 acres)

PLANT-
LOVER'S
GUIDES

NCCPG NATIONAL COLLECTIONS

ABELIA
Pleasant View Nursery & Garden
Devon, England

ABIES
Ardkinglas Woodland Garden
Strathclyde, Scotland

ACACIA
Tresco Abbey
Cornwall, England

ACER
Hergest Croft Gardens
Herefordshire, England

ACER (Japanese cvs.)
Westonbirt The National Arboretum
Gloucestershire, England

ACHILLEA
Capel Manor
London, England

ADIANTUM
Tatton Park
Cheshire, England

AESCULUS
West Dean Gardens
Sussex, West, England

ALCHEMILLA
Cambridge University Botanic Garden
Cambridgeshire, England

ANEMONE NEMOROSA
Kingston Lacy
Dorset, England

ANEMONE (Japanese anemones)
Heathlands
Hampshire, England

ANEMONE (Japanese)
Broadview Gardens
Kent, England

ANTHEMIS
University of Birmingham Botanic Garden at
Winterbourne
West Midlands, England

AQUILEGIA
Hardwicke House
Cambridgeshire, England

ARALIA
Powis Castle & Garden
Powys, Wales

ARBUTUS
Dunster Castle
Somerset, England

ARTEMISIA
Elsworth Herbs
Cambridgeshire, England

ASPLENIUM SCOLOPENDRIUM
Sizergh Castle
Cumbria, England

ASTER
Temple Newsam Park
Yorkshire, West, England

ASTER
Upton House
Warwickshire, England

ASTER (autumn-flowering)
The Picton Garden
Herefordshire, England

ASTILBE
Holehird Gardens
Cumbria, England

ASTILBE
Marwood Hill Gardens
Devon, England

ASTRANTIA
Warren Hills Cottage
Leicestershire, England

AUBRIETA
University of Leicester Botanic Garden
Leicestershire, England

AZARA
Exeter University Gardens
Devon, England
Trelissick Garden
Cornwall, England

BEGONIA
Glasgow Botanic Garden
Strathclyde, Scotland
Rhodes & Rockliffe
Essex, England

BERBERIS
Mill Hill Plants
Nottinghamshire, England

BERGENIA
Greenbank Garden
Strathclyde, Scotland

BERGENIA (species & primary hybrids)
Cambridge University Botanic Garden
Cambridgeshire, England

BETULA
Hergest Croft Gardens
Herefordshire, England
Wakehurst Place
Sussex, West, England

BONSAI
Birmingham Botanical Gardens & Glasshouses
West Midlands, England

BRACHYGLOTTIS
Inverewe
Highland, Scotland

BUDDLEJA
Longstock Water Gardens
Hampshire, England

BUXUS
Ickworth
Suffolk, England
Langley Boxwood Nursery
Hampshire, England

CALLUNA VULGARIS
RHS Garden Wisley
Surrey, England

CALTHA
Rowden Gardens
Devon, England

CAMELLIA JAPONICA
Antony Woodland Garden
Cornwall, England

CAMELLIA
Mount Edgcumbe Gardens
Cornwall, England

CAMELLIA X WILLIAMSII
Wentworth Castle Gardens
Yorkshire, South, England

CAMPANULA
Burton Agnes Hall Gardens
Yorkshire, East Riding of, England
Lingen Nursery and Gardens
Shropshire, England

CARPINUS BETULUS cvs.
Beale Arboretum
Hertfordshire, England

CARPINUS
The Sir Harold Hillier Gardens
Hampshire, England

CASSIOPE
Branklyn Garden
Tayside, Scotland

CATALPA
Cliveden
Buckinghamshire, England

CEANOTHUS (deciduous)
Knoll Gardens
Dorset, England

CELMISIA
St Luke's Cottage
Northumberland and Tyne & Wear, England

CENTAUREA
Bide-a-Wee Cottage
Northumberland and Tyne & Wear, England

CHAMAECYPARIS LAWSONIANA
University of Leicester Botanic Garden
Leicestershire, England

CHAMAECYPARIS LAWSONIANA cvs.
Bedgebury National Pinetum
Kent, England

CHRYSANTHEMUM (Charms & Cascade)
Temple Newsam Park
Yorkshire, West, England

CITRUS
Hales Hall Gardens & Reads Nursery
Norfolk, England

CLEMATIS VITICELLA
Longstock Water Gardens
Hampshire, England

CLEMATIS
Burford House Gardens
Shropshire, England

COLCHICUM
Felbrigg Hall
Norfolk, England

CONOPHYTUM
Abbey Brook Cactus Nursery
Derbyshire, England

CONVALLARIA
Kingston Lacy
Dorset, England

COPROSMA
County Park Nursery
Essex, England

CORIARIA
Crûg Farm Plants
Gwynedd, Wales

CORNUS
The Sir Harold Hillier Gardens
Hampshire, England
RHS Garden Rosemoor
Devon, England

CORNUS (excluding *C. florida* cvs.)
Newby Hall
Yorkshire, North, England

CORYLUS
The Sir Harold Hillier Gardens
Hampshire, England

CORYLUS (cobnuts & filberts)
Brogdale
Kent, England

COTONEASTER
The Sir Harold Hillier Gardens
Hampshire, England

CROCUS
RHS Garden Wisley
Surrey, England

x CUPRESSOCYPARIS
Bedgebury National Pinetum
Kent, England

CYDONIA OBLONGA
Norton Priory Museum & Gardens
Cheshire, England

CYSTOPTERIS
Sizergh Castle
Cumbria, England

DABOECIA
RHS Garden Wisley
Surrey, England

DAPHNE
Brandy Mount House
Hampshire, England

DELPHINIUM
Rougham Hall Nurseries
Suffolk, England
Temple Newsam Park
Yorkshire, West, England

DENDROBIUM
Glasgow Botanic Garden
Strathclyde, Scotland

DEUTZIA
The Hollies Park
Yorkshire, West, England

DIANELLA
Mount Stewart
Co. Down, Northern Ireland

DIANTHUS
Kingstone Cottage Plants
Herefordshire, England

DIANTHUS (Malmaison carnations)
Crathes Castle
Grampian, Scotland

DICKSONIACEAE
Glasgow Botanic Garden
Strathclyde, Scotland

DIGITALIS
The Botanic Nursery
Wiltshire, England

DRYOPTERIS
RHS Garden Harlow Carr
Yorkshire, North, England
Sizergh Castle
Cumbria, England

DWARF & SLOW-GROWING CONIFERS
Savill Garden
Surrey, England
Valley Gardens
Surrey, England

ECHINOPSIS HYBRIDS
Abbey Brook Cactus Nursery
Derbyshire, England

ELAEAGNUS
Beale Arboretum
Hertfordshire, England

EMBOTHRIUM
Bodnant Gardens
Clwyd, Wales

ENKIANTHUS
Clyne Gardens
Glamorgan, Wales

EPIMEDIUM
Lilliesleaf Nursery
Borders, Scotland
RHS Garden Wisley
Surrey, England

ERICA
Bell's Cherrybank Centre
Tayside, Scotland
RHS Garden Wisley
Surrey, England

ERYTHRONIUM
Greencombe Gardens
Somerset, England
R.V. Roger Ltd
Yorkshire, North, England

EUCALYPTUS
Meon Orchard
Hampshire, England

EUCRYPHIA
Bodnant Gardens
Clwyd, Wales
Seaforde Gardens
Co. Down, Northern Ireland

EUPHORBIA
Oxford Botanic Garden
Oxfordshire, England

FAGUS
Kirkley Hall Gardens
Northumberland and Tyne & Wear, England

FERNS
Savill Garden
Surrey, England
Valley Gardens
Surrey, England

FICUS
Hales Hall Gardens & Reads Nursery
Norfolk, England

FRAXINUS
The Quinta
Cheshire, England
Thorp Perrow Arboretum & Woodland Garden
Yorkshire, North, England

FRITILLARIA (EUROPEAN SPECIES)
Cambridge University Botanic Garden
Cambridgeshire, England

FUCHSIA
Margam Park
Glamorgan, Wales
University of Leicester Botanic Garden
Leicestershire, England

FUCHSIA (hardy)
Croxteth Hall & Country Park
Lancashire, Merseyside & Greater Manchester, England
Kathleen Muncaster Fuchsias
Lincolnshire, England

FUCHSIA section Quelusia
RHS Garden Harlow Carr
Yorkshire, North, England

GALANTHUS
Brandy Mount House
Hampshire, England

GALANTHUS
RHS Garden Wisley
Surrey, England

GARRYA
National Botanic Gardens
Co. Dublin, Republic of Ireland

GAULTHERIA
Greencombe Gardens
Somerset, England

GENTIANA
Christie's Nursery
Tayside, Scotland

GERANIUM
Catforth Garden
Lancashire, Merseyside & Greater Manchester, England
East Lambrook Manor
Somerset, England

GERANIUM (cvs)
Coombland Gardens & Nursery
Sussex, West, England

GERANIUM (species & primary hybrids)
Cambridge University Botanic Garden
Cambridgeshire, England

GREVILLEA
Pine Lodge Gardens & Nursery
Cornwall, England

GYMNOCALYCIUM
Abbey Brook Cactus Nursery
Derbyshire, England

HAMAMELIS
The Sir Harold Hillier Gardens
Hampshire, England
Swallow Hayes
Shropshire, England

HAWORTHIA
Abbey Brook Cactus Nursery
Derbyshire, England

HEDERA
Erddig
Clwyd, Wales
Fibrex Nurseries Ltd
Warwickshire, England

HELIOTROPIUM
Hampton Court Palace
London, England

HELLEBORUS
Broadview Gardens
Kent, England

HELLEBORUS (part)
Longthatch
Hampshire, England

White Windows
Hampshire, England

HEMEROCALLIS
Antony
Cornwall, England

HEMEROCALLIS (Coe hybrids)
The Hollies Park
Yorkshire, West, England

HEMEROCALLIS cvs. post-1970
Rosewood Daylilies
Kent, England

HIBISCUS SYIACUS cvs.
Notcutts Nurseries
Suffolk, England

HILLIER' PLANTS
The Sir Harold Hillier Gardens
Hampshire, England

HOHERIA
Abbotsbury Sub-Tropical Gardens
Dorset, England

HOSTA (large-leaved)
The Hollies Park
Yorkshire, West, England

HOSTA (modern hybrids)
Ann & Roger Bowden
Devon, England

HYACINTHUS ORIENTALIS
Ripley Castle Gardens
Yorkshire, North, England

HYDRANGEA
Holehird Gardens
Cumbria, England

HYPERICUM
Wakehurst Place
Sussex, West, England

ILEX
RHS Garden Rosemoor
Devon, England
Savill Garden
Surrey, England
Valley Gardens
Surrey, England

INULA
Bluebell Cottage Gardens & Lodge Lane Nursery
Cheshire, England

IRIS ENSATA
Marwood Hill Gardens
Devon, England

IRIS SIBIRICA
Lingen Nursery and Gardens
Shropshire, England

IRIS SPURIA
Belsay Hall
Northumberland and Tyne & Wear, England

IRIS
Myddelton House
London, England

IRIS (fulva, pseudacorus, versicolor, virginica & laevigata cvs)
Rowden Gardens
Devon, England

JUGLANS
Thorp Perrow Arboretum & Woodland Garden
Yorkshire, North, England
Wimpole Hall
Cambridgeshire, England

JUNIPERUS
Bedgebury National Pinetum
Kent, England

KNIPHOFIA
Barton Manor
Isle of Wight, England

LABURNUM
Powis Castle & Garden
Powys, Wales
Thorp Perrow Arboretum & Woodland Garden
Yorkshire, North, England

LAVANDULA
Downderry Nursery
Kent, England

LEWISIA
Ashwood Nurseries Ltd
Staffordshire, England

LIBERTIA
Mount Stewart
Co. Down, Northern Ireland

LIGUSTRUM
The Sir Harold Hillier Gardens
Hampshire, England

LIRIODENDRON
West Dean Gardens
Sussex, West, England

LITHOCARPUS
The Sir Harold Hillier Gardens
Hampshire, England

LITHOPS
Abbey Brook Cactus Nursery
Derbyshire, England

LONICERA (shrubby species & primary hybrids)
Cambridge University Botanic Garden
Cambridgeshire, England

LUPINUS (Russell strains)
Swallow Hayes
Shropshire, England

LYSIMACHIA
Cotswold Garden Flowers
Worcestershire, England

MAGNOLIA
Sherwood
Devon, England
Caerhays Castle Gardens
Cornwall, England
Savill Garden
Surrey, England
Valley Gardens
Surrey, England

MAGNOLIA (spp.)
Bodnant Gardens
Clwyd, Wales

MAGNOLIA species
Wentworth Castle Gardens
Yorkshire, South, England

MAHONIA
Savill Garden
Surrey, England

MAHONIA
Valley Gardens
Surrey, England

MALUS
Granada Arboretum
Cheshire, England

MALUS (apples, ornamental cvs. & cider apples)
Brogdale
Kent, England

MECONOPSIS
East Durham & Houghall Community College
Co. Durham, England

MENTHA
Iden Croft Herbs
Kent, England

MONARDA
Leeds Castle
Kent, England

NARCISSUS
Brodie Castle
Grampian, Scotland
Guy Wilson Daffodil Garden
Co. Derry, Northern Ireland

NARCISSUS (miniature)
Broadleigh Gardens
Somerset, England

NERIUM OLEANDER
Elsworth Herbs
Cambridgeshire, England

NOTHOFAGUS
Crarae Gardens
Strathclyde, Scotland
Wakehurst Place
Sussex, West, England

NYMPHAEA
Bennetts Water Lily Farm
Dorset, England
Burnby Hall Gardens
Yorkshire, East Riding of, England
Kenchester Water Gardens
Herefordshire, England
Stapeley Water Gardens
Cheshire, England

OENOTHERA
Old Vicarage
Wiltshire, England

OLEARIA
Inverewe
Highland, Scotland
Talbot Botanic Gardens
Co. Dublin, Republic of Ireland

ORIGANUM
Chesters Walled Garden
Northumberland and Tyne & Wear, England
Iden Croft Herbs
Kent, England

OSMUNDA
Sizergh Castle
Cumbria, England

PAEONIA LACTIFLORA
Kelways Ltd
Somerset, England

PAPAVER ORIENTALE
Water Meadow Nursery and Herb Farm
Hampshire, England

PARIS
Crûg Farm Plants
Gwynedd, Wales

PELARGONIUM
Fibrex Nurseries Ltd
Warwickshire, England

PENNISETUM
Knoll Gardens
Dorset, England

PENSTEMON
Kingston Maurward Gardens
Dorset, England
Pershore College
Worcestershire, England
Rowallane Garden
Co. Down, Northern Ireland

PERNETTYA
Savill Garden
Surrey, England
Valley Gardens
Surrey, England

PHILADELPHUS
The Hollies Park
Yorkshire, West, England
Pershore College
Worcestershire, England

PHLOX PANICULATA
Temple Newsam Park
Yorkshire, West, England

PHORMIUM
Mount Stewart
Co. Down, Northern Ireland

PHOTINIA
The Sir Harold Hillier Gardens
Hampshire, England
Trelissick Garden
Cornwall, England

PHYGELIUS
Knoll Gardens
Dorset, England

PICEA
Ardkinglas Woodland Garden
Strathclyde, Scotland

PIERIS
Clyne Gardens
Glamorgan, Wales

PINUS
The Quinta
Cheshire, England

PINUS (excl. dwarf cvs.)
The Sir Harold Hillier Gardens
Hampshire, England

PLANTS INTRODUCED BY SIR FREDERICK STERN
Highdown
Sussex, West, England

PLATANUS
Mottisfont Abbey
Hampshire, England

PLEIONE
Butterfields Nursery
Buckinghamshire, England

POLYGONUM (i.e. *Fagopyrum, Fallopia* & *Persicaria*)
Rowden Gardens
Devon, England

POLYPODIUM
RHS Garden Harlow Carr
Yorkshire, North, England
Rickard's Hardy Ferns Ltd
Worcestershire, England

POLYSTICHUM
Greencombe Gardens
Somerset, England
Holehird Gardens
Cumbria, England

POPULUS
Wiltshire College Lackham
Wiltshire, England

POTENTILLA FRUTICOSA cvs.
Webbs of Wychbold
Worcestershire, England

PONTENTILLA
Ardgillan Park
Co. Dublin, Republic of Ireland

PRIMULA AURICULA
Golden Acre Park
Yorkshire, West, England

PRIMULA AURICULA
Martin Nest Nurseries
Lincolnshire, England

PRIMULA (Cortusoides section)
Plant World Botanic Gardens
Devon, England

PRUNUS (cherries)
Brogdale
Kent, England

PRUNUS (plums)
Brogdale
Kent, England

PRUNUS (sato-sakura group)
Batsford Arboretum
Gloucestershire, England

PULMONARIA
Stillingfleet Lodge Nurseries
Yorkshire, North, England

PYRUS
Brogdale
Kent, England

QUERCUS
The Sir Harold Hillier Gardens
Hampshire, England

RANUNCULUS FICARIA
Rowden Gardens
Devon, England

RHEUM
RHS Garden Harlow Carr
Yorkshire, North, England

RHEUM (culinary)
RHS Garden Wisley
Surrey, England

RHODODENDRON FORRESTII
Bodnant Gardens
Clwyd, Wales

RHODODENDRON (Barbatum, Glischra & Maculifera sections)
Inverewe
Highland, Scotland

RHODODENDRON (Ghent azaleas)
Sheffield Park Garden
Sussex, East, England

RHODODENDRON (Knap Hill azaleas)
Sherwood
Devon, England

RHODODENDRON (Kurume azaleas, the Wilson 50)
Isabella Plantation
London, England

RHODODENDRON (species & Glenn Dale azaleas)
Savill Garden
Surrey, England
Valley Gardens
Surrey, England
Rhododendron (subsections Falconera, Grandia and Maddenia)
Brodick Castle
Strathclyde, Scotland

RHODODENDRON (Triflora & Falconera subsections)
Clyne Gardens
Glamorgan, Wales

RHODODENDRON species
Wentworth Castle Gardens
Yorkshire, South, England

RIBES GROSSULARIA (gooseberries)
Brogdale
Kent, England
Rougham Hall Nurseries
Suffolk, England

RIBES NIGRUM (blackcurrants)
Brogdale
Kent, England

RIBES SATIVUM (currants other than blackcurrants)
Brogdale
Kent, England

RIBES (species & primary hybrids)
Cambridge University Botanic Garden
Cambridgeshire, England

RODGERSIA
Hadspen Garden
Somerset, England

ROSA
Mottisfont Abbey
Hampshire, England

ROSA (19th-century shrubs)
Malleny House Garden
Lothian, Scotland

ROSA (Austin 'English' cultivars)
David Austin Roses
Shropshire, England

ROSA (History of European roses)
University of Birmingham Botanic Garden at Winterbourne
West Midlands, England

ROSA (species)
Peter Beales Roses
Norfolk, England

ROSMARINUS
Downderry Nursery
Kent, England

RUSCUS
Cambridge University Botanic Garden
Cambridgeshire, England

SALIX
Westonbirt The National Arboretum
Gloucestershire, England

SALVIA
Kingston Maurward Gardens
Dorset, England
Pleasant View Nursery & Garden
Devon, England

SAMBUCUS
Wallington
Northumberland and Tyne & Wear, England

SARCOCOCCA
Capel Manor
London, England

SAXIFRAGA
Waterperry Gardens
Oxfordshire, England

SAXIFRAGA (European species)
Cambridge University Botanic Garden
Cambridgeshire, England

SKIMMIA
University of Leicester Botanic Garden
Leicestershire, England

SKIMMIA
Wakehurst Place
Sussex, West, England

SOLENOSTEMON
Temple Newsam Park
Yorkshire, West, England

SORBUS
East Durham & Houghall Community College
Co. Durham, England
Granada Arboretum
Cheshire, England

SORBUS (Aria & Micromeles groups)
Winkworth Arboretum
Surrey, England

STEWARTIA
High Beeches
Sussex, West, England

STREPTOCARPUS
Dibleys Nurseries
Clwyd, Wales

STYRACACEAE (incl. *Halesia,Pterostyrax, Styrax, Sinojackia*)
Holker Hall
Cumbria, England

SYRINGA
Golden Acre Park
Yorkshire, West, England
The Hollies Park
Yorkshire, West, England

TAXUS
Bedgebury National Pinetum
Kent, England

THUJA
Bedgebury National Pinetum
Kent, England

THYMUS
Chesters Walled Garden
Northumberland and Tyne & Wear, England

TILIA
Thorp Perrow Arboretum & Woodland Garden
Yorkshire, North, England

TRADESCANTIA ANDERSONIANA GROUP
Kayes Garden Nursery
Leicestershire, England

TRILLIUM
Spinners
Hampshire, England

TROPAEOLUM species
Inveresk Lodge
Lothian, Scotland

TULBAGHIA
Marwood Hill Gardens
Devon, England

TULIPA (species & primary hybrids)
Cambridge University Botanic Garden
Cambridgeshire, England

VACCINIUM
Greencombe Gardens
Somerset, England

VIBURNUM
RHS Garden Hyde Hall
Essex, England

VITIS VINIFERA (grapes)
Brogdale
Kent, England

VITIS VINIFERA (grapes)
Hales Hall Gardens & Reads Nursery
Norfolk, England

YUCCA
Renishaw Hall
Derbyshire, England

ZELKOVA
Hergest Croft Gardens
Herefordshire, England

WHERE TO SEE PARTICULAR PLANTS

ALPINES

Brandy Mount House
Hampshire, England
Cambridge University Botanic Garden
Cambridgeshire, England
Glen Chantry
Essex, England
Hillside
Co. Cork, Republic of Ireland
W.E.Th. Ingwersen Ltd
Sussex, West, England
Jack Drake
Highland, Scotland
National Botanic Gardens
Co. Dublin, Republic of Ireland
Pershore College
Worcestershire, England
Pottertons Nursery
Lincolnshire, England
RHS Garden Wisley
Surrey, England
Royal Botanic Garden Edinburgh
Lothian, Scotland
Royal Botanic Gardens, Kew
London, England
St Luke's Cottage
Northumberland and Tyne & Wear, England
University of Leicester Botanic Garden
Leicestershire, England

ARBORETA

Abbotsbury Sub-Tropical Gardens
Dorset, England
Antony
Cornwall, England
Arley Arboretum
Worcestershire, England
Bath Botanic Gardens
Somerset, England
Batsford Arboretum
Gloucestershire, England
Bicton Park Gardens
Devon, England
Bluebell Arboretum & Nursery
Derbyshire, England

Bodenham Arboretum
Worcestershire, England
Caerhays Castle Gardens
Cornwall, England
Cambridge University Botanic Garden
Cambridgeshire, England
Chatsworth
Derbyshire, England
Chyverton
Cornwall, England
Cowdray Park
Sussex, West, England
Cruickshank Botanic Garden
Grampian, Scotland
Dawyck Botanic Garden
Borders, Scotland
Earlscliffe
Co. Dublin, Republic of Ireland
East Bergholt Place
Suffolk, England
Exbury Gardens
Hampshire, England
Exeter University Gardens
Devon, England
Fota Arboretum & Garden
Co. Cork, Republic of Ireland
Golden Acre Park
Yorkshire, West, England
Granada Arboretum
Cheshire, England
Hergest Croft Gardens
Herefordshire, England
Highclere Castle
Hampshire, England
Landford Trees
Wiltshire, England
Lynford Arboretum
Norfolk, England
Marwood Hill Gardens
Devon, England
Melbury House
Dorset, England
National Botanic Gardens
Co. Dublin, Republic of Ireland
Nymans
Sussex, West, England

Pencarrow
Cornwall, England
Pershore College
Worcestershire, England
RHS Garden Wisley
Surrey, England
RHS Garden Hyde Hall
Essex, England
RHS Garden Rosemoor
Devon, England
Rowallane Garden
Co. Down, Northern Ireland
Royal Botanic Garden Edinburgh
Lothian, Scotland
Royal Botanic Gardens, Kew
London, England
Saling Hall
Essex, England
Seaforde Gardens
Co. Down, Northern Ireland
Sheffield Park Garden
Sussex, East, England
Talbot Botanic Gardens
Co. Dublin, Republic of Ireland
Tatton Park
Cheshire, England
Thorp Perrow Arboretum & Woodland Garden
Yorkshire, North, England
Torosay Castle & Gardens
Strathclyde, Scotland
Westonbirt The National Arboretum
Gloucestershire, England
Whitfield
Herefordshire, England
Winkworth Arboretum
Surrey, England
Woburn Abbey
Bedfordshire, England

BEGONIA
Blackmore & Langdon
Somerset, England
Glasgow Botanic Garden
Strathclyde, Scotland

BLUEBELLS
Emmetts Garden
Kent, England
Fairhaven Woodland & Water Garden
Norfolk, England
Furzey Gardens
Hampshire, England
Galloway House Gardens
Dumfries & Galloway, Scotland
Haughley Park
Suffolk, England

High Beeches
Sussex, West, England
Hole Park
Kent, England
Killerton
Devon, England
Lanhydrock
Cornwall, England
Leonardslee Lakes & Gardens
Sussex, West, England
Lydney Park Gardens
Gloucestershire, England
Royal Botanic Gardens, Kew
London, England
Sheffield Park Garden
Sussex, East, England
Stourhead
Wiltshire, England
Thorp Perrow Arboretum & Woodland Garden
Yorkshire, North, England
Wakehurst Place
Sussex, West, England
Winkworth Arboretum
Surrey, England

BORDER AND HERBACEOUS PLANTS
Arley Hall
Cheshire, England
Barrington Court
Somerset, England
Beningbrough Hall & Gardens
Yorkshire, North, England
Beth Chatto Gardens
Essex, England
Bressingham Gardens
Norfolk, England
Buscot Park
Oxfordshire, England
Castle Drogo
Devon, England
Clare College Fellows' Garden
Cambridgeshire, England
Cottesbrooke Hall
Northamptonshire, England
The Courts Garden
Wiltshire, England
East Ruston Old Vicarage
Norfolk, England
Felley Priory
Nottinghamshire, England
Forde Abbey
Dorset, England
Garsington Manor
Oxfordshire, England

Goodnestone Park
Kent, England
Great Dixter
Sussex, East, England
Hatfield House
Hertfordshire, England
Helmingham Hall
Suffolk, England
Hestercombe Gardens
Somerset, England
Hinton Ampner House
Hampshire, England
Hoveton Hall
Norfolk, England
Kingston Maurward Gardens
Dorset, England
Leeds Castle
Kent, England
The National Botanic Garden of Wales
Dyfed, Wales
National Botanic Gardens
Co. Dublin, Republic of Ireland
Ness Botanic Gardens
Cheshire, England
Newby Hall
Yorkshire, North, England
Nymans
Sussex, West, England
Packwood House
Warwickshire, England
Parham
Sussex, West, England
Pashley Manor Gardens
Sussex, East, England
Pershore College
Worcestershire, England
RHS Garden Wisley
Surrey, England
RHS Garden Hyde Hall
Essex, England
Rodmarton Manor
Gloucestershire, England
Royal Botanic Gardens, Kew
London, England
Sandringham House
Norfolk, England
Savill Garden
Surrey, England
Tintinhull House
Somerset, England
Upton House
Warwickshire, England
Wallington
Northumberland and Tyne & Wear, England

White Windows
Hampshire, England

CACTI
Abbey Brook Cactus Nursery
Derbyshire, England
Birmingham Botanical Gardens & Glasshouses
West Midlands, England
Cambridge University Botanic Garden
Cambridgeshire, England
Holly Gate Cactus Nursery
Sussex, West, England
National Botanic Gardens
Co. Dublin, Republic of Ireland
RHS Garden Wisley
Surrey, England
Royal Botanic Garden Edinburgh
Lothian, Scotland
Royal Botanic Gardens, Kew
London, England
Toobees Exotics
Surrey, England

CAMELLIAS
Bodnant Gardens
Clwyd, Wales
Burncoose Gardens & Nurseries
Cornwall, England
Coleton Fishacre Garden
Devon, England
Galloway House Gardens
Dumfries & Galloway, Scotland
Glendurgan
Cornwall, England
Greenway
Devon, England
Lydney Park Gardens
Gloucestershire, England
Marwood Hill Gardens
Devon, England
Mount Edgcumbe Gardens
Cornwall, England
RHS Garden Wisley
Surrey, England
Rotherview Nursery with Coghurst Camellias
Sussex, East, England
Savill Garden
Surrey, England
Trehane Camellia Nursery
Dorset, England
Trewidden Gardens
Cornwall, England
Wentworth Castle Gardens
Yorkshire, South, England

CARNATIONS

Crathes Castle
Grampian, Scotland
RHS Garden Wisley
Surrey, England

CHRYSANTHEMUMS

Halls of Heddon
Northumberland and Tyne & Wear, England
RHS Garden Wisley
Surrey, England

CLEMATIS

Burford House Gardens
Shropshire, England
Elworthy Cottage Plants
Somerset, England
Helmsley Walled Garden
Yorkshire, North, England
Thorncroft Clematis Nursery
Norfolk, England

CONIFERS

Ascott
Buckinghamshire, England
Batsford Arboretum
Gloucestershire, England
Benmore Botanic Garden
Strathclyde, Scotland
Bressingham Gardens
Norfolk, England
Brodsworth Hall & Gardens
Yorkshire, South, England
Chatsworth
Derbyshire, England
Clumber Park
Nottinghamshire, England
Cragside
Northumberland and Tyne & Wear, England
Dawyck Botanic Garden
Borders, Scotland
Eastnor Castle
Herefordshire, England
Elvaston Castle
Derbyshire, England
Fota Arboretum & Garden
Co. Cork, Republic of Ireland
Great Comp
Kent, England
Hergest Croft Gardens
Herefordshire, England
Kingston Lacy
Dorset, England
Mount Stuart
Strathclyde, Scotland

National Botanic Gardens
Co. Dublin, Republic of Ireland
Nymans
Sussex, West, England
Pencarrow
Cornwall, England
RHS Garden Wisley
Surrey, England
Royal Botanic Gardens, Kew
London, England
Scone Palace
Tayside, Scotland
Sheffield Park Garden
Sussex, East, England
Thorp Perrow Arboretum & Woodland Garden
Yorkshire, North, England
Trelissick Garden
Cornwall, England
Wakehurst Place
Sussex, West, England
Westonbirt The National Arboretum
Gloucestershire, England
Winkworth Arboretum
Surrey, England

CYCLAMEN

Ashwood Nurseries Ltd
Staffordshire, England
Cadenza
Surrey, England
Foxgrove
Berkshire, England
RHS Garden Wisley
Surrey, England
Tile Barn Nursery
Kent, England

DAFFODILS

Acorn Bank Garden
Cumbria, England
Broadleigh Gardens
Somerset, England
Brodie Castle
Grampian, Scotland
Chenies Manor
Buckinghamshire, England
Clandon Park
Surrey, England
Erddig
Clwyd, Wales
Escot
Devon, England
Felley Priory
Nottinghamshire, England
Fota Arboretum & Garden
Co. Cork, Republic of Ireland

Guy Wilson Daffodil Garden
Co. Derry, Northern Ireland
Hever Castle
Kent, England
Overbury Court
Worcestershire, England
Petworth House
Sussex, West, England
RHS Garden Wisley
Surrey, England
Stourhead
Wiltshire, England
Stourton House Flower Garden
Wiltshire, England
Thorp Perrow Arboretum & Woodland Garden
Yorkshire, North, England
Threave Garden
Dumfries & Galloway, Scotland

DAHLIAS

Anglesey Abbey
Cambridgeshire, England
Biddulph Grange
Staffordshire, England
Butterfields Nursery
Buckinghamshire, England
Halls of Heddon
Northumberland and Tyne & Wear, England
Hever Castle
Kent, England
Orchid Paradise
Devon, England
Port Lympne
Kent, England
Savill Garden
Surrey, England
Valley Gardens
Yorkshire, North, England

DELPHINIUMS

8 Dunstarn Lane
Yorkshire, West, England
Blackmore & Langdon
Somerset, England
Cambridge University Botanic Garden
Cambridgeshire, England
Falkland Palace
Fife, Scotland
Godinton Park
Kent, England
Haddon Hall
Derbyshire, England
RHS Garden Wisley
Surrey, England
Rougham Hall Nurseries
Suffolk, England

FERNS

Abbey Cottage
Hampshire, England
The Abbey House
Wiltshire, England
Brodsworth Hall & Gardens
Yorkshire, South, England
Fibrex Nurseries Ltd
Warwickshire, England
Glasgow Botanic Garden
Strathclyde, Scotland
National Botanic Gardens
Co. Dublin, Republic of Ireland
The Ornamental Grass & Plant Nursery
Yorkshire, North, England
RHS Garden Harlow Carr
Yorkshire, North, England
Rickard's Hardy Ferns Ltd
Worcestershire, England
Royal Botanic Garden Edinburgh
Lothian, Scotland
Royal Botanic Gardens, Kew
London, England
Sherborne Garden
Somerset, England
Sizergh Castle
Cumbria, England

FRUIT

Beningbrough Hall & Gardens
Yorkshire, North, England
Berrington Hall
Herefordshire, England
Blackthorn Nursery
Hampshire, England
Brogdale
Kent, England
Broughton House Gardens
Dumfries & Galloway, Scotland
Croxteth Hall & Country Park
Lancashire, Merseyside & Greater Manchester, England
Deacon's Nursery
Isle of Wight, England
Erddig
Clwyd, Wales
Felbrigg Hall
Norfolk, England
Hales Hall Gardens & Reads Nursery
Norfolk, England
Heligan Gardens
Cornwall, England
Keepers Nursery
Kent, England
Osborne House
Isle of Wight, England

Pershore College
Worcestershire, England
Reaseheath College
Cheshire, England
RHS Garden Wisley
Surrey, England
Rougham Hall Nurseries
Suffolk, England
Ryton Organic Gardens
Warwickshire, England
Thornhayes Nursery Ltd.
Devon, England
Upton House
Warwickshire, England
West Dean Gardens
Sussex, West, England
Westbury Court
Gloucestershire, England

FUCHSIAS
Duchy of Cornwall Nursery
Cornwall, England
Margam Park
Glamorgan, Wales
The Vernon Geranium Nursery
Surrey, England

GLADIOLI
RHS Garden Wisley
Surrey, England

GLASSHOUSES
Bicton Park Gardens
Devon, England
Birmingham Botanical Gardens & Glasshouses
West Midlands, England
Cambridge University Botanic Garden
Cambridgeshire, England
Duthie Park
Grampian, Scotland
The Eden Project
Cornwall, England
Houghton Lodge
Hampshire, England
The Living Rainforest
Berkshire, England
The National Botanic Garden of Wales
Dyfed, Wales
National Botanic Gardens
Co. Dublin, Republic of Ireland
Ness Botanic Gardens
Cheshire, England
Oxford Botanic Garden
Oxfordshire, England
Plantasia
Glamorgan, Wales

RHS Garden Wisley
Surrey, England
Roundway Park & Tropical World
Yorkshire, West, England
Royal Botanic Garden Edinburgh
Lothian, Scotland
Royal Botanic Gardens, Kew
London, England
Sir George Staunton Country Park
Hampshire, England
Stapeley Water Gardens
Cheshire, England
Stowell Park
Gloucestershire, England
University of Leicester Botanic Garden
Leicestershire, England
Wentworth Castle Gardens
Yorkshire, South, England

HEATHERS
The Abbey House
Wiltshire, England
The Bannut
Herefordshire, England
Bell's Cherrybank Centre
Tayside, Scotland
Champs Hill
Sussex, West, England
Exeter University Gardens
Devon, England
Floraldene
Sussex, West, England
Furzey Gardens
Hampshire, England
Jack Drake
Highland, Scotland
National Botanic Gardens
Co. Dublin, Republic of Ireland
Ness Botanic Gardens
Cheshire, England
RHS Garden Wisley
Surrey, England
Royal Botanic Garden Edinburgh
Lothian, Scotland
Royal Botanic Gardens, Kew
London, England
Threave Garden
Dumfries & Galloway, Scotland
Valley Gardens
Surrey, England

HEBES
University of Bristol Botanic Garden
Gloucestershire, England

HEMEROCALLIS
Apple Court
Hampshire, England
Ann & Roger Bowden
Devon, England
Goldbrook Plants
Suffolk, England
Rosewood Daylilies
Kent, England

HERBS
The Abbey House
Wiltshire, England
Acorn Bank Garden
Cumbria, England
Buckland Abbey
Devon, England
Chesters Walled Garden
Northumberland and Tyne & Wear, England
Downderry Nursery
Kent, England
Iden Croft Herbs
Kent, England
The National Botanic Garden of Wales
Dyfed, Wales
RHS Garden Wisley
Surrey, England
RHS Garden Rosemoor
Devon, England
Royal Botanic Gardens, Kew
London, England
Ryton Organic Gardens
Warwickshire, England
Salley Gardens
Nottinghamshire, England
University of Leicester Botanic Garden
Leicestershire, England
The Walled Garden
Worcestershire, England
York Gate
Yorkshire, West, England

HOSTAS
Apple Court
Hampshire, England
Ann & Roger Bowden
Devon, England
Goldbrook Plants
Suffolk, England
Longthatch
Hampshire, England
Mill Hill Plants
Nottinghamshire, England
The Ornamental Grass & Plant Nursery
Yorkshire, North, England

Park Green Nurseries
Suffolk, England
Rushfields of Ledbury
Herefordshire, England

IRISES
The Abbey House
Wiltshire, England
Broadleigh Gardens
Somerset, England
Kelways Ltd
Somerset, England
Lingen Nursery and Gardens
Shropshire, England
Marwood Hill Gardens
Devon, England
Mill Hill Plants
Nottinghamshire, England
Myddelton House
London, England
Rowden Gardens
Devon, England
Wakehurst Place
Sussex, West, England

LILIES
Wakehurst Place
Sussex, West, England

MAGNOLIAS
Batsford Arboretum
Gloucestershire, England
Bodnant Gardens
Clwyd, Wales
Caerhays Castle Gardens
Cornwall, England
Chyverton
Cornwall, England
Glendurgan
Cornwall, England
Lanhydrock
Cornwall, England
Marwood Hill Gardens
Devon, England
Millais Nurseries
Surrey, England
RHS Garden Wisley
Surrey, England
Savill Garden
Surrey, England
Sherwood
Devon, England
Trewidden Gardens
Cornwall, England
Trewithen
Cornwall, England

Valley Gardens
Surrey, England
Wentworth Castle Gardens
Yorkshire, South, England

ORCHIDS
Butterfields Nursery
Buckinghamshire, England
Glasgow Botanic Garden
Strathclyde, Scotland
Kelways Ltd
Somerset, England
RHS Garden Wisley
Surrey, England
Royal Botanic Garden Edinburgh
Lothian, Scotland
Royal Botanic Gardens, Kew
London, England
Scone Palace
Tayside, Scotland

PLANTSMAN'S GARDENS
Antony
Cornwall, England
Beth Chatto Gardens
Essex, England
Biddulph Grange
Staffordshire, England
Birkheads Cottage Garden Nursery
Northumberland and Tyne & Wear, England
Bishop Burton Botanic Garden
Yorkshire, East Riding of, England
Bluebell Cottage Gardens & Lodge Lane Nursery
Cheshire, England
The Botanic Nursery
Wiltshire, England
Bressingham Gardens
Norfolk, England
Brook Cottage
Oxfordshire, England
Cally Gardens
Dumfries & Galloway, Scotland
Cambridge University Botanic Garden
Cambridgeshire, England
Cannington College Heritage Garden
Somerset, England
Capel Manor
London, England
Castle Howard
Yorkshire, North, England
Chelsea Physic Garden
London, England
Church Hill Cottage Gardens
Kent, England
Chyverton
Cornwall, England

Coleton Fishacre Garden
Devon, England
Copton Ash Gardens
Kent, England
Cotswold Garden Flowers
Worcestershire, England
The Courts Garden
Wiltshire, England
Crûg Farm Plants
Gwynedd, Wales
Cruickshank Botanic Garden
Grampian, Scotland
The Dillon Garden
Co. Dublin, Republic of Ireland
Dundee Botanic Garden
Tayside, Scotland
Earlscliffe
Co. Dublin, Republic of Ireland
East Ruston Old Vicarage
Norfolk, England
The Garden House
Devon, England
Glen Chantry
Essex, England
Gravetye Manor Hotel
Sussex, West, England
Great Dixter
Sussex, East, England
Greencombe Gardens
Somerset, England
Heathlands
Hampshire, England
Herterton House Gardens & Nursery
Northumberland and Tyne & Wear, England
Hidcote Manor Garden
Gloucestershire, England
High Beeches
Sussex, West, England
Highdown
Sussex, West, England
Hinton Ampner House
Hampshire, England
Hodnet Hall Gardens
Shropshire, England
Holehird Gardens
Cumbria, England
Home Covert Garden & Arboretum
Wiltshire, England
Howick Hall
Northumberland and Tyne & Wear, England
Hunts Court
Gloucestershire, England
W.E.Th. Ingwersen Ltd
Sussex, West, England

Kiftsgate Court
Gloucestershire, England
Killerton
Devon, England
Lamorran House
Cornwall, England
Leonardslee Lakes & Gardens
Sussex, West, England
Longstock Water Gardens
Hampshire, England
Longthatch
Hampshire, England
Marwood Hill Gardens
Devon, England
Meon Orchard
Hampshire, England
Myddelton House
London, England
National Botanic Gardens
Co. Dublin, Republic of Ireland
Newby Hall
Yorkshire, North, England
North Court
Isle of Wight, England
Nymans
Sussex, West, England
Old Vicarage
Wiltshire, England
Oxford Botanic Garden
Oxfordshire, England
Plant World Botanic Gardens
Devon, England
Ramster
Surrey, England
RHS Garden Wisley
Surrey, England
RHS Garden Harlow Carr
Yorkshire, North, England
RHS Garden Hyde Hall
Essex, England
RHS Garden Rosemoor
Devon, England
Rock Farm
Kent, England
Rowallane Garden
Co. Down, Northern Ireland
Royal Botanic Garden Edinburgh
Lothian, Scotland
Royal Botanic Gardens, Kew
London, England
Saling Hall
Essex, England
Sausmarez Manor
Guernsey, Channel Islands

Savill Garden
Surrey, England
Scotney Castle Garden
Kent, England
Sheffield Park Garden
Sussex, East, England
Sherborne Garden
Somerset, England
Snape Cottage
Dorset, England
Spetchley Park
Worcestershire, England
Spinners
Hampshire, England
St Andrews Botanic Garden
Fife, Scotland
Sticky Wicket
Dorset, England
Stillingfleet Lodge Nurseries
Yorkshire, North, England
Stone House Cottage Garden
Worcestershire, England
Talbot Botanic Gardens
Co. Dublin, Republic of Ireland
Trebah Garden Trust
Cornwall, England
Tregrehan
Cornwall, England
Trelissick Garden
Cornwall, England
Trengwainton Garden
Cornwall, England
Tresco Abbey
Cornwall, England
Trewithen
Cornwall, England
University of Birmingham Botanic Garden at Winterbourne
West Midlands, England
University of Leicester Botanic Garden
Leicestershire, England
Valley Gardens
Surrey, England
Ventnor Botanic Garden
Isle of Wight, England
Wakehurst Place
Sussex, West, England
Waterperry Gardens
Oxfordshire, England
West Dean Gardens
Sussex, West, England
White Hall Plants
Suffolk, England
Wiltshire College Lackham
Wiltshire, England

PRIMROSES

Edrom Nurseries
Borders, Scotland

RHODODENRONS AND AZALEAS

Achamore Gardens
Strathclyde, Scotland

Benmore Botanic Garden
Strathclyde, Scotland

Blackhills
Grampian, Scotland

Bodnant Gardens
Clwyd, Wales

Borde Hill Garden
Sussex, West, England

Bosahan
Cornwall, England

Brodick Castle
Strathclyde, Scotland

Cannizaro Park
London, England

Chyverton
Cornwall, England

Clyne Gardens
Glamorgan, Wales

Cragside
Northumberland and Tyne & Wear, England

Crarae Gardens
Strathclyde, Scotland

Dawyck Botanic Garden
Borders, Scotland

Dorothy Clive Garden
Staffordshire, England

Exbury Gardens
Hampshire, England

Furzey Gardens
Hampshire, England

Glenarn
Strathclyde, Scotland

Glendoick Gardens
Tayside, Scotland

Glendurgan
Cornwall, England

Glenveagh Castle
Co. Donegal, Republic of Ireland

Gresgarth Hall
Lancashire, Merseyside & Greater Manchester, England

Hergest Croft Gardens
Herefordshire, England

High Beeches
Sussex, West, England

Highclere Castle
Hampshire, England

Higher Knowle
Devon, England

Hodnet Hall Gardens
Shropshire, England

Hydon Nurseries
Surrey, England

Isabella Plantation
London, England

Knap Hill Nursery Ltd
Surrey, England

Lanhydrock
Cornwall, England

Lea Gardens
Derbyshire, England

Leonardslee Lakes & Gardens
Sussex, West, England

Lukesland
Devon, England

Lydney Park Gardens
Gloucestershire, England

Marwood Hill Gardens
Devon, England

Millais Nurseries
Surrey, England

Minterne
Dorset, England

Mount Stewart
Co. Down, Northern Ireland

Muncaster Castle
Cumbria, England

National Botanic Gardens
Co. Dublin, Republic of Ireland

Ness Botanic Gardens
Cheshire, England

Notcutts Nurseries
Suffolk, England

Nymans
Sussex, West, England

The Old Glebe
Devon, England

Plas Newydd
Gwynedd, Wales

Ramster
Surrey, England

RHS Garden Wisley
Surrey, England

Rowallane Garden
Co. Down, Northern Ireland

Royal Botanic Gardens, Kew
London, England

Savill Garden
Surrey, England

Scotney Castle Garden
Kent, England

Sheffield Park Garden
Sussex, East, England

Sherwood
Devon, England
Stourhead
Wiltshire, England
Tournaig House
Highland, Scotland
Trengwainton Garden
Cornwall, England
Trewithen
Cornwall, England
Valley Gardens
Surrey, England
Wakehurst Place
Sussex, West, England
Wentworth Castle Gardens
Yorkshire, South, England

ROCK GARDENS
Cambridge University Botanic Garden
Cambridgeshire, England
Cruickshank Botanic Garden
Grampian, Scotland
Dorothy Clive Garden
Staffordshire, England
Mount Ephraim
Kent, England
Mount Stuart
Strathclyde, Scotland
National Botanic Gardens
Co. Dublin, Republic of Ireland
Ness Botanic Gardens
Cheshire, England
RHS Garden Wisley
Surrey, England
Royal Botanic Garden Edinburgh
Lothian, Scotland
Royal Botanic Gardens, Kew
London, England

ROSES, MODERN
The Abbey House
Wiltshire, England
Benvarden Garden & Grounds
Co. Antrim, Northern Ireland
Chartwell
Kent, England
David Austin Roses
Shropshire, England
Hever Castle
Kent, England
Longleat House
Wiltshire, England
Mattocks Roses
Oxfordshire, England
Nunwell House
Isle of Wight, England

Polesden Lacey
Surrey, England
Queen Mary's Gardens
London, England
RHS Garden Wisley
Surrey, England
RHS Garden Hyde Hall
Essex, England
RHS Garden Rosemoor
Devon, England
Royal Botanic Gardens, Kew
London, England
Savill Garden
Surrey, England
Sledmere House
Yorkshire, East Riding of, England
University of Birmingham Botanic Garden at Winterbourne
West Midlands, England

ROSES, OLD
Arley Hall
Cheshire, England
Castle Howard
Yorkshire, North, England
Coombland Gardens & Nursery
Sussex, West, England
Coton Manor
Northamptonshire, England
Cruickshank Botanic Garden
Grampian, Scotland
David Austin Roses
Shropshire, England
Drum Castle
Grampian, Scotland
Elsing Hall
Norfolk, England
Felley Priory
Nottinghamshire, England
Hardwick Hall
Derbyshire, England
Helmingham Hall
Suffolk, England
Highnam Court
Gloucestershire, England
The Hiller Garden
Warwickshire, England
Hunts Court
Gloucestershire, England
Kiftsgate Court
Gloucestershire, England
Mannington Gardens
Norfolk, England
Mottisfont Abbey
Hampshire, England

Myddelton House
London, England
Nymans
Sussex, West, England
Peter Beales Roses
Norfolk, England
RHS Garden Rosemoor
Devon, England
Royal Botanic Gardens, Kew
London, England
University of Birmingham Botanic Garden at Winterbourne
West Midlands, England
Westbury Court
Gloucestershire, England
Wiltshire College Lackham
Wiltshire, England

SNOWDROPS
Anglesey Abbey
Cambridgeshire, England
Attingham Park
Shropshire, England
Benington Lordship
Hertfordshire, England
Birr Castle Demesne
Co. Offaly, Republic of Ireland
Brandy Mount House
Hampshire, England
Cambo Gardens
Fife, Scotland
Colzium Walled Garden
Strathclyde, Scotland
East Lambrook Manor
Somerset, England
Easton Walled Gardens
Lincolnshire, England
Fairhaven Woodland & Water Garden
Norfolk, England
Foxgrove
Berkshire, England
Galloway House Gardens
Dumfries & Galloway, Scotland
Heale House Garden
Wiltshire, England
Hever Castle
Kent, England
Hodsock Priory
Nottinghamshire, England
Lacock Abbey
Wiltshire, England
Monksilver Nursery
Cambridgeshire, England
Myddelton House
London, England

Painswick Rococo Garden
Gloucestershire, England
Penrhyn Castle
Gwynedd, Wales
Plas-yn-Rhiw
Gwynedd, Wales
Polesden Lacey
Surrey, England
Snape Cottage
Dorset, England
Studley Royal
Yorkshire, North, England

SUB-TROPICAL PLANTS
Abbotsbury Sub-Tropical Gardens
Dorset, England
Achamore Gardens
Strathclyde, Scotland
Antony
Cornwall, England
Bosahan
Cornwall, England
Coleton Fishacre Garden
Devon, England
Derreen
Co. Kerry, Republic of Ireland
Dunster Castle
Somerset, England
Earlscliffe
Co. Dublin, Republic of Ireland
East Ruston Old Vicarage
Norfolk, England
The Eden Project
Cornwall, England
Exeter University Gardens
Devon, England
Fota Arboretum & Garden
Co. Cork, Republic of Ireland
Glendurgan
Cornwall, England
Greenway
Devon, England
Greenways
Oxfordshire, England
Knoll Gardens
Dorset, England
Lamorran House
Cornwall, England
Logan Botanic Garden
Dumfries & Galloway, Scotland
Meon Orchard
Hampshire, England
Mount Stewart
Co. Down, Northern Ireland

Mount Stuart
Strathclyde, Scotland
North Court
Isle of Wight, England
Overbeck Museum & Garden
Devon, England
The Palm Centre
London, England
Penrhyn Castle
Gwynedd, Wales
Rowallane Garden
Co. Down, Northern Ireland
Royal Botanic Gardens, Kew
London, England
Sausmarez Manor
Guernsey, Channel Islands
Talbot Botanic Gardens
Co. Dublin, Republic of Ireland
Torosay Castle & Gardens
Strathclyde, Scotland
Trebah Garden Trust
Cornwall, England
Trelissick Garden
Cornwall, England
Trengwainton Garden
Cornwall, England
Tresco Abbey
Cornwall, England
University of Bristol Botanic Garden
Gloucestershire, England
Ventnor Botanic Garden
Isle of Wight, England
Westdale Nurseries
Wiltshire, England

TOPIARY
Abbotsford
Borders, Scotland
Athelhampton
Dorset, England
Avebury Manor Garden
Wiltshire, England
Brodsworth Hall & Gardens
Yorkshire, South, England
Burton Agnes Hall Gardens
Yorkshire, East Riding of, England
Chirk Castle
Clwyd, Wales
Drummond Castle Gardens
Tayside, Scotland
Elvaston Castle
Derbyshire, England
Garsington Manor
Oxfordshire, England

Graythwaite Hall
Cumbria, England
Hatfield House
Hertfordshire, England
Hutton-in-the-Forest
Cumbria, England
Langley Boxwood Nursery
Hampshire, England
Levens Hall
Cumbria, England
Mount Ephraim
Kent, England
Packwood House
Warwickshire, England
Pitmedden
Grampian, Scotland
Renishaw Hall
Derbyshire, England
The Romantic Garden Nursery
Norfolk, England

VIOLAS
Elizabeth MacGregor
Dumfries & Galloway, Scotland
C. W. Groves & Son
Dorset, England

VEGETABLES
Beningbrough Hall & Gardens
Yorkshire, North, England
Croxteth Hall & Country Park
Lancashire, Merseyside & Greater Manchester, England
Felbrigg Hall
Norfolk, England
Heligan Gardens
Cornwall, England
Le Manoir aux Quat'Saisons
Oxfordshire, England
Mertoun Gardens
Borders, Scotland
Pershore College
Worcestershire, England
Reaseheath College
Cheshire, England
RHS Garden Wisley
Surrey, England
RHS Garden Rosemoor
Devon, England
Ryton Organic Gardens
Warwickshire, England
Upton House
Warwickshire, England
West Dean Gardens
Sussex, West, England

WILDFLOWERS

The Garden House
Devon, England
Naturescape
Nottinghamshire, England

WOODLAND GARDENS

Broadleas
Wiltshire, England
Heligan Gardens
Cornwall, England
High Beeches
Sussex, West, England
Hodnet Hall Gardens
Shropshire, England
Home Covert Garden & Arboretum
Wiltshire, England
Leonardslee Lakes & Gardens
Sussex, West, England
Mount Stewart
Co. Down, Northern Ireland
Muncaster Castle
Cumbria, England

RHS Garden Wisley
Surrey, England
Rowallane Garden
Co. Down, Northern Ireland
Savill Garden
Surrey, England
Trebah Garden Trust
Cornwall, England
Trelissick Garden
Cornwall, England
Trengwainton Garden
Cornwall, England
Trewithen
Cornwall, England
Valley Gardens
Surrey, England
Wakehurst Place
Sussex, West, England
Westonbirt The National Arboretum
Gloucestershire, England

UNITED KINGDOM & REPUBLIC OF IRELAND

ATLANTIC OCEAN

NORTH SEA

MAP 20

SCOTLAND

MAP 19

MAP 18

NORTHERN IRELAND

MAP 22

MAP 17

ENGLAND

Irish Sea

MAP 16

MAP 15

REPUBLIC OF IRELAND

MAP 12

MAP 13

MAP 14

MAP 21

MAP 11

WALES

MAP 8

MAP 10

MAP 9

MAP 7

Celtic Sea

MAP 5

MAP 6

MAP 4

MAP 2

MAP 3

MAP 1

English Channel

0 40 80 Km
0 20 40 Miles

N

Key To Garden Location Maps

Coastline	M1 Motorway	Urban Area
International Border	A5 Dual Carriageway	Settlement
Regional Border	A15 Main Road	Garden Location
County Border	Minor Road	

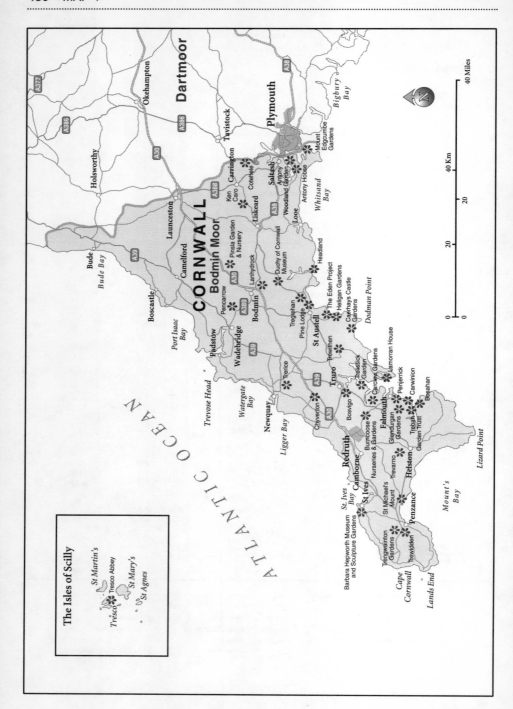

MAP 2 • 481

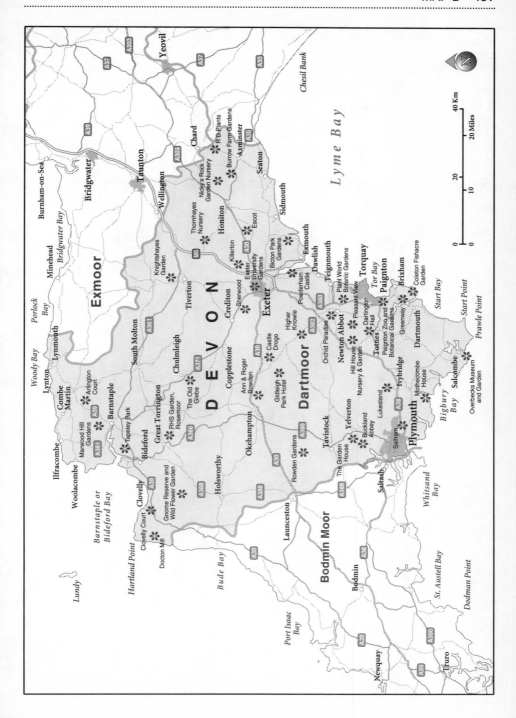

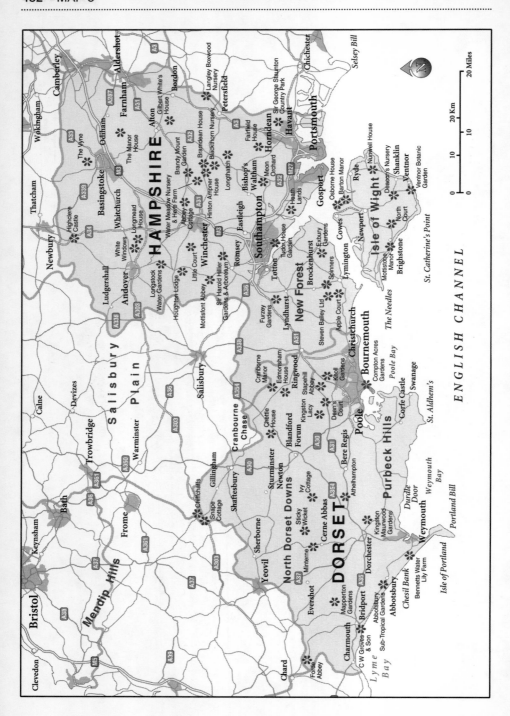

MAP 4 • 483

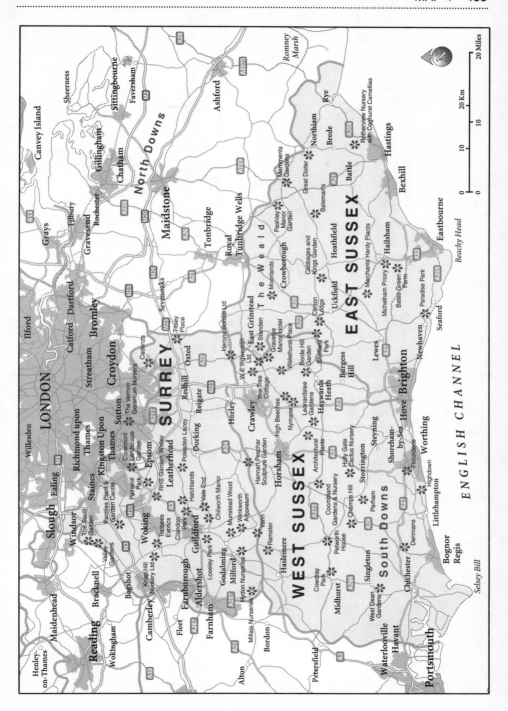

20 Miles

20 Km

Sheerness

Canvey Island

Ilford

LONDON

Willesden

Ealing

Richmond upon Thames

Kingston Upon Thames

Slough

Windsor

Bracknell

Wokingham

Reading

Henley-on-Thames

Maidenhead

Camberley

Bagshot

Staines

Sutton

Epsom

Leatherhead

Woking

Guildford

Aldershot

Farnham

Fleet

Farnborough

Godalming

Milford

Haslemere

Bordon

Alton

Petersfield

Waterlooville

Havant

Portsmouth

Bognor Regis

Selsey Bill

Chichester

Midhurst

Singleton

West Dean Gardens

Cowdray Park

Petworth Gardens & Nursery

Coompland

Champs Hill

Parham

Storrington

Steyning

Shoreham-by-Sea

Worthing

Littlehampton

Floraldene

Highdown

Hove

Brighton

Newhaven

Seaford

ENGLISH CHANNEL

Beachy Head

Eastbourne

Bexhill

Hastings

Rye

Northiam

Brede

Battle

Heathfield

Hailsham

Uckfield

Crowborough

Royal Tunbridge Wells

Tonbridge

Sevenoaks

Maidstone

Ashford

Romney Marsh

Faversham

Sittingbourne

Gillingham

Chatham

Rochester

Gravesend

Tilbury

Grays

Dartford

Catford

Bromley

Streatham

Croydon

Redhill

Reigate

Oxted

Dorking

Horley

Crawley

Horsham

Haywards Heath

Burgess Hill

Lewes

East Grinstead

SURREY

WEST SUSSEX

EAST SUSSEX

North Downs

The Weald

South Downs

Knap Hill Nursery Ltd

Valley Gardens

The Savill Garden

Pantiles Plant & Garden Centre

Toobees Exotics

Painshill Park

Claremont Landscape Garden

RHS Garden Wisley

The Vernon Geranium Nursery

Cadenza

Titsey Place

Herons Bonsai Ltd

W E Ingwersen Ltd

Yew Tree Cottage

High Beeches

Nymans

Leonardslee Gardens

Borde Hill Garden

Sheffield Park

Graveye Manor Hotel

Wakehurst Place

Standen

Clinton Lodge

Cabbages and Kings Garden

Modflands

Pashley Manor Garden

Merriments Gardens

Batemans

Great Dixter

Marchants Hardy Plants

Michelham Priory

Bates Green Farm

Paradise Park

Rotherview Nursery with Coghurst Camellias

Polesden Lacey

Hatchlands

Vale End

Clandon Park

Chilworth Manor

Munstead Wood

Winkworth Arboretum

Vann

Ramster

Loseley Park

Hydon Nurseries

Millais Nurseries

Architectural Plants

Hannah Peschar Sculpture Garden

Holly Gate Cactus Nursery

Denmans

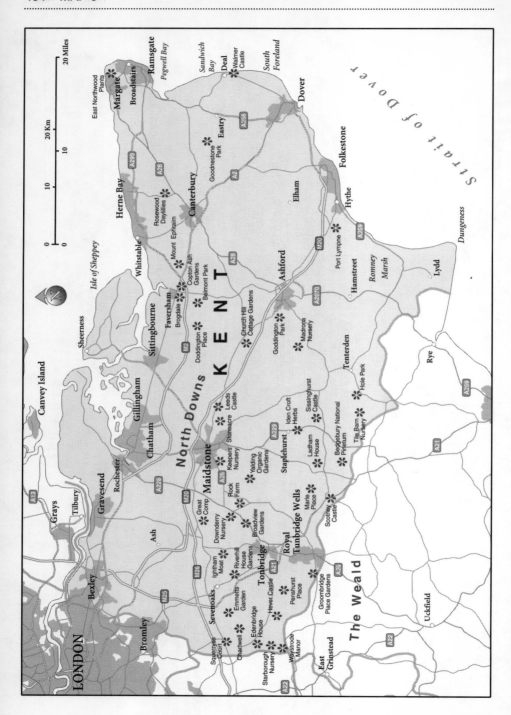

MAP 6 • 485

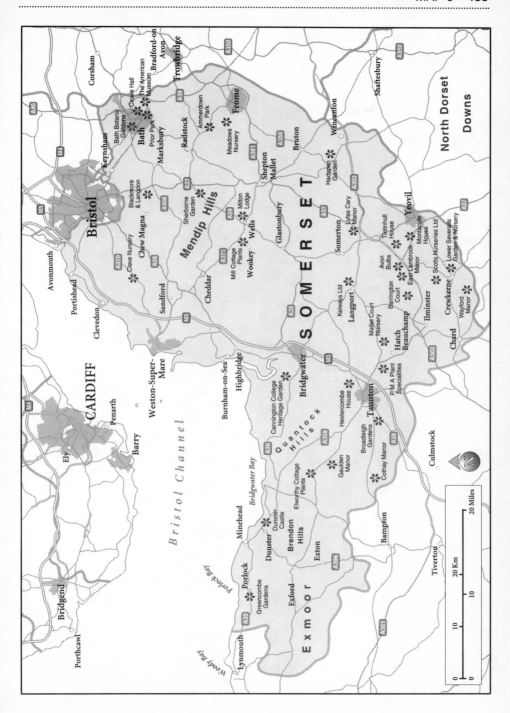

Corsham

Bradford-on Avon

Trowbridge

A350

Shaftesbury

North Dorset Downs

A46

Crowe Hall

The American Museum

A36

Frome

Bath Botanic Gardens

Bath

Prior Park

Marksbury

Keynsham

Ammerdown Park

Meadows Nursery

Wincanton

A350

Bristol

M4

Radstock

A37

A361

Bruton

A359

Shepton Mallet

Hadspen Garden

A303

Yeovil

A37

Blackmore & Langdon

Sherborne Garden

Milton Lodge

Glastonbury

Lytes Cary Manor

Tintinhull House

Montacute House

A303

Cleve Nursery

Chew Magna

A368

Mendip Hills

A39

A371

Wells

Somerton

Lower Severalls Garden & Nursery

A303

A370

Wookey

Scotts Nurseries Ltd

Avonmouth

A38

Sandford

Mill Cottage Plants

Avon Bulbs

East Lambrook Manor

Crewkerne

Portishead

Cheddar

Langport

Barrington Court

Ilminster

Wayford Manor

Clevedon

M5

Kelways Ltd

Mallet Court Nursery

Hatch Beauchamp

Chard

SOMERSET

A39

M5

A303

Weston-Super-Mare

Highbridge

Bridgwater

P M A Plant Specialities

Burnham-on-Sea

CARDIFF

M4

Penarth

Barry

Ely

Cannington College Heritage Garden

Hestercombe House

Taunton

A38

Culmstock

A38

Quantock Hills

Bristol Channel

A358

Broadleigh Gardens

Cothay Manor

Bridgwater Bay

Gauden Manor

Bridgend

Elworthy Cottage Plants

Bampton

Portcawl

Minehead

Dunster Castle

Brendon Hills

Exton

Tiverton

A396

Porlock

Dunster

Exmoor

A361

Greencombe Gardens

Exford

A39

Lynmouth

Woody Bay

Porlock Bay

N

20 Miles

20 Km

10

10

0

0

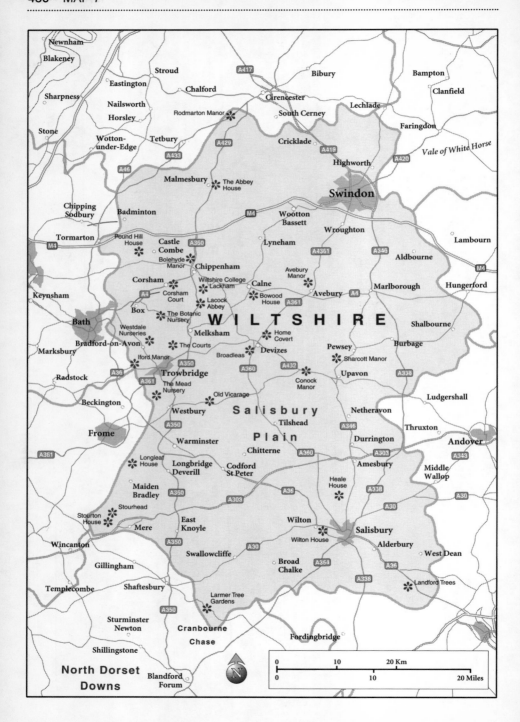

MAP 8 • 487

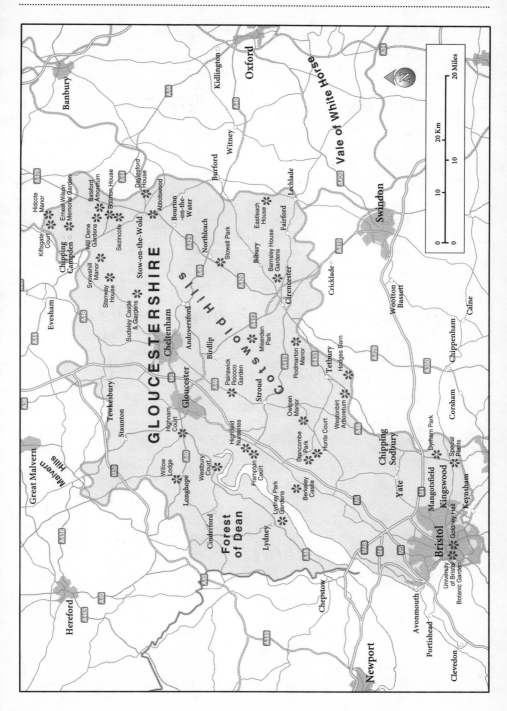

MAP 10 • 489

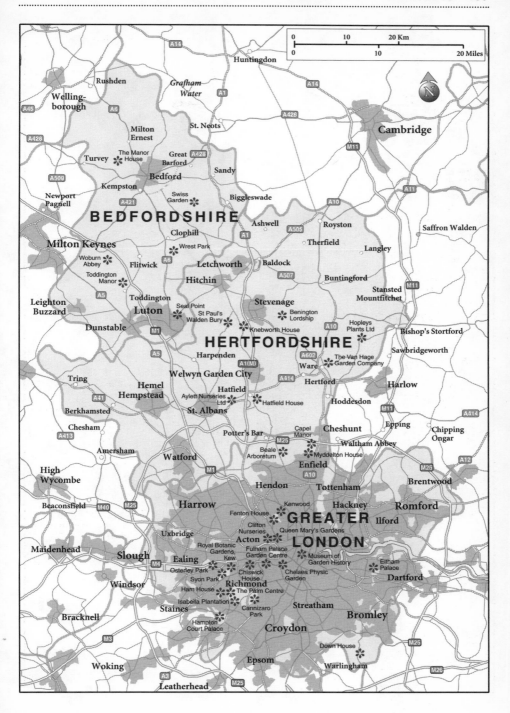

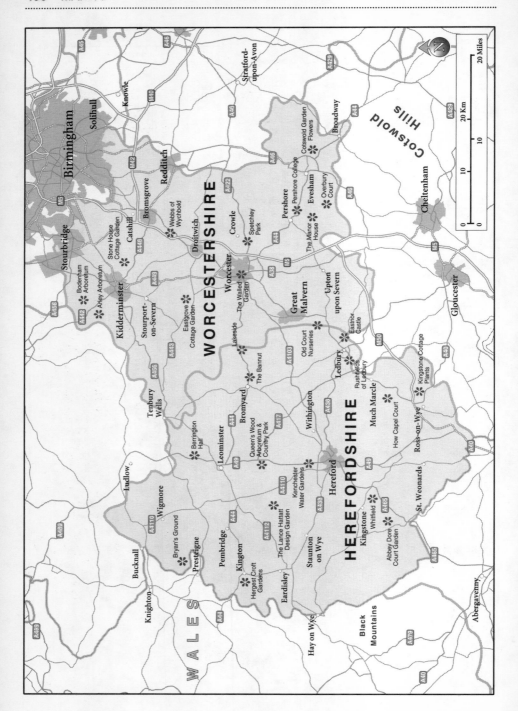

MAP 12 • 491

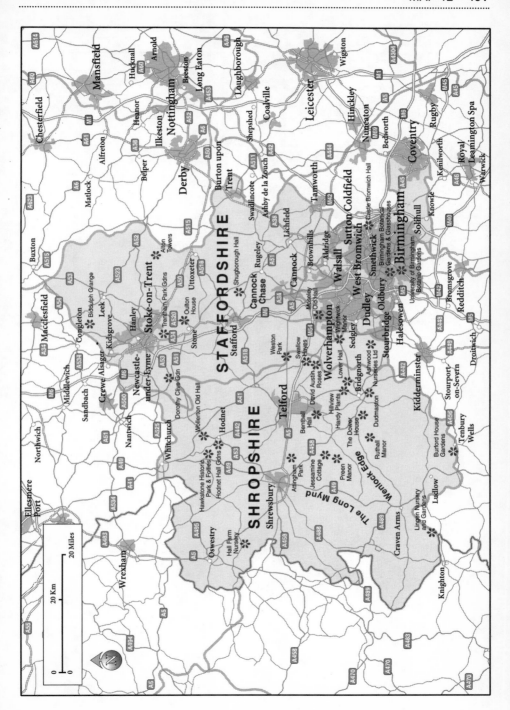

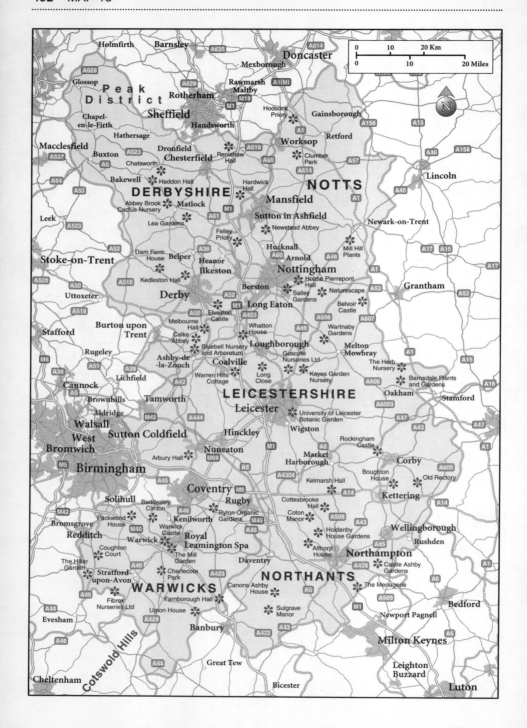

MAP 14 • 493

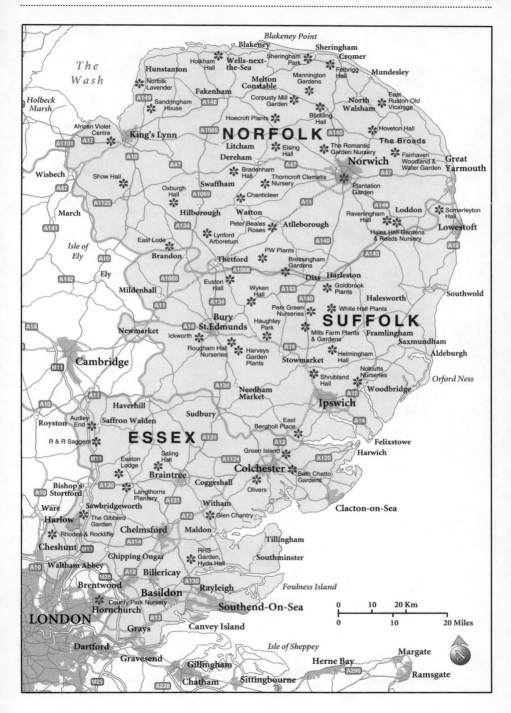

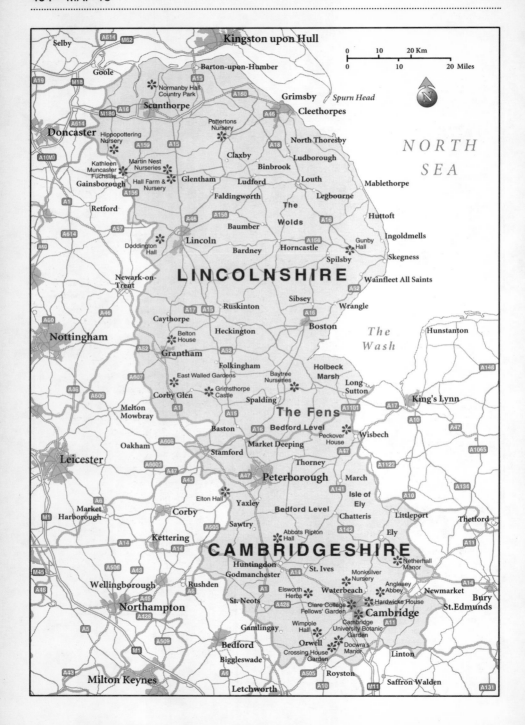

Selby • A614 M62
Goole
A19 M18 M180 A18
Doncaster A614 M180 A18
A1(M) A159 A15
Gainsborough A156
Retford
A1
A614
A46
A57
Newark-on-Trent
A46
A60
Nottingham A52
A38 A46
Leicester A6003
Market Harborough M1
Wellingborough A508 A43
A45 A46
Northampton A428
A5
A43 A509
Milton Keynes

Kingston upon Hull
Barton-upon-Humber
Normanby Hall Country Park
Scunthorpe
Grimsby   Spurn Head
Cleethorpes
Pottertons Nursery
Hippopottering Nursery
North Thoresby
Claxby   Ludborough
Kathleen Muncaster Fuchsias
Martin Nest Nurseries
Binbrook
Hall Farm & Nursery   Glentham   Ludford   Louth
Faldingworth   Legbourne
The
Baumber   Wolds
Doddington Hall   Lincoln
Bardney   Horncastle
Gunby Hall
Spilsby
Newark-on-Trent
LINCOLNSHIRE   Wainfleet All Saints
Mablethorpe
Huttoft
Ingoldmells
Skegness
Sibsey   A52
Ruskinton   Wrangle
Caythorpe   A17 A15   A16
Belton House   Heckington   Boston
Grantham   A52   The Wash   Hunstanton
Folkingham   Holbeck Marsh
East Walled Gardens   Baytree Nurseries   Long Sutton
Corby Glen   Grimsthorpe Castle
Melton Mowbray   Spalding   King's Lynn
Oakham   Baston   The Fens
Baston   Bedford Level   Peckover House   Wisbech
Market Deeping   A47
Stamford   Thorney   A1122
Peterborough   March
Elton Hall   Yaxley   A141
Corby   Bedford Level   Isle of Ely
Sawtry   Chatteris   Littleport   Thetford
Kettering   Abbots Ripton Hall   Ely   A11
CAMBRIDGESHIRE   Netherhall Manor
Huntingdon   St. Ives
Godmanchester   Monksilver Nursery
Rushden   Elsworth Herbs   Waterbeach   Anglesey Abbey   Newmarket
St. Neots   A426   Clare College Fellows' Garden   Hardwicke House   Bury St.Edmunds
Gamlingay   Wimpole Hall   Cambridge University Botanic Garden   Cambridge
Bedford   Orwell   Docwra's Manor
Biggleswade   Crossing House Garden   Linton
Royston
Letchworth   A10   M11   Saffron Walden   A131

NORTH SEA

0   10   20 Km
0   10   20 Miles

N

MAP 16 • 495

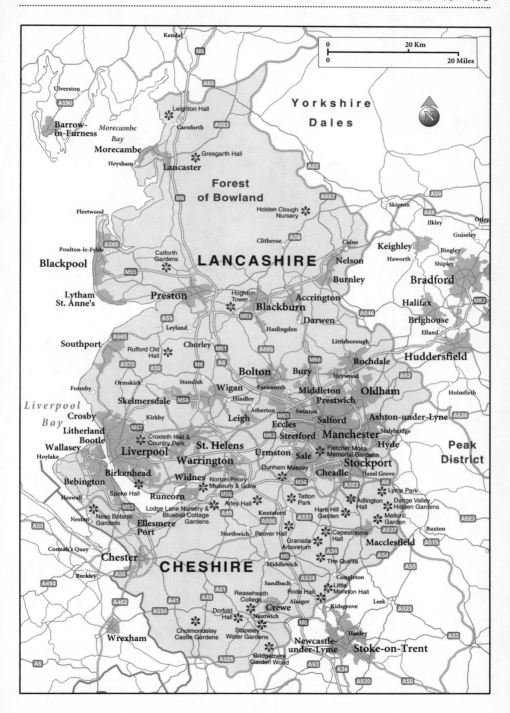

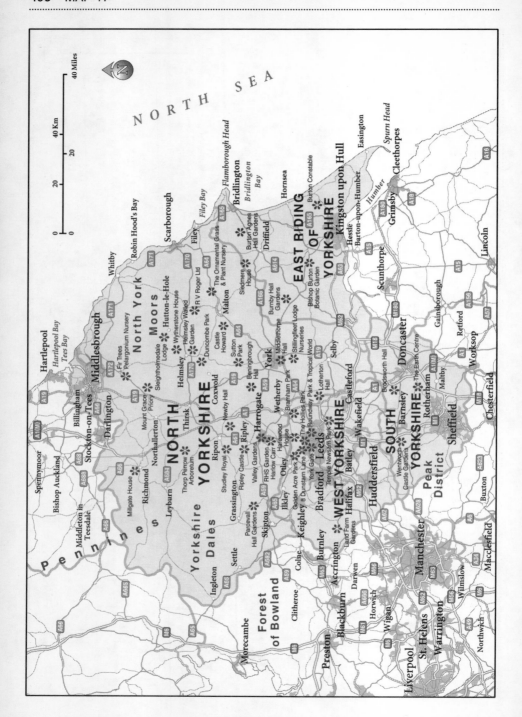

40 Miles

40 Km

20

20

20

0

0

NORTH SEA

Pennines

Middleton in Teesdale

Spennymoor

Bishop Auckland

Hartlepool
Hartlepool Bay
Tees Bay

Billingham

Stockton-on-Tees

Middlesbrough

Darlington

Whitby

Robin Hood's Bay

Scarborough

Filey
Filey Bay

Flamborough Head

Bridlington
Bridlington Bay

Hornsea

North York Moors

Hutton-le-Hole

Pelargonium Nursery

Fir Trees

Sleightholmedale Lodge

Helmsley
Helmsley Walled Garden

Witherstone House

R V Roger Ltd

The Ornamental Grass & Plant Nursery

Burton Agnes Hall Gardens

Driffield

Sledmere House

Malton

Duncombe Park

Castle Howard

Sutton Park

Beningbrough Hall

Mount Grace Priory

Northallerton

Richmond

Leyburn

Millgate House

Thirsk

Coxwold

Newby Hall

NORTH YORKSHIRE

Yorkshire Dales

Grassington

Ripon

Studley Royal

Ripley Castle

Ripley

Valley Gardens

Thorp Perrow Arboretum

York

Wetherby

Middlethorpe Hall

Stillingfleet Lodge Nurseries

Selby

Bumby Hall Gardens

Bishop Burton

Botanic Garden

Burton Constable

EAST RIDING OF YORKSHIRE

Kingston upon Hull

Barton-upon-Humber

Hessle

Humber

Easington

Spurn Head

Cleethorpes

Grimsby

Scunthorpe

Gainsborough

Retford

Worksop

Lincoln

Harrogate

RHS Garden

Harlow Carr

Otley

Harewood House

Ilkley

Golden Acre Park

8 Dunstan Lane

York Gate

The Hollies Park

Roundhay Park & Tropical World

Temple Newsam Park

Lotherton Hall

Castleford

Wakefield

Leeds

Bradford

WEST YORKSHIRE

Batley

Halifax

Huddersfield

Bradsworth Hall

Doncaster

Barnsley

Wentworth Castle Gardens

The Earth Centre

Rotherham

Maltby

SOUTH YORKSHIRE

Sheffield

Chesterfield

Peak District

Buxton

Macclesfield

Northwich

Wilmslow

Manchester

Warrington

St. Helens

Liverpool

Wigan

Horwich

Blackburn

Darwen

Accrington

Burnley

Colne

Clitheroe

Forest of Bowland

Preston

Morecambe

Settle

Ingleton

Skipton

Keighley

Land Farm Gardens

Parceval Hall Gardens

Braeham Park

Valley Gardens

Northwich

A1(M)

A66

A68

A688

A1(M)

A66

A19

A171

A170

A172

A64

A165

A166

A64

A19

A170

A59

A58

A1

A65

A6

A56

A59

A61

A58

A59

A1

A64

A63

A1079

A19

A18

A15

A57

A159

A161

A16

A46

A1(M)

A638

A161

A628

A616

A623

A515

A6

A54

A34

A556

A49

A580

A57

A635

A628

A616

A59

M62

M62

M1

M18

M180

M56

M60

M61

M6

M65

M66

M58

MAP 18 • 497

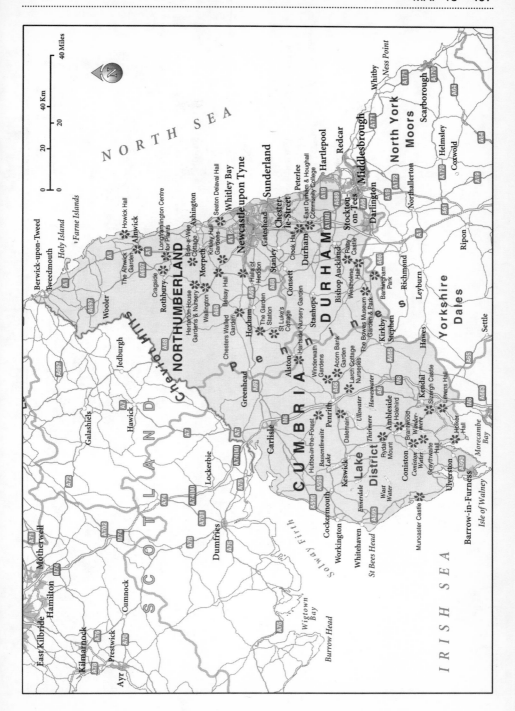

40 Miles

40 Km

20

20

0

0

N O R T H   S E A

Holy Island

Farne Islands

Berwick-upon-Tweed
Tweedmouth

Howick Hall
The Alnwick
Garden
Alnwick
Longframlington Centre
for Plants
Cragside
Rothbury
Wooler
Herterton House
Gardens & Nursery
Wallington
Belsay Hall
Gardens
Chesters Walled
Garden
Hexham
The Garden
Station
St Luke's
Cottage
Halls of
Heddon
Kirkley Hall
Gardens
Seaton Delaval Hall
Whitley Bay
Newcastle upon Tyne
Gateshead
Crook Hall
Stanley
Chester-
le-Street
Consett
Durham
East Durham & Houghall
Community College
Sunderland
Peterlee
Hartlepool
Redcar
Middlesbrough
Whitby
Ness Point
Scarborough
North York
Moors
Helmsley
Coxwold
Ripon

D U R H A M

N O R T H U M B E R L A N D

The Bowes Museum
Garden & Park
Bishop Auckland
Westholme
Hall
Raby
Castle
Barnard
Castle
Barningham
Park
Stanhope
Haristale Nursery Garden
Acorn Bank
Garden
Larch Cottage
Nurseries
Winderwath
Gardens
Alston
Greenhead
Northallerton
Stockton-
on-Tees
Darlington
Richmond
Leyburn
Hawes
Kirkby
Stephen
Settle
Yorkshire
Dales

C U M B R I A

P   e   n   n   i   n   e   s

Carlisle
Hutton-in-the-Forest
Bassenthwaite
Lake
Keswick
Ennerdale
Wast
Water
Thirlmere
Dalemain
Penrith
Ullswater
Rydal
Mount
Coniston
Water
Coniston
Graythwaite
Hall
Muncaster Castle
Ulverston
Brantwood
Holehird
Ambleside
Winder-
mere
Kendal
Sizergh Castle
Levens Hall
Holker
Hall
Barrow-in-Furness
Isle of Walney
Morecambe
Bay
Lake
District
Hawkshead
Cockermouth
Workington
Whitehaven
St Bees Head

S C O T L A N D

C h e v i o t   H i l l s

Jedburgh
Hawick
Galashiels
Lockerbie
Dumfries
Motherwell
Hamilton
East Kilbride
Kilmarnock
Ayr
Prestwick
Cumnock

Solway Firth
Wigtown
Bay
Burrow Head

I R I S H   S E A

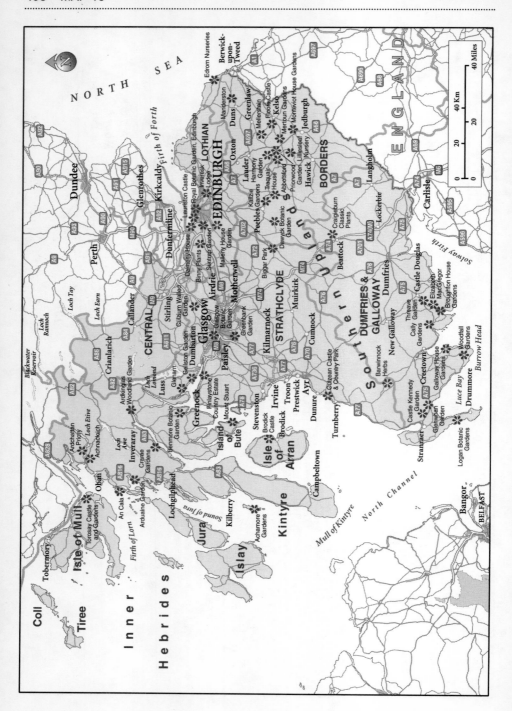

MAP 20 • 499

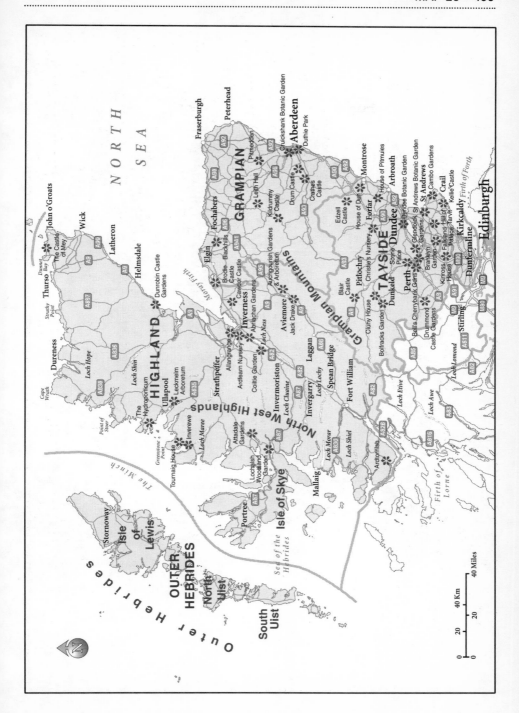

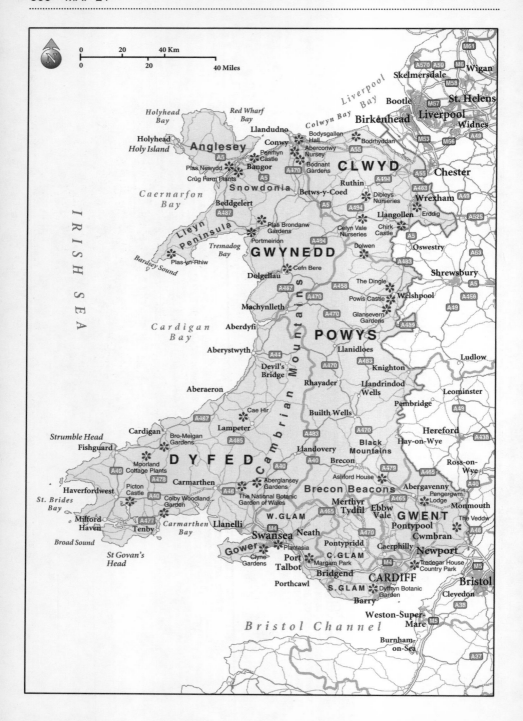

MAP 22 • 501

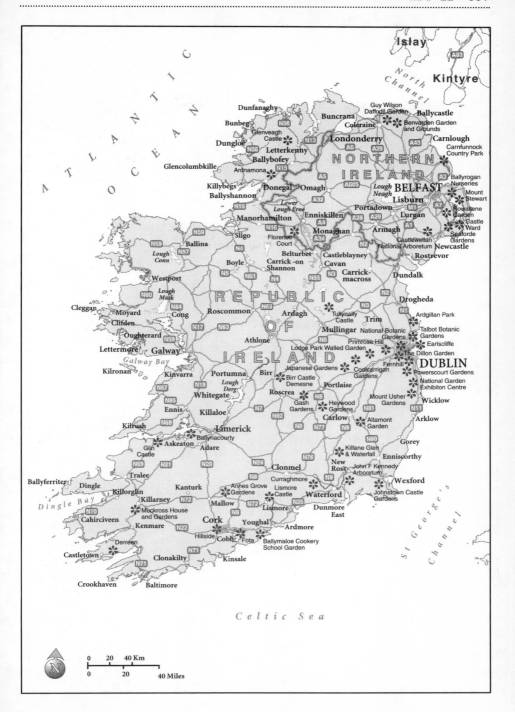

Islay

North
Channel

Kintyre

A83

Dunfanaghy

Bunbeg
Glenveagh
Castle
N56
N13

Guy Wilson
Daffodil Garden
Buncrana
Coleraine
Ballycastle
Benvarden Garden
and Grounds

Dungloe
Letterkenny
Ballybofey
N55

Londonderry
A5
Carnlough
A43
Carnfunnock
Country Park

NORTHERN

Glencolumbkille
Ardnamona
N15

IRELAND
A2
Ballyrogan
Nurseries

Killybegs
Donegal
Omagh
A505
Lough
Neagh
BELFAST
Lisburn
Mount
Stewart

Ballyshannon
A32
Portadown
Rowallene
Garden

Lower
Lough Erne
Manorhamilton
Enniskillen
A4
A28
A29
Lurgan
Armagh
A1
Castle
Ward
Seaforde
Gardens

N15
N16
Florence
Court
Monaghan
A34

Castlewellan
National Arboretum
Newcastle

Sligo
N4
Belturbet
Castleblayney
Castlewellan

Ballina
N59
N57
Carrick-on
Shannon
Cavan
Rostrevor

Lough
Conn
Boyle
N5
N61
N55
N3
Carrick-
macross
Dundalk

Westport
N60
Lough
Mask
N84

Roscommon
N63
Ardagh
Trim
Drogheda
M1
Ardgillan Park

Cleggan
Moyard
Clifden
N59
Cong
N17

N63
Mullingar
Tullynally
Castle
National Botanic
Gardens
N2
Talbot Botanic
Gardens

Oughterard
N59
Athlone
Lodge Park Walled Garden
Primrose Hill
Earlscliffe

Lettermore
Galway
Galway Bay
Japanese Gardens
Coolcarrigan
Gardens
Fernhill
The Dillon Garden
DUBLIN

Kilronan
Kinvarra
Portumna
Birr
Birr Castle
Demesne
Powerscourt Gardens

N67
Lough
Derg
Roscrea
Portlaise
Mount Usher
Gardens
National Garden
Exhibiton Centre

Ennis
N85
Whitegate
Killaloe
N7
N62
Gash
Gardens
Heywood
Gardens
N8
N81
Wicklow
Arklow
N11

Kilrush
N68
Limerick
N52
Carlow
Altamont
Garden
N80
Gorey

Kilrush
Ballynacourty
Askeaton
Adare
N6
N77
N9
Kilfane Glen
& Waterfall
Enniscorthy

Glin
Castle
N69
N21
N20
N24
Clonmel
New
Ross
John F Kennedy
Arboretum
Wexford

Tralee
Dingle
Killorglin
Kanturk
N8
Annes Grove
Gardens
Curraghmore
Lismore
Castle
N25
Johnstown Castle
Gardens

Ballyferriter
Dingle Bay
Killarney
N72
Mallow
N72
Lismore
Waterford
Dunmore
East

Cahirciveen
Muckross House
and Gardens
N8
Youghal
Ardmore

Kenmare
N22
Cork
Cobh
Fota
Ballymaloe Cookery
School Garden

Derreen
Hillside
N71
N73

Castletown
N70
Clonakilty
Kinsale

Crookhaven
Baltimore

St George's
Channel

Celtic Sea

REPUBLIC OF IRELAND

ATLANTIC OCEAN

0   20   40 Km
0   20   40 Miles

INDEX

The page numbers in **bold** refer to main entries.